MACROECONOMICS

CANADA IN THE GLOBAL ENVIRONMENT

SECOND EDITION

MACROECONOMICS

CANADA IN THE GLOBAL ENVIRONMENT

SECOND EDITION

MICHAEL PARKIN ◆ ROBIN BADE

University of Western Ontario

 ADDISON-WESLEY PUBLISHERS LIMITED

DON MILLS, ONTARIO ◆ READING, MASSACHUSETTS ◆ MENLO PARK, CALIFORNIA
◆ NEW YORK ◆ WOKINGHAM, ENGLAND ◆ AMSTERDAM ◆ BONN
SYDNEY ◆ SINGAPORE ◆ TOKYO ◆ MADRID ◆ SAN JUAN

Canadian Cataloguing in Publication Data

Parkin, Michael, 1939–
  Macroeconomics: Canada in the global
    environment

2nd ed.
Includes index.
ISBN 0-201-44320-1

1. Macroeconomics.   2. Canada — Economic
conditions.   I. Bade, Robin.   II. Title.

HB172.5.P363 1994   339   C93-095297-9

Executive Editor:	**Joseph Gladstone**
Managing Editor:	**Linda Scott**
Sponsoring Editor:	**Shirley Tessier**
Editorial Team:	**Kathie Mac Neil**
	Kateri Lanthier
	Katherine Goodes
	Mei Lin Cheung
Cover Design:	**Anthony Leung**
Production Team:	**Roberta Dick**
	Melanie Pequeux
	Linda Allison

Art developed by RWP Graphics, London, Ontario

ISBN 0-201-44320-1

To Our Students

ABOUT THE AUTHORS

MICHAEL PARKIN was educated at the University of Leicester. Currently in the Department of Economics at the University of Western Ontario, Professor Parkin has held faculty appointments at the Universities of Sheffield, Leicester, Essex, and Manchester, and has lectured extensively throughout Canada, the United States, Europe, Australia, and Japan. He has served as managing editor of the *Canadian Journal of Economics* and on the editorial boards of the *American Economic Review* and the *Journal of Monetary Economics*. Professor Parkin's research on macroeconomics, monetary economics, and international economics has resulted in 160 publications in the *American Economic Review*, the *Journal of Political Economy*, the *Review of Economic Studies*, the *Journal of Monetary Economics*, the *Journal of Money, Credit and Banking*, and dozens of other journals and edited volumes.

ROBIN BADE teaches at the University of Western Ontario. She earned degrees in mathematics and economics at the University of Queensland and her Ph.D. at the Australian National University. She has held faculty appointments in the business school at the University of Edinburgh and in the economics departments at the University of Manitoba and the University of Toronto. Her research on international capital flows appears in the *International Economic Review* and the *Economic Record*.

Professor Parkin and Dr. Bade are joint authors of *Modern Macroeconomics* (Prentice-Hall), an intermediate text, and have collaborated on many research and textbook writing projects. They are both experienced and dedicated teachers of introductory economics.

PREFACE

To change the way students see the world—this is our purpose in teaching economics and our goal in preparing this revision. There is no greater satisfaction for a teacher than to share the joy of a student who has started to think like an economist. But economics is not easy to master. Everyday in our classrooms, we relearn the challenges of gaining the insights we call the economist's way of thinking and recall our own struggles to master this discipline. In preparing this revision, we have drawn on the experiences of our own students and of students and instructors who used the first edition.

Three assumptions guided the choices we faced in writing this book. First, students are eager to learn but they have many claims on their time. They want to see the relevance of what they are studying to their own everyday experiences. Second, students want thoughtful and straightforward explanations. Third, students want to be equipped for tomorrow's world. They want to learn the economics of the 1990s and the relevant lessons of the past so they will be able to understand the world of the twenty-first century.

Approach

The core of the principles course has been around for more than one hundred years, and other important elements, especially parts of the theory of the firm and Keynesian macroeconomics, have been with us for more than fifty years. But economics has also been developing and changing rapidly during the past few decades. All principles texts pay some attention to recent developments, but they have not succeeded in integrating the new and traditional. Our goal has been to incorporate new ideas into the body of timeless principles—ideas such as game theory, the modern theory of the firm, information, public choice, and the real business cycle.

The presence of modern topics does not translate into "high level." Nor does it translate into "bias." We make recent developments in economics thoroughly accessible to beginning students. Where modern theories are controversial, alternative approaches are presented, evaluated, and compared. For example, all the macroeconomics "schools"—Keynesian, monetarist, and New Classical—are given a thoughtful and even-handed treatment.

But this book does have a point of view. It is that economics is a serious, lively, and evolving science—a science that seeks to develop a body of theory powerful enough to explain the economic world around us and that pursues its task by building, testing, and rejecting economic models. In some areas the science has succeeded in its task, but in others controversy persists. Where issues are settled, we present what is known; where controversy persists, we present the alternative viewpoints. This positive approach to economics is, we believe, especially valuable for our students as they prepare to function in a world in which simple ideologies have become irrelevant and in which familiar patterns in the economic landscape have shifted and blurred.

Macroeconomics and Changes in the Second Edition

Our goals in revising the macroeconomics coverage have been to extend and improve the positive, fact-driven approach of the first edition; to make the complexities of macroeconomic models and events relevant and understandable to students; and to address the global macroeconomic issues of the 1990s.

We have changed the balance of the coverage of national income accounting (Chapter 23), giving greater prominence to a discussion of the validity of the GDP as a measure of economic well-being. We have simplified and streamlined the initial presentation of aggregate demand-aggregate supply (Chapter 24) so that students can make effective and immediate use of this model.

In light of the 1990–1991 recession and the ongoing federal deficit, it is clear that a clear understanding of fiscal policy and monetary policy is essential. The role of fiscal policy is thoroughly discussed throughout the text (especially in Chapters 24, 26, 29, and 32), and is illustrated through issues drawn from the 1990 recession. The presentation of monetary theory and policy has been reorganized to parallel that of expenditure theory and fiscal policy. Chapter 27 now covers the demand for and supply of money and the determination of interest rates,

and Chapter 28 explains how the Bank of Canada influences the economy by manipulating interest rates.

Open economy issues are introduced as briefly as possible, and a full explanation of the balance of payments and exchange rate appears in Chapter 36. This chapter can be covered much earlier if desired.

Our coverage of aggregate supply and unemployment has been thoroughly revised. We have more on productivity and growth and on alternative theories of unemployment in Chapter 30. The theory of inflation is now treated separately from theories of expectations (Chapter 31). The coverage of stabilization policy has been revised and extended to include a discussion of the political business cycle.

Finally, the problems faced by economies making the transition from planned to market economy has been completely revised. Chapter 38 provides a framework for understanding events in Eastern Europe, the former Soviet Union, and China as these countries change their economic systems and open their markets to international influences.

Flexibility

We have chosen to present microeconomics first, but the book has been written to accommodate courses that are sequenced in either order. The microeconomics and macroeconomics chapters do not depend on each other; concepts and terms are defined and ideas are developed independently in each of the two halves.

We have accommodated a wide range of teaching approaches by building flexibility and optionality into the book. The core chapters (see p.xv) can form the basis of a one-year course that covers both macro and micro. Non-core chapters may be omitted with no loss of continuity. And the *AD–AS* model can be covered later in the macro sequence than it appears in the book (see p. xv).

Special Features

The second edition, like its predecessor, is packed with special features designed to enhance the learning process.

Art Program

A highly successful feature in the first edition was the outstanding art. The art was not only visually attractive and engaging, but also communicated the economic principles clearly. We received enormously positive feedback on the art, which confirmed our belief that one of the most important tools for economists is graphical analysis. Also, this is precisely an area that gives many students much difficulty. In the second edition, we have refined the data-based art further by deriving a style that clearly reveals the data and trends.

Our goal is to show clearly "where the economic action is." To achieve this, we observe a consistent protocol in style, notation, and use of colour, including:

◆ Highlighting shifted curves, points of equilibrium, and the most important features in red

◆ Using arrows in conjunction with colour to lend directional movement to what are usually static presentations

◆ Pairing graphs with data tables from which the curves have been plotted

◆ Using colour consistently to underscore the content, and referring to such colour in the text and captions

◆ Labelling key pieces of information in graphs with boxed notes

◆ Rendering each piece electronically so that precision is achieved

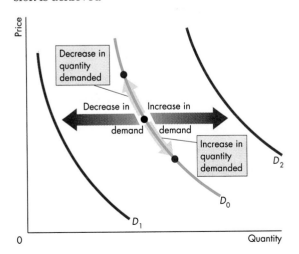

The entire art program has been developed with the study and review needs of the student in mind. We have retained the following features:

◆ Marking the most important figures and tables with a red key ◆ and listing them at the end of the chapter as "Key Figures and Tables"

◆ Using complete, informative captions that encapsulate major points in the graph so that students can preview or review the chapter by skimming through the art

The Interviews

Interviews with famous economists was another popular feature in the first edition, which we are continuing. But we have talked with an entire new cast of economists who have contributed significantly to advancing the thinking and practice in our discipline—four of whom are Nobel laureates (Kenneth Arrow, Ronald Coase, Franco Modigliani, and Robert Solow). The interviews help students to see the human face of economists as they discuss their areas of specialization, their unique contributions to economics, and their general insights which are relevant to beginning students.

An interview opens each part of the book and covers topics that are developed in the following chapters. Students can use the interviews to preview the issues and terminology they are about to encounter. A more careful reading afterwards will give a fuller appreciation of the discussion. Finally, the whole series of interviews can be approached as an informal symposium on the subject matter of economics as it is practised today.

Reading Between the Lines

Another feature that was well received in the previous edition was "Reading Between the Lines." This feature helps students to build critical thinking skills and to interpret daily news events (and their coverage in the media) using economic principles.

We have updated all the news articles and have deliberately selected topics that appeal to students, such as baseball bats, "Ice" beer, cable television, and unemployment. Each "Reading Between the Lines" spread contains three passes at a story. It begins with a facsimile of an actual (usually excerpted) newspaper or magazine article. It then presents a digest of the article's essential points. Finally, it provides an economic analysis of the news story, based on the economic models presented in that chapter.

Our Advancing Knowledge

"Our Advancing Knowledge" essays have been revised to help students trace the evolution of path-breaking economic ideas and recognize the universality of their application, not only to the past but also to the present. For example, Adam Smith's powerful ideas about the division of labour apply to the creation of the computer chip with even more force than to the pin factory of the eighteenth century. And Dionysius Lardner's 1850s application of demand and supply theory to railway pricing applies with equal force to airline pricing today. A new visual design brings excitement and vitality to these inserts, much in the way the ideas have brought excitement and vitality to economics.

Learning Aids

We have refined our careful pedagogical plan to ensure that this book complements and reinforces classroom learning. Each chapter contains the following pedagogical elements:

Objectives   Each chapter opens with a list of objectives that enables students to set their goals as they begin the chapter.

Chapter openers   Puzzles, paradoxes, or metaphors frame the important questions that are unravelled and resolved as the chapter progresses.

Highlighted in-text reviews   Succinct summaries are interspersed through the chapter for review at the end of main sections.

Key terms   Highlighted within the text, these concepts form the first part of a three-tiered review of economic vocabulary. These terms are repeated with page references at the end of each chapter and compiled in the glossary.

Key figures and tables   These are identified with the key logo ◆ and listed at the end of each chapter.

End-of-chapter study material   Summaries organized around major headings; lists of key terms with page references; lists of key figures and tables with page references; review questions; and problems.

The Teaching and Learning Package

Our fully integrated text and supplements package provides students and instructors with a seamless teaching and learning experience. The authors of these components are outstanding educators and scholars and have brought their own human capital (and those of their students!) to the job of improving the quality and value of the ancillaries for the second edition.

Study Guide   Available in microeconomics and macroeconomics split versions, the revised Study Guide was written by Avi J. Cohen of York University and Harvey B. King of the University of Regina. Carefully coordinated with both the main textbook and the Test Bank, each chapter of the Study Guide contains: Key Concepts (a one-page "crib-note" summary of key definitions, concepts, and material in the textbook chapter), Helpful Hints (to help students avoid common mistakes and to help them understand the most important concepts, graphs, equations, and techniques for problem solving), and a Self-Test (to allow students to practise exam-style questions).

The Self-Test has fifteen True/False/Uncertain and Explain questions, thirty Multiple-Choice questions (five choices per question), five Short Answer questions, and six Problems (graphical, numerical, analytical, and policy-oriented). There are complete answers to all questions, including brief explanations. All Multiple-Choice questions are in the Test Bank. Finally, at the end of every textbook "Part" there is a two-page Part Overview Problem (with answer) that integrates concepts from the chapters in the "Part." These problems are policy-oriented and help students integrate concepts they have learned and apply them to real-world situations.

Test Bank   Thoroughly revised test items were prepared by Harvey B. King of the University of Regina. The Test Bank includes over 4,600 multiple-choice questions, over one-third of which are new to this edition. All questions have been reviewed carefully for accuracy. All Multiple-Choice questions in the Study Guide are identified by the symbol (SG).

Computerized Test Bank   Testing software with graphics capability is available to qualified adopters for IBM–PC and compatible PCs.

Instructor's Manual   A brand new Instructor's Manual has been prepared by Ron Kessler of the British Columbia Institute of Technology. It includes chapter outlines, a summary of changes in the second edition, teaching suggestions, a list of colour acetates for each chapter, answers to all review questions and problems in the textbook, and additional discussion questions.

Acetates   Four-colour acetates have been developed especially for the Canadian edition, and are available upon adoption of this book.

Graphpad   The Graphpad contains reproductions of all the acetates of key figures. This eliminates tedious copying by students and allows them more time to focus on understanding the course material.

Economics in Action Software   New to this edition is a truly interactive tutorial software available for both IBM compatible and Macintosh computers. Created specifically for this text by Douglas McTaggart (co-author of the Australian edition of this book), David Gould of Bond University, Paul Davis (formerly of Bond University), and by us with a great deal of help from many other people. The software includes modules on core concepts such as graphing, production possibilities and opportunity cost, demand and supply, elasticity, utility and demand, product curves and cost curves, perfect competition, monopoly, macroeconomic performance, aggregate demand and aggregate supply, expenditure multipliers, money and banking, and international trade.

Four interactive modes take full advantage of the computer's capability to facilitate critical thinking skills. First, a tutorial mode walks students through the central concepts. Second, a quiz mode enables guided self-testing. Third, a free mode allows students and professors to interact with economic models by changing parameters and observing the effects on the graphs. Fourth, an evaluation mode allows students to construct and complete a multiple-choice test and keep a (read-only) record their score.

In addition to its emphasis on interaction, the software is also closely integrated with the text. The art style is the same, the terminology is consistent, and supporting material in the text is cross-referenced in the software. The software has a user's manual and has been tested and reviewed for accuracy.

Acknowledgments

Creating a principles textbook involves the collaboration and contribution of many individuals. Although the extent of our debts cannot be fully acknowledged here, it is nevertheless a joy to record our gratitude to the many people who have helped, some without realizing just how helpful they have been.

We want to thank those of our colleagues at the University of Western Ontario who have taught us a great deal that can be found in these pages: Jim Davies, Jeremy Greenwood, Ig Horstmann, Peter Howitt, Greg Huffman, David Laidler, Phil Reny, Chris Robinson, John Whalley, and Ron Wonnacott. We want to extend a special thanks to Glenn MacDonald, who worked well beyond the call of duty discussing this project with us from its outset, helping us develop many of its pedagogical features, and reading and commenting in detail on all the micro chapters. Special thanks also go to Doug McTaggart of Bond University and Christopher Findlay of the University of Adelaide, co-authors on the Australian edition, and David King, co-author of the European edition. Their suggestions arising from their adaptation of the first edition have been extremely helpful in fine-tuning this edition. More than that, we worked with Doug on the early drafts of the new chapter on uncertainty and information (Chapter 17) in the perfect Queensland winter of 1991.

We also want to acknowledge those who have had a profound influence on our whole view of and approach to economics and whose influence we can see in these pages. Although we never sat in their classrooms, they are in a very real sense our teachers. We are especially grateful to John Carlson (Purdue University), Carl Christ (Johns Hopkins

University), Robert Clower (University of South Carolina), Ed Feige (University of Wisconsin at Madison), Herschel Grossman (Brown University), Ronald Jones (University of Rochester), Richard Lipsey (Simon Fraser University), and Sam Wu (University of Iowa). We also want to place on record our enormous debt to the late Karl Brunner. The energy, drive, and entrepreneurship of this outstanding economist provided us and our generation of economists with incredible opportunities to interact and learn from each other in a wide variety of conference settings both in the United States and in Europe.

It is also a pleasure to acknowledge our debt to the several thousand students to whom we have been privileged to teach introductory economics. The instant feedback that comes from the look of puzzlement or enlightenment has taught us, more than anything else, how to teach economics. We are especially grateful to the several thousand students who have used this book either in its various manuscript forms or in its first edition in Economics 20 at the University of Western Ontario. The enthusiasm and care with which they have used this book have been an inspiration to us and we have benefited immeasurably from their comments, criticisms, and suggestions. We dedicate this book to them.

This book is thoroughly Canadian. It was written and developed at the University of Western Ontario, class-tested by Canadian students and, wherever possible, uses Canadian issues and problems to illustrate economic concepts. Nevertheless, the enterprise on which we embarked in 1985 when we began writing the first edition was and has remained a truly international one. At the same time as this book was being revised, a second U.S. edition was also produced as was a French-Canadian edition. We are now working, with co-authors, on second editions for the United Kingdom and Australia and on a Spanish edition.

Producing a text such as this is a team effort and the members of the Addison-Wesley Canada team are genuine co-producers of this book. We are especially grateful to George McD. Bryson, Chairman of the Board of Addison-Wesley Canada until 1989, for his enthusiasm, support, and encouragement, and for the role he played in ensuring this book's multinational dimension. We are also grateful to Tony Vander Woude, President of Addison-Wesley Canada, for his continued support for this project, to John More, Director and Vice-President of Addison-Wesley's college division, for his overall direction of the project and for his specific help in finding good news articles for "Reading Between the Lines," to Joseph Gladstone, our Executive Editor, and Linda Scott, our Managing Editor. To publish a book of this magnitude and complexity would not be possible without the dedication and commitment of many outstanding people. We acknowledge with gratitude and admiration the work of the members of our editorial team, Mei Lin Cheung, Katherine Goodes, Kateri Lanthier, Kathie Mac Neil, and Shirley Tessier, and our production team, Roberta Dick, Melanie Pequeux, Linda Allison, and Anthony Leung. They all gave unstintingly of their time, energy, and enthusiasm.

We also thank our secretary, Bronwyn Cribbes, and our librarian and general intelligence officer, Jane McAndrew, for creative help in tracking down sources and for taking care of couriers, fax messages, and a host of other details.

This edition has some common parentage with the second U.S. edition and we want to place on record our gratitude to Marilyn Freedman, Cindy Johnson, Barbara Rifkind, and Marjorie Williams, our editors at Addison-Wesley in the United States.

Throughout the revision process, Avi Cohen and Harvey King acted as constant consultants and instant sounding boards, both for us and our editors, and we want to place on record our admiration and thanks for the outstanding job they did.

We want to give special thanks to Catherine Baum and Richard and Ann Parkin. Through the years that we were developing and writing the first edition, they were going through various stages of high school and college. They forced us to craft a book that they could understand and found interesting. In preparing this edition, we have been especially helped by Catherine who gave us some editorial help and who prepared the index, and by Richard who created our electronic art manuscript and provided outstanding research assistance.

The empirical test of this textbook's value continues to be made in the classroom. We would appreciate hearing from instructors and students about how we might continue to improve the book in future editions.

Michael Parkin
Robin Bade
Department of Economics
University of Western Ontario
London, Ontario, N6A 5C2

Core Chapters and Flexibility

T he following chapters cover the core material and can form the basis of a one-year course in micro and macro. In our experience, it is possible to get through around twenty chapters in a thirteen-week term. Any chapter not listed below may be added as time permits.

Core Chapters

Introductory Core	1. What Is Economics? 3. Production, Specialization, and Exchange 4. Demand and Supply
Micro Core	5. Elasticity 7. Utility and Demand 9. Organizing Production 10. Output and Costs 11. Competition 12. Monopoly 14. Pricing and Allocating Factors of Production 19. Market Failure
Macro Core	22. Inflation, Unemployment, Cycles, and Deficits 23. Measuring Output and the Price Level 24. Aggregate Demand and Aggregate Supply 25. Expenditure Decisions and GDP 26. Expenditure Fluctuations and Fiscal Policy 27. Money, Banking, and Interest Rates 28. The Bank of Canada and Monetary Policy 33. Stabilizing the Economy
International Core	35. Trading with the World

Flexibility Chapters

| AD–AS Flexibility
We do AD–AS early. But some teachers prefer to develop the Keynesian expenditure system and monetary theory *before* deriving the AD curve. We have written the macro chapters so that this alternative sequence can be used. The sequence on the right presumes that AD–AS will be done *after* the core Keynesian theory. | 25. Expenditure Decisions and GDP (omit "Real GDP and the Price Level," pp. 706–708)
26. Expenditure Fluctuations and Fiscal Policy (omit "Multipliers and the Price Level," pp. 726–731)
27. Money, Banking, and Interest Rates
28. The Bank of Canada and Monetary Policy (omit "Money, Real GDP, and the Price Level," pp. 779–787) |
| AD–AS Optional Chapter

NOTE: Return to Chapter 24 and the omitted parts of Chapters 25 to 29. | 29. Fiscal and Monetary Influences on Aggregate Demand (omit "Real GDP, the Price Level, and Interest Rates," pp. 810–812) |

Reviewers

Addison-Wesley Publishers would like to express appreciation for the invaluable advice and encouragement received from educators across Canada during the revision of this book. We particularly wish to thank the following people:

Torben Andersen, Red Deer College
Andy Baziliauskas, University of Winnipeg
Karl Bennett, University of Waterloo
Francois Casas, University of Toronto
Avi J. Cohen, York University
Peter Fortura, Algonquin College
David M. Gray, University of Ottawa
Rod Hill, University of New Brunswick
Susan Kamp, University of Alberta
Harvey B. King, University of Regina
Robert Kunimoto, Mt. Royal College
Eva Lau, University of Waterloo
Dan MacKay, SIAST
A. Gyasi Nimarko, Vanier College
Sonja Novkovic, McGill University
A. Paus-Jenssen, University of Saskatchewan
Don Reddick, Kwantlen College
G. E. Riser, Memorial University
Nick Rowe, Carleton University
Michael Rushton, University of Regina
Marlyce Searcy, SIAST
Judith Skuce, Georgian College

CREDITS

Care has been taken to determine and locate ownership of copyright material used in this text. In the case of any errors or omissions, please advise the publisher.

PART 1: TALKING WITH ROBERT SOLOW, © **L. Barry Hetherington.**

CHAPTER 1: Cartoon, Drawing by Modell; © 1985, **The New Yorker Magazine, Inc.** Cartoon, Drawing by H. Martin; © 1987, **The New Yorker Magazine Inc.** Pin factory, **Culver Pictures, Inc.** Woman holding silicon wafer, **Bruce Ando/Tony Stone Images.** Adam Smith, **The Bettmann Archive.**

CHAPTER 2: Kids cost a lot, **Bruce Cohen, The Financial Post, 3/6/93.**

CHAPTER 3: Improving links across Pacific, **Michael Bociurkiw, The Globe and Mail, 10/5/93.**

CHAPTER 4: The railroad suspension bridge near Niagara Falls, anonymous, **gift of Maxim Karolik for the M. and M. Karolik Collection of American Paintings, 1815-1865; courtesy Museum of Fine Arts, Boston.** Antoine-Augustin Cournot, **Historical Pictures/Stock Montage.** Alfred Marshall, **Historical Pictures/Stock Montage.** Slide of Toronto Airport, **Courtesy of Air Canada.** Train, **Courtesy of Stoddart Publishing Co. Limited, Don Mills, Ontario,** from *Canada: The Missing Years.* A shocking speculation about the price of oil, **Courtesy of The Economist, 9/18/93.**

PART 9: TALKING WITH FRANCO MODIGLIANI, **L. Barry Hetherington.**

CHAPTER 22: CN chopping 11,000 jobs at a cost of $900 million, **Kevin Dougherty, The Financial Post, 3/2/93.**

CHAPTER 23: Tableau Économique, **The Economist.** Four teens washing a car, **Jeffrey Myers, Stock Boston.** Automatic car wash, **Copyright Marc Teatum/Lightstream.** Sir William Petty, **The Bettmann Archive.**

CHAPTER 24: Cartoon, Drawing by Mankoff; © 1991, **The New Yorker Magazine Inc.** Economy jumps 3.5%, **Alan Freeman, The Globe and Mail, 3/2/93.**

PART 10: TALKING WITH SYLVIA OSTRY, **Ian Crysler, Addison-Wesley Publishers Ltd.**

CHAPTER 25: Young couple in kitchen, **Peter Menzel, Stock Boston.** College students buying CDs, **John Coletti, The Picture Cube Inc.** John Maynard Keynes,

The Bettmann Archive. CMHC's expectations for housing starts dim, **The Halifax Herald, 3/9/93.**

CHAPTER 26: Tax changes are too late to help business this year, **Jay Bryan, The Montreal Gazette, 4/27/93.**

CHAPTER 28: Interest rates targeted, **Greg Ip, The Financial Post, 5/25/93.** Woman burning marks, **The Bettmann Archive.** David Hume, **The Bettman Archive.**

CHAPTER 29: Budgets hit recovery, **Jill Vardy, The Financial Post, 5/22-24/93.**

PART 11: TALKING WITH EDMUND PHELPS, **Courtesy of Joe Pineiro/Columbia University.**

CHAPTER 30: Labor productivity shows strong gains, **Greg Ip, The Financial Post, 5/18/93.**

CHAPTER 31: Can't just cut interest rates to spur economy, Crow insists, **Shawn McCarthy, The Toronto Star Syndicate, 6/3/93.**

CHAPTER 32: Robert E. Lucas, **Paul K. Dzus/Addison-Wesley, Reading, MA.** Gains from '80s boom are almost wiped out, **Greg Ip, The Financial Post, 5/4/93.** The Great Depression, **Courtesy of Canapress Photo Service.**

PART 12: TALKING WITH GOVERNOR JOHN CROW, **Courtesy of Photo Features Ltd.**

CHAPTER 33: James Coyne, Bank of Canada Governor, July, 1961, **Courtesy of Canapress Photo Services.** John Diefenbaker, **Courtesy of Canapress Photo Services.** John Crow and Michael Wilson, **Courtesy of Canapress Photo Services.** Harry Johnson, **Courtesy of Lakehead University.** Rates won't be forced up: Crow, **Heather D. Whyte, The Financial Post, 6/10/93.**

CHAPTER 34: Canada's debt near $700B, **Catherine Harris, The Financial Post, 5/29-31/93.**

PART 13: TALKING WITH LAURA TYSON, **Courtesy of University of California, BRIE.**

CHAPTER 35: David Ricardo, **Stock Montage, Inc.** Canada's market share up under free trade: StatCan, **Alan Toulin, The Financial Post, March 4, 1993.** Photo of east view of Montreal, **National Archives of Canada.** Photo of cargo hold of Air Canada, **Courtesy of Air Canada.**

BRIEF CONTENTS

Part 1 INTRODUCTION 1

Chapter 1 What Is Economics? 5
Chapter 2 Making and Using Graphs 27
Chapter 3 Production, Specialization, and Exchange 49
Chapter 4 Demand and Supply 71

Part 9 INTRODUCTION TO MACROECONOMICS 593

Chapter 22 Inflation, Unemployment, Cycles, and Deficits 597
Chapter 23 Measuring Output and the Price Level 621
Chapter 24 Aggregate Demand and Aggregate Supply 648

Part 10 AGGREGATE DEMAND FLUCTUATIONS 676

Chapter 25 Expenditure Decisions and GDP 680
Chapter 26 Expenditure Fluctuations and Fiscal Policy 712
Chapter 27 Money, Banking, and Interest Rates 736
Chapter 28 The Bank of Canada and Monetary Policy 763
Chapter 29 Fiscal and Monetary Influences on Aggregate Demand 790

Part 11 AGGREGATE SUPPLY, INFLATION, AND RECESSION 824

Chapter 30 Productivity, Wages, and Unemployment 828
Chapter 31 Inflation 860
Chapter 32 Recessions and Depressions 887

Part 12 MACROECONOMIC POLICY 911

Chapter 33 Stabilizing the Economy 915
Chapter 34 The Federal Deficit 939

Part 13 INTERNATIONAL ECONOMICS 961

Chapter 35 Trading with the World 965
Chapter 36 The Balance of Payments and the Dollar 993

Part 14 GROWTH, DEVELOPMENT, AND REFORM 1020

Chapter 37 Growth and Development 1024
Chapter 38 Economic Systems in Transition 1041

CONTENTS

PART 1

INTRODUCTION
TALKING WITH ROBERT SOLOW   **1**

CHAPTER 1   WHAT IS ECONOMICS?   5

Choice and Change   **6**

Wages and Earnings   **7**
Government, Environment, and Economic Systems   **7**
Unemployment   **7**
Inflation   **8**
International Trade   **8**
Wealth and Poverty   **8**

Scarcity   9
Economic Activity   **9**
Choice   **10**
Opportunity Cost   **10**
Competition and Cooperation   **11**

The Economy   12
What Is the Economy?   **12**
Decision Makers   **13**
Markets   **14**
Decisions   **14**
Coordination Mechanisms   **14**
The Global Economy   **16**

Economic Science   17
What Is and What Ought to Be   **17**
Observation and Measurement   **18**
Economic Theory   **18**
Economic Model   **18**
Microeconomic and Macroeconomic Models   **20**
Model, Theory, and Reality   **21**

OUR ADVANCING KNOWLEDGE
UNDERSTANDING THE SOURCES OF ECONOMIC WEALTH   **22**

Summary   **24**
Review Questions   **25**
Problems   **26**

Summary, Key Elements, Review Questions, and Problems appear at the end of each chapter.

CHAPTER 2 MAKING AND USING GRAPHS   27

Three Kinds of Lies   **28**

Graphing Data   29
Two-Variable Graphs   **29**
Scatter Diagrams   **30**
Time-Series Graphs   **32**

Graphs Used in Economic Models   38
Variables That Go Up and Down Together   **38**
Variables That Move in Opposite Directions   **38**
Relationships That Have a Maximum and a
    Minimum   **40**
Variables That Are Independent   **41**

The Slope of a Relationship   42
Calculating the Slope of a Straight Line   **42**
Calculating the Slope of a Curved Line   **43**

**Graphing Relationships among More Than Two
Variables   44**
Other Things Being Equal   **44**

READING BETWEEN THE LINES
GRAPHS IN ACTION   **36**

**CHAPTER 3 PRODUCTION, SPECIALIZATION, AND
                EXCHANGE   49**

Making the Most of It   **50**

The Production Possibility Frontier   51
A Model Economy   **51**
Jane's Preferences   **52**

Opportunity Cost   54
The Best Alternative Forgone   **54**
Measuring Opportunity Cost   **54**
Increasing Opportunity Cost   **54**
The Shape of the Frontier   **54**
Everything Has an Increasing Opportunity
    Cost   **54**
Production Possibilities in the Real World   **56**
Increasing Opportunity Cost in the Real
    World   **56**

Economic Growth   57
The Cost of Economic Growth   **57**
Capital Accumulation and Technological
    Change   **57**
Economic Growth in the Real World   **59**

Gains from Trade   60
Comparative Advantage: Jane Meets Joe   **60**
Achieving the Gains from Trade   **61**
Productivity and Absolute Advantage   **62**

Exchange in the Real World   63
Property Rights   **63**
Money   **66**

READING BETWEEN THE LINES
THE GAINS FROM SPECIALIZATION AND EXCHANGE   **64**

CHAPTER 4 DEMAND AND SUPPLY   71

Slide, Rocket, and Roller Coaster   **72**

Demand   73
What Determines Buying Plans?   **73**
The Law of Demand   **73**
Demand Schedule and Demand Curve   **73**
Willingness to Pay   **74**
A Change in Demand   **75**
Movement along versus a Shift in the Demand
Curve   **76**

Supply   78
What Determines Selling Plans?   **78**
The Law of Supply   **78**
Supply Schedule and Supply Curve   **78**
Minimum Supply Price   **78**
A Change in Supply   **79**
Movement along versus a Shift in the Supply
Curve   **80**

Price Determination   82
Price as a Regulator   **82**
Equilibrium   **83**

Predicting Changes in Price and Quantity   84
A Change in Demand   **84**
A Change in Supply   **85**
Changes in Both Supply and Demand   **88**
Walkmans, Apartments, and Coffee   **92**

OUR ADVANCING KNOWLEDGE
DISCOVERING THE LAWS OF DEMAND AND SUPPLY   **86**

READING BETWEEN THE LINES
DEMAND AND SUPPLY IN ACTION   **90**

CHAPTER 22 UNEMPLOYMENT, INFLATION, CYCLES, AND DEFICITS   597

Jobs, Prices, and Incomes   **598**

Unemployment   599
What Is Unemployment?   **599**
Measuring Unemployment   **599**
The Unemployment Record   **599**
Types of Unemployment   **600**
Full Employment   **601**
The Costs of Unemployment   **601**

Inflation   604
The Inflation Rate and the Price Level   **605**
The Recent Inflation Record   **605**
Inflation and the Value of Money   **606**
Is Inflation a Problem?   **606**
The Problem of Unanticipated Inflation   **607**
The Problem of Anticipated Inflation   **607**
High and Variable Inflation   **607**

Gross Domestic Product   608
Nominal GDP and Real GDP   **608**
Real GDP—the Record   **608**
The Benefits and Costs of Real GDP
Growth   **609**

The Business Cycle   612
Unemployment and the Business Cycle   **613**
The Stock Market and the Business Cycle   **614**
Inflation and the Business Cycle   **615**

Government Deficit and International Deficit   616
Government Deficit   **616**
International Deficit   **616**

READING BETWEEN THE LINES
STRUCTURAL UNEMPLOYMENT   **602**

CHAPTER 23 MEASURING OUTPUT AND THE PRICE LEVEL 621

Economic Barometers **622**

The Circular Flow of Expenditure and Income 623
Circular Flows in a Simplified Economy **623**
Income and Expenditure Accounts **627**

Canada's National Income and Expenditure Accounts 629
The Expenditure Approach **629**
The Factor Incomes Approach **630**
The Output Approach **633**
Aggregate Expenditure, Income, and Output **634**

The Price Level and Inflation 635
Consumer Price Index **636**
GDP Deflator **637**
Inflation and Relative Price Changes **638**
The Consumer Price Index and the Cost of Living **639**

Real GDP, Aggregate Economic Activity, and Economic Well-Being 640
Underground Real GDP **641**
Household Production **641**
Environmental Damage **641**
Leisure Time **641**
Economic Equality **644**
Are the Omissions a Problem? **644**

OUR ADVANCING KNOWLEDGE
THE DEVELOPMENT OF ECONOMIC ACCOUNTING **642**

CHAPTER 24 AGGREGATE DEMAND AND AGGREGATE SUPPLY 648

What Makes Our Garden Grow? **649**

Aggregate Demand 650
Changes in the Quantity of Real GDP Demanded **651**
Why the Aggregate Demand Curve Slopes Downward **651**
Changes in Aggregate Demand **652**
Fiscal Policy **652**
Monetary Policy **653**
International Factors **653**
Expectations **654**
Time Lags in Influences on Aggregate Demand **654**
Shifts of the Aggregate Demand Curve **655**

Aggregate Supply 656
Two Macroeconomic Time Frames **656**
Short-Run Aggregate Supply **656**
The Physical Limit to Real GDP **658**
Long-Run Aggregate Supply **658**
Changes in Short-Run Aggregate Supply **659**
Changes in Both Long-Run and Short-Run Aggregate Supply **660**

Macroeconomic Equilibrium 661
Determination of Real GDP and the Price Level **661**
Macroeconomic Equilibrium and Full Employment **662**
Aggregate Fluctuations and Changes in Aggregate Demand **663**
Aggregate Fluctuations and Changes in Aggregate Supply **665**

Recent Trends and Cycles in the Canadian Economy 666
The Economy in 1992 **666**
Growth, Inflation, and Cycles **667**
The Evolving Economy: 1971–1992 **668**
The Canada –United States Free Trade Agreement **669**
The Goods and Services Tax **669**

READING BETWEEN THE LINES
THE 1993 RECOVERY **670**

PART 10

AGGREGATE DEMAND FLUCTUATIONS
TALKING WITH SYLVIA OSTRY **676**

CHAPTER 25 EXPENDITURE DECISIONS AND GDP **680**

Fear and Trembling in the Shopping Aisles **681**

The Components of Aggregate Expenditure **682**
Magnitudes **682**
Fluctuations **683**

Consumption Expenditure and Saving **684**
The Consumption Function and the Saving Function **684**
The Average Propensities to Consume and to Save **688**
The Marginal Propensities to Consume and to Save **688**
The Canadian Consumption Function **690**

Investment **692**
Firms' Investment Decisions **692**
Investment Demand **694**
Investment Demand in Canada **696**

Government Purchases of Goods and Services **697**

Net Exports **700**
Exports **700**
Imports **700**
Net Export Function **700**

Aggregate Expenditure and Real GDP **702**
Aggregate Expenditure Schedule **702**
Aggregate Expenditure Curve **702**

Equilibrium Expenditure **704**
Actual Expenditure, Planned Expenditure, and Real GDP **704**
When Planned Expenditure Equals Real GDP **704**

Real GDP and the Price Level **706**
Aggregate Expenditure and Aggregate Demand **706**
Aggregate Planned Expenditure and the Price Level **706**

OUR ADVANCING KNOWLEDGE
DISCOVERING THE CONSUMPTION FUNCTION **686**

READING BETWEEN THE LINES
INVESTMENT PICKS UP SLOWLY **698**

CHAPTER 26 EXPENDITURE FLUCTUATIONS AND FISCAL POLICY **712**

Economic Amplifier or Shock Absorber? **713**

Expenditure Multipliers **714**
Autonomous Expenditure **714**
Induced Expenditure **714**
The Marginal Propensity to Buy Domestic Goods and Services **714**
A Change in Autonomous Expenditure **716**
The Multiplier Effect **716**
The Size of the Multiplier **716**
The Multiplier and the Marginal Propensity to Buy Domestic Goods and Services **719**
Why Is the Multiplier Greater than 1? **720**

Fiscal Policy Multipliers **722**
Government Purchases Multiplier **722**
Transfer Payments Multiplier **722**
Tax Multipliers **723**
Balanced Budget Multiplier **723**
Automatic Stabilizers **725**
Automatic Stabilizers and the Government Budget **725**

Multipliers and the Price Level **726**
Fiscal Policy and Aggregate Demand **726**
Equilibrium GDP and the Price Level **727**

The Multiplier in Canada **731**
The Canadian Multiplier in 1992 **731**
Econometric Models and the Canadian Multiplier **731**
The Multiplier in Recession and Recovery **731**
The Declining Canadian Multiplier **732**

READING BETWEEN THE LINES
NO FISCAL STIMULUS? **728**

CHAPTER 27 MONEY, BANKING, AND INTEREST RATES 736

Money Makes the World Go Round **737**

What Is Money? **738**
The Definition of Money **738**
The Functions of Money **738**
Different Forms of Money **739**
Money in Canada Today **742**

Financial Intermediaries **745**
Chartered Banks **746**
Trust and Mortgage Loan Companies **747**
Local Credit Unions and Caisses Populaires **747**
Financial Legislation **747**
The Economc Functions of Financial
Intermediaries **747**

How Banks Create Money **749**
Creating Money by Making Loans **749**
Actual and Desired Reserves **749**
The Limit to Bank Lending **749**
The Deposits Multiplier **751**
Canadian Deposits Multiplier **751**

The Demand for Money **752**
The Motives for Money Holding **752**
The Influences on Money Holding **753**
Shifts in the Demand Curve for Real
Money **755**
Financial Innovation **755**
The Demand for Money in Canada **757**

Interest Rate Determination **757**
Interest Rates and Asset Prices **757**
Money Market Equilibrium **758**

CHAPTER 28 THE BANK OF CANADA AND MONETARY POLICY 763

Fiddling with the Knobs **764**

The Bank of Canada **765**
The Origins of the Bank of Canada **765**
The Structure of the Bank of Canada **765**
The Bank of Canada and the Federal
Government **766**
International Constraints on the Bank of
Canada **767**
The Bank of Canada's Policy Tools **767**
The Bank of Canada's Balance Sheet **768**

Controlling the Money Supply **769**
How Open Market Operations Work **769**
Monetary Base and Bank Reserves **769**
The Multiplier Effect of an Open Market
Operation **771**
The Canadian Money Multiplier **773**

The Money Supply and Interest Rates **774**
Changing the Interest Rate **774**
The Bank of Canada in Action **775**
Profiting by Predicting the Bank of Canada **778**
Interest Rates and the Dollar **779**

Money, Real GDP, and the Price Level **779**
Money in the *AD–AS* Model **779**
The Quantity Theory of Money **781**
The Quantity Theory and the *AD–AS*
Model **781**
Historical Evidence on the Quantity Theory of
Money **782**
International Evidence on the Quantity Theory of
Money **786**
Correlation and Causation **786**

READING BETWEEN THE LINES
MONETARY POLICY STIMULUS **776**

OUR ADVANCING KNOWLEDGE
UNDERSTANDING THE CAUSES OF INFLATION **784**

CHAPTER 29   FISCAL AND MONETARY INFLUENCES ON AGGREGATE DEMAND   790

Sparks Fly in Ottawa   **791**

Money, Interest, and Aggregate Demand   792
Spending Decisions, Interest, and Money   **792**
Equilibrium Expenditure and the Interest Rate   **792**

Fiscal Policy and Aggregate Demand   794
First Round Effects of Fiscal Policy   **795**
Second Round Effects of Fiscal Policy   **795**
Crowding Out and Crowding In   **798**
International Crowding Out   **798**

Monetary Policy and Aggregate Demand   798
First Round Effects of a Change in the Money Supply   **799**
Second Round Effects of a Change in Money Supply   **800**
The Exchange Rate and Exports   **802**

The Relative Effectiveness of Fiscal and Monetary Policy   802
The Effectiveness of Fiscal Policy   **802**
The Effectiveness of Monetary Policy   **804**
Interest Sensitivity of Investment Demand and the Demand for Money   **806**
The Keynesian–Monetarist Controversy   **806**
Influencing the Composition of Aggregate Expenditure   **810**
Politics of Fiscal and Monetary Policy   **810**

Real GDP, the Price Level, and Interest Rates   810
The Short-Run Effects on Real GDP and the Price Level   **810**
The Long-Run Effects on Real GDP and the Price Level   **811**

READING BETWEEN THE LINES
FISCAL AND MONETARY POLICY   **808**

Appendix: The *IS–LM* Model of Aggregate Demand   **816**

CHAPTER 30   PRODUCTIVITY, WAGES AND UNEMPLOYMENT   828

Incomes and Jobs   **829**

Productivity and Income Growth   830
The Marginal Product of Labour   **830**
Diminishing Marginal Product of Labour   **831**
Economic Growth   **831**
Variable Growth Rates   **832**
Canadian Productivity Growth   **832**
The Productivity Slowdown   **832**

The Demand for Labour   834
Diminishing Marginal Product and the Demand for Labour   **834**
The Demand for Labour in a Pop Factory   **835**
The Demand for Labour in the Economy   **835**
Changes in the Demand for Labour   **835**
The Canadian Demand for Labour   **836**

The Supply of Labour   837
Hours per Worker   **837**
The Participation Rate   **840**
Intertemporal Substitution   **840**

Wages and Employment   841
The Flexible Wage Theory   **841**
Aggregate Supply with Flexible Wages   **842**
Real Business Cycle Theory   **844**
The Sticky Wage Theory   **844**
Aggregate Supply with Sticky Wages   **846**

Why Wages Are Sticky   848
Minimum Wage Regulations   **848**
Implicit Risk-Sharing Contracts   **848**
Incomplete Price Level Information   **849**
Menu Costs   **850**

Unemployment   850
Job Search   **850**
Unemployment with Flexible Wages   **852**
Job Creation and Job Destruction   **853**
Efficiency Wages   **854**
Insiders and Outsiders   **854**
Unemployment with Sticky Wages   **855**

READING BETWEEN THE LINES
PRODUCTIVITY GROWTH   **838**

CHAPTER 31 INFLATION 860

From Rome to Russia **861**

Inflation and the Price Level 862

Demand–Pull Inflation 862
Inflation Effect of an Increase in Aggregate
    Demand **862**
Wage Response **863**
A Price–Wage Inflation Spiral **864**

Supply Inflation and Stagflation 865
Inflation Effect of a Decrease in Aggregate
    Supply **865**
Aggregate Demand Response **865**
A Cost–Price Inflation Spiral **866**

Anticipating Inflation 867
Labour Market Consequences of Unanticipated
    Inflation **868**
How People Forecast Inflation **868**
How Economics Predict People's Forecasts **868**
Rational Expectation of the Price Level **869**
Model, Theory, and Reality **871**
Anticipated Inflation **871**
The Costs of Anticipated Inflation **872**
Stopping an Anticipated Inflation **872**

**Inflation over the Business Cycle: The Phillips
Curve 873**
The Short-Run Phillips Curve **873**
The Long-Run Phillips Curve **874**
Changes in the Natural Rate of
    Unemployment **875**
The Phillips Curve in Canada **875**

Interest Rates and Inflation 877
Interest Rates and Unanticipated Inflation **877**
Interest Rates and Anticipated Inflation **878**
The Effect of Unanticipated Inflation on
    Borrowers and Lenders **878**
The Effect of Anticipated Inflation on Borrowers
    and Lenders **878**
Inflation and Interest Rates in Canada **879**

The Politics of Inflation 882
Inflation Tax **882**
Contest for Income Shares **882**
Errors in Forecasting the Natural Unemployment
    Rate **883**

READING BETWEEN THE LINES
INFLATION **880**

CHAPTER 32 RECESSIONS AND DEPRESSIONS 887

What Goes Up Must Come Down **888**

The Canadian Economy 889
The Origins of the 1990 Recession **890**
Aggregate Demand and Aggregate Supply in the
    1990 Recession **891**
Expenditure in the 1990 Recession **892**
The Money Market in the 1990 Recession **893**
The Labour Market in the 1990s **894**
Sticky Wage Theory **894**
Flexible Wage Theory **896**
Which Theory of the Labour Market Is
    Correct? **898**

Another Great Depression? 899
What the Great Depression Was Like **899**
Why the Great Depression Happened **900**
Can It Happen Again? **904**

READING BETWEEN THE LINES
DEPRESSION PERSISTS **902**

OUR ADVANCING KNOWLEDGE
UNDERSTANDING BUSINESS CYCLES **906**

PART 12

MACROECONOMIC POLICY

TALKING WITH JOHN CROW   **911**

CHAPTER 33   STABILIZING THE ECONOMY   915

Jump Start or Cruise Control?   **916**

The Stabilization Problem   **917**
Real GDP Growth   **917**
Inflation   **917**

Players and Policies   **918**
The Government of Canada   **918**
The Bank of Canada   **918**
Fiscal and Monetary Policy Performance   **918**
Alternative Stabilization Policies   **921**

Stabilization Policy and Aggregate Demand Shocks   **924**
Aggregate Demand Shock with a Fixed
 Rule   **925**
Aggregate Demand Shock with a Feedback
 Rule   **925**
The Two Rules Compared   **925**
So Feedback Rules Are Better?   **926**

Stabilization Policy and Aggregate Supply Shocks   **928**
Cost–Push Inflation   **929**
Slowdown in Productivity Growth   **930**
Nominal GDP Targeting   **931**

Taming Inflation   **934**
A Surprise Inflation Reduction   **934**
A Credible Announced Inflation Reduction   **934**
Inflation Reduction in Practice   **934**
A Truly Independent Bank of Canada   **936**

READING BETWEEN THE LINES
STABILIZING THE CANADIAN ECONOMY   **922**

OUR ADVANCING KNOWLEDGE
EVOLVING APPROACHES TO ECONOMIC
STABILIZATION   **932**

CHAPTER 34   THE FEDERAL DEFICIT   939

Ottawa Spendthrifts   **940**

The Sources of the Deficit   **941**
The Federal Budget: 1969–1992   **941**
Federal Government Revenue   **942**
Federal Government Expenditure   **942**
The Story of the Deficit   **944**
The Deficit and the Business Cycle   **944**

The Real Deficit   **948**
The Real Deficit of a Family   **948**
The Government's Real Deficit   **948**
The Federal Government's Real and Nominal
 Deficit   **949**

Deficits and Inflation   **950**
Financing the Deficit   **950**
International Evidence   **952**

A Burden on Future Generations?   **953**
Crowding Out   **953**
Ricardian Equivalence   **955**

Eliminating the Deficit   **956**
Reducing Expenditure   **956**
Increasing Revenue   **957**

READING BETWEEN THE LINES
GOVERNMENT DEFICITS   **946**

PART 13

INTERNATIONAL ECONOMICS
TALKING WITH LAURA TYSON 961

CHAPTER 35 TRADING WITH THE WORLD 965

Silk Routes and Rust Belts 966

Patterns and Trends in International Trade 967
Canada's International Trade 967
Balance of Trade and International Borrowing 969

Opportunity Cost and Comparative Advantage 970
Opportunity Cost in Farmland 970
Opportunity Cost in Mobilia 970
Comparative Advantage 970

The Gains from Trade 971
Reaping the Gains from Trade 971
Balanced Trade 972
Changes in Production and Consumption 972
Calculating the Gains from Trade 974
Wages and Costs 974
Productivity 974
Gains from Trade in Reality 975
Trade in Similar Goods 975
Adjustment Costs 978

Trade Restrictions 979
The History of Tariffs 979
How Tariffs Work 980
Nontariff Barriers 982
How Quotas and VERs Work 983
Why Quotas and VERs Might Be Preferred to Tariffs 984
Dumping and Countervailing Duties 984
Why Is International Trade Restricted? 984
Compensating Losers 985
Political Outcomes 985

The Canada–United States Free Trade Agreement 985
Terms of Agreement 985

OUR ADVANCING KNOWLEDGE
UNDERSTANDING THE GAINS FROM INTERNATIONAL TRADE 976

READING BETWEEN THE LINES
NORTH AMERICAN FREE TRADE 986

CHAPTER 36 THE BALANCE OF PAYMENTS AND THE DOLLAR 993

The Global Economy 994

Financing International Trade 995
Balance of Payments Accounts 995
International Borrowing and Lending 996
Current Account Balance 997
The Twin Deficits 999
Effects of Government Deficit on Private Surplus 1000
Effects of Government Deficit on Current Account Deficit 1000
Does the Current Account Deficit Matter? 1000
Is Canada Borrowing for Consumption or Investment? 1000

Foreign Exchange and the Dollar 1001
Foreign Exchange Regimes 1001
Recent Exchange Rate History 1003

Exchange Rate Determination 1004
The Quantity of Dollars 1004
The Demand for Dollars 1004
Changes in the Demand for Dollars 1005
The Supply of Dollars 1006
Changes in the Supply of Dollars 1006
The Market for Dollars 1007
Why Is the Exchange Rate So Volatile? 1009

Exchange Rate, Prices, and Interest Rates 1011
Arbitrage 1011
Purchasing Power Parity 1012
Interest Rate Parity 1012
A World Market 1013
Monetary Independence 1013

READING BETWEEN THE LINES
DEFENDING THE DOLLAR 1014

PART 14

GROWTH, DEVELOPMENT, AND REFORM
TALKING WITH JEFFREY SACHS **1020**

CHAPTER 37 GROWTH AND DEVELOPMENT 1024

Feed the World **1025**

The International Distribution of Income 1026
    Poorest Countries **1026**
    Developing Countries **1026**
    Newly Industrialized Countries **1026**
    Industrial Countries **1026**
    Oil-Rich Countries **1026**
    Communist and Former Communist
        Countries **1026**
    The World Lorenz Curve **1027**

Growth Rates and Income Levels 1028

Resources, Technological Progress, and Economic Growth 1029
    Capital Accumulation **1029**
    Technological Change **1030**

Obstacles to Economic Growth 1032
    Absence of Property Rights and the Rule of
        Law **1032**
    Rapid Population Growth **1032**
    Low Saving Rate **1033**
    Heavy International Debt Burden **1034**
    The Underdevelopment Trap **1035**

Overcoming the Obstacles to Economic Development 1035
    Establishment of Property Rights and the Rule
        of Law **1035**
    Population Control **1035**
    Foreign Aid **1035**
    Removal of Trade Restrictions **1036**
    Aggregate Demand Stimulation **1036**

CHAPTER 38 ECONOMIC SYSTEMS IN TRANSITION 1041

The Market Bandwagon **1042**

The Economic Problem and Its Alternative Solutions 1043
    Alternative Economic Systems **1043**
    Alternative Systems Compared **1045**

Economic Change in the Former Soviet Union 1048
    History of the Soviet Union **1048**
    Soviet–Style Central Planning **1048**
    The Market Sector **1050**
    Money in the Soviet Union **1050**
    Soviet Union Decline **1050**
    Transition from Investment to Consumption
        Economy **1050**
    Map of Eastern Europe and the former Soviet
        Union **1052**
    Living Standards in the Late 1980s **1054**
    Market Economy Reforms **1054**
    Transition Problems **1054**

Economic Transition in Eastern Europe 1058
    East Germany **1059**
    Czech Republic, Slovakia, Hungary, and
        Poland **1059**

Economic Transition in China 1060
    The Great Leap Forward **1060**
    The 1978 Reforms **1060**
    Map of China **1062**
    China's Success **1064**
    Growing Out of the Plan **1065**

The Transition from Central Plan to Market 1068
    Styles of Market Economy **1068**
    The Sequence of Reform **1069**
    The Speed of Reform **1070**

OUR ADVANCING KNOWLEDGE
UNDERSTANDING THE LIMITS OF CENTRAL
    PLANNING **1056**

READING BETWEEN THE LINES
SUCCESS AND FAILURE IN EASTERN EUROPE **1066**

GLOSSARY 1073
INDEX 1080

PART 1

INTRODUCTION

Talking with Robert Solow

Robert M. Solow was born in New York City in 1924. He was an undergraduate and graduate student at Harvard University, where he obtained his Ph.D. in 1951. Professor Solow is an Institute Professor at MIT and has received all the honours possible for his outstanding contributions, including the John Bates Clark Medal (awarded to the best economist under 40) in 1961, President of the Econometrics Society, and President of the American Economics Association. In 1987, he was awarded the Nobel Memorial Prize in Economics. Professor Solow has studied a wide range of problems, including the links between unemployment and inflation, the theory of long-run economic growth, and the role of nonrenewable natural resources. Michael Parkin talked with Professor Solow about some of these issues and the economic landscape of the 1990s.

Professor Solow, why and how did you get into economics?

I grew up during the Depression of the 1930s and went to college in 1940 just before the outbreak of the Second World War. Our economy and our society were functioning badly, so it was hard *not* to be interested in economics. As a freshman and sophomore, I studied a little of all the social sciences. Then I joined the Army. When I came back to the university, I had to choose an area of study. I chose economics because it combined analytical precision with a focus on what seemed the central social problems.

Today there is a lot of anxiety about the prospects for income growth in the United States in the 1990s. Is the anxiety justified?

There is plenty of reason to be anxious about growth income in the 1990s. You only have to look at the 1970s and 1980s to understand why. So far nothing has happened to suggest that the near stagnation of the past two decades will give way to something better. There are no signs of greater investment and no particular reasons to expect the rate of

> "It is a fantasy. . .that a handful of space-age engineers simply have to apply themselves. . .to revolutionize civilian technology."

technological progress to improve. Perhaps we will be able to release much of the first-class science and engineering talent that has been used in weapons systems and divert it to advancing civilian technology. But that hasn't happened yet; and when it does happen, there will not be some instantaneous golden age. Good people will eventually produce good results, but it is a fantasy to believe that a handful of space-age engineers simply have to apply themselves in order to revolutionize civilian technology. They will have some old habits to unlearn and new ones to acquire. My guess is that we will scrape along in the 1990s.

Does the same prediction hold true for jobs in the 1990s?

Jobs present an altogether more complicated question. An economy can grow slowly and generate plenty of jobs, and I expect that our economy will do so. There is a lot of talk about whether it will produce "good" jobs. In a sense, the answer is no, if by good jobs one means jobs with good wages and rising wages. On average, income will follow productivity. For example, if productivity rises only very slowly, then incomes will also rise only very slowly on

the average. I doubt that the range of unemployment rates will be very different from the recent past. So there will be about the usual number of jobs, paying about what productivity will permit.

Remember that it is not quite right to speak of "jobs" as if they are all the same. In the 1980s, Americans with good education and advanced skills did well, even if not quite as well as earlier. It is the uneducated with limited skills who find themselves falling behind, forced to compete with low-wage labour elsewhere.

Does creating jobs inevitably create more inflation? Or can we have steady growth *and* stable prices?

We can probably have reasonably steady growth and reasonably stable prices. The harder question is whether we can do it with a low unemployment rate. I am something of a pessimist here. It seems to me that no one has yet found a way to achieve price stability in an economy that runs along with very little unemployment and excess industrial capacity. Japan may be an exception, but I don't pretend to understand how the Japanese economy works in this respect. Anyway, there is no guarantee that the Japanese secret, if

there is one, could be transferred elsewhere. The tendency of modern macroeconomics is to define the problem away, I fear: "low unemployment" *is* whatever is compatible with stable prices. To my mind, the "natural rate of unemployment" is an analytically and empirically flimsy concept. There is room for different models of the way the labour market works, with quite different implications for the understanding of inflation. This is an active subject of research right know.

How should we view international competition from Japan?

I think there are two sides to the Japan problem. The important thing to keep in mind is that no one is forced to buy a Japanese car or VCR. Many Americans do so because they prefer the combination of price and quality. North American manufacturing can get a lot better. It has already started to do so. From that point of view, competition from Japan and Europe is a good thing. Eliminate it and there is danger that our own producers will backslide. Between exchange rate movements and productivity improvements at home, we will come to an equilibrium.

I also think that evidence

> " The various scenarios in which the world economy runs out of resources and then falls into a tailspin are neither valid nor helpful."

suggests that the Japanese do not play completely by the free-trade rules. I suspect that Japanese institutions, policies, and habits contribute to the large Japanese trade surplus. Of course, a country that saves a lot more than it can invest at home is bound to have a current-account surplus. We should keep pressuring Japan, hard, to abide by the norms. But we would not kid ourselves: the main part of the problem and its solution lie at home.

Has the federal government deficit got in the way of using tax cuts to stimulate our economy?

It certainly has. You can make a case that the Reagan administration intended the massive tax cuts of 1981–1983 to do just that, to leave the federal government without the resources to undertake any positive action at all. There is no doubt that the Congress today feels that there is no elbow room. Some may think that was a good idea. I have no doubt that micromanagement by government is a loser. But I think that passive macroeconomic policy will occasionally get us what we have now—three years of stagnation, apparently to be followed by a period of weak growth.

What is an appropriate goal of macroeconomic policy?

Prolonged budget deficits that persist even when the economy is doing well present a real problem. They are a drain on the national saving, and they imply some combination of low investment and large current-account deficits. So it should be a goal of macroeconomic policy to move towards budget balance or even a surplus, depending on how much we value investment and growth compared with current consumption. But when the economy is weak, when there is plenty of idle labour and capacity, the situation is different. There is no need for investment to displace consumption. There is room for both, and consumption spending stimulates investment. Both fiscal and monetary policy stimuli would be a good thing, even at the expense of a temporary increase in the deficit.

Are there any limits to economic growth? Are we going to run Spaceship Earth out of fuel?

Finding a route to sustainable growth or sustainable development or even to a sustainable state will not be easy. First of all, I think the various scenarios in which the world economy runs out of resources and then falls

> "**I**t may be a mistake to think in terms of Great Unsolved Problems and Sensational Breakthroughs."

into a tailspin are neither valid nor helpful. My reading is that they are poor science and poor economics. We are more likely to experience rising costs of fuel and materials than to run out. We simply cannot know what tastes and technology will be like 50 or 100 years from now.

There are, however, plenty of things that people and policy should be concerned with now. Ensure that full environmental costs are reckoned into economic decision making. Impose the taxes or regulations that are needed for efficient long-run use of fish stocks and other renewable resources. Subsidize scientific and technological research that can find or create new materials and energy sources. Help and induce poor countries to control their populations. I really don't think that Doomsday scenarios move us in these directions.

What are the most important economic questions that have not been answered and that the next generation of economists will work on and possibly solve?

It may be a mistake to think in terms of Great Unsolved Problems and Sensational Breakthroughs. Instead, the next generation of economists would be wise to direct themselves towards slowly coming to understand the way the economy works. I have already mentioned the behaviour of the labour market as a fertile field for research: flows into and out of employment, how they and the stocks of employed and unemployed workers relate to the level of wages. Those are traditional questions. But more and more data accumulate, and models are improved. A lot of purely techni-

cal finger exercises get done on the way.

Another, less traditional, set of questions emerges from growth theory. Once upon a time, it was customary to treat technological change as exogenous. No one believed that, of course, but economics seemed to have little to say about the pace and direction of invention and innovation. It is now fashionable to go a step further and try to understand the allocation of resources to research and development and the payoff to resources invested. It is far from clear that this work will get very far. But it is obviously important, so the effort has to be made.

How would you advise a student to prepare for a career in economics today? What subjects are the most important to study while an undergraduate? Math? History? Politics?

Certainly an undergraduate interested in economics has no choice but to learn a little mathematics. Better to get it done before graduate school. Then some probability, statistics, and econometrics. Those are indispensable research tools. Then what? Almost anything, I would say. These days you meet too many economists who don't seem to know anything else—not history, not literature, not anything. I think anyone would be a better economist for knowing that there are other things in the world. My own favourite, I will admit, is history, especially social history and economic history. What I am hoping for is some grasp of the many ways in which people have managed to organize themselves and their societies, to give some insight into our own.

CHAPTER 1

WHAT IS ECONOMICS?

After studying this chapter, you will be able to

◆ State the kinds of questions that economics tries to answer

◆ Explain why all economic questions and economic activity arise from scarcity

◆ Explain why scarcity forces people to make choices

◆ Define opportunity cost

◆ Describe the function and the working parts of an economy

◆ Distinguish between positive and normative statements

◆ Explain what is meant by an economic theory and how economic theories are developed by building and testing economic models

F YOU WANTED TO WATCH A MOVIE IN YOUR HOME IN 1975, you had to rent a movie projector and screen—as well as the movie itself. The cost of such entertainment was as high as that incurred by a theatre showing the same movie to several hundred people. Only the rich chose to watch movies in the comfort of their own homes ◆ ◆ In 1976, the video cassette recorder (VCR) became available to consumers. Its typical price tag was $2,000 ($4,000 in today's dollars). Even at such a high price, the VCR slashed the cost of home movie watching. Since that time, the price of VCRs has steadily fallen, so that today you can buy a reliable machine for $200. A video can be rented for $1.00 a day and can be bought for less than $30. In just a few years, watching a movie at home has changed from a luxury available to the richest few to an event enjoyed by millions.

Choice and Change

◆ ◆ Advances in technology affect the way we consume. We now watch far more movies at home than we did a decade ago because new technologies have lowered the cost. ◆ ◆ We hear a great deal these days about lasers. Their most dramatic use is in weapon systems such as those used in "Desert Storm" in 1991. But lasers affect us every day: they scan prices at the supermarket checkout; they create holograms on credit cards, making them harder to forge; neurosurgeons and eye surgeons use them in our hospitals. These advances in technology affect the way we produce.

Ever-changing technology raises the first big economic question:

How do people choose what to consume and how to produce, and how are these choices affected by the discovery of new technologies?

Wages and Earnings

On a crisp, bright winter day on the ski slopes at Banff, a bronzed 23-year-old instructs some beginning skiers in the snowplow turn. For this pleasant and uncomplicated work, the young man, who quit school after grade 11, is paid $10 an hour.

In a lawyer's office in the centre of a busy city, a 23-year-old secretary handles a large volume of correspondence, filing, scheduling, and meetings. She arrives home most evenings exhausted. She has a bachelor's degree in English and has taken night courses in computer science and word processing. She receives $8 an hour for her work.

On July 3, 1993, Steffi Graf and Jana Novotna played a superb tennis match in the final at Wimbledon. At the end of the hard-fought match, the winner, Steffi Graf, received almost $540,000; Jana Novotna collected only half that amount. A similar phenomenon can be seen in the headquarters of large corporations. Chief executive officers who work no harder (and in some cases even less hard) than the people immediately beneath them receive far higher salaries than their subordinates.

Situations like these raise the second big economic question:

What determines people's incomes, and why do some people receive much larger rewards than others whose efforts appear to be similar?

Government, Environment, and Economic Systems

At the beginning of this century, government economic activity was limited to little more than providing law and order. Over the years, the scope of government has expanded to include the provision of health care, social insurance, education, national defence, equalization payments to the provinces, the regulation of food and drug production, nuclear energy, and agriculture.

Also, over the years, we've become more aware of our fragile environment. Chlorofluorocarbons (CFCs), used in a wide variety of products from coolants in refrigerators and air conditioners to plastic phones and cleaning solvents for computer circuits, are believed to damage the atmosphere's protective ozone layer. Burning fossil fuels—coal and oil—adds carbon dioxide and other gases to the atmosphere, which prevents infrared radiation from escaping, resulting in what has been called the "greenhouse effect."

We've been hearing a lot recently about alternative economic systems and the proper role of government in economic life. The former Soviet Union and the countries of Eastern Europe are shaking off decades of central economic planning and public ownership of their farms and factories. Bit by bit, they are moving towards the type of economic system and organization that is familiar to us in Canada—an economic system in which the government does not plan all the details of what is produced and does not own the nation's farms and factories. Instead, each individual farmer and business owner decides what to produce and seeks out the best profit opportunities.

These facts about government, the environment, and the dramatic changes taking place in Eastern Europe raise the third big economic question:

What is the most effective role for government in economic life, and can government help us protect our environment and do as good a job as private enterprise at producing goods and services?

Unemployment

During the Great Depression, the four years from 1929 to 1933, unemployment afflicted almost one-fifth of the labour force in the industrial world. For months and in some cases years on end, many families had no income other than meagre payments from the government or from private charities. In the 1950s and 1960s, unemployment rates stayed below 5 percent in most industrialized countries. During the 1970s and early 1980s, unemployment steadily increased so that by 1983 almost 12 percent of the Canadian labour force was looking for work. The Canadian unemployment rate fell to 7.5 percent during the 1980s but increased again to almost 12 percent in 1992.

Unemployment hurts different groups unequally. When the average unemployment rate in Canada was 11.8 percent in 1992, the unemployment rate among young people 15 to 24 years old was close to 20 percent. The unemployment rate has a regional variation as well, being especially high in Newfoundland and the Maritimes. These facts raise the fourth big economic question:

What are the causes of unemployment, and why are some groups more severely affected than others?

Inflation

Between August 1945 and July 1946, prices in Hungary rose by an average of 20,000 percent per month. In the worst month, July 1946, they rose 419 quadrillion percent (a quadrillion is the number 1 followed by 15 zeros).

In 1985, the cost of living in Bolivia rose by 11,750 percent. This meant that in downtown La Paz a McDonald's hamburger that cost 20 bolivianos on January 1 cost 2,370 bolivianos by the end of the year. That same year, prices rose only 2.9 percent in Canada. But in the late 1970s, prices in Canada were rising at a rate well in excess of 10 percent a year. These facts raise the fifth big economic question:

Why do prices rise, and why do some countries sometimes experience rapid price increases while others have stable prices?

International Trade

In the 1960s, almost all the cars and trucks on the highways of Canada and the United States were Fords, Chevrolets, and Chryslers. By the 1980s, Toyotas, Hondas, Volkswagens, and BMWs were a common sight. In fact, in 1990, more than one-third of all new cars sold in North America were imported, compared with less than 1 percent in 1950.

Cars are not exceptional. The same can be said of television sets, clothing, and computers.

Governments regulate international trade in cars and in most other commodities. They impose taxes on imports, called tariffs, and also establish quotas, which restrict the quantities that may be imported. These facts raise the sixth big economic question:

What determines the pattern and the volume of trade between nations, and what are the effects of tariffs and quotas on international trade?

Wealth and Poverty

At the mouth of the Pearl River in southeast China is a small rocky peninsula and a group of islands with virtually no natural resources. But this bare land supports more than 5 million people who, though not excessively rich, live in rapidly growing abundance. They produce much of the world's fashion goods and electronic components. They are the people of Hong Kong.

On the eastern edge of Africa bordering the Red Sea, a tract of land a thousand times larger supports a population of 34 million people—only seven times that of Hong Kong. Its people suffer such abject poverty that in 1985 rock singers from Europe and North America organized one of the most spectacular worldwide fund-raising efforts ever seen—Live Aid—to help them. These are the desperate and dying people of Ethiopia.

Hong Kong and Ethiopia, two extremes in income and wealth, are not isolated examples. The poorest two-thirds of the world's population consumes less than one-fifth of all things produced. A middle income group accounts for almost one-fifth of the world's population and consumes almost one-fifth of the world's output. A further one-fifth of the world's population—living in rich countries such as Canada, the United States, Western Europe, Japan, Australia, and New Zealand—consumes two-thirds of the world's output.

These facts raise the seventh big economic question:

What causes differences in wealth among nations, making the people in some countries rich and those in other countries poor?

These seven big questions provide an overview of economics. They are *big* questions for two reasons. First, they have an enormous influence on the quality of human life. Second, they are hard questions to answer. They generate passionate argument and debate, and just about everybody has an opinion about them. One of the hardest things for students of economics, whether beginners or seasoned practitioners, is to stand clear of the passion and emotion and to approach their work with the detachment, rigour, and objectivity of a scientist.

Later in this chapter we'll explain how economists try to find answers to economic questions. But before doing that, let's go back to the big questions. What do these questions have in common? What makes them *economic* questions? What distinguishes them from non-economic questions?

Scarcity

All economic questions arise from a single and inescapable fact: you can't always get what you want. We live in a world of scarcity. An economist defines **scarcity** to mean that wants always exceed the resources available to satisfy them. A child wants a 75¢ can of soft drink and a 50¢ pack of gum but has only $1.00 in her pocket. She experiences scarcity. A student wants to go to a party on Saturday night but also wants to spend that same night catching up on late assignments. He also experiences scarcity. Rich and poor alike face scarcity. The government of Canada with its $120 billion budget faces scarcity. The total amount that the government wants to spend on defence, health, education, welfare, and other services exceeds what it collects in taxes. Even parrots face scarcity—there just aren't enough crackers to go around.

Wants do not simply exceed resources; they are unlimited. People want good health and a long life, material comfort, security, physical and mental recreation and, finally, an awareness and understanding of themselves and their environment.

None of these wants is satisfied for everyone; everyone has some unsatisfied wants. While many Canadians have all the material comforts they want, many do not. No one feels entirely satisfied with his or her state of health and length of life. No one feels entirely secure, even in this post-Cold War era, and no one—not even the wealthiest person—has the time to enjoy all the travel, vacations, and art that he or she would like. Not even the wisest and most knowledgeable philosopher or scientist knows as much as he or she would like to know.

We can imagine a world that satisfies people's wants for material comfort and, perhaps, even security. But we cannot imagine a world in which people live as long and in as good a state of health as they would like. Nor can we imagine people having all the time, energy, and resources to enjoy all the sports, travel, vacations, and art that they would like. Natural resources and human resources—in the form of time, muscle-power, and brain-power—as well as all the dams, highways, buildings, machinery, tools, and other equipment that have been created by past human efforts amount to an enormous heritage, but they are limited. Our unlimited wants will always outstrip the limited resources available to satisfy them.

Economic Activity

The confrontation of unlimited wants with limited resources results in economic activity. **Economic activity** is what people do to cope with scarcity. **Economics** is the study of how people use their limited resources to try to satisfy unlimited wants. Defined in this way, economic activity and economics deal with a wide range of issues and problems. The seven big questions posed earlier are examples of the more important problems economists study. Let's see how those questions could not arise if resources were infinitely abundant and scarcity did not exist.

With unlimited resources, there would be no need to devise better ways of producing more goods. Studying how we all spend our time and expend our efforts would not be interesting because we would simply do what we enjoyed without restriction. We would do only what we enjoyed because there would be enough goods and services to satisfy everyone without effort. Unemployment would not be an issue because no one would work—except for people who worked simply for the pleasure it gave them. There would be no wages. Inflation—rising prices—would not be a problem because no one would care about prices. Questions about government intervention in

"Not only do I want a cracker—we all want a cracker!"

Drawing by Modell; © 1985 The New Yorker Magazine, Inc.

economic life would not arise because there would be no need for government-provided goods and no taxes. We would simply take whatever we wanted from the infinite resources available. There would be no international trade since, with complete abundance, it would be pointless to transport things from one place to another. Finally, differences in wealth among nations would not arise because we would all have as much as we wanted. There would be no such thing as rich and poor countries—all countries would be infinitely wealthy.

You can see that this science fiction world of complete abundance would give rise to no economic questions. It is the universal fact of scarcity that produces economic questions.

Choice

Faced with scarcity, people must make *choices*. When we cannot have everything we want, we must choose among the available alternatives. Because scarcity forces us to choose, economics is sometimes called the science of choice—the science that explains the choices people make and predicts how changes in circumstances affect these choices.

To make a choice, we balance the benefits of having more of one thing against the costs of having less of something else. Balancing benefits against costs and doing the best within the limits of what is possible is called **optimizing**. There is another word that has a similar meaning—*economizing*. **Economizing** is making the best use of the resources available. Once people have made a choice and have optimized, they cannot have more of *everything*. Having more of one thing means having less of something else. Expressed in another way: in making choices, we face costs. Whatever we choose to do, we could always have chosen to do something else instead.

Opportunity Cost

Economists use the term "opportunity cost" to emphasize that making choices in the face of scarcity implies a cost. The **opportunity cost** of any action is the best alternative forgone. If you cannot have everything you want, then you have to choose among the alternatives. The best thing that you choose not to do—the forgone alternative—is the cost of the thing that you choose to do.

Dollar Cost We often express opportunity cost in terms of dollars, but this is just a convenient unit of measure. The dollars spent on a book are not available for spending on a compact disc (CD). The opportunity cost of the book is not the dollars spent on it but the CD forgone.

Time Cost The opportunity cost of a good includes the value of the time spent obtaining it. If it takes an hour to visit your dentist, the value of that hour must be added to the amount you pay your dentist. We can convert time into a dollar cost by using a person's hourly wage rate. If you take an hour off work to visit your dentist, the opportunity cost of that visit (expressed in units of dollars) is the amount you paid to your dentist plus the wages you lost by not being at work. Again, it's important to keep reminding yourself that the opportunity cost is not the dollars involved but the goods you could have bought with those dollars.

External Cost Not all of the opportunity costs you incur are the result of your own choices. Sometimes others make choices that impose opportunity costs on you, and your own choices can impose opportunity costs on others. For example, when you take a ride in a bus, train, or car, part of the opportunity cost (borne by others) of the ride is the increased carbon dioxide in the atmosphere resulting from the burning of fuel used to power the bus, train, or car.

Best Alternative Forgone It's important, in measuring opportunity cost, to value only the *best* alternative forgone. To make this clear, consider the following example: You are to attend a lecture at 8:30 on Monday morning. There are two alternatives to attending this lecture: staying in bed for an hour or going jogging for an hour. You cannot stay in bed *and* go jogging for that same hour. The opportunity cost of attending the lecture is not the cost of an hour in bed *and* the cost of jogging for an hour. If these are the only two alternatives that you would contemplate, then you have to decide which one you would do if you did not go to the lecture. For a jogger, the opportunity cost of attending a lecture is an hour of exercise; for a sleeper, the opportunity cost of attending a lecture is an hour in bed.

Scarcity implies cost—opportunity cost. It also implies one other fundamental feature of human life—competition.

Competition and Cooperation

Competition   If wants exceed resources, wants must compete against each other for what is available. **Competition** is a contest for command over scarce resources. In the case of the child with $1.00 who wants a soft drink and gum that add up to $1.25, the soft drink and gum compete for the $1.00 in her pocket. For the student who has allowed assignments to accumulate, the party and the assignments compete with each other for his Saturday night. For the government, defence and social services compete with each other for limited tax dollars.

Scarcity also implies competition among people. Because it is not possible to have everything you want, you must compete with others for what is available. In modern societies, competition has been organized within a framework of almost universally accepted rules that have evolved. This evolution of rules is itself a direct response to the problem of scarcity. Not all societies, even modern societies, employ identical rules to govern competition. For example, the way economic life is organized in Canada differs greatly from the way it is organized in the former Soviet Union. In Chapter 38, we examine these differences and compare alternative economic systems. For now, we will restrict our attention to the rules that govern competition in Canada.

A key rule of economic competition in Canada is that people own what they have acquired through voluntary exchange. People can compete with each other by offering more favourable exchanges—for example, selling something for a lower price or buying something for a higher price. But they cannot compete with each other by simply taking something from someone else.

Cooperation   Perhaps you are thinking that scarcity does not make competition inevitable and that cooperation would better solve economic problems. **Cooperation** means working with others to achieve a common end. If instead of competing with each other we cooperated, wouldn't that solve our economic problems? Unfortunately, cooperation does not eliminate economic problems, because it does not eliminate economic scarcity. But cooperation is part of the solution to scarcity. We cooperate, for example, when we agree to rules of the game that limit competition to avoid violence and when we agree to participate in an economic system based on the rule of law and voluntary exchange.

Examples of solving economic problems through cooperation abound. Marriage partners cooperate. Most forms of business also entail cooperation. Workers cooperate with each other on the production line; members of a management team cooperate with each other to design, produce, and market their products; management and workers cooperate; business partners cooperate.

Common as it is, cooperative behaviour neither solves the economic problem nor eliminates competition. Almost all cooperative behaviour implies some prior competition to find the best individuals with whom to cooperate. Marriage provides a good example. Although marriage is a cooperative affair, unmarried people compete to find a marriage partner. Similarly, although workers and management cooperate with each other, firms compete for the best workers and workers compete for the best employers. Professionals such as lawyers and doctors compete with each other for the best business partners.

Competition does not end when a partner has been found. Groups of people who cooperate together compete with other groups. For example, although a group of lawyers may have formed a partnership and may work together, they will be in competition with other lawyers.

REVIEW

S carcity is the confrontation of unlimited wants with limited resources. Scarcity forces people to make choices. To make choices, people evaluate the costs of alternative actions. We call these opportunity costs, to emphasize that doing one thing removes the opportunity to do something else. Scarcity also implies that people must compete with each other. Economics studies the activities arising from scarcity. ◆

You now know the types of questions that economists try to answer and that all economic questions and economic activity arise from scarcity. In the following chapters, we are going to study economic activity and discover how a modern economy such as that of Canada works. But first, we need to stand back and take an overview of our economy.

The Economy

What do we mean by "the economy"? And how does an economy work? Rather than try to answer these questions directly, let's begin by asking similar questions about a more familiar subject: What is an airplane? How does an airplane work?

Without delving into the detail that would satisfy an aeronautical engineer, most of us could take a shot at answering these two questions. We would describe an airplane as a flying machine that transports people and cargo. To explain how an airplane works, we would describe its key components—fuselage (or body), wings, and engines, and also perhaps its flaps, rudder, and control and navigation systems. We would also explain that as its powerful engines move the machine forward, its wings create an imbalance in air pressure that lifts it into the air.

This example nicely illustrates four things. First, it is hard to explain what something is without saying what it does. To say that an airplane is a machine does not tell us much. We have to go beyond that and say what the machine is for and how it works.

Second, it is hard to explain how something works without dividing it up into components. Once we have described something in terms of its components, we can explain how those components work and how they interact with each other.

Third, it is hard to explain how something works without leaving out some details. Notice that we did not describe an airplane in all its detail. Instead, we isolated the most important parts in order to explain how the whole works. We did not mention the in-flight movie system, the seat belts, or the colour of the paint on the wings. We supposed that these things were irrelevant to an explanation of how an airplane works.

Fourth and finally, there are different levels to understanding how something works. We gave a superficial account of how an airplane works. An aeronautical engineer would have given a deeper explanation. Experts in the individual components—engines, navigation systems, control systems, and so on—would have given an even more detailed and precise explanation than a general engineer.

Now let's return to the questions about the economy. What is the economy? How does it work?

What Is the Economy?

The **economy** is a mechanism that allocates scarce resources among competing uses. This mechanism achieves three things:

◆ What
◆ How
◆ For whom

1. *What* goods and services will be produced and in *what* quantities? Will more VCRs be made or will more movie theatres be built? Will young professionals vacation in Europe or live in large houses? Will more high performance sports cars or more trucks and station wagons be built?

2. *How* will the various goods and services be produced? Will a supermarket operate with three checkout lines and clerks using laser scanners or six checkout lines and clerks keying in prices by hand? Will workers weld station wagons by hand or will robots do the job? Will farmers keep track of their livestock feeding schedules and inventories by using paper and pencil records or personal computers? Will credit card companies use computers to read charge slips in Toronto or ship paper records to Barbados for hand processing?

3. *For whom* will the various goods and services be produced? The distribution of economic benefits depends on the distribution of income. People with high incomes are able to consume more goods and services than people with low incomes. Who gets to consume what thus depends on income. Will the ski instructor consume more than the lawyer's secretary? Will the people of Hong Kong consume more than the people of Ethiopia?

To understand how an economy works, we must identify its main components and see how they interact with each other. Figure 1.1 shows a picture of the economy. It contains two types of components:

◆ Decision makers
◆ Markets

FIGURE 1.1

A Picture of the Economy

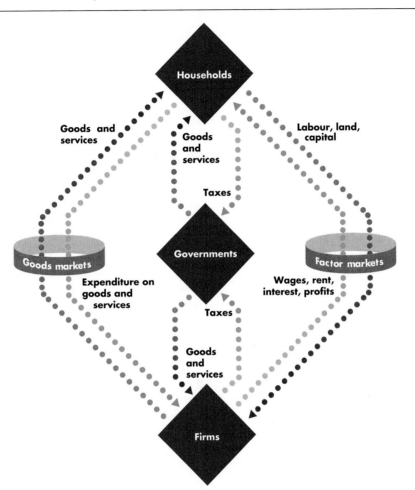

Households, firms, and governments make economic decisions. Households decide how much of their labour, land, and capital to sell or rent in exchange for wages, rent, interest, and profits. They also decide how much of their income to spend on the various types of goods and services available. Firms decide how much labour, land, and capital to hire and how much of the various types of goods and services to produce. Governments decide which goods and services they will provide and the taxes that households and firms will pay.

These decisions by households, firms, and governments are coordinated in markets—the goods markets and factor markets. In these markets, prices constantly adjust to keep buying and selling plans consistent.

Decision Makers

Decision makers are the economic actors. They make the economizing choices. Figure 1.1 identifies three types of decision makers:

1. Households
2. Firms
3. Governments

A **household** is any group of people living together as a decision-making unit. Every individual in the economy belongs to a household. Some households consist of a single person, while others consist either of families or of groups of unrelated individuals, such as two or three students sharing an apartment. Each household has unlimited wants and limited resources.

A **firm** is an organization that uses resources to produce goods and services. All producers are called firms, no matter how big they are or what they produce. Car makers, farmers, banks, and insurance companies are all firms.

A **government** is an organization that provides goods and services and redistributes income and wealth. The most important service provided by government is a framework of laws and a mechanism for their enforcement (courts and police forces). But governments also provide such services as national defence, public health, transportation, and education.

Markets

In ordinary speech, the word *market* means a place where people buy and sell goods such as fish, meat, and fruits and vegetables. In economics, *market* has a more general meaning. A **market** is any arrangement that facilitates buying and selling. An example is the market in which oil is bought and sold—the world oil market. The world oil market is not a place; It is the arena in which the many firms—oil producers, oil users, wholesalers, and brokers—who buy and sell oil interact. In this market, decision makers do not meet physically. They make deals by telephone, fax, and direct computer link.

Figure 1.1 identifies two types of market: goods markets and factor markets. **Goods markets** are those in which goods and services are bought and sold. **Factor markets** are those in which factors of production are bought and sold.

Factors of production are the economy's productive resources. They are classified under three headings:

1. Labour

2. Land

3. Capital

Labour is the brain-power and muscle-power of human beings; **land** includes natural resources of all kinds; **capital** is all the equipment, buildings, tools, and other manufactured goods that can be used in production.

Decisions

Households and firms make decisions that result in the transactions in the goods markets and factor

markets shown in Fig. 1.1. Households decide how much of their labour, land, and capital to sell or rent on factor markets. In return, they receive incomes in the form of wages, interest, and rent. Households also decide how to spend their incomes on goods and services produced by firms.

Firms decide the quantities of factors of production to hire, how to use them to produce goods and services, what goods and services to produce, and in what quantities. They sell their output on goods markets.

The flows resulting from these decisions by households and firms are shown in Fig. 1.1. The red flows are the factors of production that go from households to firms and the goods and services that go from firms to households. The green flows in the opposite direction are the payments made in exchange for these items.

Governments decide what goods and services to provide to households and firms, as well as the rates of taxes that create the funds to pay for them. These activities by governments are also shown in Fig. 1.1.

Coordination Mechanisms

Perhaps the most striking thing about the choices made by households, firms, and governments is that they must surely come into conflict with each other. For example, households choose how much work to do and what type of work to specialize in, but firms choose the type and quantity of labour to employ in the production of various goods and services. In other words, households choose the types and quantities of labour to sell, and firms choose the types and quantities of labour to buy. Similarly, in markets for goods and services, households choose the types and quantities of goods and services to buy, while firms choose the types and quantities to sell. Government choices regarding taxes and the provision of goods and services also enter the picture. Taxes taken by the government affect the amount of income that households and firms have available for spending. Also, decisions by firms and households depend on the types and quantities of goods and services that governments make available. For example, if the government provides excellent highways but a dilapidated railway system, households will allocate more of their income to buying motor vehicles and less to buying train rides.

How is it possible for the millions of individual decisions made by households, firms, and governments to be consistent with each other? What makes households want to sell the same types and quantities of labour that firms want to buy? What happens if the number of households wanting to work as economics professors exceeds the number that universities want to hire? How do firms know what to produce so that households will buy their output? What happens if firms want to sell more hamburgers than households want to buy?

Markets Coordinate Decisions   Markets coordinate individual decisions through price adjustments. To see how, think about the market for hamburgers in your local area. Suppose that the quantity of hamburgers being offered for sale is less than the quantity that people would like to buy. Some people who want to buy hamburgers will not be able to do so. To make the choices of buyers and sellers compatible, buyers will have to scale down their appetites and more hamburgers will have to be offered for sale. An increase in the price of hamburgers will produce this outcome. A higher price will encourage producers to offer more hamburgers for sale. It will also curb the appetite for hamburgers and change some lunch plans. Fewer people will buy hamburgers and more will buy hot dogs (or some other alternative to hamburgers). More hamburgers (and more hot dogs) will be offered for sale.

Now imagine the opposite situation. More hamburgers are available than people want to buy. In this case, the price is too high. A lower price will discourage the production and sale of hamburgers and encourage their purchase and consumption. Decisions to produce and sell, and to buy and consume, are continuously adjusted and kept in balance with each other by adjustments in prices.

In some cases, prices get stuck or fixed. When this happens, some other adjustment has to make the plans and choices of individuals consistent. Customer waiting lines and inventories of goods operate as a temporary safety valve when the market price is stuck. If people want to buy more than the quantity that firms have decided to sell, and if the price is temporarily stuck, then one of two things can happen. Sometimes, firms wind up selling more than they would like and their inventories shrink. At other times, lines of customers develop and only those who get to the head of the line before the goods run out are able to make a purchase. The longer the line or the bigger the decline in inventories, the more prices adjust to keep buying

and selling decisions in balance.

We have now seen how the market determines *what* to produce—how many hamburgers to make. The market also determines *how* to produce. For example, hamburger producers can use gas, electric power, or charcoal to cook their hamburgers. Which fuel is used depends in part on the flavour that the producer wants to achieve and on the cost of the different fuels. If a fuel becomes very expensive, as did oil in the 1970s, less of it is used and more of other fuels are used in its place. By substituting one fuel for another as the costs of the different fuels change, the market determines how to produce.

Finally, the market determines *for whom* to produce. Skills, talents, and resources that are in short supply command a higher price than those in greater abundance. The owners of rare resources and skills obtain a larger share of the output of the economy than the owners of abundant resources.

Alternative Coordination Mechanisms   The market is one of two alternative coordination mechanisms. The other is a command mechanism. A **command mechanism** is a method of determining *what*, *how*, and *for whom* goods and services are produced, using a hierarchical organization structure in which people carry out the instructions given to them. The best example of a hierarchical organization structure is the military. Commanders make decisions requiring actions that are passed down a chain of command. Soldiers on the front line take the actions they are ordered to take.

An economy that relies on a command mechanism is called a **command economy**. Examples of command economies in today's world are those of China, North Korea, Vietnam, and Cambodia. Before they embarked on programs of reform in the late 1980s, the former Soviet Union and other countries of Eastern Europe also had command economies.

In a command economy, a central planning bureau makes decisions about *what*, *how*, and *for whom* goods and services are to be produced. We will study command economies and compare them with other types of economies at the end of our study of economics, in Chapter 38.

An economy that determines *what*, *how*, and *for whom* goods and services are produced by coordinating individual choices through markets is called a **market economy**. But most real-world economies use both markets and commands to coordinate economic activity. An economy that relies on both markets and command mechanisms is called a **mixed economy**.

The Canadian economy relies extensively on the market as a mechanism for coordinating the decisions of individual households and firms. But the Canadian economy also uses command mechanisms. The economy of the armed forces is a command economy. Command mechanisms are also employed in other government organizations and within large firms. There is also a command element in our legal system. By enacting laws and establishing regulations and agencies to monitor the market economy, governments influence the economic decisions of households and firms and change our economic course.

Thus *what*, *how*, and *for whom* goods and services are produced in Canada depend mainly on the market mechanism, but also partly on a command mechanism, so the Canadian economy is a mixed economy.

The Global Economy

The Canadian economy is just one small part of the global economy. In 1992, Canada's 27 million people produced goods and services valued at almost $700 billion. But in the global economy during 1992, some 5 billion people produced goods and services valued at more than $20 trillion. And today, an increasing proportion of each nation's production is exchanged for the production of other nations. Also, nations with a large thirst for capital satisfy that thirst in global capital markets, markets in which funds flow to find the highest available return, with great speed and ease. The world has evolved into a closely integrated economic machine that links the economies of the individual nations.

A national economy, such as that of Canada, is an open economy. An **open economy** is an economy that has trading and financial links with other economies. In the modern world, all the national economies are open economies. But some are more open than others. The Canadian economy is especially open and undertakes a large amount of business with other economies. In contrast to the national economies, the global economy—the aggregate of all the national economies—is a closed economy. A **closed economy** is an economy that has no links with any other economy. It is a closed system.

The economic links between Canada and the rest

FIGURE 1.2

International Linkages

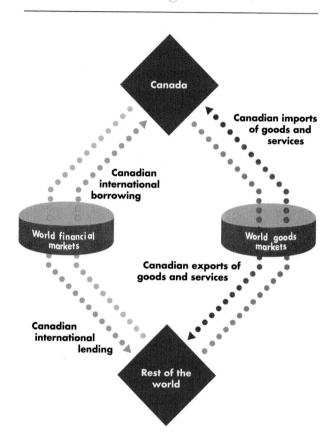

The Canadian economy buys and sells goods and services on world goods markets. What it buys are Canadian imports, and what it sells are Canadian exports. The Canadian economy also borrows from and lends to the rest of the world. These transactions take place on world financial markets.

of the world are illustrated in Fig. 1.2. Firms in the open Canadian economy sell some of their production to the rest of the world. These sales are Canadian exports of goods and services. Also, firms, households, and governments in Canada buy goods and services from firms in other countries. These purchases are Canadian imports of goods and services. Such export and import transactions take place on world goods markets and are illustrated in the figure.

The total values of exports and imports are not

necessarily equal to each other. When Canadian exports exceed Canadian imports, we have a surplus. When Canadian imports exceed Canadian exports, we have a deficit. A country with a surplus lends to the rest of the world; a country with a deficit borrows from the rest of the world. These international lending and borrowing transactions take place on the world financial markets and are also illustrated in Fig. 1.2.

Canada has had an international deficit in recent years. As a consequence, Canada has borrowed from the rest of the world. Other countries, notably those of the European Community and Japan, have international surpluses, and these countries use their surpluses to lend to the rest of the world.

During the 1980s, the global economy became a highly integrated mechanism for allocating scarce resources and deciding *what* will be produced, *how* it will be produced, and *for whom* it will be produced. It is also a mechanism that decides *where* the various goods and services will be produced and consumed.

R E V I E W

An economy is a mechanism that determines what is produced, how it is produced, and for whom it is produced. Choices are made by households, firms, and governments. These choices are coordinated through markets—markets for goods and services and markets for factors of production—or by command mechanisms. The Canadian economy relies mainly on markets but to a degree on command mechanisms. The global economy became increasingly integrated during the 1980s. ◆

We have now described an economy in about as much detail as we described an airplane. But we're about to become the economic equivalent of aeronautical engineers! We're going to build economies that fly! To do that, we have to understand the principles of economics as thoroughly as aeronautical engineers understand the principles of flight. To discover these principles, economists approach their work with the rigour and objectivity of natural scientists—they do economic science.

Economic Science

Economic science, like the natural sciences (such as physics and biology) and the other social sciences (such as political science, psychology, and sociology), is an attempt to find a body of laws or patterns that enable us to make predictions.

All sciences distinguish between two types of statements:

◆ Statements about what *is*
◆ Statements about what *ought* to be

What Is and What Ought to Be

Statements about what *is* are **positive statements**. Statements about what *ought* to be are **normative statements**. Let's illustrate the distinction between positive and normative statements with two examples.

"Our planet is warming because of an increased carbon dioxide buildup in the atmosphere" is a positive statement. "We ought to cut back on our use of carbon-based fuels such as coal and oil" is a normative statement. "Lower taxes and less generous social programs will make people work harder" is a positive statement. "Taxes and social programs should be cut" is a normative statement.

Positive statements can be shown to be wrong. And it is the job of scientists—whether natural, social, or economic—to discover positive statements that are consistent with observations. Normative statements are matters of opinion. You agree or disagree with them. Science is silent on normative questions. It is not that such questions are unimportant. On the contrary, they are often the most important questions of all. Nor is it that scientists as people do not have opinions on such questions. It is simply that the activity of doing science cannot settle a normative matter, and the possession of scientific knowledge does not equip a person with superior morals or norms. A difference of opinion on a positive matter can ultimately be settled by careful observation and measurement. A difference of opinion on a normative matter cannot be settled in that way. We settle normative disagreements in the political and legal arenas, not in the scientific area. The scientific community can, and often does, contribute to the normative debates of political life. And even though scientists have opinions about what ought to be, those opinions have no part in science itself.

Now let's see how economists attempt to discover and catalogue positive statements that are consistent with their observations and that enable them to answer economic questions such as the seven big questions we reviewed earlier.

All sciences share two other features:

◆ Observation and measurement

◆ Creation of theories

Observation and Measurement

Economic phenomena can be observed and measured in great detail. For example, we can catalogue the amounts and locations of natural and human resources. We can describe who does what kind of work, for how many hours, and how they are paid. We can catalogue the things that people produce, consume, and store, and their prices. We can describe in detail who borrows and who lends and at what interest rates. We can also catalogue the things that government taxes and at what rates, the programs it finances and at what cost.

Our list is not exhaustive. It gives a flavour, though, of the array of things that economists can describe through careful observation and measurement of economic activity.

In today's world, computers have given us access to an enormous volume of economic description. Government agencies around the world, national statistical bureaus, private economic consultants, banks, investment advisors, and research economists working in universities generate an astonishing amount of information about economic behaviour.

But economists do more than observe and measure economic activity, crucial as that is. Describing something is not the same as understanding it. You can describe your digital watch in great detail, but that does not mean you can explain what makes it work. Understanding what makes things work requires the discovery of laws. That is the main task of economists—the discovery of laws governing economic behaviour. How do economists go about this task?

Economic Theory

We can describe in great detail the ups and downs, or cycles, in unemployment, but can we explain *why* unemployment fluctuates? We can describe the fall in the price of a VCR or a pocket calculator and the dramatic increase in its use, but can we explain the low price and popularity of such items? Did the fall in the price lead more people to use pocket calculators, or did their popularity lower the costs of production and make it possible to lower the price? Or did something else cause both the fall in the price and the increase in use?

Questions like these can be answered only by developing a body of economic theory. An **economic theory** is a generalization that enables us to understand and predict the economic choices that people make. We develop economic theories by building and testing economic models. What is an economic model?

Economic Model

You have just seen an economic model. To answer the question "What is an economy and how does it work?", we built a model of an economy. We did not describe in detail all the economic activity that takes place in Canada. We concentrated our attention only on those features that seemed important for understanding economic choices, and we ignored everything else. You will perhaps better appreciate what we mean by an economic model if you think about more familiar models.

We have all seen model trains, cars, and airplanes. Although we do not usually call dolls and stuffed animals models, we can think of them in this way. Architects make models of buildings, and biologists make models of DNA (the double helix carrier of the genetic code).

A model is usually smaller than the real thing that it represents, though some models are larger (e.g., the biologist's model of the components of cells). In any case, the scale of a model is not its most important feature. A model shows less detail than its counterpart in reality. For example, all the models we have mentioned resemble the real things in *appearance*, but they are not usually made of the same substance, nor do they work like the real things that they represent. The architect's model of a new high-rise shows us what the building will look like and how it will conform with the buildings around it—but it does not contain plumbing, telephone cables, elevator shafts, air-conditioning plants, and other interior workings.

All the models we have discussed (including those typically used as toys) represent something that is real but they lack some key features, and deliberately so. The model abstracts from the detail of the real thing. It includes only those features needed for the purpose at hand. It leaves out the inessential or unnecessary. What a model includes and what it leaves out is not arbitrary; it results from a conscious and careful decision.

The models that we have just considered are all physical models. We can see the real thing and we can see the model. Indeed, the purpose of each of those models is to enable us to visualize the real thing. Some models, including economic models, are not physical. We cannot look at the real thing and look at the model and simply decide whether the model is a good or bad representation of the real thing. But the idea of a model as an abstraction from reality still applies to an economic model.

An economic model has two components:

◆ Assumptions

◆ Implications

Assumptions form the foundation on which a model is built. They are propositions about what is important and what can be ignored, about what can be treated as being constant and, therefore, reliably used to make predictions. **Implications** are the outcome of a model. The link between a model's assumptions and its implications is a process of logical deduction.

Let's illustrate these components of a model by building a simple model of your daily journey to school. The model has three assumptions:

1. You want to be in class when it begins at 9:00 a.m.

2. The bus ride to school takes 30 minutes.

3. The walk from the bus to class takes 5 minutes.

The implication of this model is that you will be on the bus no later than 8:25 a.m. With knowledge of the bus timetable we could use this model to predict the bus that you catch to school.

The assumptions of a model depend on the model's purpose. The purpose of an economic model is to understand how people make choices in the face of scarcity. Thus, in building an economic model, we abstract from the rich detail of human life and focus only on behaviour that is relevant for coping with scarcity. Everything else is ignored. Economists know that people fall in love and form deep friendships, that they experience great joy and security or great pain and anxiety. But economists assume that in seeking to understand economic behaviour, they may build models that ignore many aspects of life. They focus on one and only one feature of the world: people have wants that exceed their resources and so, by their choices, have to make the best of things.

Assumptions of an Economic Model   Economic models are based on four key assumptions:

1. *People have preferences*. Economists use the term **preferences** to denote likes and dislikes and the intensity of those likes and dislikes. People can judge whether one situation is better, worse, or just as good as another one. For example, you can judge whether, for you, one loaf of bread and no cheese is better, worse, or just as good as half a loaf of bread and 100 grams of cheese.

2. *People are endowed with a fixed amount of resources and technologies that can transform those resources into goods and services*. Economists use the term **endowment** to refer to the resources that people have and the term **technology** to describe the methods of converting those endowments into goods and services.

3. *People economize*. They choose how to use their endowments and technologies in order to make themselves as well-off as possible. Such a choice is called a rational choice. A **rational choice** is one which, among all possible choices, best achieves the goals of the person making the choice. Each choice, no matter what it is or how foolish it may seem to an observer, is interpreted, in an economic model, as a rational choice. Choices are made on the basis of the information available. With hindsight, and with more information, people may well feel that some of their past choices were bad ones. This fact does not make such choices irrational. Again, a rational choice is the best possible course of action, from the point of view of the person making the choice, given

that person's preferences and *given the information available when the choice is made*.

4. *People's choices are coordinated*. One person's choice to buy something must be matched by another person's choice to sell that same thing. One person's choice to work at a particular job must be matched by another person's choice to hire someone to do that job. The coordination of individual choices is made by either a market mechanism or a command mechanism.

Implications of an Economic Model   The implications of an economic model are the equilibrium values of various prices and quantities. An **equilibrium** is a situation in which everyone has economized—that is, all individuals have made the best possible choices in the light of their own preferences and given their endowments, technologies, and information—and in which those choices have been coordinated and made compatible with the choices of everyone else. Equilibrium is the solution or outcome of an economic model.

The term *equilibrium* conjures up the picture of a balance of opposing forces. For example, a balance scale can be said to be in equilibrium if a kilogram of butter is placed on one side of the balance and a one-kilogram weight is placed on the other side. The two masses are exactly equal and so offset each other, leaving the balance arm horizontal. A soap bubble provides another excellent physical illustration of equilibrium. The delicate spherical film of soap is maintained a balance of forces of the air inside the sphere and the air outside it.

This second physical analogy illustrates a further important feature of an equilibrium. An equilibrium is not necessarily static but may be dynamic—constantly changing. By squeezing or stretching the bubble, you can change its shape, but its shape is always determined by the balance of forces acting upon it (including the forces that you exert).

An economic equilibrium has a great deal in common with that of the soap bubble. First, it is in a constant state of motion. At each point in time, each person makes the best possible choice, given the endowments and actions of others. But changing circumstances alter those choices. For example, on a busy day in New York City, there are more cars looking for parking spaces than the number of spaces available. But people do get to park. Individual cars are leaving and arriving at a steady pace. As soon as one car vacates a parking space, another instantly

"And now a traffic update: A parking space has become available on Sixty-fifth Street between Second and Third. Hold it! A bulletin has just been handed me. That space has been taken."

Drawing by H. Martin; © 1987 The New Yorker Magazine, Inc.

fills it. In this situation, the equilibrium number of free spaces is zero. But being in equilibrium does not mean that everyone gets to park instantly. There is an equilibrium amount of time spent finding a vacant space. People hunting for a space are frustrated and experience rising blood pressure and increased anger. But there is still an equilibrium in the hunt for available parking spaces.

Similarly, an economic equilibrium does not mean that everyone is experiencing economic prosperity. The constraints may be such that some people are very poor. Nevertheless, given their preferences, endowments, the available technologies, and the actions of everyone else, each person has made the best possible choice and sees no advantage in modifying his or her current action

Microeconomic and Macroeconomic Models

Economic models fall into two categories: microeconomic and macroeconomic. **Microeconomics** is the branch of economics that studies the decisions of individual households and firms. Microeconomics also studies the way that individual markets work and the detailed way that regulation and taxes affect the allocation of labour and of goods and services.

Macroeconomics is the branch of economics that studies the economy as a whole. It seeks to understand the big picture rather than detailed individual choices. In particular, it studies the determination of the overall level of economic activity—of unemployment, aggregate income, average prices, and inflation.

Of the seven big questions, those dealing with technological change, production and consumption, and wages and earnings are microeconomic. Those dealing with unemployment, inflation, and differences in wealth among nations are macroeconomic.

Model, Theory, and Reality

People who build models often get carried away and start talking as if their model *is* the real world—as if their model is reality. No matter how useful it is, there is no sense in which a model can be said to be reality.

A model is abstract. It lists assumptions and their implications. When economists talk about people who have made themselves as well-off as possible, they are not talking about real people. They are talking about artificial people in an economic model. Do not lose sight of this important but easily misunderstood fact.

Economic theory is the bridge between economic models and the real world. Economic theory is a catalogue of models that seem to work—that seem to enable us to understand and interpret the past and to predict some aspects of the future. Economic theory evolves from a process of building and testing economic models.

To test an economic model, its implications are matched against actual events in the real world. That is, the model is used to make predictions about the real world. The model's predictions may correspond to or be in conflict with the facts. It is by comparing the model's predictions with the facts that we are able to test a model. The process of developing economic theories by using models is illustrated in Fig. 1.3. We begin by building a model. The model's implications are used to generate predictions about the world. These predictions and their testing form the basis of a theory. When predictions are in

FIGURE 1.3

How Theories Are Developed

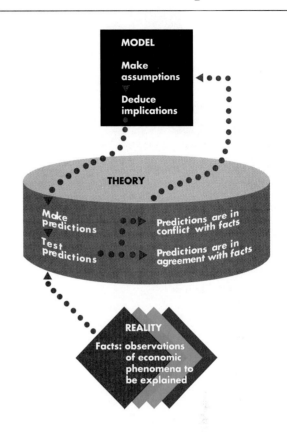

Economic theories are developed by building and testing economic models. An economic model is a set of *assumptions* about what is important and what can be ignored and the *implications* of those assumptions. The implications of a model form the basis of *predictions* about the world. These predictions are tested by being checked against the facts. If the predictions are in conflict with the facts, the model-building process begins again with new assumptions. It is only when predictions are in agreement with the facts that a useful theory has been developed.

conflict with the facts, either a theory is discarded in favour of a superior alternative or we return to the model-building stage, modifying our assumptions and creating a new model. Economics itself provides guidance on how we might discover a better model. It prompts us to look for some aspect of preferences, endowments, technology, or the coordination mechanism that has been overlooked.

UNDERSTANDING the Sources of ECONOMIC WEALTH

In 1776, new technologies were being invented and applied to the manufacture of cotton and wool, iron, transportation, and agriculture in what came to be called the "Industrial Revolution."

Adam Smith was keenly interested in these events. He wanted to understand the sources of economic wealth and he brought his acute powers of observation and abstraction to bear on this question. His answer:

◆ The division of labour

◆ Free domestic and international markets

The division of labour, said Smith, is the source of "the greatest improvement in the productive powers of labour." And he was right. Over the two centuries that followed, the division of labour enabled scientists and engineers to become specialists at inventing. Their powerful skills produced machines that could make consumer goods and other machines far faster than people could make them. And in the twentieth century, this same division of labour enabled us to make machines that perform memory and logical operations faster and more accurately than a large army of human computers.

But, said Smith, the fruits of the division of labour are limited by the extent of the market. To make the market as large as possible, there must be no impediments to free trade both within a country and among countries. Smith argued that when each person makes the best possible economic choice, that choice leads as if by "an invisible hand" to the best outcome for society as a whole.

> "It is not from the benevolence of the butcher, the brewer, or the baker that we expect our dinner, but from their regard to their own interest."
>
> ADAM SMITH
> *The Wealth of Nations*

Adam Smith speculated that one person, working hard, using the hand tools available in the 1770s, might possibly make 20 pins a day. Yet, by using those same hand tools, but breaking the process into a number of individually small operations in which people specialize—by the *division of labour*—he observed that ten people could make a staggering 48,000 pins a day. One draws out the wire, another straightens it, a third cuts it, a fourth points it, a fifth grinds it. Three specialists make the head and a fourth attaches it. Finally, the pin is polished and wrapped in paper.

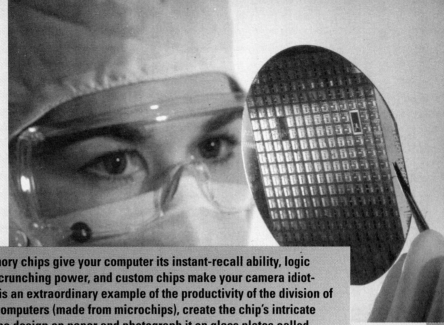

Memory chips give your computer its instant-recall ability, logic chips provide its number-crunching power, and custom chips make your camera idiot-proof. The computer chip is an extraordinary example of the productivity of the division of labour. Designers, using computers (made from microchips), create the chip's intricate circuits. Machines print the design on paper and photograph it on glass plates called masks that work like stencils. Workers prepare silicon wafers on which the circuits are printed. Some slice the wafers, others polish them, others bake them, and yet others coat them with a light-sensitive chemical. Technicians put masks and wafers into a machine that shines light through the mask, imprinting a copy of the circuit onto the wafer. Chemicals eat the unexposed portion of the wafer. A further series of passes through gas-filled ovens deposits atoms that act as transistors. Aluminum is deposited on the wafer to connect the transistors. Finally, a diamond saw or laser separates the hundreds of chips on the wafer.

ADAM SMITH AND **T**HE *Wealth of Nations*

Adam Smith, born in 1723 in Kirkcaldy, a small fishing town near Edinburgh, Scotland, and the only child of the town's customs officer (who died before his son was born), was a giant of a scholar who made extraordinary contributions in ethics and jurisprudence as well as economics.

His first academic appointment, at age 28, was as Professor of Logic at the University of Glasgow. He subsequently became tutor to a wealthy Scottish duke whom he accompanied on a two-year grand European tour, following which he received a pension of £300 a year— ten times the average income at that time.

With the financial security of his pension, Smith devoted ten years to writing the treatise that founded economic science, *An Inquiry into the Nature and Causes of the Wealth of Nations*, which was published to great acclaim in 1776.

Many had written on economic issues before Adam Smith, but it was he who made economics a science. His account of what was then known was so broad and authoritative that no subsequent writer on economics could advance his own ideas while ignoring the state of general knowledge.

Economics is a young science and a long way from having achieved its goal of understanding and explaining economic activity. It began in the eighteenth century with the publication of Adam Smith's *The Wealth of Nations* (see Our Advancing Knowledge, p. 22). In the closing years of the twentieth century, economic science has managed to discover a sizeable number of useful generalizations. In many areas, however, we are still going around the circle—changing assumptions, performing new logical deductions, generating new predictions, and getting wrong answers yet again. The gradual accumulation of correct answers gives most practitioners some faith that their methods will, eventually, provide usable answers to the big economic questions.

As we make progress, more and more pieces of the puzzle seem to fit together. Theoretical advances lead to deeper understanding. This feature of economics is shared by scientists in all fields. As Albert Einstein, the great physicist, said:

Creating a new theory is not like destroying an old barn and erecting a skyscraper in its place. It is rather like climbing a mountain, gaining new and wider views, discovering new connections between our starting point and its rich environment. But the point from which we started still exists and can be seen, although it appears smaller and forms a tiny part of our broad view gained by the mastery of the obstacles on our adventurous way up.[1]

◆ ◆ ◆ ◆ In the next chapter, we will study some of the tools that economists use to build economic models. In Chapter 3, we will build an economic model and use that model to understand the world around us and to start to answer some of the seven big economic questions.

---

[1]These words are attributed to Einstein in a letter by Oliver Sacks to *The Listener* 88, 2279 (November 30, 1972), 756.

S U M M A R Y

Scarcity

All economic questions arise from the fundamental fact of scarcity. Scarcity means that wants exceed resources. Human wants are effectively unlimited but the resources available to satisfy them are finite.

Economic activity is what people do to cope with scarcity. Scarcity forces people to make choices. Making the best choice possible from what is available is called optimizing or economizing. In order to make the best possible choice, a person weighs the costs and benefits of the alternatives—optimizes,

Opportunity cost is the cost of one choice in terms of the best forgone alternative. The opportunity cost of any action is the best alternative action that could have been undertaken in its place. Attending class instead of staying in bed has an opportunity cost—the cost of one hour of rest.

Scarcity forces people to compete with each other for scarce resources. People may cooperate in certain areas, but all economic activity ultimately results in competition among individuals acting alone or in groups. (pp. 9–11)

The Economy

People have unlimited wants but limited resources or factors of production—labour, land, and capital. The economy is a mechanism that allocates scarce resources among competing uses, determining *what*, *how*, and *for whom* the various goods and services will be produced.

The economy's two key components are decision makers and markets. Economic decision makers are households, firms, and governments. Households decide how much of their labour, land, and capital to sell or rent and how much of the various goods and services to buy. Firms decide what factors of production to employ and which goods and services to produce. Governments decide what goods and services to provide to households and firms and how much to raise in taxes.

The decisions of households, firms, and governments are coordinated through markets in which prices adjust to keep buying plans and selling plans consistent. Alternatively, coordination can be achieved by a command mechanism. The Canadian economy relies mainly on markets, but there is a command element in the actions taken by governments that also influences the allocation of scarce resources. The Canadian economy is therefore a mixed economy. (pp. 12–17)

Economic Science

Economic science, like the natural sciences and the other social sciences, attempts to discover a body of laws. Economic science makes only *positive* statements—statements about what is. It does not make *normative* statements—statements about what ought to be. Economists try to find economic laws by developing a body of economic theory, and economic theory, in turn, is developed by building and testing economic models. Economic models are abstract, logical constructions that contain two components: assumptions and implications. An economic model has four key assumptions:

1. People have preferences.
2. People have a given endowment of resources and technology.
3. People economize.
4. People's choices are coordinated through market or command mechanisms.

The implications of an economic model are the equilibrium values of various prices and quantities that result from each individual doing the best that is possible, given the individual's preferences, endowments, information, and technology and given the coordination mechanism. (pp. 17–24)

K E Y   E L E M E N T S

Key Terms

Assumptions, 19
Capital, 14
Closed economy, 16
Command economy, 15
Command mechanism, 15
Competition, 11
Cooperation, 11
Economic activity, 9
Economic theory, 18
Economics, 9
Economizing, 10
Economy, 12
Endowment, 19
Equilibrium, 20
Factor market, 14
Factors of production, 14
Firm, 14
Goods market, 14
Government, 14
Household, 13

Implications, 19
Labour, 14
Land, 14
Macroeconomics, 21
Market, 14
Market economy, 15
Microeconomics, 20
Mixed economy, 16
Normative statement, 17
Open economy, 16
Opportunity cost, 10
Optimizing, 10
Positive statement, 17
Preferences, 19
Rational choice, 19
Scarcity, 9
Technology, 19

Key Figure

Figure 1.1 A Picture of the Economy, 13

R E V I E W   Q U E S T I O N S

1 Give two examples, different from those in the chapter, that illustrate each of the seven big economic questions.

2 Why does scarcity force us to make choices?

3 What do we mean by "rational choice"? Give examples of rational and irrational choices.

4   Why does scarcity force us to economize?

5   Why does optimization require us to calculate costs?

6   Why does scarcity imply competition?

7   Why can't we solve economic problems by cooperating with each other?

8   Name the main economic decision makers.

9   List the economic decisions made by households, firms, and governments.

10   What is the difference between a command mechanism and a market?

11   Distinguish between positive and normative statements by listing three examples of each type of statement.

12   What are the four key assumptions of an economic model?

13   Explain the difference between a model and a theory.

P R O B L E M S

1   You plan to go to school this summer. If you do, you won't be able to take your usual job, which pays $6,000 for the summer, and you won't be able to live at home for free. The cost of your tuition will be $2,000, textbooks $200, and living expenses $1,400. What is the opportunity cost of going to summer school?

2   On Valentine's Day, Bernie and Catherine exchanged gifts: Bernie sent Catherine red roses and Catherine bought Bernie a box of chocolates. They each spent $15. They also spent $50 on dinner and split the cost evenly. Did either Bernie or Catherine incur any opportunity costs? If so, what were they? Explain your answer.

3   Nancy asks Beth to be the maid-of-honour at her wedding. Beth accepts. Which of the following are part of Beth's opportunity cost of being Nancy's maid-of-honour? Explain why they are or are not.

a   The $200 she spent on a new outfit for the occasion

b   The $50 she spent on a party for Nancy's friends

c   The money she spent on a haircut a week before the wedding

d   The weekend visit she missed for her grandmother's seventy-fifth birthday—the same weekend as the wedding

e   The $10 she spent on lunch on the way to the wedding

4   The local mall has free parking, but the mall is always very busy and it usually takes 30 minutes to find a parking spot. Today when you found a vacant spot Harry also wanted it. Is parking really free at this mall? If not, what did it cost you to park today? When you parked your car today did you impose any costs on Harry? Explain your answers.

5   Which of the following statements are positive and which are normative?

a   A cut in wages will reduce the number of people willing to work.

b   High interest rates prohibit many young people from buying their first home.

c   No family ought to pay more than 25 percent of their income in taxes.

d   The government should reduce its expenditure on highways and increase its expenditure on railways.

e   The government ought to supply a medical insurance scheme for everyone free of charge.

6   You have been hired by Soundtrend, a company that makes and markets tapes, records, and compact discs (CDs). Your employer is going to start selling these products in a new region that has a population of 10 million people. A survey has indicated that 50 percent of people buy only popular music, 10 percent buy only classical music, and no one buys both types of music. Another survey suggests that the average income of a pop music fan is $10,000 a year and that of a classical fan is $50,000 a year. Based on a third survey, it appears that, on average, people with low incomes spend one quarter of 1 percent of their income on tapes, records, and CDs, while people with high incomes spend 2 percent of their income on these products.

Build a model to enable Soundtrend to predict how much will be spent on pop music and classical music in this region in one year. In doing so,

a   List your assumptions.

b   Work out the implications of your assumptions.

c   Highlight the potential sources of errors in your predictions.

CHAPTER 2

MAKING AND USING GRAPHS

After studying this chapter, you will be able to

- ◆ Make and interpret a scatter diagram and a time-series graph
- ◆ Distinguish between linear and nonlinear relationships and relationships that have a maximum and a minimum
- ◆ Define and calculate the slope of a line
- ◆ Graph relationships among more than two variables

THERE ARE THREE KINDS OF LIES, SAID BENJAMIN DISRAELI, a nineteenth-century British prime minister: lies, damned lies, and statistics. One of the most powerful ways of conveying statistics is in the form of a graph. And like statistics, graphs can lie. But the right graph does not lie. It reveals a relationship that would otherwise be obscure. ◆ ◆ Graphs are a modern invention. They first appeared in the late eighteenth century, long after the discovery of logarithms and calculus. But today, in the age of personal computer and video display, graphs have become as important as words and numbers. ◆ ◆ How do economists use graphs? What types of graphs do economists use? What do economic graphs reveal and what can they hide? ◆ ◆ It is often said that in economics, everything depends on everything else. Changes in the quantity of ice cream bought are caused by changes in the temperature, the price of cream, and many other factors. How can we make and interpret graphs of relationships of several variables?

Three Kinds of Lies

◆ ◆ ◆ ◆ In this chapter, we look at the kinds of graphs that are used in economics. We are going to learn how to make them and read them. We are going to look at examples of useful graphs as well as misleading graphs. We are also going to study how we can calculate the strength of the effect of one variable on another. ◆ ◆ If you are familiar with graphs, you may want to skip (or skim) this chapter. Whether you study this chapter thoroughly or give it a quick pass, you can use it as a handy reference.

Graphing Data

G raphs represent a quantity as a distance. Figure 2.1 gives two examples. Part (a) shows temperature, measured in degrees Celsius, as the distance on a scale. Movements from left to right represent increases in temperature. Movements from right to left represent decreases in temperature. The point marked zero represents zero degrees Celsius. To the right of zero, the temperatures are positive. To the left of zero, the temperatures are negative (as indicated by the minus sign in front of the numbers).

Figure 2.1(b) provides another example. This time altitude, or height, is measured in thousands of metres above sea level. The point marked zero represents sea level. Points to the right of zero represent metres above sea level. Points to the left of zero (indicated by a minus sign) represent depths below sea level. There are no rigid rules about the scale for a graph. The scale is determined by the range of the variable being graphed and the space available for the graph.

The two graphs in Fig. 2.1 show just a single variable. Marking a point on either of the two scales indicates a particular temperature or a particular height. Thus the point marked a represents 100°C, the boiling point of water. The point marked b represents 6,194 metres, the height of Mount McKinley, the highest mountain in North America.

Graphing a single variable as we have done does not usually reveal much. Graphs become powerful when they show how two variables are related to each other.

Two-Variable Graphs

To construct a two-variable graph, we set two scales perpendicular to each other. Let's use the same two variables as those in Fig. 2.1. We will measure temperature in exactly the same way, but we will turn the height scale to a vertical position. Thus temperature is measured exactly as it was before, but height is now represented by movements up and down a vertical scale.

FIGURE 2.1

FIGURE 2.1

Graphing a Single Variable

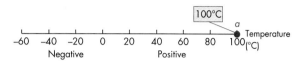

(a) Temperature

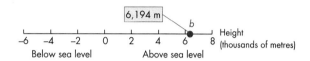

(b) Height

All graphs have a scale that measures a quantity as a distance. The two scales here measure temperature and height. Numbers to the right of zero are positive. Numbers to the left of zero are negative.

The two scale lines in Fig. 2.2 are called **axes**. The vertical line is called the **y-axis** and the horizontal line is called the **x-axis**. The letters x and y appear on the axes of Fig. 2.2. Each axis has a zero point shared by the two axes. The zero point, common to both axes, is called the **origin**.

To represent something in a two-variable graph, we need two pieces of information. For example, Mount McKinley is 6,194 metres high and, on a particular day, the temperature at its peak is –20°C. We can represent this information in Fig. 2.2 by marking the height of the mountain on the y-axis at 6,194 metres and the temperature on the x-axis at –20°C. We can now identify the values of the two variables that appear on the axes by marking point c.

Two lines, called coordinates, can be drawn from point c. **Coordinates** are lines running from a point on a graph perpendicularly to its axis. The line running from c to the x-axis is the **y-coordinate**, because its length is the same as the value marked off on the y-axis. Similarly, the line running from c to the vertical axis is the **x-coordinate**, because its length is the same as the value marked off on the x-axis.

FIGURE 2.2

Graphing Two Variables

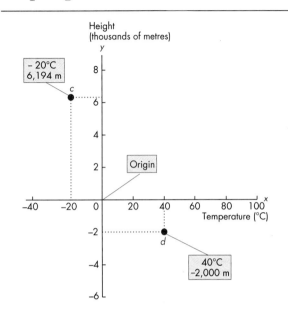

The relationship between two variables is graphed by drawing two axes perpendicular to each other. Height is measured here on the *y*-axis and temperature on the *x*-axis. Point *c* represents the top of Mount McKinley, 6,194 metres above sea level (measured on the *y*-axis), with a temperature of –20°C (measured on the *x*-axis). Point *d* represents the inside temperature in a submarine, 40°C, exploring the depths of an ocean, 2,000 metres below the sea.

Now let's leave the top of Mount McKinley, at 6,194 metres and –20°C, and take a trip on a submarine. You are exploring the depths of the ocean, 2,000 metres below the sea at a sweltering 40°C. You are at point *d* in the figure. Your *y*-coordinate is –2,000 metres and your *x*-coordinate is 40°C.

Economists use graphs similar to this one in a variety of ways. Let's look at two examples.

Scatter Diagrams

Economists use graphs to reveal whether a relationship exists between two economic variables and to describe such a relationship. The most important type of graph used for these purposes is the scatter diagram. A **scatter diagram** plots the value of one economic variable associated with the value of

another. It measures one of the variables on the *x*-axis and the other variable on the *y*-axis.

The Relationship between Consumption and Income
Figure 2.3 uses a scatter diagram to show the relationship between consumption and income. The *x*-axis measures average income, and the *y*-axis measures average consumption. Each point represents average consumption and average income in Canada in a given year between 1977 and 1988. The points for all twelve years are "scattered" within the graph. Each point is labelled with a two-digit number that tells us its year. For example, the point marked 83 tells us that in 1983, average consumption was $8,400 and average income was $15,500.

FIGURE 2.3

A Scatter Diagram: Consumption and Income

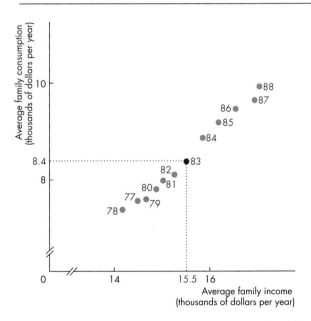

A scatter diagram shows the relationship between two variables. This scatter diagram shows the relationship between average consumption and average income during the years 1977 to 1988. Each point shows the values of the two variables in a specific year and the year is identified by the two-digit number. For example, in 1983 average consumption was $8,400 and average income was $15,500. The pattern formed by the points shows that as income increases, so does consumption.

Figure 2.3 reveals that a relationship *does* exist between average income and average consumption. The pattern formed by the points in Fig. 2.3 tells us that when income increases, consumption also increases.

Breaks in the Axes   Notice that each axis in Fig. 2.3 has a break in it—illustrated by the small gaps. The breaks indicate that there are jumps from the origin, 0, to the first values recorded. The breaks are used because, in the period covered by the graph, average consumption was never less than $7,000 and average income was never less than $14,000. With no breaks in the axes of this graph, there would be a lot of empty space, all the points would be crowded into the top right corner, and we would not be able to see whether a relationship existed between these two variables. By breaking the axes, we are able to bring the relationship into view. In effect, we use a zoom lens to bring the relationship into the centre of the graph and magnify it so that it fills the graph.

The range of the variables plotted on the axes of a graph is an important feature of a graph, and it is a good idea to get into the habit of always looking closely at the values and labels on the axes before you start to interpret a graph.

Other Relationships   Figure 2.4 shows two other scatter diagrams. In part (a), the *x*-axis shows the percentage of households owning a video cassette recorder, and the vertical axis shows its average price. Each point with its two-digit number represents a year. Thus the point marked 81 tells us that the average price of a VCR in 1981 was $600 and that VCRs were owned by 20 percent of all households. The pattern formed by the points in part (a) tells us that as the price of a VCR falls, a larger percentage of households own one.

In Figure 2.4(b), the *x*-axis measures unemployment in Canada, and the *y*-axis measures inflation. Again, each point with its two-digit number represents a year. The point marked 82 tells us that in 1982 unemployment was 11 percent and inflation was 9 percent. The pattern formed by the points in part (b) does not reveal a clear relationship between the two variables. The graph thus informs us, by its lack of a distinct pattern, that there is no relationship between these two variables.

A scatter diagram enables us to see the relationship between two economic variables. But it does

FIGURE 2.4

More Scatter Diagrams

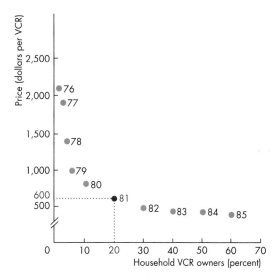

(a) VCR ownership and price

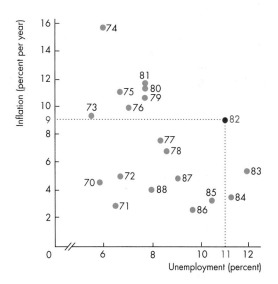

(b) Unemployment and inflation

Part (a) is a scatter diagram showing the relationship between the percentage of households owning a VCR and the average price of a VCR. It shows that as the price of a VCR has fallen, the percentage of households owning a VCR has increased. Part (b) is a scatter diagram showing inflation and unemployment. It shows that there is no clear relationship between these two variables.

not give us a clear picture of how those variables evolve over time. To see the evolution of economic variables, we use a different but common kind of graph—the time-series graph.

Time-Series Graphs

A **time-series graph** measures time (for example, years or months) on the x-axis and the variable or variables in which we are interested on the y-axis.

Figure 2.5 illustrates a time-series graph. Time is measured in years on the x-axis. The variable that we are interested in—the Canadian unemployment rate (the percentage of the labour force unemployed)—is measured on the y-axis. The time-series graph conveys an enormous amount of information quickly and easily:

1. It tells us the *level* of the unemployment rate— when it is *high* and *low*. When the line is a long way from the x-axis, the unemployment rate is high. When the line is close to the x-axis, the unemployment rate is low.

2. It tells us how the unemployment rate *changes*— whether it *increases* or *decreases*. When the line slopes upward, as in the early 1930s, the unemployment rate is increasing. When the line slopes downward, as in the early 1940s, the unemployment rate is decreasing.

3. It tells us the *speed* with which the unemployment rate is *changing*—whether it is increasing or decreasing *quickly* or *slowly*. If the line rises or falls very steeply, then the unemployment rate is changing quickly. If the line is not steep, the unemployment rate is increasing or decreasing slowly. For example, unemployment increased very quickly between 1930 and 1932. Unemployment went up again in 1933 but more slowly. Similarly, when unemployment was decreasing in the 1960s, it fell quickly between 1961 and 1962, but then it began to decrease much more slowly in 1963 and 1964.

FIGURE 2.5

A Time-Series Graph

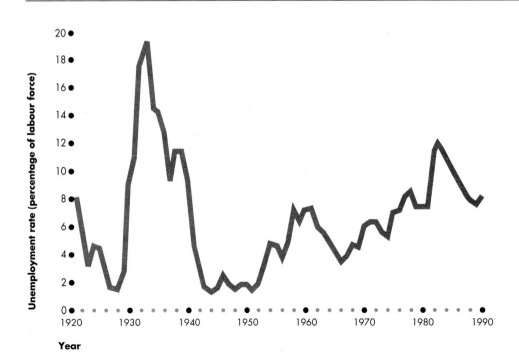

A time-series graph plots the level of a variable on the y-axis against time (day, week, month, or year) on the x-axis. This graph shows the Canadian unemployment rate each year from 1921 to 1990.

A time-series graph can also be used to depict a trend. A **trend** is a general tendency for a variable to rise or fall. You can see that unemployment had a general tendency to increase from the mid-1940s to the mid-1980s. That is, although there were ups and downs in the unemployment rate, there was an upward trend.

Graphs also allow us to compare different periods quickly. It is apparent, for example, that the 1930s were different from any other period in the twentieth century because of exceptionally high unemployment.

Thus we can see that Fig. 2.5 conveys a wealth of information, and it does so in much less space than we have used to describe only some of its features. Reading Between the Lines on pp. 36-37 shows another example of the power of graphs and their ability to reveal the relationships that might otherwise be obscure.

Misleading Time-Series Graphs   Although time-series graphs are powerful devices for conveying a large amount of information, they can also be used to distort data and to create a misleading picture. The two most commonly used ways of distorting

data are stretching and squeezing the scales on the y-axis and omitting the origin—the zero point—on the y-axis.

Figure 2.6 illustrates the first of these devices. It contains exactly the same information as Fig. 2.5, but the information is packaged in a different way. In part (a) the scale on the y-axis has been compressed; in part (b) it has been expanded. When we look at these two parts as a whole, they suggest that unemployment was pretty stable from 1921 to 1954 but that it has trended upward dramatically in the last 35 years or so.

You might think that this graphical way of distorting data is so outrageous that no one would ever attempt to use it. If you scrutinize the graphs that you see in newspapers and magazines, you will be surprised how common this device is.

Figure 2.7 illustrates the effect of omitting the origin on the y-axis. Sometimes, omitting the origin is precisely the correct thing to do, as it enables the graph to reveal its information. But there are also times when omitting the origin is misleading. In parts (a) and (b), you can see two graphs of the unemployment rate between 1970 and 1990. Part (a) includes the origin, and part (b) does not. The

FIGURE 2.6

Misleading Graphs: Squeezing and Stretching Scales

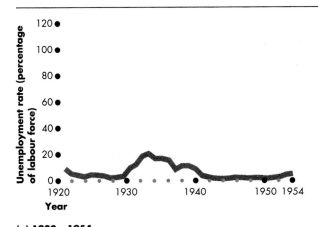

(a) 1920 – 1954

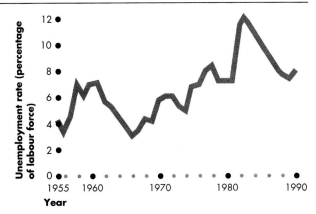

(b) 1955 – 1990

Graphs can mislead by squeezing and stretching the scales. These two graphs show exactly the same thing as Fig. 2.5—Canadian unemployment from 1921 to 1990. Part (a) has squeezed the y-axis, while part (b) has stretched that axis. The result appears to be a low and

stable unemployment rate before 1955 and an increasing, highly volatile unemployment rate after that date. Contrast the lie of Fig. 2.6 with the truth of Fig. 2.5.

graph in part (a) provides a clear account of what happened to unemployment over the time period in question. You can use that graph in the same way that we used Fig. 2.5 to describe all the features of unemployment during that time period. But the

graph in part (b) is less revealing and distorts the picture. It fails to reveal the *level* of unemployment. It focuses only on, and exaggerates, the magnitude of the increases and decreases in its rate. In particular, the increases in the unemployment rate in the

---

FIGURE 2.7

Omitting the Origin

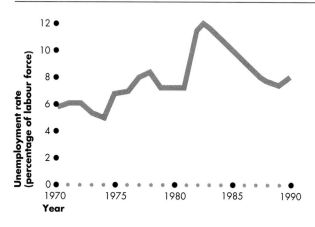

(a) Revealing graph with origin

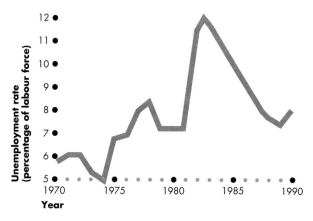

(b) Misleading graph with origin omitted

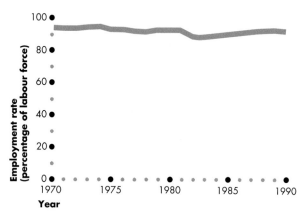

(c) Uninformative graph with origin

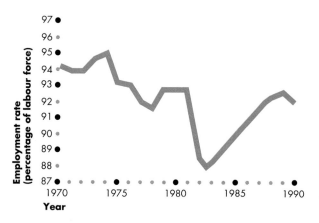

(d) Revealing graph with origin omitted

Sometimes the origin is omitted from a graph. This practice can be either revealing or misleading, depending on how it is used. Parts (a) and (b) graph the Canadian unemployment rate between 1970 and 1990. Part (a) is graphed with the origin and part (b) without it. Part (a) reveals a large amount of information about the level and changes in the unemployment rate over this time period. Part (b) overdramatizes the increases and decreases in unemployment and gives no direct visual information about its level.

Parts (c) and (d) graph the employment rate. Part (c) contains an origin and part (d) does not. In this case, the graph with the origin is uninformative and shows virtually no variation in the employment rate. The graph in part (d) gives a clear picture of fluctuations in the employment rate and is more informative than part (c) about those fluctuations.

late 1970s and early 1980s look enormous when compared with the increases that appear in part (a). By omitting the origin, small percentage changes in unemployment look like many hundredfold changes.

Parts (c) and (d) of Fig. 2.7 graph the employment rate—the percentage of the labour force employed. Part (c) includes the origin, and part (d) omits it. As you can see, the graph in part (c) reveals very little about movements in the employment rate. It seems to suggest that the employment rate was pretty constant, lying between 90 and 95 percent. The main feature of part (c) is an enormous amount of empty space and an inefficient use of the space available. Part (d) shows the same information but with the origin omitted. The scale begins at 90 percent. In this case, we can see very clearly the ups and downs in the employment rate. This graph does not provide a visual impression of the level of employment, but it does provide a clear picture of variations in its rate.

The decision about whether to include or exclude the origin of the graph depends on what the graph is designed to reveal. To convey information about the levels of employment and unemployment and variations in their rates, the graphs in parts (a) and (d) of Fig. 2.7 are almost equally revealing. By comparison, the graphs in parts (b) and (c) convey almost no information.

Comparing Two Time Series   Sometimes we want to use a time-series graph to compare two different variables. For example, suppose you wanted to know how the balance of the government's budget—its surplus or deficit—fluctuated and how those fluctuations compared with fluctuations in the unemployment rate. You can examine two such series by drawing a graph of each of them in the manner shown in Fig. 2.8(a). The scale for the unemployment rate appears on the left side of the figure, and the scale for the government's budget surplus appears on the right. The orange line shows unemployment, and the blue line shows the government's budget. You will probably agree that it is pretty hard work figuring out from Fig. 2.8(a) just what the relationship is between the unemployment rate and the government's budget. But it does look as if there is a tendency for the budget to go into a bigger deficit (blue line goes downward) when the unemployment rate increases (orange line goes upward). In other words, it seems as if these two variables have a tendency to move in opposite directions.

FIGURE 2.8

Time-Series Relationships

(a) Unemployment and budget surplus

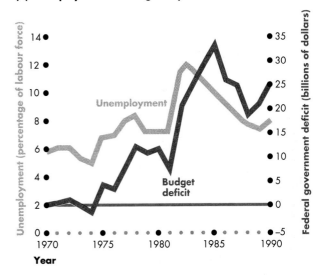

(b) Unemployment and budget deficit

A time-series graph reveals relationships between two variables. These two graphs show the unemployment rate and the balance of the government's budget between 1970 and 1990. The unemployment line is identical in the two parts. In part (a), the budget balance measures surpluses upward and deficits downward (as negative numbers) on the right scale. It looks as if the budget goes into a bigger deficit when unemployment rises. Part (b) inverts the scale on which the budget is measured. Now a deficit is measured in the up direction and a surplus in the down direction on the right scale. The relationship between the budget deficit and unemployment is now easier to see.

Graphs in Action

Home economists at Agriculture Manitoba have kept records for more than ten years on the costs of raising children.

These costs range from $5,818 a year for a 12 year-old girl to $9,679 for a 1 year-old girl.

The detailed costs at each age, for both boys and girls, separated into the costs of food, clothes, health care, personal care, recreation and school, transportation, child care and shelter, are set out in the table accompanying the article.

THE FINANCIAL POST, MARCH 6, 1993

Kids cost a lot, but just how much?

By Bruce Cohen

Any parent will tell you it costs a lot to raise a child. Onalee Nagler, whose daughter is now a second-year university student, can tell you right down to the penny.

Depending on the child's age and sex, that should range this year from at least $5,880.76 to $9,678.67.

Nagler is a Winnipeg-based family-resource management specialist in the home-economics section of Manitoba's Agriculture Ministry. For more than a decade her unit has done detailed family budgeting studies.

THE COST OF RAISING A CHILD

Age	Food Boy	Food Girl	Clothes Boy	Clothes Girl	Health care Boy	Health care Girl	Personal care Boy	Personal care Girl	Recreation/school Boy	Recreation/school Girl	Transportation Boy	Transportation Girl	Child care Boy	Child care Girl	Shelter Boy	Shelter Girl	Total Boy	Total Girl
Infant	1,411	1,411	1,654	1,654	182	182	0	0	0	0	0	0	3,961	3,961	1,800	1,800	9,008	9,008
1	903	903	403	434	182	182	78	78	307	307	0	0	5,825	5,825	1,949	1,949	9,647	9,679
2	973	973	431	449	182	182	78	78	307	307	0	0	4,850	4,850	1,925	1,925	8,746	8,765
3	973	973	431	449	243	243	78	78	307	307	0	0	4,850	4,850	1,902	1,902	8,784	8,802
4	1,326	1,326	430	448	243	243	78	78	307	307	0	0	4,850	4,850	1,902	1,902	9,137	9,154
5	1,326	1,326	430	448	243	243	78	78	388	388	31	31	4,850	4,850	1,902	1,902	9,249	9,266
6	1,326	1,326	633	648	243	243	78	78	499	499	31	31	3,453	3,453	1,902	1,902	8,165	8,180
7	1,436	1,355	633	648	243	243	75	75	707	707	31	31	3,453	3,453	1,902	1,902	8,480	8,414
8	1,436	1,355	633	648	243	243	75	75	707	707	31	31	3,453	3,453	1,902	1,902	8,480	8,414
9	1,436	1,355	659	651	243	243	75	75	707	707	31	31	3,453	3,453	1,902	1,902	8,507	8,417
10	1,618	1,436	659	651	243	243	75	75	707	707	31	31	3,453	3,453	1,902	1,902	8,689	8,499
11	1,618	1,436	659	651	243	243	75	75	707	707	31	31	3,453	3,453	1,902	1,902	8,689	8,499
12	1,618	1,436	986	1,002	243	243	133	236	723	723	276	276	0	0	1,902	1,902	5,881	5,818
13	1,764	1,550	986	1,002	243	243	133	236	723	723	276	276	0	0	1,902	1,902	6,026	5,931
14	1,764	1,550	986	1,002	243	243	133	236	815	815	276	276	0	0	1,902	1,902	6,118	6,023
15	1,764	1,550	957	1,047	243	243	267	293	973	973	276	276	0	0	1,902	1,902	6,381	6,284
16	2,068	1,555	957	1,047	243	243	267	293	973	973	276	276	0	0	1,902	1,902	6,685	6,289
17	2,068	1,555	957	1,047	243	243	267	293	973	973	276	276	0	0	1,902	1,902	6,685	6,289
18	2,068	1,555	957	1,047	243	243	267	293	813	813	276	276	0	0	1,902	1,902	6,525	6,129

Source: Manitoba Agriculture

Background and Analysis

If you study the data in the table closely, you discover that the total cost of raising a child decreases with the age of the child, but the cost of most items rises with age.

The reason why the total cost falls is that the cost of child care, the largest cost item, falls with age.

The graph in Fig. 1 shows these two facts instantly, and much more clearly than the mass of data in the table.

Figure 1 also shows the relative magnitudes of the various cost items much more quickly than you can see them in the table.

The cost of raising a child depends on the child's sex. A boy costs more to feed, and increasingly so as he gets older. A girl has higher personal care costs. Clothing also costs more for girls, except for ages 9 through 12.

Figure 2 shows the facts in the data table. If you compare the graph and the data table, you can see the power of the graph to show what the data table can reveal only with some effort.

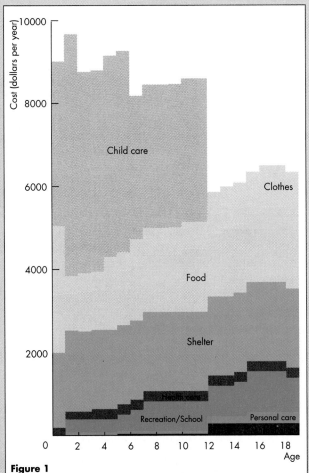

Figure 1

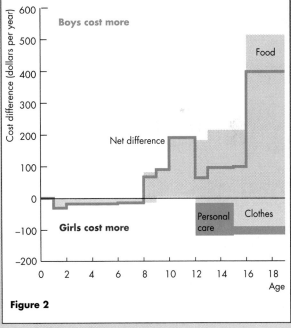

Figure 2

In a situation such as this, it is often more reveal-ing to flip the scale of one of the variables over and graph it upside-down. Figure 2.8(b) does this. The unemployment rate in part (b) is graphed in exactly the same way as in part (a), but the government's budget has been flipped over. Now, instead of mea-suring the deficit (a negative number) in the down direction and the surplus (a positive number) in the up direction, we measure the deficit upward and the surplus downward. You can now "see" very clearly the relationship between these two variables. There is indeed a tendency for the government's deficit to get bigger when the unemployment rate gets higher. But the relationship is by no means an exact one. There are significant periods, clearly revealed in the graph, when the deficit and the unemployment rate move apart. You can "see" these periods as those in which the gap between the two lines widens.

Now that we have seen how we can use graphs in economics to represent economic data and to show the relationship between variables, let us examine how economists use graphs in a more abstract way to construct and analyse economic models.

Graphs Used in Economic Models

The graphs used in economics are not always designed to show data. Instead their purpose is to illustrate the rela-tionships among the variables in an economic model. Although you will encounter many different kinds of relationships in economic models, there are some patterns. And once you have learned to recognize them, they will instantly convey to you the meaning of a graph. There are graphs that show each of the following:

♦ Variables that go up and down together

♦ Variables that move in opposite directions

♦ Relationships that have a maximum or a minimum

♦ Variables that are independent

Let's look at these four cases.

Variables That Go Up and Down Together

Graphs that show the relationship between two vari-ables that move up and down together are shown in Fig. 2.9. The relationship between two variables that move in the same direction is called a **positive rela-tionship**. Such a relationship is shown by a line that slopes upward.

Part (a) shows the relationship between the num-ber of kilometres travelled in 5 hours and speed. For example, the point marked a tells us that we will travel 200 kilometres in 5 hours if our speed is 40 kilometres an hour. If we double our speed and travel at 80 kilometres an hour, we will cover a dis-tance of 400 kilometres. The relationship between the number of kilometres travelled in 5 hours and speed is represented by an upward-sloping straight line. A relationship depicted by a straight line is called a **linear relationship**. A linear relationship is one that has a constant slope.

Part (b) shows the relationship between distance sprinted and exhaustion (exhaustion being mea-sured by the time it takes the heart rate to return to normal). This relationship is an upward-sloping one depicted by a curved line that starts out with a gen-tle slope but then becomes steeper as we move along the curve away from the origin.

Part (c) shows the relationship between the num-ber of problems worked by a student and the amount of study time. This relationship is illustrated by an upward-sloping curved line that starts out with a steep slope but then becomes more gentle as we move away from the origin.

There are three types of upward-sloping lines in the graphs in Fig. 2.9: one straight and two curved. But they are all called curves. Any line on a graph—no matter whether it is straight or curved—is called a **curve**.

Variables That Move in Opposite Directions

Figure 2.10 shows relationships between variables that move in opposite directions. A relationship between variables that move in opposite directions is called a **negative relationship**.

Part (a) shows the relationship between the num-ber of hours available for playing squash and the number of hours for playing tennis. One extra hour spent playing tennis means one hour less playing squash, and vice versa. This relationship is negative and linear. Part (b) shows the relationship between

FIGURE 2.9

Positive Relationships

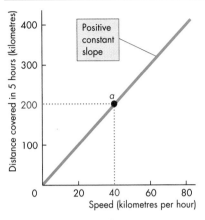

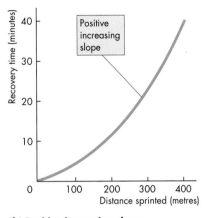

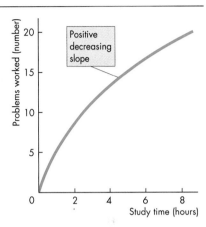

(a) Positive constant slope   **(b) Positive increasing slope**   **(c) Positive decreasing slope**

Each part of this figure shows a positive relationship between two variables. That is, as the value of the variable measured on the *x*-axis increases, so does the value of the variable measured on the *y*-axis. Part (a) illustrates a linear relationship—a relationship whose slope is constant as we move along the curve. Part (b) illustrates a positive relationship whose slope becomes steeper as we move along the curve away from the origin. It is a positive relationship with an increasing slope. Part (c) shows a positive relationship whose slope becomes flatter as we move away from the origin. It is a positive relationship with a decreasing slope.

FIGURE 2.10

Negative Relationships

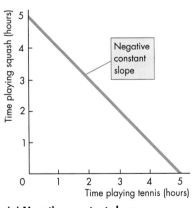

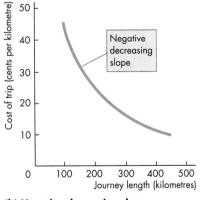

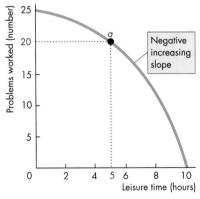

(a) Negative constant slope   **(b) Negative decreasing slope**   **(c) Negative increasing slope**

Each part of this figure shows a negative relationship between two variables. Part (a) shows a linear relationship—a relationship whose slope is constant as we travel along the curve. Part (b) shows a negative relationship of decreasing slope. That is, the slope of the relationship gets less steep as we travel along the curve from left to right. Part (c) shows a negative relationship of increasing slope. That is, the slope becomes steeper as we travel along the curve from left to right.

the cost per kilometre travelled and the length of a journey. The longer the journey, the lower is the cost per kilometre. But as the journey length increases, the cost per kilometre decreases at a decreasing rate. This feature of the relationship is illustrated by the fact that the curve slopes downward, starting out steep at a short journey length and then becoming flatter as the journey length increases.

Part (c) shows the relationship between the amount of leisure time and the number of problems worked by a student. If the student takes no leisure, 25 problems can be worked. If the student takes 5 hours of leisure, only 20 problems can be worked (point a). Increasing leisure time beyond 5 hours produces a large reduction in the number of problems worked, and if the student takes 10 hours of leisure a day, no problems get worked. This relationship is a negative one that starts out with a gentle slope at a low number of leisure hours and becomes increasingly steep as leisure hours increase.

Relationships That Have a Maximum and a Minimum

Economics is about optimizing, or doing the best with limited resources. Making the highest possible profits or achieving the lowest possible costs of production are examples of optimizing. Economists make frequent use of graphs depicting relationships that have a maximum or a minimum. Figure 2.11 illustrates such relationships.

Part (a) shows the relationship between rainfall and wheat yield. When there is no rainfall, wheat will not grow, so the yield is zero. As the rainfall increases up to 10 days a month, the wheat yield also increases. With 10 rainy days each month, the wheat yield reaches its maximum at 1.8 tonnes a per hectare (point a). Rain in excess of 10 days a month starts to lower the yield of wheat. If every day is rainy, the wheat suffers from a lack of sunshine and the yield falls back almost to zero. This relationship is one that starts out positive, reaches a maximum, and then becomes negative.

FIGURE 2.11

Maximum and Minimum Points

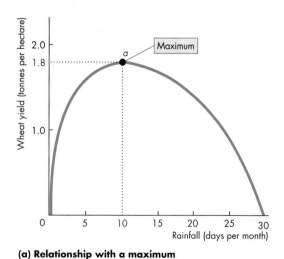

(a) Relationship with a maximum

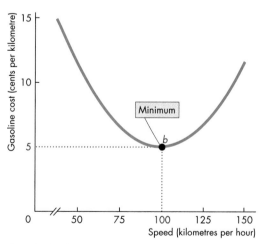

(b) Relationship with a minimum

Part (a) shows a relationship with a maximum point, a. As rainfall increases up to 10 days a month, the wheat yield increases, but as rainfall increases above 10 days a month, the wheat yield decreases. The maximum wheat yield is 1.8 tonnes a month.

Part (b) shows a relationship with a minimum point, b. As speed increases up to 100 kilometres an hour, the gasoline cost decreases, but as speed increases above 100 kilometres an hour, the gasoline cost increases. The minimum gasoline cost is 5¢ a kilometre.

Part (b) shows the reverse case—a relationship that begins with a negative slope, falls to a minimum, and then becomes positive. An example of such a relationship is the gasoline cost per kilometre as the speed of travel varies. At low speeds, the car is creeping along in a traffic snarl-up. The number of kilometres per litre is low so the gasoline cost per kilometre is high. At very high speeds, the car is operated beyond its most efficient rate, and again the number of kilometres per litre is low and the gasoline cost per kilometre is high. At a speed of 100 kilometres an hour, the gasoline cost per kilometre travelled is at its minimum (point *b*).

Variables That Are Independent

There are many situations in which one variable is independent of another. No matter what happens to the value of one variable, the other variable remains constant. Sometimes we want to show the independence between two variables in a graph. Figure 2.12 shows two ways of achieving this. In part (a), your grade in economics is shown on the vertical axis against the price of bananas on the horizontal axis. Your grade (75 percent in this example) does not depend on the price of bananas. The relationship between these two variables is shown by a horizontal straight line. In part (b), the output of French wine is shown on the horizontal axis and the number of rainy days a month in British Columbia is shown on the vertical axis. Again, the output of French wine (15 billion litres a year in this example) does not change when the number of rainy days in British Columbia changes. The relationship between these two variables is shown by a vertical straight line.

Figures 2.9 through 2.12 illustrate ten different shapes of graphs that we will encounter in economic models. In describing these graphs, we have talked about curves that slope upward or slope downward and slopes that are steep or gentle. The concept of slope is an important one. Let's spend a little time discussing exactly what we mean by slope.

FIGURE 2.12

Variables with No Relationship

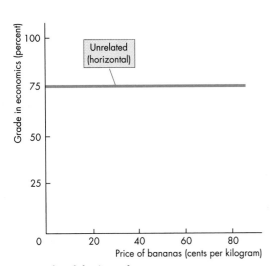

(a) Unrelated: horizontal

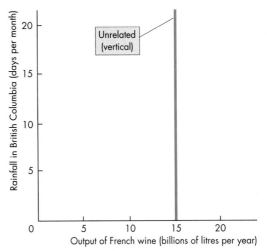

(b) Unrelated: vertical

This figure shows how we can graph two variables that are unrelated to each other. In part (a), a student's grade in economics is plotted at 75 percent regardless of the price of bananas on the *x*-axis. In part (b), the output of the vineyards of France does not vary with the rainfall in British Columbia.

The Slope of a Relationship

The **slope** of a relationship is the change in the value of the variable measured on the y-axis divided by the change in the value of the variable measured on the x-axis. We use the Greek letter Δ to represent "change in." Thus Δy means the change in the value of the variable measured on the y-axis, and Δx means the change in the value of the variable measured on the x-axis. Therefore the slope of the relationship is

$$\Delta y/\Delta x.$$

If a large change in the variable measured on the y-axis (Δy) is associated with a small change in the variable measured on the x-axis (Δx), the slope is large and the curve is steep. If a small change in the variable measured on the y-axis (Δy) is associated with a large change in the variable measured on the x-axis (Δx), the slope is small and the curve is flat.

We can make the idea of slope sharper by doing some calculations.

Calculating the Slope of a Straight Line

The slope of a straight line is the same regardless of where on the line you calculate it. Thus the slope of a straight line is constant. Let's calculate the slopes of the lines in Fig. 2.13. In part (a), when x increases from 2 to 6, y increases from 3 to 6. The change in x is +4—that is, Δx is 4. The change in y is +3—that is, Δy is 3. The slope of that line is

$$\frac{\Delta y}{\Delta x} = \frac{3}{4}.$$

FIGURE 2.13

The Slope of a Straight Line

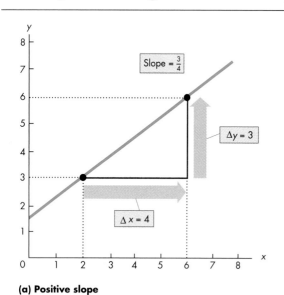

(a) Positive slope

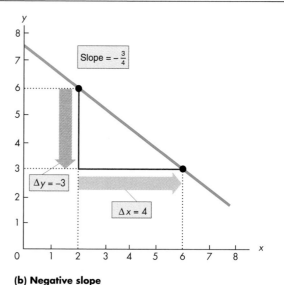

(b) Negative slope

To calculate the slope of a straight line, we divide the change in value of the variable measured on the y-axis by the change in value of the variable measured on the x-axis. Part (a) shows the calculation of a positive slope (when x goes up, y goes up). When x goes up from 2 to 6, the change in x is 4—that is, Δx equals 4. That change in x brings about an increase in y from 3 to 6, so that Δy equals 3. The slope ($\Delta y/\Delta x$) equals $3/4$. Part (b) shows a negative slope (when x goes up, y goes down). When x goes up from 2 to 6, Δx equals 4. That change in x brings about a decrease in y from 6 to 3, so that Δy equals –3. The slope ($\Delta y/\Delta x$) equals $-3/4$.

In part (b), when x increases from 2 to 6, y decreases from 6 to 3. The change in y is *minus* 3—that is, Δy is –3. The change in x is *plus* 4—that is, Δx is +4. The slope of the curve is

$$\frac{\Delta y}{\Delta x} = \frac{-3}{4}.$$

Notice that the two slopes have the same magnitude (3/4), but the slope of the line in part (a) is positive (+3/+4 = 3/4), while that in part (b) is negative (–3/+4 = –3/4). The slope of a positive relationship is positive; the slope of a negative relationship is negative.

Calculating the Slope of a Curved Line

Calculating the slope of a curved line is trickier. The slope of a curved line is not constant. Its slope depends on where on the line we calculate it. There are two ways to calculate the slope of a curved line: you can calculate the slope at a point on the line or you can calculate the slope across an arc of the line. Let's look at the two alternatives.

Slope at a Point   To calculate the slope at a point on a curved line, you need to construct a straight line that has the same slope as the curve at the point in question. Figure 2.14 shows how such a

---

FIGURE 2.14

The Slope of a Curve

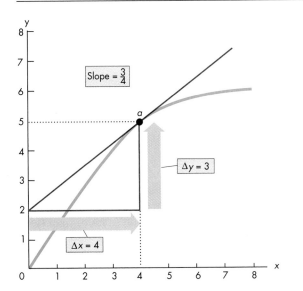

(a) Slope at a point

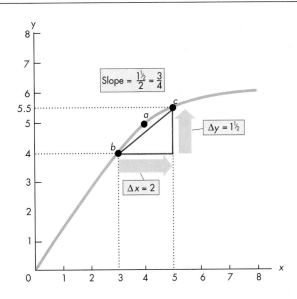

(b) Slope across an arc

The slope of a curve can be calculated either at a point, as in part (a), or across an arc, as in part (b). The slope at a point is calculated by finding the slope of a straight line that touches the curve at only one point. To calculate the slope of the curve at point *a*, draw a straight line such that it touches the curve at point *a*. The slope of that straight line is calculated by dividing the change in *y* by the change in *x*. When *x* increases from 0 to 4, Δx equals 4. That change in *x* is associated with an increase in *y* from 2 to 5, so Δy equals 3. The slope of the line at point *a* is 3/4. So the slope of the curve at point *a* is 3/4.

To calculate the slope across an arc, we place a straight line across the curve from one point to another and then calculate the slope of that straight line. To calculate the slope across the arc *bc*, draw a straight line from *b* to *c* in part (b). The slope of the straight line *bc* is calculated by dividing the change in *y* by the change in *x*. In moving from *b* to *c*, *x* increases by 2 (Δx equals 2), and *y* increases by 1½ (Δy equals 1½). The slope of the line *bc* is 1½ divided by 2, or 3/4. So the slope of the curve across the arc *bc* is 3/4.

calculation is made. Suppose you want to calculate the slope of the curve at the point marked a. Place a ruler on the graph so that it touches point a and no other point on the curve; then draw a straight line along the edge of the ruler. The straight red line in part (a) is such a line. If the ruler touches the curve only at point a, then the slope of the curve at point a must be the same as the slope of the edge of the ruler. If the curve and the ruler do not have the same slope, the line along the edge of the ruler will cut the curve instead of just touching it.

Having now found a straight line with the same slope as the curve at point a, you can calculate the slope of the curve at point a by calculating the slope of the straight line.

We already know how to calculate the slope of a straight line, so the task is straightforward. In this case, as x increases from 0 to 4 ($\Delta x = 4$), y increases from 2 to 5 ($\Delta y = 3$). Therefore the slope of the straight line is

$$\frac{\Delta y}{\Delta x} = \frac{3}{4}.$$

Thus the slope of the curve at point a is $3/4$.

Slope across an Arc   Calculating a slope across an arc is similar to calculating an average slope. An arc of a curve is a piece of the curve. In Fig. 2.14(b), we are looking at the same curve as in part (a) but instead of calculating the slope at point a, we calculate the slope across the arc from b to c. Moving along the arc from b to c, x increases from 3 to 5 and y increases from 4 to $5\frac{1}{2}$. That is, the change in x is $+2(\Delta x = 2)$, and the change in y is $-1\frac{1}{2}$ ($\Delta y = -1\frac{1}{2}$). Therefore the slope of the line is

$$\frac{\Delta y}{\Delta x} = \frac{-1\frac{1}{2}}{2} = \frac{-3}{4}.$$

Thus the slope of the curve across the arc bc is $3/4$.

This calculation gives us the slope of the curve between points b and c. The actual slope calculated is the slope of the straight line from b to c. This slope approximates the average slope of the curve along the arc bc. In this particular example, the slope across the arc bc is identical to the slope of the curve at point a, in both part (a) and part (b). But calculating the slope does not always work out so neatly. You might have some fun constructing counterexamples.

Graphing Relationships among More Than Two Variables

We have seen that we can graph a single variable as a point on a straight line and we can graph the relationship between two variables as a point formed by the x- and y-coordinates in a two-dimensional graph. You may be suspecting that although a two-dimensional graph is informative, most of the things in which you are likely to be interested involve relationships among many variables, not just two.

Relationships among more than two variables abound. For example, consider the relationship among the price of ice cream, the air temperature, and the amount of ice cream eaten. When ice cream is expensive and the temperature is low, people eat much less ice cream than when ice cream is inexpensive and the temperature is high. For any given price of ice cream, the quantity consumed varies with the temperature, and for any given temperature, the quantity of ice cream consumed varies with its price.

Other Things Being Equal

Figure 2.15 illustrates such a situation. The table shows the number of litres of ice cream that will be eaten each day at various temperatures and ice cream prices. How can we graph all these numbers? To graph a relationship that involves more than two variables, we consider what happens if all but two of the variables are held constant. This device is called *ceteris paribus*. **Ceteris paribus** is a Latin phrase that means "other things being equal." For example, in part (a) you can see what happens to the quantity of ice cream consumed when the price of ice cream varies while the temperature is held constant. The line labelled 21°C shows the relationship between ice cream consumption and the price of ice cream when the temperature stays at 21°C. The numbers used to plot that line are those in the third column of the table in Fig. 2.15. For example, when the temperature is 21°C, 18 litres are consumed when the price is 30¢ a scoop and 13 litres are consumed when the price is 45¢. The curve labelled 32°C shows the consumption of ice cream when the price varies and the temperature is 32°C.

FIGURE 2.15

Graphing a Relationship among Three Variables

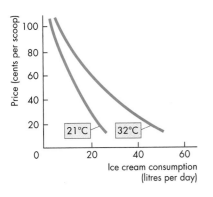

(a) Price and consumption at a given temperature

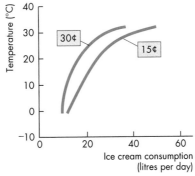

(b) Temperature and consumption at a given price

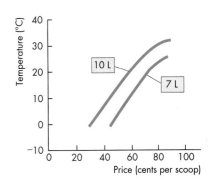

(c) Temperature and price at a given consumption

Price (cents per scoop)	Ice cream consumption (litres per day)			
	−1°C	10°C	21°C	32°C
15	12	18	25	50
30	10	12	18	37
45	7	10	13	27
60	5	7	10	20
75	3	5	7	14
90	2	3	5	10
105	1	2	3	6

The quantity of ice cream consumed (one variable) depends on its price (a second variable) and the air temperature (a third variable). The table provides some hypothetical numbers that tell us how many litres of ice cream are consumed each day at different prices and different temperatures. For example, if the price is 45¢ a scoop and the temperature is 10°C, 10 litres of ice cream will be consumed. In order to graph a relationship among three variables, the value of one variable must be held constant.

Part (a) shows the relationship between price and consumption, holding temperature constant. One curve holds temperature constant at 32°C and the other at 21°C. Part (b) shows the relationship between temperature and consumption, holding price constant. One curve holds the price at 30¢ a scoop and the other at 15¢ a scoop. Part (c) shows the relationship between temperature and price, holding consumption constant. One curve holds consumption constant at 10 litres and the other at 7 litres.

Alternatively, we can show the relationship between ice cream consumption and temperature while holding the price of ice cream constant, as shown in Fig. 2.15(b). The curve labelled 30¢ shows how the consumption of ice cream varies with the temperature when ice cream costs 30¢, and a second curve shows the relationship when ice cream costs 15¢. For example, at 30¢ a scoop, 12 litres are consumed when the temperature is 10°C and 18 litres when the temperature is 21°C.

Figure 2.15(c) shows the combinations of temperature and price that result in a constant consumption of ice cream. One curve shows the

combination that results in 10 litres a day being consumed and the other shows the combination that results in 7 litres a day being consumed. A high price and a high temperature lead to the same consumption as a lower price and lower temperature. For example, 7 litres are consumed at 10°C and 60¢ a scoop and at 21°C and 75¢ a scoop.

◆ ◆ ◆ ◆ With what you have now learned about graphs, you can move forward with your study of economics. There are no graphs in this book that are more complicated than those that have been explained here.

SUMMARY

Graphing Data

Two main types of graphs are used to represent economic data: scatter diagrams and time-series graphs. A scatter diagram plots the value of one economic variable associated with the value of another. Such a diagram reveals whether or not there is a relationship between two variables and, if there is a relationship, its nature.

A time-series graph plots the value of one or more economic variables on the vertical axis (y-axis) and time on the horizontal axis (x-axis). A well-constructed time-series graph quickly reveals the level, direction of change, and speed of change of a variable. It also reveals trends. Graphs sometimes mislead, especially when the origin is omitted or when the scale is stretched or squeezed to exaggerate or understate a variation. (pp. 29–38)

Graphs Used in Economic Models

Graphs are used in economic models to illustrate relationships between variables. There are four types: positive relationships, negative relationships, relationships that have a maximum or a minimum, and variables that are not related to each other.

Examples of these different types of relationships are summarized in Figs. 2.9 through 2.11. (pp. 38–41)

The Slope of a Relationship

The slope of a relationship is calculated as the change in the value of the variable measured on the y-axis divided by the change in the value of the variable measured on the x-axis—$\Delta y/\Delta x$. A straight line has a constant slope, but a curved line has a varying slope. To calculate the slope of a curved line, we calculate the slope either at a point or across an arc. (pp. 42–44)

Graphing Relationships among More Than Two Variables

To graph a relationship among more than two variables, we hold constant the values of all the variables except two. We then plot the value of one of the variables against the value of another. Holding constant all the variables but two is called the *ceteris paribus* assumption—other things being equal. (pp. 44–45)

KEY ELEMENTS

Key Terms

Axes, 29
Ceteris paribus, 44
Coordinates, 29
Curve, 38
Linear relationship, 38
Negative relationship, 38
Origin, 29
Positive relationship, 38
Scatter diagram, 30
Slope, 42
Time-series graph, 32
Trend, 33
x-axis, 29

x-coordinate, 29
y-axis, 29
y-coordinate, 29

Key Figures

Figure 2.9   Positive Relationships, 39
Figure 2.10   Negative Relationships, 39
Figure 2.11   Maximum and Minimum Points, 40
Figure 2.12   Variables with No Relationship, 41
Figure 2.13   The Slope of a Straight Line, 42
Figure 2.14   The Slope of a Curve, 43
Figure 2.15   Graphing a Relationship among Three Variables, 45

REVIEW QUESTIONS

1 Why do we use graphs?

2 What are the two scale lines on a graph called?

3 What is the origin on a graph?

4 What do we mean by the y-coordinate and the x-coordinate?

5 What is a scatter diagram?

6 What is a time-series graph?

7 List three things that a time-series graph shows quickly and easily.

8 What do we mean by trend?

9 Sketch some graphs to illustrate the following:

a Two variables that move up and down together

b Two variables that move in opposite directions

c A relationship between two variables that has a maximum

d A relationship between two variables that has a minimum

10 Which of the relationships in question 9 is a positive relationship and which a negative relationship?

11 What is the definition of the slope of a relationship?

12 What are the two ways of calculating the slope of a curved line?

13 How do we graph relationships among more than two variables?

PROBLEMS

1 The inflation rate in Canada between 1979 and 1992 was as follows:

Year	Inflation rate (percent per year)
1979	1.0
1980	10.6
1981	10.8
1982	8.7
1983	5.0
1984	3.1
1985	2.6
1986	2.4
1987	4.7
1988	4.6
1989	4.8
1990	3.3
1991	2.7
1992	1.0

Draw a time-series graph of these data, and use your graph to answer the following questions:

a In which year was inflation highest?

b In which year was inflation lowest?

c In which years did inflation increase?

d In which years did inflation decrease?

e In which year did inflation change the fastest?

f In which year did inflation change the slowest?

d What have been the main trends in inflation?

2 Interest rates on Government of Canada treasury bills between 1979 and 1992 were as follows:

Year	Interest rate (percent per year)
1979	11.6
1980	12.7
1981	17.8
1982	13.8
1983	9.3
1984	11.1
1985	9.5
1986	9.0
1987	8.2
1988	9.4
1989	12.0
1990	12.8
1991	8.8
1992	5.8

Use these data together with those in problem 1 to draw a scatter diagram showing the relationship between inflation and the interest rate. Use this diagram to determine whether there is a relationship between inflation and the interest rate and whether it is positive or negative.

3 Use the following information to draw a graph showing the relationship between two variables x and y:

x	0	1	2	3	4	5	6	7	8
y	0	1	4	9	16	25	36	49	64

a Is the relationship between x and y positive or negative?

b Does the slope of the relationship rise or fall as the value of x rises?

4 Using the data in problem 3,

a Calculate the slope of the relationship between x and y when x equals 4.

b Calculate the slope of the arc when x rises from 3 to 4.

c Calculate the slope of the arc when x rises from 4 to 5.

d Calculate the slope of the arc when x rises from 3 to 5.

e What do you notice that is interesting about your answers to (b), (c), and (d) compared with your answer to (a)?

5 Calculate the slopes of the following two relationships between two variables x and y:

a
x	0	2	4	6	8	10
y	20	16	12	8	4	0

b
x	0	2	4	6	8	10
y	0	8	16	24	32	40

6 Draw a graph showing the following relationship between two variables x and y:

x	0	1	2	3	4	5	6	7	8	9
y	0	2	4	6	8	10	8	6	4	2

a Is the slope positive or negative when x is less than 5?

b Is the slope positive or negative when x is greater than 5?

c What is the slope of this relationship when x equals 5?

d Is y at a maximum or at a minimum when x equals 5?

7 Draw a graph showing the following relationship between two variables

x	0	1	2	3	4	5	6	7	8	9
y	10	8	6	4	2	0	2	4	6	8

a Is the slope positive or negative when x is less than 5?

b Is the slope positive or negative when x is greater than 5?

c What is the slope of this relationship when x equals 5?

d Is y at a maximum or at a minimum when x equals 5?

8 The table gives information about the number of Walkmans that people buy in different circumstances.

Price (dollars per Walkman)	Price (dollars per tape)			
	$1	$2	$3	$4
$20	1,000	900	800	700
$25	900	800	700	600
$30	800	700	600	500
$35	700	600	500	400
$40	600	500	400	300
$45	500	400	300	200
$50	400	300	200	100

a Draw a graph of the relationship between the quantity of Walkmans that people buy and the price of a Walkman, holding the price of a tape constant. What does the graph tell you?

b Draw a graph of the relationship between the quantity of Walkmans that people buy and the price of a tape, holding the price of a Walkman constant. What does the graph tell you?

c Draw a graph of the relationship between the price of a Walkman and the price of a tape, holding the quantity of Walkmans that people buy constant. What does the graph tell you?

CHAPTER 3

PRODUCTION, SPECIALIZATION, AND EXCHANGE

After studying this chapter, you will be able to

◆ Define the production possibility frontier

◆ Calculate opportunity cost

◆ Explain why economic growth and technical change do not provide free gifts

◆ Explain comparative advantage

◆ Explain why people specialize and how they gain from trade

◆ Explain why property rights and money have evolved

W E LIVE IN A STYLE THAT MOST OF OUR GRANDPARENTS could not have imagined. Advances in medicine have cured diseases that terrified them. Our parents are amazed at the matter-of-fact way we handle computers. We casually use products such as microwave ovens, graphite tennis rackets, and digital watches that didn't exist in their youth. Economic growth has made us richer than our parents and grandparents. ◆ ◆ But economic growth and technological change have not liberated us from scarcity. Why not? Why, despite our immense wealth, must we still make choices and face costs? Why are there no "free lunches"? ◆ ◆ We see an incredible amount of specialization and trading in the world. Each one of us specializes in a particular job—as lawyer, car maker, homemaker. Only one in five Canadians works in manufacturing and more than half work in wholesale and retail trade, banking and finance, government, and other services. How do we benefit from specialization and exchange? ◆ ◆ Over many centuries, institutions and social arrangements have evolved that we take for granted. One of them is a legal system that enforces contracts and protects private property rights. Another is money. ◆ ◆ Why have these institutions evolved? And how do they extend our ability to specialize and increase production?

Making the Most of It

◆ ◆ ◆ ◆ These are the questions that we tackle in this chapter. We begin by studying the limits to what we can produce. We next learn how to measure opportunity cost. We also discover how people benefit from specialization and trade.

The Production Possibility Frontier

What do we mean by production? **Production** is the conversion of *land*, *labour*, and *capital* into goods and services. We defined the factors of production in Chapter 1. Let's briefly recall what they are.

Land is all the gifts of nature. It includes the air, the water, and the land, as well as the minerals that lie beneath the surface of the earth. *Labour* is all the muscle-power and brain-power of human beings. The voices and artistry of singers and actors, the strength and coordination of athletes, the daring of astronauts, the political skill of diplomats, as well as the physical and mental skills of the many millions of people who make cars and cola, gum and glue, wallpaper and watering cans, are included in this category.

Capital is all the goods that have been produced and can now be used in the production of other goods and services. Examples include the Trans-Canada highway system, the Saddledome and the SkyDome, dams and power projects, airports and jumbo jets, car production lines, shirt factories, and cookie shops. A special kind of capital is called human capital. **Human capital** is the accumulated skill and knowledge of human beings, which arise from their training and education.

Goods and services are all the valuable things that people produce. Goods are tangible—cars, spoons, VCRs, and bread. Services are intangible—haircuts, amusement park rides, and telephone calls. There are two types of goods: capital goods and consumption goods. **Capital goods** are goods that are used in the production process and can be used many times before they eventually wear out. Examples of capital goods are buildings, computers, automobiles, and telephones. **Consumption goods** are goods that can be used just once. Examples are dill pickles and toothpaste. **Consumption** is the process of using up goods and services.

The amount that we can produce is limited by our resources and the technologies available for transforming those resources into goods and services. That limit is described by the production possibility frontier. The **production possibility frontier** (PPF) marks the boundary between those combinations of goods and services that can be produced and those that cannot. It is important to understand the production possibility frontier in the real world, but in order to achieve that goal more easily, we will first study an economy that is simpler than the one in which we live—a model economy.

A Model Economy

Instead of looking at the real-world economy with all its complexity and detail, we will build a model of an economy. The model will have features that are essential to understanding the real economy, but we will ignore most of reality's immense detail. Our model economy will be simpler in three important ways:

1. Everything that is produced is also consumed so that in our model, capital resources neither grow nor shrink. (Later we will examine what happens if we consume less than we produce and add to capital resources.)
2. There are only two goods, corn and cloth. (In the real world we use our scarce resources to produce countless goods and services.)
3. There is only one person, Jane, who lives on a deserted island and has no dealings with other people. (Later we will see what happens when Jane's island economy has links with another economy. Also, we'll extend our view to the real world with its five billion people.)

Jane uses all the resources of her island economy to produce corn and cloth. She works 10 hours each day. The amount of corn and cloth that Jane produces depends on how many hours she devotes to producing them. Table 3.1 sets out Jane's production possibilities for corn and cloth. If she does no work, she produces nothing. Two hours a day devoted to corn farming produces 6 kilograms of corn per month. Devoting more hours to corn increases the output of corn, but there is a decline in the extra amount of corn that comes from extra effort. The reason for this decline is that Jane has to use increasingly unsuitable land for growing corn. At first, she plants corn on a lush, flat plain. Eventually, when she has used all the arable land, she has to

TABLE 3.1

Jane's Production Possibilities

Hours worked (per day)		Corn grown (kilograms per month)		Cloth produced (metres per month)
0	either	0	or	0
2	either	6	or	1
4	either	11	or	2
6	either	15	or	3
8	either	18	or	4
10	either	20	or	5

If Jane does no work, she produces no corn or cloth. If she works for 2 hours per day and spends the entire amount of time on corn production, she produces 6 kilograms of corn per month. If that same time is used for cloth production, 1 metre of cloth is produced but no corn. The last four rows of the table show the amounts of corn or cloth that can be produced per month as more hours are devoted to each activity.

start planting on the rocky hills and at the edge of the beach. The numbers in the second column of the table show how the output of corn rises as the hours devoted to cultivating it rise.

To produce cloth, Jane gathers wool from sheep that live on the island. As she devotes more hours to collecting wool and making cloth, her output rises. The numbers in the third column of Table 3.1 show how the output of cloth rises as the number of hours devoted to this activity rises.

If Jane devotes all her time to growing corn, she can produce 20 kilograms of corn in a month. In that case, however, she cannot produce any cloth. Conversely, if she devotes all her time to making cloth, she can produce 5 metres a month but will have no time left for growing corn. Jane can devote some of her time to corn and some to cloth but not more than 10 hours a day total. Thus she can spend 2 hours growing corn and 8 hours making cloth or 6 hours on one and 4 hours on the other (or any other combination of hours that adds up to 10 hours).

We have defined the production possibility frontier as the boundary between what is attainable and

what is not attainable. You can calculate Jane's production possibility frontier by using the information in Table 3.1. These calculations are summarized in the table in Fig. 3.1 and graphed in that figure as Jane's production possibility frontier. To see how we calculated that frontier, let's concentrate first on the table in Fig. 3.1.

Possibility *a* shows Jane devoting no time to cloth and her entire 10-hour working day to corn. In this case, she can produce 20 kilograms of corn per month and no cloth. For possibility *b*, she spends 2 hours a day making cloth and 8 hours growing corn, to produce a total of 18 kilograms of corn and 1 metre of cloth a month. The pattern continues to possibility *f*, where she devotes 10 hours a day to cloth and no time to corn. These numbers are plotted in the graph shown in Fig. 3.1. Metres of cloth are measured on the horizontal axis and kilograms of corn on the vertical axis. Points *a*, *b*, *c*, *d*, *e*, and *f* represent the numbers in the corresponding rows of the table.

Of course, Jane does not have to work in blocks of 2 hours, as in our example. She can work 1 hour or 1 hour and 10 minutes growing corn and devote the rest of her time to making cloth. All other feasible allocations of Jane's 10 hours enable her to produce the combinations of corn and cloth described by the line that joins points *a*, *b*, *c*, *d*, *e*, and *f*. This line shows Jane's production possibility frontier. She can produce at any point on the frontier or inside it, within the orange area. These are attainable points. Points outside the frontier are unattainable. To produce at points beyond the frontier, Jane needs more time than she has—more than 10 hours a day. By working 10 hours a day producing both corn and cloth, Jane can choose any point she wishes on the frontier. And by working less than 10 hours a day or by not putting her resources to their best possible use—by wasting some of her resources—she can produce at a point inside the frontier.

Jane's Preferences

Jane produces corn and cloth, not for the fun of it, but so that she can eat and keep warm. She wants much more corn and cloth than she can produce, and the more of each she has, the better she likes it.

Because Jane wants as much as possible of both corn and cloth, the best she can do is to produce—and therefore consume—at a point *on* her

FIGURE 3.1

Jane's Production
Possibility Frontier

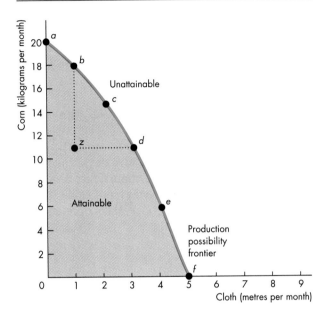

Possibility	Corn (kilograms per month)		Cloth (metres per month)
a	20	and	0
b	18	and	1
c	15	and	2
d	11	and	3
e	6	and	4
f	0	and	5

The table lists six points on Jane's production possibility frontier. Row *e* tells us that if Jane produces 6 kilograms of corn, the maximum cloth production that is possible is 4 metres. These same points are graphed as points *a, b, c, d, e,* and *f* in the figure. The line passing through these points is Jane's production possibility frontier, which separates the attainable from the unattainable. The attainable orange area contains all the possible production points. Jane can produce anywhere inside this area or on the production possibility frontier. Points outside the frontier are unattainable. Jane prefers any point between *b* and *d* to point *z* because it gives her more of both goods.

production possibility frontier. To see why, consider a point such as *z* in the attainable region. At point *z*, Jane is wasting resources. She may be taking time off work, but leisure time on the island is not worth anything to Jane. Or she may not be using her sheep and her corn fields as effectively as possible. Jane can improve her situation by moving from point *z* to a point such as *b* or *d* or to a point on the frontier between *b* and *d*, such as point *c*. Jane can have more of both goods on the frontier than at points inside it. At point *b*, she can consume more corn and no less cloth than at point *z*. At point *d*, she can consume more cloth and no less corn than at point *z*. At point *c*, she can consume more corn and more cloth than at point *z*. Jane will never choose a point such as *z* because preferred points, such as *b, c,* and *d*, are available to her. That is, Jane will always choose a point on the frontier in preference to a point inside it.

We have just seen that Jane wants to produce at some point on her production possibility frontier, but she is still faced with the problem of choosing her preferred point. In choosing between one point on her production possibility frontier and another, Jane is confronted with opportunity costs. At point *c*, for example, she has less cloth and more corn than at point *d*. If Jane moves along her production possibility frontier from point *c* to point *d*, she pays for the one additional metre of cloth by giving up some corn—4 kilograms of corn. If Jane chooses point *d*, she does so because she figures that the extra metre of cloth is worth the 4 kilograms of corn forgone.

R E V I E W

The production possibility frontier is the boundary between the outputs of goods and services that are the attainable and the unattainable. There is always a point on the production possibility frontier that is preferred to any point inside it. But moving from one point on the frontier to another involves an opportunity cost—having less of one good to get more of another. ◆

Let's go on to explore Jane's opportunity cost more closely and see how we can measure it.

Opportunity Cost

We've defined opportunity cost as the best alternative forgone: for a late sleeper, the opportunity cost of attending an early morning class is an hour in bed; for a jogger, it is an hour of exercise. We can make the concept of opportunity cost more precise by using a production possibility frontier such as the one shown in Fig. 3.1. Let's see what that curve tells us.

The Best Alternative Forgone

The production possibility frontier in Fig. 3.1 traces the boundary between attainable and unattainable combinations of corn and cloth. Since there are only two goods, there is no difficulty in working out what is the best alternative forgone. More corn can be grown only by paying the price of having less cloth, and more cloth can be made only by bearing the cost of having less corn. Thus the opportunity cost of an additional metre of cloth is the amount of corn forgone, and the opportunity cost of producing an additional kilogram of corn is the amount of cloth forgone. Let's put numerical values on the opportunity costs of corn and cloth.

Measuring Opportunity Cost

We are going to measure opportunity cost by using Jane's production possibility frontier. We will calculate how much cloth she has to give up to get more corn and how much corn she has to give up to get more cloth.

If all Jane's time is used to produce corn, she produces 20 kilograms of corn and no cloth. If she decides to produce 1 metre of cloth, how much corn does she have to give up? You can see the answer in Fig. 3.2. To produce 1 metre of cloth, Jane moves from a to b and gives up 2 kilograms of corn. Thus the opportunity cost of the first metre of cloth is 2 kilograms of corn. If she decides to produce an additional metre of cloth, how much corn does she give up? This time, Jane moves from b to c and gives up 3 kilograms of corn to produce the second metre of cloth.

These opportunity costs are set out in the table of Fig. 3.2. The first two rows set out the opportunity costs that we have just calculated. The table also lists the opportunity costs of moving between points c, d, e, and f on Jane's production possibility frontier of Fig. 3.1. You might want to work out another example on your own to be sure that you understand what is going on. Calculate Jane's opportunity cost of moving from e to f.

Increasing Opportunity Cost

As you can see, opportunity cost varies with the quantity produced. The first metre of cloth costs 2 kilograms of corn. The next metre of cloth costs 3 kilograms of corn. The last metre of cloth costs 6 kilograms of corn. Thus the opportunity cost of cloth increases as Jane produces more cloth. Figure 3.2(a) illustrates the increasing opportunity cost of cloth.

The Shape of the Frontier

Pay special attention to the shape of the production possibility frontier in Fig. 3.1. When a large amount of corn and not much cloth is produced—between points a and b—the frontier has a gentle slope. When a large amount of cloth and not much corn is produced—between points e and f—the frontier is steep. The whole frontier bows outward. These features of the production possibility frontier are a reflection of increasing opportunity cost. You can see the connection between increasing opportunity cost and the shape of the production possibility frontier in Fig. 3.2(b). Between points a and b, 1 metre of cloth can be obtained by giving up a small amount of corn. Here the opportunity cost of cloth is low and the opportunity cost of corn is high. Between points e and f, a large amount of corn must be given up to produce 1 extra metre of cloth. In this region, the opportunity cost of cloth is high and the opportunity cost of corn is low.

Everything Has an Increasing Opportunity Cost

We've just worked out the opportunity cost of cloth. But what about the opportunity cost of corn? Does it also increase as more of it is produced? You can see the answer in Fig. 3.2. By giving up 1 metre of cloth to produce some corn, Jane moves from f to e and

FIGURE 3.2

Jane's Opportunity Cost of Cloth

The table records Jane's opportunity cost of cloth. The first metre of cloth costs 2 kilograms of corn. The next metre of cloth costs 3 kilograms of corn. The opportunity cost of cloth rises as Jane produces more cloth, with the last metre of cloth costing 6 kilograms of corn. Part (a) of the figure shows the increasing opportunity cost of cloth, and part (b) shows the increasing opportunity cost as Jane moves along her outward-bowed production possibility frontier, increasing her production of cloth and decreasing her production of corn.

As Jane increases her cloth production

First **1** metre of cloth costs **2** kilograms of corn
Next **1** metre of cloth costs **3** kilograms of corn
Next **1** metre of cloth costs **4** kilograms of corn
Next **1** metre of cloth costs **5** kilograms of corn
Last metre of cloth costs **6** kilograms of corn

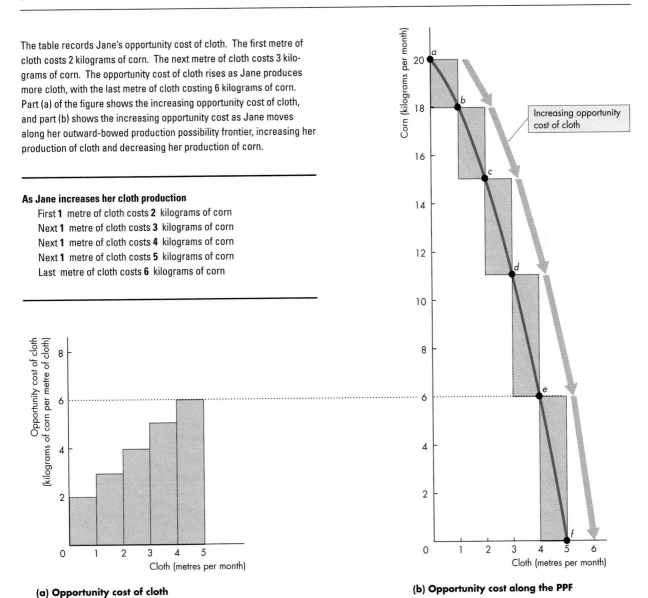

(a) Opportunity cost of cloth

(b) Opportunity cost along the PPF

produces 6 kilograms of corn. Thus the opportunity cost of the first 6 kilograms of corn is 1 metre of cloth. Moving from e to d, you can see that the next 5 kilograms of corn cost 1 metre of cloth. Thus the opportunity cost of corn also increases as Jane produces more corn.

Increasing opportunity cost and the outward bow of the production possibility frontier arise from the fact that scarce resources are not equally useful in all activities. For instance, some of the land on Jane's island is extremely fertile and produces a high crop yield, while other land is rocky and barren. The sheep on the island, however, prefer the rocky, barren land.

Jane uses the most fertile land for growing corn and the most barren areas for raising sheep. Only if she wants a larger amount of corn does she try to cultivate relatively barren areas. If she uses all her time to grow corn, she has to use some very unsuitable, low-yielding land. Devoting some time to making cloth, and reducing the time spent growing corn by the same amount, produces a small drop in corn production but a large increase in the output of cloth. Conversely, if Jane uses all her time to make cloth, a small reduction in the amount of time spent raising sheep yields a large increase in corn production and a small drop in the output of cloth.

Production Possibilities in the Real World

Jane's island is dramatically different from the world in which we live. The fundamental lesson it teaches us, however, applies to the real world. The world has a fixed number of people endowed with a given amount of human capital and limited time. The world also has a fixed amount of land and capital equipment. These limited resources can be employed, using the available but limited technology, to produce goods and services. But there is a limit to the goods and services that can be produced, a boundary between what is attainable and what is not attainable. That boundary is the real-world economy's production possibility frontier. On that frontier, producing more of any one good requires producing less of some other good or goods.

For example, if the federal government makes available more child-care services, it must at the same time cut the scale of spending on other programs, increase taxes, or borrow more. Higher taxes and more government borrowing mean less money left over for vacations and other consumption goods and services. The cost of more child-care services is less of other goods. On a smaller scale but equally important, each time you decide to rent a video you decide not to use your limited income to buy pizza, popcorn, or some other good. The cost of one more video is less of something else.

Given our limited resources, more of one thing always means less of something else. Also, the more of anything that we have or do, the higher is its opportunity cost. Let's consider a real-world example of increasing opportunity cost.

Increasing Opportunity Cost in the Real World

On Jane's island, we saw that the opportunity cost of a good increased as the output of the good increased. Opportunity costs in the real world increase for the same reasons that Jane's opportunity costs increase.

Consider, for example, two goods vital to our well-being: food and health care. In allocating our scarce resources, we use the most fertile land and the most skilful farmers to produce food. We use the best doctors and the least fertile land to produce health care services.

If we shift fertile land and tractors away from farming and ask farmers to practise medicine, the production of food drops drastically and the increase in the production of health-care services is small. The opportunity cost of health-care services rises.

Similarly, if we shift our resources away from health care towards farming, we have to use more doctors and nurses as farmers and more hospitals as hydroponic tomato factories. The drop in health-care services is large, but the increase in food production small. The opportunity cost of producing more food rises.

This example is extreme and unlikely, but these same considerations apply to any pair of goods that you can imagine: guns and butter, housing for the needy and Cadillacs for the rich, wheelchairs and golf carts, television programs and breakfast cereals. We cannot escape from scarcity and opportunity cost.

REVIEW

O pportunity cost is the value of the best alternative forgone. Opportunity cost is measured along the production possibility frontier by calculating the number of units of one good that must be given up to obtain one more unit of the other good. The production possibility frontier is bowed outward because not all resources are equally useful for producing all goods. The most useful resources are employed first. Because the production possibility frontier is bowed outward, the opportunity cost of each good increases as more of it is produced. ◆

Economic Growth

Although the production possibility frontier defines the boundary between what is attainable and what is unattainable, that boundary is not static. It is constantly changing. Sometimes the production possibility frontier shifts *inward*, reducing our production possibilities. For example, droughts or other extreme climatic conditions shift the frontier inward. Sometimes the frontier moves outward. For example, excellent growing and harvest conditions have this effect. Sometimes the frontier shifts outward because we get a new idea. It suddenly occurs to us that there is a better way of doing something that we never before imagined possible—we invent the wheel.

Over the years, our production possibilities have undergone enormous expansion. The expansion of our production possibilities is called **economic growth**. As a consequence of economic growth, we can now produce much more than we could a hundred years ago and quite a bit more than we could even ten years ago. By the late 1990s, if the same pace of growth continues, our production possibilities will be even greater. By pushing out the frontier, can we avoid the constraints imposed on us by our limited resources? That is, can we get our free lunch after all?

The Cost of Economic Growth

We are going to discover that although we can and do shift the production possibility frontier outward over time, we cannot have economic growth without incurring costs. The faster the pace of economic growth, the less we can consume at the present time. Let's investigate the costs of growth by examining why economies grow and prosper.

Two key activities generate economic growth: capital accumulation and technological progress. **Capital accumulation** is the growth of capital resources. **Technological progress** is the development of new and better ways of producing goods and services. As a consequence of capital accumulation and technological progress, we have an enormous quantity of cars and airplanes that enable us to produce more transportation than when we had only horses and carriages; we have satellites that make transcontinental communications possible on a scale much larger than that produced by the earlier cable technology. But accumulating capital and developing new technology is costly. To see why, let's go back to Jane's island economy.

Capital Accumulation and Technological Change

So far, we've assumed that Jane's island economy can produce only two goods, corn and cloth. But let's now suppose that while pursuing some of the sheep, Jane stumbles upon an outcrop of flint stone and a forest that she did not know about before. She realizes that she can now make flint tools and start building fences around the corn and sheep, thereby increasing production of both of these goods. But to make tools and build fences, Jane has to devote time to these activities. Let's continue to suppose that there are only 10 hours of working time available each day. Time spent making tools and building fences is time that could have been spent growing corn and making cloth. Thus to expand her future production, Jane must produce less corn and cloth today so that some of her time can be devoted to making tools and building fences. The decrease in her output of corn and cloth today is the opportunity cost of expanding her production of these two goods in the future.

Figure 3.3 provides a concrete example. The table sets out Jane's production possibilities for producing capital—tools and fences—as well as current consumption goods—corn and cloth. If she devotes all her working hours to corn and cloth production (row e), she produces no capital—no tools or fences. If she devotes enough time to producing one unit of capital each month (row d), her corn and cloth production is cut back to 90 percent of its maximum possible level. She can devote still more time to capital accumulation and, as she does so, her corn and cloth production falls by successively larger amounts.

The numbers in the table are graphed in Fig. 3.3. Each point, a through e, represents a row of the table. Notice the similarity between Fig. 3.3 and Fig. 3.1. Each shows a production possibility frontier. In the case of Fig. 3.3, the frontier is that between producing capital equipment (tools and

FIGURE 3.3

Economic Growth on Jane's Island

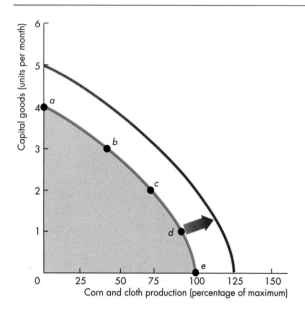

Possibility	Capital (units per month)	Corn and cloth production (percentage of maximum)
a	4	0
b	3	40
c	2	70
d	1	90
e	0	100

If Jane devotes all her time to corn and cloth production, she produces no capital equipment (row *e* of the table). If she devotes more time to capital accumulation, she produces successively smaller amounts of corn and cloth. The curve *abcde* is Jane's production possibility frontier for capital goods (tools and fences) and consumption goods (corn and cloth). If Jane produces no capital (point *e*), her production possibility frontier remains fixed at *abcde*. If she cuts her current production of corn and cloth and produces one unit of capital (point *d*), her future production possibility frontier lies outside her current frontier. The more time Jane devotes to accumulating capital and the less time she devotes to producing corn and cloth, the farther out her frontier shifts. The decreased output of corn and cloth is the opportunity cost of increased future production possibilities.

fences) and producing current consumption goods (corn and cloth). If Jane produces at point *e* in Fig. 3.3, she produces no capital goods and remains stuck on the production possibility frontier for corn and cloth shown in Fig. 3.1. But if she moves to point *d* in Fig. 3.3, she can produce one unit of capital each month. To do so, Jane reduces her current production of corn and cloth to 90 percent of what she can produce if all her time is devoted to those activities. In terms of Fig. 3.1, Jane's current production possibility frontier for corn and cloth shifts leftward as she devotes less time to corn and cloth production and some time to producing capital goods.

By decreasing her production of corn and cloth and producing tools and building fences, Jane is able to increase her future production possibilities. An increasing stock of tools and fences makes her more productive at growing corn and producing cloth. She can even use tools to make better tools.

As a consequence, Jane's production possibility frontier shifts outward as shown by the shift arrow. Jane experiences economic growth.

But how far Jane's production possibility frontier shifts outward depends on how much time she devotes to accumulating capital. If she devotes no time to this activity, the frontier remains at *abcde*— the original production possibility frontier. If she cuts back on current production of corn and cloth and produces one unit of capital each month (point *d*), her frontier moves out in the future to the red curve in Fig. 3.3. The less time she devotes to corn and cloth production and the more time to capital accumulation, the farther out the frontier shifts.

But economic growth is not a free gift for Jane. To make it happen, she has to devote more time to producing tools and building fences and less to producing corn and cloth. Economic growth is no magic formula for abolishing scarcity.

Economic Growth in the Real World

The ideas that we have explored in the setting of Jane's island also apply to our real-world economy. If we devote all our resources to producing food, clothing, housing, vacations, and the many other consumer goods that we enjoy and none to research, development, and accumulating capital, we will have no more capital and no better technologies in the future than we have at present. Our production possibilities in the future will be exactly the same as those we have today. If we are to expand our production possibilities in the future, we must produce fewer consumption goods today. The resources that we free up today will enable us to accumulate capital and to develop better technologies for producing consumption goods in the future. The cut in the output of consumption goods today is the opportunity cost of economic growth.

The recent experience of Canada and Japan provides a striking example of the effects of our choices on the rate of economic growth. In 1965, the production possibilities per person in Canada were much larger than those in Japan (see Fig. 3.4). Canada devoted one-fifth of its resources to producing capital goods and the other four-fifths to producing consumption goods, as illustrated by point *a* in Fig. 3.4(a). But Japan devoted one-third of its resources to producing capital goods and only two-thirds to producing consumption goods, as illustrated by point *a* in Fig. 3.4(b). Both countries experienced economic growth, but the growth in Japan was much more rapid than the growth in Canada. Because Japan devoted a bigger fraction of its resources to producing capital goods, its stock of

FIGURE 3.4

Economic Growth in Canada and Japan

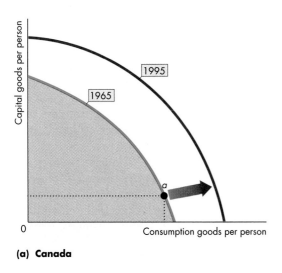

(a) Canada

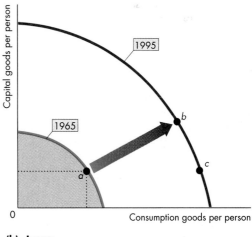

(b) Japan

In 1965, the production possibilities per person in Canada, part (a), were much larger than those in Japan, part (b). But Japan devoted one-third of its resources to producing capital goods, while Canada devoted only one-fifth—point *a* in each part of the figure. Japan's more rapid increase in capital resources resulted in its production possibility frontier shifting out more quickly than that of Canada.

The two production possibilities per person in 1995 are similar to each other. If Japan produces at point *b* on its 1995 frontier, it will continue to grow more quickly than Canada. If Japan increases consumption and produces at point *c* on its 1995 frontier, its growth rate will slow down to that of Canada.

capital equipment grew more quickly than ours, and its production possibilities expanded more quickly. As a result, Japanese production possibilities per person are now so close to those in Canada that it is hard to say which country has the larger per person production possibilities. If Japan continues to devote a third of its resources to producing capital goods (at point *b* on its 1995 production possibility frontier), it will continue to grow much more rapidly than Canada and its frontier will move out beyond our own. If Japan increases its production of consumption goods and reduces its production of capital goods (moving to point *c* on its 1995 production possibility frontier), then its rate of economic expansion will slow down to that of our own.

R E V I E W

Economic growth results from the accumulation of capital and the development of better technologies. To reap the fruits of economic growth, we must incur the cost of fewer goods and services for current consumption. By cutting the current output of consumption goods, we can devote more resources to accumulating capital and to the research and development that lead to technological change—the engines of economic growth. Thus economic growth does not provide a free lunch. It has an opportunity cost—the fall in the current output of consumption goods. ◆

Gains from Trade

No one excels at everything. One person is more athletic than another; another person may have a quicker mind or a better memory. What one person does with ease, someone else may find difficult.

Comparative Advantage: Jane Meets Joe

Differences in individual abilities mean that there are also differences in individual opportunity costs of producing various goods. Such differences give rise to **comparative advantage**—we say that a person has a comparative advantage in producing a particular good if that person can produce the good at a lower opportunity cost than anyone else.

People can produce for themselves all the goods that they consume or they can concentrate on producing one good (or perhaps a few goods) and then exchange some of their own products for the output of others. Concentrating on the production of only one good or a few goods is called **specialization**. We are going to discover how people can gain by specializing in that good at which they have a comparative advantage and trading their output with others.

Let's return again to our island economy. Suppose that Jane has discovered another island very close to her own and found that it too has only one inhabitant—Joe. Jane and Joe each have access to a simple boat that is adequate for transporting themselves and their goods between the two islands.

Joe's island, too, can produce only corn and cloth, but its terrain differs from that of Jane's island. While Jane's island has a lot of fertile corn-growing land and a small sheep population, Joe's island has little fertile corn-growing land and plenty of hilly land and sheep. This important difference between the two islands means that Joe's production possibility frontier is different from Jane's. Figure 3.5 illustrates these production possibility frontiers. Jane's frontier is labelled "Jane's PPF," and Joe's frontier is labelled "Joe's PPF."

Jane and Joe can be self-sufficient in corn and cloth. **Self-sufficiency** is a situation in which people produce only enough for their own consumption. Suppose that Jane and Joe are each self-sufficient. Jane chooses to produce and consume 3 metres of cloth and 11 kilograms of corn a month, point *d*. Joe chooses to produce and consume 2 metres of cloth and 7 kilograms of corn a month, point *b'*. These choices are identified on their respective production possibility frontiers in Fig. 3.5. (Each could have chosen any other point on their own production possibility frontier.) Total production of corn and cloth is the sum of Jane's and Joe's production: 18 kilograms of corn and 5 metres of cloth. Point *n* in the figure represents this total production.

Jane's Comparative Advantage   In which of the two goods does Jane have a comparative advantage? We have defined comparative advantage as a situation in which one person's opportunity cost of producing a good is lower than another person's opportunity cost of producing that same good. Jane, then, has a comparative advantage in producing whichever good she produces at a lower opportunity cost than Joe. What is that good?

You can answer the question by looking at the production possibility frontiers for Jane and Joe in Fig. 3.5. At the points at which they are producing and consuming, Jane's production possibility frontier is much steeper than Joe's. To produce one more kilogram of corn, Jane gives up less cloth than Joe. Hence Jane's opportunity cost of a kilogram of corn is lower than Joe's. This means that Jane has a comparative advantage in producing corn.

Joe's Comparative Advantage   Joe's comparative advantage is in producing cloth. His production possibility frontier at his consumption point is flatter than Jane's. This means that Joe has to give up less corn to produce one more metre of cloth than Jane does. Joe's opportunity cost of a metre of cloth is lower than Jane's, so Joe has a comparative advantage in cloth production.

Achieving the Gains from Trade

Can Jane and Joe do better than be self-sufficient? In particular, what would happen if each were to specialize in producing the good at which each has a comparative advantage and then trade with the other?

If Jane, who has a comparative advantage in corn production, puts all her time into growing corn, she can grow 20 kilograms. If Joe, who has a comparative advantage in cloth production, puts all his time into making cloth, he can make 9 metres. By specializing, Jane and Joe together can produce 20 kilograms of corn and 9 metres of cloth (the amount labelled *s* in the figure). Point *s* shows the production of 20 kilograms of corn (all produced by Jane) and 9 metres of cloth (all produced by Joe). Clearly, Jane and Joe produce more cloth and corn at point *s* than they were producing at point *n*, when each took care only of his or her own requirements. Jane and Joe prefer point *s* to point *n* because, between them, they have more of both corn and cloth at point

FIGURE 3.5

The Gains from Specialization and Exchange

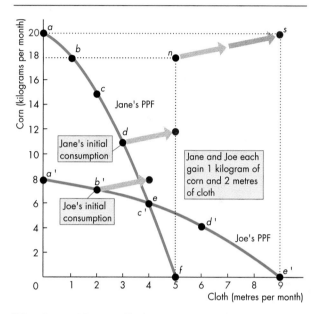

When Jane and Joe are self-sufficient, Joe consumes 7 kilograms of corn and 2 metres of cloth (point *b'*), and Jane consumes 11 kilograms of corn and 3 metres of cloth (point *d*). Their total production is 18 kilograms of corn and 5 metres of cloth (point *n*). Joe and Jane can do better by specialization and exchange. Jane, whose comparative advantage is in corn production, specializes in that activity, producing 20 kilograms a month (point *a*). Joe, whose comparative advantage is in cloth production, specializes in that activity, producing 9 metres of cloth a month (point *e'*). Total production is then 20 kilograms of corn and 9 metres of cloth (point *s*). If Jane gives Joe 8 kilograms of corn in exchange for 5 metres of cloth, they each enjoy increased consumption of both corn and cloth. They each gain from specialization and exchange.

s than at point *n*. They have an additional 2 kilograms of corn and 4 metres of cloth.

To obtain the gains from trade, Jane and Joe must do more than specialize in producing the good at which each has a comparative advantage. They must exchange the fruits of their specialized production. Suppose that Jane and Joe agree to exchange 5 metres of cloth for 8 kilograms of corn. Jane has 20 kilograms of corn and Joe has 9 metres of cloth before any exchange takes place. After the exchange takes place, Joe consumes 8 kilograms of corn and Jane 12 kilograms of corn; Joe consumes 4 metres of cloth and Jane 5 metres of cloth. Compared to the time when they were each self-sufficient, Jane now has 1 extra kilogram of corn and 2 extra metres of cloth, and Joe has 1 extra kilogram of corn and 2 extra metres of cloth. The gains from trade are represented by the increase in consumption of both goods that each obtains. Each consumes at a point outside their individual production possibility frontier.

Productivity and Absolute Advantage

Productivity is the amount of output produced per unit of inputs used to produce it. For example, Jane's productivity in making cloth is measured as the amount of cloth she makes per hour of work. If one person has greater productivity than another in the production of all goods, that person is said to have an **absolute advantage**. In our example, neither Jane nor Joe has an absolute advantage. Jane is more productive than Joe in growing corn, and Joe is more productive than Jane in making cloth.

It is often suggested that people and countries that have an absolute advantage can outcompete others in the production of all goods. For example, it is often suggested that Canada cannot compete with Japan because the Japanese are more productive than we are. This conclusion is wrong, as you are about to discover. To see why, let's look again at Jane and Joe.

Suppose that a volcano engulfs Jane's island, forcing her to search for a new one. And suppose further that disaster leads to good fortune. Jane stumbles onto a new island that is much more productive than the original one, enabling her to produce twice as much of either corn or cloth with each hour of her labour. Jane's new production possibilities appear in Table 3.2. Notice that she now has an absolute advantage.

We have already worked out that the gains from trade arise when each person specializes in producing the good in which he or she has a comparative advantage. Recall that a person has a comparative advantage in producing a particular good if that person can produce it at a lower opportunity cost than anyone else. Joe's opportunity costs remain exactly the same as they were before. What has happened to Jane's opportunity costs now that she has become twice as productive?

Table 3.2

Jane's New Production Possibilities

Possibility	Corn (kilograms per month)		Cloth (metres per month)
a	40	and	0
b	36	and	2
c	30	and	4
d	22	and	6
e	12	and	8
f	0	and	10

You can work out Jane's opportunity costs by using exactly the same calculation that was used in the table of Fig. 3.2. Start by looking at Jane's opportunity cost of corn. The first 12 kilograms of corn that Jane grows cost her 2 metres of cloth. So the opportunity cost of 1 kilogram of corn is 1/6 of a metre of cloth—the same as Jane's original opportunity cost of corn. If you calculate Jane's opportunity costs for her production possibilities a through f, you will discover that her opportunity costs have remained the same.

Since the opportunity cost of cloth is the inverse of the opportunity cost of corn, Jane's opportunity costs of cloth also have remained unchanged. Let's work through one example. If Jane moves from a to b to make 2 metres of cloth, she will have to reduce her corn production by 4 kilograms—from 40 to 36 kilograms. Thus the first 2 metres of cloth cost 4 kilograms of corn. The cost of 1 metre of cloth is therefore 2 kilograms of corn—exactly the same as before.

When Jane becomes twice as productive as before, each hour of her time produces more output, but her opportunity costs remain the same. One more unit of corn costs the same in terms of cloth forgone as it did previously. Since Jane's opportunity costs have not changed and since Joe's have not changed, Joe continues to have a comparative advantage in producing cloth. Both Jane and Joe can have more of both goods if Jane specializes in corn production and Joe in cloth production.

The key point to recognize is that it is *not* possible for a person having an absolute advantage to have a comparative advantage in everything.

R E V I E W

Gains from trade come from comparative advantage. A person has a comparative advantage in producing a good if that person can produce the good at a lower opportunity cost than anyone else. Thus differences in opportunity cost are the source of gains from specialization and exchange. Each person specializes in producing the good at which he or she has a comparative advantage and then exchanges some of that output for the goods produced by others.   ◆ ◆   If a person can produce a good with fewer inputs than someone else—is more productive—that person has an absolute advantage but not necessarily a comparative advantage. Even a person with an absolute advantage gains from specialization and exchange.   ◆

Exchange in the Real World

In the real world, countries can gain by specializing in the production of those goods and services at which they have a comparative advantage. An example is given in Reading Between the Lines on pp.64–65. But to obtain the gains from trade in the real world, where billions of people specialize in millions of different activities, trade has to be organized. To organize trade, we have evolved rules of conduct and mechanisms for enforcing those rules. One such mechanism is private property rights. Another is the institution of money. In the island economy of Jane and

Joe, direct exchange of one good with another is feasible. In the real-world economy, direct exchange of one good for another would be very cumbersome. To lubricate the wheels of exchange, societies have created money—a medium that enables indirect exchange of goods for money and money for goods. Let's examine these two aspects of exchange arrangements—private property rights and money—in more detail.

Property Rights

Property rights are social arrangements that govern the ownership, use, and disposal of property. **Property** is anything of value: it includes land and buildings, the things we call property in ordinary speech; it includes stocks and bonds, durable goods, plant and equipment; it also includes intellectual property. **Intellectual property** is the intangible product of creative effort, protected by copyrights and patents. This type of property includes books, music, computer programs, and inventions of all kinds.

What if property rights did not exist? What would such a social science fiction world be like?

A World without Property Rights   Without property rights, people could take possession of whatever they had the strength to obtain for themselves. In such a world, people would have to devote a good deal of their time, energy, and resources to protecting what they had produced or acquired.

In a world without property rights, it would not be possible to reap all the gains from specialization and exchange. People would have little incentive to specialize in producing those goods in which they each had a comparative advantage. In fact, the more of a particular good someone produced, the bigger is the chance that others would simply help themselves to it. Also, if a person could take the goods of others without giving up something in exchange, then there would be no point to specializing in producing something for exchange. In a world without property rights, no one would enjoy the gains from specialization and exchange, and everyone would specialize only in unproductive acts of piracy.

It is to overcome the problems we have just described that property rights have evolved. Let's examine these property rights as they operate to govern economic life in Canada today.

The Gains from Specialization and Exchange

The Essence of the Story

Hong Kong is Canada's 15th-largest market.

In 1992, Hong Kong exported $1.1-billion worth of goods—mainly clothes, toys, textiles, travel goods, footwear, and household equipment—to Canada.

Canada exported $822 million worth of goods to Hong Kong.

One Canadian export that grew quickly in 1992 was salmon heads, a popular item in Southern China.

THE GLOBE AND MAIL, OCTOBER 5, 1993

Improving links across Pacific

Canadian presence is significant

By Michael Bociurkiw

HONG KONG—In 1992, according to Statistics Canada, Hong Kong ranked as Canada's 15th-largest market. The colony's exports to Canada increased 11.1 per cent to $1.1-billion—mainly in the area of clothes, toys, textiles, travel goods, footwear and household equipment.

In turn, Canada exported $822-million worth of goods to Hong Kong, compared with $821-million in 1991....

Studying Canada's trade profile with Hong Kong, one unusual statistic that pops out pertains to seafood exports, which last year alone jumped 80 per cent to $26-million.

Scott Mullin, the Canadian trade commissioner in Hong Kong, said the huge increase was mostly because of the growing popularity of salmon heads in Southern China. Canadian food and agricultural products of all kinds exported to Hong Kong totalled $93-million in 1992....

Background and Analysis

Hong Kong has a comparative advantage in (among other things) clothes, toys, textiles, travel goods, footwear, and household equipment.

Canada has a comparative advantage in (among other things) seafood.

Canada and Hong Kong each gain by specializing in the goods in which they have a comparative advantage and by trading with each other.

The figure shows these gains. With no trade between Canada and Hong Kong, Canada produces 1 million salmon heads and 3 million T-shirts a month on its production possibility frontier, PPF, and Hong Kong produces 2 million salmon heads and 1 million T-shirts on its PPF.

With no trade, each country consumes what it produces. That is, Canada consumes 1 million salmon heads and 3 million T-shirts. Hong Kong consumes 2 million salmon heads and 1 million T-shirts.

With no trade, Hong Kong and Canada together produce the quantities shown by point n in the figure.

With specialization and exchange, Canada specializes in producing salmon heads, in which it has a comparative advantage, and Hong Kong specializes in producing T-shirts, in which it has a comparative advantage.

With specialization, Canada and Hong Kong together produce 6 million salmon heads and 6 million T-shirts a month—as shown by point s.

Each country consumes more of both goods as a result of specialization and exchange. Canada consumes 2 million salmon heads and 4 million T-shirts—at the red dot outside its PPF—and Hong Kong consumes 4 million salmon heads and 2 million T-shirts—at the red dot outside its PPF.

The red arrows show the gains from trade for Canada and Hong Kong. Both countries gain from specialization and trade.

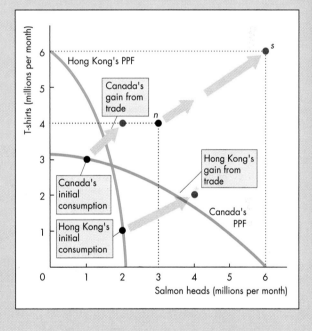

Property Rights in Private Enterprise Capitalism

The Canadian economy operates for the most part on the principles of private enterprise capitalism. **Private enterprise** is an economic system that permits individuals to decide on their own economic activities. **Capitalism** is an economic system that permits private individuals to own the capital resources used in production.

Under the property rights in such an economic system, individuals own what they have made, what they have acquired in a voluntary exchange with others, and what they have been given. Any attempt to remove the property of someone against that person's will is considered theft, a crime punished by a sufficiently severe penalty to deter most people from becoming thieves.

It is easy to see that property rights based on these ideas can generate gainful trade: people can specialize in producing those goods that, for them, have the least opportunity cost. Some people will specialize in enforcing and maintaining property rights (for example, politicians, judges, and police officers), and all individuals will have the incentive to trade with each other, offering the good in which they have a comparative advantage in exchange for the goods produced by others.

The Canadian economic system is based on private property rights and voluntary exchange. But there are important ways in which private property rights are modified in our country.

Taxes Modify Private Property Rights

Taxes on expenditure, income, and wealth transfer property from individuals to governments. Such transfers limit people's efforts to create more property and reduce their gains from specialization and exchange. But the taxes themselves are not arbitrary. Everyone faces the same rules and can calculate the effects of their own actions on the taxes for which they will be liable.

Regulation Modifies Private Property Rights

Some voluntary exchanges are prohibited or regulated. For example, food and drug manufacturers cannot place a product on the market without first obtaining approval from a government agency. The government controls or prohibits the sale of many types of drugs, and also restricts trading in human beings and their component parts—that is, it prohibits the selling of slaves, children, and human organs.

These restrictions on the extent of private property and on the legitimacy of voluntary exchange, though important, do not for the most part seriously impede specialization and gainful trade. Most people take the view that the benefits of regulation—for example, prohibiting the sale of dangerous drugs—far outweigh the costs imposed on the sellers.

Let's now turn to the other social institution that permits specialization and exchange—the development of an efficient means of exchange.

Money

We have seen that well-defined property rights based on voluntary exchange allow individuals to specialize and exchange their output with each other. In our island economy, we studied only two people and two goods. Exchange in such a situation was a simple matter. In the real world, however, how can billions of people exchange the millions of goods that are the fruits of their specialized labour?

Barter   Goods can be simply exchanged for goods. The direct exchange of one good for another is known as **barter**. However, barter severely limits the amount of trading that can take place. Imagine that you have roosters, but you want to get roses. First, you must look for someone with roses who wants roosters. Economists call this a **double coincidence of wants**—when person A wants to sell exactly what person B wants to buy, and person B wants to sell exactly what person A wants to buy. As the term implies, such occurrences are coincidences and will not arise frequently. A second way of trading by barter is to undertake a sequence of exchanges. If you have oranges and you want apples, you might have to trade oranges for plums, plums for pomegranates, pomegranates for pineapples, and then eventually pineapples for apples.

Cumbersome though it is, quite a large amount of barter does take place. For example, when British rock star Rod Stewart played in Budapest, Hungary, in 1986, he received part of his $30,000 compensation in Hungarian sound equipment, electrical cable, and the use of a forklift truck. And before the recent changes in Eastern Europe, hairdressers in Warsaw, Poland, obtained their barbershop equipment from England in exchange for hair clippings that they supplied to London wigmakers. Today, Australian meat processors swap cans of meat for Russian salmon, crabmeat, and scallops, and Australian wool growers swap wool for Russian electrical motors.

Although barter does occur, it is an inefficient means of exchanging goods. Fortunately, a better alternative has been invented.

Monetary Exchange   An alternative to barter is **monetary exchange**—a system in which some commodity or token serves as the medium of exchange. A **medium of exchange** is anything that is generally acceptable in exchange for goods and services. **Money** can also be defined as a medium of exchange—something that can be passed on to others in exchange for goods and services.

Money lowers the cost of transacting and makes posssible millions of transactions that simply would not be worth undertaking by barter. Can you imagine the chain of barter transactions you'd have to go through every day to get your coffee, cola, textbooks, professor's time, video, and all the other goods and services you consume? In a monetary exchange system, you exchange your time and effort for money and use that money to buy the goods and services you consume, cutting out the incredible hassle you'd face each day in a world of barter.

Metals such as gold, silver, and copper have long served as money, most commonly when they are stamped as coins. Primitive societies have traditionally used various commodities, such as seashells, as money. Prisoners of war in German camps in World War II used cigarettes as money. Using cigarettes as a medium of exchange should not be confused with barter. When cigarettes play the role of money, people buy and sell goods by using cigarettes as a medium of exchange.

In modern societies, governments provide paper money. The banking system also provides money in the form of chequing accounts. Chequing accounts can be used for settling debts simply by writing an instruction—writing a cheque—to the bank requesting that funds be transferred to another chequing account. Electronic links between bank accounts, now becoming more widespread, enable direct transfers between different accounts without any cheques being written.

◆ ◆ ◆ ◆ You have now begun to see how economists go about the job of trying to answer some important questions. The simple fact of scarcity and the associated concept of opportunity cost allow us to understand why people specialize, why they trade with each other, why they have social conventions that define and enforce private property rights, and why they use money. One simple idea—scarcity and its direct implication, opportunity cost—explains so much!

S U M M A R Y

The Production Possibility Frontier

The production possibility frontier is the boundary between what is attainable and what is not attainable. Production can take place at any point inside or on the production possibility frontier, but it is not possible to produce outside the frontier. There is always a point on the production possibility frontier that is better than a point inside it. (pp. 51–53)

Opportunity Cost

The opportunity cost of any action is the best alternative action forgone. The opportunity cost of acquiring one good is equivalent to the amount of another good that must be given up. The opportunity cost of a good increases as the quantity of it produced increases. (pp. 54–56)

Economic Growth

Although the production possibility frontier marks the boundary between the attainable and the unattainable, that boundary does not remain fixed. It changes over time, partly because of natural forces (for example, changes in climate and the accumulation of ideas about better ways of producing) and partly by the choices that we make (choices about consumption and saving). If we use some of today's resources to produce capital goods and for research and development, we will be able to produce more goods and services in the future. The economy will grow. But growth cannot take place without incurring costs. The opportunity cost of more goods and services in the future is consuming fewer goods and services today. (pp. 57–60)

Gains from Trade

A person has a comparative advantage in producing a good if that person can produce the good at a lower opportunity cost than anyone else. People can gain from trade if they each specialize in the activity at which they have a comparative advantage. Each person produces the good for which his or her opportunity cost is lower than everyone else's. They then exchange part of their output with each other. By this activity, each person is able to consume at a point *outside* his or her individual production possibility frontier.

When one person is more productive than another person (can produce more output from fewer inputs), that person has an absolute advantage. But having an absolute advantage does not mean there are no gains from trade. Even if someone is more productive than other people in all activities, as long as the other person has a lower opportunity cost of some good, then gains from specialization and exchange are available. (pp. 60–63)

Exchange in the Real World

Exchange in the real world involves the specialization of billions of people in millions of different activities. To make it worthwhile for each individual to specialize and to enable societies to reap the gains from trade, institutions and mechanisms have evolved. The most important of these are private property rights, with a political and legal system to enforce them, and a system of monetary exchange. These institutions enable people to specialize, exchanging their labour for money and their money for goods, thereby reaping the gains from trade. (pp. 63–67)

K E Y   E L E M E N T S

Key Terms

Absolute advantage, 62
Barter, 66
Capital accumulation, 57
Capital goods, 51
Capitalism, 66
Comparative advantage, 60
Consumption, 51
Consumption goods, 51
Double coincidence of wants, 66
Economic growth, 57
Goods and services, 51
Human capital, 51
Intellectual property, 63
Medium of exchange, 67
Monetary exchange, 67
Money, 67
Private enterprise, 66
Production, 51

Production possibility frontier, 51
Productivity, 62
Property, 63
Property rights, 63
Self-sufficiency, 60
Specialization, 60
Technological progress, 57

Key Figures

Figure 3.1 Jane's Production Possibility Frontier, 53
Figure 3.2 Jane's Opportunity Cost of Cloth, 55
Figure 3.3 Economic Growth on Jane's Island, 58
Figure 3.5 The Gains from Specialization and Exchange, 61

R E V I E W   Q U E S T I O N S

1 How does the production possibility frontier illustrate scarcity?

2 How does the production possibility curve illustrate opportunity cost?

3 Explain what shifts the production possibility frontier outward and what shifts it inward.

4 Explain how our choices influence economic growth. What is the cost of economic growth?

5 Why does it pay people to specialize and trade with each other?

6 What are the gains from trade? How do they arise?

7 Why do social contracts such as property rights and money become necessary?

8 What is money? Give some examples of money. In the late 1980s, people in Rumania could use Kent cigarettes to buy almost anything. Was this monetary exchange or barter? Explain your answer.

9 What are the advantages of monetary exchange over barter?

P R O B L E M S

1 Suppose there is a change in the weather conditions on Jane's island that makes the corn yields much higher. This enables Jane to produce the following amounts of corn:

Hours worked (per day)	Corn (kilograms per month)
0	0
2	60
4	100
6	120
8	130
10	140

Her cloth production possibilities are the same as those that appeared in Table 3.1.

a   What are six points on Jane's new production possibility frontier?

b   What are Jane's opportunity costs of corn and cloth? List them at each of the five levels of output.

c   Compare Jane's opportunity cost of cloth with that in the table in Fig. 3.2. Has her opportunity cost of cloth gone up, gone down, or remained the same? Explain why.

2 Amy lives with her parents and attends the community college. The college is operated by the provincial government, and tuition is free. Jobs that pay $7 an hour are available to high school graduates in the town. Amy's mother, a high school graduate, takes a part-time job so that Amy can go to school. Amy's textbooks cost $280, and Amy gets an allowance of $140 a month from her mother. List the items that make up Amy's opportunity cost of attending college.

3 Suppose that Leisureland produces only two goods—food and suntan oil. Its production possibilities are

Food (kilograms per month)		Suntan oil (litres per month)
300	and	0
200	and	50
100	and	100
0	and	150

Busyland also produces only food and suntan oil, and its production possibilities are

Food (kilograms per month)		Suntan oil (litres per month)
150	and	0
100	and	100
50	and	200
0	and	300

a What are the opportunity costs of food and suntan oil in Leisureland? List them at each output given in the table.

b Why are the opportunity costs the same at each output level?

c What are the opportunity costs of food and suntan oil in Busyland? List them at each output level given in the table.

4 Suppose that in problem 3 Leisureland and Busyland do not specialize and trade with each other—each country is self-sufficient. Leisureland produces and consumes 50 kilograms of food and 125 litres of suntan oil per month. Busyland produces and consumes 150 kilograms of food per month and no suntan oil. The countries begin to trade with each other.

a What good does Leisureland export, and what good does it import?

b What good does Busyland export, and what good does it import?

c What is the maximum quantity of food and suntan oil that the two countries can produce if each country specializes in the activity at which it has the lower opportunity cost?

5 Suppose that Busyland becomes three times as productive as in problem 3.

a Show, on a graph, the effect of the increased productivity on Busyland's production possibility frontier.

b Does Busyland now have an absolute advantage in producing both goods?

c Can Busyland gain from specialization and trade with Leisureland now that it is three times as productive? If so, what will it produce?

d What are the total gains from trade? What do these gains depend on?

6 Andy and Bob work at Mario's Pizza Palace. In an eight-hour day, Andy can make 240 pizzas or 100 ice cream sundaes, and Bob can make 80 pizzas or 80 ice cream sundaes. Who does Mario get to make the ice cream sundaes? Who makes the pizzas? Explain your answer.

CHAPTER 4

DEMAND AND SUPPLY

After studying this chapter, you will be able to

◆ Construct a demand schedule and a demand curve

◆ Construct a supply schedule and a supply curve

◆ Explain how prices are determined

◆ Explain how quantities bought and sold are determined

◆ Explain why some prices rise, some fall, and some fluctuate

◆ Make predictions about price changes using the demand and supply model

SLIDE, ROCKET, AND ROLLER COASTER—RIDES AT CANADA'S Wonderland? No. Commonly used descriptions of the behaviour of prices. An example of a slide is the price of the Walkman. In 1979, when Sony began to market the Walkman, its price tag was $300—more than $500 in today's money. Now you can buy a Walkman for less than one-tenth of the original price. During the time that the Walkman has been with us, the quantity bought has increased steadily. Why has there been a slide in the price of the Walkman? Why hasn't the increase in the quantity bought kept its price high? ◆ ◆ An example of rocketing prices is that of rents paid for apartments and houses in the centres of big cities. Increases in rents and house prices have not deterred people from living in the centres of cities—on the contrary, their numbers have increased slightly in recent years. Why do people continue to seek housing in city cen-

Slide, Rocket, and
Roller Coaster

tres when rents have rocketed? ◆ ◆ The prices of coffee, strawberries, and other agricultural commodities are examples of roller coasters. Why does the price of coffee roller-coaster even when people's taste for coffee hardly changes at all? ◆ ◆ The price of the audio cassette tapes that we play in a Walkman has barely changed over the past ten years. But the number of tapes bought has increased each year. Why do firms sell more tapes, even though they're not able to get a higher price for them, and why do people buy more tapes even though their price is no lower than it was a decade ago?

◆ ◆ ◆ ◆ We'll discover the answers to these and similar questions by studying the theory of demand and supply.

Demand

The **quantity demanded** of a good or service is the amount that consumers plan to buy in a given period of time at a particular price. Demands are different from wants. **Wants** are the unlimited desires or wishes that people have for goods and services. How many times have you thought that you would like something "if only you could afford it" or "if it weren't so expensive"? Scarcity guarantees that many—perhaps most—of our wants will never be satisfied. Demand reflects a decision about which wants to satisfy. If you demand something, then you've made a plan to buy it.

The quantity demanded is not necessarily the same amount as the quantity actually bought. Sometimes the quantity demanded is greater than the amount of goods available, so the quantity bought is less than the quantity demanded.

The quantity demanded is measured as an amount per unit of time. For example, suppose a person consumes one cup of coffee a day. The quantity of coffee demanded by that person can be expressed as 1 cup per day or 7 cups per week or 365 cups per year. Without a time dimension, we cannot tell whether a particular quantity demanded is large or small.

What Determines Buying Plans?

The amount that consumers plan to buy of any particular good or service depends on many factors. The main ones are

◆ The price of the good

◆ The prices of related goods

◆ Income

◆ Expected future prices

◆ Population

◆ Preferences

The theory of demand and supply makes predictions about prices and quantities bought and sold. Let's begin by focusing on the relationship between the quantity demanded and the price of a good. To study this relationship, we hold constant all other influences on consumers' planned purchases. We can then ask: how does the quantity demanded of the good vary as its price varies?

The Law of Demand

The law of demand states:

Other things remaining the same, the higher the price of a good, the lower is the quantity demanded.

Why does a higher price reduce the quantity demanded? The key to the answer lies in *other things remaining the same*. Because other things are being held constant, when the price of a good rises, it rises *relative* to the prices of all other goods. Although each good is unique, it has substitutes—other goods that serve almost as well. As the price of a good climbs higher, relative to the prices of its substitutes, people buy less of that good and more of its substitutes.

Let's consider an example—blank audio cassette tapes, which we'll refer to as "tapes." Many different goods provide a similar service to a tape: for example, records, compact discs, prerecorded tapes, radio and television broadcasts, and live concerts. Tapes sell for about $3 each. If the price of a tape doubles to $6 while the prices of all the other goods remain constant, the quantity of tapes demanded decreases. People buy more compact discs and prerecorded tapes and fewer blank tapes. If the price of a tape falls to $1 while the prices of all the other goods stay constant, the quantity of tapes demanded increases and the demand for compact discs and prerecorded tapes decreases.

Demand Schedule and Demand Curve

A **demand schedule** lists the quantities demanded at each different price, when all other influences on consumers' planned purchases—such as the prices of related goods, income, expected future prices, population, and preferences—remain the same.

The table in Fig. 4.1 sets out a demand schedule for tapes. For example, if the price of a tape is $1, the quantity demanded is 9 million tapes a week. If the price of a tape is $5, the quantity demanded is 2 million tapes a week. The other rows of the table show us the quantities demanded at prices between $2 and $4.

A demand schedule can be illustrated by drawing a demand curve. A **demand curve** graphs the relationship between the quantity demanded of a good and its price, holding constant all other influences on consumers' planned purchases. The graph in Fig. 4.1 illustrates the demand curve for tapes. By convention, the quantity demanded is always measured on the horizontal axis, and the price is measured on the vertical axis. The points on the demand curve labelled *a* through *e* represent the rows of the demand schedule. For example, point *a* on the graph represents a quantity demanded of 9 million tapes a week at a price of $1 a tape.

Willingness to Pay

Another way of looking at the demand curve is as a willingness-to-pay curve. It tells us the highest price that will be paid for the last unit available. If a large quantity is available, that price is low; if a small quantity is available, that price is high. In Fig. 4.1, if 9 million tapes are available each week, the highest price that consumers are willing to pay for the 9 millionth tape is $1. But if only 2 million tapes are available each week, consumers are willing to pay $5 for the last tape available.

To understand this view of the demand curve, think about your own demand for tapes. If you are given a list of possible prices for tapes, you can write down alongside each price your planned weekly purchase of tapes—your demand schedule for tapes. Alternatively, if you are told that you can buy just one tape a week, you can say how much you would be willing to pay for it. The price you would be willing to pay for one tape is the same as the price at which your quantity demanded is one tape a week. If you are then told you can buy a second tape, you can say how much you would be willing to pay for that tape. The amount you would be willing to pay is the same as the price at which you would buy two tapes a week. This process can continue—you are asked how much you are willing to pay for one more tape—and the resulting list of quantities of tapes and maximum prices you would be willing to pay is the same list as your demand schedule.

FIGURE 4.1

The Demand Curve and the Demand Schedule

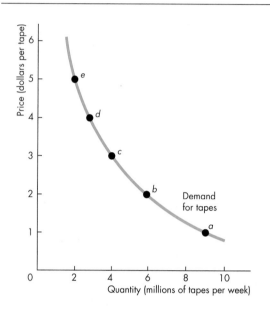

	Price (dollars per tape)	Quantity (millions of tapes per week)
a	1	9
b	2	6
c	3	4
d	4	3
e	5	2

The table shows a demand schedule listing the quantity of tapes demanded at each price if all other influences on buyers' plans are held constant. At a price of $1 a tape, 9 million tapes a week are demanded; at a price of $3 a tape, 4 million tapes a week are demanded. The demand curve shows the relationship between quantity demanded and price, holding everything else constant. The demand curve slopes downward: as price decreases, the quantity demanded increases. The demand curve can be read two ways. For a given price, it tells us the quantity that people plan to buy. For example, at a price of $3 a tape, the quantity demanded is 4 million tapes a week. For a given quantity, the demand curve tells us the maximum price consumers are willing to pay for the last tape bought. For example, the maximum price consumers will pay for the 6 millionth tape is $2.

A Change in Demand

The term **demand** refers to the entire relationship between the quantity demanded and the price of a good. The demand for tapes is described by both the demand schedule and the demand curve in Fig. 4.1. To construct a demand schedule and demand curve, we hold constant all the other influences on consumers' buying plans. But what are the effects of each of those other influences?

1. Prices of Related Goods   The quantity of tapes that consumers plan to buy does not depend only on the price of tapes. It also depends in part on the prices of related goods. These related goods fall into two categories: substitutes and complements.

A **substitute** is a good that can be used in place of another good. For example, a bus ride substitutes for a train ride; a hamburger substitutes for a hot dog; a pear substitutes for an apple. As we have seen, tapes have many substitutes—records, prerecorded tapes, compact discs, radio and television broadcasts, and live concerts. If the price of one of these substitutes increases, people economize on its use and buy more tapes. For example, if the price of records doubles, fewer records are bought and the demand for tapes increases—there is much more taping of other people's records. Conversely, if the price of one of these substitutes decreases, people use the now cheaper good in larger quantities, and they buy fewer tapes. For example, if the price of prerecorded tapes decreases, people play more of these tapes and make fewer of their own tapes—the demand for blank tapes falls.

The effects of a change in the price of a substitute occur no matter what the price of a tape. Whether tapes have a high or a low price, a change in the price of a substitute encourages people to make the substitutions that we've just reviewed. As a consequence, a change in the price of a substitute changes the entire demand schedule for tapes and shifts the demand curve.

A **complement** is a good used in conjunction with another good. Some examples of complements are hamburgers and french fries, party snacks and drinks, spaghetti and meat sauce, running shoes and jogging pants. Tapes also have their complements: Walkmans, tape recorders, and stereo tape decks. If the price of one of these complements increases, people buy fewer tapes. Conversely, if the price of one of these complements decreases, people buy more tapes.

2. Income   Another influence on demand is consumer income. Other things remaining the same, when income increases, consumers buy more of most goods, and when income decreases, they buy less of most goods. Consumers with higher incomes demand more of most goods. Consumers with lower incomes demand less of most goods. Rich people consume more food, clothing, housing, art, vacations, and entertainment than do poor people.

Although an increase in income leads to an increase in the demand for most goods, it does not lead to an increase in the demand for all goods. Goods that do increase in demand as income increases are called **normal goods**. Goods that decrease in demand when income increases are called **inferior goods**. Examples of inferior goods are rice and potatoes. These two goods are a major part of the diet of people with very low incomes. As incomes increase, the demand for these goods declines as more expensive meat and dairy products are substituted for them.

3. Expected Future Prices   If the price of a good is expected to rise, it makes sense to buy more of the good today and less in the future when its price is higher. Similarly, if its price is expected to fall, it pays to cut back on today's purchases and buy more later when the price is expected to be lower. Thus the higher the expected future price of a good, the larger is today's demand for the good.

4. Population   Demand also depends on the size of the population. Other things remaining the same, the larger the population, the greater is the demand for all goods and services, and the smaller the population, the smaller is the demand for all goods and services.

5. Preferences   Finally, demand depends on preferences. *Preferences* are an individual's attitudes towards goods and services. For example, a rock music fanatic has a much greater taste for tapes than does a tone-deaf workaholic. As a consequence, even if they have the same incomes, their demands for tapes will be very different.

Preferences are not observed. But preferences *change* slowly and so have little influence on *changes* in demand.

A summary of the influences on demand and the directions of those influences is presented in Table 4.1.

TABLE 4.1

The Demand for Tapes

THE LAW OF DEMAND

The quantity of tapes demanded

Decreases if

- The price of a tape rises

Increases if

- The price of a tape falls

CHANGES IN DEMAND

The demand for tapes

Decreases if

- The price of a substitute falls
- The price of a complement rises
- Income falls*
- The price of a tape is expected to fall in the future
- The population decreases

Increases if

- The price of a substitute rises
- The price of a complement falls
- Income rises*
- The price of a tape is expected to rise in the future
- The population increases

*A tape is a normal good

FIGURE 4.2

A Change in the Demand Schedule and a Shift in the Demand Curve

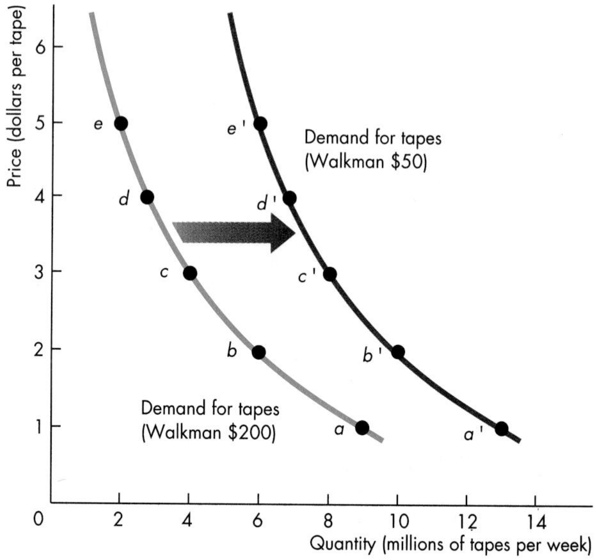

	Original demand schedule (Walkman $200)		New demand schedule (Walkman $50)	
	Price (dollars per tape)	Quantity (millions of tapes per week)	Price (dollars per tape)	Quantity (millions of tapes per week)
a	1	9	*a'* 1	13
b	2	6	*b'* 2	10
c	3	4	*c'* 3	8
d	4	3	*d'* 4	7
e	5	2	*e'* 5	6

A change in any influence on buyers other than the price of the good itself results in a new demand schedule and a shift in the demand curve. Here, a fall in the price of a Walkman—a complement of tapes—increases the demand for tapes. At a price of $3 a tape (third row of the table), 4 million tapes a week are demanded when the Walkman costs $200 and 8 million tapes a week are demanded when the Walkman costs only $50. A fall in the price of a Walkman increases the demand for tapes. The demand curve shifts rightward, as shown by the shift arrow and the resulting red curve.

Movement along versus a Shift in the Demand Curve

Changes in the influences on buyers' plans cause either a movement along the demand curve or a shift in it. Let's discuss each case in turn.

Movement along the Demand Curve If the price of a good changes but everything else remains the same, there is a movement along the demand curve. For example, if the price of a tape changes from $3 to $5, the result is a movement along the demand curve, from point *c* to point *e* in Fig. 4.1.

A Shift in the Demand Curve If the price of a good remains constant but some other influence on buyers' plans changes, we say that there is a change in demand for that good. We illustrate the change in demand as a shift in the demand curve. For example, a fall in the price of the Walkman—a complement of tapes—increases the demand for tapes. We illustrate this increase in demand for tapes with a new demand schedule and a new demand curve.

Consumers demand a larger quantity of tapes at each and every price.

The table in Fig. 4.2 provides some hypothetical numbers that illustrate such a shift. The table sets out the original demand schedule when the price of a Walkman is $200 and the new demand schedule when the price of a Walkman is $50. These numbers record the change in demand. The graph in Fig. 4.2 illustrates the corresponding shift in the demand curve. When the price of the Walkman falls, the demand curve for tapes shifts rightward.

A Change in Demand versus a Change in Quantity Demanded   A point on the demand curve shows the quantity demanded at a given price. A move-

ment along the demand curve shows a **change in the quantity demanded**. The entire demand curve shows demand. A shift in the demand curve shows a **change in demand**.

Figure 4.3 illustrates and summarizes these distinctions. If the price of a good falls but nothing else changes, then there is an increase in the quantity demanded of that good (a movement down the demand curve D_0). If the price rises but nothing else changes, then there is a decrease in the quantity demanded (a movement up the demand curve D_0). When any other influence on buyers' planned purchases changes, the demand curve shifts and there is a *change* (an increase or a decrease) *in demand*. A rise in income (for a normal good), in population, in the price of a substitute, or in the expected future price of the good or a fall in the price of a complement shifts the demand curve rightward (to the red demand curve D_2). This represents an *increase in demand*. A fall in income (for a normal good), in population, in the price of a substitute, or in the expected future price of the good or a rise in the price of a complement shifts the demand curve leftward (to the red demand curve D_1). This represents a *decrease in demand*. For an inferior good, the effects of changes in income are in the opposite direction to those described above.

FIGURE 4.3

A Change in Demand versus a Change in the Quantity Demanded

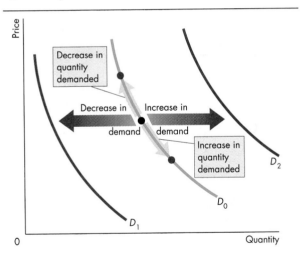

When the price of a good changes, there is a movement along the demand curve and a *change in the quantity of the good demanded*. For example, if the demand curve is D_0, a rise in the price of the good produces a decrease in the quantity demanded, and a fall in the price of the good produces an increase in the quantity demanded. The blue arrows on demand curve D_0 represent these movements along the demand curve. If some other influence on demand changes, increasing the quantity that people plan to buy, the demand curve shifts rightward (from D_0 to D_2) and demand *increases*. If some other influence on demand changes, reducing the quantity people plan to buy, the demand curve shifts leftward (from D_0 to D_1) and demand *decreases*.

REVIEW

O ther things remaining the same, the quantity demanded of a good increases if its price falls. Also, other things remaining the same, the greater the quantity available, the lower is the price that consumers are willing to pay for the last unit.
◆ ◆   Demand increases if the price of a substitute rises, if the price of a complement falls, if income rises (for a normal good), if the expected future price rises, or if the population increases; demand decreases if the price of a substitute falls, if the price of a complement rises, if income falls (for a normal good), if the expected future price falls, or if the population decreases. ◆ ◆   If the price of a good changes but all other influences on buyers' plans remain the same, there is a change in the quantity demanded and a movement along the demand curve. All other influences on consumers' planned purchases shift the demand curve. ◆

Supply

The **quantity supplied** of a good is the amount that producers plan to sell in a given period of time. The quantity supplied is not the amount a firm would like to sell but the amount it definitely plans to sell. However, the quantity supplied is not necessarily the same as the quantity actually sold. If consumers do not want to buy the quantity a firm plans to sell, the firm's sales plans will be frustrated. Like quantity demanded, the quantity supplied is expressed as an amount per unit of time.

What Determines Selling Plans?

The amount that firms plan to sell of any particular good or service depends on many factors. The main ones are

◆ The price of the good

◆ The prices of factors of production

◆ The prices of related goods

◆ Expected future prices

◆ The number of suppliers

◆ Technology

Because the theory of demand and supply makes predictions about prices and quantities bought and sold, we focus first on the relationship between the price of a good and the quantity supplied. In order to study this relationship, we hold constant all the other influences on the quantity supplied. We ask: how does the quantity supplied of a good vary as its price varies?

The Law of Supply

The law of supply states:

Other things remaining the same, the higher the price of a good, the greater is the quantity supplied.

Why does a higher price lead to a greater quantity supplied of a good? It is because the cost of producing an additional unit of the good increases (at least eventually) as the quantity produced increases. To induce them to incur a higher cost and increase production, firms must be compensated with a higher price.

Supply Schedule and Supply Curve

A **supply schedule** lists the quantities supplied at each different price, when all other influences on the amount firms plan to sell are held constant. Let's construct a supply schedule. To do so, we examine how the quantity supplied of a good varies as its price varies, holding constant the prices of other goods, the prices of factors of production used to produce it, expected future prices, and the state of technology.

The table in Fig. 4.4 sets out a supply schedule for tapes. It shows the quantity of tapes supplied at each possible price. For example, if the price of a tape is $1, no tapes are supplied. If the price of a tape is $4, 5 million tapes are supplied each week.

A supply schedule can be illustrated by drawing a supply curve. A **supply curve** graphs the relationship between the quantity supplied and the price of a good, holding everything else constant. Using the numbers listed in the table, the graph in Fig. 4.4 illustrates the supply curve for tapes. For example, point *d* represents a quantity supplied of 5 million tapes a week at a price of $4 a tape.

Minimum Supply Price

Just as the demand curve has two interpretations, so too does the supply curve. So far we have thought about the supply curve and the supply schedule as showing the quantity that firms will supply at each possible price. But we can also think about the supply curve as showing the minimum price at which the last unit will be supplied. Looking at the supply schedule in this way, we ask: what is the minimum price that brings forth a supply of a given quantity? For firms to supply the 3 millionth tape each week, the price has to be at least $2 a tape. For firms to supply the 5 millionth tape each week, they have to get at least $4 a tape.

A Change in Supply

The term **supply** refers to the entire relationship between the quantity supplied of a good and its price. The supply of tapes is described by both the supply schedule and the supply curve in Fig. 4.4. To construct a supply schedule and supply curve, we hold constant all the other influences on suppliers' plans. Let's now consider these other influences.

1. Prices of Factors of Production   The prices of the factors of production used to produce a good influence its supply. For example, an increase in the prices of the labour and the capital equipment used to produce tapes increases the cost of producing tapes, so the supply of tapes decreases.

2. Prices of Related Goods   The supply of a good can be influenced by the prices of related goods. For example, if an automobile assembly line can produce either sports cars or sedans, the quantity of sedans produced will depend on the price of sports cars and the quantity of sports cars produced will depend on the price of sedans. These two goods are *substitutes in production*. An increase in the price of a substitute in production lowers the supply of the good. Goods can also be complements in production. *Complements in production* arise when two things are, of necessity, produced together. For example, extracting chemicals from coal produces coke, coal tar, and nylon. An increase in the price of any one of these by-products of coal increases the supply of the other by-products.

Tapes have no obvious complements in production, but they do have substitutes in production: prerecorded tapes. Suppliers of tapes can produce blank tapes and prerecorded tapes. An increase in the price of prerecorded tapes encourages producers to increase the supply of prerecorded tapes and decrease the supply of blank tapes.

3. Expected Future Prices   If the price of a good is expected to rise, it makes sense to sell less of the good today and more in the future, when its price is higher. Similarly, if its price is expected to fall, it pays to expand today's supply and sell less later, when the price is expected to be lower. Thus, other things remaining the same, the higher the expected future price of a good, the smaller is today's supply of the good.

FIGURE 4.4

The Supply Curve and the Supply Schedule

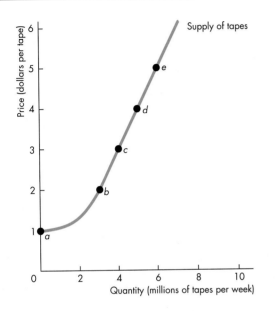

	Price (dollars per tape)	Quantity (millions of tapes per week)
a	1	0
b	2	3
c	3	4
d	4	5
e	5	6

The table shows the supply schedule of tapes. For example, at $2 a tape, 3 million tapes a week are supplied; at $5 a tape, 6 million tapes a week are supplied. The supply curve shows the relationship between the quantity supplied and price, holding everything else constant. The supply curve usually slopes upward: as the price of a good increases, so does the quantity supplied. A supply curve can be read in two ways. For a given price, it tells us the quantity that producers plan to sell. For example, at a price of $3 a tape, producers plan to sell 4 million tapes a week. The supply curve also tells us the minimum acceptable price at which a given quantity will be offered for sale. For example, the minimum acceptable price that will bring forth a supply of 4 million tapes a week is $3 a tape.

4. The Number of Suppliers   Other things remaining the same, the larger the number of firms supplying a good, the larger is the supply of the good.

5. Technology   New technologies that enable producers to use fewer factors of production will lower the cost of production and increase supply. For example, the development of a new technology for tape production by companies such as Sony and Minnesota Mining and Manufacturing (3M) has lowered the cost of producing tapes and increased their supply.

A summary of influences on supply and the directions of those influences is presented in Table 4.2. Over the long term, changes in technology are the major influence on supply.

Changes in the factors that influence producers alter the amount supplied and influence the supply

---

TABLE 4.2

The Supply of Tapes

THE LAW OF SUPPLY

The quantity of tapes supplied

Decreases if	*Increases if*
◆ The price of a tape falls	◆ The price of a tape rises

CHANGES IN SUPPLY

The supply of tapes

Decreases if	*Increases if*
◆ The price of a factor of production used to produce tapes increases	◆ The price of a factor of production used to produce tapes decreases
◆ The price of a substitute in production rises	◆ The price of a substitute in production falls
◆ The price of a complement in production falls	◆ The price of a complement in production rises
◆ The price of a tape is expected to rise in the future	◆ The price of a tape is expected to fall in the future
◆ The number of firms supplying tapes decreases	◆ The number of firms supplying tapes increases
	◆ More efficient technologies for producing tapes are discovered

---

curve in one of two ways. One possibility is that there is a movement along a supply curve. The other possibility is that the supply curve shifts. Let's look at these two cases.

Movement along versus a Shift in the Supply Curve

Whether there is a movement along the supply curve or a shift in the supply curve depends on the source of the change in supply plans.

Movement along the Supply Curve   If the price of a good changes but everything else influencing suppliers' planned sales remains constant, there is a movement along the supply curve. For example, if the price of tapes increases from $3 to $5 a tape, there will be a movement along the supply curve from point *c* (4 million tapes a week) to point *e* (6 million tapes a week) in Fig. 4.4.

A Shift in the Supply Curve   If the price of a good remains constant but another influence on suppliers' planned sales changes, then there is a change in supply and a shift in the supply curve. For example, as we have already noted, technological advances lower the cost of producing tapes and increase their supply. As a result, the supply schedule changes. The table in Fig. 4.5 provides some hypothetical numbers that illustrate such a change. The table contains two supply schedules: the original, based on "old" technology, and one based on "new" technology. With the new technology, more tapes are supplied at each price. The graph in Fig. 4.5 illustrates the resulting shift in the supply curve. When tape-producing technology improves, the supply curve of tapes shifts rightward, as shown by the shift arrow and the red supply curve.

A Change in Supply versus a Change in Quantity Supplied   A point on the supply curve shows the quantity supplied at a given price. A movement along the supply curve shows a **change in the quantity supplied**. The entire supply curve shows supply. A shift in the supply curve shows a **change in supply**.

Figure 4.6 illustrates and summarizes these distinctions. If the price of a good falls but nothing else changes, then there is a decrease in the quantity supplied of that good (a movement down the supply

FIGURE 4.5

A Change in the Supply Schedule and a Shift in the Supply Curve

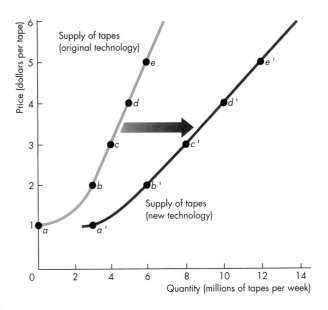

curve S_0). If the price of a good rises but nothing else changes, there is an increase in the quantity supplied (a movement up the supply curve S_0). When any other influence on sellers changes, the supply curve shifts and there is a *change in supply*. If the supply curve is S_0 and there is, say, a technological change that reduces the amounts of the factors of production needed to produce the good, then supply increases and the supply curve shifts rightward to the red supply curve S_2. Alternatively, if production costs rise, supply decreases and the supply curve shifts leftward to the red supply curve S_1.

FIGURE 4.6

A Change in Supply versus a Change in the Quantity Supplied

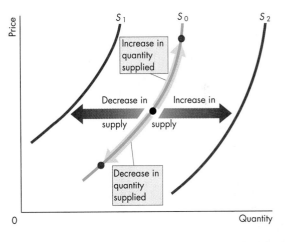

When the price of a good changes, there is a movement along the supply curve and a *change in the quantity of the good supplied*. For example, if the supply curve is S_0, a rise in the price of the good produces an increase in the quantity supplied, and a fall in the price produces a decrease in the quantity supplied. The blue arrows on curve S_0 represent these movements along the supply curve. If some other influence on supply changes, increasing the quantity that producers plan to sell, the supply curve shifts rightward (from S_0 to S_2) and *supply increases*. If some other influence on supply changes, reducing the quantity producers plan to sell, the supply curve shifts leftward (from S_0 to S_1) and *supply decreases*.

	Original technology			New technology	
	Price (dollars per tape)	Quantity (millions of tapes per week)		Price (dollars per tape)	Quantity (millions of tapes per week)
a	1	0	a'	1	3
b	2	3	b'	2	6
c	3	4	c'	3	8
d	4	5	d'	4	10
e	5	6	e'	5	12

If the price of a good remains constant but another influence on its supply changes, there will be a new supply schedule and the supply curve will shift. For example, if Sony and 3M invent a new, cost-saving technology for producing tapes, the supply schedule changes, as shown in the table. At $3 a tape, producers plan to sell 4 million tapes a week with the old technology and 8 million tapes a week with the new technology. Improved technology increases the supply of tapes and shifts the supply curve of tapes rightward.

REVIEW

T he quantity supplied is the amount of a good that producers plan to sell in a given period of time. Other things remaining the same, the quantity supplied of a good increases if its price rises. ◆ ◆ Supply can be represented by a schedule or a curve that shows the relationship between the quantity supplied of a good and its price. Supply describes the quantity that will be supplied at each possible price. Supply also describes the lowest price at which producers will supply the last unit. ◆ ◆ Supply increases if the prices of the factors of production used to produce the good fall, the prices of substitutes in production fall, the prices of complements in production rise, the expected future price of the good falls, or when technological advances lower the cost of production. ◆ ◆ If the price of a good changes but all other influences on producers' plans remain the same, there is a change in the quantity supplied and a movement along the supply curve but *no change in supply.* ◆ ◆ A change in any other influence on producers' plans changes supply and shifts the supply curve. Changes in the prices of factors of production, in the prices of substitutes in production and complements in production, in expected future prices, or in technology shift the supply curve and change supply. ◆

Let's now bring the two concepts of demand and supply together and see how prices are determined.

Price Determination

W e have seen that when the price of a good rises, the quantity demanded decreases and the quantity supplied increases. Conversely, when the price of a good falls, the quantity demanded increases and the quantity supplied decreases. We are now going to see how adjustments in price coordinate the choices of buyers and sellers.

Price as a Regulator

The price of a good regulates the quantities demanded and supplied. If the price is too high, the quantity supplied exceeds the quantity demanded. If the price is too low, the quantity demanded exceeds the quantity supplied. There is one price, and only one price, at which the quantity demanded equals the quantity supplied. We are going to work out what that price is. We are also going to discover that natural forces operating in a market move the price towards the level that makes the quantity demanded equal the quantity supplied. These forces arise from the attempts by demanders to buy at the lowest possible price and by suppliers to sell for the highest possible price. To study these forces, let's look again at the market for tapes.

The demand schedule shown in the table in Fig. 4.1 and the supply schedule shown in the table in Fig. 4.4 appear together in the table in Fig. 4.7. If the price of a tape is $1, the quantity demanded is 9 million tapes a week, but no tapes are supplied. The quantity demanded exceeds the quantity supplied by 9 million tapes a week. In other words, at a price of $1 a tape, there is a shortage of 9 million tapes a week. This shortage is shown in the final column of the table. At a price of $2 a tape, there is still a shortage but only of 3 million tapes a week. If the price of a tape is $5, the quantity supplied exceeds the quantity demanded. The quantity supplied is 6 million tapes a week, but the quantity demanded is only 2 million. There is a surplus of 4 million tapes a week. There is one price and only one price at which there is neither a shortage nor a surplus. That price is $3 a tape. At that price, the quantity of tapes demanded is equal to the quantity supplied—4 million tapes a week.

The market for tapes is illustrated in the graph in Fig. 4.7. The graph shows both the demand curve of Fig. 4.1 and the supply curve of Fig. 4.4. The demand curve and the supply curve intersect when the price is $3 a tape. At that price, the quantity demanded and supplied is 4 million tapes a week. At each price *above* $3 a tape, the quantity supplied exceeds the quantity demanded. There is a surplus of tapes. For example, at $4 a tape, the surplus is 2 million tapes a week, as shown by the blue arrow in the figure. At each price *below* $3 a tape, the quantity demanded exceeds the quantity supplied. There is a shortage of tapes. For example, at $3 a tape, the shortage is 3 million tapes a week, as shown by the red arrow in the figure.

Equilibrium

We defined *equilibrium* in Chapter 1 as a situation in which opposing forces balance each other and in which no one is able to make a better choice given the available resources and actions of others. In an equilibrium, the price is such that opposing forces balance each other exactly. The **equilibrium price** is the price at which the quantity demanded equals the quantity supplied. The **equilibrium quantity** is the quantity bought and sold at the equilibrium price. To see why equilibrium occurs where the quantity demanded equals the quantity supplied, we need to examine the behaviour of buyers and sellers a bit more closely. First, let's look at the behaviour of buyers.

The Demand Curve and the Willingness to Pay

Suppose the price of a tape is $2. In such a situation, producers plan to sell 3 million tapes a week. Consumers cannot force producers to sell more than they want to sell, so the quantity sold is also 3 million tapes a week. What is the highest price that buyers are willing to pay for the 3 millionth tape each week? The answer can be found on the demand curve in Fig. 4.7—it is $4 a tape.

If the price remains at $2 a tape, the quantity demanded is 6 million tapes a week—3 million more than are available. In such a situation, the price of a tape does not remain at $2. Because people want more tapes than are available at that price and because they are willing to pay up to $4 a tape, the price rises. If the quantity supplied stays at 3 million tapes a week, the price rises all the way to $4 a tape.

In fact, the price doesn't have to rise by such a large amount because at higher prices the quantity supplied increases. The price will rise from $2 a tape to $3 a tape. At that price, the quantity supplied is 4 million tapes a week, and $3 a tape is the highest price that consumers are willing to pay. At $3 a tape, buyers are able to make their planned purchases and producers are able to make their planned sales. Therefore no buyer has an incentive to bid the price higher.

The Supply Curve and the Minimum Supply Price

Suppose the price of a tape is $4. In such a situation, the quantity demanded is 3 million tapes a week. Producers cannot force consumers to buy more than they want, so the quantity bought is 3 million tapes a week. Producers are willing to sell 3 million tapes a week for a price lower than $4 a tape. In fact, you

FIGURE 4.7

Equilibrium

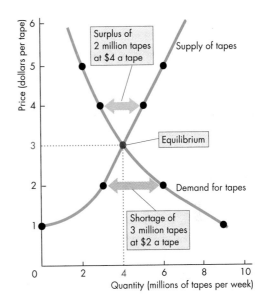

Price (dollars per tape)	Quantity demanded (millions of tapes per week)	Quantity supplied (millions of tapes per week)	Shortage (–) or surplus (+) (millions of tapes per week)
1	9	0	–9
2	6	3	–3
3	4	4	0
4	3	5	+2
5	2	6	+4

The table lists the quantities demanded and quantities supplied as well as the shortage or surplus of tapes at each price. If the price of a tape is $2, 6 million tapes a week are demanded and 3 million are supplied. There is a shortage of 3 million tapes a week, and the price rises. If the price of a tape is $4, 3 million tapes a week are demanded but 5 million are supplied. There is a surplus of 2 million tapes a week, and the price falls. If the price of a tape is $3, 4 million tapes a week are demanded and 4 million are supplied. There is neither a shortage nor a surplus. Neither buyers nor sellers have any incentive to change the price. The price at which the quantity demanded equals the quantity supplied is the equilibrium price.

can see on the supply curve in Fig. 4.7 that suppliers are willing to sell the 3 millionth tape each week at a price of $2. At $4 a tape, they would like to sell 5 million tapes each week. Because they want to sell more than 3 million tapes a week at $4 a tape, and because they would be willing to sell the 3 millionth tape for as little as $2, they will continually undercut each other to get a bigger share of the market. They will cut their price all the way to $2 a tape if only 3 million tapes a week can be sold.

In fact, producers don't have to cut their price to $2 a tape because the lower price brings forth an increase in the quantity demanded. When the price falls to $3, the quantity demanded is 4 million tapes a week, which is exactly the quantity that producers want to sell at that price. So when the price reaches $3 a tape, producers have no incentive to cut the price any further.

The Best Deal Available for Buyers and Sellers

Both situations we have just examined result in price changes. In the first case, the price starts out at $2 and is bid upward. In the second case, the price starts out at $4 and producers undercut each other. In both cases, prices change until they hit the price of $3 a tape. At that price, the quantity demanded and the quantity supplied are equal, and no one has any incentive to do business at a different price. Consumers are paying the highest acceptable price and producers are selling at the lowest acceptable price.

When people can freely make bids and offers and when they seek to buy at the lowest price and sell at the highest price, the price at which they trade is the equilibrium price—the quantity demanded equals the quantity supplied.

R E V I E W

T he equilibrium price is the price at which the plans of buyers and sellers match each other—the price at which the quantity demanded equals the quantity supplied. If the price is below equilibrium, the quantity demanded exceeds the quantity supplied, buyers offer higher prices, sellers ask for higher prices, and the price rises. If the price is above equilibrium, the quantity supplied exceeds the quantity demanded, buyers offer lower prices, sellers ask for lower prices, and the price falls. Only when the price is such that the quantity demanded and the quantity supplied are equal are there no forces acting on the price to make it change. Therefore that price is the equilibrium price. At that price, the quantity actually bought and sold is also equal to the quantity demanded and the quantity supplied. ◆

The theory of demand and supply that you have just studied is now a central part of economics. But that was not always so. Only 100 years ago, the best economists of the day were quite confused about these matters, which today even students in introductory courses find relatively easy to get right (see Our Advancing Knowledge on pp. 86–87).

As you'll discover in the rest of this chapter, the theory of demand and supply enables us to understand and make predictions about changes in prices—including the price slides, rockets, and roller coasters described in the chapter opener.

Predicting Changes in Price and Quantity

T he theory we have just studied provides us with a powerful way of analysing influences on prices and the quantities bought and sold. According to the theory, a change in price stems from either a change in demand or a change in supply or a change in both. Let's look first at the effects of a change in demand.

A Change in Demand

What happens to the price and quantity of tapes if demand for tapes increases? We can answer this question with a specific example. If the price of a Walkman falls from $200 to $50, the demand for tapes increases, as is shown in the table in Fig. 4.8. The original demand schedule and the new one are set out in the first three columns of the table. The table also shows the supply schedule.

The original equilibrium price was $3 a tape. At that price, 4 million tapes a week were demanded and supplied. When demand increases, the price that makes the quantity demanded equal the quantity supplied is $5 a tape. At this price, 6 million tapes are bought and sold each week. When demand increases, both the price and the quantity increase.

We can illustrate these changes in the graph in Fig. 4.8. The graph shows the original demand for and supply of tapes. The original equilibrium price is $3 a tape and the quantity is 4 million tapes a week. When demand increases, the demand curve shifts rightward. The equilibrium price rises to $5 a tape and the quantity supplied increases to 6 million tapes a week, as highlighted in the figure. The quantity supplied increases but there is *no change in supply*.

The exercise that we've just conducted can easily be reversed. If we start at a price of $5 a tape, trading 6 million tapes a week, we can then work out what happens if demand falls back to its original level. You can see that the fall in demand decreases the equilibrium price to $3 a tape and decreases the equilibrium quantity to 4 million tapes a week. Such a fall in demand could arise from a decrease in the price of compact discs or of CD players.

We can now make our first two predictions. Holding everything else constant,

◆ When demand increases, both the price and the quantity increase.

◆ When demand decreases, both the price and the quantity decrease.

A Change in Supply

Suppose that Sony and 3M have just introduced a new cost-saving technology in their tape-production plants. The new technology changes the supply. The new supply schedule (the same one as shown in Fig. 4.5) is presented in the table in Fig. 4.9. What is the new equilibrium price and quantity? The answer is highlighted in the table: the price falls to $2 a tape and the quantity increases to 6 million a week. You can see why by looking at the quantities demanded and supplied at the old price of $3 a tape. With the new technology, the quantity supplied at that price is 8 million tapes a week. There is a surplus of tapes, and the price falls. Only when the price is $2 a tape does the quantity supplied equal the quantity demanded.

FIGURE 4.8

The Effects of a Change in Demand

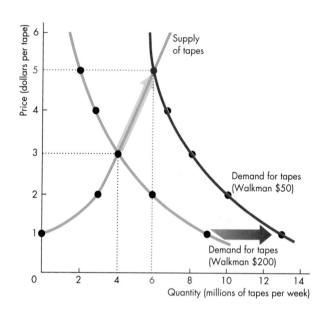

Price (dollars per tape)	Quantity demanded (millions of tapes per week)		Quantity supplied (millions of tapes per week)
	Walkman $200	Walkman $50	
1	9	13	0
2	6	10	3
3	4	8	4
4	3	7	5
5	2	6	6

With the price of a Walkman at $200, the demand for tapes is the blue curve. The equilibrium price is $3 a tape and the equilibrium quantity is 4 million tapes a week. When the price of a Walkman falls from $200 to $50, there is an increase in the demand for tapes and the demand curve shifts rightward—the red curve. At $3 a tape, there is now a shortage of 4 million tapes a week. The quantities of tapes demanded and supplied are equal at a price of $5 a tape. The price rises to this level and the quantity supplied increases. But there is no change in supply. The increase in demand increases the equilibrium price to $5 and increases the equilibrium quantity to 6 million tapes a week.

DISCOVERING the Laws of DEMAND AND SUPPLY

Railways and bridge building in the 1850s were as close to the cutting edge of technology as airlines are today. Railway investment was profitable but, as in the airline industry today, competition was fierce.

The theory of demand and supply was being developed at the same time as the railways were expanding, and it was their economic problems that gave the newly emerging theory its first practical applications.

In France, Jules Dupuit worked out how to use demand theory to calculate the value of railway bridges. His work was the forerunner of what we now call *cost-benefit analysis*. Working with the very same principles invented by Dupuit, economists today calculate the costs and benefits of highways and airports, of dams and power stations.

In England, Dionysius Lardner showed railway companies how they could increase their profits by cutting rates on long-distance business, where competition was fiercest, and raising rates on short-haul business, where they had less to fear from other suppliers. The principles first worked out by Lardner in the 1850s are used by economists working for the major airline companies today to work out the freight rates and passenger fares that will give the airline the largest possible profit. And the rates that result have a lot in common with those railway rates of the nineteenth century. On local routes that feed like the spokes of a wheel into a hub and on which there is little competition, the fares per kilometre are highest. On long-distance routes between hubs and on which there is fierce competition among airlines, the fares per kilometre are lowest.

> **"When demand and supply are in stable equilibrium, if any accident should move the scale of production from its equilibrium position, there will be instantly brought into play forces tending to push it back to that position; just as, if a stone hanging by a string is displaced from its equilibrium position, the force of gravity will at once tend to bring it back to its equilibrium position."**
>
> ALFRED MARSHALL
> *Principles of Economics*

When the first train crossed the South Saskatchewan River in 1902, the principles discovered by Dupuit had determined that a rail bridge would bring benefits valued high enough to justify the cost of the bridge. The principles first worked out by Lardner determined the freight rates charged by the railway company

Today, using the same principles devised by Dupuit, economists calculate whether the benefits of expanding airports and air traffic control facilities are sufficient to cover their costs; and airline companies use the principles developed by Lardner to set their prices and to decide when to offer "seat sales."

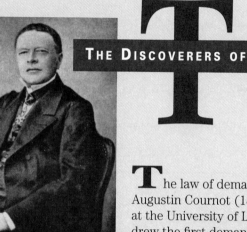

Antoine-Augustin Cournot

THE DISCOVERERS OF THE *Laws of Demand and Supply*

The law of demand was discovered by Antoine-Augustin Cournot (1801-1877), professor of mathematics at the University of Lyon, France, and it was he who drew the first demand curve in the 1830s. The first practical application of demand theory, by Jules Dupuit (1804-1866), a French engineer/economist, was the calculation of the benefits from building a bridge—and, given that a bridge had been built, of the correct toll to charge for its use.

The laws of demand *and* supply, and the connection between the costs of production and supply were first worked out by Dionysius Lardner (1793-1859), an Irish professor of philosophy at the University of London. Known satirically among scientists of the day as "Dionysius Diddler," Lardner worked on an amazing range of problems from astronomy to railway engineering to economics. A colourful character, he would have been a regular guest of Shirley Solomon and Dini Petty if their talk shows had been around in the 1850s. He visited the École des Ponts et Chaussées (the School of Bridges and Roads) in Paris and must have learned a great deal from Dupuit who was doing his major work on economics at the time.

Many others had a hand in refining the theory of demand and supply, but the first thorough and complete statement of the theory as we know it today was Alfred Marshall's (1842-1924), professor of political economy at the University of Cambridge. In 1890, he published a monumental treatise—*Principles of Economics*—a work that became *the* textbook on economics for almost half a century. Marshall was an outstanding mathematician, but he kept mathematics and even diagrams in the background. His own supply and demand diagram (reproduced here at its original size) appears only in a footnote.

Alfred Marshall

Figure 4.9 illustrates the effects of an increase in supply. It shows the demand curve for tapes and the original and new supply curves. The initial equilibrium price is $3 a tape and the original quantity is 4 million tapes a week. When the supply increases, the supply curve shifts rightward. The equilibrium price falls to $2 a tape and the quantity demanded increases to 6 million tapes a week, as highlighted in the figure. The quantity demanded increases but there is *no change in demand.*

The exercise we've just conducted can easily be reversed. If we start out at a price of $2 a tape with 6 million tapes a week being bought and sold, we can work out what happens if the supply curve shifts back to its original position. You can see that the fall in supply increases the equilibrium price to $3 a tape and decreases the equilibrium quantity to 4 million tapes a week. Such a fall in supply could arise from an increase in the cost of labour and raw materials.

We can now make two more predictions. Holding everything else constant,

◆ When supply increases, the quantity increases and the price falls.

◆ When supply decreases, the quantity decreases and the price rises.

Reading Between the Lines on pp. 90–91 shows the effect of a decrease in the supply of oil in the fall of 1993 on the price of oil and predictions about the price of oil as demand falls in the short run and increases in the long run.

Changes in Both Supply and Demand

So far we've looked at a change in demand with no change in supply and we've looked at a change in supply with no change in demand. In each case we can predict the direction of change of the price and the quantity. But if demand and supply change at the same time, we cannot always predict what will happen to both the price and the quantity.

As an example of a change in both supply and demand, let's take one final look at the market for tapes. We've seen how demand and supply determine the price and quantity of tapes, how an increase in demand resulting from a fall in the price of a Walkman both raises the price of tapes and increases the quantity bought and sold, and how an

FIGURE 4.9

The Effects of a Change in Supply

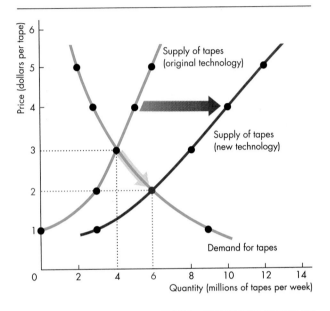

Price (dollars per tape)	Quantity demanded (millions of tapes per week)	Quantity supplied (millions of tapes per week)	
		Original technology	New technology
1	9	0	3
2	6	3	6
3	4	4	8
4	3	5	10
5	2	6	12

With the original technology, the supply of tapes is shown by the blue curve. The equilibrium price is $3 a tape and the equilibrium quantity is 4 million tapes a week. When the new technology is adopted, there is an increase in the supply of tapes. The supply curve shifts rightward —the red curve. At $3 a tape, there is now a surplus of 4 million tapes a week. The quantities of tapes demanded and supplied are equal at a price of $2 a tape. The price falls to this level and the quantity demanded increases. But there is no change in demand. The increase in supply lowers the price of tapes to $2 and increases the quantity to 6 million tapes a week.

increase in the supply of tapes resulting from an improved technology lowers the price of tapes and increases the quantity bought and sold. Let's now examine what happens when both of these changes—a fall in the price of a Walkman (which increases the demand for tapes) and an improved production technology (which increases the supply of tapes)—occur together.

The table in Fig. 4.10 brings together the numbers that describe the original quantities demanded and supplied and the new quantities demanded and supplied after the fall in the price of the Walkman and the improved tape-production technology. These same numbers are illustrated in the graph. The original demand and supply curves intersect at a price of $3 a tape and a quantity of 4 million tapes a week. The new supply and demand curves also intersect at a price of $3 a tape but at a quantity of 8 million tapes a week.

In this example, the increases in demand and supply are such that the rise in price brought about by the increase in demand is offset by the fall in price brought about by the increase in supply—so the price does not change. An increase in either demand or supply increases the quantity bought and sold. Therefore when both demand and supply increase, so does the quantity bought and sold. Note that if demand had increased slightly more than shown in the figure, the price would have risen. If supply had increased by slightly more than shown in the figure, the price would have fallen. But in both cases, the quantity bought and sold would have increased.

We've now seen that when demand and supply increase together, both the demand curve and the supply curve shift rightward. The quantity bought and sold increases, but we cannot predict whether the price will rise or fall until we know the relative magnitudes of the increases in demand and supply.

Another possibility is that demand increases and, at the same time, supply decreases. With these changes in demand and supply, the demand curve shift rightward and the supply curve shifts leftward. In this case, we know that the price rises, but we cannot predict whether the quantity will increase or decrease. To predict the change in quantity, we need to know the relative magnitudes of the changes in demand and supply.

FIGURE 4.10

The Effects of a Change in Both Demand and Supply

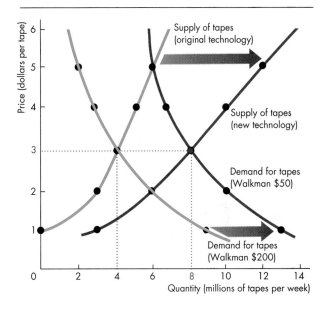

	Original quantities (millions of tapes per week)		New quantities (millions of tapes per week)	
Price (dollars per tape)	Quantity demanded (Walkman $200)	Quantity supplied (original technology)	Quantity demanded (Walkman $50)	Quantity supplied (new technology)
1	9	0	13	3
2	6	3	10	6
3	4	4	8	8
4	3	5	7	10
5	2	6	6	12

When a Walkman costs $200, the price of a tape is $3 and the equilibrium quantity is 4 million tapes a week. A fall in the price of a Walkman increases the demand for tapes, and improved technology increases the supply of tapes. The new technology supply curve intersects the higher demand curve at $3, the same price as before, but the quantity increases to 8 million tapes a week. The increase in both demand and supply increases the quantity but leaves the price unchanged.

Demand and Supply in Action

THE ECONOMIST, SEPTEMBER 18, 1993

A shocking speculation about the price of oil

On September 25th, the Organisation for Petroleum Exporting Countries will meet in Geneva. Its pressing subject: the immediate threat of a further collapse in the oil price because the cartel's members are pumping around 25m barrels per day instead of their agreed limit of 23.6m barrels per day. Oil is now trading at less than $16 a barrel, well down on OPEC's target of $21, and—in the short term—it may well fall further....

It seems foolish, against this background, to fear another oil shock. But the shock could come. Despite OPEC's difficulties, the tables in the oil market look set to turn. Demand is now poised to grow more rapidly than supply. And supply may be tighter in the second half of the 1990s than at any time over the past decade....

Cambridge Energy Research Associates (CERA), an American consultancy, says that...Asian demand will...grow by 500,000 barrels per day or more each year.... In June the OECD predicted GDP growth next year of 2.7%—enough to increase oil demand from its members by just under 1 million barrels per day each year. By the time the growth in oil demand from Latin America and the Middle East is added in, the likely growth in demand outside the former Soviet Union could be more than 2m barrels per day...by mid-1994.

Can the oil industry cope with this new demand? At present, there is perhaps only 1 million barrels per day of sustainable spare capacity... So the missing barrels must come from new oil developments. Given that it takes roughly five years to bring all but the most accessible new oil fields into production, work must begin soon. Unfortunately, the oil industry has seldom looked less adventurous...

The Organisation for Petroleum Exporting Countries (OPEC) is worried because the price of oil, at less than $16 a barrel, is below the target it would like to see of $21 a barrel. And OPEC fears that the price may fall further in the short term.

The members of OPEC are producing 25 million barrels a day instead of an agreed limit of 23.6 million barrels a day.

In the longer term, the price of oil is predicted to rise because demand will grow faster than supply.

Demand is expected to grow by more than 2 million barrels a day by mid-1994.

Supply is expected to grow by 1 million barrels a day.

Background and Analysis

In 1993, OPEC pumped about 25 million barrels of oil a day and other oil producers pumped about 35 million barrels a day, making world production about 60 million barrels a day.

The world market for oil in 1993 is shown in part (a) of the figure. The demand curve is D_0 and the supply curve is S_0. The equilibrium price is $16 a barrel and the equilibrium quantity is 60 million barrels a day.

Part (a) of the figure also shows OPEC's target. If OPEC's members cut production to 23.6 million barrels a day—a decrease of 1.4 million barrels a day—supply would decrease and the supply curve would shift leftward to S_1. The price would rise to $21 a barrel.*

The equilibrium quantity of oil does not decrease by 1.4 million barrels a day because, at a price of $21 a barrel, the *quantity of oil supplied* by non-OPEC producers increases.

Part (b) of the figure shows the predictions contained in the news article. In the short-term, demand is expected to fall—shown by the shift in the demand curve from D_0 to D_1— and the price is expected to fall. But in the longer term, demand is expected to increase— shown as the shift in the demand curve from D_0 to D_2—and the price is expected to increase.

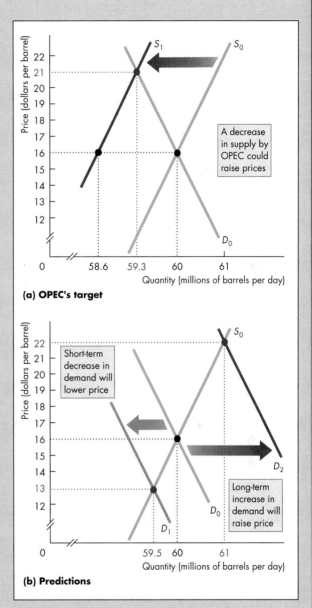

A decrease in supply by OPEC could raise prices

(a) OPEC's target

Short-term decrease in demand will lower price

Long-term increase in demand will raise price

(b) Predictions

*The slopes of the demand curve D_0 and the supply curve S_0 have been fixed on the *assumption* that the price rises to OPEC's target of $21 a barrel when supply is decreased by 1.4 million barrels a day.

Walkmans, Apartments, and Coffee

At the beginning of this chapter, we looked at some facts about prices and quantities of Walkmans, apartments, and coffee. Let's use the theory of demand and supply we have just studied to explain the movements in the prices and the quantities of those goods. Figure 4.11 illustrates the analysis.

First, let's consider the Walkman, shown in part (a). In 1980, using the original technology, the supply of Walkmans is described by the supply curve S_0. The 1980 demand curve is D_0. The quantities

supplied and demanded in 1980 are equal at Q_0, and the price is P_0. Advances in technology and the building of additional production plants increase supply and shift the supply curve from S_0 to S_1. At the same time, rising incomes increase the demand for Walkmans, but not by nearly as much as the increase in supply. The demand curve shifts from D_0 to D_1. With the new demand curve D_1 and supply curve S_1, the equilibrium price is P_1 and the quantity is Q_1. The combination of a large increase in supply with a small increase in demand results in an

FIGURE 4.11

More Changes in Supply and Demand

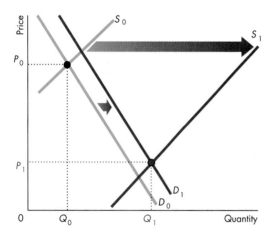

(a) Walkmans

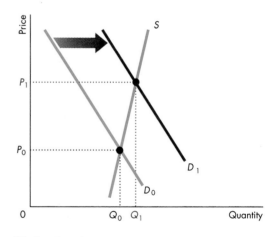

(b) Apartments

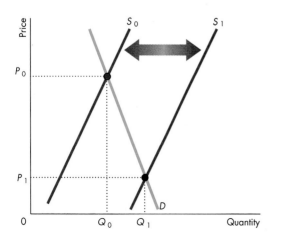

(c) Coffee

A large increase in the supply of Walkmans, from S_0 to S_1, combined with a small increase in demand, from D_0 to D_1, results in a fall in the price of the Walkman, from P_0 to P_1, and an increase in the quantity, from Q_0 to Q_1 (part a).

An increase in the demand for apartments produces a large increase in the price, from P_0 to P_1, but only a small increase in the quantity, from Q_0 to Q_1 (part b).

Variations in the weather and in growing conditions lead to fluctuations in the supply of coffee, between S_0 and S_1, which produce fluctuations in the price of coffee, between P_0 and P_1, and in the quantity, between Q_0 and Q_1 (part c).

increase in the quantity of Walkmans and a dramatic fall in their price.

Next, let's consider apartments in the centre of the city, as in part (b). The supply of apartments is described by supply curve S. The supply curve is steep, reflecting the fact that there is a fixed number of apartments. As the number of young professionals increases and the number of two-income families increases, the demand for city apartments increases sharply. The demand curve shifts from D_0 to D_1. As a result, the price increases from P_0 to P_1 and the quantity also increases, but not as much as price.

Finally, let's consider the market for coffee, shown in part (c). The demand for coffee is described by curve D. The supply of coffee fluctuates between S_0 and S_1. When growing conditions are good, the supply curve is S_1. When there are adverse growing conditions such as frost, the supply

decreases and the supply curve is S_0. As a consequence of fluctuations in supply, the price of coffee fluctuates between P_0 (the maximum price) and P_1 (the minimum price). The quantity fluctuates between Q_0 and Q_1.

◆ ◆ ◆ ◆ By using the theory of demand and supply, you will be able to explain past fluctuations in prices and quantities and also make predictions about future fluctuations. But you will want to do more than predict whether prices are going to rise or fall. In your study of microeconomics, you will learn to predict *by how much* they will change. In your study of macroeconomics, you will learn to explain fluctuations in the economy as a whole. In fact, the theory of demand and supply can help answer almost every economic question.

S U M M A R Y

Demand

The quantity demanded of a good or service is the amount that consumers plan to buy in a given period of time at a particular price. Demands are different from wants. Wants are unlimited, whereas demands reflect decisions to satisfy specific wants. The quantity that consumers plan to buy of any good depends on

◆ The price of the good

◆ The prices of related goods—substitutes and complements

◆ Income

◆ Expected future prices

◆ Population

◆ Preferences

Other things remaining the same, the higher the price of a good, the smaller is the quantity of that good demanded. The relationship between the quantity demanded and price, holding constant all other influences on consumers' planned purchases, is illustrated by the demand schedule or demand curve. A change in the price of a good produces movement

along the demand curve for that good. Such a movement is called a change in the quantity demanded.

Changes in all other influences on buying plans are said to change demand. When demand changes, there is a new demand schedule and the demand curve shifts. When there is an increase in demand, the demand curve shifts rightward; when there is a decrease in demand, the demand curve shifts leftward. (pp. 73–77)

Supply

The quantity supplied of a good or service is the amount that producers plan to sell in a given period of time. The quantity that producers plan to sell of any good or service depends on

◆ The price of the good

◆ The prices of factors of production

◆ The prices of related goods

◆ Expected future prices

◆ The number of suppliers

◆ Technology

Other things remaining the same, the higher the price of a good, the larger is the quantity of that good supplied. The relationship between the quantity supplied and price, holding constant all other influences on firms' planned sales, is illustrated by the supply schedule or supply curve. A change in the price of a good produces movement along the supply curve for that good. Such a movement is called a change in the quantity supplied.

Changes in all other influences on selling plans change supply. When supply changes, there is a new supply schedule and the supply curve shifts. When there is an increase in supply, the supply curve shifts rightward; when there is a decrease in supply, the supply curve shifts leftward. (pp. 78–82)

Price Determination

Price regulates the quantities supplied and demanded. The higher the price, the greater is the quantity supplied and the smaller is the quantity demanded. At high prices, there is a surplus—an excess of the quantity supplied over the quantity demanded. At low prices, there is a shortage—an excess of the quantity demanded over the quantity supplied. There is one price and only one price at which the quantity demanded equals the quantity supplied. That price is the equilibrium price. At that price, buyers have no incentive to offer a higher price and suppliers have no incentive to sell at a lower price. (pp. 82–84)

Predicting Changes in Price and Quantity

Changes in demand and supply lead to changes in price and in the quantity bought and sold. An increase in demand leads to a rise in price and an increase in quantity. A decrease in demand leads to a fall in price and a decrease in quantity. An increase in supply leads to an increase in quantity and a fall in price. A decrease in supply leads to a decrease in quantity and a rise in price.

A simultaneous increase in demand and supply increases the quantity bought and sold, but can raise or lower the price. If the increase in demand is larger than the increase in supply, the price rises. If the increase in demand is smaller than the increase in supply, the price falls. (pp. 84–93)

K E Y   E L E M E N T S

Key Terms

Change in demand, 77
Change in supply, 80
Change in the quantity demanded, 77
Change in the quantity supplied, 80
Complement, 75
Demand, 75
Demand curve, 74
Demand schedule, 73
Equilibrium price, 83
Equilibrium quantity, 83
Inferior good, 75
Normal good, 75
Quantity demanded, 73
Quantity supplied, 78
Substitute, 75
Supply, 79

Supply curve, 78
Supply schedule, 78
Wants, 73

Key Figures and Tables

Figure 4.1   The Demand Curve and the Demand Schedule, 74
Figure 4.3   A Change in Demand versus a Change in the Quantity Demanded, 77
Figure 4.4   The Supply Curve and the Supply Schedule, 79
Figure 4.6   A Change in Supply versus a Change in the Quantity Supplied, 81
Figure 4.7   Equilibrium, 83
Table 4.1   The Demand for Tapes, 76
Table 4.2   The Supply of Tapes, 80

R E V I E W   Q U E S T I O N S

1 Define the quantity demanded of a good or service.

2 Define the quantity supplied of a good or service.

3 List the main factors that influence the amount that consumers plan to buy and say whether an increase in the factor increases or decreases consumers' planned purchases.

4 List the main factors that influence the amount that firms plan to sell and say whether an increase in each factor increases or decreases firms' planned sales.

5 State the law of demand and the law of supply.

6 If a fixed amount of a good is available, what does the demand curve tell us about the price that consumers are willing to pay for that fixed quantity?

7 If consumers are willing to buy only a certain fixed quantity, what does the supply curve tell us about the price at which firms will supply that quantity?

8 Distinguish between:
a   A change in demand and a change in the quantity demanded
b   A change in supply and a change in the quantity supplied

9 Why is the price at which the quantity demanded equals the quantity supplied the equilibrium price?

10 What happens to the price of a tape and the quantity of tapes sold if:
a   The price of CDs increases?
b   The price of a Walkman increases?
c   The supply of live concerts increases?
d   Consumers' incomes increase and firms producing tapes switch to new cost-saving technology?
e   The prices of the factors of production used to make tapes increase?
f   A new good comes onto the market that makes tapes obsolete?

P R O B L E M S

1 Suppose that one of the following events occurs:
a   The price of gasoline rises.
b   The price of gasoline falls.
c   All speed limits on highways are abolished.
d   A new fuel-effective engine that runs on cheap alcohol is invented.
e   The population doubles.
f   Robotic production plants lower the cost of producing cars.
g   A law banning car imports from Japan is passed.
h   The rates for auto insurance double.
i   The minimum age for drivers is increased to 19 years.
j   A massive and high-grade oil supply is discovered in Mexico.
k   The environmental lobby succeeds in closing down all nuclear power stations.
l   The price of cars rises.
m   The price of cars falls.
n   The summer temperature is 10 degrees lower than normal and the winter temperature is 10 degrees higher than normal.

State which of the above events will produce
1   A movement along the demand curve for gasoline.
2   A shift of the demand curve for gasoline rightward.
3   A shift of the demand curve for gasoline leftward.
4   A movement along the supply curve of gasoline.
5   A shift of the supply curve of gasoline rightward.
6   A shift of the supply curve of gasoline leftward.
7   A movement along the demand curve for cars.

8 A movement along the supply curve of cars.

9 A shift of the demand curve for cars rightward.

10 A shift of the demand curve for cars leftward.

11 A shift of the supply curve of cars rightward.

12 A shift of the supply curve of cars leftward.

13 An increase in the price of gasoline.

14 A decrease in the quantity of oil bought and sold.

2 The demand and supply schedules for gum are as follows:

Price (cents per week)	Quantity demanded	Quantity supplied
	(millions of packs a week)	
10	200	0
20	180	30
30	160	60
40	140	90
50	120	120
60	100	140
70	80	160
80	60	180
90	40	200

a What is the equilibrium price of gum?

b How much gum is bought and sold each week?

Suppose that a huge fire destroys one-half of the gum-producing factories. Supply decreases to one-half of the amount shown in the supply schedule.

c What is the new equilibrium price of gum?

d How much gum is now bought and sold each week?

e Has there been a shift of or a movement along the supply curve of gum?

f Has there been a shift of or a movement along the demand curve for gum?

g As the gum factories destroyed by fire are rebuilt and gradually resume gum production, what will happen to:

(1) The price of gum?

(2) The quantity of gum bought?

(3) The demand curve for gum?

(4) The supply curve of gum?

3 Suppose the demand and supply schedules for gum are those in problem 2.

An increase in the teenage population increases the demand for gum by 40 million packs per week.

a Write out the new demand schedule for gum.

b What is the new quantity of gum bought and sold each week?

c What is the new equilibrium price of gum?

d Has there been a shift of or a movement along the demand curve for gum?

e Has there been a shift of or a movement along the supply curve of gum?

4 Suppose the demand and supply schedules for gum are those in problem 2.

An increase in the teenage population increases the demand for gum by 40 million packs per week, and simultaneously the fire described in problem 2 occurs, wiping out one-half of the gum-producing factories.

a Draw a graph of the original and new demand and supply curves.

b What is the new quantity of gum bought and sold each week?

c What is the new equilibrium price of gum?

PART 9

INTRODUCTION TO MACROECONOMICS

Talking

with

Franco

Modigliani

Franco Modigliani was born in Rome, Italy, in 1918. He was an undergraduate in Italy and obtained his B.A. in 1939 as World War II was beginning. He spent the war years in the United States, which has been his professional base ever since. He obtained his Ph.D. in 1944 at the New School for Social Research in New York. He worked at Carnegie-Mellon University in the 1950s and became Professor of Economics and Finance and Institute Professor at the Massachusetts Institute of Technology in 1960. Professor Modigliani was awarded the Nobel Memorial Prize in Economics in 1985 for his pioneering work on consumption and saving—the development of the life-cycle hypothesis—and for his contributions to the theory of finance.

What attracted you to economics?

I studied economics at the University of Rome as part of the requirements for the degree of Doctor in Law. However, the teaching environment under fascism was terrible, and I learned very little, except by studying on my own. I became interested in economics by a fluke: I participated in a national competition in economics and won first prize. I concluded that economics was for me.

Why did you study at the New School?

I took advantage of the New School in New York to make up for all that I had not been able to learn in Italy. But my greatest interest was in Keynes and the newly born field of macroeconomics. I also pursued mathematical economics and econometrics—also in its beginning at that time—under the guidance of a great teacher, Jacob Marshack.

> "The differences . . . spring . . . from different value judgments about the cost of unemployment or the dangers of allowing the government to have any discretionary power."

You are an "activist" in contrast to a "monetarist" and you've had many notable battles with the monetarists, especially with Milton Friedman. Yet some of your work and some of Friedman's work are remarkably similar—especially the life-cycle hypothesis and the permanent income hypothesis of consumption expenditure. What is it about economics that unites your work and Friedman's, and what is it that divides you and Friedman on policy questions?

I generally agree with Friedman and other reputable economists on basic economic theory. For instance, we agree on the nature of the mechanism through which money affects the economy or on the way consumers choose to allocate their life resources over their lifetime.

The differences arise, typically, at the level of the economic policies we advocate. They spring to an important extent from different value judgments about the cost of unemployment or the dangers of allowing the government to have any discretionary power. Thus Friedman, who profoundly distrusts government, finds that the system is sufficiently stable when left to itself, that we do not

need to take the risk of giving government discretionary power, and indeed that discretionary policies, in the hands of an incompetent government, may be destabilizing.

My value judgments and assessment are very different. I believe that instability is extremely costly, and I find that the economy, when left to itself, is not sufficiently stable. I believe that there exist good governments and central banks and that even an average policy-maker can successfully contribute to the stabilization of the economy. Thus, in contrast to Friedman, I conclude that the relevant authorities should be given the discretion necessary for a stabilization policy, but with appropriate checks.

You were one of the pioneers of large-scale econometric models. These models are now routinely used for commercial forecasting but don't appear much in the academic journals. How useful are these models?

I have not followed any of the econometric models from the "inside," that is, in terms of model upkeep and testing, since completing work on the model for the

Federal Reserve. However, from what I have been able to observe, the leading models, such as DRI, Wharton, and Michigan, have been quite useful. The forecasting record of these models is, of course, far from perfect, and at times it is outright disappointing. Yet there is considerable evidence to suggest that at least these models perform appreciably better than known alternatives. They have also proved useful in testing hypotheses and in working out the short-run effects of alternative policies.

Suppose you were given carte blanche by the president and Congress to fix the American economy and deliver a prosperous closing decade of the twentieth century. What would you recommend?

In my view, the American economy is not in significantly bad shape for the coming years. At the moment, of course, we are in the midst of a slowdown, but it is of modest magnitude, and it should not take long to get over it. For the longer run, the more serious concerns seem to be the slow growth of productivity, the deterioration in the economic welfare of the lowest income and skill classes, and a continuing substantial balance of payments deficit. All these symptoms bear a relation to one underlying cause: the great decline in national saving, initiated by the Reagan administration's fiscal deficit policy. It has hardly been corrected by the Bush administration, with the result that national saving has been reduced to about one-fourth of what it used to be for many years. The decline in national saving in turn has contributed to the large decline in domestic investment, which in turn contributed to poor productivity performance and to lower incomes of future generations. These future generations will foot the bill for our failure to pay for what we are consuming now.

The decline in investment also very likely accounts for some of the economic deterioration of the lower economic fringe. To be sure, the decline in investment was not as dramatic as that in national saving because the fiscal deficit served to attract foreign capital; but that is precisely what caused the deterioration of the current account and our growing indebtedness to foreigners.

I would therefore give high priority to eliminating the deficit—exclusive of the current social security surplus—preferably by expenditure cuts but if necessary by higher taxes. Americans pay less taxes than most citizens in other industrialized countries and can certainly afford to pay a little more in favour of future generations. The reduction in deficit could be used to expand investment and reduce the foreign deficit. The expansion of investment should include public investments in infrastructures. This expenditure would not add to the deficit if it were classified as an investment, as would be proper, and as is the prevailing practice in other countries. Productivity growth might also be helped by better education, especially at lower levels, even if it is costly.

> " The most basic principle in economics is the postulate of rational behaviour."

What other counsel would you give the president and Congress for economic policy?

I would stop the current drift towards protectionism and recommend taking a strong lead in opening up economies to international trade. I would also give high priority to a serious policy of environmental protection, despite its costs. On the other hand, I am not a great believer in government industrial policies and would rather trust the economy to the "invisible hand" except in the case of monetary policy where, as indicated, I believe that some discretion for the monetary authority is essential to the achievement of macroeconomic stability and stable prices.

What are the major principles of economics that you keep returning to and finding the most useful in your work?

The most basic principle in economics is the postulate of rational behaviour. Many of the important propositions in economics rest on that principle. However, it must be used with full awareness of its limitations. For instance, I do not necessarily include in rational behaviour "rational expectations" as defined and used by the rational expectations school. More generally, I believe that there are circumstances in which agents' behaviour is not adequately described by rationality and one must be prepared to formulate alternative hypotheses.

What advice would you give to students starting out in economics today? What other subjects should they study along with economics?

Anyone interested in becoming a professional economist, whether an academic economist or a business one, should acquire a good preparation in the quantitative methods—mathematics, statistics, and econometrics. Without this background, you will miss much of the interesting literature. There are many other subjects that can be useful, depending on one's long-run interests—for instance, social psychology, law, or political science. From my experience, I can say that whatever "extracurricular" subjects I have been exposed to have turned out to be helpful at some point in my career.

CHAPTER 22

UNEMPLOYMENT, INFLATION, CYCLES, AND DEFICITS

After studying this chapter, you will be able to

- ◆ Define unemployment and explain its costs
- ◆ Define inflation and describe its effects
- ◆ Define gross domestic product (GDP)
- ◆ Distinguish between nominal GDP and real GDP
- ◆ Explain the importance of changes in real GDP
- ◆ Define the business cycle
- ◆ Describe how unemployment, stock prices, and inflation fluctuate over the business cycle
- ◆ Define the government budget deficit and the country's international deficit

GOOD JOBS ARE HARD TO FIND. IN 1993, MORE THAN ONE person in nine was looking for a job and many more people were so discouraged about their chances of finding one that they had stopped looking. Why are jobs so hard to find? ◆ ◆ People who do find jobs worry about what their wages will buy, and for good reason. A shopping cart of groceries that cost $20 in 1963 costs more than $100 today, and prices continue to rise. What are the effects of persistently rising prices? ◆ ◆ Prices rise, but so does the value of the things we produce. From 1963 to 1993, the value of Canadian production increased fifteen-fold. How much of that growth is real and how much of it is an illusion created by inflation? ◆ ◆ From 1983 to 1987, output expanded quickly and unemployment fell. From 1990 to 1993, output at first shrank and then began to grow again, but slowly and unemployment increased. Why do we have waves of expansion and contraction? ◆ ◆ We hear a lot

Jobs, Prices, and Incomes

these days about deficits—both the federal government's deficit and Canada's international deficit. What are these deficits, how big are they, and have they been getting bigger?

◆ ◆ ◆ ◆ These questions are the subject matter of macroeconomics. With what you learn in this and the following chapters, you will be better able to understand the macroeconomic problems we face today. We'll begin by looking at our most pressing problem, unemployment.

Unemployment

At many times in Canada's history, unemployment has been a serious problem. The 1990s are such a time. In 1993, more than 1.5 million people were seeking jobs. What exactly is unemployment? How is it measured? How has its rate fluctuated? What is full employment? What are the costs of unemployment?

What Is Unemployment?

Unemployment is a state in which there are qualified workers who are available for work at the current wage rate and who do not have jobs. The total number of people who do have jobs—the employed—plus the total number of people who do not have jobs—the unemployed—is called the **labour force**. The **unemployment rate** is the number of people unemployed expressed as a percentage of the labour force.

Measuring Unemployment

Unemployment is measured in Canada every month by the Canadian Labour Force Survey. The results of this survey appear in a publication called *The Labour Force* and are reported each month in the news media.

To be counted as unemployed in the Labour Force Survey, a person must be available for work and must be in one of three categories:

1. Without work, but has made specific efforts to find a job within the previous four weeks
2. Waiting to be called back to a job from which he or she has been laid off for 26 weeks or less
3. Waiting to start a new job within the next four weeks

Anyone surveyed who satisfies one of these three criteria is counted as unemployed. Part-time workers are counted as being employed.

There are three reasons why the unemployment level as measured by the Labour Force Survey may be misleading. Let's examine these.

Unrealistic Wage Expectations A student who says that she is willing to work at McDonald's, but only for $25 an hour, is not actually available for work on the conditions being offered. It does not make sense to count her as unemployed, but in the official data, this person is counted as one of the unemployed.

Correcting the unemployment data to take account of wage and job expectations would result in a lower measured unemployment rate. How much lower we do not know. A second factor works in the opposite direction.

Discouraged Workers Some people who fail to find a suitable job after prolonged and extensive search effort come to believe that there is no work available for them. They become discouraged and stop looking for work. Such people are called discouraged workers. **Discouraged workers** are people who do not have jobs and would like work but have stopped seeking work. Discouraged workers are not counted as unemployed by the Labour Force because they have not actively sought work within the previous 4 weeks. If discouraged workers were counted as unemployed, the unemployment rate would be higher than that currently measured.

Part-Time Workers Part-time workers are counted as employed. But many part-time workers are available for and seeking full-time work. The measured unemployment rate does not capture this element of part-time unemployment.

The Unemployment Record

The Canadian unemployment record between 1926 and 1993 is set out in Fig. 22.1. The average unemployment rate over this 67-year period is approximately 6.5 percent. The dominant feature of the unemployment record is the Great Depression of the early 1930s. During that period of our history, almost 20 percent of the labour force was unemployed. Although in recent years we have not experienced anything as devastating as the Great Depression, we have experienced some high unemployment rates, and three such periods are highlighted in the figure.

Unemployment is a highly charged topic. We chart the course of the unemployment rate as a measure of economic health with the intensity with which a physician keeps track of a patient's

Figure 22.1

Unemployment: 1926–1993

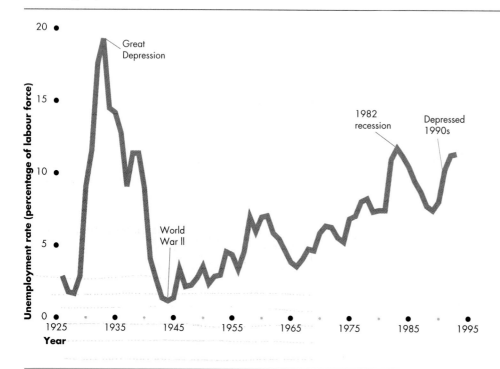

Unemployment is a persistent feature of economic life, but its rate varies. At its worst—during the Great Depression—20 percent of the labour force was unemployed. Even in the recession of 1982, its rate reached 13 percent. Since the end of World War II, there has been a general tendency for the unemployment rate to increase.

Sources: 1926-1952: F. H. Leacy, ed., *Historical Statistics of Canada,* 2nd ed. (Ottawa, Statistics Canada and the Social Science Federation of Canada, 1983), Series D-132 as a percentage of Series D-127. 1953-1965: CANSIM series D755041. 1966-1993: CANSIM series D767611.

temperature. What does the unemployment rate tell us? Does all unemployment have the same origin, or are there different types of unemployment? In fact, there are three main sources of variation in unemployment and they give rise to three types of unemployment. Let's see what they are.

Types of Unemployment

The three types of unemployment are

◆ Frictional

◆ Structural

◆ Cyclical

Frictional Unemployment   The unemployment arising from normal labour market turnover is called **frictional unemployment**. Normal labour market turnover arises from two sources. First, people are constantly changing their economic activities— young people are leaving school and joining the labour force; old people are retiring and leaving the

labour force; some people are leaving the labour force temporarily, perhaps to raise children or for some other reason, and then rejoining it. Second, the fortunes of businesses are constantly changing— some are closing down and laying off their workers; new firms are starting up and are hiring.

These persistent changes result in frictional unemployment. There are always some firms with unfilled vacancies and some people looking for work. Unemployed people don't usually take the first job that comes their way. Instead, they spend time searching out what they believe will be the best job available to them. By doing so, they can match their own skills and interests with the available jobs, finding a satisfying job and income.

It is unlikely that frictional unemployment will ever disappear. The amount of frictional unemployment depends on the rate at which people enter and leave the labour force and on the rate at which jobs are created and destroyed. For example, the postwar baby boom of the late 1940s brought a bulge in the number of people entering the labour force in the 1960s and an increase in the amount of frictional unemployment. When a major new shopping mall is built, jobs become available in the mall and a similar number of jobs are lost in the older part of town where shops are struggling to survive. The people who lose jobs aren't always the first to get the new jobs, and while they are between jobs, they are frictionally unemployed.

The length of time that people take to find a job is influenced by the scale of unemployment benefits. The more generous the unemployment benefit, the longer is the average time taken in job search and the higher is the rate of frictional unemployment.

Structural Unemployment   The unemployment that arises when there is a decline in the number of jobs available in a particular region or industry is called **structural unemployment**. Such a decline might occur because of permanent technological change—for example, the automation of a steel plant. It might also occur because of a permanent change in international competition—for example, the decline of the number of jobs in the Canadian auto industry resulting from Japanese competition.

The distinction between structural and frictional unemployment is not always a sharp one, but some cases are clear. A person who loses a job in a suburban shopping centre and gets a job a few weeks later in a new mall has experienced frictional unemployment. An auto worker who loses his job and, after a period of retraining and prolonged search, perhaps lasting more than a year, eventually gets a job as an insurance salesperson has experienced structural unemployment.

Structural unemployment has become a serious problem in the 1990s. It has arisen partly from the ongoing search for greater efficiency (see Reading Between the Lines on pp. 602–603). But structural unemployment is particularly acute today because an increasingly competitive international environment has decreased the number of jobs in traditional industries, such as autos and steel, and increased the number of jobs in new industries, such as electronics and bio-engineering, as well as in the service industries such as banking and insurance.

Cyclical Unemployment   The unemployment arising from a slowdown in the pace of economic expansion is called **cyclical unemployment**. The pace of economic expansion is ever-changing—rapid at times, slow at others, and even negative on occasion. When the economy is expanding rapidly, cyclical unemployment disappears, and when the economy is expanding slowly or contracting, cyclical unemployment can become extremely high. For example, an auto worker who is laid off because the economy is going through a slow period and who gets rehired some months later when economic activity speeds up has experienced cyclical unemployment.

Full Employment

Full employment is a state in which the quantity of labour demanded equals the quantity of labour supplied. Full employment occurs when all unemployment is frictional and there is no structural or cyclical unemployment. There is always *some* frictional unemployment, so there is always some unemployment, even at full employment.

Another unemployment concept is the natural rate of unemployment. The **natural rate of unemployment** is the sum of frictional and structural unemployment. Equivalently, it is the unemployment rate when there is no cyclical unemployment. There is controversy about the magnitude of the natural unemployment rate. Some economists believe that the natural rate of unemployment in Canada is around 6 percent of the labour force. Other economists believe not only that the natural rate of unemployment varies, but that it can be quite high, especially at times when demographic and technological factors point to a high frictional and structural unemployment rate.

What are the costs of unemployment?

The Costs of Unemployment

There are four main costs of unemployment. They are

◆ Loss of output and income

◆ Loss of human capital

◆ Increase in crime

◆ Loss of human dignity

Loss of Output and Income   The most obvious costs of unemployment are the loss of output and the loss of income that the unemployed would have produced had they had jobs. The size of these costs depends on the natural rate of unemployment. If the natural rate of unemployment is between 5 and 6 percent, as some economists believe, the lost output from unemployment is enormous.

Structural Unemployment

THE FINANCIAL POST, FEBRUARY 25, 1993

GM Canada layoffs to top 8,000

By Laura Fowlie

AUTOMAKER General Motors of Canada Ltd. has handed layoff notices to another 450 workers, pushing the planned number of permanent and temporary layoffs at its Ontario facilities to more than 8,000 by 1995....

When they leave....
- 2,500 permanent when the company's Scarborough, Ont., van plant closes this spring.
- 1,450 temporary when plant No. 1 in Oshawa goes to one shift next month. As many as 1,400 will become permanent

layoffs when the plant resumes production of the next generation Lumina in early 1994.
- 225 permanent with closure of Oshawa radiator plant in September.
- 2,200 permanent with closure of St. Catharines, Ont., foundry in fall 1994.
- 800 permanent layoffs are likely if a St. Catharines rear axle facility cannot be sold by the end of the year.
- 1,500 temporary layoffs when Windsor, Ont., transmission plant closes for a year this summer. About 400 jobs will not return.

THE FINANCIAL POST, MARCH 2, 1993

CN chopping 11,000 jobs

By Kevin Dougherty

MONTREAL—Canadian National Railway Co. said yesterday it will cut 11,000 jobs in Canada and the U.S. over the next three years....

CN is cutting 3,000 Canadian jobs this year, another 3,500 in 1994 and again in 1995— and about 1,000 of its 3,300 positions in the U.S.—bringing its workforce down to 22,300 by the end of 1995.

CN president Paul Tellier said the cuts were "one of the most important decisions ever for CN." He added that even with the cuts, CN would still offer the same level of

service and would invest $2 billion over the five-year period. He stressed that CN's goal is to offer comparable service to the large U.S. railways, at a competitive cost....

"Last year for every dollar we collected, we lost 50¢," Tellier said....

Wages and staff benefits account for 52% of CN's operating costs. Without the cuts, Tellier said, CN would have been poised to lose $1.5 billion in the period 1992-97 and its debt would likely have doubled to $4 billion....

General Motors of Canada plans to lay off the following numbers of workers before 1995:
- 2,500 permanent in Scarborough, Ont., spring 1993
- 1,450 temporary in Oshawa, Ont., spring 1993
- 1,400 permanent in Oshawa, Ont., early 1994
- 225 permanent in Oshawa in September 1993
- 2,200 permanent in St. Catharines, Ont., fall 1994
- 800 permanent in St. Catharines, end 1993
- 1,500 temporary in Windsor, Ont., summer 1993
- 400 permanent in Windsor, summer 1994

Canadian National Railway Co. lost 50¢ for every dollar of revenue in 1992.

Wages and benefits are 52% of CN's operating costs, and projected losses were $1.5 billion for the period 1992-1997.

To avoid this loss, CN plans to cut 3,000 jobs in Canada in 1993, another 3,500 in 1994, and 3,500 in 1995. It also plans to cut 1,000 jobs in the United States.

CN aims to maintain its service by investing $2 billion in plant and equipment over the five-year period and to cut its costs and eliminate its loss.

Background and Analysis

The Canadian economy is in a constant state of change. One feature of this change is the on-going destruction and creation of jobs.

During 1993, the rate of job destruction was high. And many of the jobs destroyed were lost *permanently*.

Permanent job losses lead to *structural unemployment*.

Temporary job losses lead to *cyclical unemployment*.

Of the job losses at GM and CN reported in these news articles, 2,950 are temporary and 18,525 are permanent.

Jobs are destroyed mainly by big firms such as GM and CN as these firms use more cost-effective technology.

Jobs are created mainly by small firms as these firms try new ideas and create new products. Many of these ideas and products fail, but those that succeed bring job growth and income growth.

At any point in time, a large number of Canadians are in a state of transition from one job to another, some remaining unemployed for a relatively short period, but others remaining unemployed for many months. The figure shows the anatomy of unemployment resulting from job losses such as those described in these news articles.

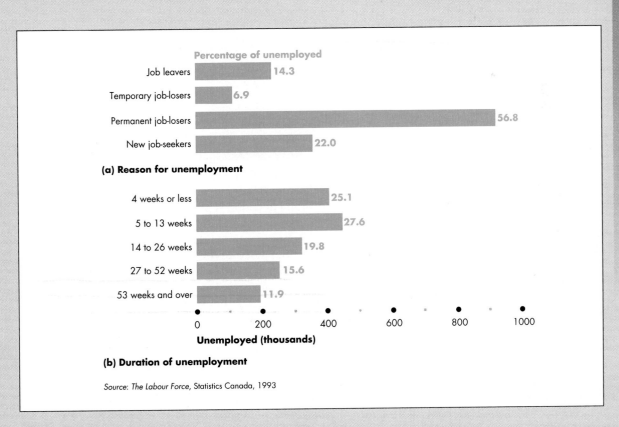

Source: *The Labour Force*, Statistics Canada, 1993

Arthur Okun, a well-known U.S. economist, estimated that for every 1 percentage point rise in the unemployment rate, a nation's output of goods and services falls by 3 percentage points. One percent of aggregate output in Canada in 1993 was $7 billion. Thus getting the unemployment rate down from 10 percent to 6 percent raises output by $28 billion. With a population of 28 million, the average person could buy an additional $1,000 worth of goods and services each year.

Those economists who believe that the natural rate of unemployment itself varies think that the lost output cost of unemployment is small. They regard the fluctuations in the unemployment rate as arising from fluctuations in structural unemployment. With rapid structural change, people need to find their most productive new jobs. A period of high unemployment is like an investment in the future. It is the price paid today for a larger future income.

Loss of Human Capital   Unemployment can do permanent damage to a worker by hindering his or her career development and acquisition of human capital. **Human capital** is the value of a person's education and acquired skills. For example, Jody finishes law school at a time when unemployment is high, and she just can't find a job in a law office. Desperately short of income, she becomes a taxi driver. After a year in this work, she discovers that it is impossible to compete with the new crop of law graduates and is stuck with cab driving. Her human capital as a lawyer has been wiped out by high unemployment.

Increase in Crime   A high unemployment rate usually leads to a high crime rate. There are two reasons. First, when people cannot earn an income from legal work, they sometimes turn to illegal work, and the amount of theft increases sharply. Second, with low incomes and increased frustration, family life begins to suffer, and there are increases in crimes such as child beating, wife assault, and suicide.

Loss of Human Dignity   A final cost that is difficult to quantify, but that is large and very important, is the loss of self-esteem that afflicts many who suffer prolonged periods of unemployment. It is probably this aspect of unemployment that makes it so highly charged with political and social significance.

R E V I E W

The unemployment rate fluctuates but no matter how low it becomes, unemployment never disappears. Some unemployment is frictional, arising from labour market turnover. Some is structural, arising from the decline in certain industries and regions. And some is cyclical, arising from a slowdown in the pace of economic expansion. Full employment occurs when the only unemployment is frictional. The natural rate of unemployment is the unemployment rate when there is no cyclical unemployment. This rate fluctuates with changes in the frictional and structural unemployment rate. The costs of unemployment include lost output and income, loss of human capital, an increase in crime, and a loss of human dignity. ◆

Unemployment is not the only indicator of the state of the nation's economic health. Another is inflation. Let's now examine that.

Inflation

Inflation is an upward movement in the average level of prices. Its opposite is deflation, a downward movement in the average level of prices. The boundary between inflation and deflation is price stability. Price stability occurs when the average level of prices is moving neither up nor down. The average level of prices is called the **price level**. It is measured by a price index. A **price index** measures the average level of prices in one period as a percentage of their average level in an earlier period called the base period.

Canadian price indexes that go back to Confederation have been compiled, and the story they tell is shown in Fig. 22.2. Over the 126 year period shown in that figure, prices have risen seventeen-fold—an average annual rate of increase of 2.3 percent. But prices have not moved upward at a constant and steady pace. In some periods, such as World War I and the years 1974 to 1982, the increase was sharp

FIGURE 22.2

The Price Level: 1867–1993

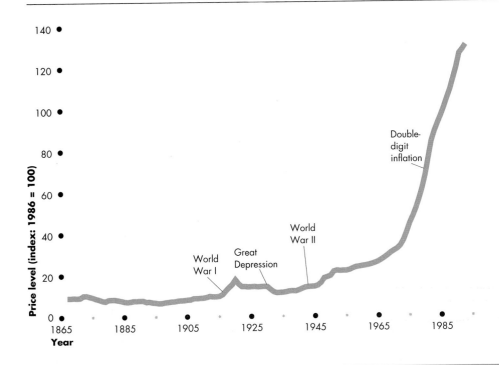

Between 1867 and 1993, prices, on the average, increased seventeen-fold. In some periods, such as the years of World War II, price increases were rapid. In other periods, such as the 1970s, a period of sustained increases occurred. At yet other times, such as the years of the Great Depression during the 1930s, prices fell.

Sources: 1867-1912, *Historical Statistics,* Series K-33; 1913-1975, *Historical Statistics,* Series K-8; 1976-1993, CANSIM series D484000. The raw data were spliced and converted to a base of 1981 = 100.

and pronounced—at times exceeding 10 percent a year. In other periods, such as the 1960s and 1970s, the increase was prolonged and steady. At yet other times, there have been periods of falling prices—in the early 1920s and during the Great Depression.

The Inflation Rate and the Price Level

The **inflation rate** is the percentage change in the price level. The formula for the annual inflation rate is

$$\text{Inflation rate} = \frac{\text{Current year's price level} - \text{Last year's price level}}{\text{Last year's price level}} \times 100.$$

A common way of measuring the price level is to use the *Consumer Price Index* (the CPI). (We'll learn more about the CPI in Chapter 23.) We can illustrate the calculation of the annual inflation rate by using the CPI. In December 1992, the CPI was 129.5. In December 1991, it was 126.8. Substituting

these values into the formula gives the inflation rate for 1992 as:

$$\text{Inflation rate} = \frac{129.5 - 126.8}{126.8} \times 100$$

$$= 2.1\%$$

The Recent Inflation Record

Recent Canadian economic history has seen some dramatic changes in the inflation rate. The inflation rate between 1960 and 1993, as measured by the CPI, is shown in Fig. 22.3.

During the early 1960s the inflation rate was low, lying between 1 and 2 percent a year. It began to increase in the late 1960s at the time of the Vietnam War. But the largest increases in inflation occurred in 1974 and again in 1980, years in which the actions of the Organization of Petroleum Exporting Countries (OPEC) resulted in exceptionally large increases in the price of oil. Inflation decreased

FIGURE 22.3

Inflation: 1960–1993

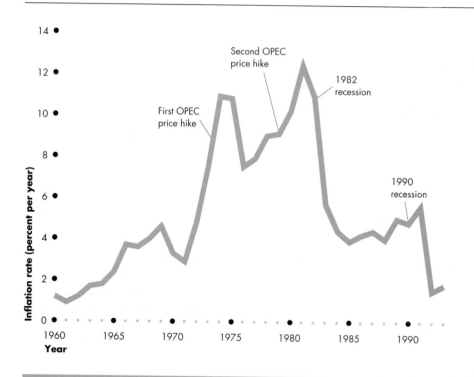

Inflation is a persistent feature of modern economic life in Canada. The inflation rate was low in the first half of the 1960s, but it moved upward in the late 1960s. It increased further with the OPEC oil price hikes but eventually declined through the 1980s and into the 1990s.

Sources: See Fig. 22.2.

through the 1980s and, in recent years, price stability has become the official policy goal.

The inflation rate rises and falls over the years. But since the 1930s the price level has generally risen (see Fig. 22.2). The price level falls only when the inflation rate is negative. Thus, even in years such as 1961 and 1986 when the inflation rate was low, the price level was rising.

Inflation and the Value of Money

When inflation is present, money is losing value. The **value of money** is the amount of goods and services that can be bought with a given amount of money. When an economy experiences inflation, the value of money falls—you cannot buy as many groceries with $50 this year as you could last year. The rate at which the value of money falls is equal to the inflation rate. When the inflation rate is high, as it was in 1980, money loses its value at a rapid pace. When inflation is low, as it was in 1961, the value of money falls slowly.

Inflation is a phenomenon that all countries experience. But inflation *rates* vary from one country to another. When inflation rates differ over a prolonged period of time, the result is a change in the foreign exchange value of money. A **foreign exchange rate** is the rate at which one country's money (or currency) exchanges for another country's money. For example, in March 1993, one Canadian dollar bought 95 Japanese yen. But in January 1971, you could get 360 yen for a dollar. The value of the Canadian dollar, in terms of the Japanese yen, has fallen over the years because our inflation rate has been higher than that in Japan. We'll learn more about exchange rates and how they are influenced by inflation in Chapter 36.

Is Inflation a Problem?

Is it a problem if money loses its value and does so at a rate that varies from one year to another? It is, but to describe the problem, we need to distinguish between anticipated and unanticipated inflation.

When prices are rising, people are aware of the fact and have some idea about the rate at which prices are rising. The rate at which people believe that the price level is rising is called the **expected inflation rate**. But expectations may be right or wrong. If they turn out to be right, the actual inflation rate equals the expected inflation rate, and inflation is anticipated. **Anticipated inflation** is an inflation rate that has been correctly forecasted. To the extent that the inflation rate is misforecasted, it is said to be unanticipated. That is, **unanticipated inflation** is the part of the inflation rate that has caught people by surprise.

The problems arising from inflation differ depending on whether it is anticipated or unanticipated.

The Problem of Unanticipated Inflation

With unanticipated inflation, it is as if the economy were a giant casino in which some people gain and some lose, and no one can predict where the gains and losses will fall. Gains and losses occur because of unanticipated changes in the value of money. Money is used as a measuring rod of the value of the transactions that we undertake. Borrowers and lenders, workers and their employers, all make contracts in terms of money. If the value of money varies unexpectedly over time, then the amounts *really* paid and received differ from those that people intended to pay and receive when they signed the contracts. Measuring value with a measuring rod whose units vary is a bit like trying to measure a piece of cloth with an elastic ruler. The size of the cloth depends on how tightly the ruler is stretched.

The Problem of Anticipated Inflation

Anticipated inflation is a problem when the inflation rate is high. At high inflation rates, people know that money is losing value quickly, so they try to avoid holding on to money for too long. The inflation rate—the rate at which money is losing value—is part of the *opportunity cost* of holding money. Instead of having a wallet stuffed with $20 bills and a big chequing account balance, people spend their incomes as soon as they receive them. The same is true for firms. Instead of hanging on to the money they receive from the sale of their goods and services, they pay it out in wages as quickly as possible.

In Germany, Poland, and Hungary in the 1920s, inflation rates reached extraordinary heights—in excess of 50 percent a month. Such high inflation rates are called *hyperinflations*. At the height of these hyperinflations, firms paid out wages twice a day. As soon as they were paid, workers spent their wages before they lost too much value. To buy a handful of groceries, they needed a shopping cart of currency. People who lingered too long in the coffee shop found that the price of their cup of coffee had increased between the time they placed their order and when the check was presented. Such anticipated inflation brings economic chaos.

High and Variable Inflation

Even if inflation is reasonably well anticipated, and even if its rate is not as high as during a period of hyperinflation, it can still impose very high costs. A high and variable inflation rate causes resources to be diverted from productive activities to forecasting inflation. It becomes more profitable to forecast the inflation rate correctly than to invent a new product. Doctors, lawyers, accountants, farmers—just about everyone—can make themselves better off, not by practising the profession for which they have been trained, but by becoming amateur economists and inflation forecasters. From a social perspective, this diversion of talent and resources is like throwing our scarce resources onto the garbage heap. This waste of resources is a cost of inflation.

REVIEW

T he inflation rate rises and falls, but since the 1930s, the *price level* has only risen. The effects of inflation depend on whether it is unanticipated or anticipated. Unanticipated inflation brings unpredictable gains and losses to borrowers and lenders, workers and employers. Anticipated inflation becomes a problem when its rate is high and people spend money as soon as they receive it. Inflation also is a problem when its rate is variable, because resources are diverted to predicting inflation. ◆

A third indicator of a nation's economic health is its gross domestic product. Let's now examine that.

Gross Domestic Product

The value of all the final goods and services produced in the economy in a year is called **gross domestic product** or GDP. **Final goods and services** are goods and services that are bought by their final user and are not used as inputs in the production of other goods and services. Such goods include consumption goods and services and also new durable goods. Examples of final goods are cans of pop and cars. Examples of final services are automobile insurance and haircuts.

Goods and services used as inputs in production are called **intermediate goods and services**. Examples of intermediate goods are the windshields, batteries, and gearboxes used by car producers and the paper and ink used by newspaper manufacturers. Examples of intermediate services are the banking and insurance services bought by car producers and news printers. Whether a good or service is intermediate or final depends on who buys it and for what purpose. For example, electric power bought by a car producer or a printer is an intermediate good. Electric power bought by you is a final good.

When we measure gross domestic product, we do not include the value of intermediate goods and services produced. If we did, we would be counting the same thing more than once. When someone buys a new car from the local Chrysler dealer, that is a final transaction and the value of the car is counted as part of GDP. But we must not also count as part of GDP the amount the dealer paid to Chrysler for the car or the amount paid by Chrysler to all its suppliers for the car's various parts.

If we want to measure GDP, we somehow have to add together all the *final* goods and services produced. Obviously, we can't achieve a useful measure by simply adding together the number of cars, newspapers, kilowatts of electric power, haircuts, and automobile insurance policies. To determine GDP, we first calculate the dollar *value* of the output of each final good or service. This calculation simply involves multiplying the quantity produced of each final good or service by its price. That is, we measure the output of each good and service in the common unit of dollars. We then add up the dollar values of the outputs of the different goods to arrive at

their total value, which is GDP. Although we measure GDP in dollars, it is a mixture of real quantities (the numbers of final goods and services produced) and dollar quantities (the prices of the goods and services). A change in GDP, therefore, contains a mixture of the effects of changes in prices and changes in the quantities of final goods and services. For many purposes, it is important to distinguish price changes from quantity changes. To do so, we use the concepts of nominal GDP and real GDP. Let's examine these concepts.

Nominal GDP and Real GDP

Nominal GDP measures the value of the output of final goods and services using *current* prices. It is sometimes called *current dollar GDP*. **Real GDP** measures the value of the output of final goods and services using the prices that prevailed in a given base period. An alternative name for real GDP is *constant dollar GDP*.

Comparing real GDP from one year to another enables us to say whether the economy has produced more or fewer goods and services. Comparing nominal GDP from one year to another does not permit us to compare the quantities of goods and services produced in those two years. Nominal GDP may be higher in 1993 than 1992, but that might reflect only higher prices (inflation), not more production.

The distinction between real GDP and nominal GDP is illustrated in Fig. 22.4. In any year, real GDP is measured by the height of the red area and nominal GDP by the height of the green area. The difference between the height of the green area and the height of the red area shows the inflation component in nominal GDP. In 1962, GDP was $44 billion. By 1992, it had grown to $690 billion. But only part of that increase represents an increase in goods and services available—an increase in real GDP. Most of the increase came from inflation. Notice that nominal GDP increases every year in the figure but that real GDP sometimes falls, such as in 1975, 1982, and 1991.

Real GDP—the Record

Estimates of real GDP in Canada go back to 1926. Figure 22.5 illustrates the real GDP record. Two facts stand out. First, there has been a general tendency for real GDP to increase. Second, the rate of upward movement is not uniform, and sometimes

FIGURE 22.4

Gross Domestic Product: 1960–1993

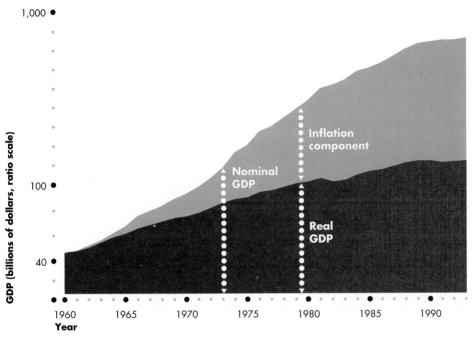

Gross domestic product increased fifteen-fold between 1963 and 1993. But much of that increase was the result of inflation. Real GDP, the increase in GDP attributable to the increase in the volume of goods and services produced, increased but at a more modest pace. The figure shows how real GDP and the inflation component of nominal GDP have evolved. Nominal GDP has increased in every year, but real GDP fell in 1982 and again in 1991.

Source: CANSIM series D20000 and D20031.

real GDP has actually declined. The most precipitous decline occurred in the early 1930s during the Great Depression. But declines also occurred in recent times, during the 1982 and 1990 recessions. There were also periods when real GDP grew extremely quickly—for example, the years during World War II.

We can get a clearer picture of the changes in real GDP if we separate the two features we've just identified. The first of these features is the general upward movement of real GDP. This feature of real GDP is called trend real GDP. Trend real GDP rises for three reasons:

◆ Growing population

◆ Growing stock of capital equipment

◆ Advances in technology

These forces have produced the general upward tendency that you can see in Fig. 22.5. Trend real GDP is illustrated in Fig. 22.5 as the thin black line passing through the middle of the path followed by real

GDP in its meanderings above trend (blue areas) and below trend (red areas).

The second feature of real GDP is its periodic fluctuation around its trend. Real GDP fluctuations are measured as percentage deviations of real GDP from trend. They are illustrated in Fig. 22.6. As you can see, real GDP fluctuations show distinct cycles in economic activity. At times such as the Great Depression, the mid-1970s, the early 1980s, and 1990s, real GDP was below trend, and during the years of World War II it was above trend.

The Benefits and Costs of Real GDP Growth

The upward trend in real GDP is the major source of improvements in living standards. The pace of this upward movement has a powerful effect on the standard of living of one generation compared with its predecessor. For example, if real GDP trends upward at 1 percent a year, it takes 70 years for real GDP to double. But a growth trend of 10 percent a year will double real GDP in just seven years. With an average

Figure 22.5

Real GDP: 1926–1993

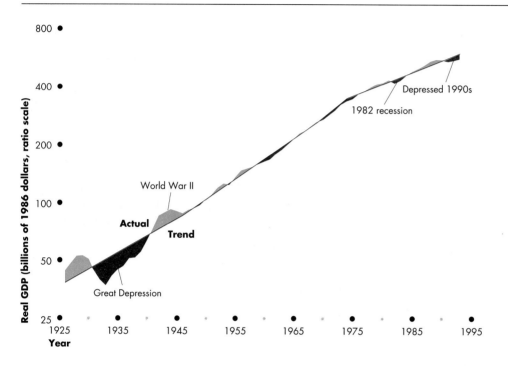

Between 1926 and 1993, real GDP grew at an annual average rate of 4.2 percent. This general tendency of real GDP to grow is shown by the thin black trend line. But the growth rate was not the same in each year. In some periods, such as the years during World War II, real GDP expanded quickly. In other periods, such as the Great Depression and, more recently, in the 1982 recession and the depressed 1990s, real GDP declined.

Sources: Historical Statistics, Series F-55 and CANSIM series D20031.

trend increase of between 2 and 3 percent a year, which is commonly experienced in industrial countries and which has also been the long-term experience of Canada, real GDP doubles approximately every generation (every 25 years or so).

Rapid growth in real GDP brings enormous benefits. It enables us to consume more goods and services of all kinds. It enables us to spend more on health care for the poor and old, and on cancer and AIDS research, on research and exploration, and on roads and housing. It even enables us to spend more on the environment, cleaning our lakes and protecting our air.

But an upward trend in real GDP has its costs. The more quickly we increase real GDP, the faster are exhaustible resources such as oil and natural gas depleted, and the more severe our environmental and atmospheric pollution problems become. Although we have more to spend on these problems, they become bigger problems requiring higher expenditures. Furthermore, the more quickly real GDP increases, the more we have to accept change, both in what we consume and in the jobs we do.

The benefits of more rapid growth in real GDP have to be balanced against the costs. The choices that people make to balance these benefits and costs, acting individually and through government institutions, determine the actual pace at which real GDP increases.

As we have seen, real GDP does not increase at an even pace. Are the fluctuations in real GDP important? Economists do not agree on the answer to this question. Some economists believe that real GDP fluctuations are costly. With real GDP below trend, unemployment is above its natural rate and output is lost forever. With real GDP above trend, inflationary bottlenecks and shortages arise. If a downturn can be avoided, average consumption levels can be increased, and if rises above trend can be avoided, inflation can be kept under control.

Other economists believe that fluctuations are the best possible response to the uneven pace and direction of technological change. At some times, technological change is rapid and at other times it is slow. At some times, new technologies increase the productivity of workers in their existing jobs, and at

---

FIGURE 22.6

Real GDP Fluctuations: 1926–1993

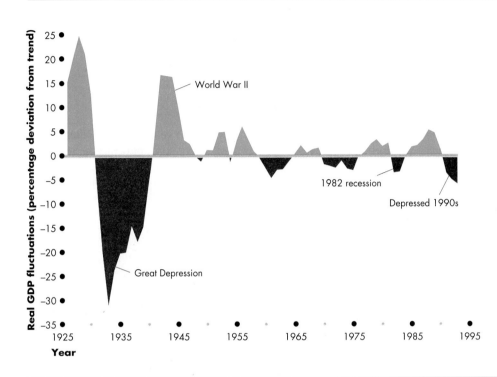

The uneven pace of increase of real GDP is illustrated by tracking its fluctuation measured as the percentage deviation of real GDP from trend. Rapid expansion of real GDP, which occurred during World War II, puts real GDP above trend. Decreases in real GDP, which occurred during the Great Depression and the two most recent recessions, put real GDP below trend. The real GDP fluctuations describe the course of the business cycle.

Source: See Fig. 22.5.

---

other times new technologies increase productivity only after massive structural change has taken place. Real GDP growth fluctuates with the pace of technological change—faster technological change brings faster real GDP growth. But structural change complicates the relationship. Rapid technological and structural changes at first bring structural unemployment and slow real GDP growth. Since we are not able to order the pace and direction of technological change to be smooth, we can smooth the pace of economic growth only by *delaying* the implementation of new technologies. Such delays would result in never-to-be-recovered waste.

Regardless of which position economists take, they all agree that depressions as deep and long as that which occurred in the early 1930s result in extraordinary waste and human suffering. The disagreements concern the more common and gentler ebbs and flows of economic activity that have occurred in the years since World War II, which we saw earlier in Fig. 22.6.

R E V I E W

G ross domestic product is the dollar value of all the final goods and services produced in the economy. Nominal GDP measures the value of the output of final goods and services using current prices. Real GDP measures the value of the output using the prices that prevailed in a given base period. Nominal real GDP increases more quickly than real GDP because of inflation. The general tendency for real GDP to increase is called trend real GDP. Economic fluctuations can be measured by departures from trend real GDP. The upward trend in real GDP is the major source of improved living standards. However, the upward trend has costs in terms of depletion of exhaustible resources and environmental pollution. ◆

Let's now take a more systematic look at the ebbs and flows of economic activity.

The Business Cycle

The **business cycle** is the periodic but irregular up-and-down movement in economic activity, measured by fluctuations in real GDP and other macroeconomic variables. As we've just seen, real GDP can be divided into two components:

◆ Trend real GDP

◆ Real GDP fluctuations

To identify the business cycle, we focus our attention on the real GDP fluctuations, since this variable gives a direct measure of the uneven pace of economic activity, separate from its underlying trend growth path.

A business cycle is not a regular, predictable, or repeating phenomenon like the swing of the pendulum of a clock. Its timing is random and, to a large degree, unpredictable. A business cycle is identified as a sequence of four phases:

◆ Contraction

◆ Trough

◆ Expansion

◆ Peak

These four phases are shown in Fig. 22.7. This figure, which is an enlargement of part of Fig. 22.6, shows the business cycle for 1980 to 1991. Notice the four phases of the cycle. A **contraction** is a slowdown in the pace of economic activity, such as occurred between 1981 and 1982. An **expansion** is a speedup in the pace of economic activity, such as occurred between 1983 and 1988. A **trough** is the lower turning point of a business cycle, where a

FIGURE 22.7

The Business Cycle

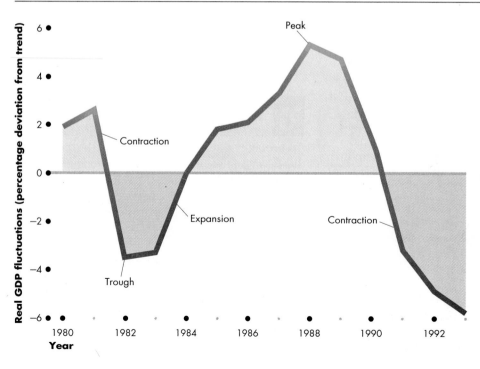

The business cycle has four phases: contraction, trough, expansion, and peak. Our experience in the 1980s and early 1990s is used to illustrate these phases. There was a contraction from 1981 to 1982. In 1982, the trough was reached and an expansion began. That expansion reached a peak in 1988, when a new contraction set in.

contraction turns into an expansion. A trough occurred in 1982. A **peak** is the upper turning point of a business cycle, where an expansion turns into a contraction. A peak occurred in 1988.

A recession occurs if a contraction is severe enough. A **recession** is a downturn in the level of economic activity in which real GDP declines in two successive quarters. A deep trough is called a slump or a **depression**.

Unemployment and the Business Cycle

Real GDP is not the only variable that fluctuates over the course of the business cycle. Its fluctuations are matched by related fluctuations in a wide range of other economic variables. One of the most important of these is unemployment. In the contraction phase of a business cycle, unemployment increases; in the expansion phase, unemployment decreases; at the peak, unemployment is at its lowest; at the trough, unemployment is at its highest. This relationship between unemployment and the

phases of the business cycle is illustrated in Fig. 22.8.

That figure shows real GDP fluctuations and unemployment in Canada since 1926. The Great Depression, World War II, the 1982 recession, and the depressed 1990s are highlighted in the figure. The figure also shows the unemployment rate. So that we can see how unemployment lines up with real GDP fluctuations, the unemployment rate has been measured with its scale inverted. That is, the unemployment rate *increases* as we move *down* the vertical axis on the right-hand side of the figure.

Fluctuations in unemployment closely follow those in real GDP. That is, the cycle in unemployment rate follows the business cycle. But some changes in unemployment are unrelated to the business cycle. They are the persistent increases in unemployment that occurred in the 1970s and 1980s. These persistent increases, visible in Fig. 22.8, took the boom-time unemployment rate of the late 1980s to a level that exceeded the recession unemployment rate of the 1970s.

Unemployment and the Business Cycle

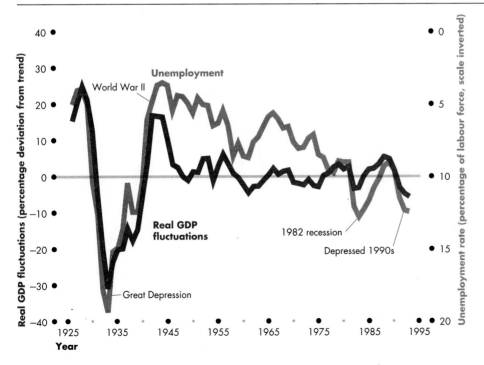

This figure shows the relationship between unemployment and the business cycle. Real GDP fluctuations tell us when the economy is in a contraction or expansion phase. Unemployment is plotted on the same figure but with its scale inverted. The line measuring unemployment is high when unemployment is low, and the line is low when unemployment is high. As you can see, the cycle in real GDP is closely matched by the cycle in unemployment.

Source: See Figs. 22.1 and 22.6.

The Stock Market and the Business Cycle

We've seen that unemployment fluctuations mirror the business cycle quite closely, but that inflation does not. Another indicator of the state of the economy, and perhaps the most visible of all such indicators, is the performance of the stock market. Every weekday evening, newscasts tell us of the day's events on the Toronto, Montreal, and world stock exchanges. Movements in share prices attract attention partly for their own sake and also partly for what they may foretell about our *future* economic fortunes.

Do stock prices move in sympathy with fluctuations in real GDP and unemployment? Is a stock price downturn a predictor of economic contraction? Is a stock price boom a predictor of economic expansion? To answer these questions, let's take a look at the behaviour of stock prices and see how they relate to the expansions and contractions of economic activity.

Figure 22.9 tracks the course of stock prices from 1914 to 1993. The prices plotted in this figure are inflation adjusted. Actual stock prices increased much more than indicated here because of inflation, but the purely inflationary parts of the price increases have been removed so that we can see what has *really* been happening to stock prices—that is, the path of *real* stock prices.

The most striking feature of stock prices is their volatility and lack of any obvious cyclical patterns. Two stock price crashes are highlighted in the figure: those of 1929 and 1987. The 1929 crash was a sharp one, and it was followed by two successive years of massive stock price decline. The 1987 crash was much smaller, and the decline in prices was short-lived. There have also been periods of rapid increases in stock price, the most dramatic being that which preceded the 1929 crash. There were also strong increases in stock prices before the 1987 crash.

How do fluctuations in stock prices correspond with the business cycle? Sometimes they correspond quite closely, and at other times they do not. For example, the movements in stock prices through the Great Depression and the recovery from it suggest

---

FIGURE 22.9

Stock Prices: 1914–1993

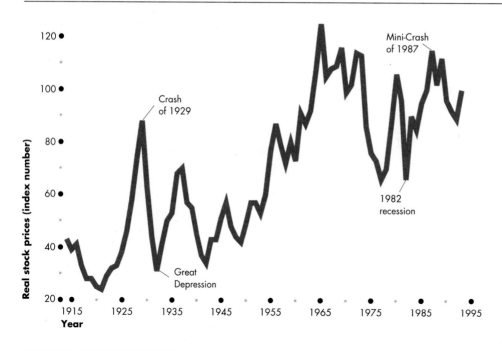

Stock prices are among the most volatile elements of our economy. Real stock prices (stock prices measured to take out the effects of changes in the value of money) climbed strongly in the late 1920s. Then, in 1929, came the crash that preceded the Great Depression. Stock prices began a new climb after World War II, reaching a peak in 1965. They gradually fell to a trough in 1977, rebounded for two years, and returned to their trough level in 1982. They then climbed to a new peak in 1987 before the October crash of that year.

Source: 1914-1955: *Historical Statistics* Series J-494: 1955-1993: CANSIM series B4237.

that the stock market tells us where the economy is heading. The stock market moved in sympathy with, but slightly ahead of, the contraction and expansion of real GDP and the rise and fall in the unemployment rate.

But do turning points in the stock market always reliably predict the turning points in the economy? The answer is no. In some periods the stock market and real GDP move together, but in others the movements oppose each other. For example, the mini-crash of 1987 occurred at a time when the economy, both in Canada and in the rest of the world, was expanding strongly.

When stock prices collapsed in October 1987, many people drew parallels between that episode and the 1929 stock price crash. In 1930, the economy collapsed. In 1988, the economy continued to grow. Why were the two episodes so different? The answer is that stock prices are determined by *expectations* about economic growth and those expectations are sometimes right and sometimes wrong. In 1929, expectations correctly anticipated the Great Depression. In 1987, expectations were more pessimistic than the performance of the economy justified. On the average, expectations turn out to be wrong about as often as they turn out to be right. Thus the movement in stock prices is not an entirely reliable predictor of the state of the economy.

Inflation and the Business Cycle

We've looked at the fluctuations in real GDP and unemployment and seen a relationship between these variables. How does inflation behave over the business cycle? Are fluctuations in inflation related to the fluctuations in real GDP and unemployment or is inflation independent of the business cycle?

To answer these questions, look at Figure 22.10. That figure shows a scatter diagram of the inflation rate plotted against the deviation of real GDP from its trend. Each point in the figure represents a year. The pattern made by the points tells us how the inflation rate relates to the business cycle.

Two features of the relationship between inflation and real GDP fluctuations are visible in the figure. They are

◆ A tendency, on the average, for inflation to be higher, the further real GDP is above its trend

FIGURE 22.10

Inflation and the Business Cycle

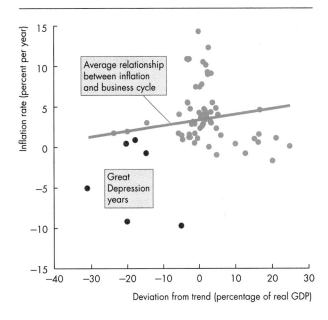

This figure shows a scatter diagram of inflation (on the vertical axis) plotted against the deviation of real GDP from trend (on the horizontal axis). Each dot in the figure represents a year. The red dots are the Great Depression years of the 1930s and the blue dots represent the other years. On the average, the further real GDP is above its trend, the higher is the inflation rate. This average tendency is shown by the green line. But the relationship between inflation and the business cycle is a loose one, as is shown by the large spread in the red and blue dots.

Source: See Figs. 22.2 and 22.5.

◆ Large fluctuations in inflation that are independent of the state of real GDP

The average relationship between inflation and real GDP fluctuations is shown by the green line in the figure. The independence of inflation is shown by the fact that the dots do not lie very close to the green line. For example, when real GDP is close to trend (when the deviation from trend is close to zero) the inflation rate varies between –2 percent and +14 percent a year. These years are illustrated by the blue dots. In the Great Depression years, shown by the red dots, inflation ranged between +5 and –10 percent a year.

R E V I E W

The business cycle is the periodic but irregular up-and-down movement in economic activity. It has four phases: contraction, trough, expansion, and peak. A recession is a contraction in which real GDP declines for at least two quarters. Over the business cycle, real GDP and unemployment fluctuate together. During a contraction, the unemployment rate rises, and during an expansion it falls. Inflation can also move in sympathy with the business cycle but there are important fluctuations in the inflation rate that are not related to the business cycle. Although the stock market sometimes moves in sympathy with the business cycle, it does not reliably predict turning points in the economy. ◆

We've studied unemployment, inflation, real GDP fluctuations, and business cycles. Let's now turn to our final topic, deficits.

Government Deficit and International Deficit

If you spend more than you earn in a given period, you have a deficit. To cover your deficit, you have to borrow or sell off some of the things that you own. Just as individuals have deficits, so can governments and entire nations. These deficits—the government deficit and the international deficit—have attracted a lot of attention recently.

Government Deficit

The **government deficit** is the total expenditure of the government sector minus the total revenue of that sector in a given period. The government sector is composed of the federal government and the provincial and local governments. These governments spend on a variety of public and social programs and obtain their revenue from taxes.

Sometimes the government sector is in surplus, and at other times it is in deficit. Occasionally, the deficit is a very large one, as it was in 1975. Since 1980, the government sector has had a persistent deficit, averaging about 3 percent of GDP.

To some degree, the balance of the government budget is related to the business cycle. When the economy is expanding quickly, incomes grow quickly and so do tax receipts. At the same time, unemployment decreases, and so do unemployment benefits. The government deficit shrinks through this phase of the business cycle. When the economy is in a contraction phase, tax receipts decline and unemployment benefits increase. The government budget deficit increases. What is significant about the budget deficit in the 1980s is that it persisted despite the fact that the economy experienced strong and prolonged expansion.

We'll study the government deficit more closely and at greater length in Chapter 34. In that chapter, we'll discuss its sources and consequences.

International Deficit

The value of all the goods and services we sell to other countries (exports) minus the value of all the goods and services we buy from foreigners (imports) is called our **trade balance**. If we add to our trade balance the interest payments we receive from other countries and subtract the interest payments we make to the rest of the world (and add net gifts), we arrive at our **current account balance**. If we spend less in the rest of the world than we receive from it, we have a current account surplus. If we spend more in the rest of the world than we receive from it, we have a current account deficit.

Most of the time since 1950, Canada has had small current account balances that have alternated between surpluses and deficits. But in the late 1980s, a large current account deficit emerged. That deficit was not only persistent but also gradually increased in magnitude.

When we have a current account deficit, we have to borrow from the rest of the world to pay for the goods and services that we are buying in excess of the value of those we are selling. Mirroring our current account deficit is a current account surplus in some other countries. The most notable country on the opposite side of our international payments balance is Japan. That country has been operating a current account surplus and, in recent years, an increasing surplus. To finance our deficit, we borrow from the rest of the world and the rest of the world lends to us.

The causes of these international surpluses and deficits and their consequences will be discussed at greater length in Chapter 36.

◆ ◆ ◆ ◆ In our study of macroeconomics, we're going to find out what economists currently know about the causes of unemployment and of variations in its rate; we're also going to discover what economists know about the causes of inflation and

business cycle fluctuations. We're going to discover why sometimes inflation and the business cycle move in sympathy with each other, and why at other times these variables follow separate courses. We're also going to discover why at certain times the stock market is a good predictor of the state of the economy and at others it is not. Finally, we will learn more about deficits—the government deficit and the international deficit—and their causes, their importance, and their consequences. ◆ ◆ The next step in our study of macroeconomics is to learn more about macroeconomic measurement—about how we measure GDP, the price level, and inflation.

S U M M A R Y

Unemployment

Unemployment is a state in which there are qualified workers who are available for work at the current wage rate and who do not have jobs. The labour force is the sum of those who are unemployed and those who are employed. The unemployment rate is the percentage of the labour force that is unemployed. Unemployment is measured each month by a survey of households.

Unemployment was a major problem in Canada during the Great Depression years of the early 1930s, and again became a serious problem in the 1980s and 1990s.

There are three types of unemployment: frictional, structural, and cyclical. Frictional unemployment arises from normal labour market turnover and the fact that people take time to find the job that best matches their skills. Structural unemployment arises when technological change causes a decline in jobs that are concentrated in particular industries or regions. Cyclical unemployment arises when the pace of economic expansion slows down. Full employment is a state in which all unemployment is frictional. The natural rate of unemployment is the sum of the frictional and structural unemployment rates.

The major costs of unemployment are the lost output and earnings that could have been generated if the unemployed had been working. Other major costs include the deterioration of human capital and, when unemployment is prolonged, increased crime and

severe social and psychological problems for unemployed workers and their families. (pp. 599–604)

Inflation

Inflation is an upward movement in the average level of prices. To measure the average level of prices, we calculate a price index. The inflation rate is the percentage change in the value of a price index.

Inflation is a persistent feature of economic life in Canada, but the rate of inflation fluctuates. In the early 1960s, inflation was between 1 and 2 percent a year. By 1981, its rate exceeded 13 percent a year. There was an upward trend in inflation through the 1960s and 1970s, but inflation has been on a downward trend since 1981.

Inflation is a problem because it brings a fall in the value of money at an unpredictable rate. The more unpredictable the inflation rate, the less useful is money as a measuring rod for conducting transactions. Inflation makes money especially unsuitable for transactions that are spread out over time, such as borrowing and lending or working for an agreed wage rate. A rapid anticipated inflation is a problem because it makes people get rid of money as quickly as possible, disrupting economic life. (pp. 604–607)

Gross Domestic Product

The nation's total output is measured by gross domestic product (GDP). GDP is the dollar value of all final goods and services produced in the economy in a given time period. Changes in GDP reflect both changes in prices and changes in the quantity of goods and services produced. To separate the effects of prices from real quantities, we distinguish between nominal GDP and real GDP. Nominal GDP is measured by using current prices. Real GDP is measured by using prices for a given base year.

Real GDP grows, on average, every year, so that the trend of real GDP is upward. But real GDP does not increase at a constant rate. Its rate of expansion fluctuates, so real GDP fluctuates around its trend value. Increases in real GDP bring rising living standards, but not without costs. The main costs of fast economic growth are resource depletion, environmental pollution, and the need to face rapid and often costly changes in job type and location. The benefits of higher consumption levels have to be balanced against such costs. (pp. 608–611)

The Business Cycle

The business cycle is the periodic but irregular up and down movement in macroeconomic activity. The cycle has four phases: contraction, trough, expansion, and peak. When real GDP falls for two quarters, the economy is in a recession.

Unemployment fluctuates closely with real GDP fluctuations. When real GDP is above trend, the unemployment rate is low; when real GDP is below trend, the unemployment rate is high. Stock prices do not fluctuate in line with the business cycle. Sometimes a stock market crash precedes a recession, but it does not always do so. There is no simple relationship between the inflation rate and the business cycle. Sometimes the inflation rate increases in an expansion phase and decreases in a contraction phase. At other times, inflation moves independently of the business cycle.(pp. 612–616)

Government Deficit and International Deficit

The government deficit is the total expenditure of the government sector minus the total revenue of that sector. The government deficit fluctuates over the course of the business cycle. But in the 1980s, the government sector operated with a persistent deficit even though the economy underwent a strong and persistent expansion.

A country's current account balance is the difference between what it receives from and what it spends in the rest of the world. Canada has had a small current account balance that alternates between deficit and surplus, but in the 1980s a deficit emerged. Mirroring Canada's current account deficit is a current account surplus in some other countries. Japan is one of the countries that had a large surplus in the 1980s. (pp. 616–617)

K E Y   E L E M E N T S

Key Terms

Anticipated inflation, 607
Business cycle, 612
Contraction, 612
Current account balance, 616
Cyclical unemployment, 601
Depression, 613
Discouraged workers, 599
Expansion, 612
Expected inflation rate, 607
Final goods and services, 608

Foreign exchange rate, 606
Frictional unemployment, 600
Full employment, 601
Government deficit, 616
Gross domestic product, 608
Human capital, 604
Inflation, 604
Inflation rate, 605
Intermediate goods and services, 608
Labour force, 599
Natural rate of unemployment, 601

Nominal GDP, 608
Peak, 613
Price index, 604
Price level, 604
Real GDP, 608
Recession, 613
Structural unemployment, 601
Trade balance, 616
Trough, 612
Unanticipated inflation, 607
Unemployment, 599
Unemployment rate, 599
Value of money, 606

Key Figures

Figure 22.1   Unemployment: 1926–1993, 600
Figure 22.2   The Price Level: 1867–1993, 605
Figure 22.4   Gross Domestic Product: 1960–1993, 609
Figure 22.5   Real GDP: 1926–1993, 610
Figure 22.6   Real GDP Fluctuations: 1926–1993, 611
Figure 22.7   The Business Cycle, 612
Figure 22.8   Unemployment and the Business Cycle, 613
Figure 22.10 Inflation and the Business Cycle, 615

R E V I E W   Q U E S T I O N S

1 What is the definition of unemployment?

2 How is the unemployment rate measured in Canada?

3 Why may the measured unemployment rate understate or overstate the true extent of unemployment?

4 What are the different types of unemployment?

5 What are the main costs of unemployment?

6 What is inflation?

7 What are some of the costs of inflation?

8 What, if any, are the benefits from inflation? If there are none, explain why.

9 Why is inflation like a national casino?

10 Why might anticipated inflation be a problem?

11 What makes GDP grow?

12 What are the costs and benefits of a high average increase in real GDP?

13 What are the costs and benefits of fluctuations in real GDP?

14 What is a business cycle? Describe the four phases of a business cycle. What was the phase of the Canadian business cycle in 1977? In 1982? In 1985? In 1991?

15 When the economy is in a recovery phase, what is happening to the unemployment rate?

16 How does the inflation rate fluctuate over the business cycle?

17 Compare the fluctuations in inflation and unemployment.

18 What happens to stock prices over the business cycle?

19 What is the government budget deficit?

20 What is the current account balance?

P R O B L E M S

1 In a month in 1933, the number of people counted as unemployed was 800,000 and the number counted as employed was 3,400,000. What was the unemployment rate in that month?

2 At the end of 1993, the price index was 150. At the end of 1992, the price index was 125. What was the inflation rate in 1993?

3 Obtain data on unemployment in your province. If your school library has the Statistics Canada publication *The Labour Force Survey*, you can get the data from there. Otherwise, you might have to call your local newspaper business desk for the information. Compare the behaviour of unemployment in your province with that in Canada as a whole. Why do you think your province might have a higher or a lower unemployment rate than the Canadian average?

4 Obtain data on inflation in Canada, the United States, Japan, and Germany since 1980. You will find these data in *International Financial Statistics* in your school library. Draw a graph of the data and answer the following questions:

a   Which country had the highest inflation rate?
b   Which country had the lowest inflation rate?
c   Which country had the fastest-rising inflation rate?
d   Which country had the fastest-falling inflation rate?

5 On the basis of your discovery in answering problem 4, what do you expect happened to the foreign exchange rates between the Canadian dollar and the Japanese yen, the U.S. dollar, and the German mark? Check your expectation by finding these exchange rates in the *International*

Financial Statistics from which you got the inflation rates.

6 You are given the following information about the economy of Macrominor:

Year/quarter	Real GDP (billions of 1993 dollars)	Price level (index, 1993 = 100)	Unemployment rate (percentage of labour force)	Stock market price (index, 1993 = 100)
1994/1	101	104	5	104
1994/2	102	105	5	106
1994/3	103	108	5	108
1994/4	104	110	5	100
1995/1	103	111	6	102
1995/2	102	112	7	110
1995/3	106	115	5	112
1995/4	108	119	4	114

a   In which period did Macrominor have a recession?
b   Did the stock market anticipate the recession?
c   When recession hit Macrominor, did the unemployment rate increase or decrease?
d   When the recession hit Macrominor, did the inflation rate increase or decrease?
e   When did Macrominor begin its recovery from recession?
f   Did the stock market anticipate the recovery?
g   When the recovery began in Macrominor, did the unemployment rate decrease right away?
h   When the recovery began in Macrominor, did the inflation rate increase or decrease?

CHAPTER 23

MEASURING OUTPUT AND THE PRICE LEVEL

After studying this chapter, you will be able to

◆ Describe the flows of expenditure and income

◆ Explain why aggregate expenditure and income are equal to each other

◆ Explain how gross domestic product (GDP) is measured

◆ Describe two common measures of the price level—the Consumer Price Index (CPI) and the GDP deflator

◆ Explain how real GDP is measured

◆ Distinguish between inflation and changes in relative prices

◆ Explain why real GDP is not a good measure of economic well-being

EVERY THREE MONTHS, STATISTICS CANADA PUBLISHES ITS latest estimates of gross domestic product, or GDP—a barometer of our nation's economy. Analysts pore over the data, trying to understand the past and peer into the future. How do government accountants add up all the blooming, buzzing economic activity of the country to arrive at the number called GDP? And what exactly *is* GDP? ◆ ◆ From economists to homemakers, inflation watchers of all types pay close attention to another economic barometer, the Consumer Price Index, or CPI. Statistics Canada publishes new figures each month, and analysts in newspapers and on TV quickly leap to conclusions. How does the government determine the CPI? How well does it measure the consumer's living costs? ◆ ◆ Our economy grows. But to reveal the rate of growth, we must remove the effects of inflation on GDP and assess how GDP has changed because of changing

Economic Barometers

production. How do we remove the inflation component of GDP? ◆ ◆ Some people make a living from crime. Others, although doing work that is legal, try to hide the payment they receive to evade taxes or other regulations. Most people undertake some economic activity inside their homes. Fixing meals, laundering shirts, mowing the lawn, and washing the car are examples. Are any of these activities measured in GDP? How important are the activities not counted as part of GDP?

◆ ◆ ◆ ◆ In this chapter, we're going to learn more about GDP and the price level. But first we'll describe the flows of expenditure and income.

The Circular Flow of Expenditure and Income

The circular flow of expenditure and income provides the conceptual basis for measuring gross domestic product. We'll see some of the key ideas and relationships more clearly if we begin with a model economy that is simpler than the one in which we live. We'll then add some features to make our simplified economy correspond with that of the real economy.

Circular Flows in a Simplified Economy

Our simplified economy has just two kinds of economic decision makers: households and firms.

Households

◆ Receive incomes in exchange for the supply of factors of production to firms

◆ Make expenditures on consumption goods and services bought from firms

◆ Save some of their incomes

Firms

◆ Pay incomes to households in exchange for the factors of production hired (these payments include wages paid for labour, interest paid for capital, rent paid for land, and profits)

◆ Make investment expenditures—purchases of capital goods from other firms and changes in their inventories

◆ Receive revenue from the sale of consumption goods and services to households

◆ Receive revenue from other firms' investment expenditures

◆ Borrow to finance investment expenditures

The economy has three types of markets:

◆ Goods (and services) markets

◆ Factor markets

◆ Financial markets

Transactions between households and firms take place in these markets. In factor markets, households sell the services of labour, capital, and land to firms. In exchange, firms make income payments to households. These payments are wages for labour services, interest for the use of capital, rent for the use of land, and profits to the owners of firms. These payments for factor services are households' incomes. **Aggregate income** is the amount received by households in payment for the services of factors of production.

In the markets for goods and services, firms sell consumer goods and services—such as popcorn and movies, microwave ovens and dry cleaning services—to households. In exchange, households make payments to firms. The total payment made by households on consumption goods and services is called **consumption expenditure**.

Firms do not sell all their output to households. Some of what they produce is new capital equipment, and it is sold to other firms. For example, IBM sells a mainframe computer to General Motors. Also, some of what firms produce might not be sold at all, but added to inventory. For example, if General Motors produces 1,000 cars and sells 950 of them to households, 50 cars remain unsold and GM's inventory of cars increases by 50. When a firm adds unsold output to inventory, we can think of the firm as buying goods from itself. The purchase of new plant, equipment, and buildings and additions to inventories are called **investment**. To finance investment, firms borrow from households in financial markets.

These transactions between households and firms result in flows of income and expenditure, as shown in Fig. 23.1. To help you keep track of the different types of flows, they have been colour-coded. The blue flow represents aggregate income, which we denote by Y. The red flows represent expenditures on goods and services. Consumption expenditure is denoted by C. Investment is denoted by I. Notice that investment is illustrated in the figure as a flow from firms through the goods markets and back to firms. It is illustrated in this way because some firms produce capital goods and other firms buy them (and firms "buy" inventories from themselves).

There are two additional flows in the figure, shown in green. These flows do not represent payments for the services of factors of production or for the purchases of goods and services. They represent saving and borrowing. Households do not spend all

FIGURE 23.1

The Circular Flow of Expenditure and Income between Households and Firms

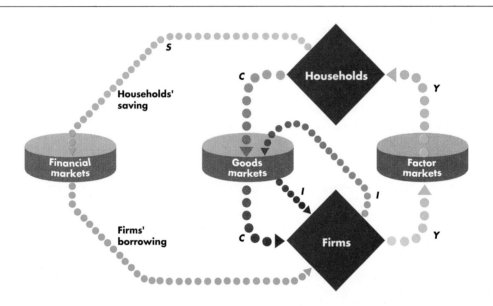

Transactions between households and firms in goods markets and factor markets generate the circular flow of expenditure and income. Households receive factor incomes (Y) from firms in exchange for factor services they supply (blue flow). Households purchase consumer goods and services (C) from firms; and firms purchase capital goods from other firms and inventories from themselves—investment (I)—

(red flows). Outside the circular flow, households save part of their income (S) and firms borrow to finance their investment expenditures (green flows). Firms' receipts from the sale of goods and services are paid to households as wages, interest, rent, or profit. Aggregate expenditure (consumption expenditure plus investment) equals aggregate income, which equals GDP.

their income—they save some of it. In this simplified economy, saving, denoted by S, is the difference between aggregate income and consumption expenditure. Saving gets channelled through financial markets, in which firms borrow the funds needed to finance their investment.

The most important of the flows illustrated in Fig. 23.1 are aggregate income (the blue flow) and expenditures (the red flows). We're going to discover that the blue flow and the two red flows in aggregate are equal. Let's see why.

Equality of Aggregate Income and Aggregate Expenditure

The sum of consumption expenditure (C) and investment (I) is aggregate expenditure on final goods and services (more briefly, aggregate expenditure). To see the equality of aggregate

income and aggregate expenditure, look again at Fig. 23.1 and focus on firms. Notice that there are two red arrows indicating flows of revenue to firms. They are consumption expenditure (C) and investment (I), or aggregate expenditure. Everything that a firm receives from the sale of its output it also pays out for the services of the factors of production that it hires. To see why, recall that payments for factors of production include not only wages, interest, and rent paid for the services of labour, capital, and land, but also profits. Any difference between the amount received by a firm for the sale of its output and the amount paid to its suppliers of labour, capital, and land is a profit (or loss) for the owner of the firm. The owner of the firm is a household, and the owner receives the firm's profit (or makes good the firm's loss). Thus the total income that each firm pays out to households equals its revenue from the sale of final goods and services. Since this reasoning applies to each and every firm in the economy, then

Aggregate expenditure = Aggregate income.

Gross Domestic Product in the Simplified Economy

Gross domestic product (GDP) is the value of all the final goods and services produced in the economy. In the simplified economy that we are studying, the final goods and services produced are the consumption goods and services and capital goods produced by firms. There are two ways in which we can value that production. One is to value it on the basis of what buyers have paid. This amount is aggregate expenditure. The other is to value it on the basis of the cost of the factors of production used to produce it. This amount is aggregate income. But we've just discovered that aggregate expenditure equals aggregate income. That is, the total amount spent on the goods and services produced equals the total amount paid for the factors of production used to produce them. Thus GDP equals aggregate expenditure, which in turn equals aggregate income. That is,

GDP = Aggregate expenditure = Aggregate income.

Government and Foreign Sectors

In the simplified economy we've just examined, we focused only on the behaviour of households and firms. In real-world economies, there are two other sectors that contribute additional flows to the circular flow of expenditure and income: the government and the rest of the world. These sectors do not change the fundamental results we've just obtained. GDP equals aggregate expenditure or aggregate income, no matter how many sectors we consider and how complicated a range of flows we consider between them. Nevertheless, we must add the government and the rest of the world to our model so we can see the additional expenditure and income flows that they generate.

The government

◆ Makes expenditures on goods and services bought from firms

◆ Receives tax revenue from and makes transfer payments to households and firms

◆ Borrows to finance the difference between its revenue and spending

The rest of the world

◆ Makes expenditures on goods and services bought from domestic firms and receives revenue from the sale of goods and services to domestic firms

◆ Lends to (or borrows from) households and firms in the domestic economy

The additional flows arising from the transactions among the government, the rest of the world, and households and firms, along with the original flows we've already considered, are illustrated in Fig. 23.2.

Let's first focus on the flows involving the government. Government purchases of goods and services from firms are shown as the flow G. This flow is shown in red (like consumption expenditure and investment) to indicate that it is an expenditure on goods and services.

Net taxes are the net flow from households to the government.[1] This net flow is the difference between the taxes paid and transfer payments received. **Transfer payments** are flows of money from the government such as pensions and unemployment insurance benefits. Don't confuse transfer payments with government purchases of goods and services. The term "transfer payments" is designed to remind us that these items are transfers of money and, as such, are similar to taxes except that they flow in the opposite direction—they flow from government to households. Net taxes (T) are illustrated in the figure as a green flow to remind you that this flow does not represent a payment in exchange for goods and services or a factor income. It is simply a transfer of financial resources from households to the government.

The difference between the net taxes received by government and government expenditure on goods and services is the government's budget deficit. The government covers its deficit by borrowing in financial markets. Such borrowing is illustrated by the green flow in the figure.

---

[1] The figure does not show firms paying any taxes. You can think of taxes paid by firms as being paid on behalf of the households that own the firms. For example, a tax on a firm's profit means that the households owning the firm receive less income. It is as if the households receive all the profit and then pay the tax on it. This way of looking at taxes simplifies Fig. 23.2 but does not change any conclusions.

FIGURE 23.2

The Circular Flow Including Government and the Rest of the World

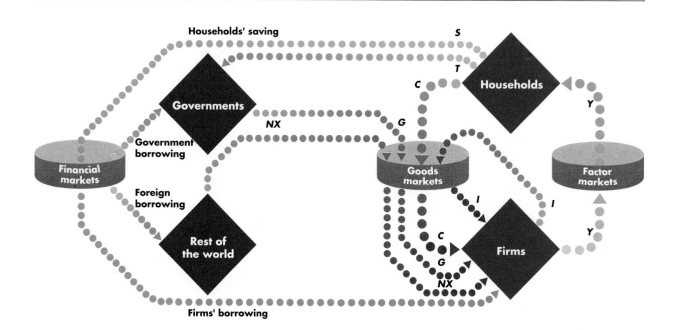

Transactions between households, firms, governments, and the rest of the world in goods markets and factor markets generate the circular flow of expenditure and income. Households receive factor incomes (*Y*) from firms in exchange for factor services they supply (blue flow). Households purchase consumer goods and services (*C*) from firms; firms purchase capital goods from other firms and inventories from themselves (*I*); governments purchase goods and services (*G*); the rest of the world purchases goods and services from firms, and firms purchase goods and services from the rest of the world (*NX*)—(red flows).

Outside the circular flow, households save part of their income (*S*) and pay net taxes (*T*) to governments; firms borrow to finance their investment expenditures; governments borrow to finance their deficits; and the rest of the worlds borrows (or lends)—(green flows).

Firms' receipts from the sale of goods and services are paid to households as wages, interest, rent, or profit. Aggregate expenditure (consumption expenditure plus investment plus government purchases plus net exports) equals aggregate income, which equals GDP.

Next, look at transactions with the rest of the world. The red flow in Fig. 23.2 labelled *NX* is net exports. **Net exports** equals exports of goods and services to the rest of the world minus imports of goods and services from the rest of the world. This flow represents the expenditure by the rest of the world on goods and services produced by domestic firms (exports) minus the expenditure of domestic firms on goods and services produced in the rest of the world (imports).

If exports exceed imports, net exports is positive. There is a net flow into the domestic economy. To finance that net inflow, the rest of the world borrows from the domestic economy in financial markets. This flow is illustrated by the green flow labelled "Foreign borrowing." If imports exceed exports, net exports is negative and there is a flow from domestic firms to the rest of the world. In this case, the domestic economy borrows from the rest of the world in financial markets. To illustrate this case in the figure, we would reverse the directions of the flows of net exports and foreign borrowing.

Now that we have introduced more elements of the real world into our model economy, let's check that aggregate expenditure still equals aggregate income.

Expenditure Equals Income Again   Aggregate expenditure equals aggregate income in this more complicated economy just as it does in the economy that has only households and firms. To see this equality, focus on the expenditures on goods and services (the red flows) received by firms and on firms' payments for factor services (the blue flow). We now have four flows representing firms' revenues from the sale of goods and services—consumption expenditure (C), investment (I), government purchases of goods and services (G), and net exports (NX). The sum of these four flows is equal to aggregate expenditure on final goods and services. As before, everything that a firm receives from the sale of its output is paid out as income to the owners of the factors of production that it employs and to the households that have a claim on its profits. The blue factor income flow therefore equals the sum of the red expenditure flows. That is,

$$Y = C + I + G + NX.$$

Thus, as we discovered in the case of the simpler model economy, aggregate income equals aggregate expenditure.

GDP also equals aggregate expenditure, or aggregate income. This equality occurs because we can measure the value of output either as the sum of the incomes paid to the factors of production or as the expenditure on that output.

GDP, Consumption Expenditure, Saving, and Taxes
Another equation links GDP, consumption expenditure, saving, and taxes. To discover this equation, look at households in Fig. 23.2. There is one flow into households and three flows out. The flow in is aggregate income (Y), which we've seen is equal to GDP. The flows out are consumption expenditure (C), saving (S), and net taxes (T). Aggregate income minus net taxes (equivalently GDP minus net taxes) is called **disposable income**. Disposable income is either spent on consumption goods and services or saved. Thus **saving** equals disposable income minus consumption expenditure. Equivalently, everything received by households is either spent on consumption goods and services, saved, or paid in taxes. That is,

$$Y = C + S + T.$$

Income and Expenditure Accounts

We can record the transactions shown in the circular flow diagram in a set of accounts, one for firms and one for households. Table 23.1(a) shows the firms' revenue and expenditure account. The first two sources of revenue are the sale of consumption goods and services to households (C) and the sale of capital goods to other firms (I). In addition, firms now receive revenue from the sale of goods and services to the government (G) and from their sale of goods and services (net of purchases) to the rest of the world (NX). The sum of all their sources of revenue ($C + I + G + NX$) equals the payments made to the owners of factors of production (Y).

The households' income and expenditure account is shown in Table 23.1(b). Households receive income (Y) in payment for the factors of production supplied and spend that income on consumption goods (C). They also pay net taxes (T) and, as before, the balancing item is household saving (S).

Injections and Leakages   The flow of income from firms to households and of consumption expenditure from households to firms is the circular flow of income and expenditure. **Injections** into the circular flow of income and expenditure are expenditures that do not originate with households. Investment, government purchases of goods and services, and exports are injections into the circular flow of expenditure and income. **Leakages** from the circular flow of income and expenditure are income that is not spent on domestically produced goods and services. Net taxes, saving, and imports are leakages from the circular flow of expenditure and income. Let's take a closer look at these injections and leakages.

We have seen from the firms' accounts that

$$Y = C + I + G + NX.$$

Let's break net exports into its two components, exports of goods and services (EX) and imports of goods and services (IM). That is,

$$NX = EX - IM.$$

Substituting this equation into the previous one, you can see that

$$Y = C + I + G + EX - IM.$$

TABLE 23.1

Firms' and Households' Accounts

(a) FIRMS

Revenue		Expenditure	
Sale of consumption goods and services	C	Payments to factors of production	Y
Sale of capital goods and changes in inventories	I		
Sale of goods and services to government	G		
Sale of goods and services to rest of world (EX)			
minus Purchases of goods and services from rest of world (IM)	NX		
Total	Y		Y

(b) HOUSEHOLDS

Income		Expenditure	
Payments for supplies of factors of production	Y	Purchases of consumption goods and services	C
		Taxes paid (TAX)	
		minus Transfer payments received (TR)	T
		Saving	S
Total	Y		Y

Firms, shown in part (a), receive revenue from consumption expenditure (C), investment (I), government purchases of goods and services (G), and net exports (NX). Firms make payments for the services of factors of production (Y). The total income firms pay equals their total revenue: $Y = C + I + G + NX$. Households, shown in part (b), receive an income for the factors of production supplied (Y). They buy consumption goods and services from firms (C) and pay net taxes (taxes minus transfer payments) to the government (T). The part of households' income that is not spent on consumption goods or paid in net taxes is saved (S). Consumption expenditure plus net taxes plus saving is equal to income: $Y = C + T + S$.

We have also seen from the households' accounts that

$$Y = C + S + T.$$

Since the left side of these two equations is the same, it follows that

$$I + G + EX - IM = S + T.$$

If we add IM to both sides of this equation, we get

$$I + G + EX = S + T + IM.$$

The left side shows the injections into the circular flow, and the right side shows the leakages from the circular flow. *The injections into the circular flow equal the leakages from the circular flow.*

REVIEW

A ggregate expenditure is the sum of consumption expenditure, investment, government purchases of goods and services, and exports of goods and services minus imports of goods and services. Aggregate expenditure equals the value of the final goods and services produced. It also equals the aggregate income of the factors of production used to produce these goods and services. That is,

$$Y = C + I + G + EX - IM.$$

Households allocate aggregate income to three

activities: consumption expenditure, taxes (net of transfer payments), and saving. That is,

$$Y = C + S + T.$$

Investment, government purchases, and exports are *injections* into the circular flow of expenditure and income. Saving, net taxes (taxes minus transfer payments), and imports are *leakages* from the circular flow. Injections equal leakages. That is,

$$I + G + EX = S + T + IM. \quad \blacklozenge$$

The circular flow of income and expenditure and the income and expenditure accounts of firms and households are our tools for measuring GDP. Let's now see how the accountants at Statistics Canada use these concepts to measure Canada's GDP.

Canada's National Income and Expenditure Accounts

S tatistics Canada collects data to measure GDP and publishes its

findings in Canada's *National Income and Expenditure Accounts*. The data are collected by using three approaches:

- ◆ Expenditure approach
- ◆ Factor incomes approach
- ◆ Output approach

Let's look at what is involved in using these three alternative ways of measuring GDP.

The Expenditure Approach

The **expenditure approach** measures GDP by collecting data on consumption expenditure (C), investment (I), government purchases of goods and services (G), and net exports (NX). This approach is illustrated in Table 23.2. The numbers refer to 1992 and are in billions of dollars. To measure GDP using the expenditure approach, we add together consumption expenditure (C), investment (I), government purchases of goods and services (G), and net exports of goods and services (NX). There is a statistical discrepancy that we'll explain shortly.

Consumption expenditure is the expenditure on goods and services produced by firms and sold to households. It includes goods such as pop, compact

---

TABLE 23.2

GDP: The Expenditure Approach

Item	Symbol	Amount in 1992 (billions of dollars)	Percentage of GDP
Personal consumption expenditures	C	420	60.9
Gross private domestic investment	I	111	16.2
Government purchases of goods and services	G	165	23.9
Net exports of goods and services	NX	–4	–0.6
Statistical discrepancy	___	–3	–0.4
Gross domestic product	Y	689	100.0

The expenditure approach measures GDP by adding together personal consumption expenditures, gross private domestic investment, government purchases of goods and services, and net exports. In 1992, GDP measured by the expenditure approach was $689 billion. The largest component of aggregate expenditure was on personal consumption of goods and services—almost 61 percent of GDP.

Source: Statistics Canada, *National Income and Expenditure Accounts.*

discs, books, and magazines, as well as services such as insurance, banking, and legal advice. It does not include the purchase of new residential houses, which is counted as part of investment.

Investment is expenditure on capital equipment by firms and expenditure on new residential houses by households. It also includes the change in firms' inventories. **Inventories** are the stocks of raw materials, semifinished products, and unsold final products held by firms. Inventories are an essential input into the production process. If a firm does not hold inventories of raw materials, its production process can operate only as quickly as the rate at which new raw materials can be delivered. Similarly, if a firm does not have inventories of semifinished goods, processes at later stages of production may become disrupted as a result of breakdowns or accidents at earlier stages. Finally, by holding inventories of finished goods, firms can respond to fluctuations in sales, standing ready to meet an exceptional surge in demand.

The stock of plant, equipment, buildings (including residential housing), and inventories is called the **capital stock**. Additions to the capital stock are investment.

Government purchases of goods and services are the purchases of goods by all levels of government—from Ottawa to the local town hall. This item of expenditure includes the cost of providing national defence, law and order, street lighting, and garbage collection. It does not include *transfer payments*. As we have seen, such payments do not represent a purchase of goods and services but rather a transfer of money from government to households.

Net exports of goods and services is the value of exports minus the value of imports. When Northern Telecom sells telephone equipment to Volkswagen, the German car producer, the value of that equipment is part of Canada's exports. When you buy a new Mazda RX7, your expenditure is part of Canada's imports. The difference between what the country earns by selling goods and services to the rest of the world and what it pays for goods and services bought from the rest of the world is the value of net exports.

Table 23.2 shows the relative magnitudes of the four items of aggregate expenditure. As you can see, consumption expenditure is by far the largest component of the expenditures that add up to GDP.

Statistical discrepancy is the difference between GDP as measured by the expenditure approach and GDP as measured by the factor incomes approach (described below). Although these two approaches rarely give the same numerical estimate of GDP, the discrepancy is usually small relative to the aggregates being measured. In 1992, it was $3 billion.

The Factor Incomes Approach

The **factor incomes approach** measures GDP by adding together all the incomes paid by firms to households for the services of the factors of production they hire—wages for labour, interest for capital, rent for land, and profits. But this addition, on its own, does not give GDP. Some further adjustments have to be made. Let's see how the factor incomes approach works.

The National Income and Expenditure Accounts divide factor incomes into five components:

♦ Wages, salaries, and supplementary labour income

♦ Corporate profits

♦ Interest and miscellaneous investment income

♦ Farmers' income

♦ Income of non-farm unincorporated business

Wages, salaries, and supplementary labour income is the total payment by firms for labour services. This item includes the net wages and salaries (called take-home pay) that workers receive each week or month, plus taxes withheld on earnings, plus all fringe benefits such as social security and pension fund contributions.

Corporate profits are the total profits made by corporations. Some of these profits are paid out to households in the form of dividends, and some are retained by the corporations as undistributed profits.

Interest and miscellaneous investment income is the total interest payments received by households on loans made by them minus the interest payments made by households on their own borrowing. This item includes, on the plus side, payments of interest by firms to households on bonds and, on the minus side, households' interest payments on the outstanding balances on their credit cards.

Farmers' income and the *income from non-farm unincorporated businesses* can be added together and called proprietors' income. These items are a mixture of the elements that we have just reviewed. The proprietor of an owner-operated business supplies labour, capital, and perhaps land and buildings to the business. National income accountants find it difficult to split up the income earned by an owner-operator into its component parts—compensation for labour, payment for the use of capital, rent payments for the use of land or buildings, and profit. As a consequence, the national income accounts lump all these separate factor incomes earned by proprietorships into a single category. Rental income—the payment for the use of land and other rented inputs—is also included in this category. It is the payments for rented housing and imputed rent for owner-occupied housing. (Imputed rent is an estimate of what homeowners would pay to rent the housing they own. By including this item in the national income accounts, we measure the total value of housing services, whether they are owned or rented.)

Net domestic income at factor cost is the sum of all factor incomes. Thus if we add together the items that we have just reviewed, we arrive at this measure of aggregate income. To measure GDP using the factor incomes approach, we have to make two adjustments to *net domestic income at factor cost*. Let's see what these adjustments are.

Market Price and Factor Cost   To calculate GDP using the expenditure approach, we add together expenditures on *final goods and services*. These expenditures are valued at the prices people pay for the various goods and services. The price that people pay for a good or service is called the **market price**.

Another way of valuing a good is factor cost. **Factor cost** is the value of a good measured by adding together the costs of all the factors of production used to produce it. If the only economic transactions were between households and firms, the market price and factor cost methods of measuring value would be identical. But the presence of indirect taxes and subsidies makes these two methods of valuation diverge.

An **indirect tax** is a tax paid by consumers when they purchase goods and services. (In contrast, a *direct* tax is a tax on income.) Examples of indirect taxes are the Goods and Services Tax (GST), provincial sales taxes, and taxes on alcohol, gasoline, and tobacco products. Indirect taxes result in the con-

sumer paying more than the producer receives for a good. For example, suppose that in your province there is a sales tax of 7 percent so that the GST and provincial sales tax total 14 percent. If you buy a $1 chocolate bar, it costs you $1.14. The total cost, including profit, of all the inputs used to produce the chocolate bar, is $1. The market price of the chocolate bar is $1.14. The factor cost value of the chocolate bar is $1.

A **subsidy** is a payment made by the government to producers. Examples are subsidies paid to grain growers and dairy farmers. A subsidy also drives a wedge between the market price value and the factor cost value, but in the opposite direction to indirect taxes. A subsidy lowers the market price below the factor cost—consumers pay less for the good than it costs the producer to make the good.

To use the factor incomes approach to measure gross domestic product, we need to add indirect taxes to total factor incomes and to subtract subsidies. Making this adjustment still does not quite get us to GDP. There is one further adjustment needed.

Net Domestic Product and Gross Domestic Product

If we total all the factor incomes and add indirect taxes minus subsidies to that total, we arrive at **net domestic product at market prices**. What do the words *gross* and *net* mean, and what is the distinction between the two terms *gross domestic product* and *net domestic product*?

The difference between these two terms is accounted for by the depreciation of capital. **Depreciation** is the decrease in the value of the capital stock that results from wear and tear and the passage of time. We've seen that investment is the purchase of new capital equipment. Depreciation is the opposite—the wearing out or destruction of capital equipment. Part of investment represents the purchase of capital equipment to replace equipment that has worn out. That investment does not add to the capital stock, it simply maintains the capital stock. The other part of investment represents additions to the capital stock—the purchase of new additional plant, equipment, and inventories. Total investment is called gross investment. **Gross investment** is the amount spent on replacing depreciated capital and on making net additions to the capital stock. Gross investment minus depreciation is called **net investment**. Net investment is the net addition to the capital stock. Let's illustrate these ideas with an example.

TABLE 23.3

Capital Stock, Investment, and Depreciation for Swanky, Inc.

Capital stock on January 1, 1992 (value of knitting machines owned at beginning of 1992)	$7,500
Gross investment (value of new knitting machine bought in 1992)	+3,000
minus Depreciation (fall in value of knitting machines during 1992)	−1,000
equals Net investment	2,000
Capital stock on December 31, 1992 (value of knitting machines owned at end of 1992)	9,500

Swanky, Inc.'s capital stock at the end of 1992 equals its capital stock at the beginning of the year plus net investment. Net investment is equal to gross investment minus depreciation. Gross investment is the value of new machines bought during the year, and depreciation is the fall in the value of Swanky's knitting machines over the year.

TABLE 23.4

GDP: The Factor Incomes Approach

Item	Amount in 1992 (billions of dollars)	Percentage of GDP
Wages, salaries, and supplementary labour income	392	56.9
Corporate profits	32	4.6
Interest and miscellaneous investment income	57	8.3
Farmers' income	4	0.6
Income of non-farm unincorporated businesses	37	5.4
Indirect taxes *minus* Subsidies	85	12.3
Depreciation (capital consumption)	82	11.9
Gross domestic product	689	100.0

(Handwritten note: "Only included in gross DP")

The sum of all factor incomes equals net domestic income at factor cost. GDP equals net domestic income at factor cost plus indirect taxes minus subsidies plus capital consumption (depreciation). In 1992, GDP measured by the factor incomes approach was $689 billion. The wages, salaries, and supplementary labour income—labour income—was by far the largest part of total factor incomes.

Source: Statistics Canada, *National Income and Expenditure Accounts.*

On January 1, 1992, Swanky, Inc. had a capital stock consisting of three knitting machines that had a market value of $7,500. In 1992, Swanky bought a new machine for $3,000. But during the year the machines owned by Swanky depreciated by a total of $1,000. By December 31, 1992, Swanky's stock of knitting machines was worth $9,500. Swanky's purchase of a new machine for $3,000 is the firm's gross investment. The firm's net investment—the difference between gross investment ($3,000) and depreciation ($1,000)—is $2,000. These transactions and the relationship among gross investment, net investment, and depreciation are summarized in Table 23.3.

Gross domestic product equals net domestic product plus depreciation. (Depreciation is called *capital consumption* by the income accountants of Statistics Canada.) Total expenditure *includes* depreciation—because it includes *gross investment*. Total factor incomes plus indirect taxes minus subsidies *excludes* depreciation—because when

firms calculate their profit, they make an allowance for depreciation and so subtract from their gross profit their estimate of the decrease in the value of their capital stock. As a result, adding up factor incomes gives a measure of domestic product that is net of the depreciation of the capital stock. To reconcile the factor incomes and expenditure approaches, we must add capital consumption (depreciation) to net domestic product. Table 23.4 summarizes these calculations and shows how the factor incomes approach leads to the same estimate of GDP as the expenditure approach. The table also shows the relative magnitudes of the various factor incomes. As you can see, wages, salaries, and supplementary labour income (wages and salaries) is by far the largest factor income.

The Output Approach

The **output approach** measures GDP by summing the value of output in each sector of the economy. This approach breaks down real GDP into broad product categories such as agriculture, construction, manufacturing, and services. In constructing the output measure for each sector, we must be careful to count only the value added by that sector.

Value added is the value of a firm's output minus the value of *intermediate goods* bought from other firms. Equivalently, it is the sum of the incomes (including profits) paid to the factors of production used by a firm to produce its output. Let's illustrate value added by looking at the production of a loaf of bread.

Figure 23.3 takes you through the brief life of a loaf of bread. It starts with the farmer, who grows the wheat. To do so, the farmer hires labour, capital equipment, and land, paying wages, interest, and rent. The farmer also receives a profit. The entire value of the wheat produced is the farmer's value

added. The miller buys wheat from the farmer and turns it into flour. To do so, the miller hires labour and uses capital equipment, paying wages and interest, and receives a profit. The miller has now added some value to the wheat bought from the farmer. The baker buys flour from the miller. The flour includes value added by the farmer and by the miller. The baker adds more value by turning the flour into bread. Wages are paid to bakery workers, interest is paid on the capital used by the baker, and the baker makes a profit. The bread is bought from the baker by the grocery store. The bread now has value added by the farmer, the miller, and the baker. At this stage, the value of the loaf is its *wholesale* value. The grocery store adds further value by making the loaf available in a convenient place at a convenient time. The consumer buys the bread for a price—its *retail price*—that includes the value added by the farmer, the miller, the baker, and the grocery store.

Final Goods and Intermediate Goods   In valuing output, we count only *value added*. The sum of the value added at each stage of production equals expenditure on the *final good*. In the above example, the only thing that has been produced and consumed is one loaf of bread. But many transactions occurred in the process of producing the loaf of bread. The miller bought grain from the farmer, the baker bought flour from the miller, and the grocer bought bread from the baker. These transactions were the purchase and sale of *intermediate goods*. To count the expenditure on intermediate goods and services as well as the expenditure on the final good involves counting the same thing twice, or more than twice when there are several intermediate stages, as there are in this example. Counting both expenditure on final goods and intermediate goods is known as **double counting**. Wheat, flour, and even the finished loaf bought by the grocery store are all intermediate goods in the production of a loaf of bread bought by a final consumer.

Many goods are sometimes intermediate goods and sometimes final goods. For example, the electric power used by General Motors to produce automobiles is an intermediate good, but the electric power that you buy to use in your home is a final good. Whether a good is intermediate or final depends not on what it is, but on what it is used for.

Table 23.5 shows the output approach to measuring GDP in Canada. This approach adds together the value added in all sectors of the economy. This sum

FIGURE 23.3

Value Added in the Life of a Loaf of Bread

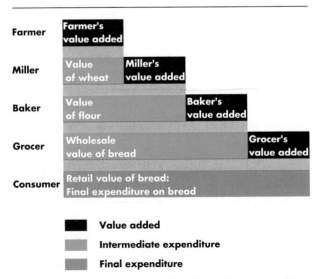

■ Value added

■ Intermediate expenditure

■ Final expenditure

A consumer's expenditure on a loaf of bread is equal to the sum of the value added at each stage in its production. Intermediate expenditure—for example, the purchase of flour by the baker from the miller—already includes the value added by the farmer and the miller. Including intermediate expenditure double counts the value added.

TABLE 23.5

GDP: The Output Approach

Sector	Value added in 1992 (billions of dollars)
Agriculture, fishing, and trapping	14
Logging and forestry	3
Mines, quarries, and oil wells	24
Construction	35
Manufacturing	103
Transportation, storage, and communications	50
Other utilities	19
Trade (wholesale and retail)	71
Finance, insurance, and real estate	101
Community, business, and personal services	73
Nonbusiness sector	111
Gross domestic product at factor cost	604
Indirect taxes *minus* subsidies	85
Gross domestic product at market prices	689

The output approach adds together the value added in each sector of the economy, which is gross domestic product at factor cost. To measure GDP, indirect taxes minus subsidies is added to gross domestic product at factor cost. In 1992, GDP measured by the output approach was $689 billion.

Source: Statistics Canada, *National Income and Expenditure Accounts.*

FIGURE 23.4

Aggregate Expenditure, Output, and Income

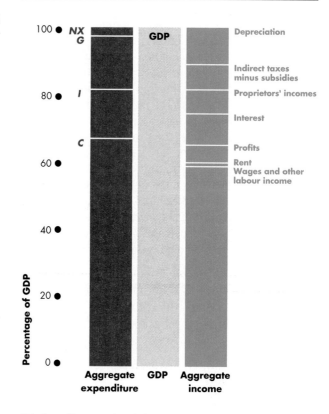

This figure illustrates the relative magnitudes of the main components of aggregate expenditure and aggregate income and also illustrates the equality among aggregate expenditure, aggregate income, and GDP.

is gross domestic product at factor cost. To calculate GDP, add indirect taxes minus subsidies to gross domestic product at factor cost.

Aggregate Expenditure, Income, and Output

We've now studied the concepts of aggregate expenditure, aggregate income, and the value of output, and we've seen that these concepts are alternative measures of GDP. We've also seen how these concepts are measured by Statistics Canada.

The equality of the three concepts and the relative magnitudes of their components are illustrated in Fig. 23.4. This figure provides a snapshot summary of the entire description of the national accounting concepts that you've studied in this chapter.

REVIEW

G DP is measured by three methods: the *expenditure approach* (the sum of consumption expenditure, investment, government purchases of goods and services, and exports minus imports), the *factor incomes approach* (the sum of wages, interest, rent, and profit with the adjustment for indirect taxes, subsidies, and depreciation), and the *output approach* (the sum of the value added in each sector of the economy). ◆

So far, in our study of GDP and its measurement, we've been concerned with the dollar value of GDP and its components. But GDP can change either because prices change or because there is a change in the volume of goods and services produced—a change in *real* GDP. Let's now see how we measure the price level and distinguish between price changes and changes in real GDP.

The Price Level and Inflation

T he *price level* is the average level of prices measured by a *price index*. To construct a price index, we take a basket of goods and services and calculate its value in the current period and in a base period. The price index is the ratio of its value in the current period to its value in the base period. The price index tells us how much more expensive the basket is in the current period than it was in the base period, expressed as a percentage.

Table 23.6 shows you how to calculate a price index for the basket of goods that Tom buys. His basket is a simple one. It contains four movies and two six-packs of pop. The value of Tom's basket, shown in the table, in 1991 was $30. The same basket in 1992 cost $35.40. Tom's price index is $35.40 expressed as a percentage of $30. That is,

$$\frac{\$35.4}{\$30} \times 100 = 118.$$

Notice that if the current period is also the base period, the price index is 100.

There are two main price indexes used to measure the price level in Canada today: the Consumer Price Index and the GDP deflator. The **Consumer Price Index** (CPI) measures the average level of prices of the goods and services typically consumed by an urban Canadian family. The **GDP deflator** measures the average level of prices of all the goods and services that are included in GDP. We are now going to study the method used for determining these price indexes. In calculating the actual indexes, Statistics Canada processes millions of pieces of information. But we can learn the principles involved in those calculations by working through some simple examples.

TABLE 23.6

Calculating a Price Index

Items in the basket	1991 (base period)			1992 (current period)	
	Quantity bought	Price	Expenditure	Price	Expenditure
Movies	4	$6	$24	$6.75	$27.00
Six-packs of pop	2	$3	$ 6	$4.20	$ 8.40
			$30		$35.40

Price index for 1992 $= \dfrac{\$35.40}{\$30.00} \times 100 = 118$

A price index for 1992 is calculated in two steps. The first step is to value the goods bought in 1991, the base period, at the prices prevailing in both 1991 and 1992. The second step is to divide the value of those goods in 1992 by their value in 1991 and multiply the result by 100.

Consumer Price Index

Every month, Statistics Canada calculates and publishes the *Consumer Price Index*. To construct the CPI, Statistics Canada first selects a base period. Currently, the base period is 1986. Then, on the basis of surveys of consumer spending patterns, it selects a basket of goods and services—the quantities of approximately 490 different goods and services that were typically consumed by urban households in the base period.

Every month, Statistics Canada sends a team of observers to 64 urban centres across Canada to record the prices for these 490 items. When all the data are collected, the CPI is calculated by valuing the base-period basket of goods and services at the current month's prices. That value is expressed as a percentage of the value of the same basket in the base period.

To see more precisely how the CPI is calculated, let's work through an example. Table 23.7 summarizes our calculations. Let's suppose that there are only three goods in the typical consumer's basket: oranges, haircuts, and bus rides. The quantities bought and the prices prevailing in the base period

are shown in the table. Total expenditure in the base period is also shown: the typical consumer buys 200 bus rides at 70¢ each and so spends $140 on bus rides. Expenditure on oranges and haircuts is worked out in the same way. Total expenditure is the sum of expenditures on the three goods, which is $210.

To calculate the price index for the current period, we only need to discover the prices of the goods in the current period. We do not need to know the quantities bought. Let's suppose that the prices are those given in the table under "Current period." To calculate the current period's value of the basket of goods we use the current period's prices. For example, the current price of oranges is $1.20 a kilogram, so the current period's value of the base-period quantity (5 kilograms) is 5 multiplied by $1.20, which is $6. The base-period quantities of haircuts and bus rides are valued at this period's prices in a similar way. In the current period, the total value of the base-period basket is $231.

We can now calculate the CPI—the ratio of this period's value of the goods to the base period's value, multiplied by 100. In this example, the CPI for the current period is 110. The CPI for the base period is, by definition, 100.

TABLE 23.7

The Consumer Price Index: A Simplified Calculation

Items in the basket	Base period			Current period	
	Quantity	Price	Expenditure	Price	Expenditure on base-period quantities
Oranges	5 kg	$0.80/kg	$4	$1.20/kg	$6
Haircuts	6	$11.00 each	$66	$12.50 each	$75
Bus rides	200	$0.70 each	$140	$0.75 each	$150
Total expenditure			$210		$231
CPI		$\frac{\$210.00}{\$210.00} \times 100 = 100$			$\frac{\$231.00}{\$210.00} \times 100 = 110$

A fixed basket of goods—5 kilograms of oranges, 6 haircuts, and 200 bus rides—is valued in the base period at $210. Prices change, and that same basket is valued at $231 in the current period. The CPI is equal to the current-period value of the basket divided by the base-period value of the basket multiplied by 100. In the base period the CPI is 100, and in the current period the CPI is 110.

GDP Deflator

The *GDP deflator* measures the average level of prices of all the goods and services that make up GDP. You can think of GDP as being like a balloon that is being blown up by growing production of goods and services and rising prices. Figure 23.5 illustrates this idea. The purpose of the GDP deflator is to let some air out of the GDP balloon—the contribution of rising prices—so that we can see what has happened to *real* GDP. Real GDP is a measure of the physical volume of output arrived at by valuing the current period output at prices that prevailed in a *base period*. Currently, the base period for calculating real GDP is 1986. We refer to the units in which real GDP is measured as "1986 dollars." The red balloon for 1986 shows real GDP in that year. The green balloon shows *nominal* GDP in 1992. We use the term "nominal GDP" because it measures the money value of output.) The red balloon for 1992 shows real GDP for that year. To see real GDP in 1992, we *deflate* nominal GDP using the GDP deflator. Let's see how we calculate real GDP and the GDP deflator.

We are going to learn how to calculate the GDP deflator by studying an imaginary economy. We will calculate nominal GDP and real GDP as well as the GDP deflator.

To make our calculations simple, let's imagine an economy that has just three final goods: the con-

FIGURE 23.5

The GDP Balloon

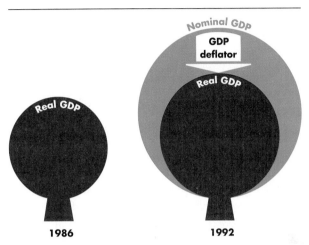

GDP is like a balloon that gets bigger because of growing output and rising prices. The GDP deflator is used to let the air resulting from higher prices out of the balloon so that we can see the extent to which production has grown.

sumption good is oranges; the capital good is computers; and the government purchases red tape. (Net exports is zero in this example.) Table 23.8

TABLE 23.8

Nominal GDP, Real GDP, and the GDP Deflator: Simplified Calculations

Item	Current period Quantity	Current period Price	Current period Expenditure	Base period Price	Base period Expenditure
Oranges	4,240 kg	$1.05/kg	$4,452	$1/kg	$4,240
Computers	5	$2,100 each	$10,500	$2,000 each	$10,000
Red tape	1,060 metres	$1/metre	$1,060	$1/metre	$1,060
		Nominal GDP	$16,012	Real GDP	$15,300

$$\text{GDP deflator} = \frac{\$16,012}{\$15,300} \times 100 = 104.7$$

An imaginary economy produces only oranges, computers, and red tape. In the current period, nominal GDP is $16,012. If the current-period quantities are valued at the base-period prices, we obtain a

measure of real GDP, which is $15,300. The GDP deflator in the current period—which is calculated by dividing nominal GDP by real GDP in that period and multiplying by 100—is 104.7.

summarizes the calculations of nominal GDP, real GDP, and the GDP deflator in this economy.

Let's focus first on calculating nominal GDP. We'll use the expenditure approach. The table shows the quantities of the final goods and their prices. To calculate nominal GDP, let's work out the expenditure on each good and then total the three expenditures. Consumption expenditure (purchases of oranges) is $4,452, investment (purchases of computers) is $10,500, and government purchases of red tape are $1,060, so nominal GDP is $16,012.

Next, let's calculate real GDP. This is calculated by valuing the current-period quantities at the base-period prices. The table shows the prices for the base period. Real expenditure on oranges for the current period is 4,240 kilograms of oranges valued at $1 a kilogram, which is $4,240. If we perform the same types of calculations for computers and red tape and total the real expenditures, we arrive at a real GDP of $15,300.

To calculate the GDP deflator for the current period, we divide nominal GDP ($16,012) by real GDP ($15,300) and multiply the result by 100. The GDP deflator that we obtain is 104.7. If the current period is also the base period, nominal GDP equals real GDP and the GDP deflator is 100. Thus the GDP deflator in the base period is 100, just as for the CPI.

Inflation and Relative Price Changes

The inflation rate is calculated as the percentage increase in the price index. For example, in the case we studied in Table 23.7, the CPI rose by 10 percent from the base period to the current period. Underlying that change in the CPI were the individual changes in the prices of oranges, haircuts, and bus rides. No individual price rose by 10 percent. The price of oranges rose by 50 percent, the price of haircuts by 13.6 percent, and the price of bus rides by 7.1 percent. This example captures a common feature of the world we live in: it is rarely the case that all prices change by the same percentage amount. When the prices of goods rise by different percentages, there is a change in relative prices. A **relative price** is the ratio of the price of one good to the price of another good. For example, if the price of oranges is 80¢ a kilogram and the price of a haircut is $11, the relative price of a haircut is 13.75 kilograms of oranges. It costs 13.75 kilograms of oranges to buy one haircut.

Prices and inflation mean a great deal to people. But many people are confused by the difference between the inflation rate and relative price changes. Inflation and relative price changes are separate phenomena. To see why this is so, we will work through an example showing that, for the same relative price changes, we can have two entirely different inflation rates.

We will first learn how to calculate a change in relative prices. The percentage change in a relative price is the percentage change in the price of one good minus the percentage change in the price of another good. For example, if the price of oranges increases from 80¢ a kilogram to 88¢ a kilogram—an increase of 10 percent—and if the price of a haircut remains constant at $11—an increase of zero percent—the relative price of a haircut falls from 13.75 kilograms of oranges to 12.5 kilograms of oranges—a decrease of (approximately) 10 percent.

For practical calculations of relative price changes, we use the inflation rate—the percentage change in prices on the average—as the reference point. That is, we calculate the rate of change of the price of a good minus the inflation rate. Goods whose prices rise at a higher rate than the inflation rate experience a rising relative price, and goods whose prices rise at a rate below the inflation rate experience a falling relative price.

Let's work out some relative price changes, using again the calculations that we worked through in Table 23.7, now presented in Table 23.9(a). The price of oranges rises from 80¢ to $1.20, or by 50 percent. We have already calculated that the inflation rate is 10 percent. That is, prices on the average rise by 10 percent. To calculate the percentage change in the relative price of oranges, subtract the inflation rate from the percentage change in the price of oranges. The price of oranges increased relative to the price level by 50 percent minus 10 percent, which is 40 percent. The price of bus rides falls relative to the price level by 2.9 percent.

In Table 23.9(b), we see that relative prices can change without inflation. In fact, part (b) illustrates the same changes in relative prices that occur in part (a), but with no inflation. In this case, the price of oranges increases by 40 percent to $1.12, the price of haircuts increases by 3.6 percent to $11.40, and the price of bus rides falls by 2.9 percent to 68¢. If you calculate the current and base-period values of the basket in part (b), you will find that consumers spend exactly the same at the new prices as

TABLE 23.9

Relative Price Changes with or without Inflation

(a) 10 PERCENT INFLATION

Item	Base-period price	New price	Percentage change in price	Percentage change in relative price
Oranges	$0.80	$1.20	+50.0	+40.0
Haircuts	$11.00	$12.50	+13.6	+3.6
Bus rides	$0.70	$0.75	+7.1	−2.9

(b) NO INFLATION

Item	Base-period price	New price	Percentage change in price	Percentage change in relative price
Oranges	$ 0.80	$1.12	+40.0	+40.0
Haircuts	$11.00	$11.40	+3.6	+3.6
Bus rides	$0.70	$0.68	−2.9	−2.9

A relative price is the price of one good divided by the price of another good. Relative prices change whenever the price of one good changes by a different percentage than the price of some other good. Relative price changes do not cause inflation. They can occur with or without inflation. In part (a), the price index rises by 10 percent. In part (b), the price index remains constant. In both parts, the relative price of oranges increases by 40 percent and that of haircuts by 3.6 percent, and the relative price of bus rides falls by 2.9 percent. The rise in the price of oranges cannot be regarded as the cause of the rise in the price index in part (a), because that same rise in the price of oranges occurs with no change in the price index in part (b).

they do at the base-period prices. There is no inflation, even though relative prices have changed.

We've now looked at two cases in which the relative price of oranges increases by 40 percent. In one, inflation is 10 percent; in the other, there is no inflation. In the first case, the price of each good increases by 10 percent more than it does in the second case. Singling out the good whose *relative* price has increased most does not explain why *all* prices are rising by 10 percent more in the first case than in the second case. To explain an increase (or decrease) in the inflation rate, we have to explain why *all* prices are inflating at a different rate and not why *some* prices are increasing faster than others.

The Consumer Price Index and the Cost of Living

Does the Consumer Price Index measure the cost of living? Does a 5 percent increase in the CPI mean that the cost of living has increased by 5 percent? It does not, and for three reasons. They are

◆ Substitution effects

◆ Arrival of new goods and disappearance of old ones

◆ Quality improvements

Substitution Effects   A change in the CPI measures the percentage change in the price of a *fixed* basket of goods and services. The actual basket of goods and services bought depends on relative prices and on consumers' tastes. Changes in relative prices will lead consumers to economize on goods that have become relatively expensive and to buy more of those goods whose relative prices have fallen. If chicken doubles in price but the price of beef increases by only 5 percent, people will substitute the now relatively less expensive beef for the relatively more expensive chicken. Because consumers make such substitutions, a price index based on a fixed basket will overstate the effects of a given price change on the consumer's cost of living.

Arrival and Disappearance of Goods   Discrepancies between the CPI and the cost of living also arise from the disappearance of some commodities and the emergence of new ones. For example, suppose you want to compare the cost of living in 1992 with that in 1892. Using a price index that has horse feed in it will not work. Though that price featured in people's transportation costs in 1892, it plays no role today. Similarly, a price index with gasoline in it will be of little use, since gasoline, while relevant today, did not feature in people's spending in 1892. Even comparisons between 1992 and 1980 suffer from this same problem. Compact discs and microwave pop-corn that featured in our budgets in 1992 were not available in 1980.

Quality Improvements   The Consumer Price Index can overstate a true rise in prices by ignoring quality improvements. Most goods undergo constant quality improvement. Automobiles, computers, CD players, even textbooks, get better year after year. Part of the increase in price of these items reflects the improvement in the quality of the product. Yet the CPI regards such a price change as inflation. Attempts have been made to assess the contribution of this factor, and some economists estimate that it accounts for as much as 2 percent a year on the average of the measured inflation rate.

Substitution effects, the arrival of new goods and the departure of old ones, and quality changes make the connection between the CPI and the cost of living imprecise. To reduce the problems that arise from this source, Statistics Canada from time to time updates the weights used for calculating the CPI. Even so, the CPI is of limited value for making comparisons of the cost of living over long periods of time. But for the purpose for which it was devised—calculating month-to-month and year-to-year rates of inflation—the CPI does a pretty good job.

R E V I E W

The Consumer Price Index is a price index based on the consumption expenditures of a typical urban family. It is calculated as the ratio of the value of a base-period basket in the current

period to its value in the base period (multiplied by 100). The GDP deflator is a price index calculated as the ratio of nominal GDP to real GDP (multiplied by 100). Real GDP values the current period's output at base-period prices.   ◆ ◆   A relative price is the price of one good relative to the price of another good. Relative prices are constantly changing but are independent of the inflation rate. Any pattern of relative price changes can take place at any inflation rate.   ◆ ◆   The CPI has limitations as a means of comparing the cost of living over long periods but does a good job of measuring year-to-year changes in the inflation rate.   ◆

Now that we've studied the measurement of GDP and the price level and know how *real* GDP is measured, let's take a look at what real GDP tells us about the aggregate value of economic activity, the standard of living, and economic well-being.

Real GDP, Aggregate Economic Activity, and Economic Well-Being

What does real GDP really measure? How good a measure is it? What does it tell us about aggregate economic activity? And what does it tell us about the standard of living and economic welfare? Some of these questions are discussed further in Our Advancing Knowledge on pp. 642–643.

Economic welfare is a comprehensive measure of the general state of well-being and standard of living. Economic welfare depends on the following factors:

1. The quantity and quality of goods and services available

2. The amount of leisure time available

3. The degree of equality among individuals

Real GDP does not accurately measure all the goods and services that we produce, and it provides no information on the amount of leisure time and the degree of economic equality. Its mismeasurement of production has errors in both directions. We'll examine five factors that limit the usefulness of real GDP as a measure of economic welfare. They are

◆ Underground real GDP

◆ Household production

◆ Environmental damage

◆ Leisure time

◆ Economic equality

Underground Real GDP

The **underground economy** is all economic activity that is legal but unreported. Underground economic activity is unreported because participants in the underground economy withhold information to evade taxes or regulations. For example, avoiding safety regulations, minimum wage laws, or GST payments are motives for operating in the underground economy. Attempts have been made to assess the scale of the underground economy, and estimates range between 5 and 15 percent of GDP ($30 billion to $90 billion).

Although not usually regarded as part of the underground economy, a great deal of other unreported activity takes place—economic activity that is illegal. In today's economy, various forms of illegal gambling, prostitution, and drug trading are omitted components of economic activity. It is impossible to measure the scale of illegal activities, but estimates range between 1 and 5 percent of GDP (between $6 billion and $30 billion).

Household Production

An enormous amount of economic activity that no one is obliged to report takes place every day in our own homes. Changing a light bulb, cutting the grass, washing the car, laundering a shirt, painting a door, and teaching a child to catch a ball are all examples of productive activities that do not involve market transactions and that are not counted as part of GDP.

Household production has become much more capital intensive over the years. As a result, less labour is used in household production than in earlier periods. For example, a microwave meal that takes just a few minutes to prepare uses a great deal of capital and almost no labour. Because we use less labour and more capital in household production, it is not easy to work out whether this type of

production has increased or decreased over time. It is likely, however, that it has decreased as more and more people have joined the labour force.

Household production is almost certainly cyclical. When the economy is in recession, household production increases since households whose members are unemployed buy fewer goods in the marketplace and provide more services for themselves. When the economy is booming, employment outside the home increases and household production decreases.

Environmental Damage

The environment is directly affected by economic activity. The burning of hydrocarbon fuels is the most visible activity that damages our environment. But it is not the only example. The depletion of exhaustible resources, the mass clearing of forests, and the pollution of lakes and rivers are other environmental consequences of industrial production.

Resources used to protect the environment are valued as part of GDP. For example, the value of catalytic converters that help to protect the atmosphere from automobile emissions is part of GDP. But if we did not use such pieces of equipment and instead polluted the atmosphere, we would not count the deteriorating air that we were breathing as a negative part of GDP.

It is obvious that an industrial society produces more atmospheric pollution than a primitive or agricultural society. But it is not obvious that such pollution increases as we become wealthier. One of the things that wealthy people value is a clean environment, and they devote resources to protecting it. Compare the pollution that was discovered in East Germany in the late 1980s with pollution in Canada. East Germany, a relatively poor country, polluted its rivers, lakes, and atmosphere in a way that is unimaginable in Canada.

Leisure Time

Leisure time is obviously an economic good that adds to our economic welfare. Other things remaining the same, the more leisure we have, the better off we are. Our time spent working is valued as part of GDP, but our leisure time is not. Yet from the point of view of economic welfare, that leisure time must be at least as valuable to us as the wage we earn on the last hour worked. If it were not, we would work instead of taking the leisure.

THE Development of ECONOMIC ACCOUNTING

National income was first measured in England by William Petty in 1665. But it was not until the 1930s, when it was needed to test and use the new Keynesian theory of economic fluctuations, that national income measurement became a routine part of the operation of Statistics Canada.

With one exception, the national income accounts measure only *market transactions*. The exception is owner-occupied housing. National income includes an estimate of the amount that homeowners would have received (and paid) in rent if they had rented their homes rather than owned them. The idea is that regardless of whether a home is rented or owned, it provides a service, and the rent (actual or implicit) measures the value of that service.

But owner-occupied housing is not really so exceptional. We produce lots of services at home—called *home production*—that are not recorded in the national accounts. Watching a video is an example. If you go to the movies, the price you pay for the ticket includes the cost of the movie, the rent of the seat, the cost of heating or cooling the theatre, the wages of the theatre workers, and the profit (or loss) of the theatre owner—the full cost of your entertainment. The price of your ticket is measured as part of national income. But if you watch a home video, only the video rental is measured as part of national income. The rental cost of the television, VCR, arm chair, and sitting room (you rent them from yourself so there's no market transaction) are not measured.

The amount of home production has increased over the years. Kitchens equipped with microwaves and dishwashers, automated laundries, and living rooms containing more audio and video equipment than a 1970s' TV studio, have turned the home into a capital-intensive production centre.

Partly because of all this capital equipment, women spend more time outside the home earning a wage and what they earn does get measured as part of national income. Both women and men are more productive in the home now than ever before, but the value of this production does not get measured as part of national income.

> "To express my self in Terms of Number, Weight, or Measure; to use only Arguments of Sense, and to consider only such Causes as have visible Foundations in Nature"
>
> SIR WILLIAM PETTY
> *Political Arithmetick*

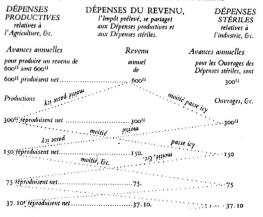

TABLEAU ÉCONOMIQUE.

ts à considérer, 1°. *Trois sortes de dépenses;* 2°. *leur source;* 3°. *leurs avances* leur distribution; 5°. *leurs effets;* 6°. *leur reproduction;* 7°. *leurs rapports entr'elles* leurs rapports avec la population; 9°. *avec l'Agriculture;* 10°. *avec l'industrie* avec le commerce; 12°. *avec la masse des richesses d'une Nation.*

DÉPENSES PRODUCTIVES relatives à l'Agriculture, &c.	DÉPENSES DU REVENU, l'Impôt prélevé, se partaget aux Dépenses productives et aux Dépenses stériles.	DÉPENSES STÉRILES relatives à l'industrie, &c.
Avances annuelles pour produire un revenu de 600ll sont 600ll	Revenu annuel de	Avances annuelles pour les Ouvrages des Dépenses stériles, sont
600ll produisent net.............600ll		300ll
Productions		Ouvrages, &c.
300ll reproduisent net.............300ll		300ll
150 reproduisent net.............150.		150
75 reproduisent net.............75.		75
37. 10 reproduisent net.............37.10		37.10

One of the earliest national economic accounts was Quesnay's *Tableau Économique* used to measure economic activity in France in 1758. One of Quesnay's "disciples" was so impressed with the *Tableau* that he described it as being worthy of being ranked, along with writing and money, as one of the three greatest inventions of the human race. Quesnay's *Tableau* was praised by Karl Marx, the founder of socialism, and is regarded as the forerunner of the types of input-output tables used in the former Soviet Union to construct annual economic plans. Modern national accounts are less like Quesnay's *Tableau* and more like the income and expenditure accounts of large corporations. They record the incomes of factors of production and the expenditures on final goods and services.

Regardless of the method used, the output is a clean car. And regardless of whether the factors of production are teenagers, rags, a hose and a bucket, or an automated machine, these factors of production have created a good that is valued. Yet the teenagers' efforts are not measured in the national accounts, while that of the automatic car wash is. As services bought from others (market transactions) replace do-it-yourself (home production), national income increases. But part of the increase is just an illusion arising from the way we keep the books. To avoid this illusion, we need to develop methods of national income accounting that estimate the value of home production using a method similar to that used to estimate the rental value of owner-occupied homes.

SIR WILLIAM PETTY: A PIONEER *of Economic Statistics*

William Petty was born in England in 1623. He was a cabin boy on a merchant ship at 13, a student in a Jesuit college in France at 14, a successful doctor of medicine in his early 20s, a professor of anatomy at Oxford University at 27, and a professor of music at 28. As chief medical officer of the British army in Ireland at age 29, he organized a topographical survey of Ireland, from which he emerged as a substantial owner of Irish land!

Petty was also an economic thinker and writer of considerable repute. He was the first person to measure national income and one of the first to propose that a government department be established for the collection of reliable and timely economic statistics. He believed that economic policy could only improve economic performance if it was based on an understanding of cause-and-effect relations discovered by the systematic measurement of economic activity—a process he called "Political Arithmetick."

Economic Equality

A country might have a very large real GDP per person, but with a high degree of inequality. A few people might be extremely wealthy while the vast majority live in abject poverty. Such an economy would generally be regarded as having less economic welfare than one in which the same amount of real GDP was more equally shared. For example, average GDP per person in the oil-rich countries of the Middle East is similar to that of several countries in Western Europe, but much less equally distributed. Economic welfare is higher in those Western European countries.

Are the Omissions a Problem?

If real GDP increases at the expense of other factors that affect economic welfare, there is no change in economic welfare. But if real GDP increases with no reduction (or even an increase) in the other factors, then economic welfare increases. Whether we get the wrong message from changes (or differences) in real GDP depends on the questions being asked. There are two main types of questions:

◆ Business cycle questions

◆ Standard of living and economic welfare questions

Business Cycle Questions   The fluctuations in economic activity measured by real GDP probably overstate the fluctuations in total production and economic welfare. When there is an economic downturn, household production increases and so does leisure time, but real GDP does not record these changes. When real GDP is growing quickly, leisure time and household production probably decline. Again, this change is not recorded as part of real GDP. But the directions of change of real GDP and economic welfare are likely to be the same.

Standard of Living and Economic Welfare Questions
The factors omitted from real GDP make standard-of-living comparisons misleading. For example, in developing countries the underground economy and the amount of household production are a much higher fraction of economic activity than in developed countries. This fact makes comparisons of GDP between countries such as Canada and Nigeria, for example, unreliable measures of comparative living standards unless the GDP data are supplemented with other information.

Using GDP data to gauge changes in living standards over time is also unreliable. Living standards depend only partly on the value of output. They also depend on the composition of that output. For example, two economies may have the same GDP, but one economy may produce more weapons and the other more music. Consumers will not be indifferent as to which of these two economies they live in.

Other factors affecting living standards include the amount of leisure time available, the quality of the environment, the security of jobs and homes, the safety of city streets, and so on. It is possible to construct broader measures that combine the many factors that contribute to human happiness. Real GDP will be one element in that measure, but it will by no means be the whole of it.

◆ ◆ ◆ ◆ In Chapter 22, we examined the macroeconomic performance of Canada in recent years and over a longer sweep of history. In this chapter, we studied in some detail the methods used for measuring the macroeconomy and, in particular, the average level of prices and the overall level of real economic activity. In the following chapters, we're going to study some macroeconomic models—models designed to explain and predict the behaviour of real GDP, the price level, employment and unemployment, the stock market, and other related phenomena. We start this process in the next chapter by examining a macroeconomic model of demand and supply—a model of *aggregate* demand and *aggregate* supply.

S U M M A R Y

The Circular Flow of Expenditure and Income

All economic agents—households, firms, government, and the rest of the world—interact in the circular flow of income and expenditure. Households sell factors of production to firms and buy consumption goods and services from firms. Firms hire factors of production from households and pay incomes to households in exchange for factor services. Firms sell consumption goods and services to households and capital goods to other firms. Government collects taxes from households and firms, makes transfer payments under various social programs to households, and buys goods and services from firms. Foreigners buy goods from domestic firms and sell goods to them.

The flow of expenditure on final goods and services winds up as somebody's income. Therefore

Aggregate income = Aggregate expenditure.

Furthermore, expenditure on final goods and services is a method of valuing the output of the economy. Therefore

GDP = Aggregate expenditure = Aggregate income.

From the firms' accounts we know that

$$Y = C + I + G + EX - IM,$$

and from the households' accounts we know that

$$Y = C + S + T.$$

Combining these two equations, we obtain

$$I + G + EX = S + T + IM.$$

This equation tells us that injections into the circular flow (left side) equal the leakages from the circular flow (right side). (pp. 623–629)

Canada's National Income and Expenditure Accounts

Because aggregate expenditure, aggregate income, and the value of output are equal, national income accountants can measure GDP using one of three approaches: the expenditure approach, the factor incomes approach, and the output approach.

The expenditure approach totals consumption expenditure, investment, government purchases of goods and services, and net exports to arrive at an estimate of GDP.

The factor incomes approach totals the incomes paid to the various factors of production plus profit paid to the owners of firms. To use the factor incomes approach, it is necessary to make an adjustment from the factor cost value of GDP to the market price value by adding indirect taxes and subtracting subsidies. It is also necessary to add capital consumption in order to arrive at GDP.

The output approach totals the value of output of each firm or sector in the economy. To measure the value of output, we measure the value added. Using value added avoids double counting. (pp. 629–635)

The Price Level and Inflation

There are two major price indexes that measure the price level and inflation: the Consumer Price Index and the GDP deflator.

The CPI measures the average level of prices of goods and services typically consumed by an urban family in Canada. The CPI is the ratio of the value of a base-period basket of commodities at current-period prices to the same basket valued at base-period prices, multiplied by 100.

The GDP deflator is nominal GDP divided by real GDP, multiplied by 100. Nominal GDP is calculated by valuing current quantities produced at current-period prices. Real GDP is calculated by valuing the quantities produced in the current period at the prices that prevailed in the base period.

In interpreting changes in prices, we need to distinguish between inflation and relative price changes. A relative price is the price of one good in terms of another good. Relative prices are constantly changing. We cannot tell anything about the sources of inflation by studying which relative prices have changed most. Any relative price changes can occur with any inflation rate.

The CPI is an imperfect measure of the cost of living, especially when comparisons are made across a long time span, for three reasons. First, relative prices change and cause consumers to substitute less expensive items for more expensive items. Second, the range of goods available changes. And third, the quality of goods changes. None of these changes is captured by the CPI. (pp. 635–640)

Real GDP, Aggregate Economic Activity, and Economic Well-Being

Real GDP is not a perfect measure of aggregate economic activity or of economic welfare. It excludes production in the underground economy, household production, environmental damage, and the contribution to economic welfare of equality and leisure. (pp. 640–644)

K E Y   E L E M E N T S

Key Terms

Aggregate income, 623
Capital stock, 630
Consumer Price Index, 635
Consumption expenditure, 623
Depreciation, 631
Disposable income, 627
Double counting, 633
Economic welfare, 640
Expenditure approach, 629
Factor cost, 631
Factor incomes approach, 630
GDP deflator, 635
Gross investment, 631
Indirect tax, 631
Injections, 627
Inventories, 630
Investment, 623
Leakages, 627
Market price, 631
Net domestic income at factor cost, 631
Net domestic product at market prices, 631

Net exports, 626
Net investment, 631
Output approach, 633
Relative price, 638
Saving, 627
Subsidy, 631
Transfer payments, 625
Underground economy, 641
Value added, 633

Key Figures and Tables

Figure 23.1   The Circular Flow of
              Expenditure and Income between
              Households and Firms, 624
Figure 23.2   The Circular Flow Including
              Government and the Rest of the
              World, 626
Table 23.2   GDP: The Expenditure Approach, 629
Table 23.4   GDP: The Factor Incomes Approach,
              632
Table 23.5   GDP: The Output Approach, 634

R E V I E W   Q U E S T I O N S

1 List the components of aggregate expenditure.

2 What are the components of aggregate income?

3 Why does aggregate income equal aggregate expenditure?

4 Why does the value of output (or GDP) equal aggregate income?

5 Distinguish between government purchases of goods and services and transfer payments.

6 What are injections into the circular flow of expenditure and income? What are leakages?

7 Explain why injections into the circular flow of income and expenditure equal leakages from it.

8 How does Statistics Canada measure GDP?

9 Explain the expenditure approach to measuring GDP.

10 Explain the factor incomes approach to measuring GDP.

11 Distinguish between expenditure on final goods and expenditure on intermediate goods?

12 What is value added? How is it calculated? What does the sum of value added by all firms equal?

13 What are the two main price indexes used to measure the price level and inflation?

14 How is the Consumer Price Index calculated?

15 How is the basket of goods and services used in constructing the CPI chosen? Is it the same basket in 1992 as it was in 1952? If not, how is it different?

16 How is the GDP deflator calculated?

17 Explain what a relative price change is.

18 How can relative price changes be identified in periods when the inflation rates are different?

19 Can we use the CPI to compare the cost of living today with that in the 1930s? If not, why not?

20 Is GDP a good measure of economic welfare? If not, why not?

P R O B L E M S

1 The following transactions took place in Ecoland last year:

Item	Billions of dollars
Wages paid to labour	800,000
Consumption expenditure	600,000
Taxes paid on wages	200,000
Government transfer payments	50,000
Firms' profits	200,000
Investment	250,000
Taxes paid on profits	50,000
Government purchases of goods and services	200,000
Export earnings	300,000
Saving	250,000
Import payments	250,000

a   Calculate Ecoland's GDP.

b   Did you use the expenditure approach or the factor incomes approach to make this calculation?

c   Does your answer to part (a) value output in terms of market prices or factor cost? Why?

d   What extra information do you need in order to calculate net domestic product?

2 Cindy, the owner of The Great Cookie, spends $100 on eggs, $50 on flour, $45 on milk, $10 on utilities, and $60 on wages to produce 200 great cookies. Cindy sells her cookies for $1.50 each. Calculate the value added per cookie at The Great Cookie.

3 A typical family living on Sandy Island buys only apple juice, bananas, and cloth. Prices in the base year are $4 a litre for apple juice, $3 a kilogram for bananas, and $5 a metre for cloth. The typical family spends $40 on apple juice, $45 on bananas, and $25 on cloth. In the current year, apple juice costs $3 a litre, bananas cost $4 a kilogram, and cloth costs $7 a metre. Calculate the CPI on Sandy Island in the current year and the inflation rate between the base year and the current year.

4 The newspaper on Sandy Island, commenting on the inflation figures that you have just calculated, runs the headline "Inflation Results from Increases in Cloth Prices." Write a letter to the editor pointing out the weakness in the economic reasoning of that paper's business reporter.

5 An economy has the following real GDP and nominal GDP in 1991 and 1992:

Year	Real GDP	Nominal GDP
1990	$1,000 billion	$1,000 billion
1991	$1,050 billion	$1,200 billion
1992	$1,200 billion	$1,500 billion

a   What was the GDP deflator in 1991?

b   What was the GDP deflator in 1992?

c   What is the inflation rate as measured by the GDP deflator between 1991 and 1992?

d   What is the percentage increase in the price level between 1990 and 1992 as measured by the GDP deflator?

CHAPTER 24

AGGREGATE DEMAND AND AGGREGATE SUPPLY

After studying this chapter, you will be able to

- ◆ Define aggregate demand and explain what determines it

- ◆ Explain why aggregate demand grows and fluctuates

- ◆ Define aggregate supply and explain what determines it

- ◆ Explain why aggregate supply grows and fluctuates

- ◆ Define macroeconomic equilibrium

- ◆ Predict the effects of changes in aggregate demand and aggregate supply on real GDP and the price level

- ◆ Explain why real GDP grows

- ◆ Explain why inflation rises and falls

- ◆ Explain why we sometimes have severe recessions

URING THE PAST 20 YEARS, CANADIAN REAL GDP HAS more than doubled. In fact, a doubling of real GDP every 20 years has been routine. What forces drive our economy to grow? ◆ ◆ At the same time as real GDP has been growing, we've experienced persistent inflation. Today, you need $300 to buy what $100 would have bought 20 years ago. Most of this inflation occurred during the 1970s, when the price level doubled. What causes inflation? And why did inflation explode during the 1970s? ◆ ◆ The Canadian economy ebbs and flows over a business cycle. For example, in 1984, real GDP grew by 6 percent, while in 1991, a recession brought a fall in real GDP. What makes real GDP grow unevenly, sometimes speeding up and sometimes slowing down or even shrinking? ◆ ◆ Our economy is influenced by events in other parts of the world, such as the 1991–1992 recessions in the United States, Europe, and Japan. It is also influenced by govern-

What Makes Our Garden Grow?

ment policies such as the Canada–United States Free Trade Agreement and the introduction of the Goods and Services Tax (GST). And our economy is influenced by changes in interest rates and the exchange rate brought about by the actions of the Bank of Canada. How do the world economy, the government, and Bank of Canada affect prices and production?

◆ ◆ ◆ ◆ To answer these questions, we need a macroeconomic model. This chapter presents such a model—the *aggregate demand–aggregate supply model.* We'll use this model to explain real GDP growth, inflation, and fluctuations in the Canadian economy.

Aggregate Demand

The **aggregate quantity of goods and services demanded** is the quantity of real GDP demanded. That is, it is the sum of the quantities of consumption goods and services households plan to buy, of investment goods firms plan to buy, of goods and services governments plan to buy, and of net exports foreigners plan to buy. Thus the quantity of real GDP demanded depends on decisions made by households, firms, governments, and foreigners. To study the forces influencing aggregate buying plans, we summarize the decisions of households, firms, governments, and foreigners by using an aggregate demand schedule and an aggregate demand curve.

An **aggregate demand schedule** lists the quantity of real GDP demanded at each price level, holding all other influences on buying plans constant. (The price level is measured by the GDP deflator.) The **aggregate demand curve** plots the quantity of real GDP demanded against the price level. **Aggregate demand** is the entire relationship between the quantity of real GDP demanded and the price level.

Figure 24.1 shows an aggregate demand schedule and aggregate demand curve. Each row of the table corresponds to a point in the figure. For example, row c of the aggregate demand schedule tells us that if the price level (GDP deflator) is 130, the level of real GDP demanded is 600 billion 1986 dollars. This row is plotted as point c on the aggregate demand curve. You can see from the downward slope of the aggregate demand curve, and from the numbers that describe the aggregate demand schedule, that the higher the price level, the smaller is the quantity of real GDP demanded.

In constructing the aggregate demand schedule and aggregate demand curve, we hold constant all the influences on the quantity of real GDP demanded other than the price level. The effect of a change in the price level is shown as a movement along the aggregate demand curve. A change in any of the other influences on the quantity of real GDP demanded results in a new aggregate demand schedule and a shift in the aggregate demand curve.

FIGURE 24.1

The Aggregate Demand Curve and Aggregate Demand Schedule

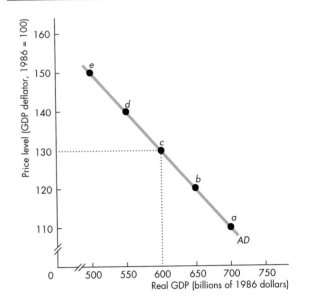

	Price level (GDP deflator)	Real GDP (billions of 1986 dollars)
a	110	700
b	120	650
c	130	600
d	140	550
e	150	500

The aggregate demand curve (*AD*) traces the quantity of real GDP demanded as the price level varies, holding everything else constant. The aggregate demand curve is derived from the schedule in the table. Each point—a through e—on the curve corresponds to the row in the table identified by the same letter. Thus when the price level is 130, the quantity of real GDP demanded is 600 billion 1986 dollars, illustrated by point c in the figure.

First, we'll look at the effects of a change in the price level on the quantity of real GDP demanded. In particular, we'll examine the reasons why the aggregate demand curve slopes downward—why an increase in the price level, other things remaining the same, decreases the quantity of real GDP demanded.

Changes in the Quantity of Real GDP Demanded

When the price level rises, other things remaining the same, the quantity of real GDP demanded decreases. When the price level falls, other things remaining the same, the quantity of real GDP demanded increases. These changes result in movements along the aggregate demand curve and are illustrated in Fig. 24.2.

Figure 24.2 also summarizes the reasons why the aggregate demand curve slopes downward. Let's look at those reasons.

Why the Aggregate Demand Curve Slopes Downward

If the price of Coca-Cola rises, the quantity of Coca-Cola demanded falls because some people switch to drinking Pepsi-Cola and other substitutes. The demand curve for Coca-Cola slopes downward because of a substitution effect. If the prices of Coca-Cola, Pepsi-Cola, and all other brands of pop rise, the quantity of pop demanded falls because some people switch from drinking pop to other substitute drinks and other goods. The demand curve for pop slopes downward because of a substitution effect. If the prices of all goods increase—the price level increases—people demand less of *all* goods. But what do they demand more of? What do people substitute for real GDP?

Real GDP has three main substitutes: money, future real GDP, and foreign real GDP. And these three substitutes give rise to three effects on the demand for real GDP. They are the following:

◆ Real money balances effect
◆ Intertemporal substitution effect
◆ International substitution effect

Real Money Balances Effect The **real money balances effect** is the change in the quantity of real GDP demanded resulting from a change in the quantity of real money. Real money? What's that?

Money is notes and coins and bank deposits—the things you use to buy goods and pay bills. **Real money** is the quantity of goods and services that money will buy. The higher the price level, the smaller is the quantity of *real* money—the less money you *really* have. With a smaller amount of

FIGURE 24.2

Changes in the Quantity of Real GDP Demanded

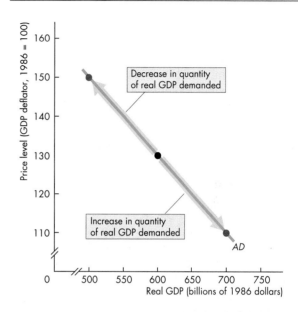

THE QUANTITY OF REAL GDP DEMANDED

Decreases if the price level *increases*	*Increases* if the price level *decreases*
	because of the:
Real money balances effect	
◆ An increase in the price level decreases the real money supply	◆ A decrease in the price level increases the real money supply
Intertemporal substitution effect	
◆ An increase in the price level increases the cost of current goods and services relative to future goods and services	◆ A decrease in the price level decreases the cost of current goods and services relative to future goods and services
International substitution effect	
◆ An increase in the price level increases the cost of domestic goods and services relative to foreign goods and services	◆ A decrease in the price level decreases the cost of domestic goods and services relative to foreign goods and services

real money, you plan to spend less on goods and services and to keep more money in the bank.

Intertemporal Substitution Effect

The **intertemporal substitution effect** is the change in the quantity of real GDP demanded resulting from a change in the *relative price* of goods now and goods in the future.

If you can buy something next year for less than the sum of today's price and the interest you earn by delaying your purchase, you might think it is worth waiting. The higher the price level, other things remaining the same, the more likely you will wait and buy later.

International Substitution Effect

The **international substitution effect** is the change in the quantity of real GDP demanded resulting from a change in the *relative price* of domestic goods and services and foreign goods and services.

If you can buy a foreign-made product for less than an equivalent Canadian-made product, you will probably buy the foreign product. The higher the Canadian price level, other things remaining the same, the more foreign goods and services and the fewer Canadian goods and services you will buy.

For the three reasons we've just reviewed, the higher the price level in Canada, the less is the quantity demanded of Canadian-made goods and services—Canadian real GDP. And the lower the price level in Canada, the greater is the quantity demanded of Canadian-made goods and services—Canadian real GDP.

REVIEW

The aggregate demand curve traces the effects of a change in the price level (the GDP deflator) on the aggregate quantity of goods and services demanded—that is, real GDP demanded. The effect of a change in the price level is shown as a movement along the aggregate demand curve. Other things remaining the same, the higher the price level, the smaller is the quantity of real GDP demanded—the aggregate demand curve slopes downward. ◆ ◆ The aggregate demand curve slopes downward for three reasons: money and goods are substitutes (*real money balances effect*);

goods today and goods in the future are substitutes (*intertemporal substitution effect*); domestic goods and foreign goods are substitutes (*international substitution effect*). ◆

Changes in Aggregate Demand

The aggregate demand schedule and aggregate demand curve describe aggregate demand at a point in time. But aggregate demand does not remain constant. It frequently changes. As a consequence, the aggregate demand curve frequently shifts. The main influences on aggregate demand that shift the aggregate demand curve are

◆ Fiscal policy

◆ Monetary policy

◆ International factors

◆ Expectations

Let's examine each of these influences.

Fiscal Policy

The government's attempt to influence the economy using its spending and taxes is called **fiscal policy**. We'll study the effects of fiscal policy by looking at two actions the government can take. They are

◆ Changes in government purchases of goods and services

◆ Changes in taxes and transfer payments

Changes in Government Purchases of Goods and Services The scale of government purchases of goods and services has a direct effect on aggregate demand. If taxes are held constant, the more hospitals, highways, schools, colleges, and universities the government demands, the larger are government purchases of goods and services and so the larger is aggregate demand. The largest changes in government purchases of goods and services arise from international tensions and conflict. In times of war, government purchases increase dramatically. In this century, government purchases increased sharply during World War II and then declined. They increased again during the Cold War era and then decreased as part of the "peace dividend." These changes in spending exerted a large influence on aggregate demand.

Changes in Taxes and Transfer Payments A decrease in taxes increases aggregate demand. An increase in transfer payments—unemployment benefits and other welfare payments—also increases aggregate demand. Both of these influences operate by increasing households' *disposable* income. The larger the disposable income, the greater is the demand for goods and services. Since lower taxes and higher transfer payments increase disposable income, they also increase aggregate demand.

This source of changes in aggregate demand has been an important one in recent years. Through the late 1960s, there was a large increase in government payments under various social programs, and these led to a sustained increase in aggregate demand.

Monetary Policy

Decisions made by the Bank of Canada about the money supply and interest rates affect aggregate demand. The Bank of Canada's attempt to influence the economy by varying the money supply and interest rates is called **monetary policy.**

Money Supply The money supply is determined by the Bank of Canada and the banks (in a process described in Chapters 27 and 28). The greater the *quantity of money*, the greater is the level of aggregate demand. An easy way to see why money affects aggregate demand is to imagine what would happen if the Bank of Canada borrowed the armed forces' helicopters, loaded them with millions of dollars worth of new $10 bills, and sprinkled the bills like confetti across the nation. We would all stop whatever we were doing and rush out to pick up our share of the newly available money. But we wouldn't just put the money we picked up in the bank. We would spend some of it, so our demand for goods and services would increase. Although this story is pretty extreme, it does illustrate that an increase in the quantity of money increases aggregate demand.

In practice, changes in the quantity of money change interest rates and so have an additional influence on aggregate demand by affecting investment and the demand for consumer durables. When the Bank of Canada speeds up the rate at which new money is being injected into the economy, interest rates tend to fall. When the Bank of Canada slows down the pace at which it is creating money, interest rates tend to rise. Thus a change in the quantity of money has a second effect on aggregate demand, operating through its effects on interest rates.

Interest Rates If the Bank of Canada increases interest rates, households and firms change their borrowing, lending, and spending plans. They try to borrow less, lend more, and cut back their spending on durable goods—investment. The cut in spending on durable goods is a decrease in aggregate demand.

Fluctuations in the quantity of money and interest rates have been important sources of changes in aggregate demand. Sustained increases in the quantity of money through the 1970s increased aggregate demand, contributing to the inflation of those years; decreases in the growth rate of the quantity of money slowed aggregate demand growth, contributing to the recessions of 1982 and 1991.

International Factors

There are two main international factors that influence aggregate demand. They are

◆ The foreign exchange rate

◆ The state of the world economy

The Foreign Exchange Rate A change in the Canadian price level, other things remaining the same, changes the prices of Canadian-produced goods and services *relative* to the prices of goods and services produced in other countries. Another influence on the price of Canadian-produced goods and services relative to those produced abroad is the *foreign exchange rate*. The foreign exchange rate affects aggregate demand because it affects the prices that foreigners have to pay for Canadian-produced goods and services and the prices that we have to pay for foreign-produced goods and services.

Suppose that the dollar is worth 125 Japanese yen. You can buy a Fujitsu cellular telephone (made in Japan) that costs 125,000 yen for $1,000. What if for $900 you can buy a Northern Telecom phone (made in Canada) that is just as good as the more expensive Fujitsu? In such a case, you will buy the Northern Telecom phone.

But which phone will you buy if the value of the Canadian dollar rises to 150 yen and everything else remains the same? Let's work out the answer. At 150 yen per dollar, you pay only $833.33 to buy the 125,000 yen needed to buy the Fujitsu phone. Since the Northern Telecom phone costs $900, the Fujitsu is now cheaper and you will substitute the Fujitsu phone for the Northern Telecom phone. The demand for Canadian-made phones falls as the foreign exchange value of the dollar rises. So, as the foreign exchange value of the dollar rises, everything else remaining the same, aggregate demand decreases.

There have been huge swings in the foreign exchange value of the dollar through the 1980s, leading to large swings in aggregate demand.

The State of the World Economy   The main feature of the world economy that affects Canada is the level of income in the rest of the world. The income of foreigners affects the aggregate demand for domestically produced goods and services. For example, an increase in income in the United States, Japan, and Germany increases the demand by U.S., Japanese, and German consumers and producers for Canadian-made consumption goods and capital goods. These sources of change in aggregate demand have been important ones since World War II. The rapid economic growth of Japan and Western Europe and of some of the newly industrializing countries of the Pacific Rim, such as Korea and Singapore, has led to a sustained increase in demand for Canadian-made goods and services.

Expectations

Expectations about all aspects of future economic conditions play a crucial role in determining current decisions. But three expectations are especially important. They are

◆ Expected inflation

◆ Expected future incomes

◆ Expected future profits

Expected Inflation   An increase in the expected inflation rate, other things remaining the same, leads to an increase in aggregate demand. The higher the expected inflation rate, the higher is the expected price of goods and services in the future and the lower is the expected real value of money and other assets in the future. As a consequence, when people expect a higher inflation rate, they plan to buy more goods and services in the present and hold smaller quantities of money and other financial assets.

Inflation expectations changed during the 1980s. At the beginning of the decade, people expected

inflation to persist at close to 10 percent a year. But a severe recession in 1982 reduced those inflation expectations. Other things remaining the same, the effect of this decrease in inflation expectations was to decrease aggregate demand.

Expected Future Incomes   An increase in expected future income, other things remaining the same, increases the amount that households plan to spend on consumption goods and consumer durables. When households expect slow future income growth, or even a decline in income, they scale back their spending plans.

Expectations about future income growth were pessimistic during 1990, and this factor contributed to the decrease in spending that brought on a recession in that year.

Expected Future Profits   A change in expected future profit changes firms' demands for new capital equipment. For example, suppose that a recent wave of technological change has increased productivity. Firms will expect that by installing new equipment that uses the latest technology, their future profit will rise. This expectation leads to an increase in demand for new plant and equipment and so to an increase in aggregate demand.

Profit expectations were pessimistic in 1981 and led to a decrease in aggregate demand. Expectations were optimistic through most of the mid-1980s, leading to sustained increases in aggregate demand.

Time Lags in Influences on Aggregate Demand

The effects of the influences on aggregate demand that we've considered do not occur instantly. They occur with time lags. A *time lag* is a delay in the response to a stimulus. For example, when you take a tablet to cure a headache, the headache doesn't go away immediately—the medication works with a time lag. In a similar way, monetary policy influences aggregate demand with a time lag and one that spreads out over many months. For example, if the Bank of Canada increases the money supply, at first there is no change in aggregate demand. A little later, as people reallocate their wealth, there is an increase in the supply of loans and interest rates fall. Later still, confronted with lower interest rates, households and firms increase their purchases of goods and services. The

FIGURE 24.3

Changes in Aggregate Demand

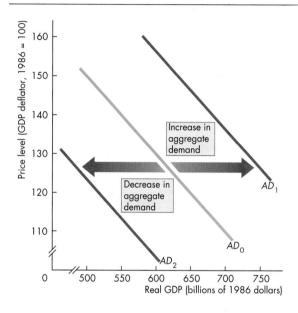

AGGREGATE DEMAND

Decreases if

- ◆ Fiscal policy decreases government spending, increases taxes, or decreases transfer payments

- ◆ Monetary policy decreases the money supply or increases interest rates

- ◆ The exchange rate increases or foreign income decreases

- ◆ Expected inflation, expected incomes, or expected profits decrease

Increases if

- ◆ Fiscal policy increases government spending, decreases taxes, or increases transfer payments

- ◆ Monetary policy increases the money supply or decreases interest rates

- ◆ The exchange rate decreases or foreign income increases

- ◆ Expected inflation, expected incomes, or expected profits increase

total effect of the initial change in the quantity of money is spread out over many months. The next time the Bank of Canada takes exactly the same action, there is no guarantee that its effects will take place with exactly the same timing as before. The time lags in the effects of monetary policy on aggregate demand are both spread out and variable and, to a degree, unpredictable.

Now that we've reviewed the factors that influence aggregate demand, let's summarize their effects on the aggregate demand curve.

Shifts of the Aggregate Demand Curve

We illustrate a change in aggregate demand as a shift in the aggregate demand curve. Figure 24.3 illustrates two changes in aggregate demand, and summarizes the factors bringing about such changes. Aggregate demand is initially AD_0, the same aggregate demand curve as that in Fig. 24.1.

Any factor that increases aggregate demand shifts the aggregate demand curve rightward. The aggregate demand curve shifts rightward, from AD_0 to AD_1, when government purchases of goods and services increase, taxes are cut, transfer payments increase, the money supply increases and interest rates decrease, the foreign exchange rate decreases, income in the rest of the world increases, expected future profits increase, or the expected future incomes increase, or the expected inflation rate increases.

Any factor that decreases aggregate demand shifts the aggregate demand curve leftward. The aggregate demand curve shifts leftward, from AD_0 to AD_2, when government purchases of goods and services decrease, taxes are increased, transfer payments decrease, the money supply decreases and interest rates increase, the foreign exchange rate increases, income in the rest of the world decreases, expected future profits decrease, or the expected inflation rate decreases.

REVIEW

A change in the price level leads to a change in the aggregate quantity of goods and services demanded. That change is shown as a movement along the aggregate demand curve. A change in any other influence on aggregate demand shifts the aggregate demand curve. These other influences include

- ◆ Fiscal policy

- ◆ Monetary policy

- ◆ International factors

- ◆ Expectations ◆

Aggregate Supply

The **aggregate quantity of goods and services supplied** is the amount of the quantities of all final goods and services that all the firms in the economy plan to produce. It is measured as real gross domestic product supplied. In studying aggregate supply, we distinguish between two macroeconomic time frames: the short run and the long run.

Two Macroeconomic Time Frames

The **macroeconomic short-run** is a period during which the prices of goods and services change in response to changes in demand and supply, but the prices of factors of production—wage rates and the prices of raw materials—do not change. The short run is an important time frame for two reasons. First, wage rates are determined by labour contracts that run for up to three years. As a result, wage rates change more slowly than prices. Second, the prices of some raw materials, especially oil, are strongly influenced by the actions of a small number of producers who keep the price steady in some periods but change it by a large amount in others.

The **macroeconomic long-run** is a period that is sufficiently long for the prices of all the factors of production—wage rates and other factor prices—to have adjusted to any disturbance so that the aggregate quantities demanded and supplied are equal in all markets—goods and services markets, labour markets, and the markets for other factors of production. In the macroeconomic long-run, with wage rates having adjusted to bring equality between the quantities of labour demanded and supplied, there is *full employment*. Equivalently, unemployment is at its *natural rate*.

Short-Run Aggregate Supply

Short-run aggregate supply is the relationship between the aggregate quantity of final goods and services (real GDP) supplied and the price level (the GDP deflator), everything else remaining the same. We can represent short-run aggregate supply either as a short-run aggregate supply schedule or a short-run aggregate supply curve. The **short-run aggregate supply schedule** lists quantities of real GDP supplied at each price level, everything else remaining the same. The **short-run aggregate supply curve** plots the relationship between the quantity of real GDP supplied and the price level, everything else remaining the same.

Figure 24.4 shows a short-run aggregate supply schedule and the corresponding short-run aggregate supply curve (labelled *SAS*). Part (a) shows the entire curve, and part (b) zooms in on the range of the curve where the economy normally operates. Each row of the aggregate supply schedule corresponds to a point in the figure. For example, row a' of the short-run aggregate supply schedule and point a' on the curve tell us that if the price level (GDP deflator) is 120, the quantity of real GDP supplied is 550 billion 1986 dollars.

Focus first on the entire short-run aggregate supply curve in Fig. 24.4(a). This curve has three ranges. It is horizontal over the depression range, upward sloping over the intermediate range, and vertical at the physical limit of the economy's ability to produce goods and services. Why is the short-run aggregate curve horizontal in the depression range? Why does it slope upward over the intermediate range? And why does it eventually become vertical?

Depression Range   When the economy is severely depressed, firms have lots of excess capacity and are anxious to sell whatever they can at the going price. They would be glad to be able to sell more and willing to offer it for sale with no inducement from a higher price. Thus each firm has a horizontal supply curve. Since each firm has a horizontal supply curve, the aggregate supply curve is also horizontal. The last time the economy was on the depression range of its *SAS* curve was in the 1930s.

The Intermediate Range   Normally, the economy operates in the upward-sloping intermediate range of its *SAS* curve. That's why we've zoomed in on this range in Fig. 24.4(b), and it is this part of the *SAS* curve that we'll use in the rest of the book.

Why does the *SAS* curve slope upward? To answer this question, think about the supply curve of tapes. If wages are constant, tape producers can make bigger profits by increasing output when the price of a tape rises. So, the higher the price of a tape, other things remaining the same, the greater is the quantity of tapes supplied. What's true for tape

FIGURE 24.4

The Aggregate Supply Curves and Aggregate Supply Schedule

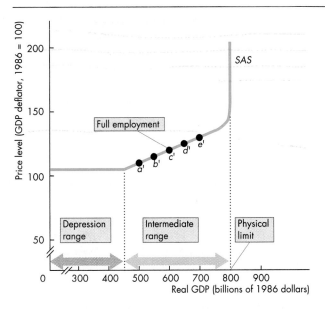

(a) The short-run aggregate supply curve

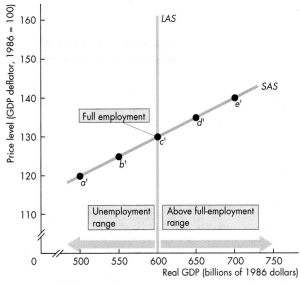

(b) The short-run and long-run aggregate supply curves

	Price level (GDP deflator)	Real GDP (billions of 1986 dollars)
Depression range	105	0 to 400
a'	120	500
b'	125	550
c'	130	600
d'	135	650
e'	140	700
Physical limit	Above 300	800

The short-run aggregate supply curve (*SAS*) traces the quantity of real GDP supplied as the price level varies, everything else remaining the same. The *SAS* curves in this figure are derived from the schedule in the table. Part (a) shows the *SAS* curve over its entire range and part (b) zooms in on the intermediate range. In a depression, firms are willing to increase the quantity sold with no increase in price and the *SAS* curve is horizontal. At its physical limit, the economy can squeeze out no more production and the *SAS* curve becomes vertical. Normally, the economy operates in the upward-sloping intermediate range. In that range, full employment occurs at *c'*, where real GDP is $600 billion.

The long-run aggregate supply curve (*LAS*) shows the relationship between full-employment real GDP and the price level. This level of real GDP is independent of the price level so the *LAS* curve is vertical, as shown in part (b). At levels of real GDP below the long-run level, unemployment is above the natural rate, and at levels of real GDP above the long-run level, unemployment is below the natural rate.

factories is also true for tomato bottling plants, auto assembly lines, and firms producing every other good and service. Thus when prices rise but wages remain constant, the aggregate quantity of goods and services supplied—real GDP supplied—increases.

To increase their output in the short run, firms hire additional labour and work their existing labour force for longer hours. Thus a change in the price level, with wage rates held constant, leads to a change in the aggregate quantity of goods and services supplied and to a change in the level of employment and unemployment. The higher the price level, the greater is the aggregate quantity of goods and services supplied, the higher is the level of employment, and the lower is the level of unemployment.

The Physical Limit to Real GDP

At some level of real GDP, the short-run aggregate supply becomes vertical because there is a physical limit to the output the economy can produce. If prices increase while wages remain constant, each firm increases its output. It does so by working its labour overtime, hiring more labour, and working its plant and equipment at a faster pace. But there is a limit to the amount of overtime workers are willing to accept. There is also a limit below which the unemployment rate cannot be pushed. And there is a limit beyond which firms are not willing to operate their plant and equipment because of the high cost of wear and tear and breakdowns. Once these limits are reached, no more output is produced, no matter how high prices rise relative to wages. At that output, the short-run aggregate supply curve becomes vertical. In the example in Fig. 24.4, when the economy is operating at its physical limit, real GDP is $800 billion.

Long-Run Aggregate Supply

Long-run aggregate supply is the relationship between the aggregate quantity of final goods and services (real GDP) supplied and the price level (GDP deflator) when there is full employment.

The Long-Run Aggregate Supply Curve   Long-run aggregate supply is represented by the long-run aggregate supply curve. The **long-run aggregate supply curve** plots the relationship between the quantity of real GDP supplied and the price level when there is full employment. The long-run aggregate supply curve is vertical and is illustrated in Fig. 24.4(b) as *LAS*. In this example, full employment occurs when real GDP is $600 billion. If real GDP is less than $600 billion, a smaller quantity of labour is required and unemployment rises above its natural rate. The economy operates in the unemployment range shown in the figure. If real GDP is greater than $600 billion, a larger quantity of labour is required and unemployment falls below its natural rate. The economy operates in the above full-employment range shown in the figure.

Pay special attention to the *position* of the *LAS* curve. It is a vertical line that intersects the short-run aggregate supply curve at point *c'* on its upward-sloping intermediate range. The *LAS* curve does not coincide with the vertical part of the *SAS* curve where the economy is operating at its physical production limit.

Why is the long-run aggregate supply curve vertical? And why is long-run aggregate supply less than the physical limit to production?

Why the Long-Run Aggregate Supply Curve Is Vertical
The long-run aggregate supply curve is vertical because there is only one level of real GDP that can be produced at full employment, no matter how high the price level. As we move along the long-run aggregate supply curve, *two* sets of prices vary: the prices of goods and services and the prices of factors of production. And they vary by the same percentage. You can see why the level of output doesn't vary in these circumstances by thinking about the tape factory again. If the price of tapes increases and the cost of producing them also increases by the same percentage, there is no incentive for tape makers to change their output level. What's true for tape producers is true for the producers of all goods and services, so the aggregate quantity supplied does not change.

Why the Long-Run Aggregate Supply Is Less than the Physical Limit of Production   Real GDP cannot be increased above its physical limit. But it can be increased above its long-run level by driving unemployment below its natural rate. But real GDP can be above its long-run level only temporarily. With output above its long-run level and unemployment below its natural rate, there are labour shortages. Firms compete with each other for labour, wages rise faster than prices, and output eventually falls to its long-run level.

R E V I E W

The short-run aggregate supply curve shows the relationship between real GDP supplied and the price level, everything else remaining the same. With no change in wage rates or other factor prices, an increase in the price level results in an increase in real GDP supplied. The short-run aggregate supply curve is horizontal in a severe depression, upward sloping in the intermediate range, and vertical when the economy is at the physical limit of its productive capacity. ◆ ◆ The long-run aggregate supply curve shows the relationship between real GDP supplied and the price level when there is full employment. This level of real GDP is independent of the price level, and the long-run aggregate supply curve is vertical. Its position tells us the level of real GDP supplied when the economy is at full employment, which is a lower level of real GDP than the physical production limit. ◆

A change in the price level, with everything else remaining the same, results in a movement along the short-run aggregate supply curve. A change in the price level, with an accompanying change in wage rates that keeps unemployment at its natural rate, results in a movement along the long-run aggregate supply curve. But there are many other influences on real GDP supplied. These influences result in a change in aggregate supply and shifts in the aggregate supply curves.

Some factors change both short-run aggregate supply and long-run aggregate supply; others affect short-run aggregate supply but leave long-run aggregate supply unchanged. Let's examine these influences on aggregate supply, starting with those that affect only short-run aggregate supply.

Changes in Short-Run Aggregate Supply

The only influences on short-run aggregate supply that do not change long-run aggregate supply are the wage rate and the prices of other factors of production. Factor prices affect short-run aggregate supply through their influence on firms' costs. The higher the level of wage rates and other factor prices, the higher are firms' costs and the lower is the quantity of output firms want to supply at each price level. Thus an increase in wage rates and other factor prices decreases short-run aggregate supply.

Why do factor prices affect short-run aggregate supply but not long-run aggregate supply? The answer lies in the definition of long-run aggregate supply. Recall that long-run aggregate supply refers to the quantity of real GDP supplied when wages and other factor prices have adjusted by the same percentage amount as the price level has changed. Faced with the same percentage increase in factor prices and the price of its output, a firm has no incentive to change its output. Thus aggregate output—real GDP—remains constant.

Shifts in the Short-Run Aggregate Supply Curve   A change in factor prices changes short-run aggregate supply and shifts the short-run aggregate supply curve. Figure 24.5 shows such a shift. Long-run

FIGURE 24.5

A Decrease in Short-Run Aggregate Supply

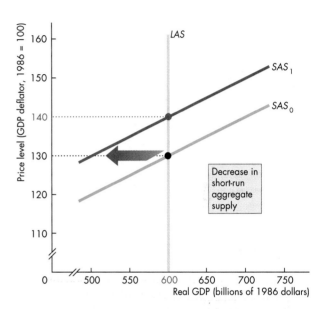

An increase in wage rates or in the prices of other factors of production decreases short-run aggregate supply but does not change long-run aggregate supply. It shifts the short-run aggregate supply curve leftward and leaves the long-run aggregate supply curve unaffected. Such a change is shown here. The original short-run aggregate supply curve is SAS_0 and, after the wage rate has increased, the new short-run aggregate supply curve is SAS_1.

aggregate supply is LAS and initially the short-run aggregate supply curve is SAS_0. These curves intersect at the price level 130. Now suppose that labour is the only factor of production and that wage rates increase from \$12 an hour to \$13 an hour. At the original level of wage rates, firms are willing to supply, in total, \$600 billion worth of output at a price level of 130. They will supply that same level of output at the higher wage rate only if prices increase in the same proportion as wages have increased. With wages up from \$12 an hour to \$13 an hour, the price level that will keep the aggregate quantity of goods and services supplied constant at \$600 billion is 140. Thus the short-run aggregate supply curve shifts to SAS_1. There is a *decrease* in short-run aggregate supply.

Changes in Both Long-Run and Short-Run Aggregate Supply

Three main factors influence both long-run and short-run aggregate supply and shift the aggregate supply curves (as shown in shown in Fig. 24.6). They are

◆ The labour force

◆ The capital stock

◆ Technology

The Labour Force   The larger the labour force, the larger is the quantity of goods and services produced. Other things remaining the same, a farm with 10 workers produces more corn than a farm with one worker. The same is true for the economy as a whole. With its labour force of more than 125 million people, the United States produces a much larger quantity of goods and services than it would if, everything else remaining the same, it had Canada's labour force of 12.5 million people.

The Capital Stock   The larger the stock of plant and equipment, the more productive is the labour force and the greater is the output that it can produce. Also, the larger the stock of *human capital*—the skills that people have acquired in school and through on-the-job training—the greater is the level of output. The capital-rich Canadian economy produces a vastly greater quantity of goods and services than it would if, everything else remaining the same, it had Ethiopia's stock of capital equipment.

Technology   Inventing new and better ways of doing things enables firms to produce more from any given amount of inputs. So, even with a constant population and constant capital stock, improvements in technology increase production and increase aggregate supply. Technological advances are by far the most important source of increased production over the past two centuries. As a result of technological advances, in Canada today, one farmer can feed 100 people, and one auto worker can produce almost 14 cars and trucks in a year.

Other Influences   Other influences on aggregate supply include incentives, the climate, and the changing composition of output.

Incentives   Aggregate supply is influenced by the incentives that people face. Two examples are unemployment benefits and investment tax credits.

In Britain, unemployment benefits are much more generous, relative to wages, than those in Canada. There is a greater incentive to find a job in Canada than in Britain. As a result, Britain's natural unemployment rate is higher and its long-run aggregate supply is lower than it would be if Britain had Canadian unemployment compensation arrangements. Investment tax credits are credits that cut business taxes in proportion to the scale of a firm's investment in new plant and equipment. Such credits provide an incentive to greater capital accumulation and, other things remaining the same, increase aggregate supply.

FIGURE 24.6

Long-Run Growth in Aggregate Supply

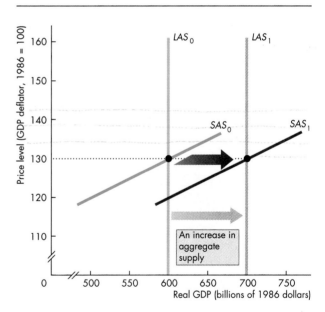

AGGREGATE SUPPLY

Increases in the long-run if

◆ The labour force increases

◆ The capital stock increases

◆ Technological change increases the productivity of labour and capital

◆ Incentives are strengthened, the climate improves, or structural change diminishes

Both the long-run and short-run aggregate supply curves shift rightward and by the same amount.

Climate   The climate has an obvious effect on output, especially in the agricultural sector. Ideal amounts of rainfall and sunshine and ideal temperatures can produce an increase in output while extreme climatic conditions restrict output.

Pace of Structural Change   If some sectors or regions expand rapidly and others decline, the economy undergoes structural change. An example of structural change was the explosive growth of banking and financial services and the relative decline of manufacturing in Canada during the 1980s. Other things remaining the same, the more rapid the pace of structural change, the larger is the amount of structural unemployment, and the lower is the level of aggregate supply.

Shifts in the Short-Run and Long-Run Aggregate Supply Curves   If any of the events that change long-run aggregate supply occur, the long-run aggregate supply curve *and the short-run aggregate supply curve* shift. Most of the factors that influence both short-run and long-run aggregate supply bring an *increase* in aggregate supply. This case is summarized in Fig. 24.6.

Initially, the long-run aggregate supply curve is LAS_0 and the short-run aggregate supply curve is SAS_0. These curves intersect at a price level of 130 and a real GDP of 600 billion 1986 dollars. An increase in productive capacity that increases full-employment real GDP to 700 billion 1986 dollars shifts the long-run aggregate supply curve to LAS_1 and the short-run aggregate supply curve to SAS_1. Long-run aggregate supply is now 700 billion 1986 dollars.

R E V I E W

A change in wage rates or in other factor prices changes short-run aggregate supply but leaves long-run aggregate supply unchanged. It shifts the short-run aggregate supply curve, but does not shift the long-run aggregate supply curve. ◆ ◆ Changes in the size of the labour force, the capital stock, and the state of technology, or changes in incentives, the climate, and the pace of structural change, change both short-run and long-run aggregate supply. Such changes shift both the short-run and the long-run aggregate supply curves, and in the same direction. ◆

Macroeconomic Equilibrium

T he purpose of the aggregate demand-aggregate supply model is to predict changes in real GDP and the price level. To make predictions about real GDP and the price level, we need to combine aggregate demand and aggregate supply and determine macroeconomic equilibrium. **Macroeconomic equilibrium** occurs when the quantity of real GDP demanded equals the quantity of real GDP supplied. Let's see how macroeconomic equilibrium is determined.

Determination of Real GDP and the Price Level

The aggregate demand curve tells us the quantity of real GDP demanded at each price level, and the short-run aggregate supply curve tells us the quantity of real GDP supplied at each price level. There is one and only one price level at which the quantity demanded equals the quantity supplied. Macroeconomic equilibrium occurs at that price level. Figure 24.7 illustrates such an equilibrium at a price level of 130 and real GDP of 600 billion 1986 dollars (points c and c').

To see why this position is an equilibrium, let's work out what happens if the price level is something other than 130. Suppose, for example, that the price level is 140. In that case, the quantity of real GDP demanded is $550 billion (point d), but the quantity of real GDP supplied is $700 billion (point e'). There is an excess of the quantity supplied over the quantity demanded, or a surplus of goods and services. Unable to sell all their output, and with inventories piling up, firms cut prices. Prices will be cut until the surplus is eliminated—at a price level of 130.

Next consider what happens if the price level is 120. In this case, the quantity of real GDP that firms supply is $500 billion worth of goods and services (point a') and the quantity of real GDP demanded is $650 billion worth (point b). The quantity demanded exceeds the quantity supplied. With inventories running out, firms raise their prices and continue to do so until the quantities demanded and supplied are in balance—again at a price level of 130.

FIGURE 24.7

Macroeconomic Equilibrium

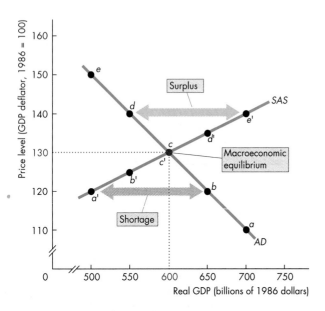

Macroeconomic equilibrium occurs when real GDP demanded equals real GDP supplied. Such an equilibrium is at the intersection of the aggregate demand curve (*AD*) and the short-run aggregate supply curve (*SAS*)—points *c* and *c'*—where the price level is 130 and real GDP is 600 billion 1986 dollars. At price levels above 130, for example 140, there is an excess of the quantity of real GDP supplied over the quantity demanded—a surplus—and the price level falls. At price levels below 130, for example 120, there is an excess of the quantity of real GDP demanded over the quantity supplied—a shortage—and the price level rises. Only when the price level is 130 is the quantity of real GDP demanded equal to the quantity supplied. This is the equilibrium price level.

Macroeconomic Equilibrium and Full Employment

Macroeconomic equilibrium does not necessarily occur at full employment. At full employment, the economy is on its *long-run* aggregate supply curve. But macroeconomic equilibrium occurs at the intersection of the *short-run* aggregate supply curve and the aggregate demand curve and can occur at, below, or above full employment. We can see this fact most clearly by considering the three possible cases shown in Fig. 24.8.

In part (a) of Fig. 24.8, the fluctuations of real GDP are shown for an imaginary economy over a five-year period. In year 2, real GDP falls below its long-run level and there is a recessionary gap. A **recessionary gap** is long-run real GDP minus actual real GDP when actual real GDP is below long-run real GDP. In year 4, real GDP rises above its long-run level and there is an inflationary gap. An **inflationary gap** is actual real GDP minus long-run real GDP when actual real GDP is above long-run real GDP. In year 3, actual real GDP and long-run real GDP are equal and the economy is at full employment.

These situations are illustrated in parts (b), (c), and (d) of Fig. 24.8 as the three types of macroeconomic equilibrium. In part (b), there is an unemployment equilibrium. An **unemployment equilibrium** is a situation in which macroeconomic equilibrium occurs at a level of real GDP below long-run GDP. In such an equilibrium, there is a recessionary gap. The unemployment equilibrium illustrated in part (b) occurs where aggregate demand curve AD_0 intersects short-run aggregate supply curve SAS_0 at a real GDP of 500 billion 1986 dollars and a price level of 130. There is a recessionary gap of 100 billion 1986 dollars. The Canadian economy was in a situation similar to that shown in part (b) in 1982. In that year, unemployment was high and real GDP was substantially below its long-run level.

Part (c) of Fig. 24.8 is an example of full-employment equilibrium. **Full-employment equilibrium** is a macroeconomic equilibrium in which actual real GDP equals long-run real GDP. In this example, the equilibrium occurs where the aggregate demand curve AD_1 intersects the short-run aggregate supply curve SAS_1 at an actual and long-run real GDP of 600 billion 1986 dollars. The Canadian economy was in a situation such as that shown in part (c) in the mid-1980s.

Finally, part (d) of Fig. 24.8 illustrates an above full-employment equilibrium. **Above full-employment equilibrium** is a situation in which macroeconomic equilibrium occurs at a level of real GDP above long-run real GDP. In such an equilibrium, there is an inflationary gap. The above full-employment equilibrium illustrated in part (d) occurs where the aggregate demand curve AD_2 intersects the short-run aggregate supply curve SAS_2 at a real GDP of 700 billion 1986 dollars and a price level of 130. There is an inflationary gap of 100 billion 1986 dollars. The Canadian economy was in a situation similar to that depicted in part (d) in 1988-1990.

FIGURE 24.8

Three Types of Macroeconomic Equilibrium

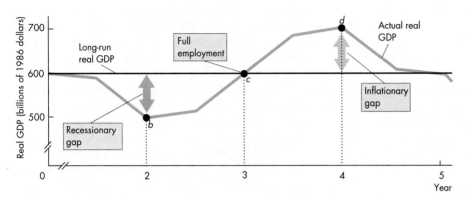

(a) Fluctuations in real GDP

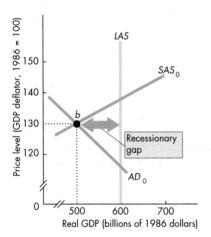

(b) Unemployment equilibrium

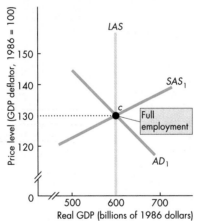

(c) Full-employment equilibrium

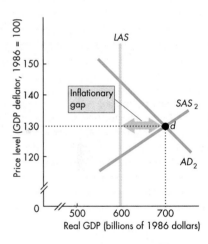

(d) Above full-employment equilibrium

In part (a), real GDP fluctuates around its long-run level. When actual real GDP is below long-run real GDP, there is a recessionary gap (as in year 2). When actual real GDP is above long-run real GDP, there is an inflationary gap (as in year 4). When actual real GDP is equal to long-run real GDP, there is full employment (as in year 3).

In year 2, there is an unemployment equilibrium, as illustrated in part (b). In year 3, there is a full employment equilibrium, as illustrated in part (c). And in year 4, there is an above full-employment equilibrium, as illustrated in part (d).

The economy moves from one type of equilibrium to another as a result of fluctuations in aggregate demand and in short-run aggregate supply. These fluctuations produce fluctuations in real GDP and the price level.

Next, we're going to put the model to work generating macroeconomic fluctuations.

Aggregate Fluctuations and Changes in Aggregate Demand

We're going to work out what happens to real GDP and the price level following a change in aggregate demand. Let's suppose that the economy starts out at full employment and, as illustrated in Fig. 24.9, is

FIGURE 24.9

The Effects of an Increase in Aggregate Demand

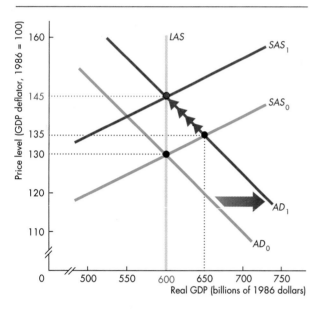

An increase in aggregate demand shifts the aggregate demand curve from AD_0 to AD_1. Real GDP increases from 600 billion to 650 billion 1986 dollars and the price level increases from 130 to 135. There is an inflationary gap. A higher price level induces higher wage rates, which in turn cause the short-run aggregate supply curve to shift leftward. As the *SAS* curve shifts leftward from SAS_0 to SAS_1, it intersects the aggregate demand curve AD_1 at higher price levels and lower real GDP levels. Eventually, the price level increases to 145 and real GDP falls back to 600 billion 1986 dollars—its full-employment level.

producing $600 billion worth of goods and services at a price level of 130. The economy is on the aggregate demand curve AD_0, the short-run aggregate supply curve SAS_0, and on its long-run aggregate supply curve *LAS*.

Now suppose that the Bank of Canada takes steps to increase the quantity of money. With more money in the economy, people increase their demand for goods and services—the aggregate demand curve shifts rightward. Suppose that the aggregate demand curve in Fig. 24.9 shifts from AD_0 to AD_1. A new equilibrium occurs, where the aggregate demand that curve AD_1 intersects the short-run aggregate supply curve SAS_0. Output rises to $650 billion (1986 dollars) and the price level rises to 135. The economy is now at an above full-employment

equilibrium. Real GDP is above its long-run level, and there is an inflationary gap.

The increase in aggregate demand has increased the prices of all goods and services. Faced with higher prices, firms have increased their output rates. At this stage, prices of goods and services have increased but wage rates have not changed. (Recall that as we move along a short-run aggregate supply curve, wage rates are constant.)

The economy cannot stay above its long-run aggregate supply and full-employment levels forever. Why not? What are the forces at work bringing real GDP back to its long-run level and restoring full employment?

If the price level has increased but wage rates have remained constant, workers have experienced a fall in the purchasing power of their wages. Furthermore, firms have experienced a fall in the real cost of labour. In these circumstances, workers demand higher wages, and firms, anxious to maintain their employment and output levels, meet those demands. If firms do not raise wage rates, they either lose workers or have to hire less productive ones.

As wage rates rise, short-run aggregate supply begins to decrease—the short-run aggregate supply curve shifts leftward. It moves from SAS_0 towards SAS_1. The rise in wages and the shift in the *SAS* curve produce a sequence of new equilibrium positions. At each point on the adjustment path, output falls and the price level rises. Eventually, wages will have risen by so much that the *SAS* curve is SAS_1. At this time, the aggregate demand curve AD_1 intersects SAS_1 at a full-employment equilibrium. The price level has risen to 145, and output is back where it started, at its long-run level. Unemployment is again at its natural rate.

Throughout the adjustment process, higher wage rates raise firms' costs and, with rising costs, firms offer a smaller quantity of goods and services for sale at any given price level. By the time the adjustment is over, firms are producing exactly the same amount as initially produced, but at higher prices and higher costs. The level of costs relative to prices will be the same as it was initially.

We've just worked out the effects of an increase in aggregate demand. A decrease in aggregate demand has similar but opposite effects to those we've just studied. That is, when aggregate demand falls, real GDP falls below its long-run level and unemployment rises above its natural rate. There is a recessionary gap. The lower price level increases the purchasing power of wages and increases firms' costs relative to their output prices. Eventually, as the slack economy leads to falling wage rates, the short-run aggregate supply curve shifts downward. Real GDP gradually returns to its long-run level and full employment is restored.

Aggregate Fluctuations and Changes in Aggregate Supply

Let's now work out the effects of a change in aggregate supply on real GDP and the price level. Figure 24.10 illustrates the analysis. Suppose that the economy is initially at full-employment equilibrium as shown in part (a). The aggregate demand curve is AD_0, the short-run aggregate supply curve is SAS_0, and the long-run aggregate supply curve is LAS. Output is 600 billion 1986 dollars and the price level is 130.

Now suppose that the price of oil increases sharply, as it did when OPEC used its market power in 1973-1974 and again in 1979-1980. With a higher price of oil, firms are faced with higher costs and they lower their output. Short-run aggregate supply decreases and the short-run aggregate supply curves shift leftward to SAS_1.

As a result of this decrease in short-run aggregate supply, the economy moves to a new equilibrium where SAS_1 intersects the aggregate demand curve AD_0. The price level rises to 140 and real GDP falls to 550 billion 1986 dollars. Because real GDP falls, the economy experiences recession. Because the price level increases, the economy experiences inflation. Such a combination of recession and inflation—called *stagflation*—actually occurred in the 1970s and 1980s at the times of the OPEC oil price hikes.

What happens next depends on the policy response of the government and the Bank of Canada.

FIGURE 24.10

The Effects of an Increase in the Price of Oil

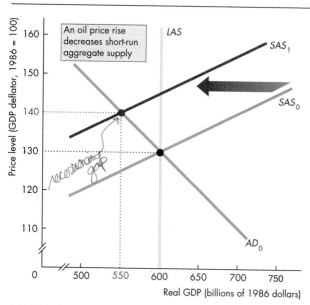

(a) In the short run

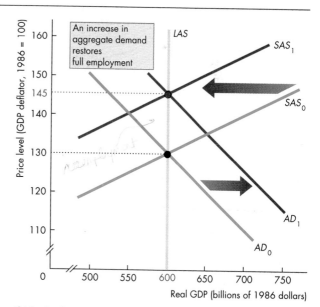

(b) In the long run

An increase in the price of oil decreases short-run aggregate supply and shifts the short-run aggregate supply curve leftward (in part a) from SAS_0 to SAS_1. Real GDP decreases from 600 billion to 550 billion 1986 dollars and the price level increases from 130 to 140. The econo-

my experiences both recession and inflation—*stagflation*. In part (b), a fiscal and monetary policy stimulates aggregate demand and shifts the aggregate demand curve rightward from AD_0 to AD_1. Real GDP returns to its original level but the price level rises still further from 140 to 145.

If the policy is to do nothing, the economy remains stuck in an unemployment equilibrium. If the government and the Bank of Canada respond with a fiscal and monetary policy package that increases aggregate demand, the aggregate demand curve shifts rightward, as shown in Fig. 24.10(b), and the economy returns to full employment, but at an even higher price level.

R E V I E W

Macroeconomic equilibrium occurs when the quantity of real GDP demanded equals the quantity of real GDP supplied. There are three types of macroeconomic equilibrium: unemployment equilibrium (a situation in which real GDP is below long-run GDP and there is a recessionary gap), full-employment equilibrium (a situation in which actual real GDP equals long-run real GDP), and above full-employment equilibrium (a situation in which real GDP is above long-run real GDP and there is an inflationary gap). As aggregate demand and aggregate supply fluctuate, the economy moves from one type of macroeconomic equilibrium to another and real GDP and the price level fluctuate. ◆

We've now seen how changes in aggregate demand and aggregate supply influence real GDP and the price level. Let's put our new knowledge to work and see how it helps us understand recent Canadian macroeconomic performance.

Recent Trends and Cycles in the Canadian Economy

We're now going to use our new tools of aggregate demand and aggregate supply to interpret some recent trends and cycles in the Canadian economy. We'll begin by looking at the state of the Canadian economy in 1992.

The Economy in 1992

In 1992, the Canadian economy was growing but real GDP had not returned to its pre-recession level. Measured in 1986 dollars, real GDP was $560 billion but long-run real GDP was $588 billion. The price level was 123. We can illustrate this state of the Canadian economy by using the aggregate demand-aggregate supply model.

In Fig. 24.11 the aggregate demand curve in 1992 is AD_{92} and the short-run aggregate supply curve in 1992 is SAS_{92}. The point at which these curves intersect determines the price level (123) and real GDP ($560 billion) in 1992. The long-run aggregate supply curve in 1992 is LAS_{92} at a real GDP of $588 billion and there is a recessionary gap—actual real GDP is below long-run real GDP.

The 1990 recession from which the economy was still recovering in 1992 and 1993 resulted from three main influences. The first was the Bank of Canada's pursuit of price stability (see Talking with John Crow on pp. 911–914). To achieve a stable price level, the Bank of Canada slowed the growth rate of

---

FIGURE 24.11

The Canadian Economy in 1992

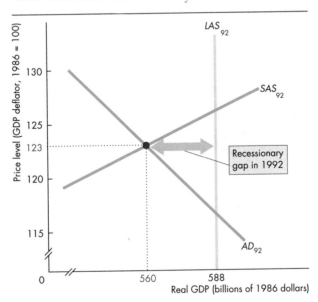

In 1992, the Canadian economy was on the aggregate demand curve AD_{92} and the aggregate supply curve SAS_{92}. The price level was 123 and real GDP was 560 billion 1986 dollars. The long-run aggregate supply curve, LAS_{92}, was at 588 billion 1986 dollars. There was a recessionary gap of 28 billion 1986 dollars.

"Please stand by for a series of tones. The first indicates the official end of the recession, the second indicates prosperity, and the third the return of the recession."

Drawing by H. Mankoff; © 1991 The New Yorker Magazine, Inc.

the money supply. This influence decreased aggregate demand and produced a leftward shift in the *AD* curve. The second influence was a slowdown in economic expansion in the United States. The slowdown of the U.S. economy brought slower growth in the demand for Canada's exports and resulted in lower aggregate demand. Like monetary policy, this influence also shifted the *AD* curve leftward. The third influence was the Canada-United States Free Trade Agreement. The initial effects of this agreement (which are explained more fully below) were to decrease both aggregate demand and short-run aggregate supply, shifting both the *AD* and *SAS* curves leftward.

The combined effect of these influences led to recession in the winter of 1990-91. Through 1991 and 1992, the economy recovered from recession but extremely slowly and unemployment remained high throughout those years. The recovery was aided by a decrease in the price of oil. It was also aided by a considerable easing of monetary restraint. The Bank of Canada engineered successive decreases in interest rates that led to a gradual increase in aggregate demand. But confidence—business confidence about profit prospects and consumer confidence about income growth—remained weak, so aggregate demand did not grow quickly.

By late 1992, the recovery had picked up some steam (see Reading Between the Lines on pp. 670–671) but doubts remained about how strong the recovery would be. Some people were optimistic that monetary and fiscal policy stimulus would be strong enough to keep aggregate demand growing

and maintain the recovery. But others (as portrayed in the cartoon) were pessimistic that, with low confidence, aggregate demand might even fall yet again, causing renewed recession.

Growth, Inflation, and Cycles

The economy is continually changing. If you imagine the economy as a video, then Fig. 24.11 is a freeze-frame. We're going to run the video again—an instant replay—but keep our finger on the freeze-frame button, looking at some important parts of the previous action. Let's run the video from 1971.

Figure 24.12 shows the state of the economy in 1971 at the point of intersection of its aggregate demand curve AD_{71} and short-run aggregate supply curve SAS_{71}. Real GDP was $287 billion and the GDP deflator was 34 (less than one-quarter of its 1992 level).

By 1992, the economy had reached the point marked by the intersection of aggregate demand curve AD_{92} and short-run aggregate supply curve SAS_{92}. Real GDP was $560 billion and the GDP deflator was 123.

There are three important features of the economy's path traced by the blue and red points:

♦ Growth

♦ Inflation

♦ Cycles

Growth   Over the years, real GDP grows—as shown in Fig. 24.12 by the rightward movement of the points. The main force generating this growth is an increase in long-run aggregate supply. Long-run aggregate supply increases because of population growth, the accumulation of capital—both physical plant and equipment and human capital—the discovery of new resources, and the advance of technology.

Inflation   The price level rises over the years—as shown in Fig. 24.12 by the upward movement of the points. The main force generating this persistent increase in the price level is a tendency for aggregate demand to increase at a faster pace than the increase in long-run aggregate supply. All of the factors that increase aggregate demand and shift the aggregate demand curve influence the pace of inflation. But one factor—the quantity of money—is the most important source of *persistent* increases in aggregate demand and persistent inflation.

FIGURE 24.12

Aggregate Demand and Aggregate Supply: 1971 to 1992

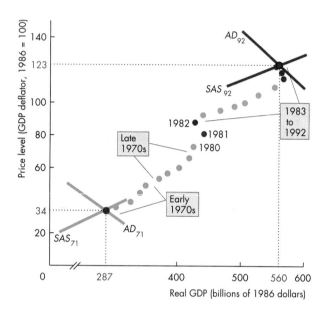

Each point indicates the value of the GDP deflator and real GDP in a given year. In 1971, these variables were determined by the intersection of the aggregate demand curve AD_{71} and the short-run aggregate supply curve SAS_{71}. Each point is generated by the gradual shifting of the AD and SAS curves. By 1992, the curves were AD_{92} and SAS_{92}. Real GDP grew and the price level increased. But growth and inflation did not proceed smoothly. Real GDP grew quickly and inflation was moderate in the early 1970s; real GDP growth sagged in 1974-1975 and again, more strongly, in 1982. The 1974-1975 slowdown was caused by an unusually sharp increase in oil prices. The 1982 recession was caused by a slowdown in the growth of aggregate demand, which resulted mainly from the Bank of Canada's monetary policy. The period from 1982 to 1989 was one of strong, persistent recovery. Inflation was rapid during the 1970s but slowed after the 1982 recession. A recession began in mid-1990.

Cycles   Over the years, the economy grows and shrinks in cycles—as shown in Fig. 24.12 by the wave-like pattern made by the points, with recessions highlighted in red. The cycles arise because both the expansion of short-run aggregate supply and the growth of aggregate demand do not proceed at a fixed, steady pace.

The Evolving Economy: 1971-1992

During the early 1970s, real GDP growth was rapid and inflation was low. This was a period of rapid increases in aggregate supply and of moderate increases in aggregate demand.

The mid-1970s were years of rapid inflation and recession—of stagflation. The major source of these developments was a series of massive oil price increases that shifted the short-run aggregate supply curve leftward, and rapid increases in the quantity of money that shifted the aggregate demand curve rightward. Recession occurred because the aggregate supply curve shifted leftward at a faster pace than the aggregate demand shifted rightward.

The rest of the 1970s saw high inflation—the price level increased quickly—and only moderate growth in real GDP. This inflation was the product of a battle between OPEC and the Bank of Canada. OPEC jacked up the price of oil and an inflationary recession ensued. Eventually, the Bank of Canada gave way and lowered interest rates to stimulate aggregate demand and bring the economy back to full employment. Then OPEC, taking advantage of oil shortages created by a crisis in the relations between the United States and Iran, played a similar hand again, pushing up the price of oil still further. The Bank of Canada was faced with a dilemma. Should it stimulate aggregate demand again to restore full employment, notching up the inflation rate yet further, or should it keep the growth of aggregate demand in check?

The answer, delivered by Bank of Canada Governor Gerald Bouey, was to keep aggregate demand growth in check. You can see the effects of Governor Bouey's actions in 1979 to 1982. In this period, most people expected high inflation to persist, and wages grew at a rate consistent with those expectations. The short-run aggregate supply curve shifted leftward. Aggregate demand increased, but not fast enough to create inflation at as fast a pace as most people expected. As a consequence, by 1982, the leftward shift of the short-run aggregate supply curve was so strong relative to the growth of aggregate demand that the economy went into a further deep recession.

During the years 1982 to 1990, capital accumulation and steady technological advance resulted in a sustained rightward shift of the long-run aggregate supply curve. Wage growth was moderate and the short-run aggregate supply curve also shifted rightward. Aggregate demand growth kept pace with the growth of aggregate supply. Sustained but steady growth in aggregate supply and aggregate demand kept real GDP growing and inflation steady. The economy moved from a recession with real GDP well below its long-run level to above full employment. It was in this condition when the events unfolded (described above) that led to the 1990 recession.

The Canada–United States Free Trade Agreement

On January 1, 1989, the Canada-United States Free Trade Agreement came into effect. The purpose of the agreement is to reduce trade barriers between the two countries so that Canadian consumers can buy U.S. goods at lower prices and Canadian firms can gain greater access to U.S. markets. What are the predicted effects of the free trade agreement on Canada's macroeconomic performance—on real GDP and the price level?

Effect on Aggregate Demand   In 1989, the first year of operation of the agreement, Canada's net exports declined sharply. Some economists attributed this decline to the effects of the free trade agreement, although others believed it was the consequence of a slowdown in the U.S. economy.

If the free trade agreement brought a decrease in net exports, it decreased aggregate demand and shifted the aggregate demand curve leftward. When aggregate demand decreases, real GDP decreases and the price level falls. (In an economy experiencing inflation, the price level does not actually fall but the inflation rate slows down.) If net exports declined because of the slowdown in the U.S. economy, then the agreement itself had no perceptible effect on aggregate demand in 1989.

What about the longer-term effects of the free trade agreement on aggregate demand? Over the longer term, the agreement will increase both U.S. imports from Canada and Canadian imports from the United States. But there is no presumption about the direction of change of net exports. The most likely outcome is that exports and imports will increase by roughly the same amounts, so that the balance of trade between the two nations is unaffected. If this outcome does occur, the long-run effects of the agreement on aggregate demand will be negligible.

Effect on Aggregate Supply   By encouraging a rationalization of economic activity and increased efficiency in both Canada and the United States, the free trade agreement will lead to a higher level of long-run aggregate supply than would otherwise have been achieved. But in the early stages of the implementation of the agreement, it is possible that aggregate supply will decrease. Some Canadian firms will go out of business in the face of tough U.S. competition and jobs will be destroyed. Other Canadian firms will expand to take advantage of new opportunities in the U.S. market and jobs will be created. But jobs may be destroyed before new ones are created. Thus, for some years, and perhaps for a relatively prolonged period, the free trade agreement may decrease aggregate supply in Canada.

Effects on Real GDP and the Price Level   Bringing together the effects of the free trade agreement on both aggregate demand and aggregate supply, we predict an initial slowdown in Canada's rate of expansion of real GDP and an increase in Canada's inflation rate. In the longer run, these effects will be reversed, with the growth rate of real GDP increasing and the inflation rate moderating.

The Goods and Services Tax

The Goods and Services Tax (GST) is a *value-added tax* on most sectors of the economy and a *transactions tax* on the sale of used physical assets such as houses. The GST was introduced on January 1, 1991, and it replaced the former Federal Sales Tax (FST). What are the effects of the GST on real GDP and the price level? To answer this question we need to look at the effects of the tax on aggregate demand and aggregate supply.

Effect on Aggregate Demand   The introduction of the GST increased the total tax receipts of the federal government by some $6 billion. This increase in taxes decreased aggregate demand and shifted the aggregate demand curve leftward. With aggregate supply unchanged, this change in aggregate demand would slow the growth of real GDP and lower the inflation rate. But was aggregate supply unchanged?

Effect on Aggregate Supply   The popular discussion of GST suggested that its introduction would be inflationary. This conclusion was based on the observation that imposing a tax on goods that were not

The 1993 Recovery

In the fourth quarter of 1992, a sharp increase in consumer spending in the United States brought faster growth of real gross domestic product (GDP) in that country and in Canada.

Real GDP grew at a 4.8 percent annual rate in the United States and at a 3.5 percent annual rate in Canada.

Canada's faster growth resulted from the growth in exports to the United States.

Canadian consumer spending and business investment fell during the final quarter of 1992.

THE GLOBE AND MAIL, MARCH 2, 1993

Economy jumps 3.5%
Surging exports to U.S. mask sluggish consumer picture

By Alan Freeman

OTTAWA—Fueled by surging exports to the United States, the Canadian economy grew at a compound annual rate of 3.5 per cent in the fourth quarter of 1992, its best performance in 18 months. But the robust figures masked the fact that Canadian consumers are not yet participating in the recovery and business investment actually fell, as non-residential construction plunged 7.2 per cent in the quarter.

"If it weren't for the U.S., we'd be in dire straits," said John Clinkard, senior economist at Canadian Imperial Bank of Commerce.

"Superficially, the numbers look very good," said Philip Cross, director of current analysis at Statistics Canada. "Under the surface, the figures are less encouraging because domestic spending is sluggish and consumer spending is flat."

Although Canada's growth rate in the fourth quarter picked up sharply, it was still considerably slower than in the United States, where GDP advanced at a 4.8-per-cent annual rate in the quarter.

"They (the U.S.) are having a consumer-led recovery," Mr. Cross said. "We're having an export-led recovery."

Background and Analysis

By the end of 1992, the economies of Canada and the United States were recovering from recession.

Part (a) of the figure shows the recovery in the United States. Aggregate demand increased from AD_0 to AD_1 as a result of an increase in consumer spending and an increase in business investment spending. As a result, real GDP increased from $4.933 trillion to $4.991 trillion (1987 U.S. dollars).

This increase is a 4.8 percent annual rate which is calculated as:

$$\{(4.991/4.933)^4 - 1\} \times 100 = 4.8 \text{ percent.}$$

The price level rose from 121.2 to 121.9, an annual inflation rate of 2.3 percent.

Part (b) of the figure shows the recovery in Canada. An increase in exports to the United States increased Canadian aggregate demand and shifted the aggregate demand curve from AD_0 to AD_1. As a result, real GDP increased from $559 billion to $563 billion (1986 Canadian dollars), an annual rate of increase of 2.9 percent. [The increase of 3.5 percent reported in the news article was subsequently revised downward by Statistics Canada.]

The price level in Canada rose from 123.1 to 123.7, an annual inflation rate of 2.3 percent—the same as in the United States.

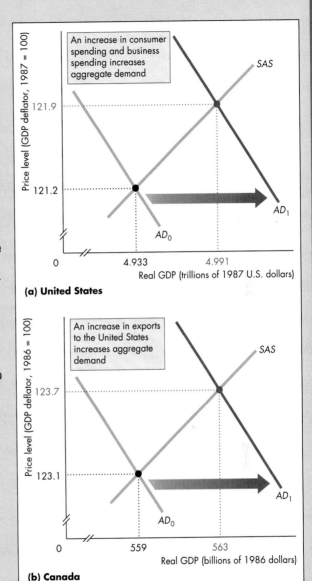

(a) United States

(b) Canada

previously taxed would result in a rise in their prices. But this conclusion ignored the effect of removing the FST. The replacement of the FST with the GST resulted in a decrease in the taxes on manufactured goods so their prices fell. Thus there was a decrease in the prices of manufactured goods and an increase in the prices of goods not previously taxed—a change in *relative prices*.

Advocates of the GST argued that the replacement of the FST (a high rate of tax on a narrow range of goods) by the GST (a lower rate of tax on a wider range of goods) would lead to increased economic efficiency and an increase in aggregate supply. If this view is correct, the GST resulted in an increase in long-run and short-run aggregate supply—a rightward shift of the aggregate supply curves.

Effects on Real GDP and the Price Level   Combining the predicted change in aggregate supply with the change in aggregate demand, the GST had an ambiguous effect on Canada's real GDP. The decrease in aggregate demand decreased real GDP, while the increase in aggregate supply worked in the opposite direction. But the decrease in aggregate demand and the increase in aggregate supply reinforced each other to slow the inflation rate. This conclusion about inflation is the opposite of the popular view.

The ultimate effects of the GST on our economy will be known only after some years of its operation. But the tools of analysis that will be used to assess its effects are the ones that we have just been working with.

◆ ◆ ◆   This chapter has provided a model of real GDP and the GDP deflator that can be used to understand the growth, inflation, and cycles that our economy follows. The model is a useful one because it enables us to keep our eye on the big picture—on the broad trends and cycles in inflation and output. But the model lacks detail. It does not tell us as much as we need to know about the components of aggregate demand—consumption, investment, government purchases of goods and services, and exports and imports. It doesn't tell us what determines interest rates or wage rates or even, directly, what determines employment and unemployment. In the following chapters, we will start to fill in that detail. ◆ ◆   In some ways, the study of macroeconomics is like doing a large jigsaw puzzle. The aggregate demand–aggregate supply model provides the entire edge of the jigsaw. We know its general shape and size but we haven't filled in the middle. One block of the jigsaw contains the story of aggregate demand. Another, the story of aggregate supply. When we place the two together, we place them in the frame of the model developed in this chapter, and the picture is completed.

S U M M A R Y

Aggregate Demand

Aggregate demand is the relationship between the quantity of real GDP demanded and the price level, holding all other influences constant. Other things remaining the same, the higher the price level, the smaller is the quantity of real GDP demanded—the aggregate demand curve slopes downward. The aggregate demand curve slopes downward for three reasons: money and goods are substitutes (*real money balances effect*); goods today and goods in the future are substitutes (*intertemporal substitution effect*); domestic goods and foreign goods are substitutes (*international substitution effect*).

The main factors that change aggregate demand—and shift the aggregate demand curve—are fiscal policy (government purchases of goods and services and taxes), monetary policy (the money supply and interest rates), international factors (economic conditions in the rest of the world and the foreign exchange rate), and expectations (especially expectations about future inflation and profits). (pp. 650–655)

Aggregate Supply

Short-run aggregate supply is the relationship between the quantity of real GDP supplied and the price level when wage rates and other factor prices are constant. The short-run aggregate supply curve is horizontal in a deep depression, vertical at the economy's physical production limit, but generally upward sloping. With factor prices and all other influences on supply held constant, the higher the price level, the more output firms plan to sell.

Long-run aggregate supply is the relationship between the quantity of real GDP supplied and the price level when there is full employment. The long-run aggregate supply curve is vertical—long-run aggregate supply is independent of the price level.

The factors that change short-run aggregate supply shift the short-run aggregate supply curve. Factors that change long-run aggregate supply also change short-run aggregate supply. Thus anything that shifts the long-run aggregate supply curve also shifts the short-run aggregate supply curve and they shift in the same direction. The most important of these factors are the size of the labour force, the capital stock, and the state of technology. (pp. 656–661)

Macroeconomic Equilibrium

Macroeconomic equilibrium occurs when the quantity of real GDP demanded equals the quantity of real GDP supplied. Macroeconomic equilibrium occurs at the intersection of the aggregate demand curve and the short-run aggregate supply curve. The price level that achieves this equality is the equilibrium price level and the output level is equilibrium real GDP.

Macroeconomic equilibrium does not always occur at long-run real GDP and full employment— that is, at a point on the long-run aggregate supply curve. Unemployment equilibrium occurs when equilibrium real GDP is less than its long-run level. There is a recessionary gap and unemployment exceeds its natural rate. When equilibrium real GDP is above its long-run level, there is an inflationary gap and unemployment is below its natural rate.

An increase in aggregate demand shifts the aggregate demand curve rightward and increases both real GDP and the price level. If real GDP is above its long-run level, wage rates begin to increase and, as

they do so, the short-run aggregate supply curve shifts leftward. The leftward shift of the short-run aggregate supply curve results in a yet higher price level and lower real GDP. Eventually, real GDP returns to its long-run level.

An increase in factor prices decreases short-run aggregate supply and shifts the short-run aggregate supply curve leftward. Real GDP decreases and the price level rises—stagflation. (pp. 661–666)

Recent Trends and Cycles in the Canadian Economy

Growth in the Canadian economy results from labour force growth, capital accumulation, and technological change. Inflation persists in the Canadian economy because of steady increases in aggregate demand brought about by increases in the quantity of money. The Canadian economy experiences cycles because the short-run aggregate supply and aggregate demand curves shift at an uneven pace.

Large oil price hikes in 1973 and 1974 resulted in stagflation. Further oil price increases in 1979 intensified the inflationary situation. Restraint in aggregate demand growth in 1980 and 1981 resulted in a severe recession in 1982. This recession resulted in lower output and a lower inflation rate. Moderate increases in wage rates and steady technological advance and capital accumulation resulted in a sustained expansion from 1982 to 1989. But a slowdown in aggregate demand growth brought recession in mid-1990.

The free trade agreement affects real GDP and the price level mainly through its effects on aggregate supply. The agreement initially decreased aggregate supply, but subsequently it will increase aggregate supply. Thus, in the short run, real GDP growth will slow down and the inflation rate will increase, but in the long run, these tendencies will be reversed, other things remaining the same.

The Goods and Services Tax affects real GDP and the price level through its effects on both aggregate demand and aggregate supply. The tax increases government revenue and decreases aggregate demand. If the replacement of the FST with the GST increases economic efficiency, it will increase aggregate supply. The combined consequences of these effects are an increase in real GDP growth and a slowdown in inflation. (pp. 666–672)

K E Y   E L E M E N T S

Key Terms

Above full-employment equilibrium, 662
Aggregate demand, 650
Aggregate demand curve, 650
Aggregate demand schedule, 650
Aggregate quantity of goods and services demanded, 650
Aggregate quantity of goods and services supplied, 656
Fiscal policy, 652
Full-employment equilibrium, 662
Inflationary gap, 662
International substitution effect, 652
Intertemporal substitution effect, 652
Long-run aggregate supply, 658
Long-run aggregate supply curve, 658
Macroeconomic equilibrium, 661
Macroeconomic long-run, 656
Macroeconomic short-run, 656
Monetary policy, 653
Money, 651
Real money, 651
Real money balances effect, 651
Recessionary gap, 662

Short-run aggregate supply, 656
Short-run aggregate supply curve, 656
Short-run aggregate supply schedule, 656
Unemployment equilibrium, 662

Key Figures and Tables

Figure 24.1   The Aggregate Demand Curve and Aggregate Demand Schedule, 650
Figure 24.2   Changes in the Quantity of Real GDP Demanded, 651
Figure 24.3   Changes in Aggregate Demand, 655
Figure 24.4   The Aggregate Supply Curves and Aggregate Supply Schedule, 657
Figure 24.5   A Decrease in Short-Run Aggregate Supply, 659
Figure 24.6   Long-Run Growth in Aggregate Supply, 660
Figure 24.7   Macroeconomic Equilibrium, 662
Figure 24.8   Three Types of Macroeconomic Equilibrium, 663
Figure 24.9   The Effects of an Increase in Aggregate Demand, 664
Figure 24.10 The Effects of an Increase in the Price of Oil, 665

R E V I E W   Q U E S T I O N S

1 What is aggregate demand?

2 What is the difference between aggregate demand and the aggregate quantity of goods and services demanded?

3 List the main factors that affect aggregate demand. Separate them into those that increase aggregate demand and those that decrease it.

4 Which of the following do not affect aggregate demand:

a   Quantity of money?
b   Interest rates?
c   Technological change?
d   Human capital?

5 Distinguish between macroeconomic short-run and long-run.

6 What is short-run aggregate supply?

7 What is the difference between short-run aggregate supply and the aggregate quantity of goods and services supplied?

8 Distinguish between short-run aggregate supply and long-run aggregate supply.

9 Consider the following events:

a   The labour force increases.
b   Technology improves.
c   The wage rate increases.
d   The quantity of money increases.
e   Foreign incomes increase.
f   The foreign exchange value of the dollar increases.

Sort these events into the following four categories:

Category A: Those that affect long-run aggregate supply but not short-run aggregate supply.

Category B: Those that affect short-run aggregate supply but not long-run aggregate supply.

Category C: Those that affect both short-run aggregate supply and long-run aggregate supply.

Category D: Those that have no effect on short-run aggregate supply or on long-run aggregate supply.

10 Define macroeconomic equilibrium.

11 Distinguish between an unemployment equilibrium and full-employment equilibrium.

12 Work out the effect of an increase in the quantity of money on the price level and real GDP.

13 Work out the effect of an increase in the price of oil on the price level and real GDP.

14 What are the main factors generating growth of real GDP in the Canadian economy?

15 What are the main factors generating persistent inflation in the Canadian economy?

16 Why does the Canadian economy experience cycles in aggregate economic activity?

P R O B L E M S

1 The economy of Mainland has the following aggregate demand and supply schedules:

Price level	Real GDP demanded	Real GDP supplied in the short run
	(billions of 1986 dollars)	
90	450	350
100	400	400
110	350	450
120	300	500
130	250	550
140	200	550

a Plot the aggregate demand curve and short-run aggregate supply curve in a figure.

b What is Mainland's real GDP and price level?

c Mainland's long-run real GDP is 500 billion 1986 dollars. Plot the long-run aggregate supply curve in the same figure in which you answered part (a).

d Is Mainland at, above, or below its natural rate of unemployment?

e What is the physical limit of the economy of Mainland?

2 In problem 1, aggregate demand is increased by 100 billion 1986 dollars. What is the change in real GDP and the price level?

3 In problem 1, aggregate supply decreases by 100 billion 1986 dollars. What is the new macroeconomic equilibrium?

4 You are the prime minister's economic advisor

and you are trying to figure out where the Canadian economy is heading next year. You have the following forecasts for the *AD*, *SAS*, and *LAS* curves:

Price level	Real GDP demanded	Short-run real GDP supplied	Long-run aggregate supply
	(billions of 1986 dollars)		
115	650	350	520
120	600	450	520
125	550	550	520
130	500	650	520

This year, real GDP is $500 billion and the price level is 120.

The prime minister wants answers to the following questions:

a What is your forecast of next year's real GDP?

b What is your forecast of next year's price level?

c What is your forecast of the inflation rate?

d Will unemployment be above or below its natural rate?

e Will there be a recessionary gap or an inflationary gap? By how much?

5 Draw some figures similar to those in this chapter and use the information in problem 4 to explain:

a What has to be done to aggregate demand to achieve full employment

b What the inflation rate is if aggregate demand is manipulated to achieve full employment

PART 10

AGGREGATE DEMAND FLUCTUATIONS

Talking with Sylvia Ostry

Sylvia Ostry, born in Winnipeg, was a student of economics at McGill (B.A.) and Cambridge (Ph.D. 1954), and is one of Canada's outstanding economists and public figures. Dr. Ostry taught at McGill, the University of Montreal, and Oxford University until she took a job at Statistics Canada. She followed this work with a succession of high level positions, a small sample of which are: Chief Statistician, Deputy Minister of Consumer and Corporate Affairs in Ottawa, Chairman of the Economic Council of Canada, Head of the Department of Economics and Statistics at the OECD (Organization for Economic Cooperation and

Development) in Paris, Deputy Minister for International Trade, and the Prime Minister's personal representative for the Economic Summit. In 1990, Dr. Ostry returned to academic life as Chairman of the Centre for International Studies at the University of Toronto. Robin Bade and Michael Parkin talked with Sylvia Ostry about her career as a national and international economic advisor.

You started out to become a doctor but you found first-year medicine a little too boring, too unexciting. What made you think of economics?

I wanted to learn more about social science and to understand more about the world in which I live—I sort of stumbled into economics.

You have spent most of your career in the public service. What attracted you to the public service?

I was at McGill when I was offered a research job at the Dominion Bureau of Statistics (now Statistics Canada). I became increasingly interested in how better research and analysis and information could improve the policy making system. And that's really been a theme of the work I've always done.

Have you always been interested in education, technological change, and competitiveness?

I've always had a strong interest in education and human capital. At the Economic Council, we looked at improving the policy-making process. At OECD, some of us focussed on micro issues of the impact of the second oil shock—micro issues of elasticities of demand response to the structural change—and also on labour market issues. We tried to look at the structural aspects of the economy and to link the structural aspects to the effectiveness of macro policy.

Are these issues related to Canada's competitiveness?

Absolutely. As Deputy Minister of Trade, I became more and more intrigued by the lack of communication and coordination among three sets of global actors: the multinational corporations, domestic governments, and the international agencies. In the 1980s, there was an enormous increase in foreign investment, which has transformed the world scene. So my projects involve the role of the multinationals, competition, foreign investment, the role of technology, the role of innovation, and so on.

What can the government of Canada do to make Canada more competitive?

One of the many characteristics of the environment in which we are living is rapid change and uncertainty. In a period of rapid change, the ability to adapt really becomes a question of survival. The government structure of Canada, decentralized federalism, increases the transactions costs of decision making. For a more effective federalism, there is a clear need to come to grips with the issue of how to improve the decision-making process.

The major elements needed to increase Canada's competitiveness are: tight effective fiscal coordination, a linkage between

> " **W**e tried to look at the structural aspects of the economy and to link the structural aspects to the effectiveness of macro policy."

monetary policy and fiscal policy, and a federal–provincial debate about the international trading system.

Medium-term fiscal target should be set, involving binding mechanisms for federal–provincial cooperation. Our current debt-GDP ratio and our foreign debt-GDP ratio indicate that there has been no coordination between the federal government and the provinces.

There are two macro policies, fiscal policy and monetary policy. And when they are at odds, there must be some means of discussing a linkage between the two.

I was in favour of the Free Trade Agreement because I thought it was a necessary insurance policy against what was clearly an enormous increase in American protectionism in the first half of the decade. The Free Trade Agreement was also essential for ensuring that Canadian firms improve their competitiveness by competing in the world's largest market. I think that, in that sense, it has operated reasonably well. But now one would want to think very seriously about what kind of options a middle-sized country like Canada has. Do we want to integrate further in a

regional block? How can we increase our linkages with the Asian countries, which are the only really rapidly growing countries? I think we need a federal–provincial debate.

The 1993 election campaign was dominated by two central issues: jobs and the deficit. Do you think that the deficit is an obstacle to job creation?

Yes, I do think the deficit is an obstacle. If you look at both levels of government, the total debt to GDP ratio as it is moving upward is a really very dangerous situation. It is more dangerous because of our heavy foreign indebtedness. The financial markets will have a referendum on that and I think the reason it is a real impediment is that the deficit is crowding out domestic investment. Tangible and intangible investment (knowledge) are the keys to growth. There is no long-term way of creating jobs without improving our capacity to invest, which means lower indebtedness. So, I find it most unfortunate that the deficit and job creation are presented as though we were back in the 1940s—as a viable tradeoff. It isn't.

677

"I do not agree with the inflation target. I prefer a national income target. Nominal income includes both growth and inflation."

The Bank of Canada is firm on its policy of price stability. Do you agree with the Bank's policy?

The impact of monetary policy is not independent of the fiscal stance. It was the asymmetry between the fiscal policy and monetary policy that has created the high real interest rates and pushed up the dollar. I think John Crow made it perfectly clear that the Bank is not going to determine the fiscal stance.

I do not agree with the inflation target. I prefer a national income target. Nominal income includes both growth and inflation. Therefore, the Bank cannot determine the division of those two. But a nominal income target has been shown to be a better indicator than any monetary target or group of eclectic targets.

The division you get with a nominal income target of 10 percent, whether you get 7 percent inflation and 3 percent real growth, cannot be handled by macro policy. The division depends on a coherent policy package including both micro policy and macro policy. Thus a nominal income target is a better device for a medium-term coherent policy approach at both the micro and macro level. However, its disadvantage is that it's a lagging statistic.

What role can international organizations, such as OECD, the IMF, and GATT, play in improving national and global economic performance? Can they make a difference to how well the world economy performs?

To answer that question, you have to ask what will happen if they don't exist. The main thing that the IMF and the OECD do is to share information among countries to illuminate domestic policy issues and to improve the possibility through information exchange and peer group pressure for more coordinated international action.

The difference between the IMF and the OECD is that the IMF has clout. If a country moves too far beyond what the international community will accept, the IMF steps in.

The OECD has no clout: it influences through the use of information, consultation, and discussion. The OECD is a more effective mechanism—the absence of the power facilitates more real discussion. The OECD has a much greater range of expertise. Its directorates deal with science and technology, the environment, labour and social policy, and developing countries.

I think what is missing is a greater linkage among the institutions. I think that the OECD as an intellectual networking organization (which is more flexible) can act as an intermediary with both the GATT and the IMF.

Students are always interested in information about careers. What kind of work do economists do at international organizations such as the OECD and the IMF?

In the OECD, the major jobs for economists are either in the macro and forecasting area or in the micro analysis area. For either, a combination of knowledge on competition policy and industrial organization is very valuable.

At the IMF, there are really two sets of jobs: ones that deal with the developed countries, the OECD countries, and international economic coordination through the G7, and the others that deal with the developing countries or the newly democratizing countries. For both jobs, you need a first-class economic background. More and more the IMF is rotating their young people in research areas and then moving them to, say, an Eastern European or Asian desk. The experience you get by working for an international institution is enormously enlightening and valuable.

Many students setting out today to do first year at the university have as their goal to be an economist, maybe to work in an international institution or the government. What would you recommend that they study at the university to prepare themselves for a career?

The major issue is not so much in what they take but in that they should strive for excellence. In the end, what you learn at university is the technical capacity.

> " think that the OECD as an intellectual networking organization (which is more flexible) can act as an intermediary with both the GATT and the IMF."

What you really learn is from applying your knowledge on a job. So the learning process really starts after you leave university. You have to have the necessary qualifications to jump, but it's the experience and how much you gain from the experience that become valuable.

So, the main feature of the university program is to develop the skill of knowing how to learn?
I think so. And striving for excellence. Because of globalization, knowing how to speak in different languages is an asset. A language skill is a good complement to the technical training one receives.

CHAPTER 25

EXPENDITURE
DECISIONS
AND
GDP

After studying this chapter, you will be able to

◆ Describe the magnitudes and
fluctuations in the components of
aggregate expenditure

◆ Explain how households make
consumption and saving decisions

◆ Explain how firms make
investment decisions

◆ Explain how governments make
decisions about the purchases
of goods and services

◆ Explain what determines exports,
imports, and net exports

◆ Derive the aggregate expenditure
schedule and aggregate
expenditure curve

◆ Explain how aggregate
expenditure is determined

◆ Explain the relationship between
aggregate expenditure and
aggregate demand

"A UTO MAKERS HOBBLE INTO THE NEW YEAR WITH LITTLE Hope for a Robust Recovery," "Consumer Borrowing Flat," "New Home Sales Down," "Consumer Confidence Slips Again," "Little Christmas Cheer for Retailers." These are headlines from the winter of 1992. Why all the fear and trembling over what happens in the shopping aisles? Besides a few manufacturers and stores, who really cares whether people buy a lot of gifts for the holidays, or whether they buy cars and new homes? How does this affect the rest of us? What makes people decide to spend less and save more? ◆ ◆ It's not only consumer spending that stirs up hope and fear in the economy. At times, firms' orders for new plant and equipment grow to a flood, and at other times they become a trickle. Government purchases of goods and services fluctuate, and our exports to the rest of the world ebb and flow with the changing economic fortunes of the United States, Europe, and Japan.

Fear and Trembling in the Shopping Aisles

How do business investment, government purchases, and exports affect us? How much of the country's spending do they make up when compared with consumer spending? Are fluctuations in these components of aggregate expenditure sources of fluctuations in our job prospects and living standards?

◆ ◆ ◆ ◆ The spending that people do in shopping aisles spreads out in waves across the economy, affecting millions of people. In this chapter, we study the composition of those waves and see why consumption has a big effect outside the stores. We also study the other components of aggregate expenditure—investment, government purchases of goods and services, and net exports.

The Components of Aggregate Expenditure

The components of aggregate expenditure are

◆ Consumption expenditure

◆ Investment

◆ Government purchases of goods and services

◆ Net exports (exports minus imports)

Magnitudes

Figure 25.1 shows the relative magnitudes of the components of aggregate expenditure between 1971 and 1991. By far the biggest portion of aggregate expenditure is consumption expenditure, which ranges between 57 and 60 percent and averages 59 percent of total expenditure. The smallest portion is net exports, which ranges between –3 and 4 percent and averages zero percent of total expenditure. Investment ranges between 13 and 22 percent of total expenditure and averages 17 percent. Government purchases of goods and services are larger than investment, ranging between 22 and 26 percent and averaging 24 percent of total expenditure.

FIGURE 25.1

The Components of Aggregate Expenditure: 1971-1992

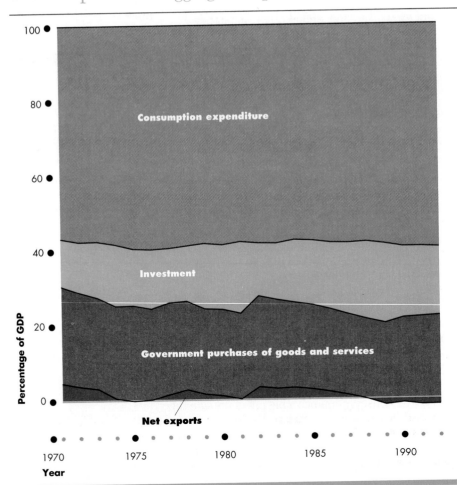

The biggest component of aggregate expenditure is consumption expenditure. It ranges between 57 and 60 percent of GDP and averages 59 percent. Investment averages 17 percent of GDP and fluctuates between 13 and 22 percent. Government expenditure on goods and services ranges between 22 and 26 percent of GDP and averages 24 percent. Net exports, the smallest item, ranges between –3 and 4 percent of GDP and averages approximately zero.

Fluctuations

Figure 25.2 shows the fluctuations in the components of aggregate expenditure. The most volatile are investment and net exports. Consumption expenditure and government purchases of goods and services fluctuate less than these two items.

Notice that although the fluctuations in consumption expenditure have a much smaller range than those in investment, the ups and downs of the two series move in sympathy with each other. Notice also that the two big declines in investment—in 1982 and 1990—occurred at precisely the time the economy was in recession (recessions that we saw in Chapter 22, pp. 613–614 and in Chapter 24, pp.668–669). Fluctuations in government purchases of goods and services are similar to those in consumption expenditure. The fluctuations in net exports are similar in magnitude to those in investment, but these two components of aggregate expenditure tend to fluctuate in opposite directions—years of high investment are years of low net exports.

Let's study the choices that determine the size and volatility of the components of aggregate expenditure, beginning with the largest component, consumption expenditure.

FIGURE 25.2

Fluctuations in the Components of Aggregate Expenditure: 1971-1992

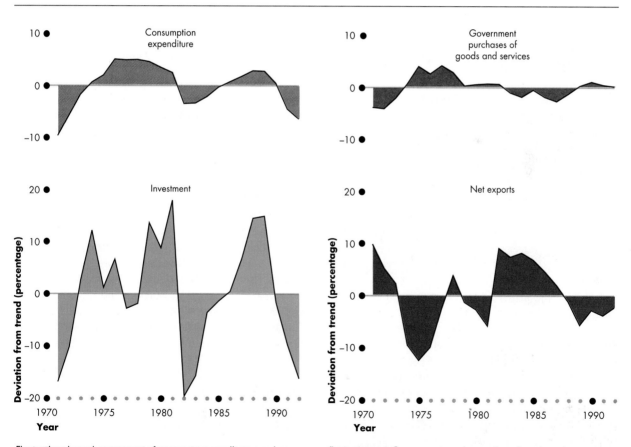

Fluctuations in each component of aggregate expenditure are shown as percentage deviations from trend. Although consumption expenditure is the biggest component of aggregate expenditure, it is the one that fluctuates least, in percentage terms. Investment and net exports fluctuate most. Government purchases of goods and services fluctuate in a similar way to consumption expenditure. Net exports tends to fluctuate in the opposite direction to investment.

Consumption Expenditure and Saving

Consumption expenditure is the value of the consumption goods and services bought by households. Many factors influence a household's consumption expenditure. But the most important is disposable income. **Disposable income** is the aggregate income that households receive in exchange for supplying the services of factors of production plus transfers from the government minus taxes. A household can do only two things with its disposable income: spend it on consumption goods and services or save it.

As a household's disposable income increases, so does its expenditure on food and beverages, clothing, accommodation, transportation, medical care, and on most other goods and services. That is, a household's consumption expenditure increases as its income increases.

The Consumption Function and the Saving Function

The relationship between consumption expenditure and disposable income, other things remaining the same, is called the **consumption function**. The consumption function has played a major role in macroeconomics over the past 50 years and the story of its discovery is told in Our Advancing Knowledge on pp. 686–687. The relationship between saving and disposable income, other things remaining the same, is called the **saving function**. The consumption function and saving function for a typical household—the Polonius household—are shown in Fig. 25.3.

The Consumption Function The Polonius household's consumption function is plotted in Fig. 25.3(a). The horizontal axis measures disposable income and the vertical axis measures consumption expenditure (both in thousands of dollars). The points labelled a through e in the figure correspond to the rows having the same letters in the table. For example, point c indicates a disposable income of $20,000 and consumption of $17,000.

The 45° Line Figure 25.3(a) also contains a line labelled "45° line." This line connects the points at which consumption, measured on the vertical axis, equals disposable income, measured on the horizontal axis. When the consumption function is above the 45° line, consumption exceeds disposable income; when the consumption function is below the 45° line, consumption is less than disposable income; and at the point where the consumption function intersects the 45° line, consumption and disposable income are equal.

The Saving Function The saving function is graphed in Fig. 25.3(b). The horizontal axis is exactly the same as that in part (a). The vertical axis measures saving. Again, the points marked a through e correspond to the rows of the table.

There are two things to note about the Polonius household's consumption and saving functions. First, even if the household has no disposable income, it still consumes. It does so by having a negative level of saving. Negative saving is called **dissaving**. Households that consume more than their disposable income do so either by living off assets or by borrowing—a situation that cannot last forever.

Second, as the Polonius household's disposable income increases, so does the amount that it plans to spend on consumption and the amount that it plans to save. Since a household can only consume or save its disposable income, these two items always add up to disposable income. That is, consumption and saving plans are consistent with disposable income.

This relationship between the consumption function and the saving function can be seen by looking at the two parts of the figure. When the saving function is below the horizontal axis, saving is negative (dissaving) and the consumption function is above the 45° line. When the saving function is above the horizontal axis, saving is positive and the consumption function is below the 45° line. When the saving function intersects the horizontal axis, saving is zero, and the consumption function intersects the 45° line.

Other Influences on Consumption Expenditure and Saving Of the many other factors that influence consumption expenditure and saving, the most important is expected future income. A household's expected future income depends on the scale of its investments, its debts, and the security and income growth prospects of the jobs that its members do. Other things remaining the same, the higher a household's expected future income, the greater is its current consumption

FIGURE 25.3

The Polonius Household's Consumption Function and Saving Function

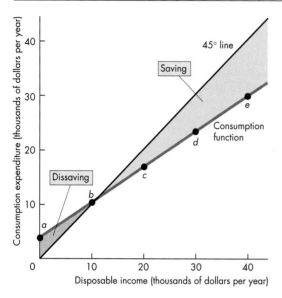

(a) Consumption function

(b) Saving function

	Disposable income	Consumption expenditure	Saving
	(thousands of dollars per year)		
a	0	4.0	−4.0
b	10	10.5	−0.5
c	20	17.0	3.0
d	30	23.5	6.5
e	40	30.0	10.0

The table sets out the consumption and saving plan of the Polonius household at various levels of disposable income. Part (a) of the figure shows the relationship between consumption expenditure and disposable income (the consumption function). Part (b) shows the relationship between saving and disposable income (the saving function). Points *a* through *e* on the consumption and saving functions correspond to the rows in the table.

The 45° line in part (a) is the line of equality between consumption expenditure and disposable income. The Polonius household's consumption expenditure and saving equals its disposable income. When the consumption function is above the 45° line, saving is negative (dissaving occurs) and the saving function is below the horizontal axis. When the consumption function is below the 45° line, saving is positive and the saving function is above the horizontal axis. At the point where the consumption function intersects the 45° line, all disposable income is consumed, saving is zero, and the saving function intersects the horizontal axis.

expenditure. That is, if there are two households that each have the same disposable income in the current year, the household with the larger expected future income will spend a larger portion of current disposable income on consumption goods and services. Consider, for example, two households whose principal income earner is a senior executive in a large corporation. One executive has just been told of a promotion that will increase the household's income by 50 per-

cent in the following years. The other has just been told that the firm has been taken over and that there will be no further employment beyond the end of the year. The first household buys a new car and takes an expensive foreign vacation, thereby increasing its current consumption expenditure. The second household sells the family's second car and cancels its winter vacation plans, thereby cutting back on its current consumption expenditure.

DISCOVERING the CONSUMPTION FUNCTION

The theory that consumption is determined by disposable income was proposed by John Maynard Keynes in 1936. With newly available national income data compiled by Simon Kuznets supporting Keynes' theory, it was instantly accepted.

During the 1940s and 1950s, a lot of additional data were collected, some of which revealed shortcomings in Keynes' theory. By the late 1940s, the Keynesian consumption function began to make forecasting errors. The propensity to consume—what Keynes had called a "fundamental psychological law"—was revealed to be increasing and to vary according to whether a person was young or old, black or white, or from an urban or rural area.

These failings brought forth two new theories—Franco Modigliani's life-cycle hypothesis and Milton Friedman's permanent income hypothesis—based on the proposition that consumption is determined by wealth and wealth depends on current and future income. Other things remaining the same, the wealthier a person, the more that person consumes. But only permanent and previously unexpected changes in income bring changes in wealth and consumption. Temporary and previously foreseen changes in income leave wealth and consumption unchanged.

The revolution in macroeconomics of the 1970s brought the next reappraisal of consumption and a rational expectations theory of consumption proposed by Robert Hall of Stanford University. Hall started from the same point as Modigliani and Friedman: consumption depends on wealth and wealth depends on future income. But to make consumption decisions, people must form expectations of future income using whatever information is available. Expectations change only as a result of new information, which arrives at random. Therefore people's estimates of how wealthy they are, together with their consumption, change at random. No variable other than current consumption is of any value for predicting future consumption. Consumption and income are correlated, but changes in income do not cause changes in consumption.

> "The fundamental psychological law, upon which we are entitled to depend with confidence ... is that [people] are disposed ... to increase their consumption as their income increases, but not by as much as the increase in their income."
>
> JOHN MAYNARD KEYNES
> *General Theory*

A family whose income is permanently low has a low consumption level. But such a family doesn't always spend all its income every week. Instead, it saves a small amount to smooth its consumption between one year and the next. The amount that such a family saves is influenced by its stage in the life cycle. A young family saves a larger fraction of its income than an older family that has exactly the same level of permanent income. For most low-income families, saving does not mean putting money in the bank, or in stocks and bonds. It means buying a home, buying life insurance, and paying taxes that partly get used to provide social benefits.

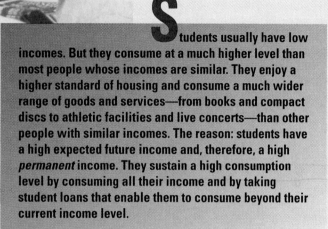

Students usually have low incomes. But they consume at a much higher level than most people whose incomes are similar. They enjoy a higher standard of housing and consume a much wider range of goods and services—from books and compact discs to athletic facilities and live concerts—than other people with similar incomes. The reason: students have a high expected future income and, therefore, a high *permanent* income. They sustain a high consumption level by consuming all their income and by taking student loans that enable them to consume beyond their current income level.

JOHN MAYNARD KEYNES:

A Macroeconomic Revolutionary

When John Maynard Keynes (1883-1946) of Cambridge, England, published his *General Theory of Employment, Interest, and Money* in 1936, he set off a revolution. The centrepieces of Keynes' theory of employment and income were the consumption function and the multiplier. As with all intellectual revolutions, the older generation rejected it and the young embraced it eagerly. The first Canadian Keynesian was Robert Bryce, an engineering graduate from the University of Toronto who studied economics at Cambridge where he was taught by Keynes. Bryce went on to become a distinguished public servant in Ottawa where he served as secretary to the cabinet and deputy minister of finance.

Keynes was one of the chief architects of the International Monetary Fund and visited the United States to finalize arrangements for the world's new monetary order as World War II was ending. He used the occasion to drop in on the Keynesians of Cambridge, Massachusetts. Asked on his return to England what he thought of his American disciples, he reported that he found them far more Keynesian than he!

Changes in factors other than disposable income that influence consumption expenditure shift both the consumption function and the saving function. For example, an increase in expected future income shifts the consumption function upward and the saving function downward. It is common for such shifts to occur when the economy begins to recover from a recession. Going into the recession, people expect lower future incomes, but when the recovery begins they expect higher future incomes. The beginning of the recovery from the 1990 recession was such an occasion.

The Average Propensities to Consume and to Save

The **average propensity to consume** (*APC*) is consumption expenditure divided by disposable income. Table 25.1(a) shows you how to calculate the average propensity to consume. Let's do a sample calculation. At a disposable income of $20,000, the Polonius household consumes $17,000. Its average propensity to consume is $17,000 divided by $20,000, which equals 0.85.

As you can see from the numbers in the table, the average propensity to consume declines as disposable income rises. At a disposable income of $10,000, the household consumes $10,500, an amount greater than its income. So its average propensity to consume is $10,500 divided by $10,000, which equals 1.05. But at a disposable income of $40,000 the household consumes only $30,000, so its average propensity to consume is $30,000 divided by $40,000, which equals 0.75.

The **average propensity to save** (*APS*) is saving divided by disposable income. Table 25.1(a) shows you how to calculate the average propensity to save. For example, when disposable income is $20,000 the Polonius household saves $3,000, so its average propensity to save is $3,000 divided by $20,000, which equals 0.15. When saving is negative, the average propensity to save is negative. As disposable income increases, the average propensity to save increases.

As disposable income increases, the average propensity to consume falls and the average propensity to save rises. Equivalently, as disposable income increases, the fraction of income saved increases and the fraction of income consumed decreases. These patterns in the average propensities to consume and save reflect the fact that people with very

low disposable incomes are so poor that their income is not even sufficient to meet their consumption requirements. Consumption expenditure exceeds disposable income. As people's incomes increase, they are able to meet their consumption requirements with a smaller fraction of their disposable income.

The sum of the average propensity to consume and the average propensity to save is one. These two average propensities add up to one because consumption and saving exhaust disposable income. Each dollar of disposable income is either consumed or saved.

You can see that the two average propensities add up to 1 by using the following equation:

$$C + S = YD$$

Divide both sides of the equation by disposable income to obtain

$$C/YD + S/YD = 1.$$

C/YD is the *average propensity to consume* and S/YD is *average propensity to save*. Thus

$$APC + APS = 1.$$

The Marginal Propensities to Consume and to Save

The last dollar of disposable income received is called the marginal dollar. Part of that marginal dollar is consumed and part of it is saved. The allocation of the marginal dollar between consumption expenditure and saving is determined by the marginal propensities to consume and to save.

The **marginal propensity to consume** (*MPC*) is the fraction of the last dollar of disposable income that is spent on consumption goods and services. It is calculated as the change in consumption expenditure divided by the change in disposable income. The **marginal propensity to save** (*MPS*) is the fraction of the last dollar of disposable income saved. The marginal propensity to save is calculated as the change in saving divided by the change in disposable income.

Table 25.1 shows the calculation of the Polonius household's marginal propensities to consume and to save. Looking at part (a), you can see that disposable income increases by $10,000 as we move from one row to the next—$10,000 is the change in

---

TABLE 25.1

Average and Marginal Propensities to Consume and to Save

(a) CALCULATING AVERAGE PROPENSITIES TO CONSUME AND TO SAVE

Disposable income (YD)	Consumption expenditure (C)	Saving (S)	APC (C/YD)	APS (S/YD)
	(thousands of dollars per year)			
0	4.0	−4.0	—	—
10	10.5	−0.5	1.05	−0.05
20	17.0	3.0	0.85	0.15
30	23.5	6.5	0.78	0.22
40	30.0	10.0	0.75	0.25

(b) CALCULATING MARGINAL PROPENSITIES TO CONSUME AND TO SAVE

Change in disposable income	ΔYD =	$10,000
Change in consumption	ΔC =	$6,500
Change in saving	ΔS =	$3,500
Marginal propensity to consume	$MPC = \Delta C/\Delta YD$ =	0.65
Marginal propensity to save	$MPS = \Delta S/\Delta YD$ =	0.35

Consumption and saving depend on disposable income. At zero disposable income, some consumption is undertaken and saving is negative (dissaving occurs). As disposable income increases, so do both consumption and saving. The average propensities to consume and to save are calculated in part (a). The average propensity to consume—the ratio of consumption to disposable income—declines as disposable income increases; the average propensity to save—the ratio of saving to disposable income—increases as disposable income

increases. These two average propensities sum to 1. Each additional—or *marginal*—dollar of disposable income is either consumed or saved.

Part (b) calculates the marginal propensities to consume and to save. The marginal propensity to consume is the change in consumption that results from a $1 change in disposable income. The marginal propensity to save is the change in saving that results from a $1 change in disposable income. The marginal propensities to consume and to save sum to 1.

---

disposable income. You can also see from part (a) that when disposable income increases by $10,000, consumption increases by $6,500. The marginal propensity to consume—the change in consumption divided by the change in disposable income—is therefore $6,500 divided by $10,000, which equals 0.65. The Polonius household's marginal propensity to consume is constant. It is the same at each level of disposable income. Out of a marginal dollar of disposable income, 65¢ is spent on consumption goods and services.

Part (b) of Table 25.1 shows the calculation of the marginal propensity to save. You can see from part (b) that when disposable income increases by $10,000, saving increases by $3,500. The marginal propensity to save—the change in saving divided by the change in disposable income—is therefore $3,500 divided by $10,000, which equals 0.35. The Polonius household's marginal propensity to save is constant. It is the same at each level of disposable income. Out of the last dollar of disposable income, 35¢ is saved.

The marginal propensity to consume plus the marginal propensity to save equals one. Each additional dollar must either be consumed or spent. In this example, when disposable income increases by $1, 65¢ more is spent and 35¢ more is saved. That is,

$$MPC + MPS = 1.$$

Marginal Propensities and Slopes The marginal propensity to consume is equal to the slope of the consumption function. You can see this equality by looking back at Fig. 25.3. In that figure, the consumption function has a constant slope that can be measured as the change in consumption divided by the change in income. For example, when income increases from $20,000 to $30,000—an increase of $10,000—consumption increases from $17,000 to $23,500, an increase of $6,500. The slope of the consumption function is $6,500 divided by $10,000, which equals 0.65—the same value as the marginal propensity to consume we calculated in Table 25.1.

The marginal propensity to save is equal to the slope of the saving function. You can see this equality by again looking at Fig. 25.3. When income increases by $10,000, saving increases by $3,500. The slope of the saving function is $3,500 divided by $10,000, which equals 0.35—the same value as the marginal propensity to save we calculated in Table 25.1.

R E V I E W

Consumption expenditure is influenced by many factors, but the most important is disposable income. Households allocate their disposable income to either consumption expenditure or saving. The relationship between consumption expenditure and disposable income, other things remaining the same, is the *consumption function*; the relationship between saving and disposable income, other things remaining the same, is the *saving function*. Changes in other factors that influence consumption expenditure, the most important of which is expected future income, shift the consumption and saving functions. ◆ ◆ The change in consumption expenditure divided by the change in disposable income, other things remaining the same, is the *marginal propensity to consume* (MPC); the change in saving divided by the change in disposable income, other things remaining the same, is

the *marginal propensity to save* (MPS). Because consumption expenditure plus saving equals disposable income, $MPC + MPS = 1$. ◆

We've studied the consumption function of a household. Let's now look at the Canadian consumption function.

The Canadian Consumption Function

Data for consumption expenditure and disposable income in Canada for the years 1971 to 1992 are shown in Fig. 25.4(a). The vertical axis measures consumption expenditure (in 1986 dollars), and the horizontal axis measures disposable income (also in 1986 dollars). Each point identified by a blue dot represents consumption expenditure and disposable income for a particular year.

The orange line highlights the average relationship between consumption expenditure and disposable income and is an estimate of the Canadian consumption function. It tells us that, on the average, consumption expenditure has been 90 percent of disposable income. The slope of this consumption function, which is also the marginal propensity to consume, is 0.9. The relationship between consumption expenditure and disposable income in any given year does not fall exactly on the orange line. The reason is that the position of the consumption function depends on the other factors that influence consumption expenditure, and as a result the consumption function shifts over time.

Consumption as a Function of GDP Our purpose in developing a theory of the consumption function is to explain the determination of aggregate expenditure and real GDP. To achieve this purpose, we need to establish the relationship between consumption expenditure and real GDP—consumption expenditure as a function of real GDP.

The blue dots in Fig. 25.4(b) show consumption expenditure and real GDP in Canada for each year between 1971 and 1992. The orange line shows consumption expenditure as a function of real GDP in 1991. Consumption expenditure is a function of real GDP because disposable income depends on real GDP. Disposable income is real GDP minus net taxes (net taxes are taxes minus transfer payments). But net taxes increase as real GDP increases. Almost all the taxes we pay—personal taxes, corporate taxes, and Canada Pension Plan and unemployment insurance contributions—increase as our incomes

FIGURE 25.4

The Canadian Consumption Function

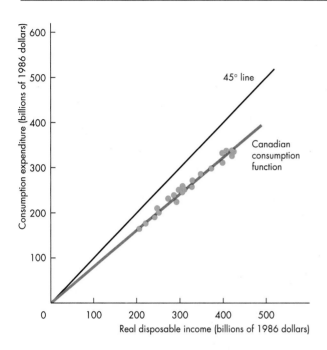

(a) Consumption as a function of disposable income

(b) Consumption as a function of real GDP

Part (a) shows the relationship between real consumption expenditure and real disposable income for each year between 1971 and 1992. Each blue point represents real consumption expenditure and real disposable income for a particular year. The orange line shows the average relationship between consumption expenditure and disposable income—an estimate of the Canadian consumption function. This consumption function has a slope and a marginal propensity to consume of approximately 0.9.

Part (b) shows the relationship between consumption expenditure and real GDP. This relationship takes into account the fact that as real GDP increases, so do net taxes. Because net taxes are a fairly stable percentage of real GDP, consumption expenditure is a fairly stable function of real GDP—shown by the orange line.

increase. Transfer payments, such as Guaranteed Income Supplement and unemployment benefits, decrease as our incomes increase. Since taxes increase and transfers decrease, net taxes increase as incomes increase.

It turns out that net taxes tend to be a fairly stable percentage of real GDP, so consumption expenditure is a fairly stable function of real GDP. The change in consumption expenditure divided by the change in real GDP is the **marginal propensity to consume out of real GDP.** It is measured by the slope of the orange line in Fig. 25.4(b).

R E V I E W

O f all the influences on consumption expenditure, disposable income is the most important. Consumption expenditure in Canada is a function of disposable income. Disposable income is, in turn, related to GDP. Therefore consumption expenditure is a function of GDP. ◆

The theory of the consumption function has an important implication. Because consumption expenditure is determined mainly by disposable income, most of the changes in consumption expenditure result from changes in income, and are not causes of those income changes. It is fluctuations in other components of aggregate expenditure that bring fluctuations in income. And the most notable of these is investment.

Investment

Gross investment is the purchase of new buildings, new plant and equipment, and additions to inventories. It has two components: *net investment* (additions to existing capital) and *replacement investment* (purchases to replace worn out or depreciated capital). As we saw in Fig. 25.2, gross investment is a volatile element of aggregate expenditure. What determines gross investment and why does it fluctuate so much? The answer lies in the investment decisions of firms—in the answers to such questions as: what determines IBM's outlays on new computer designs? How does Bell Canada choose what it will spend on fibre optic communications systems? Let's answer questions such as these.

Firms' Investment Decisions

The main influences on firms' investment decisions are

◆ Real interest rates

◆ Profit expectations

1. Real Interest Rates   The **real interest rate** is the interest rate paid by a borrower and received by a lender after taking into account changes in the value of money resulting from inflation. It is approximately equal to the agreed interest rate (called the *nominal* interest rate) minus the inflation rate. To see why, suppose that prices are rising by 10 percent a year. Each dollar borrowed for one year is repaid at the end of the year with a dollar that is worth only

90¢ today. The borrower gains and the lender loses 10¢ on each dollar. This loss must be subtracted from the agreed interest rate to find the interest *really* paid and received—the real interest rate. If the nominal interest rate is 20 percent a year, the real interest rate is only 10 percent a year.

Firms sometimes pay for capital goods with money they have borrowed, and sometimes they use their own funds—called retained earnings. But regardless of the method of financing an investment project, the real interest rate is part of its *opportunity cost*. The real interest paid on borrowed funds is a direct cost. The real interest cost of using retained earnings arises because these funds could be lent to another firm at the going real interest rate, generating income. The real interest income forgone is the opportunity cost of using retained earnings to finance an investment project.

The lower the real interest rate, the lower is the opportunity cost of any given investment project. Some investment projects that are not profitable at a high real interest rate become profitable at a low real interest rate. The lower the real interest rate, the larger is the number of investment projects that are profitable and, therefore, the greater is the amount of investment.

Let's consider an example. Suppose that Chrysler is contemplating building a new automobile assembly line in Windsor, Ontario, at a cost of $100 million. The assembly line is expected to produce cars for three years, and then it will be scrapped completely and replaced with a new line that produces an entirely new range of models. Chrysler's expected net revenue in each of the first two years is $20 million and in the third year is $100 million. Net revenue is the difference between the total revenue from car sales and the costs of producing those cars. In calculating net revenue, we do not take into account the initial cost of the assembly line or the interest that has to be paid on it. We take separate account of these costs. To build the assembly line, Chrysler plans to borrow the initial $100 million, and at the end of each year to use its expected net revenue to pay the interest on the loan outstanding along with as much of the loan as it can. Does it pay Chrysler to invest $100 million in this car assembly line? The answer depends on the real interest rate.

Case 1 in Fig. 25.5 shows what happens if the interest rate is 20 percent per year. (We'll assume the expected inflation rate to be zero so the expected real interest rate is also 20 percent a year. This is

FIGURE 25.5

FIGURE 25.5

Investment in an Automobile Assembly Line

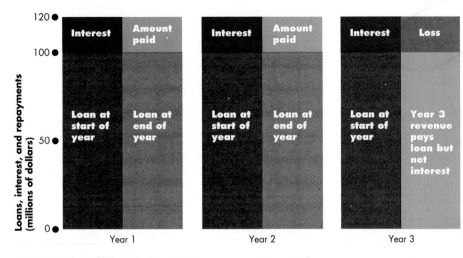

Case 1: Real interest rate is 20 percent

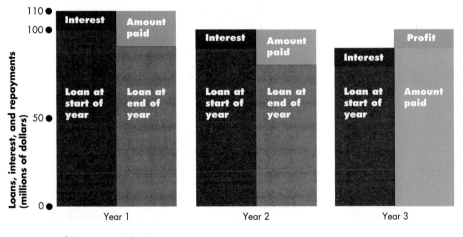

Case 2: Real interest rate is 10 percent

An automobile assembly line costs $100 million to build. It is expected to generate the following revenue:

Year 1	$20 million
Year 2	$20 million
Year 3	$100 million

The line will then be scrapped and replaced by a new one. In case 1, the interest rate is 20 percent per year. The revenue stream is too low to cover the total expense, and the project is not worth undertaking. In case 2, the interest rate is 10 percent per year, and the project is profitable. The lower the interest rate, the larger is the number of projects that are profitable and that are undertaken.

an unlikely high rate, but it makes the numbers work out easily.) Chrysler borrows $100 million and at the end of the first year has to pay $20 million in interest. It has a net revenue of $20 million and so can just meet this interest payment, but cannot reduce the size of its outstanding loan. At the end of the second year, it is in exactly the same situation as at the end of the first. It owes another $20 million on its outstanding loan. Again, its revenue just covers

the interest payment. At the end of the third year, Chrysler owes another $20 million in interest payments plus the $100 million outstanding loan. Therefore it has to pay $120 million. But net revenue in the third year is only $100 million, so Chrysler has a $20 million loss on this project.

Case 2 in Fig. 25.5 shows what happens if the real interest rate is 10 percent per year. (Again, we'll assume the expected inflation rate is zero so the expected real interest rate is also 10 percent a year.) In this case, Chrysler owes $10 million interest at the end of the first year. Since it has $20 million of revenue, it can make this interest payment and reduce its outstanding loan to $90 million. In the second year, the interest owing on the loan is $9 million (10 percent of $90 million). Again, with revenue of $20 million, Chrysler pays the interest and reduces its outstanding loan by $11 million to $79 million. In the third and final year of the project, the interest on the loan is $7.9 million (10 percent of $79 million), so the total amount owing—the outstanding loan plus the interest—is $86.9 million. Chrysler's revenue in year 3 is $100 million, so it repays the loan, pays the interest, and pockets the balance, a profit of $13.1 million. If Chrysler builds the assembly line, it expects to make a profit of $13.1 million.

You can see that at a real interest rate of 20 percent a year, it does not pay Chrysler to invest in this car assembly plant. At a 10 percent real interest rate, it does pay. The lower the real interest rate, the larger is the number of projects, such as the one considered here, that yield a positive net profit. Thus the lower the real interest rate, the larger is the amount of investment.

2. Profit Expectations   The higher the expected profitability of new capital equipment, the greater is the amount of investment. Chrysler's assembly line investment decision illustrates this effect. To decide whether or not to build the assembly line, Chrysler has to work out its net revenue. To perform that calculation, it has to work out the total revenue from car sales which, in turn, are affected by its expectations of car prices and the share of the market that it can attain. Chrysler also has to figure out its operating costs, which include the wages of its assembly workers, and the costs of the products it buys from other producers. The larger the net revenue that it anticipates, the more profitable is the investment project that generates those net revenues and the more likely it is that the project will be undertaken.

Many factors influence profit expectations themselves. Among the main ones are taxes on company profits, the degree to which existing capital is utilized, and the state of global relations and tensions. For example, the collapse of the Soviet Union and the emergence of the new republics of Eastern Europe are likely to have a large impact on profit expectations in the 1990s—positive in some industries and negative in others.

Investment Demand

Investment demand is the relationship between the level of planned investment and the real interest rate, holding all other influences on investment constant. The **investment demand schedule** is a list of the quantities of planned investment at each real interest rate, holding all other influences on investment constant. The **investment demand curve** graphs the relationship between the real interest rate and the level of planned investment, holding everything else constant. Some examples of investment demand schedules and investment demand curves appear in Fig. 25.6. The investment demand schedule and the position of the investment demand curve depend on the other major influence on investment—expected profit.

Sometimes firms are pessimistic about future profits, sometimes they are optimistic, and sometimes their expectations are average. Fluctuations in profit expectations are the main source of fluctuations in investment demand. The three investment demand schedules in the table in Fig. 25.6 give examples of investment demand under the three types of expectations. In the case of average profit expectations, if the real interest rate is 4 percent a year, investment is $100 billion. If the real interest rate decreases to 2 percent a year, investment increases to $120 billion. If the real interest rate increases to 6 percent a year, investment decreases to $80 billion. In the case of optimistic profit expectations, investment is higher at each interest rate than it is when expectations are average. In the case of pessimistic profit expectations, investment is lower at each interest rate than with average expectations.

The investment demand curve is shown in the figure. In part (a), the investment demand curve (*ID*) is that for average expected profit. Each point (*a* through *c*) corresponds to a row in the table. A change in the real interest rate causes a movement along the investment demand curve. Thus if the real interest rate is 4 percent a year, planned investment is $100 billion. If the real interest rate rises to 6 percent a year, there is a movement up the investment demand curve (see blue arrow), and planned investment decreases to $80 billion. If the real interest rate falls to 2 percent a year, there is a movement down the investment demand curve, and planned investment increases to $120 billion.

The effects of profit expectations are shown in part (b) of Fig. 25.6. A change in profit expectations

FIGURE 25.6

Investment Demand Curves and Investment Demand Schedules

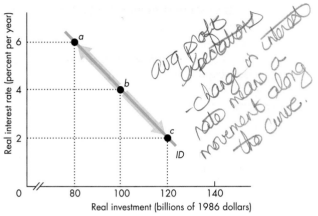

(a) The effect of a change in real interest rate

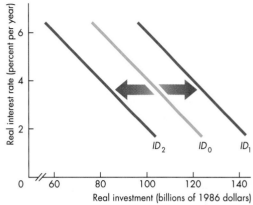

(b) The effect of a change in profit expectation

	Real interest rate (percent per year)	Investment (billions of 1986 dollars)		
		Optimistic	Average	Pessimistic
a	6	100	80	60
b	4	120	100	80
c	2	140	120	100

The table shows three investment demand schedules—for average, optimistic, and pessimistic expectations. Part (a) shows the investment demand curve for average profit expectations. Along that investment demand curve, as the real interest rate rises from 4 percent to 6 percent, planned investment decreases—there is a movement along the investment demand curve from *b* to *a*. Part (b) shows how the investment demand curve changes when expected future profits change. With average profit expectations, the investment demand curve is ID_0—the same curve as in part (a). With optimistic expectations about future profits, the investment demand curve shifts rightward, to ID_1. With pessimistic expectations about future profits, the investment demand curve shifts leftward, to ID_2.

shifts the investment demand curve. The demand curve ID_0 represents average expected profit. When profit expectations become optimistic, the investment demand curve shifts rightward, from ID_0 to ID_1. When profit expectations become pessimistic, the investment demand curve shifts leftward, from ID_0 to ID_2.

The investment demand curve also shifts when there is an increase in the amount of investment to replace depreciated capital. This influence leads to a steady rightward shift in the ID curve.

R E V I E W

Investment depends on the real interest rate and profit expectations. Other things remaining the same, the lower the real interest rate, the larger is the amount of investment. When profit expectations become optimistic, the investment demand curve shifts rightward; when profit expectations become pessimistic, it shifts leftward. Profit expectations are influenced by taxes, the degree of capacity utilization, and the global environment. ◆

We've just studied the *theory* of investment demand. Let's now see how that theory helps us to understand the fluctuations in investment that occur in the Canadian economy.

Investment Demand in Canada

As we saw in Fig. 25.2, investment is one of the most volatile components of aggregate expenditure. In some years, investment is as much as 22 percent of GDP and in others as little as 13 percent. Let's see how we can interpret these fluctuations in investment with the theory of investment demand we've just been studying.

We'll begin by looking at Fig. 25.7. It shows investment (in billions of 1986 dollars) between 1971 and 1992. It also shows the way in which investment (gross investment) is broken down between net investment and the replacement of

depreciated capital (depreciation). As you can see, both depreciation and gross investment increase steadily over time. Depreciation follows a very smooth path. It reflects the fact that the capital stock grows steadily and smoothly. Net investment is the component of investment that fluctuates. You can see that fluctuation as the blue area between gross investment and depreciation.

The theory of investment demand predicts that fluctuations in investment result from fluctuations in the real interest rate and in future profit expectations. What is the relative contribution of these two factors? Figure 25.8 answers this question. The points in the figure represent the gross investment and the real interest rate in Canada each year from 1979 to 1992. The figure also shows four Canadian investment demand curves. The curve labelled ID_0 is the investment demand curve in 1979. Profit expectations increased and by 1981, the curve had shifted rightward to ID_1. But expectations turned

FIGURE 25.7

Gross and Net Investment in Canada: 1971-1992

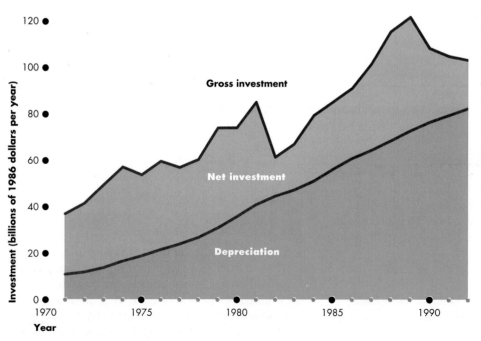

Gross investment is separated into two parts: the replacement of depreciated capital (green area) and net investment (blue area). Gross investment and depreciation increased steadily between 1971 and 1992. Depreciation follows a very smooth growth path because the capital stock grows steadily and smoothly. Net investment fluctuates.

Source: Statistics Canada, *National Income and Expenditure Accounts.*

FIGURE 25.8

The Canadian Investment Demand Curve

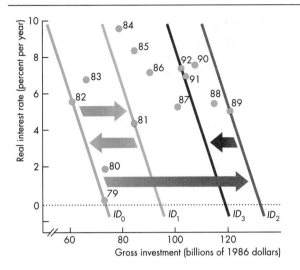

The blue points show the gross investment and real interest rate in Canada for each year between 1979 and 1992. In 1979, the investment demand curve was ID_0. As expected profits increased, the investment demand curve shifted rightward to reach ID_1, by 1981. Pessimistic expectations shifted the curve leftward in 1982 and then a period of prolonged optimism shifted the curve rightward again until by 1990 it was at ID_2. Renewed pessimism shifted the curve leftward again in 1991 to ID_3. When the real interest rate changes with given profit expectations, there is a movement along the investment demand curve. When profit expectations change, the investment demand curve shifts. Swings in profit expectations are more important than changes in interest rates in creating fluctuations in gross investment.

Source: Bank of Canada Review, Winter 1992-1993, and our calculations and assumptions.

pessimistic in 1982 and the curve shifted leftward to ID_0.

Throughout the 1980s, as the economy expanded, investment demand increased and by 1990, the investment demand curve had shifted rightward to ID_2. During the 1980s, optimistic profit expectations resulted from technological advances, especially in the electronics sector. The development of the low cost microchip opened up an amazing array of applications for computer technology in manufacturing, transportation and communication, and in consumer products. The result was an investment boom comparable to that of 200 years earlier when steam power was first harnessed.

The optimistic profit expectations of the 1980s turned pessimistic in 1991 as the economy went into recession, and the investment demand curve shifted leftward to ID_3. The fluctuations in investment in Canada are explored yet further in Reading Between the Lines, pp. 698–699, which focusses on housing investment in the recovery from the 1990 recession.

Regardless of whether the fluctuations in investments are generated by shifts in the investment demand curve or movements along it, they have far-reaching effects on the economy. We'll learn about some of those effects in Chapter 26.

Let's now turn to the third component of aggregate expenditure, government purchases of goods and services.

Government Purchases of Goods and Services

Government purchases of goods and services cover a wide range of public sector activities. They include goods and services for our national defence, international representation (embassies and delegations in other countries), and domestic programs such as health care, education, and highways. These expenditures are determined by our political institutions. They are influenced by our votes in national, provincial, and local elections, the views of the members of parliament, senators, and provincial and local legislators we elect, the actions of lobbyists, the political state of the world, and the state of the Canadian and world economies.

Although some components of government purchases do vary with the state of the economy, most do not. We will assume, therefore, that government purchases do not vary in a systematic way with the level of GDP. The level of government purchases influences GDP but it is not directly influenced by it.

The final component of aggregate expenditure is net exports. Let's now see how it is determined.

Investment
Picks up
Slowly

The Essence of the Story

The Canada Mortgage and Housing Corporation (CMHC) predicts that housing starts will rise 5.2 percent in 1993 to 177,000 units and 9 percent to 193,000 in 1994.

Increases of between 10 percent and 15 percent are more typical in a business recovery.

The reasons for slow growth in house building are

◆ a high level of consumer debt
◆ concerns about job security
◆ a small post-baby boom generation of home buyers
◆ low inflation

HALIFAX HERALD, THE CANADIAN PRESS, MARCH 9, 1993

CMHC's expectations for housing starts dim

TORONTO—The economy will get only a modest amount of help from the homebuilding industry this year and next, a new forecast from Canada Mortgage and Housing Corp. suggests.

Housing starts will rise 5.2 per cent this year to 177,000 units and nine per cent to 193,000 in 1994, CMHC said in the forecast, which was released at a homebuilders' conference Monday.

"Those kind of increases are not usual in a recovery," Gilles Proulx, the federal agency's chief economist, said in an interview. "Normally, housing goes up by double-digit jumps as you move out of a recession."

Housing starts rose 7.7 per cent in 1992 to 168,271. Proulx said increases of between 10 per cent and 15 per cent were typical in the years following the 1982–82 recession.

This year's forecast finds CMHC in a far less optimistic mood that a year ago, when it said housing starts would jump 15 per cent in 1992 to 180,000 units.

A panel of economists told homebuilders that demand for new homes this year will be limited by high levels of consumer debt and concerns about job security.

Proulx said another reason for the lack-lustre demand is that baby boomers are nearing the end of their house-buying years and are being succeeded by the smaller post-baby boom generation.

Low inflation, while a benefit to the overall economy, is also hurting demand for new homes.

"You don't have this drive to buy a house because its price will go up and you'll make a killing," Proulx said....

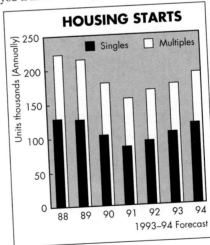

HOUSING STARTS

Units thousands (Annually)

■ Singles   □ Multiples

88 89 90 91 92 93 94
1993–94 Forecast

Source: CMHC

Background and Analysis

Expenditure on new houses is part of investment and, like other components of investment, it fluctuates a great deal.

Part (a) of the figure shows the fluctuations in housing investment since 1980. The quantity shown in this graph is total expenditure on new houses (in 1986 dollars) divided by the number of employed Canadians aged 25 to 54. This group buys most of the new houses.

One of the main influences on house buying is the mortgage interest rate, shown in part (b). But a benefit of owning a house is that its price might rise. The difference between the mortgage interest rate and the rate of increase of house prices is the *real* interest rate paid by house owners. This rate is also shown in part (b).

Part (c) shows the effect of changes in the real interest rate on housing investment. In the early 1980s, the housing investment demand curve was ID_0.

Rising incomes during the 1980s increased the demand for housing and by 1989 the investment demand curve shifted rightward to ID_1.

A rise in the real interest rate in 1990—as the Bank of Canada pursued its price stability goal—decreased the quantity of new houses demanded. This decrease is shown as a *movement along* the demand curve ID_1 in part (c).

Falling real incomes in the 1991 recession together with uncertainty about the future decreased housing investment demand in the early 1990s and the investment demand curve shifted leftward to where it had been a decade earlier.

In the business recovery of 1983, housing investment increased sharply because the real interest rate fell. In the business recovery of 1992, housing investment was stagnant because the real interest rate did not fall. Only if the real interest rate falls, or expected future income rises, can we expect a significant increase in house building.

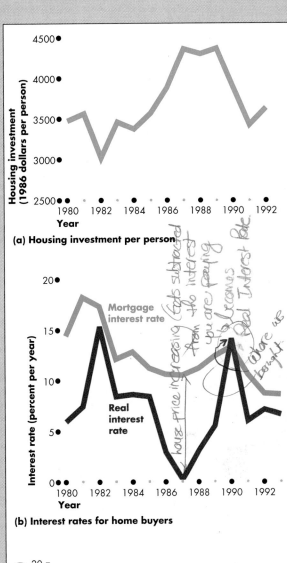

(a) Housing investment per person

(b) Interest rates for home buyers

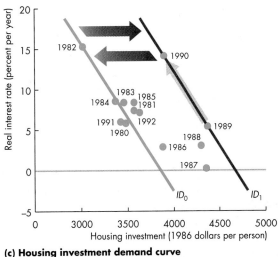

(c) Housing investment demand curve

Net Exports

Net exports is the expenditure by foreigners on Canadian-made goods and services minus the expenditure by Canadian residents on foreign-made goods and services. That is, net exports is Canadian exports minus Canadian imports. *Exports* are the sale of the goods and services produced in Canada to the rest of the world. *Imports* are the purchase of goods produced in the rest of the world by firms and households in Canada.

Exports

Exports are determined by decisions made in the rest of the world and are influenced by three main factors:

◆ Real GDP in the rest of the world

◆ Prices of Canadian-made goods and services relative to the prices of similar goods and services made in other countries

◆ Foreign exchange rates

Other things remaining the same, the higher the level of real GDP in the rest of the world, the greater is the demand by foreigners for Canadian-made goods and services. For example, an economic boom in Japan increases the Japanese demand for Canadian-made goods and services, such as B.C. lumber, Alberta wheat, and Ontario machine tools, and increases Canadian exports. A recession in Japan cuts the Japanese demand for Canadian-made goods and decreases Canadian exports.

Also, other things remaining the same, the lower the price of Canadian-made goods and services relative to the prices of similar goods and services made in other countries, the greater is the quantity of Canadian exports.

Finally, and again other things remaining the same, the lower the value of the Canadian dollar against other currencies, the larger is the quantity of Canadian exports. For example, as the Canadian dollar fell in value against the German mark and the Japanese yen in 1987, the demand for Canadian-

made goods and services by those two countries increased sharply.

Imports

Imports are determined by three main factors:

◆ Canadian real GDP

◆ Prices of foreign-made goods and services relative to the prices of similar goods and services made in Canada

◆ Foreign exchange rates

Other things remaining the same, the higher the level of Canadian real GDP, the larger is the quantity of Canadian imports. For example, the long period of sustained income growth in Canada between 1983 and 1987 brought a huge increase in Canadian imports.

Also, and again other things remaining the same, the higher the prices of Canadian-made goods and services relative to the prices of similar foreign-made goods and services, the larger is the quantity of Canadian imports.

Finally, and again other things remaining the same, the higher the value of the Canadian dollar against other currencies, the larger is the quantity of Canadian imports.

During the mid-1980s, rapid real GDP growth in Canada brought an increase in imports. But the increase was smaller than it otherwise would have been because of a fall in the value of the Canadian dollar against other currencies. The lower dollar made foreign goods and services more expensive and so slowed down, to some degree, the growth of Canadian imports.

Net Export Function

The **net export function** is the relationship between net exports and Canadian real GDP, holding constant real GDP in the rest of the world, prices, and the exchange rate. The net export function can also be described by a net export schedule, which lists the level of net exports at each level of real GDP, with everything else held constant. The table in Fig. 25.9 gives an example of a net export schedule.

In the table, exports are a constant $120 billion; they do not depend on Canadian real GDP. Imports

FIGURE 25.9

Net Export Function and Net Export Schedule

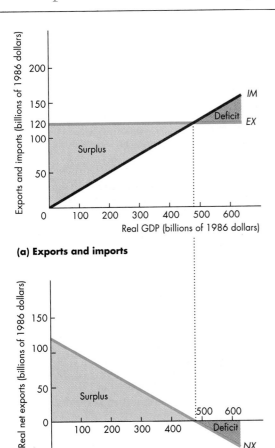

(a) Exports and imports

(b) Net exports

Real GDP (Y)	Exports (EX)	Imports (IM)	Net exports (EX – IM)
	(billions of 1986 dollars)		
0	120	0	120
200	120	50	70
400	120	100	20
600	120	150	–30
800	120	200	–80
1,000	120	250	–130

The net export schedule shows the relationship between net exports and real GDP. Net exports is equal to exports (EX) minus imports (IM). Exports are independent of real GDP, but imports increase as real GDP increases. In the table, imports are 25 percent of real GDP. Net exports decreases as GDP increases.

Part (a) graphs the export and import schedules. Since exports are independent of real GDP, they are graphed as a horizontal line. Since imports rise as real GDP rises, they appear as an upward-sloping line. The distance between the export curve and the import curve represents net exports. Net exports is graphed in part (b) of the figure. The net export function slopes downward because the import curve slopes upward. The real GDP level at which the net export function intersects the horizontal axis in part (b) is the same as that at which the imports curve intersects the exports curve in part (a). That level of real GDP is $480 billion. Below that level of real GDP there is a surplus and above it there is a deficit.

increase by 25¢ for each $1 increase in Canadian real GDP. Net exports, the difference between exports and imports, is shown in the final column of the table. When real GDP is $200 billion, net exports is $70 billion. Net exports decreases as real GDP increases. At a real GDP of $480 billion, net exports is zero; and at real GDP levels higher than that, net exports becomes increasingly negative (imports exceed exports).

Exports and imports are graphed in Fig. 25.9(a) and the net export function is graphed in Fig. 25.9(b). By comparing part (a) and part (b), you can see that when exports exceed imports, net exports is above zero (there is a surplus) and when imports exceed exports, net exports is below zero (there is a deficit). When real GDP is $480 billion, there is a balance between exports and imports.

The position of the net export function depends on real GDP in the rest of the world and on prices of Canadian-made goods and services compared with the prices of those goods and services made in the rest of the world. If real GDP in the rest of the world increases, the net export function shifts upward. If Canadian-made goods and services become cheap relative to goods and services made in the rest of the world, the net export function also shifts upward.

We've now studied the main influences on consumption expenditure, investment, and net exports. Our next task is to see how these components of aggregate expenditure interact with each other and with government purchases of goods and services to determine aggregate expenditure. Our starting point is to establish a relationship between aggregate planned expenditure and real GDP.

Aggregate Expenditure and Real GDP

There is a relationship between aggregate planned expenditure and real GDP. **Aggregate planned expenditure** is the expenditure that economic agents (households, firms, governments, and foreigners) plan to undertake in given circumstances. Aggregate planned expenditure is not necessarily equal to actual aggregate expenditure. We'll see how these two expenditure concepts—planned and actual—differ from each other later in this chapter.

The relationship between aggregate planned expenditure and real GDP may be described by either an aggregate expenditure schedule or an aggregate expenditure curve. The **aggregate expenditure schedule** lists the level of aggregate planned expenditure generated at each level of real GDP. The **aggregate expenditure curve** is a graph of the aggregate expenditure schedule.

Aggregate Expenditure Schedule

The aggregate expenditure schedule is set out in the table in Fig. 25.10. The table shows aggregate planned expenditure as well as its components. To work out the level of aggregate planned expenditure at a given real GDP, we add the various components together. The first column of the table shows real GDP and the second column shows the consumption expenditure generated by each level of real GDP. When real GDP is $200 billion, consumption

expenditure is $170 billion. A $1 increase in real GDP generates a 65¢ increase in consumption expenditure. So, when real GDP increases by $200 to $400 billion, consumption expenditure increases by $130 billion to $300 billion.

The next two columns show investment and government purchases of goods and services. Recall that investment depends on the real interest rate and the state of profit expectations. Suppose that those factors are constant and, at a given point in time, generate a level of investment of $100 billion. This investment level is independent of real GDP. Government purchases of goods and services are also fixed. Their value is also $100 billion.

The next three columns show exports, imports, and net exports. Exports are influenced by events in the rest of the world, by our prices compared with prices in other countries, and by the foreign exchange value of our dollar. They are not directly affected by the level of real GDP. In the table, exports appear as a constant $120 billion. In contrast, imports *do* increase as real GDP increases. In the table, a $1 increase in real GDP generates a 25¢ increase in imports. Net exports—exports minus imports—also varies as real GDP varies, decreasing by 25¢ for each $1 increase in real GDP.

The final column of the table shows aggregate planned expenditure. This amount is the sum of planned consumption expenditure, planned investment, planned government purchases of goods and services, and planned net exports.

Aggregate Expenditure Curve

The aggregate expenditure curve appears in the diagram in Fig. 25.10. Real GDP is shown on the horizontal axis and aggregate planned expenditure on the vertical axis. The aggregate expenditure curve is the red line labelled *AE*. Points *a* through *f* on that curve correspond to the rows in the table. The *AE* curve is a graph of the last column, "Aggregate planned expenditure," plotted against real GDP.

The figure also shows the components of aggregate expenditure. The constant components—investment, government purchases of goods and services, and exports—are indicated by the horizontal lines in the figure. Consumption is the vertical gap between the line labelled $I + G + EX + C$ and that labelled $I + G + EX$.

FIGURE 25.10

The Aggregate Expenditure Curve and Aggregate Expenditure Schedule

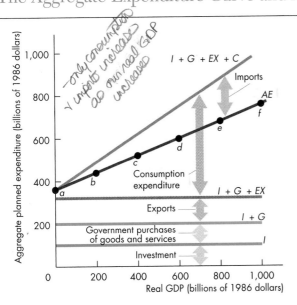

The relationship between aggregate planned expenditure and real GDP may be described by an aggregate expenditure schedule (as shown in the table) or an aggregate expenditure curve (as shown in the diagram). Aggregate planned expenditure is calculated as the sum of planned consumption expenditure, investment, government purchases of goods and services, and net exports. For example, in row *b* of the table, if real GDP is $200 billion, aggregate planned consumption is $170 billion, planned investment is $100 billion, planned government purchases of goods and services are $100 billion, and planned net exports is $70 billion. Thus when real GDP is $200 billion, aggregate planned expenditure is $440 billion ($170 + $100 + $100 + $70). The expenditure plans are graphed in the figure as the aggregate expenditure curve *AE*, the line *af*.

	Real GDP (Y)	Consumption expenditure (C)	Investment (I)	Government purchases (G)	Exports (EX)	Imports (IM)	Net exports (NX = EX − IM)	Aggregate planned expenditure (E = C + I + G + NX)
				(billions of 1986 dollars)				
a	0	40	100	100	120	0	120	360
b	200	170	100	100	120	50	70	440
c	400	300	100	100	120	100	20	520
d	600	430	100	100	120	150	−30	600
e	800	570	100	100	120	200	−80	680
f	1,000	700	100	100	120	250	−130	760

To calculate the *AE* curve, we subtract imports from the *I* + *G* + *EX* + *C* line. Imports are subtracted because they are not expenditure on Canadian real GDP. The purchase of a new car is part of consumption expenditure, but if that car is a Toyota made in Japan, expenditure on it has to be subtracted from consumption expenditure to find out how much is spent on goods and services produced in Canada—that is, on Canadian real GDP. Money paid to Toyota for car imports from Japan does not add to aggregate expenditure in Canada.

We've now seen how to calculate the aggregate expenditure schedule and the aggregate expenditure curve, and seen that aggregate planned expenditure increases as real GDP increases. This relationship is summarized in the *AE* curve. But what determines the point on the *AE* curve at which the economy operates?

Equilibrium Expenditure

E quilibrium expenditure occurs when aggregate planned expenditure equals real GDP. At levels of real GDP below equilibrium, planned expenditure exceeds real GDP; at levels of real GDP above equilibrium, planned expenditure falls short of real GDP.

To see how equilibrium expenditure is determined, we need to distinguish between actual expenditure and planned expenditure, and understand how actual expenditure, planned expenditure, and real GDP are related.

Actual Expenditure, Planned Expenditure, and Real GDP

Actual aggregate expenditure is always equal to real GDP. (We established this fact in Chapter 23, p. 627.) But *planned* expenditure is not necessarily equal to actual expenditure and, therefore, is not necessarily equal to actual real GDP. How can actual expenditure and planned expenditure differ from each other? Why don't people implement their plans? The reason is that firms may end up with unplanned excess inventories or with an unplanned shortage of inventories. People carry out their consumption expenditure plans, the government implements its planned purchases of goods and services, and net exports is as planned. Firms carry out their plans to invest in buildings, plant, and equipment. One component of investment, however, is the change in firms' inventories of goods that have not yet been sold. Inventories change when aggregate planned expenditure differs from real GDP. If real GDP exceeds planned expenditure, inventories rise, and if real GDP is less than planned expenditure, inventories fall.

When aggregate planned expenditure is equal to aggregate actual expenditure and equal to real GDP, the economy is in an expenditure equilibrium. When aggregate planned expenditure and aggregate actual expenditure are unequal, a process of convergence towards an equilibrium expenditure occurs. Let's examine equilibrium expenditure and the process that brings it about.

When Planned Expenditure Equals Real GDP

The table in Fig. 25.11 shows different levels of real GDP. Against each level of real GDP, the second column shows aggregate planned expenditure. Only when real GDP equals $600 billion is aggregate planned expenditure equal to real GDP. This level of expenditure is the equilibrium expenditure.

The equilibrium is illustrated in Fig. 25.11(a). The aggregate expenditure curve is *AE*. Since aggregate planned expenditure on the vertical axis and real GDP on the horizonal axis are measured in the same units and on the same scale, a 45° line drawn in Fig. 25.11(a) shows all the points at which aggregate planned expenditure equals real GDP. Where the aggregate expenditure curve intersects the 45° line, at point *d*, equilibrium expenditure is determined.

Convergence to Equilibrium You will get a better idea of why point *d* is the equilibrium if you consider what is happening when the economy is not at point *d*. Suppose that real GDP is $200 billion. You can see from Fig. 25.11(a) that in this situation aggregate planned expenditure is $440 billion (point *b*). Thus aggregate planned expenditure is larger than real GDP. If aggregate expenditure is actually $440 billion as planned, then real GDP would also be $440 billion, since every dollar spent by one person is a dollar of income for someone else. But real GDP is $200 billion. How can real GDP be $200 billion if people *plan* to spend $440 billion? The answer is that *actual* spending is less than *planned* spending. If real GDP is $200 billion, the value of production is also $200 billion. The only way that people can buy goods and services worth $440 billion, when the value of production is $200 billion, is if firms' inventories fall by $240 billion (point *b* in Fig. 25.11b). Since changes in inventories are part of investment, actual investment is less than planned investment.

But this is not the end of the story. Firms have target levels for inventories, and when inventories fall below those targets, they increase production to restore inventories to their target levels. To restore their inventories, firms hire additional labour and increase production. Suppose that they increase production in the next period by $200 billion. Real GDP rises by $200 billion to $400 billion. But again, aggregate planned expenditure exceeds real GDP. When real GDP is $400 billion, aggregate planned expenditure is $520 billion (point *c* in Fig. 25.11a). Again, inventories fall, but this time by less than before. With real GDP of $400 billion and planned

FIGURE 25.11

Equilibrium Expenditure and Real GDP

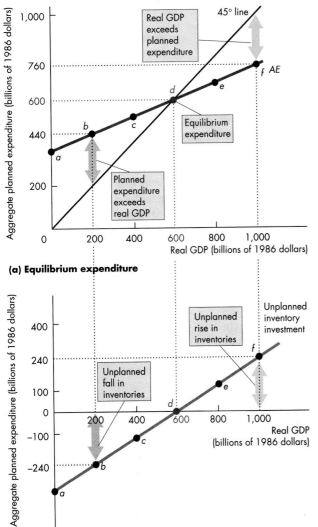

(a) Equilibrium expenditure

(b) Unplanned inventory changes

Real GDP (Y)	Aggregate planned expenditure (E)	Unplanned inventory changes (Y – E)
	(billions of 1986 dollars)	
a 0	360	–360
b 200	440	–240
c 400	520	–120
d 600	600	0
e 800	680	120
f 1,000	760	240

The table shows the aggregate expenditure schedule. When real GDP is $600 billion, aggregate planned expenditure equals real GDP. At real GDP levels below $600 billion, aggregate planned expenditure exceeds real GDP. At real GDP levels above $600 billion, aggregate planned expenditure is less than real GDP.

The diagram illustrates equilibrium expenditure in part (a). The 45° line shows those points at which aggregate planned expenditure equals real GDP. The aggregate expenditure curve is *AE*. Actual aggregate expenditure equals real GDP. Equilibrium expenditure and real GDP are $600 billion. That real GDP level generates planned expenditure that equals real GDP, shown at point *d* in part (a).

The forces bringing the equilibrium about are illustrated in parts (a) and (b). At real GDP levels below $600 billion, aggregate planned expenditure exceeds real GDP and inventories fall—for example, point *b* in both parts of the figure. In such cases, firms increase output to restore their inventories and real GDP rises. At real GDP levels higher than $600 billion, aggregate planned expenditure is less than real GDP and inventories rise—for example, point *f* in both parts of the figure. In such a situation, firms decrease output to work off excess inventories and real GDP falls. Only where the aggregate planned expenditure curve cuts the 45° line is planned expenditure equal to real GDP. This position is the equilibrium. There are no unplanned inventory changes and output remains constant.

expenditure of $520 billion, inventories fall by only $240 billion (point *b* in Fig. 25.11b). Again, firms hire additional labour, and production increases; real GDP increases yet further.

The process that we have just described— planned expenditure exceeds income, inventories fall, and production rises to restore the unplanned

inventory reduction—ends when real GDP has reached $600 billion. At this level of real GDP, there is an equilibrium. There are no unplanned inventory changes, and firms do not change their production.

Next, let's perform a similar experiment, but one starting with a level of real GDP greater than the equilibrium. Suppose that real GDP is $1,000 billion.

At this level, aggregate planned expenditure is $760 billion (point *f* in Fig. 25.11a), $240 billion less than real GDP. With aggregate planned expenditure less than real GDP, inventories rise by $240 billion (point *f* in Fig. 25.11b)—there is unplanned investment. With unsold inventories on their hands, firms cut production. They lay off workers and reduce the amount they pay out in wages; real GDP falls. If they cut production by $200 billion, real GDP falls by this amount to $800 billion. At that level of real GDP, aggregate planned expenditure is $680 billion (point *e* in Fig. 25.11a). Again, there is an unplanned increase in inventories, but it is only $120 billion (point *e* in Fig. 25.11b). Again, firms will cut production and lay off yet more workers, reducing real GDP still further. Real GDP continues to fall whenever unplanned inventories increase. As before, real GDP keeps on changing until it reaches its equilibrium level of $600 billion.

You can see that if real GDP is below equilibrium, aggregate planned expenditure exceeds real GDP, inventories fall, firms increase production to restore their inventories, and real GDP rises. If real GDP is above equilibrium, aggregate planned expenditure is less than real GDP, unsold inventories prompt firms to cut back on production, and real GDP falls.

Only if real GDP equals aggregate planned expenditure are there no unplanned inventory changes and no changes in firms' output plans. In this situation, real GDP remains constant.

REVIEW

E quilibrium expenditure occurs when aggregate planned expenditure equals real GDP. If aggregate planned expenditure exceeds real GDP, inventories fall and firms increase output to replenish inventory levels. Real GDP increases and so does planned expenditure. If aggregate planned expenditure is below real GDP, inventories accumulate and firms cut output to lower inventory levels. Real GDP and aggregate planned expenditure decline. Only when aggregate planned expenditure equals real GDP are there no unplanned changes in inventories and no changes in output. Real GDP remains constant. ◆

Real GDP and the Price Level

W hen firms find unwanted inventories piling up, they cut back on orders and decrease production. They also usually cut prices. Similarly, when firms are having trouble keeping up with sales and their inventories are falling, they increase their orders and step up production, but they also usually increase their prices. So far, we've studied the macroeconomic consequences of firms changing their production levels when their sales change, but we have not looked at the effects of price changes. When firms change their prices, for the economy as a whole the price level changes.

To study the price level, we use the *aggregate demand-aggregate supply model*. We also need to work out the relationship between the aggregate demand-aggregate supply model and the aggregate expenditure model that we've used in this chapter. The key to the relationship between these two models is the distinction between the aggregate *expenditure* curve and the aggregate *demand* curve.

Aggregate Expenditure and Aggregate Demand

The aggregate expenditure curve is the relationship between the aggregate planned expenditure and real GDP, holding all other influences constant. The aggregate demand curve is the relationship between the aggregate quantity of goods and services demanded and the price level, holding all other influences constant. Let's explore the links between these two relationships.

Aggregate Planned Expenditure and the Price Level

At a given price level, there is a given level of autonomous expenditure and a given level of aggregate planned expenditure. But if the price level changes, so does autonomous expenditure. Why? There are three main reasons, and they are explained more fully in Chapter 24. They are

◆ Real money balances effect

◆ Intertemporal substitution effect

◆ International substitution effect

A rise in the price level, other things remaining the same, decreases the quantity of real money. A smaller quantity of real money decreases aggregate planned expenditure—the *real money balances effect*. A rise in the price level, other things remaining the same, makes current goods and services more costly relative to future goods and services, resulting in a delay in purchases—the *intertemporal substitution effect*. A rise in the price level, other things remaining the same, makes Canadian-produced goods less competitive, increasing imports and decreasing exports—the *international substitution effect*.

All these effects of a rise in the price level reduce aggregate planned expenditure at each level of real GDP. As a result, when the price level rises, the aggregate expenditure curve shifts downward. A decrease in the price level has the opposite effect. When the price level falls, the aggregate expenditure curve shifts upward.

Figure 25.12(a) illustrates these effects. When the price level is 130, the aggregate expenditure curve is AE_0, which intersects the 45° line at point b. Equilibrium expenditure and real GDP are $600 billion. If the price level increases to 170, the aggregate expenditure curve shifts downward to AE_1, which intersects the 45° line at point a. Equilibrium expenditure and real GDP are $400 billion. If the price level decreases to 90, the aggregate expenditure curve shifts upward to AE_2, which intersects the 45° line at point c. Equilibrium expenditure and real GDP are $800 billion.

We've just seen that when the price level changes, other things remaining the same, the aggregate expenditure curve shifts and a new expenditure equilibrium arises. But when the price level changes, other things remaining the same, there is a movement along the aggregate demand curve. Figure 25.12(b) illustrates these movements. At a price level of 130, the aggregate quantity of goods and services demanded is $600 billion—point b on the aggregate demand curve AD. If the price level increases to 170, the aggregate quantity of goods and services demanded decreases to $400 billion. There is a movement along the aggregate demand curve to point a. If the price level decreases to 90, the aggregate quantity of goods and services demanded

FIGURE 25.12

Aggregate Demand

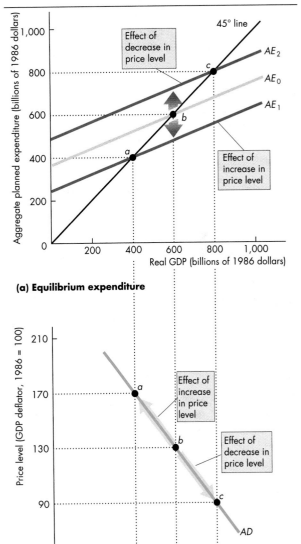

(a) Equilibrium expenditure

(b) Aggregate demand

A change in the price level shifts the aggregate expenditure curve and results in a movement along the aggregate demand curve. For example, when the price level is 130, the *AE* curve is AE_0, and equilibrium expenditure is $600 billion (point b). When the price level rises to 170, the *AE* curve is AE_1, and equilibrium expenditure is $400 billion (point a). When the price level falls to 90, the *AE* curve is AE_2, and the equilibrium is at point c.

Points a, b, and c on the aggregate demand curve correspond to the equilibrium points a, b, and c in part (a).

increases to $800 billion. There is a movement along the aggregate demand curve to point *c*.

Each point on the aggregate demand curve corresponds to an expenditure equilibrium. The expenditure equilibrium points *a*, *b*, and *c* in Fig. 25.12(a) correspond to the points *a*, *b*, and *c* on the aggregate demand curve in Fig. 25.12(b).

◆ ◆ ◆ ◆ In this chapter, we've studied the factors that influence private expenditure decisions, looking at each item of aggregate expenditure—

consumption expenditure, investment, and net exports—in isolation from the others. We've also seen how these private components of expenditure interact with each other and with government purchases of goods and services to determine equilibrium aggregate expenditure and the position of the aggregate demand curve. In the next chapter, we'll study the sources of *changes* in the equilibrium. In particular, we'll see how changes in investment, exports, and government fiscal policy actions can change equilibrium aggregate expenditure and shift the aggregate demand curve.

S U M M A R Y

The Components of Aggregate Expenditure

The components of aggregate expenditure are

◆ Consumption expenditure

◆ Investment

◆ Government purchases of goods and services

◆ Net exports

The main component of aggregate expenditure is consumption expenditure. On the average, 59 percent of total expenditure comes from consumption expenditure. Investment accounts for 17 percent and government purchases of goods and services account for 24 percent of the total. Net exports averages approximately zero.

The components of aggregate expenditure that fluctuate most are investment and net exports. (pp. 682–683)

Consumption Expenditure and Saving

Consumption expenditure is influenced by many factors, but the most important is disposable income. As disposable income increases, so do both consumption expenditure and saving. The relationship between consumption expenditure and disposable income is called the *consumption function*. The relationship between saving and disposable income is called the *saving function*. At low levels of disposable income, consumption expenditure exceeds disposable income, which means that saving is

negative (dissaving occurs). As disposable income increases, consumption expenditure increases, but by less than the increase in disposable income.

The fraction of each additional dollar of disposable income consumed is called the *marginal propensity to consume*. The fraction of each additional dollar of disposable income saved is called the *marginal propensity to save*. All influences on consumption and saving, other than disposable income, shift the consumption and saving functions. The most important of these other influences is expected future income.

Consumption expenditure is a function of real GDP because disposable income and GDP vary together. (pp. 684–692)

Investment

The amount of investment depends on

◆ Real interest rates

◆ Profit expectations

The lower the real interest rate, the greater is the amount of investment. And the higher the expected profit, the greater is the amount of investment.

The main influence on investment demand is fluctuations in profit expectations. Swings in the degree of optimism and pessimism about future profits lead to shifts in the investment demand curve. Swings in profit expectations are associated with business cycle fluctuations and the degree of capacity utilization. When the economy is in an expansion phase and capacity utilization is rising, profit expectations are optimistic and investment is high. When the economy is in a contraction phase and capacity utilization is falling, profit expectations are pessimistic and investment is low. (pp. 692–697)

Government Purchases of Goods and Services

Government purchases are determined by political processes; the amount of government purchases is determined largely independently of the current level of real GDP. (p. 697)

Net Exports

Net exports is the difference between exports and imports. Exports are determined by decisions made in the rest of the world and are influenced by real GDP in the rest of the world, the prices of Canadian-made goods and services relative to the prices of similar goods and services made in other countries, and the foreign exchange rate. Imports are determined by Canadian real GDP, the prices of foreign-made goods and services relative to the prices of goods and services produced in Canada, and the foreign exchange rate.

The net export function shows the relationship between net exports and Canadian real GDP, holding constant all the other influences on exports and imports. (pp. 700–702)

Aggregate Expenditure and Real GDP

Aggregate planned expenditure is the sum of planned consumption expenditure, planned investment, planned government purchases of goods and services, and planned net exports. The relationship between aggregate planned expenditure and real GDP can be represented by the aggregate expenditure schedule and the aggregate expenditure curve. (pp. 702–703)

Equilibrium Expenditure

Equilibrium expenditure occurs when aggregate planned expenditure equals real GDP. At real GDP levels above the equilibrium, aggregate planned expenditure is below real GDP; in such a situation, real GDP falls. At levels of real GDP below the equilibrium, aggregate planned expenditure exceeds real GDP, and real GDP rises. Only when real GDP equals aggregate planned expenditure is real GDP constant and in equilibrium. The main influence bringing real GDP and aggregate planned expenditure into balance is the behaviour of inventories. When aggregate planned expenditure exceeds real GDP, inventories fall. To restore their inventories, firms increase output, and this action increases real GDP. When planned expenditure is below real GDP, inventories accumulate and firms cut back their output. This action lowers the level of real GDP. Only when there are no unplanned inventory changes do firms keep output constant so that real GDP remains constant. (pp. 704–706)

Real GDP and the Price Level

The aggregate demand curve is the relationship between the quantity of real GDP demanded and the price level, other things remaining the same. A change in the price level brings a movement along the aggregate demand curve. The aggregate expenditure curve is the relationship between aggregate planned expenditure and real GDP, other things remaining the same. At a given price level and a given level of real GDP, there is a given aggregate expenditure curve. A change in the price level changes autonomous expenditure and shifts the aggregate expenditure curve. Thus a movement along the aggregate demand curve is associated with a shift in the aggregate expenditure curve. (pp. 706–708)

KEY ELEMENTS

Key Terms

Aggregate expenditure curve, 702
Aggregate expenditure schedule, 702
Aggregate planned expenditure, 702
Average propensity to consume, 688
Average propensity to save, 688
Consumption function, 684
Dissaving, 684
Disposable income, 684
Equilibrium expenditure, 704
Investment demand, 694
Investment demand curve, 694
Investment demand schedule, 694
Marginal propensity to consume, 688
Marginal propensity to consume out of real GDP, 691
Marginal propensity to save, 688
Net export function, 700
Real interest rate, 692
Saving function, 684

Key Figures and Tables

Figure 25.3   The Polonius Household's Consumption Function and Saving Function, 685
Figure 25.4   The Canadian Consumption Function, 691
Figure 25.6   Investment Demand Curves and Investment Demand Schedules, 695
Figure 25.10   The Aggregate Expenditure Curve and Aggregate Expenditure Schedule, 703
Figure 25.11   Equilibrium Expenditure and Real GDP, 705
Figure 25.12   Aggregate Demand, 707
Table 25.1   Average and Marginal Propensities to Consume and to Save, 689

REVIEW QUESTIONS

1 What are the components of aggregate expenditure? Which component is the largest? Which components fluctuate the most?

2 What is the consumption function?

3 What is the fundamental determinant of consumption?

4 Distinguish between disposable income and GDP.

5 What is the saving function? What is the relationship between the saving function and the consumption function?

6 What is the meaning of the term *marginal propensity to consume*? Why is it less than one?

7 Explain the relationship between the average propensity to consume and the marginal propensity to consume.

8 Explain the relationship between the marginal propensity to consume and the marginal propensity to save.

9 What determines investment? Why does investment increase as the real interest rate falls?

10 What is the effect of the following on Canadian net exports?

a An increase in Canadian real GDP

b An increase in real GDP in Japan

c A rise in the price of Japanese-made cars with no change in the price of Canadian-made cars

11 What is the aggregate expenditure schedule and aggregate expenditure curve?

12 How is equilibrium expenditure determined? What would happen if aggregate planned expenditure exceeded real GDP?

13 What is the relationship between the aggregate expenditure curve and the aggregate demand curve?

14 The price level changes and everything else is held constant. What happens to the aggregate demand curve and the aggregate expenditure curve?

P R O B L E M S

1 You are given the following information about the Batman family (Batman and Robin):

Disposable income (dollars per year)	Consumption expenditure (dollars per year)
0	5,000
10,000	10,000
20,000	15,000
30,000	20,000
40,000	25,000

a Calculate the Batman family's marginal propensity to consume.

b Calculate the average propensity to consume at each level of disposable income.

c Calculate how much the Batman family saves at each level of disposable income.

d Calculate their marginal propensity to save.

e Calculate their average propensity to save at each level of disposable income.

f Draw a diagram of the consumption function. Calculate its slope.

g Over what range of income does the Batman family dissave?

2 A car assembly plant can be built for $10 million, and it will have a life of three years. At the end of three years, the plant will have a scrap value of $1 million. The firm will have to hire labour at a cost of $1.5 million a year and will have to buy parts and fuel costing another $1.5 million. If the firm builds the plant, it will be able to produce cars that will sell for $7.5 million each year. Will it pay the firm to invest in this new production line at the following interest rates?

a 2 percent a year

b 5 percent a year

c 10 percent a year

3 You are given the following information about the economy of Dreamland. When real GDP is $100 billion, consumption expenditure is $80 billion, and when real GDP is $200 billion, consumption expenditure is $140 billion. Calculate the marginal propensity to consume out of real GDP.

4 You are given the following information about the economy of Happy Isle. When disposable income is zero, consumption is $80 billion. The marginal propensity to consume is 0.75. Investment is $400 billion; government purchases of goods and services are $600 billion; taxes are a constant $500 billion and do not vary as income varies. At the expenditure equilibrium, calculate

a Real GDP

b Consumption expenditure

c Saving

d The average and marginal propensities to consume

e The average and marginal propensities to save

5 You are given the following information about the economy of Zeeland. Autonomous consumption expenditure is $100 billion and the marginal propensity to consume is 0.9. Investment is $460 billion, government purchases of goods and services are $400 billion, taxes are a constant $400 billion—they do not vary with income. Exports are $350 billion and imports are 10 percent of real GDP. Suppose that the price level in the economy of Zeeland is 100. Find one point on Zeeland's aggregate demand curve.

CHAPTER 26

EXPENDITURE FLUCTUATIONS AND FISCAL POLICY

After studying this chapter, you will be able to

◆ Explain why a change in investment or exports has a multiplier effect on aggregate expenditure

◆ Define and calculate the multiplier

◆ Explain why a change in government purchases of goods and services has a multiplier effect on aggregate expenditure

◆ Explain why a change in taxes or transfer payments has a multiplier effect on aggregate expenditure

◆ Explain how the government might use fiscal policy in an attempt to stabilize aggregate expenditure

N TORONTO'S EXHIBITION STADIUM, BRYAN ADAMS BREATHES

into a microphone at a barely audible whisper.

Moving to a louder passage, he increases the volume

of his voice and now, through the magic of electron-

ic amplification, booms across the stadium, drown-

ing out every other sound. ◆ ◆ Gary Filmon, the

premier of Manitoba, is being driven to a business

meeting along one of Winnipeg's less well-repaired highways. (There are some

pretty badly potholed highways in Winnipeg, especially after the thaw.) The car's

wheels are bouncing and vibrating over some of the worst highway in the nation,

but its passengers are completely undisturbed, and notes are being written with-

out a ripple, thanks to the car's efficient shock absorbers. ◆ ◆ Investment

and exports fluctuate like the volume of Bryan

Adams' voice and the uneven surface of a Winnipeg

highway. How does the economy react to those fluc-

tuations? Does it react like Gary Filmon's limousine,

Economic Amplifier or Shock Absorber?

absorbing the shocks and providing a smooth ride for the economy's passengers?

Or does it behave like Bryan Adams' amplifier, blowing up the fluctuations and

spreading them out to affect the many millions of participants in an economic

rock concert? ◆ ◆ Is the economic machine built to a design that we simply

have to live with, or can we modify it, changing its amplification and shock-

absorbing powers? And can the government operate the economic machine in a

way that gives us all a smoother ride?

◆ ◆ ◆ ◆ We are now going to explore these questions. We are also going to

discover how the government can try to smooth out the economy by varying its

purchases of goods and services and by varying tax rates.

Expenditure Multipliers

In Chapter 25, we discovered what determines equilibrium expenditure. We're now going to see what happens to equilibrium expenditure when there is a *change* in investment, exports, or government purchases of goods and services. To study the effects of such changes, we classify the components of aggregate expenditure into two groups:

◆ Autonomous expenditure

◆ Induced expenditure

Autonomous Expenditure

Autonomous expenditure is the part of aggregate planned expenditure that is not influenced by real GDP. It is the amount of aggregate planned expenditure when real GDP is zero, and it is shown in row *a* of the table in Fig. 26.1. The components of autonomous expenditure are autonomous consumption expenditure, investment, government purchases of goods and services, and exports. In the table, autonomous consumption expenditure is $40 billion, investment is $100 billion, government purchases are $100 billion, and exports are $120 billion. The sum of these items is autonomous expenditure, and it is $360 billion.

Autonomous expenditure is illustrated in both parts of Fig. 26.1 as the point at which the *AE* curve touches the vertical axis—the level of aggregate planned expenditure when real GDP is zero. In part (b), autonomous expenditure is highlighted by the blue arrow.

Induced Expenditure

Induced expenditure is the part of aggregate planned expenditure that varies as real GDP varies. Induced expenditure equals induced consumption expenditure minus imports. For example, in the table in Fig. 26.1, when real GDP increases from zero (row *a*) to $800 billion (row *e*), an increase of $800 billion, consumption expenditure increases

from $40 billion to $560 billion, an increase of $520 billion. This is induced consumption expenditure. The $800 billion increase in real GDP increases imports by $200 billion. So induced expenditure is $320 billion—$520 billion of induced consumption expenditure minus $200 billion of induced imports.

Induced expenditure is illustrated in both parts of Fig. 26.1. In part (a), induced consumption expenditure is shown by the red arrow and imports are shown by the purple arrow. In part (b), induced expenditure is highlighted by the orange arrow.

The Marginal Propensity to Buy Domestic Goods and Services

The **marginal propensity to buy domestic goods and services** is the marginal propensity to consume out of real GDP minus the marginal propensity to import. The *marginal propensity to consume out of real GDP* (defined in Chapter 25) is the fraction of the last dollar of real GDP consumed and is equal to the change in consumption expenditure divided by the change in real GDP. The **marginal propensity to import** is the fraction of the last dollar of real GDP spent on imports and is equal to the change in imports divided by the change in real GDP.

In Fig. 26.1, when real GDP increases from zero (row *a*) to $200 billion (row *b*), consumption expenditure increases from $40 billion to $170 billion, an increase of $130 billion. So the marginal propensity to consume out of real GDP is $130 billion divided by $200 billion and is 0.65. The same increase in real GDP induces an increase in imports from zero to $50 billion. So the marginal propensity to import is $50 billion divided by $200 billion—that is, 0.25. The marginal propensity to buy domestic goods and services is 0.65 minus 0.25, which equals 0.4.

The marginal propensity to buy domestic goods and services is also equal to the slope of the aggregate expenditure curve. You can check this by noticing that when real GDP increases from zero to $200 billion, aggregate planned expenditure increases from $360 billion to $440 billion, an increase of $80 billion. The slope of the aggregate expenditure curve equals the increase in aggregate planned expenditure divided by the increase in real GDP—$80 billion divided by $200 billion, which equals 0.4. This value is the same as the marginal propensity to consume out of real GDP minus the marginal propensity to import that you have just calculated.

FIGURE 26.1

Aggregate Expenditure

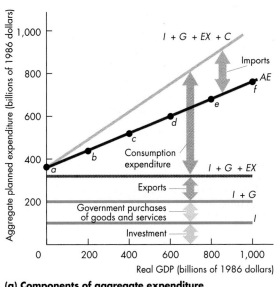

(a) Components of aggregate expenditure

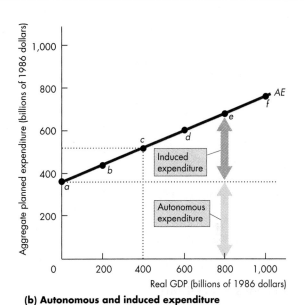

(b) Autonomous and induced expenditure

		Planned Expenditure						
	Real GDP (Y)	Consumption expenditure (C)	Investment (I)	Government purchases (G)	Exports (EX)	Imports (IM)	Net exports (NX = EX − IM)	Aggregate planned expenditure (E = C + I + G + NX)
				(billions of 1986 dollars)				
a	0	40	100	100	120	0	120	360
b	200	170	100	100	120	50	70	440
c	400	300	100	100	120	100	20	520
d	600	430	100	100	120	150	−30	600
e	800	560	100	100	120	200	−80	680
f	1,000	690	100	100	120	250	−130	760

In the table, autonomous expenditure, the amount of aggregate planned expenditure when real GDP is zero, is $360 billion. In the figure, autonomous expenditure is the sum of investment, government purchases of goods and services, exports, and autonomous consumption expenditure. It is the point at which the *AE* curve touches the vertical axis. Autonomous expenditure is shown by the blue line in part (a), and

its magnitude is highlighted by the blue arrow in part (b). Induced expenditure is equal to induced consumption expenditure minus imports. It increases as real GDP increases. In part (a), induced consumption expenditure is shown by the red arrow and imports by the purple arrow. In part (b), induced expenditure is highlighted by the orange arrow.

A Change in Autonomous Expenditure

There are many possible sources of a change in autonomous expenditure. A fall in the real interest rate might induce firms to increase their planned investment. A wave of innovation, such as occurred with the spread of computers in the 1980s, might increase expected future profits and lead firms to increase their planned investment. Stiff competition in the auto industry from Japanese and European imports might force General Motors, Ford, and Chrysler to increase their investment in robotic assembly lines. An economic boom in Western Europe and Japan might lead to a large increase in their expenditure on Canadian-produced goods and services—on Canadian exports. A worsening of international relations might lead the Canadian government to increase its expenditure on armaments—an increase in government purchases of goods and services. These are all examples of increases in autonomous expenditure. What are the effects of such increases on aggregate planned expenditure? And do increases in autonomous expenditure affect consumers? Will they plan to increase their consumption expenditure? Let's answer these questions.

Aggregate planned expenditure is set out in the table in Fig. 26.2. Autonomous expenditure initially is $360 billion. Each $1 billion increase in real GDP induces an increase in aggregate expenditure of $0.4 billion. Adding induced expenditure and autonomous expenditure together gives aggregate planned expenditure. This aggregate expenditure schedule is shown in the figure as the aggregate expenditure curve AE_0. Initially, equilibrium occurs when real GDP is $600 billion. You can see this equilibrium in row d of the table, and in the figure where the curve AE_0 intersects the 45° line at the point marked d.

Now suppose that autonomous expenditure increases by $120 billion to $480 billion. What is the new equilibrium? The answer is worked out in the final two columns of the table in Fig. 26.2. When the new level of autonomous expenditure is added to induced expenditure, aggregate planned expenditure increases by $120 billion at each level of real GDP. The new aggregate expenditure curve is AE_1. The new equilibrium, highlighted in the table (row e'), occurs where AE_1 intersects the 45° line, and is at $800 billion (point e'). At this level of real GDP, aggregate planned expenditure is equal to real GDP.

Autonomous expenditure is $480 billion and induced expenditure is $320 billion.

The Multiplier Effect

Notice in Fig. 26.2 that an increase in autonomous expenditure of $120 billion increases real GDP by $200 billion. That is, the change in autonomous expenditure leads, like Bryan Adams' music-making equipment, to an amplified change in real GDP. This is the *multiplier effect*—real GDP increases by *more than* the increase in autonomous expenditure. An increase in autonomous expenditure of $120 billion initially increases aggregate expenditure and real GDP by $120 billion. But the increase in real GDP *induces* a further increase in aggregate expenditure—an increase in consumption expenditure minus imports. Aggregate expenditure and real GDP increase by the sum of the initial increase in autonomous expenditure and the increase in induced expenditure. In this example, induced expenditure increases by $80 billion, so real GDP increases by $200 billion.

Although we have just analysed the effects of an *increase* in autonomous expenditure, the same analysis applies to a decrease in autonomous expenditure. If autonomous expenditure is initially $480 billion, the initial equilibrium real GDP is $800 billion. If, in that situation, there is a cut in government purchases, exports, or investment of $120 billion, then the aggregate expenditure curve shifts downward by $120 billion to AE_0. Equilibrium real GDP decreases from $800 billion to $600 billion. The decrease in real GDP is larger than the decrease in autonomous expenditure.

We have seen that a change in autonomous expenditure has a multiplier effect on real GDP. But how big is the multiplier effect?

The Size of the Multiplier

Suppose that the economy has been in a recession. But profit prospects start to look better and firms are making plans for large increases in investment. The world economy is also heading towards recovery, and exports are rising. The question on everyone's lips is: how strong will the recovery be? This is a hard question to answer. But an important ingredient in the answer is working out the size of the multiplier.

FIGURE 26.2

An Increase in Autonomous Expenditure

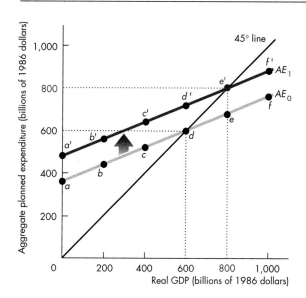

An increase in autonomous expenditure from $360 billion to $480 billion increases aggregate planned expenditure at each level of real GDP by $120 billion. As shown in the table, the initial equilibrium expenditure of $600 billion is no longer the equilibrium. At a real GDP of $600 billion, aggregate planned expenditure is now $720 billion. The new equilibrium expenditure is $800 billion, where aggregate planned expenditure equals real GDP. The increase in real GDP is larger than the increase in autonomous expenditure.

The figure illustrates the effect of the increase in autonomous expenditure. At each level of real GDP, aggregate planned expenditure is $120 billion higher than before. The aggregate planned expenditure curve shifts upward from AE_0 to AE_1—a parallel shift. The new AE curve intersects the 45° line at e' where real GDP is $800 billion—the new equilibrium.

Real GDP (Y)	Induced expenditure (N)		Original expenditure				New expenditure	
			Autonomous expenditure (A_0)	Aggregate planned expenditure (AE_0)			Autonomous expenditure (A_1)	Aggregate planned expenditure (AE_1)
				(billions of 1986 dollars)				
0	0	a	360	360		a'	480	480
200	80	b	360	440		b'	480	560
400	160	c	360	520		c'	480	640
600	240	d	360	600		d'	480	720
800	320	e	360	680		e'	480	800
1,000	400	f	360	760		f'	480	880

The **autonomous expenditure multiplier** (often abbreviated to simply the **multiplier**) is the amount by which a change in autonomous expenditure is multiplied to determine the change in equilibrium expenditure that it generates. To calculate the multiplier, we divide the change in equilibrium real GDP by the change in autonomous expenditure. Let's calculate the multiplier for the example in Fig.

26.3(a). The economy has a real GDP of $600 billion. Autonomous expenditure increases from $360 billion to $480 billion, an increase of $120 billion, and equilibrium real GDP increases from $600 billion to $800 billion, an increase of $200 billion. That is,

◆ Autonomous expenditure increases by $120 billion.

◆ Real GDP increases by $200 billion.

The multiplier is

$$\text{Multiplier} = \frac{\text{Change in equilibrium real GDP}}{\text{Change in autonomous expenditure}}$$

$$= \frac{\$200 \text{ billion}}{\$120 \text{ billion}}$$

$$= 1.67.$$

Thus a change in autonomous expenditure of $1 billion produces a change in equilibrium real GDP of $1.67 billion.

Next, look at Fig. 26.3(b). The economy has a real GDP of $400 billion. But now, autonomous expenditure increases from $120 to $240 billion, and equilibrium real GDP increases from $400 billion to $800 billion. That is,

◆ Autonomous expenditure increases by $120 billion.

◆ Real GDP increases by $400 billion.

The multiplier is

$$\text{Multiplier} = \frac{\text{Change in equilibrium real GDP}}{\text{Change in autonomous expenditure}}$$

$$= \frac{\$400 \text{ billion}}{\$120 \text{ billion}}$$

$$= 3.33.$$

Thus a change in autonomous expenditure of $1 billion produces a change in equilibrium real GDP of $3.33 billion.

FIGURE 26.3

The Multiplier and the Slope of the *AE* Curve

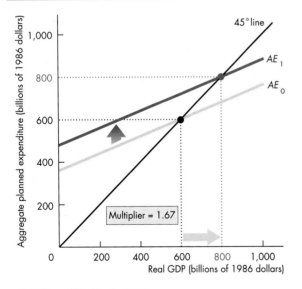

(a) The multiplier is 1.67

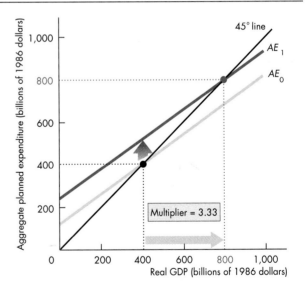

(b) The multiplier is 3.33

The size of the multiplier depends on the marginal propensity to buy domestic goods and services, g, which is also the slope of the AE curve. The multiplier formula, $1/(1 - g)$, tells us the relationship. If the slope of the AE curve (g) is 0.4, the multiplier is 1.67. In this case, an increase of autonomous expenditure of $120 billion shifts the AE curve upward from AE_0 to AE_1 in part (a). Real GDP increases from $600 billion to $800 billion, 1.67 times the increase in autonomous expenditure. If g equals 0.7, the multiplier is 3.33. In this case, a $120 billion increase in autonomous expenditure shifts the aggregate expenditure curve upward from AE_0 to AE_1 in part (b). Real GDP increases from $400 billion to $800 billion, 3.33 times the increase in autonomous expenditure.

The Multiplier and the Marginal Propensity to Buy Domestic Goods and Services

Why is the multiplier in Fig. 26.3(b) bigger than the multiplier in Fig. 26.3(a)? The reason is that the aggregate expenditure curve in part (b) is steeper than that in part (a). Equivalently, the marginal propensity to buy domestic goods and services is larger in part (b) than in part (a). The steeper the AE curve, the larger is the multiplier. In part (a), the slope of the AE curve is 0.4 and the multiplier is

1.67. In part (b), the slope of the AE curve is 0.7 and the multiplier is 3.33.

Multiplier Calculations Table 26.1 shows how to calculate the value of the multiplier. Part (a) introduces some definitions. It starts with the change in real GDP, ΔY. Our objective is to calculate the size of this change when there is a given change in autonomous expenditure, ΔA. In the example in Table 26.1, the change in autonomous expenditure is $120 billion. The slope of the aggregate expenditure curve is the marginal propensity to buy domestic

TABLE 26.1

Calculating the Multiplier

	Symbols and Formulas*	Numbers
(a) DEFINITIONS		
Change in real GDP	ΔY	
Change in autonomous expenditure	ΔA	120
Marginal propensity to buy domestic goods and services	g (slope)	0.4
Change in induced expenditure	$\Delta N = g\Delta Y$	$\Delta N = (0.4)\Delta Y$
Change in aggregate planned expenditure	$\Delta E = \Delta A + \Delta N$	
The multiplier (autonomous expenditure multiplier)	$\Delta Y/\Delta A$	
(b) CALCULATIONS		
Aggregate planned expenditure	$E = A + gY$	
Change in AE curve	$\Delta E = \Delta A + g\Delta Y$	$\Delta E = 120 + (0.4)\Delta Y$
Change in equilibrium expenditure	$\Delta E = \Delta Y$	
Replacing ΔE with ΔY	$\Delta Y = \Delta A + g\Delta Y$	$\Delta Y = 120 + (0.4)\Delta Y$
Subtracting $g\Delta Y$ or $(0.4)\Delta Y$ from both sides and factoring ΔY	$\Delta Y(1 - g) = \Delta A$	$\Delta Y(1 - 0.4) = 120$
Dividing both sides by $(1 - g)$ or $(1 - 0.4)$	$\Delta Y = \dfrac{1}{1 - g} \Delta A$	$\Delta Y = \dfrac{1}{1 - 0.4} 120$
		or $\Delta Y = \dfrac{1}{(0.6)} 120$
		or $\Delta Y = 200$
Dividing both sides by ΔA or 120 gives the multiplier	$\dfrac{\Delta Y}{\Delta Y} = \dfrac{1}{1 - g}$	$\dfrac{\Delta Y}{\Delta A} = \dfrac{200}{120} = 1.67$

*The Greek letter (Δ) stands for "change in."

goods and services and equals the marginal propensity to consume minus the marginal propensity to import. Let's call the marginal propensity to buy domestic goods and services g. In Table 26.1, g is equal to 0.4, the same as in Fig. 26.3(a). The change in aggregate planned expenditure (ΔE) is the sum of the change in autonomous expenditure (ΔA) and the change in induced expenditure (ΔN). Finally, the multiplier is defined as

$$\frac{\Delta Y}{\Delta A}.$$

Part (b) of the table sets out the calculations of the change in real GDP and the multiplier. The change in aggregate planned expenditure (ΔE) is equal to the sum of the change in autonomous expenditure (ΔA) and the change in induced expenditure ($g\Delta Y$). In the example, the change in aggregate planned expenditure is equal to $120 billion plus 0.4 of the change in real GDP. Since in equilibrium the change in aggregate planned expenditure is equal to the change in real GDP, the change in real GDP is

$$\Delta Y = \Delta A + g\Delta Y.$$

Using our numbers,

$$\Delta Y = 120 + (0.4)\Delta Y.$$

This equation has just one unknown, ΔY, and we can find its value as shown in the next two rows of the table. Finally, dividing ΔY by ΔA gives the value of the multiplier, which is

$$\text{Multiplier} = \frac{1}{(1-g)}.$$

Because g is a fraction—a number lying between 0 and 1—so $(1-g)$ is also a fraction and the multiplier is greater than 1. In the example, g is 0.4, $(1-g)$ is 0.6, and the multiplier is $1 \div 0.6$, which equals 1.67.

You can see that this formula also works for the multiplier shown in Fig. 26.3(b). In this case, the marginal propensity to buy domestic goods and services is 0.7, g is 0.7, $(1-g)$ is 0.3 and the multiplier is $1 \div 0.3$, which equals 3.33.

Why Is the Multiplier Greater than 1?

The multiplier is greater than 1 because of induced expenditure—an increase in autonomous expendi-

ture *induces* further increases in expenditure. If General Motors spends $10 million on a new car assembly line, aggregate expenditure and real GDP immediately increase by $10 million. But that is not the end of the story. Engineers and construction workers now have more income, and they spend part of the extra income on cars, microwaves, vacations, and a host of other goods and services. Real GDP now rises by the initial $10 million plus the extra expenditure induced by the $10 million increase in income. The producers of cars, microwaves, vacations, and other goods and services now have increased incomes, and they, in turn, also spend part of their increase in income on consumption goods and services. Additional income induces additional expenditure, which creates additional income.

This multiplier process is illustrated in Fig. 26.4. In this example, the marginal propensity to buy domestic goods and services (and the slope of the AE curve) is 0.4 as in Fig. 26.3(a). In round 1, there is an increase in autonomous expenditure of $120 billion. At that stage, there is no change in induced expenditure, so aggregate expenditure and real GDP increase by $120 billion. In round 2, the higher real GDP induces higher consumption expenditure. Since induced expenditure increases by 0.4 times the increase in real GDP, the increase in real GDP of $120 billion induces a further increase in expenditure of $48 billion. This change in induced expenditure, when added to the initial change in autonomous expenditure, results in an increase in aggregate expenditure and real GDP of $168 billion. The round 2 increase in real GDP induces a round 3 increase in expenditure. The process repeats through successive rounds recorded in the table. Each increase in real GDP is 0.4 times the previous increase. The cumulative increase in real GDP gradually approaches $200 billion. After 9 rounds it is within 0.1 of that level.

It appears that the economy does not operate like the shock absorbers on Gary Filmon's car. The economy's potholes and bumps are changes in autonomous expenditure—mainly brought about by changes in investment and exports. These economic potholes and bumps are not smoothed out, but instead are amplified.

FIGURE 26.4
The Multiplier Process

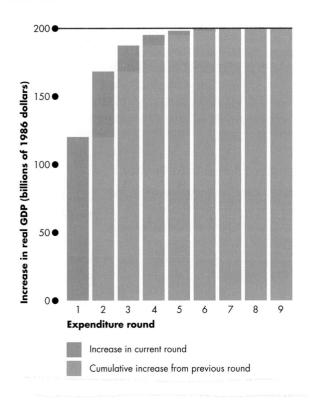

Expenditure round	Increase in aggregate expenditure	Cumulative increase in real GDP
	(billions of 1986 dollars)	
1	120.0	120.0
2	48.0	168.0
3	19.2	187.2
4	7.7	194.9
5	3.1	198.0
6	1.2	199.2
7	0.5	199.7
8	0.2	199.9
9	0.1	200.0

Autonomous expenditure increases in round 1 by $120 billion. Real GDP also increases by the same amount. Each additional dollar of real GDP induces an additional 0.4 of a dollar of aggregate expenditure—the marginal propensity to buy domestic goods and services is 0.4. In round 2, the round 1 increase in real GDP induces an increase in expenditure of $48 billion. At the end of round 2, real GDP has increased by $168 billion. The extra $48 billion of real GDP in round 2 induces a further increase in expenditure of $19.2 billion in round 3. Real GDP increases still further to $187.2 billion. This process continues until real GDP has eventually increased by $200 billion.

REVIEW

Autonomous expenditure is the part of aggregate expenditure that does not respond to changes in real GDP. Induced expenditure is the part of aggregate expenditure that does respond to changes in real GDP. A change in autonomous expenditure changes equilibrium expenditure and real GDP. The magnitude of the change in real GDP is determined by the multiplier. The multiplier, in turn, is determined by the marginal propensity to buy domestic goods and services (the slope of the aggregate expenditure curve), which equals the marginal propensity to consume out of real GDP minus the marginal propensity to import. The larger the marginal propensity to buy domestic goods and services, the larger is the multiplier. The multiplier acts like an amplifier. ◆

One of the components of autonomous expenditure that the multiplier amplifies is government purchases of goods and services. Because of this fact, the government can take advantage of the multiplier and attempt to smooth out fluctuations in aggregate expenditure. It can also vary transfer payments and taxes for this purpose. Let's see how.

Fiscal Policy Multipliers

Fiscal policy is the government's attempt to smooth the fluctuations in aggregate expenditure by varying its purchases of goods and services, transfer payments, and taxes. If the government foresees a decline in investment or exports, it may attempt to offset the effects of the decline by increasing its own purchases of goods and services, increasing transfer payments, or cutting taxes. But the government must figure out the size of the increase in purchases or transfers or the size of the tax cut needed to achieve its goal. To make this calculation, the government needs to know the multiplier effects of its own actions. Let's study the multiplier effects of changes in government purchases, transfer payments, and taxes.

Government Purchases Multiplier

The **government purchases multiplier** is the amount by which a change in government purchases of goods and services is multiplied to determine the change in equilibrium expenditure that it generates. Government purchases of goods and services are one component of autonomous expenditure. A change in government purchases has the same effect on aggregate expenditure as a change in any other component of autonomous expenditure. It sets up a multiplier effect exactly like the multiplier effect of a change in investment or exports. That is,

$$\text{Government purchases multiplier} = \frac{1}{(1-g)}.$$

By varying government purchases to offset a change in investment or exports, the government can try to keep total autonomous expenditure constant (or growing at a steady rate). Because the government purchases multiplier is the same size as the investment and exports multipliers, stabilization of autonomous expenditure can be achieved by increas-

ing government purchases by $1 for each $1 decrease in the other items of autonomous expenditure.

In practice, using variations in government purchases to stabilize aggregate expenditure is often frustrated because the legislative process operates with a long time lag. As a consequence, it is not possible to forecast changes in private expenditure far enough ahead to make this macroeconomic stabilization instrument as effective as it otherwise might be.

A second way in which the government may seek to stabilize aggregate expenditure is by varying transfer payments. Let's see how this type of policy works.

Transfer Payments Multiplier

The **transfer payments multiplier** is the amount by which a change in transfer payments is multiplied to determine the change in equilibrium expenditure that it generates. A change in transfer payments influences aggregate expenditure by changing disposable income. The change in disposable income, in turn, induces a change in purchases of domestic goods and services. This change in purchases is a change in autonomous expenditure, and it has a multiplier effect exactly like that of any other change in autonomous expenditure. But how large is the change in autonomous expenditure? It is equal to the change in transfer payments multiplied by the marginal propensity to buy domestic goods and services. Why? An additional dollar of transfer payments leads to an increase in consumption expenditure of an amount determined by the marginal propensity to consume out of real GDP. But part of the additional consumption expenditure is on imported goods and services. The amount of the additional imports is determined by the marginal propensity to import. So the additional autonomous expenditure is determined by marginal propensity to buy domestic goods and services, g.

So the increase in autonomous expenditure that results from an increase in transfer payments is equal to g times the increase in transfer payments. And the transfer payments multiplier is equal to g times the autonomous expenditure multiplier. That is,

$$\text{Transfer payments multiplier} = \frac{g}{(1-g)}.$$

In our example, the marginal propensity to buy domestic goods and services is 0.4, so the transfer payments multiplier is 0.67 (0.4/0.6 = 0.67).

The use of variations in transfer payments to stabilize the economy has the same problems as the use of variations in government purchases of goods and services. Time lags in the legislative process make it difficult to adjust the scale of transfer payments quickly enough to offset fluctuations in other components of autonomous expenditure.

Tax Multipliers

A third type of fiscal stabilization policy is to vary taxes. The **tax multiplier** is the amount by which a change in taxes is multiplied to determine the change in equilibrium expenditure that it generates. An *increase* in taxes leads to a *decrease* in disposable income and a decrease in expenditure on domestic goods and services—a decrease in autonomous expenditure. The amount by which autonomous expenditure decreases initially is determined by the marginal propensity to buy domestic goods and services. This initial response of autonomous expenditure to an increase in taxes is exactly the same as the response of autonomous expenditure to a decrease in transfer payments. Thus a change in taxes works like a change in transfer payments but in the opposite direction, and the tax multiplier equals the negative of the transfer payments multiplier. Because a tax *increase* leads to a *decrease* in equilibrium expenditure, the tax multiplier is *negative*. It is

$$\text{Tax multiplier} = \frac{-g}{(1-g)}.$$

Figure 26.5 illustrates the multiplier effect of an increase in taxes (or a decrease in transfer payments). Initially, the aggregate expenditure curve is AE_0 and equilibrium expenditure is $600 billion. The marginal propensity to buy domestic goods and services, and the slope of the aggregate expenditure curve AE_0, is 0.4. Taxes increase by $120 billion and disposable income falls by that amount. With a marginal propensity to buy domestic goods and services of 0.4, consumption expenditure decreases initially by $48 billion and the aggregate expenditure curve shifts downward by that amount to AE_1. Equilibrium expenditure and real GDP fall by $80 billion to $520 billion. The tax multiplier is −0.67.

Here, we've studied the effects of tax changes through their effects on disposable income and

FIGURE 26.5

The Tax Multiplier

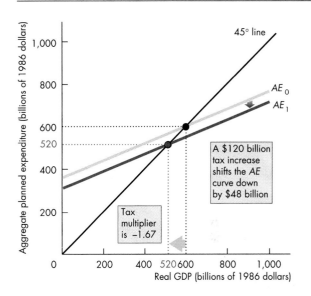

Initially, the aggregate expenditure curve is AE_0, and equilibrium expenditure is $600 billion. The marginal propensity to buy domestic goods and services is 0.4. Taxes are increased by $120 billion, so autonomous expenditure falls by $48 billion and the aggregate expenditure curve shifts downward by this amount to AE_1. Equilibrium expenditure and real GDP decrease by $80 billion to $520 billion. The tax multiplier is −0.67.

consumption. But tax cuts can also work to stimulate the economy by providing stronger investment incentives. This possible effect of a tax change is explained in Reading Between the Lines on pp. 728–729.

Balanced Budget Multiplier

A balanced budget fiscal policy action is one that keeps the government budget deficit or surplus unchanged—both government purchases and taxes change by the same amount. The **balanced budget multiplier** is the amount by which a change in government purchases of goods and services is multiplied to determine the change in equilibrium expenditure when taxes are changed by the same amount as the change in government purchases. What is the multiplier effect of this fiscal policy action?

To find out, we must combine the two multipliers that we have just worked out. We've seen that those two separate multipliers are

$$\text{Government purchases multiplier} = \frac{1}{(1-g)}$$

$$\text{Tax multiplier} = \frac{-g}{(1-g)}.$$

Adding these two multipliers together gives the balanced budget multiplier, which is

$$\text{Balanced budget multiplier} = \frac{(1-g)}{(1-g)}$$

$$= 1.$$

Figure 26.6 illustrates the balanced budget multiplier. Initially, the aggregate expenditure curve is AE_0 and real GDP is $600 billion. A $120 billion increase in taxes decreases aggregate planned expenditure by $48 billion and shifts the aggregate expenditure curve downward to AE_0'. A $120 billion increase in government purchases increases aggregate planned expenditure by the entire $120 billion and shifts the aggregate expenditure curve upward to AE_1. The net shift in the aggregate expenditure curve is upward by $72 billion (120 billion − 48 billion). The new equilibrium occurs at the intersection of AE_1 and the 45° line (highlighted by the red dot). Real GDP increases by $72 billion times the autonomous expenditure multiplier of 1.67, or $120 billion. But this amount is the same as the increase in government purchases and taxes. So the balanced budget multiplier is 1.

The balanced budget multiplier is important because it means that the government does not have to unbalance its budget and run a deficit in order to stimulate aggregate demand.

FIGURE 26.6

The Balanced Budget Multiplier ◆

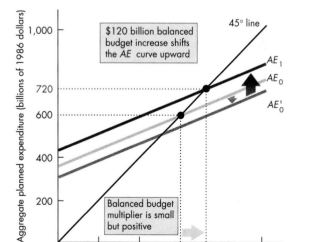

Initially, the aggregate expenditure curve is AE_0. The government increases both taxes and purchases of goods and services by $120 billion. The $120 billion tax increase shifts the aggregate expenditure curve downward by $48 billion to AE_0'. The $120 billion increase in government purchases shifts the aggregate expenditure curve upward by the entire $120 billion to AE_1. Real GDP increases by $120 billion—the balanced budget multiplier is 1.

REVIEW

T he government purchases multiplier is equal to the autonomous expenditure multiplier. By varying its purchases of goods and services, the government can try to offset fluctuations in investment and exports. The transfer payments multiplier is equal to the marginal propensity to buy domestic goods and services multiplied by the government purchases multiplier. A change in transfer payments works through a change in disposable income. Part of the change in disposable income is spent on domestic goods and services, part is saved, and part is spent on imports. Only the part that is spent on domestic goods and services, determined by the marginal propensity to buy domestic goods and services, has a multiplier effect. ◆ ◆ The tax multiplier has the same magnitude as the transfer payments multiplier but it is negative—a tax *increase* leads to a *decrease* in equilibrium expenditure. An equal change in both purchases of goods and services and taxes has a balanced budget multiplier effect on real GDP. The balanced budget multiplier is 1. This means that the government can stimulate aggregate demand without unbalancing the budget. In practice, fiscal actions are difficult to use to stabilize the economy because of time lags in the legislative process. ◆

Automatic Stabilizers

Income taxes and transfer payments act as automatic stabilizers. An **automatic stabilizer** is a mechanism that decreases the fluctuations in *aggregate* expenditure resulting from fluctuations in a *component* of aggregate expenditure. The automatic stabilizing effects of income taxes and transfer payments mean that they act like an economic shock absorber, making the aggregate effects of fluctuations in investment and exports smaller than they otherwise would be.

The scale of income taxes minus transfer payments is determined by the marginal tax rate. The **marginal tax rate** is the fraction of the last dollar of income paid to the government in net taxes (taxes minus transfer payments).

The higher the marginal tax rate, the larger is the proportion of the last dollar of real GDP that is paid to the government. And the larger proportion of the last dollar of real GDP paid to the government, the smaller is the marginal propensity to buy domestic goods and services.

To see how income taxes and transfer payments act as a shock absorber, let's see how a change in investment or exports affects equilibrium expenditure in two economies: in the first economy there are no income taxes and transfer payments, and in the second there are income taxes and transfer payments similar to those in Canada.

No Income Taxes and Transfer Payments   An economy with no taxes and transfer payments has a high marginal propensity to buy domestic goods and services. Suppose that the marginal propensity to buy domestic goods and services is 0.9. What is the size of the multiplier in this case? You can answer by using the formula

$$\text{Multiplier} = \frac{1}{(1-g)}.$$

The value of g is 0.9, so the multiplier is 10. In this economy, a \$1 billion change in autonomous expenditure produces a \$10 billion change in equilibrium expenditure. This economy has a strong amplifier.

Income Taxes and Transfer Payments   Contrast the economy we have just described with one that has income taxes and transfer payments and, therefore, a lower marginal propensity to buy domestic goods and services, g. Suppose that g is 0.4. Then the

multiplier is 1.67. The economy still amplifies shocks from changes in exports and investment, but on a smaller scale than the economy with no taxes and transfer payments. Thus to some degree, taxes and transfer payments absorb the shocks of the fluctuations in autonomous expenditure. The higher the marginal tax rate, the greater is the extent to which autonomous expenditure shocks are absorbed.

The existence of taxes and transfer payments helps the shock-absorbing capacities of the economy. They don't produce the economic equivalent of the suspension of a Lincoln Continental, but they do produce the economic equivalent of something better than the springs of a stagecoach. As the economy fluctuates, the government's budget fluctuates, absorbing some of the shocks, changing taxes and transfer payments, and smoothing the fluctuations in disposable income and aggregate expenditure.

Next, let's look at the effects of automatic stabilizers on the government's budget and its deficit or surplus.

Automatic Stabilizers and the Government Budget

Because taxes and transfer payments fluctuate with real GDP, so does the government's deficit. Figure 26.7 shows how. The level of government purchases is independent of the level of real GDP. In the figure, it is fixed at \$100 billion—shown by the horizontal red line. Taxes net of transfer payments increase as real GDP increases. In the figure, they are shown by the upward-sloping blue line. There is a particular level of real GDP at which the government's budget is balanced—the deficit is zero. In the figure, that level of real GDP is \$600 billion. When real GDP is below \$600 billion, there is a deficit. When real GDP is above \$600 billion, there is a surplus.

As investment and exports fluctuate, bringing fluctuations in real GDP, taxes and the deficit also fluctuate. For example, an increase in investment increases real GDP, increases taxes, and reduces the deficit (or creates a surplus). The higher taxes act as an automatic stabilizer. They decrease disposable income and induce a decrease in consumption expenditure. This decrease dampens the effects of the initial increase in investment and moderates the increase in aggregate expenditure and real GDP.

Conversely, when a decrease in investment is pushing the economy into recession, taxes decrease and the deficit increases (or the surplus decreases).

FIGURE 26.7

The Government Budget

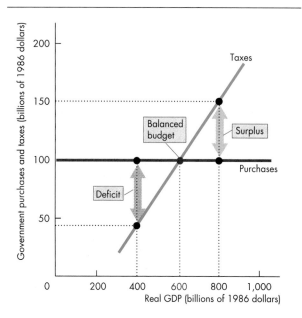

Government purchases (the red line) are independent of the level of real GDP, but income taxes (the blue line) increase as real GDP increases. When real GDP is $600 billion, the government's budget is balanced. When real GDP is below $600 billion, there is a deficit, and when real GDP is above $600 billion, there is a surplus. Fluctuations in taxes act as an automatic stabilizer when the economy is hit by changes in autonomous expenditure.

The lower taxes act as an automatic stabilizer. They limit the fall in disposable income and moderate the extent of the decline in aggregate expenditure and real GDP.

R E V I E W

T he presence of taxes and transfer payments reduces the value of the multiplier and acts as an automatic stabilizer. The higher the marginal tax rate, the smaller are the fluctuations in real GDP resulting from fluctuations in autonomous expenditure. ◆

We have studied the effects of changes in autonomous expenditure and fiscal policy on real GDP, *at a given price level*. We're now going to see how the price level itself responds to changes in autonomous expenditure and fiscal policy. We're also going to see that the autonomous expenditure and fiscal policy multiplier effects on real GDP are smaller when price level changes are taken into account.

Multipliers and the Price Level

T o see how big the multiplier is when we take changes in the price level into account, we use the aggregate demand-aggregate supply model. You learned about the relationship among the aggregate demand curve, the aggregate expenditure curve, and the equilibrium level of aggregate expenditure in Chapter 25. You are now going to use what you learned there to work out what happens to aggregate demand, the price level, and real GDP when fiscal policy changes. We'll start by looking at the effects of a change in fiscal policy on aggregate demand.

Fiscal Policy and Aggregate Demand

When the price level changes, other things remaining the same, the aggregate expenditure curve shifts and there is a movement along the aggregate demand curve. When any other influence on aggregate expenditure changes, both the aggregate expenditure curve and the aggregate demand curve shift. It is these other influences on aggregate expenditure (and sources of shifts in the aggregate expenditure curve) that you've been studying earlier in this chapter—for example, a change in investment, exports, and fiscal policy. Figure 26.8 illustrates these shifts.

Initially, the aggregate expenditure curve is AE_0 in part (a) and the aggregate demand curve is AD_0 in part (b). The price level is 130, real GDP is $600, and the economy is at point a in both parts of the figure. Now suppose that autonomous expenditure

FIGURE 26.8

Changes in Autonomous
Expenditure and
Aggregate Demand

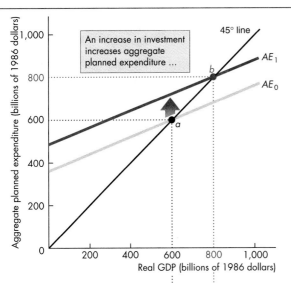

(a) Equilibrium expenditure

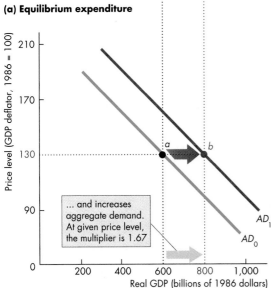

(b) Aggregate demand

The price level is 130. When the aggregate expenditure curve is AE_0 (part a), the aggregate demand curve is AD_0 (part b). An increase in autonomous expenditure shifts the aggregate expenditure upward to AE_1. In the new equilibrium (at b) real GDP is $800 billion. Since the quantity of real GDP demanded at a price level of 130 increases to $800 billion, the aggregate demand curve shifts rightward to AD_1.

increases by $120 billion. (This increase could result from an increase in investment, exports, or government purchases of goods and services, or a tax cut.) At a constant price level of 130, the aggregate expenditure curve shifts upward to AE_1. This curve intersects the 45° line at an equilibrium expenditure of $800 billion (point b). This amount is the aggregate quantity of goods and services demanded at a price level of 130, as shown by point b in part (b). Point b lies on a new aggregate demand curve. The aggregate demand curve has shifted rightward to AD_1.

The distance by which the aggregate demand curve shifted rightward is determined by the autonomous expenditure multiplier. The larger the multiplier, the larger is the shift in the aggregate demand curve resulting from a given change in autonomous expenditure. In this example, a $120 billion increase in autonomous expenditure produces a $200 billion increase in the quantity of real GDP demanded at each price level. The multiplier is 1.67. That is, a $1 billion increase in autonomous expenditure shifts the aggregate demand curve rightward by $1.67 billion.

A decrease in autonomous expenditure shifts the aggregate expenditure curve downward and shifts the aggregate demand curve leftward. You can see these effects by reversing the change that we've just studied. Suppose the economy initially is on aggregate expenditure curve AE_1 and aggregate demand curve AD_1. There is then a decrease in autonomous expenditure and the aggregate expenditure curve shifts downward to AE_0. The quantity of real GDP demanded decreases to $600 billion and the aggregate demand curve shifts leftward to AD_0.

We can summarize what we have just discovered in the following way: an increase in autonomous expenditure arising from some source other than a change in the price level shifts the AE curve upward and shifts the AD curve rightward. The magnitude of the shift of the AD curve is determined by the change in autonomous expenditure and the autonomous expenditure multiplier.

Equilibrium GDP and the Price Level

In Chapter 24, we learned how to determine the equilibrium levels of real GDP and the price level at the intersection point of the aggregate demand and short-run aggregate supply curves. We've now put aggregate demand under a more powerful

The Essence of the Story

THE MONTREAL GAZETTE, APRIL 27, 1993

Tax changes are too late to help business this year

By Jay Bryan

OTTAWA—Among the few tax changes in yesterday's budget were measures designed to make business more competitive by lowering the tax burden on investment.

But a closer look at this package, dubbed "investing in prosperity," reveals an initiative that provides more promises than investment stimulus this year.

The investment package will offer more generous tax treatment to companies that engage in research and development, buy or license technology or invest in their busi-nesses. It will cost the federal treasury $395 million in lost taxes over the next five years.

But in the current year—important since the economy is now struggling—the investment package offers just $17 million in tax cuts. The figure jumps to $84 million in the 1994–95 fiscal year, which begins next April. But by that time, both government and most private-sector economists believe the economy will already have achieved a healthy growth rate....

A tax change in the 1993 budget offered lower taxes to companies that engage in research and development, buy or license technology, or invest in their businesses.

The change will cost the federal treasury $395 million in lost taxes over the five years to 1998.

But the tax cuts in 1993 will be only $17 million. They will rise to $84 million in the 1994–95 fiscal year.

Economists believe the economy will be growing quickly by the time the tax changes are having their full effects.

Background and Analysis

The tax changes discussed in this news article are tiny, even when they begin to have their full effects. To place them in perspective, the full cost of the cuts over five years—$395 million—is 0.05 percent of gross domestic product in one year.

It is unlikely that a tax change of this small magnitude will have an observable effect on investment and real GDP.

Although the effect will be small, we can predict its direction.

The lower tax on investment will increase investment and shift the investment demand curve rightward from ID_0 to ID_1 as shown in part (a) of the figure.

With higher investment, aggregate expenditure increases and the aggregate expenditure curve shifts upward from AE_0 to AE_1 in part (b).

If the news article is correct, other factors will increase investment at the same time that the investment tax cuts are having their maximum effects. If the tax changes were large ones, this outcome could lead to a growth in aggregate demand that is too fast and that rekindles inflation.

But with tax changes of the small magnitude of those described in the article, there is no chance that they could overheat the economy.

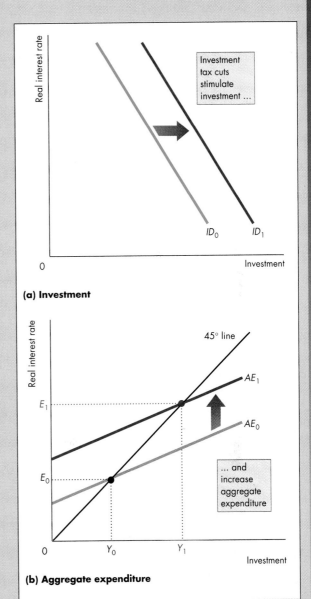

(a) Investment

(b) Aggregate expenditure

microscope and discovered that changes in autonomous expenditure and fiscal policy shift the aggregate demand curve and that the magnitude of the shift depends on the multiplier. But whether a change in autonomous expenditure results ultimately in a change in real GDP or a change in the price level or some combination of the two depends on aggregate supply. We'll look at two cases. First, we'll see what happens in the short run. Then we'll look at the long run.

An Increase in Aggregate Demand in the Short Run

The economy is illustrated in Fig. 26.9. In part (a), the aggregate expenditure curve is AE_0, and equilibrium expenditure and real GDP are $600 billion—point a. In part (b), aggregate demand is AD_0, and the short-run aggregate supply curve is SAS. (Check back to Chapter 24 if you need to refresh your understanding of this curve.) Equilibrium is at point a, where the aggregate demand and short-run aggregate supply curves intersect. The price level is 130 and real GDP is $600 billion.

Now suppose there is a tax cut that increases autonomous expenditure by $120 billion. With the price level held constant at 130, the aggregate expenditure curve shifts upward to AE_1. Equilibrium expenditure and real GDP increase to $800 billion—point b in part (a). In part (b), the aggregate demand curve shifts rightward by $200 billion, from AD_0 to AD_1. But with this new aggregate demand curve, the price level does not remain constant. It increases to 143, as determined by the point of intersection of the short-run aggregate supply curve and the new aggregate demand curve—point c. And real GDP does not increase to $800 billion, but to $733 billion.

At a price level of 143, the aggregate expenditure curve does not remain at AE_1 in part (a). It shifts downward to AE_2, which intersects the 45° line at a level of aggregate expenditure and real GDP of $733 billion (point c).

Taking price level effects into account, the tax cut still has a multiplier effect on real GDP, but the effect is smaller than it would be if the price level remained constant. The steeper the slope of the short-run aggregate supply curve, the larger is the increase in the price level and the smaller is the multiplier effect on real GDP.

An Increase in Aggregate Demand in the Long Run

In the long run, the economy is at full-employment equilibrium and on its long-run aggregate supply

FIGURE 26.9

Fiscal Policy, Real GDP, and the Price Level

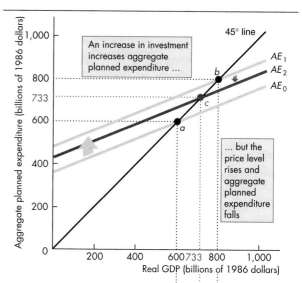

(a) Equilibrium expenditure

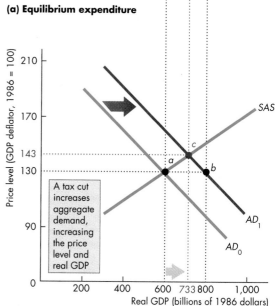

(b) Aggregate demand

A tax cut shifts the AE curve upward from AE_0 to AE_1 (part a). The AD curve shifts from AD_0 to AD_1 (part b). The economy moves from point a to point b (parts a and b), and there is excess demand. The price level rises, and the higher price level shifts the AE curve downward to AE_2. The economy moves to point c in both parts. The steeper the SAS curve, the larger is the effect on the price level change and the smaller is the change in real GDP.

curve. When the economy is at full employment, an increase in aggregate demand has the same initial effect (short-run effect) as we've just worked out, but its long-run effect is different.

To see the long-run effect, suppose that in Fig. 26.9 long-run aggregate supply is $600 billion. When aggregate demand increases, shifting the aggregate demand curve from AD_0 to AD_1, the equilibrium at point c is an above full-employment equilibrium. When the labour force is more than fully employed, there are shortages of labour and wages increase. Higher wages bring higher costs and a decrease in aggregate supply. The result is a further increase in the price level and a decrease in real GDP. Eventually, when wage rates and the price level have increased by the same percentage, real GDP is again at its full-employment level. The multiplier in the long run is zero.

We've now seen how fiscal policy multipliers can be used by the government to influence real GDP and the price level. But so far we have studied model economies. Let's now turn to the real world. How big are the multipliers in the Canadian economy?

The Multiplier in Canada

In the economy we studied earlier in this chapter, each additional dollar of income induces 40¢ of expenditure. At a given price level, the multiplier is 1.67. When induced price level changes are taken into account, the multiplier is smaller than this. But what is the value of the multiplier in the Canadian economy?

The Canadian Multiplier in 1992

In 1992, the marginal propensity to consume in Canada was 0.75 and disposable income was 0.8 of GDP. Putting these two pieces of information together, we can calculate that the marginal propensity to consume out of GDP is 0.6 (0.75 of 0.8 equals 0.6). Imports were 35 percent of GDP. Using this percentage as an estimate of the marginal propensity to import gives a value of 0.35; each additional dollar of GDP induces 35¢ of imports. Subtracting the mar-

ginal propensity to import from the marginal propensity to consume out of GDP gives the marginal propensity to buy domestic goods and services, which is 0.25 (that is, 0.6 minus 0.35). The multiplier is 1.33. That is,

$$\text{The multiplier} = \frac{1}{1 - 0.25} = \frac{1}{0.75} = 1.33.$$

This multiplier formula tells us how far the AD curve shifts when autonomous expenditure changes. But it does not tell us about the effect on real GDP when induced price level changes are taken into account. To calculate such a multiplier, we must use the estimates made by large-scale models of the Canadian economy.

Econometric Models and the Canadian Multiplier

An **econometric model** is a model economy with numerical values for the marginal propensities to consume and import, and for other economic parameters, which are estimated from data for an actual economy. Today, many such models are in use. Most of these models are commercial tools that produce forecasts used by businesses and governments. But the prototypes from which the commercial models were developed were created by research economists working in the universities, the Bank of Canada, and the Economic Council of Canada. The four main models, together with their estimates of the Canadian multiplier, are set out in Table 26.2.

The four models tell divergent stories about the magnitude of the Canadian multiplier. The largest estimate is that of TRACE at 1.87, and the smallest is that of RDX2 at 0.96. The estimate that we obtained in the previous section lies between these values. The reason for different estimates of the multiplier is that the models incorporate different assumptions about the influences on the components of aggregate expenditure. What one model assumes is a movement along the consumption function, another model assumes is a shift in the consumption function. As a consequence, estimates of the marginal propensity to consume, and therefore of the multiplier, differ.

The Multiplier in Recession and Recovery

The multiplier tends to be smaller when the economy goes into a recession than when it is in a

TABLE 26.2

Four Econometric Models' Estimates of the Multiplier in Canada

Model	Multiplier
CANDIDE — Economic Council of Canada	1.70
QFM — University of Toronto Quarterly Forecasting Model	1.37
RDX2 — Bank of Canada	0.96
TRACE — University of Toronto Institute for Policy Analysis	1.87

Four economic models estimate that the Canadian multiplier lies between 0.96 and 1.87. Differences arise mainly because different models contain different assumptions about the structure of the economy.

Source: John F. Helliwell, T. Maxwell, and H.E.L. Waslander, "Comparing the Dynamics of Canadian Macro Models," *Canadian Journal of Economics*, XII, 2 May 1979, pp. 181-194.

recovery. The reason is that there are cycles in the marginal propensity to consume. Consumption expenditure depends on both current income and expected future income. Therefore the effect of a change in current income on consumption expenditure depends on whether the change is expected to be permanent or temporary. A change in current income that is expected to be permanent has a larger effect than a change that is expected to be temporary. That is, the marginal propensity to consume is larger when there is a permanent change in income than when income changes temporarily. For this reason, the marginal propensity to consume varies and does so in a way that is connected with the business cycle.

At the start of a recovery, income gains are expected to be permanent and the marginal propensity to consume rises. When a business cycle peak is approached, and during recessions, income changes are expected to be temporary and the marginal propensity to consume falls.

The Declining Canadian Multiplier

Although the multiplier in recovery is larger than that in recession, the multiplier has declined over the years. The reason is that the marginal propensity to import has steadily increased. A higher marginal propensity to import lowers the marginal propensity to buy domestic goods and services and makes the multiplier smaller.

◆ ◆ ◆ ◆ We have now studied the forces that influence the components of aggregate expenditure and have analysed the way the components interact with each other to determine equilibrium expenditure and aggregate demand. We've seen that fluctuations in equilibrium expenditure and shifts in the aggregate demand curve are caused by fluctuations in autonomous expenditure. An important element of autonomous expenditure is investment, which in turn depends on, among other things, interest rates. But what determines interest rates? That is the question to which we turn in the next two chapters.

S U M M A R Y

Expenditure Multipliers

Aggregate expenditure is divided into two components: autonomous expenditure and induced expenditure. Autonomous expenditure is the sum of investment, government purchases, exports, and the part of consumption expenditure that does not vary with income. Induced expenditure is the part of consumption expenditure that does vary with income minus imports.

An increase in autonomous expenditure increases aggregate planned expenditure and shifts the aggregate expenditure upward. Equilibrium expenditure and real GDP increase by more than the increase in autonomous expenditure. They do so because the increased autonomous expenditure induces an increase in consumption expenditure. Aggregate expenditure increases by the sum of the initial increase in autonomous expenditure and the increase in induced expenditure.

The autonomous expenditure multiplier (or simply, the multiplier) is the change in equilibrium real GDP divided by the change in autonomous expenditure that brought it about. The size of the multiplier depends on the marginal propensity to buy domestic goods and services (g), and its value is given by the formula

$$\text{Multiplier} = \frac{1}{(1 - g)}.$$

Because g is a number between zero and 1, the multiplier is greater than 1. The larger the value of g, the larger is the multiplier. The multiplier is greater than 1 because of induced expenditure—because an increase in autonomous expenditure induces an increase in consumption expenditure. (pp. 714–722)

Fiscal Policy Multipliers

There are three main fiscal policy multipliers:

◆ Government purchases multiplier

◆ Transfer payments multiplier

◆ Tax multiplier

The government purchases multiplier is the amount by which a change in government purchases of goods and services is multiplied to determine the change in equilibrium expenditure that it generates. Because government purchases of goods and services are one of the components of autonomous expenditure, this multiplier is equal to the autonomous expenditure multiplier. That is,

$$\text{Government purchases multiplier} = \frac{1}{(1 - g)}.$$

The transfer payments multiplier is the amount by which a change in transfer payments is multiplied to determine the change in equilibrium expenditure that it generates. Because a change in transfer payments influences aggregate expenditure by changing disposable income, this multiplier is equal to the marginal propensity to buy domestic goods and services (g) multiplied by the autonomous expenditure multiplier. That is,

$$\text{Transfer payments multiplier} = \frac{g}{(1 - g)}.$$

The tax multiplier is the amount by which a change in taxes is multiplied to determine the

change in equilibrium expenditure that it generates. A tax increase brings a decrease in equilibrium expenditure. The initial response of consumption expenditure to a tax increase is exactly the same as its response to a decrease in transfer payments. Thus a tax change works like a change in transfer payments but its multiplier is negative. That is,

$$\text{Tax multiplier} = \frac{-g}{(1 - g)}.$$

If both government purchases of goods and services and taxes are changed together and by the same amount, there is a balanced budget multiplier that combines the two separate multipliers. That is,

$$\text{Balanced budget multiplier} = \frac{(1 - g)}{(1 - g)},$$

which is equal to 1.

The tax and transfer payments system acts as an automatic stabilizer—a mechanism that decreases the fluctuations in aggregate expenditure. (pp. 722–726)

Multipliers and the Price Level

A change in autonomous expenditure not caused by a change in the price level shifts the aggregate expenditure curve and also shifts the aggregate demand curve. The magnitude of the shift in the aggregate demand curve depends on the size of the multiplier and on the change in autonomous expenditure.

Real GDP and the price level are determined by both aggregate demand and aggregate supply. If an increase in aggregate demand occurs at an unemployment equilibrium, both the price level and real GDP increase. But the increase in real GDP is smaller than the increase in aggregate demand. The steeper the short-run aggregate supply curve, the larger is the change in the price level and the smaller is the change in real GDP. If an increase in aggregate demand occurs at full employment, its long-run effect is entirely on the price level. (pp. 726–731)

The Multiplier in Canada

Estimates of the multiplier in Canada range between 1.87 and 0.96. The multiplier fluctuates over the business cycle, rising during a recovery and falling during a recession. Its value has fallen, over time, because the marginal propensity to import has increased. (pp. 731–732)

KEY ELEMENTS

Key Terms

Automatic stabilizer, 725
Autonomous expenditure, 714
Autonomous expenditure multiplier, 717
Balanced budget multiplier, 723
Econometric model, 731
Government purchases multiplier, 722
Induced expenditure, 714
Marginal propensity to buy domestic goods and
  services, 714
Marginal propensity to import, 714
Marginal tax rate, 725
Multiplier, 717
Tax multiplier, 723
Transfer payments multiplier, 722

Key Figures and Table

Figure 26.1   Aggregate Expenditure, 715
Figure 26.2   An Increase in Autonomous
               Expenditure, 717
Figure 26.3   The Multiplier and the Slope of the *AE*
               Curve, 718
Figure 26.5   The Tax Multiplier, 723
Figure 26.6   The Balanced Budget Multiplier, 724
Figure 26.8   Changes in Autonomous Expenditure
               and Aggregate Demand, 727
Figure 26.9   Fiscal Policy, Real GDP, and the Price
               Level, 730
Table 26.1   Calculating the Multiplier, 719

REVIEW QUESTIONS

1 The autonomous expenditure multiplier applies to changes in which components of aggregate expenditure?

2 What is the connection between the autonomous expenditure multiplier and the slope of the *AE* curve?

3 Why is the autonomous expenditure multiplier greater than 1?

4 What is the government purchases multiplier? Is its value greater than 1?

5 What is the transfer payments multiplier?

6 What is the tax multiplier? How does it compare with the autonomous expenditure multiplier?

7 How does the transfer payments multiplier compare with the tax multiplier?

8 What is the balanced budget multiplier? Is its value greater than 1?

9 Explain how income taxes and transfer payments act as automatic stabilizers.

10 What was the size of the multiplier in Canada in 1992?

11 A change in autonomous expenditure occurs that is not produced by a change in the price level. What happens to the aggregate expenditure curve and the aggregate demand curve?

P R O B L E M S

1 You are given the following information about the economy of Zeeland. Autonomous consumption expenditure is $100 billion and the marginal propensity to consume is 0.9. Investment is $460 billion, government purchases of goods and services are $400 billion, and taxes are a constant $400 billion—they do not vary with income. Exports are $350 billion and imports are 10 percent of income.

a Calculate the slope of the *AE* curve.

b The government cuts its purchases of goods and services to $300 billion. What is the change in real GDP and the government purchases multiplier?

c The government continues to purchase $400 billion worth of goods and services and cuts taxes to $300 billion. What is the change in real GDP and the tax multiplier?

d The government simultaneously cuts both its purchases of goods and services and taxes to $300 billion. What is the change in real GDP? What is the name of the multiplier now at work and what is its value?

2 You are given the following information about the economy of Interland. Autonomous consumption expenditure is $250 billion and the marginal propensity to consume is 0.8. Investment is $560 billion, government purchases of goods and services are $400 billion, and income taxes are 10 percent of real GDP.

a Calculate the slope of the *AE* curve.

b Government purchases are cut to $300 billion. What is the change in real GDP and the government purchases multiplier?

c What is the change in consumption expenditure? Explain why consumption expenditure changes by more than real GDP changes.

d The government introduces transfer payments of $50 billion. What is the transfer payments multiplier and the change in real GDP?

3 You are given three pieces of information about the multiplier in the economy of Alphabeta. Its average value is 2, in year A it is $3\frac{1}{2}$, and in year B it is $\frac{1}{2}$.

a Was year A a recovery year or a recession year? Why?

b Was year B a recovery year or a recession year? Why?

4 Suppose that the price level in the economy of Zeeland as described in problem 1 is 100.

a If the government of Zeeland increases its purchases of goods and services by $100 billion, what happens to the quantity of real GDP demanded?

b In the short run, does equilibrium real GDP increase by more than, less than, or the same amount as the increase in the quantity of real GDP demanded?

c In the long run, does equilibrium real GDP increase by more than, less than, or the same amount as the increase in the quantity of real GDP demanded?

d In the short run, does the price level in Zeeland rise, fall, or remain unchanged?

e In the long run, does the price level in Zeeland rise, fall, or remain unchanged?

CHAPTER 27

MONEY, BANKING, AND INTEREST RATES

After studying this chapter, you will be able to

- ◆ Define money and state its functions

- ◆ Explain what money is in Canada today

- ◆ Describe the balance sheets of Canada's banks and other financial intermediaries

- ◆ Explain the functions of banks and other financial intermediaries

- ◆ Explain how banks create money

- ◆ Explain what determines the demand for money

- ◆ Explain how interest rates are determined

ONEY, LIKE FIRE AND THE WHEEL, HAS BEEN AROUND for a long time. And an incredible array of items have served as money. Muskrat pelts were used in Upper Canada, and tobacco was used by early American colonists. Today, when we want to buy something, we use coins or bank notes, write a cheque, or present a credit card. Are all these things money? ◆ ◆ When we deposit some coins or bank notes into a bank, is that still money? And what happens when the bank lends the money in our deposit account to someone else? How can we get our money back if it's been lent out? Does lending by banks create money—out of thin air? ◆ ◆ In the 1970s, you had either a savings account that earned interest or a chequing account that didn't. Today, there's a wide variety of accounts that provide the convenience of a chequing account and the income of a savings account. Why were these kinds of bank accounts introduced? ◆ ◆ There are

Money Makes the World Go Round

enough coins and bank notes circulating for every Canadian to have a wallet stuffed with $800. There are enough deposits in financial institutions for everyone to have more than $20,000 in these accounts. What determines the amount of money that people hold? ◆ ◆ In recent years, interest rates have tumbled. In the 1980s, a home loan might have cost 20 percent a year. In 1993, a home loan cost only 8 percent a year. Why?

◆ ◆ ◆ ◆ This chapter explains how interest rates are determined. But first, it looks at money—its functions and the way it is defined and measured. We'll discover that interest rates depend, in part, on the amount of money in existence.

What Is Money?

W hat do muskrat pelts, tobacco, nickels, and dimes have in common? Why are they all examples of money? To answer these questions we need a definition of money.

The Definition of Money

Money is any commodity or token that is generally acceptable as the means of payment. The **means of payment** is the method of settling a debt. When a payment has been made there is no remaining obligation between the parties to a transaction. The particular commodities and tokens that have served this purpose have varied enormously. We're going to study money and the institutions of monetary exchange that have evolved in the Canadian economy. But first, let's look at the functions of money.

The Functions of Money

Money has four functions:

◆ Medium of exchange

◆ Unit of account

◆ Store of value

◆ Standard of deferred payment

Medium of Exchange   A **medium of exchange** is a commodity or token that is generally accepted in exchange for goods and services. Money acts as such a medium. Without money, it would be necessary to exchange goods and services directly for other goods and services—an exchange known as **barter**. For example, if you wanted to buy a hamburger, you would offer the paperback novel you've just finished reading or half an hour of your labour in the kitchen in exchange for it. Barter can take place only when there is a double coincidence of wants. A **double coincidence of wants** is a situation that occurs when person A wants to buy what person B is selling, and person B wants to buy what person A is selling. That is, to get your hamburger, you have to find someone who's selling hamburgers and who wants a paperback novel or your work in the kitchen. The occurrence of a double coincidence of wants is sufficiently rare that barter would leave most potential gains from specialization and exchange unrealized.

Money guarantees that there is always a double coincidence of wants. People with something to sell will always accept money in exchange for it, and people who want to buy will always offer money. Money acts as a lubricant that smooths the mechanism of exchange. It lowers the costs of doing transactions. The evolution of monetary exchange is a consequence of our economizing activity—of getting the most possible out of limited resources.

Unit of Account   An agreed measure for stating the prices of goods and services is a **unit of account**. To get the most out of your budget, you have to figure out, among other things, whether seeing one more movie is worth the price you have to pay, not in dollars and cents, but in terms of the number of ice-cream cones, cans of pop, and cups of coffee that you have to give up. It's not hard to do such calculations when all these goods have prices in terms of dollars and cents (see Table 27.1). If a movie costs $6 and a six-pack of pop costs $3, you know right away that seeing one more movie costs you 2 six-packs of pop. If jelly beans are 50¢ a pack, one more movie costs 12 packs of jelly beans. You need only one calculation to figure out the opportunity cost of any pair of goods and services.

But imagine how troublesome it would be if your local movie house posted its price as 2 six-packs of pop; and if the convenience store posted the price of a six-pack of pop as 2 ice-cream cones; and if the ice-cream shop posted the price of a cone as 3 packs of jelly beans; and if the candy store priced jelly beans as 2 cups of coffee! Now how much running around and calculating do you have to do to figure out how much that movie is going to cost you in terms of the pop, ice cream, jelly beans, or coffee that you must give up to see it? You get the answer for pop right away from the sign posted on the movie house, but for all the other goods you're going to have to visit many different stores to establish the price of each commodity in terms of another and then calculate prices in units that are relevant for your own decision. Cover up the column labelled "Price in money units" in Table 27.1 and see how hard it is to figure out the number of local phone calls it costs to see one movie. It's enough to make a

TABLE 27.1

A Unit of Account Simplifies Price Comparisons

Good	Price in money units	Price in units of another good
Movie	$6.00 each	2 six-packs of pop
Pop	$3.00 per six-pack	2 ice-cream cones
Ice cream	$1.50 per cone	3 packs of jelly beans
Jelly beans	$0.50 per pack	2 cups of coffee
Coffee	$0.25 a cup	1 local phone call

Money as a unit of account: One movie costs $6 and one cup of coffee costs 25¢, so one movie costs 24 cups of coffee ($6.00 ÷ 25¢ = 24).

No unit of account: You go to a movie house and learn that the price of a movie is 2 six-packs of pop. You go to a candy store and learn that a pack of jelly beans costs 2 cups of coffee. But how many cups of coffee does seeing a movie cost you? To answer that question, you go to the convenience store and find that a six-pack of pop costs 2 ice-cream cones. Now you head for the ice-cream store, where an ice-cream cone costs 3 packs of jelly beans. Now you get out your pocket calculator: 1 movie costs 2 six-packs of pop, or 4 ice-cream cones, or 12 packs of jelly beans, or 24 cups of coffee!

person swear off movies! How much simpler it is for everyone to express his or her prices in terms of dollars and cents.

Store of Value Any commodity or token that can be held and exchanged later for goods and services is called a **store of value**. Money acts as a store of value. If it did not, it would not be acceptable in exchange for goods and services. The more stable the value of a commodity or token, the better it can act as a store of value, and the more useful it is as money. No stores of value are completely safe. The value of a physical object, such as a house, a car, or a work of art, fluctuates over time. The value of a commodity or token used as money also fluctuates, and when there is inflation its value falls.

Standard of Deferred Payment An agreed measure that enables contracts to be written for future receipts and payments is called a **standard of deferred payment**. If you borrow money to buy a

house or if you save money to provide for retirement, your future commitment or future receipt will be agreed to in dollars and cents. Money is used as the standard for a deferred payment.

Using money as a standard of deferred payment is not entirely without risk because, as we saw in Chapter 22, inflation leads to unpredictable changes in the value of money. But, to the extent that borrowers and lenders anticipate inflation, its rate is reflected in the interest rates paid and received. Lenders in effect protect themselves by charging a higher interest rate, and borrowers, anticipating inflation, willingly pay the higher rate.

Different Forms of Money

Money can take four different forms:

- ◆ Commodity money
- ◆ Convertible paper money
- ◆ Fiat money
- ◆ Private debt money

Commodity Money A physical commodity that is valued in its own right and also used as a means of payment is **commodity money**. An amazing array of items have served as commodity money at different times and places, several of which were described in the chapter opener. But the most common commodity monies have been coins made from metals such as gold, silver, and copper. The first known coins were made in Lydia, a Greek city-state, at the beginning of the seventh century B.C. These coins were made of electrum, a natural mixture of gold and silver.

The earliest money used in pre-Confederation Canada was commodity money. Some of this money was gold coin of British, French, Spanish, or Mexican origin. More exotic forms of commodity money were also used, including muskrat pelts.

Commodity money has considerable advantages but some drawbacks. Let's look at these.

Advantages of Commodity Money The main advantage of commodity money is that because the commodity is valued for its own sake, its value as money is readily known. This fact provides a guarantee of the value of money. For example, gold may be used to fill teeth and make rings; its value in these uses determines its value as money. Historically, gold and silver were ideal for use as money because they were in limited supply and in constant demand (by those wealthy enough to use them) for ornaments and jewellery. Further, their quality was easily verified, and they were easily divisible into units small enough to facilitate exchange.

Disadvantages of Commodity Money   Commodity money has two main disadvantages. First, there is a constant temptation to cheat on the value of the money. Two methods of cheating have been commonly used—clipping and debasement. *Clipping* is reducing the size of coins by an imperceptible amount, thereby lowering their metallic content. *Debasement* is creating a coin having a lower silver or gold content (the balance being made up of some cheaper metal).

This temptation to lower the value of money led to a phenomenon known as Gresham's Law, after the sixteenth-century English financial expert Sir Thomas Gresham. **Gresham's Law** is the tendency for bad money to drive good money out of circulation. Bad money is debased money; good money is money that has not been debased. It's easy to see why Gresham's Law works. Suppose that a person is paid with two coins, one debased and the other not. Each coin has the same value if used as money in exchange for goods. But one of the coins—the one that's not debased—is more valuable as a commodity than it is as a coin. It will not, therefore, be used as money. Only the debased coin will be used as money. It is in this way that bad money drives good money out of circulation.

A second major disadvantage of commodity money is that the commodity, valued for its own sake, could be used in ways other than as money—it has an opportunity cost. For example, gold and silver used as money cannot be used to make jewellery or ornaments. This opportunity cost creates incentives to find alternatives to the commodity itself for use in the exchange process. One such alternative is a paper claim to commodity money.

Convertible Paper Money   When a paper claim to a commodity circulates as a means of payment, that claim is called **convertible paper money**. The first known example of paper money occurred in China during the Ming dynasty (1368–1399 A.D.). This form of money was also used extensively throughout Europe in the Middle Ages.

The inventiveness of goldsmiths and their clients led to the increase and widespread use of convertible paper money. Because gold was

valuable, goldsmiths had well-guarded safes in which to keep their own gold. They also rented space to artisans and others who wanted to put their gold in safekeeping. The goldsmiths issued a receipt entitling the owner of the gold to reclaim their "deposit" on demand. These receipts were much like the coat check token that you get at a theatre or museum.

Suppose that Isabella has a gold receipt indicating that she has 100 grams of gold deposited with Samuel Goldsmith. She is going to buy a piece of land valued at 100 grams of gold from Henry. There are two ways that Isabella might undertake the transaction. The first way is to go to Samuel, hand over her receipt and collect her gold, transport the gold to Henry, and take title to the land. Henry now goes back to Samuel with the gold and deposits it there for safekeeping, leaving with his own receipt. The second way of doing this transaction is for Isabella simply to hand over her gold receipt to Henry, completing the transaction by using the gold receipt as money. Obviously, it is much more convenient to complete the transaction in the second way, provided Henry can trust Samuel. The gold receipt circulating as a means of payment is money. The paper money is *backed* by the gold held by Goldsmith. In addition, the paper money is *convertible* into commodity money.

Fractional Backing   Once the convertible paper money system is operating and people are using their gold receipts rather than gold itself as the means of payment, goldsmiths notice that their vaults are storing a large amount of gold that is never withdrawn. This gives them a brilliant idea. Why not lend people gold receipts? The goldsmith can charge interest on the loan and the loan is created just by writing on a piece of paper. As long as the number of such receipts created is not too large in relation to the stock of gold in the goldsmith's safe, the goldsmith is in no danger of not being able to honour his promise to convert receipts into gold on demand. The gold in the goldsmith's safe is a *fraction* of the gold receipts in circulation. By this device, *fractionally backed* convertible paper money was invented.

There are examples of the use of fractionally backed convertible paper money in Canada's early colonial history, as well as in the post-Confederation era. The earliest is the use of fractionally backed playing cards as money in New France in the late seventeenth century. Playing cards were declared to be money, different cards being denominated as different values. Playing cards circulated alongside gold coins and could be redeemed in Quebec when gold arrived from France.

The first fractionally backed bank notes issued in Canada began to circulate in 1817 when the Bank of Montreal was permitted to issue notes backed by gold, silver, or government bonds up to three times the value of its capital. As more banks were chartered during the nineteenth century, the volume of private bank notes issued expanded steadily. In 1870, the Dominion Bank Note Act was passed, which permitted the government to issue bank notes. Government bank notes grew at a more rapid pace than chartered bank notes and, by the beginning of this century, were the dominant form of currency in circulation in Canada.

Fractionally backed convertible paper money continued to be used in Canada until 1914. The Finance Act of that year, however, removed Canada from the gold standard. Chartered banks were no longer required to redeem their notes in gold on demand, although there was a temporary resumption of gold redemption between 1926 and 1929.

It is no accident that Canada (along with most other countries) eventually abandoned fractionally backed paper money. For even though paper money can be issued vastly in excess of the volume of commodities that back it, valuable commodities that could be used for other productive activities are tied up in the exchange process. There remains an incentive to find a yet more efficient way of facilitating exchange and of freeing up the commodities used to back the paper money. This alternative is fiat money.

Fiat Money   The term *fiat* means "let it be done" or "by order of the authority." **Fiat money** is an intrinsically worthless (or almost worthless) commodity that serves the functions of money. Some of the earliest fiat monies in North America were the continental currency issued during the American Revolution and the "greenbacks" issued during the Civil War, which circulated until 1879. Another early issue of fiat money was that of the so-called *assignats* issued during the French Revolution. These early experiments with fiat money ended in rapid inflation because the amount of fiat money created was allowed to increase at a rapid pace, causing the money to lose value.

However, provided the quantity of fiat money is not allowed to grow too rapidly, it has a reasonably steady value in terms of the goods and services that it will buy. People are willing to accept fiat money in exchange for the goods and services they sell only because they know it will be honoured when they go to buy goods and services. The bank notes and coins that we use in Canada today—collectively known as **currency**—are examples of fiat money. Because of the creation of fiat money, people are willing to accept a piece of paper with a special watermark, printed in coloured ink, and worth not more than a few cents as a commodity, in exchange for $50 worth of goods and services. The small metal alloy disk that we call a quarter is worth almost nothing as a piece of metal but it pays for a local phone call and many other small commodities. The replacement of commodity money by fiat money enables the commodities themselves to be used productively.

Fiat money in Canada had its origins in the 1914 Finance Act. That act not only freed the chartered banks from the obligation to redeem their notes in gold on demand. It also empowered the minister of finance to issue Dominion notes to banks that could themselves be used as backing for the bank's own notes in exchange for other securities held by the chartered banks. In other words, it permitted a chartered bank to make a loan to a private Canadian company and then to exchange the claim to that loan for Dominion notes against which it could issue more of its own notes. Canada's fiat money system was formalized by the establishment in 1935 of the Bank of Canada. With the passage of the Bank of Canada Act in that year, the note-issuing powers of the chartered banks were repealed and the Bank of Canada became the sole issuer of bank notes. These notes were backed by nothing other than the government debts held by the Bank of Canada, together with a small amount of gold and foreign currency held by the Bank of Canada.

Private Debt Money   In the modern world, there is a fourth type of money—private debt money. **Private debt money** is a loan that the borrower promises to repay in currency on demand. By transferring the entitlement to be repaid from one person to another, such a loan can be used as money. For example, you give me an IOU for $10; I give the IOU to a bookseller to buy a biography of Adam Smith; you pay the holder of the IOU $10—only now it's the bookseller holding the IOU. The private debts that serve as money today are deposits at chartered banks and other financial institutions.

Money in Canada Today

There are two main measures of money in Canada today: **M1** and **M2+**. They are defined in Table 27.2 and the terms used to describe the components of the two measures are set out in the compact glossary in Table 27.3. Two other measures are M2 and M3. These are also defined in Table 27.2.

Are Both M1 and M2+ Really Money? Money is the means of payment. So the test of whether an asset is money is whether it serves as a means of payment. Currency passes the test. But what about deposits? Deposits fall into three categories:

◆ Demand deposits
◆ Notice deposits
◆ Term deposits

These deposits are defined in the compact glossary in Table 27.3. Demand deposits are money because they can be transferred from one person to another

---

TABLE 27.2

Measures of Money in Canada

MAIN MEASURES

narrow money

M1 ◆ **Currency held outside banks**

◆ **Privately held demand deposits at chartered banks**

M2+ ◆ **M1**

broad money

◆ **Personal savings deposits at chartered banks**

◆ **Non-personal notice deposits at chartered banks**

◆ **Deposits at trust and mortgage companies**

◆ **Deposits at credit unions and caisses populaires**

◆ **Deposits at other financial institutions**

OTHER MEASURES

M2 ◆ **M1**

◆ **Personal savings deposits at chartered banks**

◆ **Non-personal notice deposits at chartered banks**

M3 ◆ **M2**

◆ **Non-personal term deposits at chartered banks**

◆ **Foreign currency deposits of residents booked in Canada**

TABLE 27.3

A Compact Glossary of the Components of Money

Currency	**Notes issued by the Bank of Canada and coins made at the Royal Canadian Mint in Winnipeg, issued by the government of Canada**
Demand deposit	**A deposit that may be withdrawn on demand**
Notice deposit	**A deposit that may be withdrawn after giving notice (In practice, most notice deposits are withdrawable on demand.)**
Term deposit	**A deposit that may be withdrawn on a fixed date**
Privately held demand deposit at a chartered bank	**A demand deposit held by a household, firm, or other financial institution at a chartered bank**
Deposit at a trust and mortgage loan company	**Any type of deposit (demand, notice, or term) at a trust or mortgage company**
Deposit at a credit union and caisse populaire	**Any type of deposit (demand, notice, or term) in a credit union or caisse populaire**
Personal savings deposit at a chartered bank	**A notice deposit held by a household at a chartered bank**
Non-personal notice deposit at a chartered bank	**A notice deposit held by a firm or other institution at a chartered bank**
Non-personal term deposit at a chartered bank	**A term deposit held by a firm or other institution at a chartered bank**
Foreign currency deposit of resident booked in Canada	**A deposit (demand, notice, or term) denominated in a foreign currency, held by a resident in a chartered bank in Canada**

by writing a cheque. Such a transfer of ownership is equivalent to transferring currency. So all the assets that make up M1 are money.

The notice deposits and term deposits that are added to M1 to give M2+ are technically not means of payment. But most of them are liquid assets. A **liquid asset** is one that is instantly convertible into a means of payment at a known price. Because most of the deposits in M2+ are readily converted into currency or demand deposits, they are operationally similar to M1 and are counted as money. M1 is called *narrow money* and M2+ is called *broad money*.

The Components of Canada's Money   As you can see from Fig. 27.1, currency constitutes a small part of our money. The largest part is deposits at chartered banks, but deposits at other financial institutions have also become large in recent years.

Deposits Are Money but Cheques Are Not   In defining money, we have included, along with currency, deposits at banks and other financial institutions. But we have not counted the cheques that people write as money. Why are deposits money and cheques not?

To see why deposits are money but cheques are not, consider what happens when Barb buys a bike for $200 from Rocky's Mountain Bikes. When Barb goes to the bike shop, she has $500 in her deposit account at the Laser Bank. Rocky has $1,000 in his deposit account—at the same bank, as it happens. The total deposits of these two people is $1,500. On June 11, Barb writes a cheque for $200. Rocky takes the cheque to Laser Bank right away and deposits it. Rocky's bank balance rises from $1,000 to $1,200. But the bank not only credits Rocky's account with $200, it also debits Barb's account $200 so that her balance falls from $500 to $300. The total deposits of Barb and Rocky are still the same as before, $1,500. But Rocky now has $200 more and Barb $200 less than before. These transactions are summarized in Table 27.4.

This transaction has transferred money from Barb to Rocky. The cheque itself was never money. That is, there wasn't an extra $200 worth of money while the cheque was in circulation. The cheque served as a written instruction to the bank to transfer money from Barb to Rocky.

In the example, Barb and Rocky use the same bank. The same story, though with additional steps, describes what happens if Barb and Rocky use dif-

FIGURE 27.1

Three Measures of Money

	$ billions
M2+	**$553**
Comprises all in M2, plus...	
Deposits at other financial institutions	$70
Deposits at credit unions and caisses populaires	$71
Deposits at trust and mortgage loan companies	$116
M2	**$296**
Comprises all in M1, plus...	
Personal savings deposits at chartered banks	$227
Non-personal notice deposits at chartered banks	$25
M1	**$44**
Currency	$22
Demand deposits	$22

The M1 measure of money consists of currency outside the banks and demand deposits at chartered banks. M1 makes up only 8 percent of the M2+ measure of money. M2+ consists of M1 plus personal savings deposits at chartered banks, non-personal notice deposits at chartered banks, deposits at trust and mortgage companies, deposits at credit unions and caisses populaires, and deposits at other financial institutions. The deposits at chartered banks are slightly larger than those at the other financial institutions.

Source: Bank of Canada Review, Winter 1992-1993, Table E1.

ferent banks. Rocky's bank will credit the cheque to Rocky's account and then take the cheque to a cheque-clearing centre. Barb's bank will pay Rocky's bank $200 and then debit Barb's account $200. This process can take a few days but the principles are the same as when two people use the same bank.

Credit Cards Are Not Money   So cheques are not money. But what about credit cards? Isn't presenting a credit card to pay for a bike the same thing as using money? Why aren't credit cards money?

TABLE 27.4

Paying by Cheque

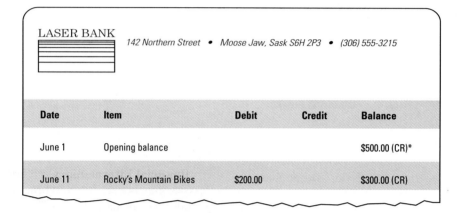

Date	Item	Debit	Credit	Balance
June 1	Opening balance			$500.00 (CR)*
June 11	Rocky's Mountain Bikes	$200.00		$300.00 (CR)

Barb's deposit account

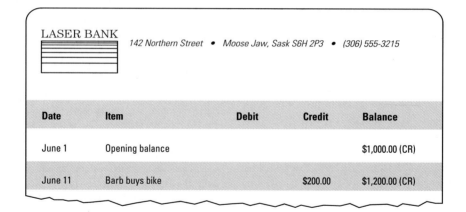

Date	Item	Debit	Credit	Balance
June 1	Opening balance			$1,000.00 (CR)
June 11	Barb buys bike		$200.00	$1,200.00 (CR)

Rocky's Mountain Bikes deposit account

When you pay by cheque you are frequently asked to prove your identity by showing your driver's licence. It would never occur to you to think of your driver's licence as money. Your driver's licence is just an ID. A credit card is also an ID card but one that enables you to borrow money at the instant a purchase is made on the promise of repaying later. When you make a purchase, you sign a credit card sales slip that creates a debt in your name. You are saying: "I agree to pay for these goods when the credit card company bills me." Once you get your statement from the credit card company, you have to make the minimum payment due. To make that payment you need money—you need to have currency or funds in your demand deposit so that you can write a cheque to pay the credit card company. Although you use a credit card to make purchases, it is not money.

M oney is anything that serves as the means of payment for goods and services or for settling debts. Any asset that serves as money performs four functions:

◆ Medium of exchange

◆ Unit of account

◆ Store of value

◆ Standard of deferred payment

In earlier times, commodities served as money but modern societies use fiat money. The components of money in Canada today are coins, Bank of Canada notes, and deposits at chartered banks and other financial institutions. Neither cheques nor credit cards are money. ◆

We've seen that the main component of money in Canada is deposits at banks and other financial institutions. Let's take a closer look at the economic activities of these financial institutions.

Financial Intermediaries

W e are going to study the banking and financial system by first describing the financial intermediaries that operate in Canada today. We'll then examine the operations of banks and other financial intermediaries. After describing the main features of financial intermediaries, we'll examine their economic functions, describing what they produce and how they make a profit.

A **financial intermediary** is a firm that takes deposits from households and firms and makes loans to other households and firms. Three types of financial intermediaries take deposits that are components of the nation's money:

◆ Chartered banks

◆ Trust and mortgage loan companies

◆ Local credit unions and caisses populaires

A compact glossary of these financial intermediaries and their relative sizes are given in Table 27.5. Let's begin by examining the chartered banks.

TABLE 27.5

A Compact Glossary of Financial Intermediaries

Financial intermediary	Total assets (billions of dollars)	Description and functions
Chartered banks	676	A private firm chartered under the Bank Act (1992) to receive deposits and make loans and to supply other financial services
Trust and mortgage loan companies	270	A private company operating under the Trust and Loan Companies Act (1992) (and corresponding provincial laws) that undertakes business almost identical to that of a chartered bank and that acts as a trustee for pension and other funds and for estates
Credit unions and caisses populaires	85	A cooperative organization operating under the Cooperative Credit Association Act (1992) (and corresponding provincial laws) that receives deposits and makes loans

Source: Bank of Canada Review, Winter 1992-1993, Tables C1, D1, D2, and D3 and pp. 21-45.

Chartered Banks

A **chartered bank** is a private firm chartered under the Bank Act of 1992 to receive deposits and make loans. In 1992, there were 10 Canadian-owned banks chartered by Parliament and 55 foreign-owned banks. These banks operated more than 7,350 banking offices in Canada, 206 of which were offices of foreign banks. The scale and scope of the operations of chartered banks can be seen by examining the balance sheet of all the chartered banks added together.

A **balance sheet** is a statement that lists a firm's assets and liabilities. **Assets** are the things of value that a firm owns. **Liabilities** are the things that a firm owes to households and other firms. The liabilities of banks are deposits. Your deposit at a bank is an asset to you, but a liability for your bank. The bank has to repay you your deposit (and sometimes interest on it too) whenever you decide to take your money out of the bank.

The balance sheet for all chartered banks in September 1992 is set out in Table 27.6. The left side—the assets—lists the items *owned* by the banks. The right side—the liabilities—lists the items that the banks *owe* to others.

The first thing to notice about the chartered banks' balance sheet is that its assets and liabilities are divided into two broad groups—those denominated in Canadian dollars and those denominated in foreign currency. Partly because of our proximity to the U.S. money and financial markets, and partly because of the enormous volume of international trade undertaken by Canadians, a large amount of banking business is done in U.S. dollars and other foreign currencies. Table 27.6 shows that one-third of the assets and liabilities of chartered banks are in foreign currencies. Foreign currency assets are loans or securities denominated in foreign currencies. Foreign currency liabilities are deposits made and repayable in the foreign currency.

Large though their foreign currency business is, it is business conducted in Canadian dollars that constitutes the bulk of the work of the chartered banks. Let's look at this aspect of their balance sheet, starting on the liability side.

TABLE 27.6

The Balance Sheet of All Chartered Banks: September 1992

Assets (billions of dollars)		Liabilities (billions of dollars)	
Canadian dollar assets		**Canadian dollar liabilities**	
Bank of Canada deposits and notes	5.7	Personal savings deposits:	
Liquid assets	49.2	Chequable	35.1
Securities	23.8	Nonchequable	71.3
Loans	316.5	Fixed term	118.2
Other assets	55.5		224.6
		Non-personal term and notice deposits	76.5
		Demand deposits	24.9
		Government of Canada deposits	2.6
		Total deposits	328.6
		Other liabilities	106.2
Total Canadian dollar assets	450.7	Total Canadian dollar liabilities	434.8
Foreign currency assets	224.9	**Foreign currency liabilities**	240.8
Total assets	675.6	Total liabilities	675.6

Source: Bank of Canada Review, Winter 1992-1993, Table C3 and C4.

Total Canadian dollar liabilities of the chartered banks in September 1992 were almost $435 billion. By far the largest component of these liabilities is deposits. You have met these deposits before in the various definitions of money. They are the personal savings deposits (notice and term), non-personal term and notice deposits, and demand deposits. An additional small item in the table is the deposits of the government of Canada.

Banks make a profit by using the funds they borrow. And the asset side of the balance sheet tells us what the banks did with the $676 billion worth of borrowed funds in September 1992.

The banks kept some of their funds as deposits at the Bank of Canada and as cash in their vaults. (We'll study the Bank of Canada in Chapter 28.) The cash in a bank's vault plus its deposits at the Bank of Canada are called its **reserves**. You can think of a chartered bank's deposit at the Bank of Canada as being similar to your deposit at your own bank. Chartered banks use these deposits in the same way that you use your bank account. A chartered bank deposits cash into or draws cash out of its account at the Bank of Canada and writes cheques on that account to settle debts with other banks.

If the banks kept all their funds as deposits at the Bank of Canada and cash in their vaults, they wouldn't make any profit. But if they didn't keep *some* of their funds in these forms, they wouldn't be able to meet the demands for cash that their customers place on them—they wouldn't be able to keep that automatic teller replenished every time you and your friends have raided it for cash for a midnight pizza.

The bulk of the banks' borrowed funds are put to work by making loans. Some of these loans are instantly convertible into cash with virtually no risk. These are the banks' *liquid assets*. An example of a liquid asset is a government of Canada Treasury bill that can be sold at a moment's notice for an almost guaranteed price.

The banks' assets also include securities. A **security** is a marketable asset that can be sold at a moment's notice but at a price that fluctuates. An example of an investment security is a government of Canada long-term bond. Such bonds can be sold instantly but their prices fluctuate. Banks earn a higher interest rate on their investment securities than they do on liquid assets, but they involve higher risk.

Most of the banks' assets are the loans that they have made. A **loan** is a commitment of a fixed amount of money for an agreed period of time. Most of the loans made by banks are used by corporations to finance the purchase of capital equipment and inventories. But banks also make loans to households—personal loans. Such loans are used to buy consumer durable goods such as cars or boats. The outstanding balances on credit card accounts are also bank loans.

Banks make a profit by earning interest on loans, investment securities, and liquid assets in excess of the interest paid on deposits and other liabilities. Also, banks receive revenue by charging fees for managing accounts.

Next, let's examine the other types of financial intermediaries.

Trust and Mortgage Loan Companies

A **trust and mortgage loan company** is a privately owned financial intermediary, operating under the Trust and Loan Companies Act of 1992, that receives deposits and makes loans and in addition acts as a trustee for pension funds and for estates. In 1992, their total deposit liabilities were $270 billion.

Local Credit Unions and Caisses Populaires

A **local credit union** is a cooperative organization, operating under the Cooperative Credit Association Act of 1992, that receives deposits and makes loans. Caisses populaires are similar institutions operating in the province of Quebec. In 1992, the total liabilities of these institutions were $84 billion.

Financial Legislation

Historically, Canada made a sharp legal distinction between banks and other deposit-taking financial institutions. But the economic functions of other financial intermediaries have grown increasingly similar to those of banks. This fact is recognized in laws governing these institutions that became effective in 1992. Today, their deposit liabilities, which are part of the M2 + definition of money, approach the same magnitude as those of the chartered banks.

The Economic Functions of Financial Intermediaries

All financial intermediaries make a profit from a spread between the interest rate they pay on deposits and the interest rate at which they lend. Why can financial intermediaries borrow at a low interest rate and lend at a higher one? What services do they perform that makes their depositors willing to put up with a low interest rate and their borrowers willing to pay a higher one?

Financial intermediaries provide four main services:

◆ Minimizing the cost of obtaining funds

◆ Minimizing the cost of monitoring borrowers

◆ Pooling risk

◆ Creating liquid assets

Minimizing the Cost of Obtaining Funds Finding someone from whom to borrow can be a costly business. Imagine how troublesome it would be if there were no financial intermediaries. A firm that was looking for $1 million to buy a new production plant would probably have to hunt around for several dozen people from whom to borrow in order to acquire enough funds for its capital project. Financial intermediaries lower those costs. The firm needing $1 million can go to a single financial intermediary to obtain those funds. The financial intermediary has to borrow from a large number of people, but it's not doing that just for this one firm and the million dollars it wants to borrow. The financial intermediary can establish an organization capable of raising funds from a large number of depositors and can spread the cost of this activity over a large number of borrowers.

Minimizing the Cost of Monitoring Borrowers Lending money is a risky business. There's always a danger that the borrower might not repay. Most of the money lent gets used by firms to invest in projects that they hope will return a profit. But sometimes those hopes are not fulfilled. And when profit expectations are not fulfilled, borrowers are often unable to repay their loans.

To minimize the chances of a loan not being repaid, lenders monitor the activites of borrowers. But checking up on the activities of a borrower and ensuring that the best possible decisions are being made to ensure a profit and avoid a loss is a costly

and specialized activity. Imagine how costly it would be if each and every household that lent money to a firm had to incur the costs of monitoring that firm directly. By depositing funds with a financial intermediary, households avoid those costs. The financial intermediary performs the monitoring activity by using specialized resources that have a much lower cost than what each household would incur if it had to undertake the activity individually.

Pooling Risk As we noted above, lending money is risky. There is always a chance of not being repaid—that is, of default. The risk of default can be reduced by lending to a large number of different individuals. In such a situation, if one person defaults on a loan, it is a nuisance but not a disaster. In contrast, if only one person borrows and that person defaults on the loan, the entire loan is a write-off. Financial intermediaries enable people to pool risk in an efficient way. Thousands of people lend money to any one financial intermediary and, in turn, the financial intermediary re-lends the money to hundreds, and perhaps thousands, of individual firms. If any one firm defaults on its loan, that default is spread across all the depositors with the intermediary and no individual depositor is left exposed to a high degree of risk.

Creating Liquid Assets Financial intermediaries create liquid assets by borrowing short and lending long. Borrowing short means taking deposits but standing ready to repay them on short notice (or on no notice in the case of demand deposits). The deposit liabilities of banks are liquid assets to the depositors. Lending long means making loan commitments for a prearranged, and often quite long, period of time.

To see that financial intermediaries create liquid assets, think about Alice who has $100,000 to lend and Jim who wants a loan of $100,000 for 15 years to buy a house. If Alice lends Jim $100,000, she has no liquidity. She can't get her money back quickly. But if Alice deposits her money in a bank and Jim gets a loan from the bank, Alice can get her funds whenever she needs them and the bank is left with the problem of finding another deposit to finance the loan to Jim. The bank has created a liquid asset for Alice.

REVIEW

Most of the nation's money is made up of deposits in financial intermediaries. Those financial intermediaries are chartered banks, trust and mortgage loan companies, credit unions, and caisse populaires. The main economic functions of financial intermediaries are minimizing the cost of obtaining funds and of monitoring borrowers, pooling risk, and creating liquid assets. ◆

Because financial intermediaries are able to create money, they occupy a unique place in our economy and influence the quantity of money in existence. Let's see how money gets created.

How Banks Create Money

Money is created by the activities of chartered banks and other financial intermediaries—by all those institutions whose deposits circulate as a means of payment. In this section, we'll use the term *banks* to refer to all these depository institutions.

Creating Money by Making Loans

When we say that banks create money, we don't mean that they have smoke-filled back rooms in which counterfeiters are busily working. Remember, most money is deposits, not currency. What banks create is deposits and they do so by making loans. To see how, just think about what happens if you decide to get a $5,000 loan from your bank to buy a car. When the bank lends you the $5,000, it credits your account with that amount. You are now ready

to go ahead and write a cheque to pay for your car. When you pay for your car, your bank deposit falls by $5,000, but the bank deposit of the car dealer rises by this amount, so bank deposits haven't changed. By lending you $5,000, the bank has created money. If creating money is so simple, why don't the banks create an unlimited amount of it? The reason is that the amount that a bank can lend is limited by its reserves. Let's see how.

Actual and Desired Reserves

As we saw in Table 27.6, banks don't have $100 in bills for every $100 that people have deposited with them. In fact, a typical bank today has $1.15 in currency and another 37¢ on deposit at the Bank of Canada for every $100 deposited in it. No need for panic. Banks have learned, from experience, that these reserve levels are adequate for ordinary business needs. The fraction of a bank's total deposits that are held in reserves is called the **reserve ratio**. The value of the reserve ratio is influenced by the actions of a bank's depositors. If a depositor withdraws currency from a bank, the reserve ratio falls. If a depositor puts currency into a bank, the reserve ratio increases.

The **desired reserve ratio** is the ratio of reserves to deposits that banks plan to hold. A bank's **desired reserves** are equal to its deposits multiplied by the desired reserve ratio. Actual reserves minus desired reserves are **excess reserves**. Only when banks have excess reserves are they able to create money. To see how much money the banks can create, we are going to look at a model of the banking system.

The Limit to Bank Lending

In the model banking system that we'll study, the desired reserve ratio is 25 percent. That is, for each dollar deposited, banks want to keep 25¢ in the form of reserves and lend the rest.

The story begins with Al, a customer of the Golden Nugget Bank, who decides to reduce his holdings of currency and put $100 in his deposit account. Suddenly, the Golden Nugget Bank has $100 of new deposits and $100 of additional reserves. But with $100 of new deposits the bank doesn't want to hold on to $100 of additional reserves. It has excess reserves. Its desired reserve ratio is 25 percent, so it plans to lend $75 of the additional $100 to another customer. Amy, a customer at the same bank, borrows $75. At this point, the Golden Nugget Bank has new deposits of $100, new loans of $75, and new reserves of $25. As far as Golden Nugget is concerned, that is the end of the story. But it's not the end of the story for the entire banking system. What happens next?

Amy uses the $75 loan to buy a jacket from Barb. She gives the $75 to Barb, who deposits it in the Laser Bank. The Laser Bank now has new deposits of $75 and an additional $75 of reserves. Bank deposits are now $175 higher than they were initially. Al has $100 more on deposit and Barb has $75 more.

The Laser Bank doesn't need to hang on to the entire $75 as reserves: it needs only a quarter of that amount—$18.75. The Laser Bank lends the additional amount, $56.25, to Bob, who buys some used stereo equipment from Carl. Bob hands the $56.25 to Carl, who deposits it in his account at the Apollo Bank. The Apollo Bank now has new deposits of $56.25, so total deposits have increased by $231.25—$100 for Al, $75 for Barb, and $56.25 for Carl.

The transactions we've just described are summarized in Table 27.7. But the story is still incomplete. The process we're describing continues through the remaining banks and their depositors and borrowers, all the way down the list in the table. By the time we get down to the Pirates Bank, Ken has paid Len $5.63 for a box of computer disks, and so the Pirates Bank has new deposits of $5.63

TABLE 27.7

Creating Money by Making Loans: Many Banks

Bank	Depositor	Borrower	New deposits	New loans	New reserves	Cumulative increase in deposits
Golden Nugget	Al	Amy	$ 100.00	$ 75.00	$ 25.00	$100.00
Laser	Barb	Bob	75.00	56.25	18.75	175.00
Apollo	Carl	Con	56.25	42.19	14.06	231.25
Monty Python	Di	Dan	42.19	31.64	10.55	273.44
Plato	Ed	Eve	31.64	23.73	7.91	305.08
J.R. Ewing	Fran	Fred	23.73	17.80	5.93	328.81
1st Madonna	Gus	Gail	17.80	13.35	4.45	346.61
Rambo	Holly	Hal	13.35	10.01	3.34	359.96
Trump	Jim	Jan	10.01	7.51	2.50	369.97
Disney	Kym	Ken	7.51	5.63	1.88	377.48
Pirates	Len	Lee	5.63	4.22	1.41	383.11
			.	.	.	.
			.	.	.	.
			.	.	.	.
All others			16.89	12.67	4.22	.
Total banking system			$400.00	$300.00	$100.00	$400.00

and additional reserves of that same amount. Since it needs only $1.41 of additional reserves, it makes a loan of $4.22 to Lee, who in turn spends the money. By this time, total bank deposits have increased by $383.11.

This process continues but with amounts that are now getting so tiny that we will not bother to keep track of them. All the remaining stages in the process taken together add up to the numbers in the second-to-last row of the table. The final tallies appear as the totals at the bottom of the table. Deposits have increased by $400, loans by $300, and reserves by $100. The banks have created money by making loans.

The Deposits Multiplier

The ability of banks to create deposits does not mean that they can create an indefinite amount of deposits. The amount that they can create depends on the size of their reserves and on the desired reserve ratio. In this example where the desired reserve ratio is 25 percent, bank deposits have increased by four times the level of reserves.

The **deposits multiplier** is the amount by which an increase in bank reserves is multiplied to calculate the increase in bank deposits. That is,

$$\text{Deposits multiplier} = \frac{\text{Change in deposits}}{\text{Change in reserves}}.$$

In the example we've just worked through, the deposits multiplier is 4—a $100 increase in reserves created the $400 increase in deposits.

The deposits multiplier is related to the desired reserve ratio. In our example, that ratio is 25 percent (or 1/4). That is,

$$\text{Desired reserves} = (1/4) \text{ Deposits}.$$

Whenever desired reserves exceed actual reserves (a situation of negative excess reserves), the banks call in loans. When desired reserves are below actual reserves (a situation of positive excess reserves), the banks make additional loans. By adjusting their loans, the banks bring their actual reserves into line with their desired reserves, eliminating excess reserves. Thus, when banks have changed their

loans and reserves to make actual reserves equal desired reserves,

$$\text{Actual Reserves} = (1/4) \text{ Deposits}.$$

Dividing both sides of this equation by 1/4, we obtain

$$\text{Deposits} = 1/(1/4) \text{ Actual reserves}.$$

When the bank s receive new deposits, actual reserves increase. If the increase in reserves occurs when desired reserves and actual reserves are equal, the banks have excess reserves. They lend these excess reserves until bank deposits have increased by enough to increase desired reserves by the same amount as the increase in actual reserves. A decrease in deposits lowers reserves and forces the banks to call in some loans. The end result of this process is a decrease in deposits by an amount that decreases desired reserves by the same amount as the decrease in actual reserves. When deposits have changed by enough to have eliminated excess reserves, the change in deposits taken place is

$$\text{Change in deposits} = 1/(1/4) \text{ Change in reserves}.$$

By definition, $1/(1/4)$ is the deposits multiplier. It is the amount by which the change in reserves is multiplied to calculate the change in deposits. In our example, this multiplier equals 4. The relationship between the deposits multiplier and the desired reserve ratio is

$$\text{Deposits multiplier} = \frac{1}{\text{Desired reserve ratio}}.$$

Canadian Deposits Multiplier

The deposits multiplier in Canada differs from the one we've just calculated for two reasons. First, the desired reserve ratio of Canadian banks is much smaller than the 25 percent we used here. Second, in Canada, not all the loans made by banks return to them in the form of reserves. Some of the loans remain outside the banks in the form of currency. These two factors work in opposing directions. The smaller desired reserve ratio makes the Canadian multiplier larger than the above example. And the fact that some currency remains outside the banks makes the Canadian multiplier smaller.

REVIEW

Banks create deposits by making loans. The amount they can lend is determined by their reserves and the desired reserve ratio. Each time they make a loan, deposits increase, and so do desired reserves. When deposits are at a level that makes desired reserves equal to actual reserves, the banks cannot increase their lending or deposits any further. An initial change in reserves brings about an eventual change in deposits equal to the change in reserves multiplied by (1/desired reserve ratio). ◆

The amount of money created by the banking system has a powerful influence on the economy. This influence begins with interest rates. To understand how the quantity of money influences interest rates, we must first study the demand for money.

The Demand for Money

The amount of money we *receive* each week in payment for our labour is income—a flow. The amount of money we hold in our wallet or in a bank account is an inventory—a stock. There is no limit to how much income—or flow—we would like to receive each week. But there is a limit to how big an inventory of money each of us would like to hold, on the average.

The Motives for Money Holding

Why do people hold an inventory of money? Why do you carry coins and bank notes in your wallet, and why do you keep money in a deposit account at your neighbourhood bank?

There are three main motives for holding money:

◆ Transactions motive

◆ Precautionary motive

◆ Speculative motive

Transactions Motive   The main motive for holding money is to be able to undertake transactions and to minimize the cost of transactions. By carrying an inventory of currency, you are able to undertake small transactions such as buying your lunch at the cafeteria. If you didn't carry an inventory of currency, you'd have to go to the bank every lunchtime in order to withdraw enough cash. The opportunity cost of these transactions, in terms of your own lost study or leisure time, would be considerable. You avoid those transactions costs by keeping an inventory of currency large enough to make your normal purchases over a period of perhaps a week in length.

You also keep an inventory of money in the form of deposits at the bank to make transactions such as paying the rent on your apartment or paying your bookstore bill. Instead of having an inventory of bank deposits for these purposes, you might put all your assets into the stock or bond market—buying IBM shares or government of Canada securities. But if you did that, you would have to call your broker and sell some stocks and bonds each time you needed to pay the rent or the bookstore. Again, you'd have to pay the opportunity cost of such transactions. Instead, those costs can be avoided by holding larger inventories of bank deposits.

Individual holdings of money for transactions purposes fluctuate during any week or month. But aggregate money balances held for transactions purposes do not fluctuate much, because what one person is spending, someone else is receiving.

Firms' money holdings are at their peak just before the moment they pay their employees' wages. Households' money holdings are at a peak just after wages have been paid. As households spend their incomes, their money holdings decline and firms' holdings of money increase. Firms' holdings of money are actually quite large and it is this fact that makes average money holdings appear to be so large. Average money holdings of households are much lower than the economy-wide averages presented in the chapter opener.

Precautionary Motive   Money is held as a precaution against unforeseen events that require unplann-ed purchases to be made. For example, on an out-of-town trip you carry some extra money in case your car breaks down and has to be fixed. Or, if you are shopping in the January sales, you take with you more money than you are planning on spending in case you come across a real bargain that you just can't pass up.

Speculative Motive   The final motive for holding money is to avoid losses from holding stocks or bonds that are expected to fall in value. Suppose, for example, that a week before the stock market crashes, you predict the crash. On the Friday afternoon before the markets close, you sell all your stocks and put the proceeds into your bank deposit account for the weekend. This temporary holding of money persists until stock prices have fallen. Only then do you reduce your bank deposit and buy stocks again.

The Influences on Money Holding

The transactions, precautionary, and speculative motives for holding money tell us *why* households and firms hold money. But the three motives do not tell us *how much* money people will choose to hold. What determines the quantity of money that households and firms choose to hold? There are three main influences on this quantity:

◆ Prices

◆ Real expenditure

◆ The opportunity cost of holding money

The higher the level of prices, other things remaining the same, the larger is the quantity of money that people will want to hold. The higher the level of real expenditure, other things remaining the same, the larger is the quantity of money that people plan to hold. The higher the opportunity cost of holding money, the smaller is the quantity of money that people plan to hold.

These influences on individual decisions about money holding translate into three macroeconomic variables that influence the aggregate quantity of money demanded:

◆ The price level

◆ Real GDP

◆ The interest rate

Let's look at each of these influences.

Price Level and the Quantity of Money Demanded   The quantity of money measured in current dollars is called the quantity of **nominal money**. The quantity of nominal money demanded is proportional to the price level. That is, other things remaining the same, if the price level (GDP deflator) increases by 10 per-

cent, people will want to hold 10 percent more nominal money than before. What matters to people is not the number of dollars they hold but the buying power of those dollars. Suppose, for example, that to undertake your weekly expenditure on movies and pop you carry an average of $20 in your wallet. If your income and the prices of movies and pop increased by 10 percent, you would increase your average cash holdings by 10 percent to $22.

The quantity of money measured in constant dollars (for example, in 1986 dollars) is called *real money*. Real money is equal to nominal money divided by the price level. The quantity of real money demanded is independent of the price level. In the above example, you held $20, on the average, at the original price level. When the price level increased by 10 percent, you increased your average cash holding by 10 percent, keeping your *real* cash holding constant. Your $22 at the new price level is the same quantity of *real money* as your $20 at the original price level.

Real GDP and the Quantity of Money Demanded
One determinant of the quantity of money demanded is the level of real income—for the aggregate economy, real GDP. As you know, real GDP and real aggregate expenditure are two sides of the same transaction. The amount of money that households and firms demand depends on the amount they are spending. The higher the expenditure—the higher the income—the larger is the quantity of money demanded. Again, suppose that you hold an average of $20 to finance your weekly purchases of movies and pop. Imagine that the prices of these goods and of all other goods remain constant but that your income increases. As a consequence, you now spend more and you also keep a larger amount of money on hand to finance your higher volume of expenditure.

The Interest Rate and the Quantity of Money Demanded
You already know the fundamental principle that as the opportunity cost of something rises, people try to find substitutes for it. Money is no exception to this principle. The higher the opportunity cost of holding money, other things remaining the same, the lower is the quantity of real money demanded. But what is the opportunity cost of holding money?

The opportunity cost of holding money is measured by the interest rate. To see why, recall that the opportunity cost of any activity is the value of the best alternative forgone. What is the best alternative to holding money, and what is the value forgone? The best alternative to holding money is holding an interest-earning financial asset such as a savings bond or Treasury bill. By holding money instead of such an asset, you forgo the interest that you otherwise would have received. This forgone interest is the opportunity cost of holding money. The higher the interest rate, the higher is the opportunity cost of holding money and the smaller is the amount of money held. At the same time, the quantity of interest-earning assets held increases. Interest-earning assets are substituted for money.

Money loses value because of inflation. Why isn't the inflation rate part of the cost of holding money? It is. Other things remaining the same, the higher the expected inflation rate, the higher are interest rates and, therefore, the higher is the opportunity cost of holding money.

The Demand for Real Money

The **demand for real money** is the relationship between the quantity of real money demanded and the interest rate, holding constant all other influences on the amount of money that people wish to hold. To make the demand for real money more concrete, let's consider an example. A household's demand for real money can be represented as a demand schedule for real money. Such a schedule sets out the quantity of real money that a person wants to hold at a given level of real income for different levels of the interest rate.

Figure 27.2 sets out some numbers for the Polonius household. The household's real income is $20,000 a year. The price level is 1, or the GDP deflator is equal to 100, so the quantity of money is the same whether we measure it in nominal terms or real terms. The table tells us how the quantity of real money demanded by the Polonius household changes as the interest rate changes. For example, in row a, when the interest rate is 7 percent a year, the Polonius household holds $2,400 of money, on the average. When the interest rate is 5 percent a year, real money holdings increase to $3,000, and when the interest rate falls to 3 percent a year, real money holdings increase to $4,000.

The figure also graphs the Polonius household's demand curve for real money (*MD*). If the interest rate increases from 5 percent to 7 percent, there is a rise in the opportunity cost of holding money and a decrease in the quantity of real money demanded—illustrated by an upward movement along the

FIGURE 27.2

The Polonius Household's Demand for Real Money

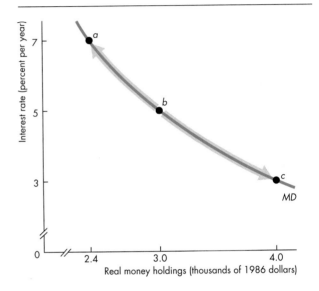

Polonius household's real income is $20,000; price level is 1.

	Interest rate (percent per year)	Real money holdings (thousands of 1986 dollars)
a	7	2.4
b	5	3.0
c	3	4.0

The table shows the Polonius household's demand schedule for real money. The lower the interest rate, the larger is the quantity of real money that the household plans to hold. The graph shows the household's demand curve for real money (*MD*). Points *a*, *b*, and *c* on the curve correspond to the rows in the table. A change in the interest rate leads to a movement along the demand curve. The demand curve for real money slopes downward because the interest rate is the opportunity cost of holding money. The higher the interest rate, the larger is the interest forgone on holding another asset.

demand curve in Fig. 27.2. If the interest rate decreases from 5 percent to 3 percent, there is a fall in the opportunity cost of holding money and an increase in the quantity of real money demanded—illustrated by a downward movement along the demand curve in Fig. 27.2.

Shifts in the Demand Curve for Real Money

The demand curve for real money shifts when

◆ Real income changes.

◆ Financial innovation occurs.

Changes in Real Income   An increase in real income shifts the demand curve for real money to the right and a decrease shifts it to the left. The effect of real income on the demand curve for real money is shown in Fig. 27.3. The table shows the effects of a change in real income on the quantity of real money demanded when the interest rate is constant at 5 percent. Look first at row *b* of the table. It tells us that when the interest rate is 5 percent and real income is $20,000, the quantity of real money demanded by the Polonius household is $3,000. This row corresponds to point *b* on the demand curve for real money MD_0. Continuing to hold the interest rate constant, if real income falls to $12,000, the quantity of real money held falls to $2,400. Thus the demand curve for real money shifts from MD_0 to MD_1 in Fig. 27.3. If the Polonius household's real income increases to $28,000, the quantity of real money held by the household increases to $3,600. In this case, the demand curve shifts rightward from MD_0 to MD_2.

Financial Innovation

Financial innovation also results in a change in the demand for real money and a shift in the demand curve for real money. One such innovation in recent years has been the development of daily interest chequing accounts with banks and other financial institutions. This innovation has been brought about partly as a result of deregulation of the financial sector and partly by the availability of low-cost computing power.

Computers are a part of the story of financial innovation because they have dramatically lowered the cost of keeping records and doing calculations. Doing the interest calculations on daily interest chequing accounts by hand, although technologically feasible, would be very costly.

Now that banks have access to a vast amount of extremely low-cost computing power, they can offer a wide variety of deposit arrangements that make it convenient to convert non-means of payment assets into means of payment assets at extremely low cost.

FIGURE 27.3

Changes in the Polonius Household's Demand for Real Money

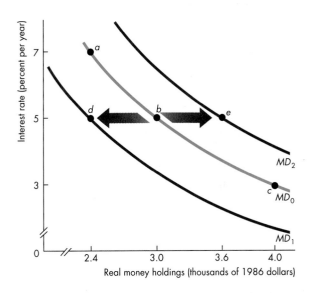

Interest rate is 5 percent; price level is 1.

	Real income (thousands of 1986 dollars)	Real money holdings (thousands of 1986 dollars)
a	12	2.4
b	20	3.0
e	28	3.6

A change in real income leads to a change in the demand for real money. The table shows the quantity of real money held by the Polonius household at three different levels of real income when the interest rate is constant at 5 percent a year. The graph shows the effects of a change in real income on the demand curve for real money. When real income is $20,000 and the interest rate is 5 percent, the household is at point *b* on the demand curve for real money MD_0. When real income falls to $12,000, the demand curve is MD_1 and, at a 5 percent interest rate, the household is at point *d*. When real income rises to $28,000, the demand curve shifts to MD_2. With an interest rate of 5 percent, the household is at point *e*.

The development of these arrangements has led to a decrease in the demand for money—a leftward shift in the demand curve for money.

The availability of low-cost computing power in the financial sector is also responsible, in large degree, for the widespread use of credit cards. Again, keeping the records and calculating the interest and outstanding debt required to operate a credit card system is feasible by hand but too costly to undertake. No one would find it worthwhile to use plastic cards, shuffle sales slips, and keep records if all the calculations had to be done by hand (or even by pre-electronic mechanical calculating machines). This innovation—low-cost computing power—has also lowered the demand for money. By using a credit card to make purchases, people can operate with a much smaller inventory of money. Instead of holding money for transactions purposes through the month, people can charge purchases to a credit card and pay the credit card bill a day or two after payday. As a consequence, the average holding of money throughout the month is much smaller.

The financial innovations we have just considered affect the demand for money. Some financial innovations have changed the composition of our money holdings but not its total amount. One of these is the automatic teller machine. On the average, we can now function efficiently with smaller currency holdings than before, simply because we can obtain currency easily at almost any time or place. Although this innovation has decreased the demand for currency and increased the demand for deposits, it has probably not affected the overall demand for real money.

FIGURE 27.4

The Demand for Money in Canada

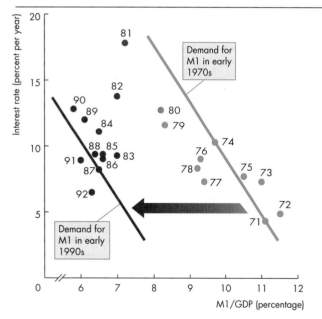

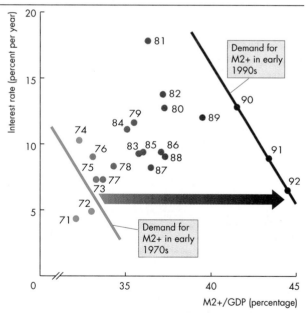

In part (a), the quantity of M1, expressed as a percentage of GDP, is graphed against the interest rate (the three-month Treasury bill rate). In the 1970s, there was a negative relationship between these two variables. That relationship shifted leftward in the 1980s—there was a decrease in the demand for M1. The decrease occurred because of financial innovation and increasingly attractive interest rates on savings deposits.

Part (b) shows the demand for M2+. The quantity of M2+ held (again, expressed as percentage of GDP) is plotted against the interest rate. There is a tendency for the amount of M2+ held to decline as the interest rate increases, other things remaining the same. The demand curve for M2+ shifted in the opposite direction to that for M1 during the 1980s. M2+ holdings increased at each interest rate. The main reason for this increase is the fact that savings deposits themselves earn interest and that the interest rate has become relatively more attractive during the 1980s.

Source: Interest rate, three-month Treasury bill rate, Cansim series B14007; M1, Cansim series B1627; M2+, Cansim series B1630, *Bank of Canada Review.*

Now that we have studied the theory of the demand for real money, let's look at the facts about money holdings in Canada and see how they relate to real income and the interest rate.

The Demand for Money in Canada

Figure 27.4 shows the relationship between the interest rate and the quantity of money demanded in Canada since 1970. Money is measured as a percentage of GDP to isolate the effects of interest rates, financial innovation, and other factors on the demand for money. Each dot shows the interest rate and the amount of money held (as a percentage of GDP) in a given year.

In the case of M1 (part a), there was a fairly clear demand curve in the 1970s that is shown in the figure. As the interest rate increased, so the quantity of M1 demanded (as a percentage of GDP) decreased. At the end of the 1970s, the demand curve for M1 shifted leftward—the demand for M1 decreased. A negative relationship between the interest rate and the quantity of M1 demanded still prevailed during the 1980s but at a lower level of money holdings than in the 1970s.

In the case of M2+ (part b), the demand curve shifted rightward between the 1970s and the 1980s. There was an increase in the demand for M2+. During the 1970s, as the interest rate increased, the quantity of M2+ demanded decreased. During the late 1970s and early 1980s, interest rates and the quantity of M2+ demanded increased together.

Why did the demand for M1 decrease and the demand for M2+ increase? The main part of the answer is that financial innovation and increasingly attractive interest rates on savings deposits encouraged people to substitute savings accounts (part of M2+) for demand deposits (part of M1). These substitutions were especially strong during the middle of the 1980s when attractive interest rates were available on savings accounts.

REVIEW

T he quantity of money demanded depends on the price level, real GDP, and the interest rate. The quantity of nominal money demanded is proportional to the price level. Real money is the quantity of nominal money divided by the price level. The quantity of real money demanded increases as real GDP increases. The opportunity cost of holding money is the interest rate. The benefit from holding money is the avoidance of frequent transactions. The higher the interest rate, the smaller is the quantity of real money demanded. ◆ ◆ The demand curve for real money shows how the quantity of real money demanded varies as the interest rate varies. When the interest rate changes, there is a movement along the demand curve for real money. Other influences on the quantity of real money demanded shift the demand curve for real money. An increase in real income shifts the demand curve rightward; financial innovations that create convenient near-money deposits shift the demand curve leftward. ◆

We've now studied the factors that determine the demand for money and discovered that one determinant of the quantity of real money demanded is the opportunity cost of holding it—the interest rate. Next, we will see how the interest rate is determined.

Interest Rate Determination

A n interest rate is the percentage yield on a financial security such as a *bond* or a *stock*. There is a relationship between the interest rate and the price of a financial asset. Let's spend a moment studying that relationship before analysing the forces that determine interest rates.

Interest Rates and Asset Prices

A bond is a promise to make a sequence of future payments. There are many different possible sequences but the most simple one, for our purposes, is the case of a bond called a perpetuity. A **perpetuity** is a bond that promises to pay a certain fixed amount of money each year forever. The issuer of such a bond will never buy the bond back (redeem it); the bond will remain outstanding

TABLE 27.8

The Interest Rate and the Price of a Bond

FORMULA FOR INTEREST RATE

r = interest rate, c = coupon, p = price of bond

$$r = \frac{c}{p} \; 100$$

EXAMPLES

	Price of bond	Coupon	Interest rate (percent per year)
a	$50	$10	20
b	100	10	10
c	200	10	5

---

forever, and will earn a fixed dollar payment each year. The fixed dollar payment is called the *coupon*. Since the coupon is a fixed dollar amount, the interest rate on the bond varies as the price of the bond varies. Table 27.8 illustrates this fact.

First, the table shows the formula for calculating the interest rate on a bond. The interest rate (r) is the coupon (c) divided by the price of the bond (p), all multiplied by 100 to convert it into a percentage. The table goes on to show some numerical examples for a bond whose coupon is $10 a year. If the bond cost $100 (row *b* of Table 27.8), the interest rate is 10 percent per year. That is, the holder of $100 worth of bonds receives $10 a year.

Rows *a* and *c* of Table 27.8 show two other cases. In row *a*, the price of the bond is $50. With the coupon at $10, this price produces an interest rate of 20 percent—$10 returned on a $50 bond holding is an interest rate of 20 percent. In row *c*, the bond costs $200 and the interest rate is 5 percent—which gives $10 return on a $200 bond holding.

There is an inverse relationship between the price of a bond and the interest rate earned on the bond. As a bond price rises, the bond's interest rate declines. Understanding this relationship will make it easier for you to understand the process whereby the interest rate is determined. Let's now turn to studying how interest rates are determined.

Money Market Equilibrium

The interest rate is determined at each point in time by equilibrium in the markets for financial assets. We study that equilibrium in the market for money.

The Supply of Money   The quantity of money supplied is determined by the actions of the banking system and the Bank of Canada. We'll assume that the amount of money in existence is fixed, so the supply of money is a fixed quantity. (Chapter 28 explains how the quantity of money is determined and how it can be changed.) The *real* quantity of money supplied is equal to the nominal quantity supplied divided by the price level. At a given moment in time, there is a particular price level and so the quantity of real money supplied is also a fixed amount. The supply curve of real money is shown in Fig. 27.5 as the vertical line labelled *MS*. The quantity of real money supplied is $500 billion.

The Demand for Money   The demand for real money depends on the level of real GDP and on the interest rate. The table in Fig. 27.5 sets out the quantity of real money demanded at three different interest rates when real GDP and the price level are constant. These quantities are graphed as the demand curve for real money, *MD*, in the figure.

Equilibrium   When the quantity of money supplied equals the quantity of money demanded, the money market is in equilibrium. This equilibrium is brought about by an adjustment in the interest rate. If the interest rate is too high, people will try to hold less money than is available. If the interest rate is too low, people will try to hold more than the amount available. When the interest rate is such that people want to hold exactly the amount of money that is available, then equilibrium prevails.

Figure 27.5 illustrates an equilibrium in the money market. The equilibrium interest rate is 5 percent, the rate at which the quantity of money demanded equals the quantity supplied. If the interest rate is above 5 percent, people will want to hold less money than is available. At an interest rate below 5 percent, people will want to hold more money than is available. At a 5 percent interest rate, the amount of money available is willingly held.

Converging to Equilibrium   How does money market equilibrium come about? To answer this question, let's perform a thought experiment. First, imagine that the interest rate is temporarily at 7 percent.

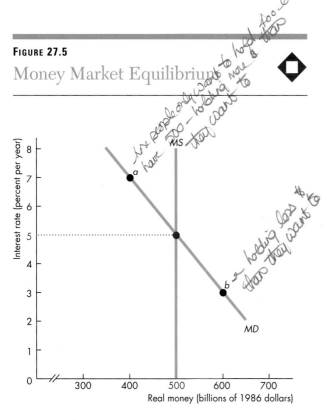

FIGURE 27.5

Money Market Equilibrium

[handwritten: bx people only wants to hold too-lrt have 500 - holding more than they want to]

[handwritten: a - holding less than they want to]

The demand for real money is given by the schedule in the table and by the curve *MD*. The supply of real money, shown in the table and by the curve *MS* in the figure, is $500 billion. Adjustments in the interest rate achieve money market equilibrium. Here, equilibrium occurs on row *b* of the table (point *b* in the figure) at an interest rate of 5 percent a year. At interest rates above 5 percent, the quantity of real money demanded is less than the quantity supplied, so the interest rate falls. At interest rates below 5 percent, the quantity of real money demanded exceeds the quantity supplied, so interest rates rise. Only at 5 percent is the quantity of real money in existence willingly held.

	Interest rate (percent per year)	Quantity of real money demanded (billions of 1986 dollars)	Quantity of real money supplied (billions of 1986 dollars)
a	7	400	500
b	5	500	500
b	3	600	500

In this situation, people will want to hold only $400 billion in real money even though $500 billion exists. But since $500 billion exists, people must be holding it. That is, people are holding more money than they want to. In such a situation, they will try to get rid of some of their money. Each individual will try to re-organize his or her affairs in order to lower the amount of money held and take advantage of the 7 percent interest rate by buying more financial assets. But everybody will be trying to buy financial assets, and nobody will be trying to sell them at a 7 percent interest rate. There is an excess demand for financial assets such as bonds. When there is an excess demand for anything, its price rises. So with an excess demand for financial assets, the prices of financial assets will rise. We saw earlier that there is an inverse relationship between the price of a financial asset and its interest rate. As the price of a financial asset rises, its interest rate falls. *[handwritten: (eg bonds)]*

As long as anyone is holding money in excess of the quantity demanded, that person will try to lower his or her money holdings by buying additional financial assets. Financial asset prices will continue to rise and interest rates will continue to fall. Only when the interest rate has moved down to 5 percent will the amount of money in existence be held willingly. That is, people's attempts to get rid of unwanted excess money do not result in reducing the amount of money held in aggregate. Instead, those efforts result in a change in the interest rate that makes the amount of money available willingly held.

The experiment we have just conducted can be performed in reverse by supposing that the interest rate is 3 percent. In this situation, people will want to hold $600 billion even though only $500 billion is available. To acquire more money, people will sell financial assets. There will be an excess supply of financial assets, so their prices will fall. As the prices of financial assets fall, the yield on them—the interest rate—rises. People will continue to sell financial assets and try to acquire money until the interest rate has risen to 5 percent, where the amount of money available is the amount they want to hold.

◆ ◆ ◆ ◆ In this chapter, we have studied the institutions that make up our banking and financial system. We've seen how the deposit liabilities of chartered banks and other financial institutions comprise our means of payment—our money. We've also seen how banks and other financial institutions create money by making loans. Finally, we've seen how interest rates adjust to make the quantity of money that firms and households are willing to hold equal to the quantity of money that the banking system has created. ◆ ◆ In the next chapter, we're going to see how the quantity of money is regulated and influenced by the actions of the Bank of Canada. We're also going to discover how, by its influence on the money supply, the Bank of Canada is able to influence interest rates, thereby affecting the level of aggregate demand. It is through its effects on the money supply and interest rates and their wider ramifications that the Bank of Canada is able to help steer the course of the economy.

S U M M A R Y

What Is Money?

Money is the means of payment. It has four functions: medium of exchange, unit of account, standard of deferred payment, and store of value. The earliest forms of money were commodities. In the modern world, we use fiat money. The biggest component of money is deposits at banks and other financial institutions.

The two main measures of money in Canada today are M1 and M2+. M1 consists of currency outside the banks and demand deposits at chartered banks. M2+ consists of M1 together with other personal deposits at chartered banks as well as deposits at trust companies, mortgage loan companies, caisses populaires, credit unions, and other institutions. Demand deposits are money but cheques and credit cards are not. (pp. 738–745)

Financial Intermediaries

The main financial intermediaries whose liabilities serve as money are chartered banks, trust and mortgage loan companies, local credit unions, and caisses populaires. These institutions take in deposits, hold cash reserves to ensure that they can meet their depositors' demands for currency, and use the rest of their funds to buy securities or make loans. Financial intermediaries make a profit by borrowing at a lower interest rate than that at which they lend. All financial intermediaries provide four main economic services: they minimize the cost of obtaining funds, minimize the cost of monitoring borrowers, pool risks, and create liquid assets. (pp. 745–749)

How Banks Create Money

Banks create money by making loans. The total quantity of deposits that can be supported by a given amount of reserves (the deposits multiplier) is equal to 1 divided by the desired reserve ratio. (pp. 749–752)

The Demand for Money

The quantity of money demanded is the amount of money that people plan to hold on the average. The quantity of nominal money demanded is proportional to the price level and the quantity of real money demanded depends on the interest rate and real GDP. A higher interest rate induces a smaller quantity of real money demanded—a movement along the demand curve for real money. A higher level of real GDP induces a larger demand for real money—a shift in the demand curve for real money. Technological changes in the financial sector also change the demand for money and shift the demand curve for real money. (pp. 752–757)

Interest Rate Determination

There is an inverse relationship between the interest rate and the price of a financial asset. The higher the interest rate, the lower is the price of a financial asset. Money market equilibrium achieves an interest rate and asset price that make the quantity of real money demanded equal to the quantity supplied. (pp. 757–760)

KEY ELEMENTS

Key Terms

Asset, 746
Balance sheet, 746
Barter, 738
Chartered bank, 746
Commodity money, 739
Convertible paper money, 740
Currency, 741
Demand for real money, 754
Deposits multiplier, 751
Desired reserve ratio, 749
Desired reserves, 749
Double coincidence of wants, 738
Excess reserves, 749
Fiat money, 741
Financial intermediary, 745
Gresham's Law, 740
Liabilities, 746
Liquid asset, 743
Loan, 747
Local credit union, 747
M1, 742
M2+, 742
Means of payment, 738

Medium of exchange, 738
Money, 738
Nominal money, 753
Perpetuity, 757
Private debt money, 741
Reserve ratio, 749
Reserves, 747
Security, 747
Standard of deferred payment, 739
Store of value, 739
Trust and mortgage loan company, 747
Unit of account, 738

Key Figures and Tables

Figure 27.1   Three Measures of Money, 743
Figure 27.5   Money Market Equilibrium, 759
Table 27.2   Measures of Money in Canada, 742
Table 27.3   A Compact Glossary of the
              Components of Money, 742
Table 27.5   A Compact Glossary of Financial
              Intermediaries, 745
Table 27.8   The Interest Rate and the Price of a
              Bond, 758

REVIEW QUESTIONS

1 What is money? What are its functions?

2 What are the different forms of money?

3 What are the two main official measures of money in Canada today?

4 Are cheques and credit cards money? Explain your answer.

5 What are financial intermediaries? What are the types of financial intermediaries in Canada? What are the main deposit-taking institutions other than chartered banks?

6 What are the main items in the balance sheet of a chartered bank?

7 What are the economic functions of financial intermediaries?

8 How do banks make a profit and how do they create money?

9 Define the deposits multiplier. Explain why it equals 1/desired reserve ratio.

10 Explain the motives for holding money.

11 Distinguish between nominal money and real money.

12 What do we mean by the demand for money?

13 What determines the demand for real money?

14 What is the opportunity cost of holding money?

15 What happens to the interest rate on a bond if the price of the bond increases?

16 How does equilibrium come about in the money market?

P R O B L E M S

1 In Canada today, money includes which of the following items?

a Bank of Canada bank notes in the Bank of Montreal's cash machines

b Your Visa card

c The quarters inside public phones

d Bank of Canada bank notes in your wallet

e The cheque you have just written to pay for your rent

f The loan you took last August to pay for your school fees

2 Which of the following items are fiat money? Which are private debt money?

a Deposits at Canada Trust

b Rogers Cable shares held by individuals

c Gold bars held by banks

d A "Loonie"

e Government of Canada securities

f Daily interest chequing accounts

3 Sara withdraws $1,000 from her account at the Lucky Trust Company, keeps $50 in cash, and deposits the balance in her demand account, which is a demand deposit at the Bank of Nova Scotia. What is the immediate change in M1 and M2+?

4 The chartered banks in Desertland have the following assets and liabilities:

Total reserves	$250 million
Loans	$1,000 million
Deposits	$2,000 million
Total assets	$2,500 million

a Construct the chartered banks' balance sheet. If you are missing any assets, call them "other assets"; if you are missing any liabilities, call them "other liabilities."

b Calculate the chartered banks' reserve ratio.

c If the reserve ratio in (b) is equal to the chartered banks' desired reserve ratio, calculate the deposits multiplier.

5 An immigrant arrives in New Transylvania with $1,200. The $1,200 is put into a bank deposit. All the banks in New Transylvania have a desired reserve ratio of 10 percent.

a What is the initial increase in the quantity of bank deposits when the immigrant arrives?

b How much does the immigrant's bank lend out?

c Using a format similar to that in Table 27.7, calculate the amount lent and the amount of deposits created at each "round," assuming that all the funds lent are returned to the banking system in the form of deposits.

d By how much has total deposits increased after 20 rounds of lending?

e What is the ultimate increase in bank loans and bank deposits?

6 You are given the following information about the economy of Miniland: For each $1 increase in real GDP, the demand for real money increases by one quarter of a dollar, other things remaining the same. Also, if the interest rate increases by 1 percentage point (for example, from 4 percent to 5 percent), the quantity of real money demanded falls by $50. If real GDP is $4,000 and the price level is 1,

a At what interest rate is no money held?

b How much real money is held at an interest rate of 10 percent?

c Draw a graph of the demand for real money.

7 Given the demand for real money in Miniland, if the price level is 1, real GDP is $4,000, and the real money supply is $750, what is the equilibrium in the money market?

CHAPTER 28

THE BANK OF CANADA AND MONETARY POLICY

After studying this chapter, you will be able to

◆ Describe the role of the Bank of Canada

◆ Describe the tools used by the Bank of Canada to influence the money supply and interest rates

◆ Explain what an open market operation is and how it works

◆ Explain how an open market changes the money supply

◆ Explain how the Bank of Canada influences interest rates and the value of the Canadian dollar

◆ Explain how the Bank of Canada influences real GDP and the level

◆ Explain the quantity theory of money

T HE YEAR IS 1982. A YOUNG COUPLE, THINKING OF BUYING A first home, has found the perfect place. But mortgage rates are 20 percent a year. Amid much gnashing of teeth, they put off their purchase until interest rates decline, making a home affordable. What determines interest rates? Are they determined by forces of nature? Or is somebody fiddling with the knobs somewhere?   ◆ ◆   You suspect that someone is indeed fiddling with the knobs. For you've just read in your newspaper: "Bank of Canada nudging interest rates down to spark recovery." And a few months earlier, you read: "The Bank of Canada doesn't plan to push interest rates higher unless it sees further rebound of inflation." What is "the Bank of Canada"? Why would the Bank of Canada want to change interest rates? And how can the Bank of Canada influence interest rates?   ◆ ◆   During the 1970s, the quantity of money in existence in Canada increased quickly, but in the 1980s it increased at a

Fiddling with the Knobs

slower pace. In Russia and in some Latin American countries, the quantity of money is increasing at an extremely rapid pace. In Switzerland and Germany, the quantity of money has increased at a slower pace. Does the rate of increase in the quantity of money matter? What are the effects of an increasing quantity of money on our economy?

◆ ◆ ◆ ◆ In this chapter, we are going to study the Bank of Canada and learn how it influences the quantity of money and interest rates in an attempt to smooth the business cycle and keep inflation in check.

The Bank of Canada

The **Bank of Canada** is Canada's central bank. A **central bank** is a public authority charged with regulating and controlling a country's monetary and financial institutions and markets. The Bank of Canada is also responsible for the nation's monetary policy. **Monetary policy** is the attempt to control inflation and the foreign exchange value of our currency, and to moderate the business cycle by changing the quantity of money in circulation and adjusting interest rates. We are going to study the tools available to the Bank of Canada in its conduct of monetary policy and also work out the effects of the Bank of Canada's actions on interest rates. But first we'll examine the origins and structure of the Bank of Canada.

The Origins of the Bank of Canada

The Bank of Canada was created by the Bank of Canada Act of 1935. Before the establishment of the Bank of Canada—for the first 68 years of Canada's history—there was no formal, central bank. The major bank at that time was the Bank of Montreal, which acted as the government's bank. But the Bank of Montreal did not act as a modern, central bank does. In effect, the minister of finance conducted Canada's monetary policy. But that monetary policy was crude and ill-suited to the conditions of the age. None of the tools of monetary policy that we're going to learn about in this chapter was employed in Canada prior to the creation of the Bank of Canada.

By the time that the Bank of Canada was created, most other countries already had a central bank. The Federal Reserve System (the central bank in the United States) had been created in 1913 and the first central banks had been established in Sweden and England as long ago as the seventeenth century. But the origins of these earliest central banks were very different from that of the Bank of Canada. They were set up as private banks designed to solve the financial problems of monarchs. These banks gradually evolved into modern central banks, eventually becoming publicly owned corporations.

The Structure of the Bank of Canada

There are three key components to the structure of the Bank of Canada. They are

◆ The governor
◆ The board of directors
◆ The senior staff

The Governor The governor of the Bank of Canada is appointed by the government of Canada for a term of seven years. There have been six governors of the Bank:

◆ 1935–54, Graham Towers
◆ 1955–61, James Coyne
◆ 1961–73, Louis Rasminsky
◆ 1973–87, Gerald Bouey
◆ 1987–94, John Crow
◆ 1994–,   Gordon Thiessen

The governor of the Bank of Canada, with the advice of the Bank's senior staff, formulates and oversees the implementation of the nation's monetary policy. In these activities, the governor consults closely with the minister of finance and the Bank's board of directors, as well as the senior staff of the Bank.

The Board of Directors The Bank's board of directors consists of the governor, the senior deputy-governor, and the deputy minister of finance, together with 11 men and women from all regions of Canada who represent a variety of commercial, legal, and financial interests. The board meets approximately every month. The minutes of those meetings are summarized and reported in the Bank of Canada's monthly *Review*. The Bank's board meetings take the form of a dialogue and exchange between the governor and the board members. The governor reviews the state of the economy and describes and explains the Bank's recent and current policy positions. The board members comment on the Bank's policy from the perspective of the wide variety of interests that they represent.

Senior Staff The senior staff members of the Bank of Canada are key players in the formulation of the Bank's monetary policy. They are economists and central bankers with considerable national and international experience in monetary and financial affairs. These are the people who, day by day and even hour by hour, monitor the Canadian and world economies. They record the ebbs and flows of economic activity, the rising and falling patterns of interest rates, exchange rates, inflation, unemployment, and GDP. Using macroeconomic models similar to those you are studying in this book, they prepare forecasts of the Canadian economy and of the other major economies of the world and analyse the effects of alternative policy measures that the Bank might take—both those that it ultimately does take and other possible policies that have to be contemplated in the process of arriving at policy decisions.

The Bank of Canada and the Federal Government

There are two different models for the relationship between a country's central bank and its central government:

◆ Independence

◆ Subservience

Independent Central Bank   An independent central bank is one that has complete autonomy to determine the nation's monetary policy. Government public servants and elected officials may comment on monetary policy but the governor of the Bank is under no obligation to take into account the views of anyone other than his own staff and board of directors.

The argument for an independent central bank is that it enables monetary policy to be formulated with a long-term view to maintaining stable prices and prevents monetary policy from being used for short-term, political advantage. Countries that have independent central banks today are Germany, the United States, and Switzerland.

When the Bank of Canada was founded in 1935, it too was established as an independent central bank. Governors Towers and Coyne enjoyed almost complete autonomy from the government of Canada in the formulation and pursuit of their monetary policies. In 1961, however, James Coyne, the governor of the Bank, had a severe clash with John Diefenbaker, the prime minister, concerning who was in charge of the nation's monetary policy. Tight, disinflationary monetary policies were being pursued at the time and, as a consequence of this clash, Coyne resigned as governor. For a period, it was not clear whether the Bank of Canada was indeed

independent as the act that established it proclaimed, or whether it was under the direct control of the government as the outcome of the Coyne-Diefenbaker affair seemed to imply. The matter was resolved in clear-cut terms, however, when a revision of the Bank of Canada Act in 1967 redefined the relationship between the Bank of Canada and the government of Canada, making the Bank a servant of the Department of Finance in monetary policy matters.

Subservient Central Bank   Most central banks are subservient to their governments. In the event of a difference of opinion between the central bank and government, it is the government that carries the day and, if necessary, the central bank governor must resign if he is unwilling to implement the policies dictated by the government. The Bank of Canada has been in such a position since 1967.

Those advocating subservience of the central bank take the view that monetary policy is essentially political in its effects and therefore must, like fiscal policy and indeed all other government policies, be subject ultimately to democratic control.

Although, ultimately, the minister of finance is responsible for Canada's monetary policy, this fact does not, by any means, reduce the governor of the Bank of Canada to a position of impotence. Because of his expertise and authority in the field and because of the quality of the advice that he receives from the Bank's staff of senior economists and advisors, the governor of the Bank has considerable power in both private and public discussions of monetary policy. Opinions would have to be sharply divided and on a range of crucial matters before a government would be willing to run the risk of seeing the governor resign on a dispute over policy. Also, there are times when a government wants to pursue unpopular monetary policies and, at such times, it is convenient for democratically elected officials to hide behind the authority of a relatively independent monetary agency such as the Bank of Canada.

The Bank of Canada is also in a strong position vis-à-vis the government of Canada because the Bank is the government's main banker and financial agent. When the government is running a deficit, the Bank of Canada has the responsibility of helping the government find a way of covering that deficit. One way of covering the deficit is simply to print more money. Another is to handle the sale of government securities. By taking a firm stand and being unwilling to print new money to cover a government's deficit, the Bank can force the government to face the higher interest rates that it brings upon itself by spending in excess of its tax receipts.

International Constraints on the Bank of Canada

The Canadian economy is closely integrated with the world economy. Economic integration has been a fact of Canadian life since long before Confederation. The sheer size and importance of the money and financial markets in New York make it essential that Canadian financial institutions seek profitable business not only in Canada but beyond its borders.

Faced with a giant for a neighbour, some countries erect large barriers that limit the giant's access to the national economy and restrict the international activities of the country's citizens. Canada is not such a country. Just as we have civil freedoms of travel between Canada and the United States, so also do we have considerable economic freedom. There are no restrictions on the movement of goods (except for illegal goods) or on borrowing and lending, imposed by the government of Canada or the Bank of Canada. Foreigners are free to place deposits in Canadian banks and Canadians are free to place deposits in foreign banks. Banks are free to make loans to foreigners or to Canadians. Furthermore, these deposits and loans may be denominated in Canadian dollars or in any other currency. As we saw in Chapter 27 (pp. 746–747), a substantial portion of the deposits and loans of chartered banks is in foreign currencies (most of it in U.S. dollars).

These facts of financial life in Canada restrict the actions that the Bank of Canada can take. It cannot, for example, ignore interest rate pressures that stem from south of the border.

The Bank of Canada is in a similar situation to a monopolist selling fresh mountain spring water. The monopolist can determine a price at which to sell the water, leaving the market to decide how much to buy at that price, or can decide on a production rate, leaving the market to determine the price at which that quantity will be sold. The monopolist cannot choose both the price at which it will sell its output and the quantity that people will buy.

The Bank of Canada is a monopolist in the supply of Canadian dollars. It can choose the quantity to supply but not the price at which it exchanges for other currencies. Alternatively, the Bank of Canada can fix the price at which the Canadian dollar exchanges for some other currency (for example, the U.S. dollar) but, in so doing, it loses control over the quantity of Canadian dollars outstanding.

The choice made by the Bank of Canada is to control the quantity of Canadian money and to let its value fluctuate on the foreign exchange market. By making this choice, the Bank of Canada retains control over Canadian interest rates. How the Bank exercises that control is the subject of the rest of this chapter. How the foreign exchange market works to determine the value of the Canadian dollar is the subject of Chapter 37.

Our next task in studying the Bank of Canada's monetary policy is to examine the policy tools that the Bank has at its disposal.

The Bank of Canada's Policy Tools

The Bank of Canada has many responsibilities, but we'll examine its most important responsibility—regulating the amount of money floating around in Canada and influencing the level of interest rates. How does the Bank of Canada control the money supply? It does so by adjusting the reserves of the banking system. It is also by adjusting the reserves of the banking system, and by standing ready to make loans to banks, that the Bank of Canada is able to prevent banking panics and bank failures. The Bank of Canada uses two main policy tools to achieve its objectives:

◆ Bank rate

◆ Open market operations

Bank Rate   The **bank rate** is the interest rate at which the Bank of Canada stands ready to lend reserves to the chartered banks. The bank rate is fixed every Tuesday and is based on a formula that relates it to movements in the interest rate on three-month government of Canada Treasury bills. The bank rate is usually about 1/4 of a percent above the Treasury bill rate. In practice, chartered banks do not borrow much from the Bank of Canada, so the bank rate does not have any practical consequences for the chartered banks' profits. Instead, it acts as a type of barometer of the attitude of the Bank of Canada towards short-term interest rates. When the bank rate moves up, this is a signal that the Bank of Canada is seeking to tighten monetary conditions.

Other interest rates move with the bank rate in response to this general signal, rather than as a consequence of borrowed reserves being more costly for the banks.

Open Market Operations

An **open market operation** is the purchase or sale of government of Canada securities—Treasury bills and bonds—by the Bank of Canada, designed to influence the money supply. When the Bank of Canada sells government securities, they are paid for with bank deposits and bank reserves, and tighter monetary and credit conditions are created. With lower reserves, the banks cut their lending, and interest rates rise. When the Bank of Canada buys government securities, the Bank of Canada's payment for them puts additional reserves in the hands of the banks and loosens credit conditions. With extra reserves, the banks increase their lending, and interest rates fall. In order to understand the Bank of Canada's open market operations, we first need to examine the structure of the Bank of Canada's balance sheet.

The Bank of Canada's Balance Sheet

The balance sheet of the Bank of Canada for September 1992 is set out in Table 28.1. The assets on the left side are what the Bank of Canada owns and the liabilities on the right side are what it owes. Most of the Bank of Canada's assets are government of Canada securities. The most significant aspect of the Bank of Canada's balance sheet is on the liabilities side.

The largest liability of the Bank of Canada is Bank of Canada notes in circulation. These are the bank notes that we use in our daily transactions. Some of these bank notes are in circulation with the public and others are in the tills and vaults of banks and other financial institutions.

You may be wondering why Bank of Canada notes are considered a liability of the Bank. Bank notes are considered a liability of the bank that issues them because, when notes were invented, they gave their owner a claim on the gold reserves of the issuing bank. Such notes are **convertible paper money**. The holder of such a note could convert the note on demand into gold (or some other commodity such as silver) at a guaranteed price. Thus when a bank issued a note, it was holding itself liable to convert that note into a commodity. Modern bank notes are nonconvertible. A **nonconvertible note** is a bank

TABLE 28.1

The Balance Sheet for the Bank of Canada: September 1992

Assets (millions of dollars)		Liabilities (millions of dollars)	
Government of Canada securities	23.6	Bank of Canada notes in circulation	23.3
		Chartered banks' deposits	2.3
		Monetary base	25.6
Other assets	3.0	Other liabilities	1.0
Total	26.6	Total	26.6

Source: *Bank of Canada Review*, Winter 1992-1993, Table B1.

note that is not convertible into any commodity and that obtains its value by government fiat—hence the term fiat money. Such bank notes are considered the legal liability of the bank that issues them, but they are backed not by commodity reserves but by holdings of securities and loans. Bank of Canada notes are backed by the Bank of Canada's holdings of government of Canada securities.

The other significant liability of the Bank of Canada is the deposits held there by chartered banks. We saw these deposits as an asset in the balance sheets of the banks. The remaining liability of the Bank of Canada consists of items such as government of Canada deposits (government bank accounts at the Bank of Canada) and accounts held by foreign central banks (such as the Bank of England and the Federal Reserve Board).

The two largest items on the liability side of the Bank of Canada's balance sheet make up most of the monetary base. The **monetary base** is the amount of Bank of Canada notes in circulation, chartered banks' deposits at the Bank, and coins in circulation. Coins are issued, not by the Bank of Canada, but by the government of Canada. They do not appear, therefore, as a liability of the Bank of Canada.

By buying or selling government securities, the Bank of Canada can directly determine the scale of its own liabilities and exert a considerable influence upon the monetary base. Such purchases and sales of government securities are the Bank of Canada's open market operations, its main method of controlling the money supply.

Controlling the Money Supply

The money supply is determined by the Bank of Canada's actions. Let's see how. We begin by looking at what happens when the Bank of Canada conducts an open market operation.

How Open Market Operations Work

When the Bank of Canada conducts an open market operation in which it buys government of Canada securities, it increases the reserves of the banking system. When it conducts an open market operation in which it sells government of Canada securities, it decreases the reserves of the banking system. Let's study the effects of an open market operation by working out what happens when the Bank of Canada buys $100 million of government of Canada securities.

Open market operations affect the balance sheets of the Bank of Canada, the banks, and the rest of the economy. Table 28.2 keeps track of the changes in these balance sheets. When the Bank of Canada buys securities, there are two possible sellers: the banks or some other agents in the economy. Part (a) of the table works out what happens when banks sell the securities that the Bank of Canada buys.

When the Bank of Canada buys securities from the banks, the Bank of Canada pays for the securities by crediting the banks' deposit accounts at the Bank of Canada. The Bank of Canada's balance sheet changes. Its assets increase by $100 million (the additional government of Canada securities bought) and its liabilities also increase by $100 million (the additional bank deposits). The banks' balance sheet also changes, but their total assets remain constant. Their deposits at the Bank of Canada increase by $100 million and their securities decrease by $100 million.

Part (b) of the table deals with the case in which the banks do not sell any securities and the Bank of Canada buys securities from agents in the rest of the economy other than the banks. The Bank of Canada's holdings of government of Canada securities increase by $100 million and other agents' holdings of government of Canada securities go down by $100 million. The Bank of Canada pays for the securities by giving cheques drawn on itself to the sellers. The sellers take the cheques to the banks and deposit them. Bank deposits increase by $100 million. The banks in turn present the cheques to the Bank of Canada, which credits the banks' accounts with the value of the cheques. Banks' deposits with the Bank of Canada—reserves—increase by $100 million.

Regardless of which of the two cases takes place, by conducting an open market purchase of securities, the Bank of Canada increases the banks' deposits with itself—increases the banks' reserves.

If the Bank of Canada conducts an open market *sale* of securities, the events that we have just traced occur in reverse. The Bank of Canada's assets and liabilities will decrease in value and so will the reserves of the banks.

The effects of an open market operation on the balance sheets of the Bank of Canada and the banks that we've traced in Table 28.2 are not the end of the story—they are just the beginning. With an increase in their reserves, the banks are now able to make more loans and by making loans they create deposits. We studied this deposit creation process in Chapter 27, where we learned that the change in deposits is a multiple of the change in reserves that brings it about. We'll look again at this multiplier process. But now that you understand the basic idea, we'll add an element of realism we ignored in Chapter 27, the distinction between the monetary base and bank reserves.

Monetary Base and Bank Reserves

We've defined the *monetary base* as the sum of Bank of Canada notes, coins, and banks' deposits at the Bank of Canada. The monetary base is held either by banks as *reserves* or outside the banks as

TABLE 28.2

An Open Market Operation

(a) BANKS SELL THE SECURITIES BOUGHT BY THE BANK OF CANADA

Effects on the balance sheet of the Bank of Canada

Change in assets (millions of dollars)		Change in liabilities (millions of dollars)	
Government of Canada securities	+100	**Banks' deposits reserves (reserves)**	+100

Effects on the balance sheet of the banks

Change in assets (millions of dollars)		Change in liabilities (millions of dollars)	
Banks' deposits (reserves)	+100		
Government of Canada securities	−100		

(b) AGENTS OTHER THAN BANKS SELL THE SECURITIES BOUGHT BY THE BANK OF CANADA

Effects on the balance sheet of the Bank of Canada

Change in assets (millions of dollars)		Change in liabilities (millions of dollars)	
Government of Canada securities	+100	**Banks' deposits (reserves)**	+100

Effects on the balance sheet of the banks

Change in assets (millions of dollars)		Change in liabilities (millions of dollars)	
Banks' deposits (reserves)	+100	**Deposits**	+100

Effects on the balance sheet of the other agents

Change in assets (millions of dollars)		Change in liabilities (millions of dollars)	
Deposits	+100		
Government of Canada securities	−100		

currency in circulation. When the monetary base increases, both bank reserves and currency in circulation increase. Only the increase in bank reserves can be used by banks to make loans and create additional money. An increase in currency held outside the banks is called a **currency drain**. A currency drain reduces the amount of additional money that can be created from a given increase in the monetary base.

The **money multiplier** is the amount by which a change in the monetary base is multiplied to determine the resulting change in the quantity of money.

It differs from the deposits multiplier that we studied in Chapter 27. The *deposits multiplier* is the amount by which a change in bank reserves is multiplied to determine the change in bank deposits.

Let's now look at the money multiplier.

The Multiplier Effect of an Open Market Operation

We'll work out the multiplier effect of an open market operation in which the Bank of Canada buys securities from the banks. In this case, although the open market operation increases the banks' reserves, it has no immediate effect on the quantity of money. The banks are holding additional reserves and fewer government of Canada securities. But they have excess reserves. When the banks have excess reserves, the sequence of events shown in Fig. 28.1 takes place. These events are

- ◆ Banks lend excess reserves.
- ◆ New loans are used to make payments.
- ◆ Households and firms receive payments from new loans.
- ◆ Part of the receipts are held as currency—a *currency drain*.
- ◆ Part of the receipts are deposited in banks.
- ◆ Bank reserves increase (by the same amount as the increase in deposits).
- ◆ Desired reserves increase (by a fraction—the desired reserve ratio—of the increase in deposits).
- ◆ Excess reserves decrease but remain positive.
- ◆ The money supply increases by the amount of the currency drain and the increase in bank deposits.

FIGURE 28.1

A Round in the Multiplier Process Following an Open Market Operation

---

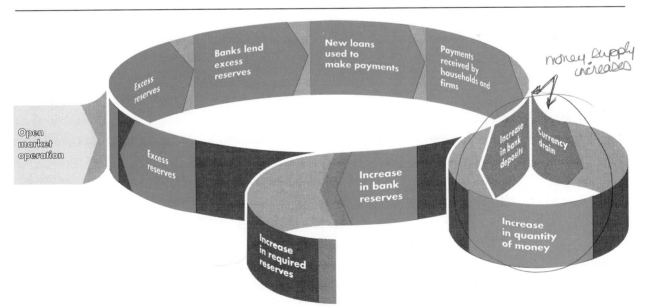

An open market purchase of government of Canada securities increases bank reserves and creates excess reserves. Banks lend the excess reserves and new loans are used to make payments. Households and firms receiving payments keep some of the receipts in the form of currency—a currency drain—and place the rest on deposit in banks. The increase in bank deposits increases banks' reserves, but also increases banks' desired reserves. Desired reserves increase by less than actual reserves, so the banks still have some excess reserves, though less than before. The process repeats until excess reserves have been eliminated. There are two components to the increase in the quantity of money: the currency drain and the increase in deposits.

The sequence just described is similar to the one we studied in Chapter 27 except that there we ignored the currency drain. As before, the sequence repeats in a series of "rounds," but each round begins with a smaller quantity of excess reserves than did the previous one. The process continues until excess reserves have finally been eliminated.

Figure 28.2 illustrates the accumulated increase in the quantity of money and in its components, bank deposits and currency, resulting from an open market operation of $100 million. In this figure, the *currency drain* is one-third and the *desired reserve ratio* is 10 percent. As you can see, when the open market operation (labelled OMO in the figure) takes place, there is no initial change in either the quantity of money or its components. After the first round of bank lending, the quantity of money increases by $100 million—the size of the open market operation. In successive rounds, the quantity of money and its components continue to increase but by successively smaller amounts until, after 10 rounds, the quantities of currency and deposits and their amount, the quantity of money, have almost reached the values to which they are ultimately heading.

The table in Fig. 28.2 keeps track of the magnitudes of new loans, the currency drain, the increases in deposits and reserves, the increase in desired

---

FIGURE 28.2

The Multiplier Effect of an Open Market Operation

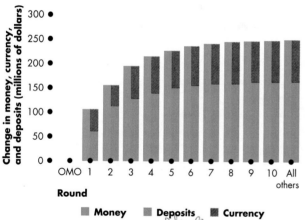

Round

■ **Money**   ■ **Deposits**   ▨ **Currency**

An open market operation (OMO) in which the Bank of Canada buys $100 million of government securities from the banks has no immediate effect on the money supply but creates excess reserves in the banking system. When loans are made with these reserves, bank deposits and currency holdings increase. Each time a new loan is made, part of the loan drains out from the banks and is held as currency and part of the loan stays in the banking system in the form of additional deposits and additional reserves. Banks continue to increase their lending until excess reserves have been eliminated. The effects for the first five "rounds" of lending and money creation are described in the table and the process is illustrated in the figure. The magnitude of the ultimate increase in the money supply is determined by the money multiplier.

Round	Excess reserves at start of round	New loans	Change in deposits	Currency drain	Change in reserves	Change in desired reserves	Excess reserves at end of round	Change in quantity of money
				(millions of dollars)				
1	100.00	100.00	66.67	33.33	66.67	6.67	60.00	100.00
2	60.00	60.00	40.00	20.00	40.00	4.00	36.00	60.00
3	36.00	36.00	24.00	12.00	24.00	2.40	21.60	36.00
4	21.60	21.60	14.40	7.20	14.40	1.44	12.96	21.60
5	12.96	12.96	8.64	4.32	8.64	0.86	7.78	12.96
⋮	⋮	⋮	⋮	⋮	⋮	⋮	⋮	⋮
All others		19.44	12.96	6.48		9.63		19.44
Total		250.00	166.67	83.33		25.00		250.00

reserves, and the change in excess reserves. The initial open market operation increases the banks' reserves, but since deposits do not change there is no change in desired reserves. The banks have excess reserves of $100 million. They lend those reserves. When the money borrowed from the banks is spent, two-thirds of it returns as additional deposits and one-third drains off as currency. Thus when the banks lend the initial $100 million of excess reserves, $66.67 million comes back in the form of deposits and $33.33 million drains off and is held outside the banks as currency. The quantity of money has increased by $100 million—the increase in deposits plus the increase in currency holdings.

The increased bank deposits of $66.67 million generates an increase in desired reserves of 10 percent of that amount, which is $6.67 million. But actual reserves have increased by the same amount as the increase in deposits—$66.67 million. The banks now have excess reserves of $60 million. At this stage we have completed round 1. We've gone around the circle shown in Fig. 28.1 once. The banks still have excess reserves, but the level has fallen from $100 million at the beginning of the round to $60 million at the end of the round. Round 2 begins.

The process we've just described keeps on repeating. The table in Fig. 28.2 shows the first five rounds in this process and collapses all the remaining ones into the next-to-last row of the table. At the end of the process, the quantity of money has increased by $250 million.

The Canadian Money Multiplier

The money multiplier is calculated as the ratio of the change in the quantity of money to the change in the monetary base. That is,

$$\text{Money multiplier} = \frac{\text{Change in the quantity of money}}{\text{Change in the monetary base}}.$$

The size of the money multiplier depends on which measure of money we use. The M1 multiplier in Canada in 1992 was 1.7 and the M2+ multiplier was 20.8. Table 28.3 also gives numbers.

The size of the money multiplier is determined by two ratios. They are

◆ The banks' desired reserve ratio

◆ The ratio of currency holdings outside the banks to bank deposits

---

TABLE 28.3

Calculating the Money Multiplier

In General		Numbers
1. THE VARIABLES		
Reserves	R	
Currency	C	
Monetary base	MB	
Deposits	D	
Money supply	M	
Money multiplier	mm	

2. DEFINITIONS

The monetary base is the sum of reserves and currency	$MB = R + C$	
The money supply is the sum of deposits and currency	$M = D + C$	
The money multiplier is the ratio of the change in the money supply to the change in the monetary base	$mm = \Delta M / \Delta MB$	

3. RATIOS

Change in reserves to change in deposits	$\Delta R / \Delta D$	0.01
Change in currency to change in deposits	$\Delta C / \Delta D$	0.04

4. CALCULATIONS

Begin with the definition	$mm = \Delta M / \Delta MB$	
Use the definitions of M and MB to give	$mm = \dfrac{\Delta D + \Delta C}{\Delta R + \Delta C}$	
Divide top and bottom by ΔD to give	$mm = \dfrac{1 + \Delta C / \Delta D}{\Delta R / \Delta D + \Delta C / \Delta D}$	$= \dfrac{1 + 0.04}{0.04 + 0.01}$
		$= \dfrac{1.04}{0.05}$
		$= 20.8$

Table 28.3 shows how the money multiplier depends on these two ratios. The size of the money multiplier also gives numbers for the M2+ money multiplier in 1992. In 1992 the bank's reserves were 1 percent (0.01) of the deposits in M2+. The currency held outside the banks was 4 percent of the deposits that make up M2+. So the ratio of currency outside the banks to bank deposits was 0.04. Combining these ratios in the formula derived in the table shows that the M2+ money multiplier was 20.8.

REVIEW

T he Bank of Canada is the nation's central bank. The Bank of Canada influences the quantity of money in circulation by changing the excess reserves of the banking system. It has two instruments at its disposal: bank rate and open market operations. Open market operations change the excess reserves of the banking system and set up a multiplier effect. When excess reserves are lent, some of the loans "drain" out of the banking system in the form of currency and others come back in the form of new deposits. The banks continue to lend until the currency drain and the increase in their desired reserves have eliminated excess reserves. The multiplier effect of an open market operation depends on the scale of the currency drain and the banks' desired reserve ratio. ◆

The Bank of Canada's objectives in conducting open market operations or taking other actions that influence the quantity of money in circulation are not simply to affect the money supply for its own sake. Its objective is to influence the course of the economy—especially the level of output, employment, and prices. But these effects are indirect. The Bank of Canada's immediate objective is to move interest rates up or down. To work out the effects of the Bank of Canada's actions on interest rates, we need to work out how interest rates change when the quantity of money changes. We'll discover the answer to this question by studying the money market.

The Money Supply and Interest Rates

I magine that the economy is slowing down and the Bank of Canada wants to encourage additional aggregate demand and spending. To do so, it wants to lower interest rates and encourage more borrowing and more expenditure on goods and services. What does the Bank of Canada do? How does it fiddle with the knobs to achieve lower interest rates?

Changing the Interest Rate

The Bank of Canada undertakes an open market operation, buying government securities from banks, households, and firms. As a consequence, the monetary base increases, and banks start making additional loans. The money supply increases.

Suppose that the Bank of Canada undertakes open market operations on a sufficiently large scale to increase the money supply from $500 billion to $600 billion. As a consequence, the supply curve of real money shifts to the right, as shown in Fig. 28.3(a), from MS_0 to MS_1. At the original interest rate, firms and households are now holding more money than they would like to hold. They attempt to lower their money holding by buying financial assets. As they do so, the prices of bonds and stocks increase and the interest rate falls. When the interest rate has fallen to 3 percent, people are willing to hold the higher $600 billion stock of real money that the Bank of Canada and the banking system has created.

Conversely, suppose that the economy is overheating and the Bank of Canada fears inflation. The Bank of Canada decides to take action to slow down spending and cuts the money supply. In this case, the Bank of Canada undertakes an open market sale of securities. As it does so, it mops up bank reserves and induces the banks to cut down the scale of their lending. The banks make a smaller quantity of new loans each day until the stock of loans outstanding has fallen to a level consistent with the new lower level of reserves. Suppose that the Bank of Canada undertakes an open market sale of securities on a scale big enough to cut the real money supply to $400 billion. Now the supply of real money curve

FIGURE 28.3

The Bank of Canada Changes
the Interest Rate

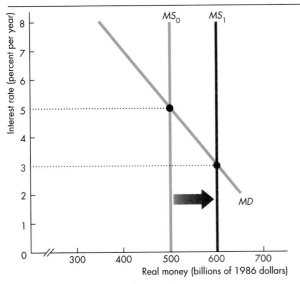

(a) An increase in the money supply

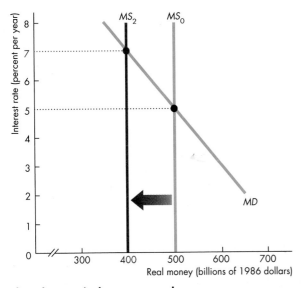

(b) A decrease in the money supply

In part (a), the Bank of Canada increases the money supply to $600 billion. The real money supply shifts rightward. The new equilibrium interest rate is 3 percent. In part (b), the Bank of Canada decreases the real money supply to $400 billion. The money supply curve shifts leftward, and the interest rate rises to 7 percent. By changing the money supply, at a given real GDP and price level, the Bank of Canada can adjust interest rates daily or weekly.

shifts leftward, as shown in Fig. 28.3(b), from MS_0 to MS_2. With less money available, people attempt to acquire additional money by selling interest-earning assets. As they do so, asset prices fall and interest rates rise. Equilibrium occurs when the interest rate has risen to 7 percent, at which point the new lower real money stock of $400 billion is willingly held.

The Bank of Canada in Action

All this sounds nice in theory, but does it really happen? Indeed, it does happen, and sometimes with dramatic effect. Let's look at two episodes in the life of the Bank of Canada, one from the turbulent years of the early 1980s and the other from the period since the stock market crash of 1987—see also Reading Between the Lines, pp. 776–777.

Gerald Bouey's Fight against Inflation   As the 1980s opened, Canada was locked in the grips of double-digit inflation. The governor of the Bank of Canada, Gerald Bouey, with some help from Paul Volcker in the United States, eradicated that inflation. He did so by forcing interest rates sharply upward in the early 1980s. This increase in interest rates resulted from the Bank of Canada (and the Federal Reserve) using open market operations to keep the banks short of reserves, which in turn held back the growth in the supply of loans and of money, relative to the growth in their demand Interest rates increased sharply. Let's relive the episode with the help of some economic analysis.

As we saw in Fig. 28.3(b), to increase interest rates, the Bank of Canada has to cut the real money supply. In practice, because the economy is growing and because prices are rising, a slowdown in nominal money supply growth is enough to increase interest rates. It is not necessary to actually cut the nominal money supply.

In 1982, money supply growth rates were slashed, as you can see from the numbers in Table 28.4. As a result of this slowdown in money supply growth, interest rates increased sharply. The Treasury bill rate—the rate at which the government borrows on a three-month basis—increased from 12 percent to almost 18 percent. Mortgage rates—the rate at which housebuyers borrow—increased to more than 20 percent. The economy went into recession. The money supply growth slowdown and interest rate hike cut back the growth of aggregate demand. Real GDP fell and the inflation rate slowed down.

Monetary Policy Stimulus

THE FINANCIAL POST, MAY 25, 1993

Interest rates targeted

By Greg Ip

Quietly but persistently, the Bank of Canada is signalling that interest rates have a lot further to fall—if it can get skittish money market investors to co-operate.

Over the past six weeks, the central bank's open market operations and cash management have persuaded many traders and analysts that it wants rates as much as a full percentage point lower.

Most analysts predict the commercial bank prime lending rate, now at a 20-year low of 6%, will fall to a 26-year low of 5.75% within the next two weeks and could hit 5.5%, or even 5.25%—a rate unseen since 1959—by summer's end....

Strongest signal
Today the bank rate is expected to fall about 20 basis points from 5.4%, but remain in the 5.2%–5.5% range that has prevailed since March. The central bank's strongest signal that it wants to break through that range is the huge spread it has allowed to open between T-bill yields and the "call" or "overnight" rate, charged on day-to-day loans between banks and other money market participants.

The bank rate is set 25 basis points (one quarter of a percentage point) above the three-month T-bill yield....

Repeated scares
The Bank of Canada's failure to get the bank rate lower in the past two months stems directly from the repeated scares money market traders have had over federal and provincial deficits and credit downgrades.

During April and May 1993, the Bank of Canada's open market operations signalled that the bank wanted interest rates to fall by as much as a full percentage point.

Analysts predicted that the commercial bank prime lending rate would fall from its 20 year low of 6% to a 26 year low of 5.75% within two weeks and could fall to a 34 year low of 5.25% by the end of the summer.

On the day of the news article, the bank rate was expected to fall about 20 basis points (two-tenths of a percentage point) from 5.4% to 5.2%.

The strongest signal that the Bank of Canada wants the bank rate to fall below 5.2% is the spread it has allowed to open between the Treasury bill yield and the overnight interest rate charged on day-to-day loans between banks.

The bank rate is set 25 basis points (one-quarter of a percentage point) above the three-month Treasury bill yield.

The Bank of Canada's failure to get the bank rate lower in the past two months stems from scares over federal and provincial deficits and the fear of credit downgrades.

Background and Analysis

Throughout the first half of 1993, the Bank of Canada increased the quantity of money and lowered interest rates.

But interest rates fell much more during February and March than in April through June. The figure explains why.

The Bank of Canada increased the money supply from January to March, shifting the money supply curve from MS_{Jan} to MS_{Mar}. The demand for money remained at MD_{Jan}, so interest rates fell from 6.7 percent in January to 5.3 percent in March.

In April, the bank increased the money supply by a similar amount to the increase of the previous two months but interest rates barely moved. They fell just 0.1 percentage points to 5.2 percent.

The reason for the small fall in the interest rate was an increase in the demand for money. The demand curve shifted rightward from MD_{Jan} to MD_{Apr}.

Further increases in the supply of money in May and June were accompanied by increases in the demand for money, so the interest rate fell, but only by moderate amounts.

The main reasons why the demand for money increased were increases in real GDP and increasing concern that Ontario's credit rating would be lowered in the international market for credit.

A downgrading of Ontario's credit rating would increase interest rates, lower bond prices, and result in capital losses for bond holders. Wealth holders reasoned that it was better to hold money and avoid the capital losses.

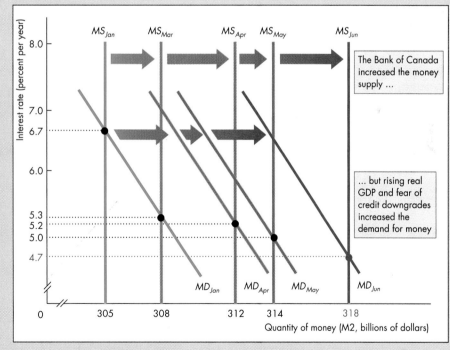

TABLE 28.4

Growth Rates of the Money Supply: 1981-1982

Monetary aggregate	1981	1982
M1	3.3	−0.1
M2+	14.4	8.0

Source: Bank of Canada Review, Winter 1992-1993.

John Crow's Bank   John Crow became governor of the Bank of Canada in January 1987. In the years preceding his appointment, money supply growth rates had been held steady and so had inflation. Crow, like his predecessor, is a fierce inflation fighter and intent on holding the money supply growth rate steady. In October 1987, however, before Crow had been in the job for a full year, he was faced with one of the most severe crises that any central banker can be faced with—a stock market crash. The Bank of Canada, in the company of other central banks around the world, feared the recession potential that might be signalled by the stock market crash. In order to avoid any hint of financial tightness that might exacerbate a recessionary situation, the Bank of Canada permitted the money supply to grow quickly. The money supply growth rate for 1987 edged upward from its 1986 level and short-term interest rates fell slightly.

As the months passed and it became increasingly clear that the October 1987 stock market crash was not signalling a recession, unemployment continued to fall, real GDP continued to be strong, and fears of recession were replaced by fears of a re-emergence of inflation.

Seeking to avoid such an event, the Bank of Canada again slowed down the money supply growth rate, just as Gerald Bouey had done eight years earlier, forcing interest rates upward again. Open market operations were targeted towards creating a shortage of reserves in the banking system to slow down the growth rate of the money supply. As a consequence, during 1988, the growth rates of all the monetary aggregates were substantially below what they had been in 1987.

The Bank of Canada continued to keep a tight reign on money supply growth through 1990 as it increasingly focussed on achieving price stability. As a result, monetary policy contributed to a deepening of Canada's recession in 1991.

Profiting by Predicting the Bank of Canada

Every day the Bank of Canada influences interest rates by its open market operations. By buying securities and increasing the money supply, the Bank of Canada can lower interest rates; by selling securities and lowering the money supply, the Bank of Canada can increase interest rates. Sometimes such actions are taken to offset other influences and keep interest rates steady. At other times the Bank of Canada moves interest rates up or down. The higher the interest rate, the lower is the price of a bond; the lower the interest rate, the higher is the price of a bond. Thus predicting interest rates is the same as predicting bond prices. Predicting that interest rates are going to fall is the same as predicting that bond prices are going to rise—a good time to buy bonds. Predicting that interest rates are going to rise is the same as predicting that bond prices are going to fall—a good time to sell bonds.

Because the Bank of Canada is the major player in bond markets, predicting the Bank of Canada is profitable and a good deal of effort goes into that activity. But people who anticipate that the Bank of Canada is about to increase the money supply buy bonds right away, pushing their prices upward and pushing interest rates downward, *before* the Bank of Canada acts. Similarly, people who anticipate that the Bank of Canada is about to decrease the money supply sell bonds right away, pushing their prices downward and pushing interest rates upward, before the Bank of Canada acts. In other words, bond prices and interest rates change as soon as the Bank of Canada's actions are foreseen. By the time the Bank of Canada actually takes its actions, if those actions are correctly foreseen, they have no effect. The effects occur in anticipation of the Bank of Canada's actions. Only changes in the money supply that are not foreseen change the interest rate at the time that those changes occur.

Interest Rates and the Dollar

We've seen that an increase in the money supply leads to lower interest rates and that a decrease in the money supply leads to higher interest rates. But a change in interest rates affects the exchange rate. Lower interest rates make the dollar fall in value against other currencies, and higher interest rates make the dollar rise in value against other currencies.

R E V I E W

A t any given moment, the interest rate is determined by the demand for and the supply of money. The interest rate makes the quantity of money demanded equal to the quantity of money supplied. Changes in the interest rate occur as a result of changes in the money supply. When the money supply change is unanticipated, interest rates change at the same time as the change in the money supply. When the money supply change is anticipated, interest rates change ahead of the change in the money supply. ◆

The money supply has a powerful effect on our economy. We're seen its influence on interest rates and the exchange rate. Our next task is to examine the effect of the money supply on real GDP and the price level.

Money, Real GDP, and the Price Level

W e now know what money *is*. We also know that in a modern economy such as that of Canada today, most of the money is made up of deposits at banks and other financial intermediaries. We've seen that these institutions can actually create money by making loans. Does the quantity of money created by the banking and financial system

matter? What effects does it have? Does it matter whether the quantity increases quickly or slowly?

We're going to address these questions first by using the aggregate demand-aggregate supply model. Then we're going to consider a special theory of money and prices—the quantity theory of money. Finally, we'll look at some historical and international evidence on the relationship between money and prices. Also, Our Advancing Knowledge on pp. 788–789 looks at the evolution of our understanding of the effects of changes in the quantity of money.

Money in the *AD-AS* Model

We've seen that the Bank of Canada uses monetary policy to steer the economy between unemployment on the one side and inflation on the other. Let's use the aggregate demand-aggregate supply model to work out the effects of the Bank's actions on real GDP and the price level.

Monetary Policy to Reduce Unemployment   In Fig. 28.4, the economy is experiencing unemployment. The long-run aggregate supply, along the *LAS* curve, is $600 billion, but actual real GDP is only $550 billion, at the intersection of the aggregate demand curve AD_0 and the short-run aggregate supply curve is *SAS*. The price level is 90 and real GDP is $4.4 billion. With a large amount of unemployment, wages will eventually fall. As a result, the *SAS* curve will shift rightward, the price level will fall and real GDP will increase, restoring full employment. But this automatic adjustment process is extremely slow.

In an attempt to bring the economy to full employment more quickly, the Bank of Canada increases the quantity of money by conducting an open market operation. Banks, flush with excess reserves, make loans and the loans create money. With more money in their bank accounts, people increase their expenditure and aggregate demand increases. The aggregate demand curve shifts rightward to become AD_1. The new equilibrium is at the intersection point of AD_1 and *SAS*. The price level rises to 130 and real GDP increases to $600 billion. The economy is now on its long-run aggregate supply curve and there is full employment.

To achieve this outcome, the Bank of Canada needs a combination of good judgement and good luck. A smaller increase in the money supply would not shift the aggregate demand curve as far

FIGURE 28.4

Monetary Policy to Reduce Unemployment

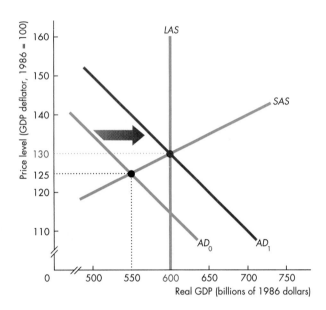

The economy is on aggregate demand curve AD_0 and short-run aggregate supply curve *SAS*. The price level is 125 and real GDP is $550 billion. Long-run aggregate supply is *LAS*, and there is unemployment. An increase in the money supply shifts the aggregate demand curve to AD_1, the price level rises to 130 and real GDP increases to $600 billion, its full-employment level.

FIGURE 28.5

Monetary Policy to Lower Inflation

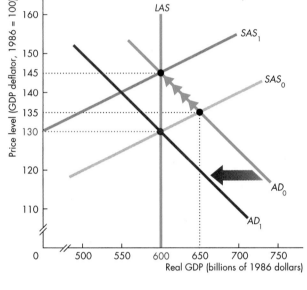

The economy is on aggregate demand curve AD_0 and short-run aggregate supply curve SAS_0. The price level is 135 and real GDP is $650 billion. Long-run aggregate supply is *LAS*, and there is above full-unemployment. With no change in aggregate demand, wages increase, the short-run aggregate supply curve shifts to SAS_1, the price level rises to 145, and real GDP decreases to $600 billion. Before this adjustment occurs, a decrease in the quantity of money shifts the aggregate demand curve to AD_1. The price level falls to 130 and real GDP decreases to $600 billion.

rightward, and the economy would remain in an unemployment equilibrium. A larger increase in the money supply would shift the aggregate demand curve too far rightward and would create an inflation problem.

Let's see how the Bank of Canada can deal with an inflationary situation.

Monetary Policy to Lower Inflation In Fig. 28.5, the economy is overheated and is experiencing inflationary pressures. Long-run aggregate supply along the *LAS* curve is $600. Initially, the short-run aggregate supply curve is SAS_0 and the aggregate demand curve is AD_0. Equilibrium occurs where the aggregate demand curve AD_0 intersects the short-run aggregate supply curve SAS_0. The price level is 135 and real GDP is $650 billion.

If the Bank of Canada does not take some action, the economy will not remain at its current position. Because real GDP is above its long-run level, there is a shortage of labour and wages will begin to rise. As they do so, the *SAS* curve will shift leftward to SAS_1. The price level will rise to 145 and real GDP will decrease to its long-run level of $600 billion.

The Bank of Canada can help to prevent rising wages and rising prices by decreasing the quantity of money. By conducting an open market operation in which it sells securities, the Bank of Canada can decrease the money supply and shift the aggregate demand curve leftward to AD_1. If it takes this action before wages have increased, the new equilibrium is at the intersection point of AD_1 and SAS_0. The price level falls to 130 and real GDP decreases to $600 billion, its long-run level.

Again, to achieve its goal, the Bank of Canada needs a combination of good judgement and good luck. A smaller decrease in the money supply would not shift the aggregate demand curve as far leftward, and the economy would remain in an inflationary situation. A larger decrease in the money supply would shift the aggregate demand curve too far to the left and would create unemployment—as it did in 1991.

The aggregate demand-aggregate supply model tells us how real GDP and the price level respond to a change in the quantity of money. There is another model of money that is more limited that the *AD-AS* model that works in some situations. It is called the quantity theory of money.

The Quantity Theory of Money

The **quantity theory of money** is the proposition that an increase in the quantity of money leads to an equal percentage increase in the price level. The original basis of the quantity theory of money is a concept known as the velocity of circulation and an equation called the equation of exchange. The **velocity of circulation** is the average number of times a dollar of money is used annually to buy the goods and services that make up GDP. GDP is equal to the price level (P) multiplied by real GDP (Y). That is,

$$GDP = PY.$$

Call the quantity of money M. The velocity of circulation, V, is determined by the equation

$$V = PY/M.$$

For example, if GDP is $600 billion and if the quantity of money is $500 billion, the velocity of circulation is 1.2. On the average, each dollar of money circulates 1.2 times in its use to purchase the final goods and services that make up GDP.

The **equation of exchange** states that the quantity of money (M) multiplied by the velocity of circulation (V) equals GDP, or

$$MV = PY.$$

Given the definition of the velocity of circulation, this equation is always true—it is true by definition. With M equal to $500 billion and V equal to 1.2, MV is equal to $600 billion, the value of GDP.

The equation of exchange becomes the quantity theory of money by making two propositions:

◆ The velocity of circulation is a constant.

◆ Real GDP is not influenced by the quantity of money.

If these two propositions are true, the equation of exchange tells us that a given percentage change in the quantity of money brings about an equal percentage change in the price level. You can see why by solving the equation of exchange for the price level. Dividing both sides of the equation by real GDP (Y) gives

$$P = (V/Y)M.$$

Because V and Y are constant, the relationship between the change in the price level (ΔP) and the change in the money supply (ΔM) is

$$\Delta P = (V/Y)\Delta M.$$

Dividing this equation by the previous one gives the quantity theory proposition, namely that the percentage increase in the price level ($\Delta P/P$) equals the percentage increase in the money supply ($\Delta M/M$). That is,

$$\Delta P/P = \Delta M/M.$$

The Quantity Theory and the *AD-AS* Model

The quantity theory of money can be interpreted in terms of the aggregate demand-aggregate supply model. The aggregate demand curve is a relationship between the quantity of real GDP demanded (Y) and the price level (P), other things remaining constant. We can obtain such a relationship from the equation of exchange,

$$MV = PY.$$

Dividing both sides of this equation by real GDP (Y) gives

$$P = MV/Y.$$

This equation may be interpreted as describing an aggregate demand curve. For a given money supply (M) and a given velocity of circulation (V), the higher the price level (*P*), the lower is the quantity of real GDP demanded (*Y*).

In general, when the quantity of money changes, the velocity of circulation might also change. But the quantity theory asserts that velocity is a constant. If velocity is constant, an increase in the quantity of money increases aggregate demand and shifts the aggregate demand curve upward by the same amount as the percentage change in the quantity of money.

The quantity theory of money also asserts that real GDP is not affected by the money supply. This assertion is only true in the aggregate demand-aggregate supply model at a full-employment equilibrium. As we saw in Fig. 28.4(a), starting out with unemployment, an increase in the quantity of money increases real GDP. And starting out at above full-employment, a decrease in the quantity of money decreases real GDP. In these cases, the price level changes by a smaller percentage than the percentage change in aggregate demand and the money supply.

Figure 28.6 uses the *AD-AS* model to get the quantity theory result. Initially the economy is at full employment on the long-run aggregate supply curve *LAS* and at the intersection of the aggregate demand curve *AD*$_0$ and the short-run aggregate supply curve *SAS*$_0$. A 10 percent increase in the quantity of money shifts the aggregate demand curve from *AD*$_0$ to *AD*$_1$. This shift, measured by the vertical distance between the two demand curves, is 10 percent. With no change in wages, the economy moves to an above full-employment equilibrium. But as wages rise, the short-run aggregate supply curve shifts leftward to *SAS*$_1$ and a new full-employment equilibrium occurs at the intersection of *AD*$_1$ and *SAS*$_1$. Real GDP is back at its original level of $600 billion and the price level has increased to 143. The new price level is 10 percent higher than the initial one (143 − 130 = 13, which is 10 percent of 130).

So, the aggregate demand-aggregate supply model predicts the same outcome as the quantity theory of money so long as the velocity of circulation is constant and so long as we compare two positions of full employment. In general, the *AD-AS* model predicts a looser relationship between the quantity of money and the price level than that implied by the quantity theory.

Which theory of the relationship between the quantity of money and the price level is correct? Is the relationship as precise as implied by the quantity

FIGURE 28.6

Money Supply Growth at Full Employment

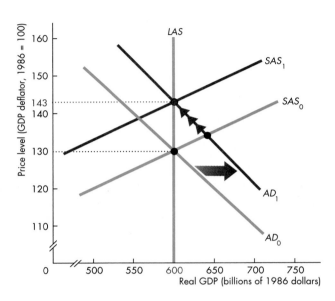

The economy is on aggregate demand curve *AD*$_0$ and short-run aggregate supply curve *SAS*$_0$. The price level is 130 and real GDP is $600 billion. Long-run aggregate supply is *LAS*, and there is full unemployment. A 10 percent increase in the quantity of money shifts the aggregate demand curve to *AD*$_1$. Wages increase by 10 percent and the short-run aggregate supply curve shifts to *SAS*$_1$. The price level rises to 143—a 10 percent increase—and real GDP remains at $600 billion. This outcome is the one predicted by the quantity theory of money.

theory, or is it a looser relationship, as implied by the aggregate demand-aggregate supply model? Let's look at the relationship between money and the price level, both historically and internationally.

Historical Evidence on the Quantity Theory of Money

The quantity theory of money can be tested on the historical data of Canada by looking at the relationship between the growth rate of the quantity of money and the inflation rate. Figure 28.7 shows this relationship for the years between 1926 and 1992.

The figure reveals four features of the relationship between money supply growth and inflation. They are

1. On the average, the quantity of money grows at a rate that exceeds the inflation rate.

2. Variations in the growth rate of the quantity of money are correlated with variations in the inflation rate.

3. During World War II and its aftermath, there was a break in the relationship between money growth and inflation.

4. During the years since 1950, inflation has been less volatile than money supply growth.

1. Average Money Growth and Inflation   You can see that the money growth rate is greater than the inflation rate, on the average, by looking at the two lines in the figure. Most of the time the money growth line is above the inflation line. The difference in the averages is accounted for by the fact that the economy expands with real GDP growing. Money

growth that matches real GDP growth does not add to inflation.

2. Correlation between Money Growth and Inflation
The correlation between money growth and inflation is most evident in the data for the years 1913 to 1940. For example, the massive buildup of inflation during the 1920s was accompanied by a huge increase in the growth rate of the quantity of money. The falling prices of the early 1920s and the Great Depression were associated with a decrease in the quantity of money. Although displaying a less strong relationship in the post-World War II years, you can see that the steadily increasing money supply growth rate through the 1960s and 1970s brought steadily rising inflation through those decades.

3. The Effects of Wars   During World War II, there was a large increase in the growth rate of the money supply but no corresponding increase in the inflation rate. Inflation was suppressed by a program of price controls and rationing. But when these measures were lifted at the end of the war, inflation

FIGURE 28.7

Money Growth and Inflation in Canada

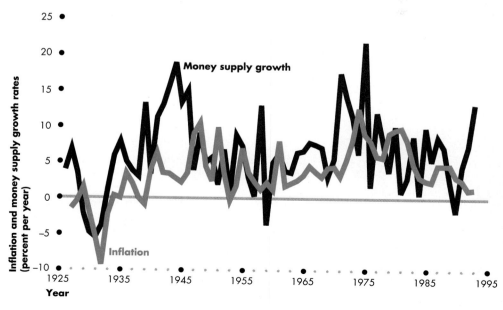

Money growth and inflation between 1926 and 1992 show that broad movements in the inflation rate are caused by changes in the money growth rate. But there are many independent changes in the inflation rate, indicating that money growth is not the only cause of inflation.

Sources: 1926-1945, F. H. Leacy (ed.), *Historical Statistics of Canada*, 2nd edition (based on M. C. Urquhart and K. A. H. Buckley, 1st edition (Statistics Canada and Social Science Federation of Canada, Ottawa, 1982, Series J9); 1946-1969, *Historical Statistics*, Series J26; 1970-1992, *Bank of Canada Review,* Summer 1993, Table K7.

UNDERSTANDING
the Causes of
INFLATION

The combination of history and economics has taught us a great deal about the causes of inflation.

Severe inflation—hyperinflation—arises from a breakdown of the normal fiscal policy processes at times of war and political upheaval. Tax revenues fall short of government spending, and the gap is filled by printing money. As inflation increases, there is a *shortage* of money, so its rate of creation is increased yet further, and prices rise yet faster. Eventually, the monetary system collapses. Such was the experience of Germany in the 1920s, and Russia is heading in this direction today.

In earlier times, when commodities were used as money, inflation resulted from the discovery of new sources of money. The most recent occurrence of this type of inflation was in the nineteenth century when gold, then used as money, was discovered in California and Australia.

In modern times, inflation has resulted from increases in the money supply that have accommodated increases in costs. The most dramatic inflation of this type occurred during the 1970s when oil price increases were accommodated by the Bank of Canada and other central banks around the world.

To avoid inflation, money supply growth must be held in check. But at times of severe cost pressure, central banks feel a strong tug in the direction of avoiding recession and accommodating the cost pressure. Yet some countries have avoided inflation more effectively than others. A key source of success is central bank independence. In low-inflation countries, such as Germany and Japan, the central bank decides how much money to create and at what level to set interest rates, and does not take instructions from the government. In high-inflation countries, such as the United Kingdom and Italy, the central bank takes direct orders from the government about interest rates and money supply growth. This connection between central bank independence and inflation has been noticed by the architects of a new monetary system for the European Community who are modelling the European Central Bank on Germany's Bundesbank, not on the Bank of England!

> "Inflation is always and everywhere a monetary phenomenon."
>
> MILTON FRIEDMAN
> *The Counter-Revolution in Monetary Thory*

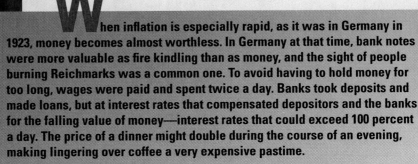

When inflation is especially rapid, as it was in Germany in 1923, money becomes almost worthless. In Germany at that time, bank notes were more valuable as fire kindling than as money, and the sight of people burning Reichmarks was a common one. To avoid having to hold money for too long, wages were paid and spent twice a day. Banks took deposits and made loans, but at interest rates that compensated depositors and the banks for the falling value of money—interest rates that could exceed 100 percent a day. The price of a dinner might double during the course of an evening, making lingering over coffee a very expensive pastime.

Hyperinflation has never occurred in a computer-age economy. But imagine the scene if hyperinflation—an inflation rate of 50 percent a month—did break out. ATMs would be refilled several times an hour, and the volume of paper (both money and receipts) spewed out would grow to astronomical proportions. But most of us would try to avoid using money. Instead, we would buy as much as possible using credit cards. But we'd be eager to pay our card balances off quickly because the interest rate on unpaid balances would be 70 percent a month. Only at such a high interest rate would it pay banks to lend to cardholders, since banks themselves would be paying interest rates of more than 50 percent a month to induce depositors to keep their money in the bank.

DAVID HUME

AND *the Quantity Theory of Money*

Born in Edinburgh, Scotland, in 1711, and a close friend of Adam Smith, David Hume was a philosopher, historian, and economist of extraordinary breadth. His first book, by his own description, "fell dead-born from the press." But his essays, on topics ranging from love and marriage, and the immortality of the soul, to money, interest, and the balance of payments, were widely read and earned him a considerable fortune.

Hume gave the first clear statement of the quantity theory of money—the theory that an increase in the quantity of money brings an equiproportional increase in the price level. His account of the way in which an increase in the quantity of money brings an increase in prices even anticipated the discovery, some 220 years later, of the Phillips curve (see pp. 873–876) and the Keynesian theory of aggregate demand.

temporarily exploded even though money growth was, by then, moderate. There was a further burst of inflation not directly triggered by additional money growth during the Korean War of the early 1950s.

4. Relative Volatility of Money Growth and Inflation

The quantity theory predicts a closer correlation between money growth and inflation than that visible in the data. In particular, it does not predict the generally observed fact that money growth is more volatile than inflation. This tendency for money growth to fluctuate more than inflation, although not consistent with the quantity theory, is predicted by the aggregate demand-aggregate supply model. The phenomenon arises from fluctuations in real GDP that accompany fluctuations in the quantity of money and from changes in the velocity of circulation.

The year-to-year fluctuations in money supply growth and inflation look different from the predictions of the quantity theory. But the longer-term fluctuations in money supply growth and inflation are similar to the predictions of the quantity theory.

International Evidence on the Quantity Theory of Money

The international evidence on the quantity theory of money is summarized in Fig. 28.8, which shows the inflation rate and the money growth rate for 60 countries. There is an unmistakable tendency for high money growth to be associated with high inflation.

But like the historical evidence for Canada, these international data also tell us that money supply growth is not the only influence on inflation. Some countries have an inflation rate that exceeds the money supply growth rate, while others have an inflation rate that falls short of the money supply growth rate.

Correlation and Causation

The fact that money growth and inflation are correlated does not mean that we can determine from that correlation the direction of causation. Money growth might cause inflation; inflation might cause money growth; or some third variable might simultaneously cause inflation and money growth. In the quantity

FIGURE 28.8

Money Growth and Inflation

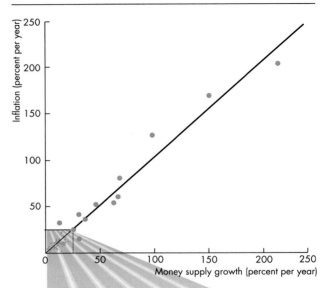

(a) All countries

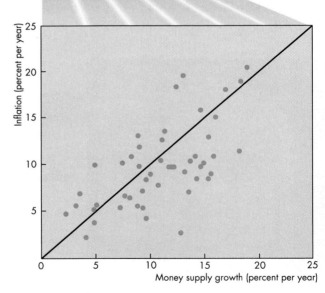

(b) Low-inflation countries

Inflation and money growth in 60 countries (in part a) and low-inflation countries (in part b) show that money growth is one influence, though not the only influence, on inflation.

Source: Federal Reserve Bank of St. Louis, *Review*, May/June 1988, p. 15.

theory and in the aggregate demand-aggregate supply model, causation runs from money growth to inflation. But neither theory denies the possibility that at different times and places, causation might run in the other direction, or that some third factor, such as a government budget deficit, might be the root cause of both rapid money growth and inflation.

There are some occasions, however, that give us an opportunity to test our assumptions about causation. One of these is World War II and the years immediately following it. Rapid money supply growth during the war years accompanied by price controls almost certainly caused the post-war inflation. The inflationary consequences of the money growth was delayed by the controls but not removed. It is inconceivable that this was an example of reverse causation—of post-war inflation causing war-time money growth.

run, an increase in aggregate demand increases both the price level and real GDP. But on the average, real GDP fluctuates around its full-employment level and increases in the quantity of money bring increases in the price level. The quantity theory of money predicts that an increase in the quantity of money produces an equivalent percentage increase in the price level. The historical and international evidence on the relationship between the quantity of money and the price level provides broad support for the quantity theory of money as a proposition about long-run tendencies, but the evidence also reveals changes in the price level that occur independently of changes in the quantity of money. ◆

◆ ◆ ◆ ◆ In this chapter, we've studied the determination of interest rates and discovered how the Bank of Canada can "fiddle with the knobs" to influence interest rates by its open market operations that change the quantity of money. In Chapters 25 and 26 we discovered that the interest rate influences investment, aggregate expenditure, and real GDP. In the next chapter, we're going to bring these two aspects of the macroeconomy together and study the wider effects of the Bank of Canada's actions—effects on investment and the level of aggregate demand.

R E V I E W

T he quantity of money exerts an influence on the price level. An increase in the quantity of money increases aggregate demand. In the short

S U M M A R Y

The Bank of Canada

The Bank of Canada is the central bank of Canada. It is headed by a governor, aided by a staff of senior economists and other advisors, and directed by a board of directors representing a variety of regional and other interests. The Bank's main instrument for influencing the economy is its open market operations. By buying government securities in the market (an open market purchase) the Bank of Canada is able to increase the monetary base and the reserves available to banks. As a result, there is an

expansion of bank lending and a fall in interest rates. By selling government securities, the Bank of Canada is able to decrease the monetary base and the reserves of banks and other financial institutions, thereby curtailing loans and putting upward pressure on interest rates. The overall effect of a change in the monetary base on the money supply is determined by the money multiplier, which in turn depends on the ratio of currency to deposits held by households and firms and the ratio of reserves to deposits held by banks and other financial institutions. (pp. 765–769)

Controlling the Money Supply

By buying government securities in the market (an open market purchase), the Bank of Canada is able to increase the monetary base and the reserves available to banks. As a result, there is an expansion of bank lending and the quantity of money increases. By selling government securities, the Bank of Canada is able to decrease the monetary base and the reserves of banks and other financial institutions, thereby curtailing loans and decreasing the quantity of money. The overall effect of a change in the monetary base on the money supply is determined by the money multiplier. The value of the money multiplier depends on the ratio of currency to deposits held by households and firms and the ratio of reserves to deposits held by banks and other financial institutions. (pp. 769–774)

The Money Supply and Interest Rates

If the quantity of real money is increased by the actions of the Bank of Canada, the interest rate falls and the prices of financial assets rise. People attempt to profit by predicting the actions of the Bank of Canada. To the extent that they can predict the Bank of Canada, interest rates and the price of financial assets move in anticipation of the Bank's actions rather than in response to them. As a consequence, interest rates change when the Bank of Canada changes the money supply only if the Bank of Canada catches people by surprise. Anticipated changes in the money supply produce interest rate changes by themselves.

Interest rates affect the value of the dollar against other currencies. That is, a change in the money supply leads to a change in interest rates and to a change in the foreign exchange value of the dollar. (pp. 774–779)

Money, Real GDP, and the Price Level

The quantity of money affects aggregate demand. An increase in the quantity of money increases aggregate demand and, in the short run, increases both the price level and real GDP. Over the long run, real GDP grows and fluctuates around its full-employment level, and increases in the quantity of money bring increases in the price level. The quantity theory of money predicts that an increase in the quantity of money increases the price level by the same percentage amount and leaves real GDP undisturbed. Both historical and international evidence suggest that the quantity theory of money is only correct in a broad average sense. The quantity of money does exert an influence on the price level but also on real GDP. There are other influences on the price level. Further, the correlation between money growth and inflation does not tell us the direction of causation. (pp. 779–787)

K E Y   E L E M E N T S

Key Terms

Bank of Canada, 765
Bank rate, 767
Central bank, 765
Convertible paper money, 768
Currency drain, 770
Equation of exchange, 781
Monetary base, 768
Money multiplier, 770
Monetary policy, 765
Nonconvertible note, 768
Open market operation, 768
Quantity theory of money, 781
Velocity of circulation, 781

Key Figures and Table

Figure 28.3   The Bank of Canada Changes the Interest Rate, 775
Figure 28.4   Monetary Policy to Reduce Unemployment, 780
Figure 28.5   Monetary Policy to Lower Inflation, 780
Figure 28.6   Money Supply Growth at Full Employment, 782
Table 28.3   Calculating the Money Multiplier, 773

REVIEW QUESTIONS

1 What are the three main elements in the structure of the Bank of Canada?

2 What are the two policy tools of the Bank of Canada? Which of these is the Bank of Canada's main tool?

3 If the Bank of Canada wants to cut the quantity of money, does it buy or sell government of Canada securities in the open market?

4 Describe the events that take place when banks have excess reserves.

5 What is the money multiplier?

6 What determines the size of the money multiplier?

7 What happens to the interest rate if the real GDP and price level are constant and the money supply increases?

8 Explain why it pays people to try to predict the Bank of Canada's actions.

9 What does the aggregate demand-aggregate supply model predict about the effects of a change in the quantity of money on the price level and real GDP

a   Starting out with unemployment?
b   Starting out with above full-employment?
c   Starting out at full employment?

10 What is the equation of exchange and the velocity of circulation? What assumptions are necessary to make the equation of exchange the quantity theory of money?

11 What is the Canadian and international evidence on the quantity theory of money?

PROBLEMS

1 You are given the following information about the economy of Nocoin: The banks have deposits of $300 billion. Their reserves are $15 billion, two-thirds of which is in deposits with the central bank. There are $30 billion notes outside the banks. There are no coins in Nocoin!

a   Calculate the monetary base.
b   Calculate the currency drain.
c   Calculate the money supply.
d   Calculate the money multiplier.

2 Suppose the Bank of Nocoin, the central bank, undertakes an open market purchase of securities of $0.5 million. What happens to the money supply? Explain why the change in the money supply is not equal to the change in the monetary base?

3 You are given the following information about the economy of Miniland: For each $1 increase in real GDP, the demand for real money increases by one quarter of a dollar, other things remaining the same. Also, if the interest rate increases by 1 percentage point (for example, from 4 percent to

5 percent), the quantity of real money demanded falls by $50. Suppose that the Bank of Miniland, the central bank, wants to lower the interest rate by 1 percentage point. By how much would it have to change the real money supply to achieve that objective?

4 Quantecon is a country in which the quantity theory of money operates. The country has a constant population, capital stock, and technology. In year 1, real GDP was $400 million, the price level was 200, and the velocity of circulation of money was 20. In year 2, the quantity of money was 20 percent higher than in year 1.

a   What was the quantity of money in Quantecon in year 1?
b   What was the quantity of money in Quantecon in year 2?
c   What was the price level in Quantecon in year 2?
d   What was the level of real GDP in Quantecon in year 2?
e   What was the velocity of circulation in Quantecon in year 2?

CHAPTER 29

FISCAL AND MONETARY INFLUENCES ON AGGREGATE DEMAND

After studying this chapter, you will be able to

◆ Explain how fiscal policy—a change in government purchases or taxes—influences interest rates and aggregate demand

◆ Explain how monetary policy—a change in the money supply—influences interest rates and aggregate demand

◆ Explain what determines the relative effectiveness of fiscal and monetary policy on aggregate demand

◆ Describe the Keynesian–monetarist controversy about the influence of fiscal and monetary policy on aggregate demand and explain how the controversy was settled

◆ Explain how the mix of fiscal and monetary policy influences the composition of aggregate expenditure

◆ Explain how fiscal and monetary policy influence real GDP and the price level in both the short run and the long run

EACH YEAR, THE FEDERAL PARLIAMENT AND PROVINCIAL legislatures approve budgets that in 1993 put taxes and spending at more than $300 billion—close to one-half of GDP. How do taxes and government spending influence aggregate demand, interest rates, and the exchange rate? ◆ ◆ Not far from Parliament Hill, on Sparks Street, the Bank of Canada pulls the nation's monetary policy levers. We've seen how the Bank of Canada influences interest rates and the exchange rate. But how do the effects of the Bank's actions ripple through to the rest of the economy? ◆ ◆ There are times when fiscal policy and monetary policy are in harmony with each other. And there are other times when they come into conflict—creating sparks on Sparks Street! Do fiscal and monetary policies need to be coordinated? Are they equivalent to each other? Does it matter whether a recession is avoided by having the Bank loosen up its monetary policy or by having Parliament cut taxes?

Sparks Fly in Ottawa

◆ ◆ ◆ ◆ We are going to answer these questions in this chapter. You already know that the effects of fiscal and monetary policy are determined by the interaction of aggregate demand and aggregate supply. And you already know quite a lot about these two concepts. But this chapter will give you a deeper understanding of aggregate demand and the way it is affected by the actions of the federal government and the Bank of Canada.

Money, Interest, and Aggregate Demand

Our goal is to understand how fiscal and monetary policy influence real GDP and the price level (as well as unemployment and inflation). Real GDP and the price level are determined by the interaction of aggregate demand and aggregate supply, as described in Chapter 24. But the main effects of fiscal and monetary policy are on aggregate *demand*. Thus we focus our attention initially on these effects.

To study the effects of fiscal and monetary policy on aggregate demand we use the aggregate expenditure model of Chapters 25 and 26. This model determines equilibrium expenditure *at a given price level*. Such an equilibrium corresponds to a point on the aggregate demand curve (see Fig. 25.12). When equilibrium expenditure changes, the aggregate demand curve shifts and by the amount of the change in equilibrium expenditure.

The aggregate expenditure model freezes the price level and asks questions about the directions and magnitudes of the shifts of the aggregate demand curve at a given price level. But the price level is not actually fixed. It is determined by aggregate demand and aggregate supply.

We begin our study of fiscal and monetary policy by discovering an interaction among aggregate expenditure decisions, the interest rate, and the supply of money.

Spending Decisions, Interest, and Money

We discovered in Chapter 26 (pp. 716–717) that equilibrium expenditure depends on the level of autonomous expenditure. We also discovered that one of the components of autonomous expenditure—investment—varies with the interest rate.[1] The higher the interest rate, other things remaining the same, the lower is investment and hence the lower is autonomous expenditure and equilibrium

expenditure. Therefore equilibrium expenditure and real GDP depend on the interest rate.

In Chapters 27 and 28, we saw how the interest rate is determined by equilibrium in the money market. We also saw that the demand for money depends on both real GDP and the interest rate. The higher the level of real GDP, other things remaining the same, the greater is the demand for money and the higher is the interest rate. Therefore the interest rate depends on real GDP.

We're now going to see how *both* real GDP and the interest rate are determined simultaneously. We'll then go on to see how the Bank's monetary policy and the government's fiscal policy affect both real GDP and the interest rate at a given price level.

Equilibrium Expenditure and the Interest Rate

Let's see how we can link together the money market, where the interest rate is determined, and the market for goods and services, where equilibrium expenditure is determined. Figure 29.1 illustrates the determination of equilibrium expenditure and the interest rate. The figure has three parts: part (a) illustrates the money market; part (b) shows investment demand; and part (c) shows aggregate planned expenditure and the determination of equilibrium expenditure. Let's begin with part (a).

The Money Market   The curve labelled *MD* is the demand for real money. The position of this curve depends on the level of real GDP. For a given level of real GDP, there is a given demand curve for real money. Suppose that the demand curve shown in the figure describes the demand for real money when real GDP is $600 billion. If real GDP is higher than $600 billion, the demand curve for real money is to the right of the one shown; if real GDP is below $600 billion, the demand curve for real money is to the left of the one shown.

The curve labelled *MS* is the supply curve of real money. Its position is determined by the monetary policy actions of the Bank of Canada, the behaviour of the banking system, and the price level. At a given point in time, all these influences determine a quantity of money supplied that is independent of the interest rate. Hence the supply curve for real money is vertical. ⤷ *fixed*

The interest rate adjusts to achieve equilibrium in the money market—equality between the quantity of real money demanded and the quantity supplied.

---

[1] Actually, investment depends on the *real* interest rate. Here, we assume there is no inflation and the real interest rate is equal to the *nominal* interest rate.

FIGURE 29.1

Equilibrium Interest Rate and Real GDP

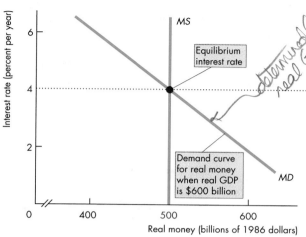

(a) Money and the interest rate

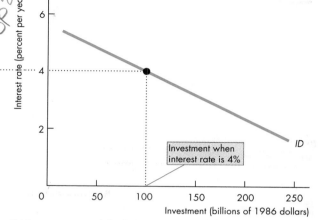

(b) Investment and the interest rate

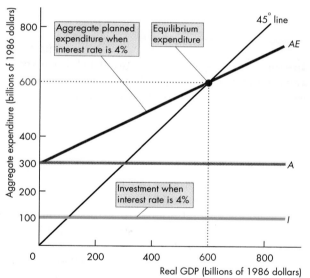

(c) Expenditure and real GDP

Equilibrium in the money market (part a) determines the interest rate. The money supply curve is *MS* and the demand curve for real money is *MD*. The position of the *MD* curve is determined by real GDP and the curve shown is for a real GDP of $600 billion. The investment demand curve (*ID*) in part (b) determines investment at the equilibrium interest rate determined in the money market.

Investment is part of autonomous expenditure and its level determines the position of the aggregate expenditure curve (*AE*) shown in part (c). Equilibrium expenditure and real GDP are determined at the point at which the aggregate expenditure curve intersects the 45° line. In equilibrium, real GDP and the interest rate are such that the quantity of real money demanded equals the quantity of real money supplied and aggregate planned expenditure equals real GDP.

This equilibrium occurs at the point of intersection of the demand and supply curves of real money. In the economy illustrated in Fig. 29.1, the equilibrium interest rate is 4 percent.

Investment and Interest Rate   Next, let's look at part (b), where investment is determined. The investment demand curve is *ID*. The position of the investment demand curve is determined by profit

expectations and, as those expectations change, the investment demand curve shifts. For given expectations, there is a given investment demand curve. This curve tells us the level of planned investment at each level of the interest rate. We already know the interest rate from equilibrium in the money market. When the investment demand curve is *ID* and the interest rate is 4 percent, the level of planned investment is $100 billion.

Equilibrium Expenditure   Part (c) shows the determination of equilibrium expenditure. This diagram is similar to the one that you studied in Chapter 25 (Fig. 25.11a). The aggregate expenditure curve (*AE*) tells us aggregate planned expenditure at each level of real GDP. Aggregate planned expenditure is made up of autonomous expenditure and induced expenditure. Investment is part of autonomous expenditure. In this example, investment is $100 billion and the other components of autonomous expenditure are $200 billion, so autonomous expenditure is $300 billion. These amounts of investment *I* and autonomous expenditure *A* are shown by the horizontal lines in part (c). Induced expenditure is the induced part of consumption expenditure minus imports. In this example, the marginal propensity to buy domestic goods and services is 0.5, therefore induced expenditure equals 0.5 multiplied by real GDP.

Equilibrium expenditure is determined at the point of intersection of the *AE* curve and the 45° line. Equilibrium expenditure occurs when aggregate planned expenditure and real GDP are each $600 billion. That is, the level of aggregate demand is $600 billion.

The Money Market Again   Recall that the demand curve *MD*, in part (a), is the demand curve for real money when real GDP is $600 billion. We've just determined in part (c) that when aggregate expenditure is at its equilibrium level, real GDP is $600 billion. What happens if the level of real GDP that we discover in part (c) is different from the value that we assumed when drawing the demand curve for real money in part (a)? Let's perform a thought experiment to answer this question.

Suppose, when drawing the demand curve for real money, we assume that real GDP is $500 billion. In this case, the demand curve for real money is to the left of the *MD* curve in part (a). The equilibrium interest rate is lower than 4 percent. With an interest rate below 4 percent, investment is not $100 billion as determined in part (b), but a larger amount. If investment is larger than $100 billion, autonomous expenditure is larger and the *AE* curve lies above the one shown in part (c). If the aggregate expenditure curve is above the *AE* curve shown, equilibrium expenditure and real GDP are larger than $600 billion. Thus if we start with the demand curve for real money for a real GDP less than $600 billion, equilibrium expenditure occurs at a real GDP that is

greater than $600 billion. There is an inconsistency: the real GDP assumed in drawing the demand curve for real money is too small.

Next, let's reverse the experiment. Assume a level of real GDP of $700 billion. In this case, the demand curve for real money lies to the right of the *MD* curve in part (a). The equilibrium interest rate is higher than 4 percent. With an interest rate higher than 4 percent, investment is less than $100 billion and the *AE* curve lies below the one shown in part (c). In this case, equilibrium expenditure occurs at a real GDP that is less than $600 billion. Again, there is an inconsistency, but now the real GDP assumed in drawing the demand curve for real money is too large.

We've just seen that for a given money supply, money market equilibrium determines an interest rate that varies with real GDP. The higher the level of real GDP, the higher is the equilibrium interest rate. But the interest rate determines investment which, in turn, determines equilibrium expenditure. The higher the interest rate, the lower is investment and the smaller is equilibrium real GDP.

There is one particular level of both the interest rate and real GDP that simultaneously gives money market equilibrium and equilibrium expenditure. In the example we are studying, that interest rate is 4 percent and real GDP is $600 billion. Only if we use a real GDP of $600 billion to determine the position of the demand curve for real money do we get a consistent story in the three parts of this figure. If the demand curve for real money is based on a real GDP of $600 billion, the interest rate determined (4 percent) delivers investment of $100 billion which, in turn, generates equilibrium expenditure at the same level of real GDP that determines the position of the demand curve for real money.

Let's now study the effects of fiscal policy on aggregate demand.

Fiscal Policy and Aggregate Demand

The government is concerned that the economy is slowing down and that a recession looks likely. To head off the recession, the government decides to stimulate aggregate demand by using fiscal policy, increasing its purchases of goods and services by $150 billion. A fiscal policy that increases aggregate demand is called an *expansionary fiscal policy*.

The effects of the government's actions are similar to those of throwing a pebble into a pond. There's an initial splash followed by a series of ever smaller ripples. The initial splash is the "first round effect" of the fiscal policy action. The ripples are the "second round effects." Let's start by looking at the first round effects of the government's fiscal policy action.

First Round Effects of Fiscal Policy

The economy starts out in the situation shown in Fig. 29.1. The interest rate is 4 percent, investment is $100 billion, and real GDP is $600 billion. In this situation, the government increases its purchases of goods and services by $150 billion.

The first round effects of this action are shown in Fig. 29.2. The increase in government purchases increases autonomous expenditure. This increase is shown in Fig. 29.2 by the shift of the line A_0 to A_1. The increase in autonomous expenditure increases aggregate planned expenditure and shifts the AE curve upward from AE_0 to AE_1. Equilibrium expenditure increases to $900 billion. This increase in aggregate planned expenditure and equilibrium expenditure sets off a multiplier process that starts real GDP increasing. We described this process in Chapter 26, pp. 716–717. These are the first round effects of an expansionary fiscal policy and they are summarized in Fig. 29.3(a).

Second Round Effects of Fiscal Policy

At the end of the first round that we've just studied, real GDP is rising. The increase in real GDP increases the demand for money. The increase in the demand for money raises the interest rate. The rise in the interest rate decreases investment, and autonomous expenditure decreases. The decrease in autonomous expenditure decreases aggregate planned expenditure, which in turn decreases equilibrium expenditure. These second round effects are summarized in Fig. 29.3(b). These effects go in the opposite direction to the first round effects, but they are smaller. They diminish the magnitude of the first

FIGURE 29.2

First Round Effects of an
Expansionary Fiscal Policy

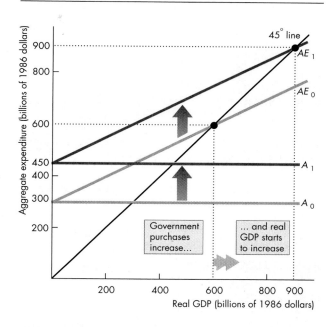

Initially, autonomous expenditure is A_0, the aggregate expenditure curve is AE_0, and real GDP is $600 billion. An increase in government purchases of goods and services increases autonomous expenditure to A_1. The aggregate expenditure curve shifts upward to AE_1 and equilibrium expenditure increases to $900 billion. A multiplier process is set off in which real GDP starts to increase. These are the first round effects of an expansionary fiscal policy.

round effects but do not change the direction of the outcome of the fiscal policy action. That outcome is an increase in real GDP, an increase in the interest rate, and a decrease in investment.

When a new equilibrium is arrived at, the new higher real GDP and higher interest rate give simultaneous money market equilibrium and equilibrium expenditure similar to that in Fig. 29.1. This equilibrium is shown in Fig. 29.4. The demand for real money has increased to MD_1 and the interest rate has risen to 5 percent in part (a). The higher interest rate has decreased investment in part (b). The increase in autonomous expenditure is $100 billion, which is equal to the initial increase in government

FIGURE 29.3

How the Economy Adjusts to an Expansionary Fiscal Policy

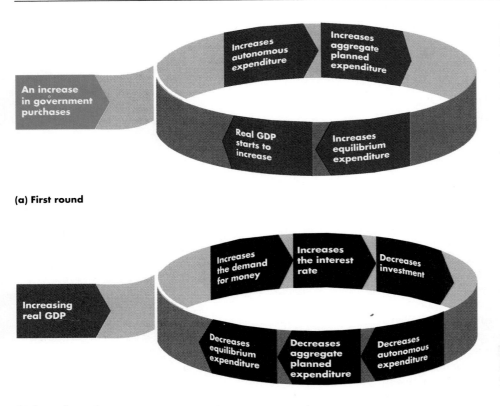

(a) First round

(b) Second round

In the first round (part a), an increase in government purchases increases autonomous expenditure. Aggregate planned expenditure and equilibrium expenditure increase. A multiplier process is set off that starts real GDP increasing.

In the second round (part b), the rising real GDP increases the demand for money, and interest rates rise. The rising interest rate decreases investment, decreases autonomous expenditure, and decreases aggregate planned expenditure and equilibrium expenditure.

The second round effects work in the opposite direction to the first round effects and are smaller in magnitude. The outcome of an increase in government purchases is an increase in real GDP, a rise in the interest rate, and a decrease in investment.

purchases of $150 billion minus the decrease in investment of $50 billion, shown in part (c). Finally, aggregate planned expenditure has increased to AE_1 and the new equilibrium expenditure is at a real GDP of $800 billion (also shown in part c).

Other Fiscal Policies   A change in government purchases is only one possible fiscal policy action. Others are a change in transfer payments, such as an increase in unemployment compensation or an increase in social benefits, and a change in taxes. All fiscal policy actions work by changing autonomous expenditure. The magnitude of the change in autonomous expenditure differs for different fiscal actions. But fiscal policy actions that change autonomous expenditure by a given amount and in a

given direction have similar effects on equilibrium real GDP and the interest rate regardless of whether they involve changes in purchases of goods and services, transfer payments, or taxes.

R E V I E W

A n expansionary fiscal policy—an increase in government purchases of goods and services or an increase in transfer payments, or a decrease in taxes—affects aggregate demand by increasing autonomous expenditure.

FIGURE 29.4

The Effects of a Change in Government Purchases

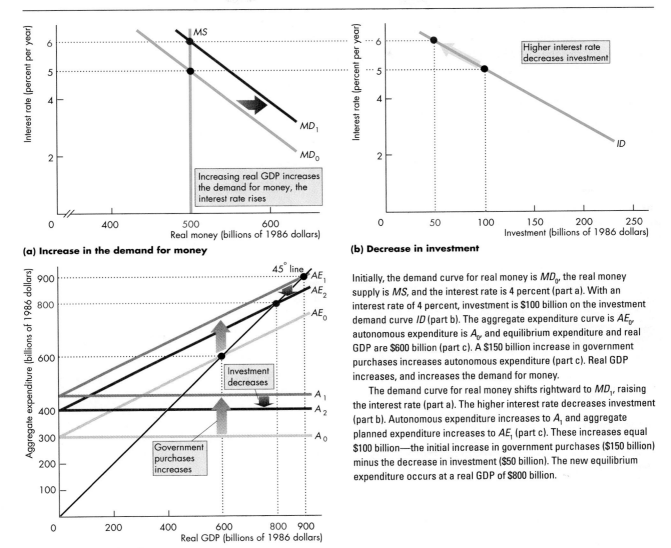

(a) Increase in the demand for money

(b) Decrease in investment

(c) Expenditure and real GDP

Initially, the demand curve for real money is MD_0, the real money supply is MS, and the interest rate is 4 percent (part a). With an interest rate of 4 percent, investment is $100 billion on the investment demand curve ID (part b). The aggregate expenditure curve is AE_0, autonomous expenditure is A_0, and equilibrium expenditure and real GDP are $600 billion (part c). A $150 billion increase in government purchases increases autonomous expenditure (part c). Real GDP increases, and increases the demand for money.

The demand curve for real money shifts rightward to MD_1, raising the interest rate (part a). The higher interest rate decreases investment (part b). Autonomous expenditure increases to A_1 and aggregate planned expenditure increases to AE_1 (part c). These increases equal $100 billion—the initial increase in government purchases ($150 billion) minus the decrease in investment ($50 billion). The new equilibrium expenditure occurs at a real GDP of $800 billion.

◆ In the first round, aggregate planned expenditure increases, real GDP increases, the demand for money increases, and the interest rate starts to rise.

◆ In the second round, the rising interest rate decreases investment, decreases autonomous expenditure, and decreases equilibrium expenditure and real GDP.

The second round effects go in the opposite direction to the first round effects but are smaller. An expansionary fiscal policy increases real GDP, raises the interest rate, and decreases investment. ◆

We've seen that an expansionary fiscal policy raises interest rates and decreases investment. Let's take a closer look at this effect of fiscal policy.

Crowding Out and Crowding In

The tendency for an expansionary fiscal policy to increase interest rates and decrease investment is called **crowding out**. Crowding out may be partial or complete. Partial crowding out occurs when the decrease in investment is less than the increase in government purchases. This is the normal case— and the case we've just seen. Increased government purchases of goods and services increase real GDP, which increases the demand for real money, and so interest rates rise. Higher interest rates decrease investment. But the effect on investment is smaller than the initial change in government purchases.

Complete crowding out occurs if the decrease in investment equals the initial increase in government purchases. For complete crowding out to occur, a small change in the demand for real money must lead to a large change in the interest rate, and the change in the interest rate must lead to a large change in investment.

Another influence of government purchases on investment that we've not considered so far works in the opposite direction to the crowding out effect and is called "crowding in." **Crowding in** is the tendency for expansionary fiscal policy to *increase* investment. This effect works in three ways.

First, in a recession, an expansionary fiscal policy might create expectations of a more speedy recovery and bring an increase in expected future profits. With higher expected profits, the investment demand curve shifts rightward and investment increases despite higher interest rates.

The second source of crowding in is increased government purchases of capital. Such expenditure might increase the profitability of privately owned capital and lead to an increase in investment. For example, suppose the government increased its expenditure and built a new highway that cut the cost of transporting a farmer's produce to a market that previously was too costly to serve. The farmer might now purchase a new fleet of refrigerated trucks to take advantage of the newly available profit opportunity.

The third source of crowding in is decreased taxes. If the expansionary fiscal policy cuts the taxes on business profits, firms' after-tax profits increase and additional investment might be undertaken.

As a practical matter, crowding out is probably more common than crowding in, and because of a persistent government deficit, crowding out is a continuing source of uneasiness in Canada.

International Crowding Out

We've seen that an expansionary fiscal policy leads to higher interest rates. And with interest rates higher in Canada than in the rest of the world, funds flow into Canada and people around the world demand more Canadian dollars. The dollar rises in value against other currencies. Foreigners now find Canadian exports more expensive and Canadians find imports less expensive. Exports fall and imports rise—net exports falls. The tendency for expansionary fiscal policy to decrease net exports is called **international crowding out**. The decrease in net exports offsets to some degree the initial increase in aggregate expenditure brought about by an expansionary fiscal policy.

REVIEW

C rowding out can be partial or complete. The normal case is partial crowding out— the decrease in investment is less than the initial increase in autonomous expenditure resulting from the fiscal action. ◆ ◆ Crowding in might occur in a recession if fiscal stimulation brings expectations of higher future profits, if the government purchases of capital hasten recovery, or if tax cuts stimulate investment. ◆ ◆ International crowding out occurs if fiscal expansion increases interest rates and makes the dollar rise in value against other currencies. A higher dollar decreases net exports. ◆

Let's now study the effects of monetary policy on aggregate demand.

Monetary Policy and Aggregate Demand

T he Bank of Canada is concerned that the economy is heading for a recession. To speed up the economy, the Bank decides to increase aggregate demand by increasing the money supply. To work out the consequences of this monetary policy action, we divide its effects into first round and second round effects (just as we did with fiscal policy). Let's look at the first round effects of the Bank's monetary policy action.

First Round Effects of a Change in the Money Supply

The economy is in the situation that we studied in Fig. 29.1. The interest rate is 4 percent, investment

is $100 billion, and real GDP is $600 billion. The Bank of Canada now increases the real money supply by $150 billion, from $500 billion to $650 billion. The first round effects of this action are shown in Fig. 29.5. The immediate effect is shown in part (a). The real money supply curve shifts rightward from MS_0 to MS_1, and the interest rate falls from 4 percent to 1 percent. The effect of the lower interest rate is shown in part (b). Investment increases from $100 billion to $250 billion—a movement along the

FIGURE 29.5

First Round Effects of an Increase in the Money Supply

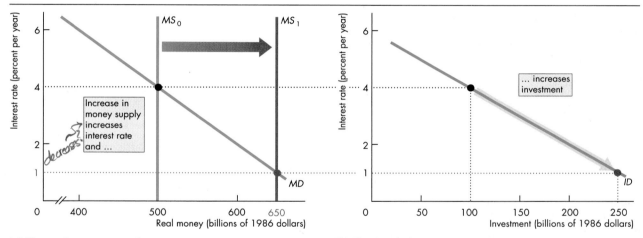

(a) Change in money supply

(b) Changes in investment

An increase in the money supply shifts the supply curve of real money from MS_0 to MS_1 (part a). Equilibrium in the money market is achieved by a fall in the interest rate from 4 percent to 1 percent. At the lower interest rate, investment increases (part b). The increase in investment increases both autonomous expenditure and aggregate planned expenditure (part c). The AE curve shifts upward from AE_0 to AE_1. Equilibrium real GDP increases from $600 billion to $900 billion. And a multiplier process is set up in which real GDP increases.

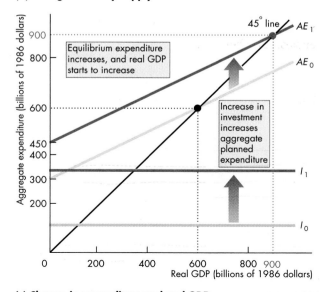

(c) Change in expenditure and real GDP

investment demand curve. The effect of an increase in investment is shown in part (c). The increase in investment increases aggregate planned expenditure—an upward shift in the AE curve from AE_0 to AE_1. The increase in aggregate planned expenditure increases equilibrium expenditure, and real GDP starts to increase. That is, a multiplier process begins in which real GDP gradually increases towards its equilibrium level. We described such a process in Chapter 26 (pp. 716–717).

We've just described the first round effects of an increase in the money supply: the interest rate falls, investment increases, and real GDP starts to increase. These effects are illustrated in Fig. 29.6(a).

Second Round Effects of a Change in Money Supply

At the end of the first round that we've just studied, real GDP is increasing. As real GDP increases it sets off the second round, which is illustrated in Fig. 29.6(b). A higher real GDP increases the demand for real money, and the interest rate rises. The higher interest rate brings a decrease in investment and a decrease in aggregate planned expenditure. With aggregate planned expenditure decreasing, equilibrium expenditure is also decreasing.

These second round effects go in the opposite direction to the first round effects, but they are smaller. They diminish the magnitude of the first

FIGURE 29.6

How the Economy Adjusts to an Increase in the Money Supply

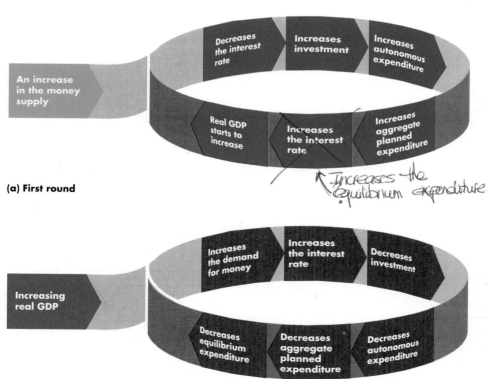

(a) First round

(b) Second round

In the first round (part a), an increase in the money supply decreases the interest rate, which increases investment, autonomous expenditure, aggregate planned expenditure, and equilibrium expenditure. Real GDP starts to increase.

In the second round (part b), the increasing real GDP increases the demand for money. The interest rate rises, and investment decreases. The decrease in investment decreases autonomous expenditure, aggregate planned expenditure, and equilibrium expenditure.

The second round effects work in the opposite direction to the first round effects but are smaller in magnitude. The outcome of an increase in the money supply is an increase in real GDP and a fall in the interest rate.

round effects, but they do not change the direction of the outcome of the monetary policy action. That outcome is an increase in real GDP and a fall in the interest rate. When a new equilibrium is arrived at, the new higher real GDP and lower interest rate give simultaneous money market equilibrium and equilibrium expenditure similar to that in Fig. 29.1. This equilibrium is shown in Fig. 29.7. The demand for real money has increased to MD_1 and the inter-

est rate has fallen to 2 percent in part (a). The lower interest rate has increased investment in part (b). The increase in investment is $100 billion, which is equal to the initial increase of $150 billion minus a decrease of $50 billion, shown in part (c). Finally, aggregate planned expenditure has increased to AE_2 and the new equilibrium expenditure is at a real GDP of $800 billion (also shown in part c).

FIGURE 29.7

The Effects of a Change in the Money Supply

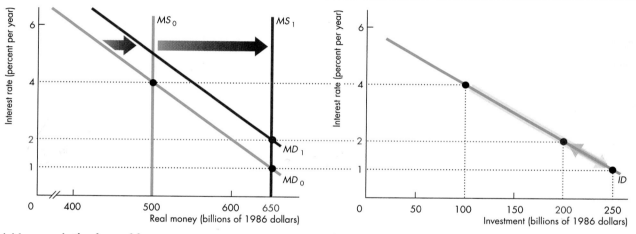

(a) Increase in the demand for money

(b) Decrease in investment

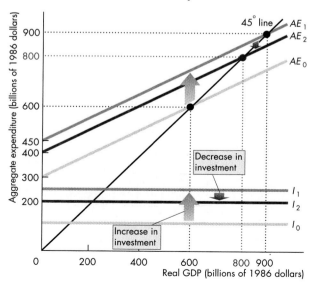

(c) Expenditure and real GDP

Initially, the demand curve for real money is MD_0, the real money supply is MS, and the interest rate is 4 percent (part a). With an interest rate of 4 percent investment is $100 billion on the investment demand curve ID (part b) and I_1 (part c). The aggregate expenditure curve is AE_0 and equilibrium expenditure and real GDP are $600 billion (part c).

A $150 billion increase in the money supply shifts the money supply curve rightward to MS_1 (part a). The increased money supply lowers the interest rate to 1 percent, and investment increases to $250 billion (part b) and I_1 (part c). The increase in investment increases aggregate planned expenditure to AE_1 (in part c). Real GDP begins to increase.

An increasing real GDP increases the demand for money. The demand curve for real money shifts rightward to MD_1, raising the interest rate (part a). The higher interest rate decreases investment (part b). The lower investment (shown as I_2 in part c) decreases aggregate planned expenditure to AE_2 (part c). The new equilibrium expenditure occurs at a real GDP of $800 billion with an interest rate of 2 percent and investment of $200 billion.

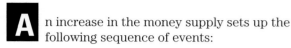

REVIEW

An increase in the money supply sets up the following sequence of events:

◆ In the first round, the interest rate decreases, investment increases, and real GDP starts to increase.

◆ In the second round, increasing real GDP increases the demand for money, increases the interest rate, decreases investment, and decreases equilibrium expenditure.

The second round effects go in the opposite direction to the first round effects but are smaller. An increase in the money supply increases real GDP and decreases the interest rate. ◆

So far, we have looked at the effects of monetary policy on the interest rate and investment. There is another effect—on the foreign exchange rate and exports.

The Exchange Rate and Exports

An increase in the money supply decreases the interest rate. If the interest rate falls in Canada but does not fall in the United States, Japan, and Western Europe, international investors sell the now lower-yielding Canadian assets and buy the relatively higher-yielding foreign assets. As they undertake these transactions, they sell Canadian dollars and buy foreign currency. These actions decrease the demand for Canadian dollars and increase the demand for foreign currencies. The result is a lower value of the Canadian dollar against other currencies. (This mechanism is discussed in greater detail in Chapter 36, pp. 1004–1010.)

With the Canadian dollar worth less, foreigners face lower prices for Canadian-produced goods and services and Canadians face higher prices for the foreign produced goods and services. Foreigners increase their imports from Canada, and Canadians reduce their imports from the rest of the world. The result is a net increase in the demand for Canadian-produced goods and services. The effects of an increase in net exports are similar to the effects of an increase in investment that we've described above.

The Relative Effectiveness of Fiscal and Monetary Policy

We've now seen that equilibrium aggregate expenditure and real GDP are influenced by both fiscal and monetary policy. But which policy is the more potent? Which has the larger "bang per buck"? This question was once at the centre of a controversy among macro-economists, and later in this section we'll look at that controversy and see how it was settled. Let's begin by discovering what determines the relative effectiveness of fiscal and monetary policy.

The Effectiveness of Fiscal Policy

The effectiveness of fiscal policy is measured by the magnitude of the increase in equilibrium real GDP resulting from a given increase in government purchases of goods and services (or decrease in taxes). The effectiveness of fiscal policy depends on the same two factors as the effectiveness of monetary policy:

◆ The sensitivity of investment demand to the interest rate

◆ The sensitivity of the demand for money to the interest rate

We'll discover how these two factors influence the effectiveness of fiscal policy by studying Fig. 29.8.

Fiscal Policy Effectiveness and Investment Demand
Other things remaining the same, the more sensitive investment demand is to the interest rate, the smaller is the effect of a change in fiscal policy on equilibrium real GDP. Figure 29.8(a) shows why.

The figure shows two investment demand curves, ID_A and ID_B. Investment is more sensitive to a change in the interest rate along the demand curve ID_A than along the demand curve ID_B. An increase in government purchases increases real GDP and increases the demand for money. The demand curve for real money shifts from MD_0 to MD_1. This increase in the demand for money increases the interest rate from 4 percent to 5 percent. If the investment demand curve is ID_A, investment decreases from $100 billion to $50 billion. Contrast this outcome with what

FIGURE 29.8

The Effectiveness of Fiscal Policy

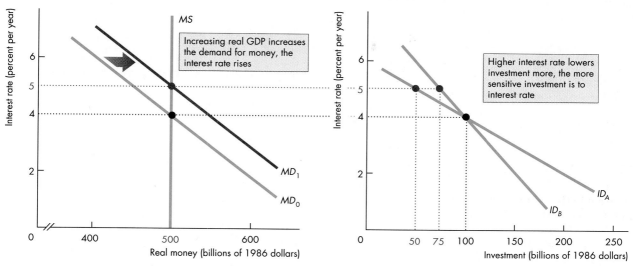

(a) Effectiveness and investment demand

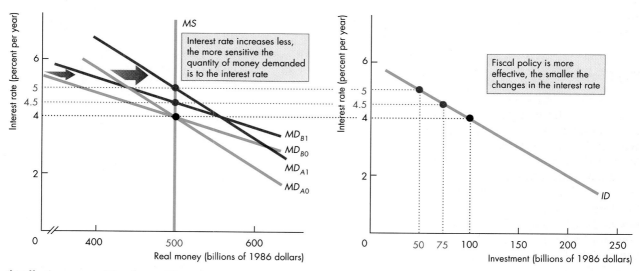

(b) Effectiveness and the demand for money

In part (a), the level of planned investment is more sensitive to a change in the interest rate along ID_A than along ID_B. An increase in government purchases increases real GDP and shifts the demand curve for real money from MD_0 to MD_1, raising the interest rate from 4 percent to 5 percent. With investment demand curve ID_A, investment decreases from $100 billion to $50 billion, but with demand curve ID_B, investment decreases to only $75 billion. So fiscal policy is less effective with investment demand curve ID_A than with ID_B.

In part (b), the demand for money is less sensitive to a change in

the interest rate along MD_{A0} than along MD_{B0}. An increase in government purchases increases real GDP and the demand curve for real money shifts rightward—MD_{A0} shifts to MD_{A1} and MD_{B0} shifts to MD_{B1}. The size of the rightward shift is the same in each case. In the case of MD_A, the interest rate rises from 4 percent to 5 percent and investment decreases from $100 billion to $50 billion. In the case of MD_B, the interest rate rises to 4.5 percent and investment decreases to only $75 billion. So fiscal policy is less effective with the demand curve for real money MD_A than with MD_B.

happens if the investment demand curve is ID_B. The same increase in the interest rate decreases investment from $100 billion to $75 billion.

The decrease in investment decreases autonomous expenditure, offsetting to some degree the increase in government purchases. Therefore the larger the decrease in investment, the smaller is the increase in equilibrium real GDP resulting from a given increase in government purchases. Thus fiscal policy is less effective with the investment demand curve ID_A than with the investment demand curve ID_B.

Fiscal Policy Effectiveness and the Demand for Money
Other things remaining the same, the more sensitive the demand for money is to the interest rate, the bigger is the effect of fiscal policy on equilibrium real GDP. Figure 29.8(b) shows why.

The figure shows two alternative initial (blue) demand curves for real money, MD_{A0} and MD_{B0}. The demand for money is less sensitive to a change in the interest rate along the demand curve MD_A than along the demand curve MD_B.

An increase in government purchases increases real GDP and increases the demand for money, shifting the demand curve for real money rightward. If the initial curve is MD_{A0}, the new curve is MD_{A1}; if the initial curve is MD_{B0}, the new curve is MD_{B1}. Notice that the size of the rightward shift is the same in each case. In the case of MD_A, the increase in the demand for money increases the interest rate from 4 percent to 5 percent, and investment decreases from $100 billion to $50 billion. In the case of MD_B, the increase in the demand for money increases the interest rate from 4 percent to 4.5 percent, and investment decreases from $100 billion to $75 billion.

A decrease in investment decreases autonomous expenditure, offsetting to some degree the increase in government purchases. Therefore the smaller the decrease in investment, the larger is the increase in equilibrium real GDP resulting from a given increase in government purchases. Thus fiscal policy is less effective with the demand for real money curve MD_A than with the demand for real money curve MD_B.

The Effectiveness of Monetary Policy

The effectiveness of monetary policy is measured by the magnitude of the increase in equilibrium real GDP resulting from a given increase in the money supply. The effectiveness of monetary policy depends on two key factors:

◆ The sensitivity of investment demand to the interest rate
◆ The sensitivity of the demand for money to the interest rate

But other things remaining the same, the more effective is monetary policy, the less effective is fiscal policy. Let's see why by studying Fig. 29.9.

Monetary Policy Effectiveness and Investment Demand
Other things remaining the same, the more sensitive investment demand is to the interest rate, the bigger is the effect of a change in the money supply on equilibrium real GDP. Figure 29.9(a) shows why.

The figure shows two investment demand curves, ID_A and ID_B. Investment is more sensitive to a change in the interest rate along the demand curve ID_A than along the demand curve ID_B.

With the demand curve for real money MD, an increase in the money supply that shifts the real money supply curve from MS_0 to MS_1 decreases the interest rate from 4 percent to 2 percent. If the investment demand curve is ID_A, investment increases from $100 billion to $200 billion. Contrast this outcome with what happens if the investment demand curve is ID_B. The same decrease in the interest rate increases investment from $100 billion to only $150 billion.

The larger the increase in investment, the larger is the resulting increase in equilibrium real GDP. Thus with the investment demand curve ID_A, monetary policy is more effective than with the investment demand curve ID_B.

Monetary Policy Effectiveness and the Demand for Money   Other things remaining the same, the less sensitive the demand for money is to the interest rate, the bigger is the effect of a change in the money supply on equilibrium real GDP. Figure 29.9(b) shows why.

The figure shows two demand curves for real money, MD_A and MD_B. The demand for money is less sensitive to a change in the interest rate along the demand curve MD_A than along the demand curve MD_B.

If the demand curve for real money is MD_A, an increase in the money supply that shifts the real money supply curve from MS_0 to MS_1 decreases the interest rate from 4 percent to 2 percent. Investment increases from $100 billion to $200 billion. Contrast this outcome with what happens if the demand curve for real money is MD_B. In this case,

FIGURE 29.9

The Effectiveness of Monetary Policy

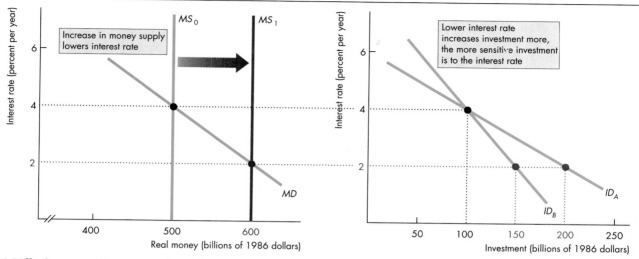

(a) Effectiveness and investment demand

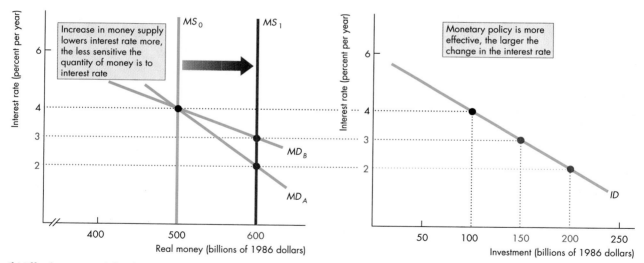

(b) Effectiveness and the demand for money

In part (a), planned investment is more sensitive to a change in the interest rate along the investment demand curve ID_A than along the demand curve ID_B. With the demand curve for real money MD, a shift in the real money supply curve from MS_0 to MS_1 lowers the interest rate from 4 percent to 2 percent. With investment demand curve ID_A, investment increases from $100 billion to $200 billion, but with investment demand curve ID_B, investment increases to only $150 billion. The larger the increase in investment, the larger is the resulting increase in equilibrium real GDP. So monetary policy is more effective with investment demand curve ID_A than with ID_B.

In part (b), the demand for money is less sensitive to a change in the interest rate along MD_A than along MD_B. With the demand curve MD_A, an increase in the money supply that shifts the real money supply curve from MS_0 to MS_1 lowers the interest rate from 4 percent to 2 percent and increases investment from $100 billion to $200 billion. With demand curve MD_B, the same increase in the money supply lowers the interest rate to only 3 percent and increases investment to only $150 billion. The larger the increase in investment, the larger is the resulting increase in equilibrium real GDP. So monetary policy is more effective with demand curve MD_A than with MD_B.

the same increase in the money supply lowers the interest rate from 4 percent to only 3 percent and investment increases to only $150 billion.

The larger the increase in investment, the larger is the resulting increase in equilibrium real GDP. Thus with the demand curve for real money MD_A, monetary policy is more effective than with the demand curve for real money MD_B.

Interest Sensitivity of Investment Demand and the Demand for Money

What determines the degree of sensitivity of investment demand and the demand for money to interest rates? The answer is the degree of substitutability between capital and labour and the degree of substitutability between money and other financial assets. Investment is the purchase of capital—of productive buildings, plant, and equipment. The substitute for capital is labour, but it is an imperfect substitute. The amount of capital used, and the amount of investment undertaken, decreases as the interest rate increases. The degree to which a change in the interest rate brings a change in investment depends on how easily labour can be substituted for capital.

Money performs a unique function that other financial assets do not perform—it facilitates the exchange of goods and services. Therefore money and other financial assets are imperfect substitutes. Holding money has an opportunity cost, which is the interest forgone by not holding other financial assets. The amount of money that we hold decreases as its opportunity cost—the interest rate—increases. The degree to which a change in the interest rate brings a change in the quantity of money held depends on how easily other financial assets can be substituted for money.

The analysis presented in this chapter of the effects of fiscal and monetary policy on aggregate expenditure was for several years in the 1950s and 1960s extremely controversial. It was at the heart of what was called the Keynesian–monetarist controversy. The Keynesian–monetarist controversy of today is different from that of the 1950s and 1960s and we'll consider that controversy (a controversy about how labour markets work) in Chapter 30. But that earlier Keynesian–monetarist controversy was an interesting episode in the development of modern macroeconomics. Let's take a look at the essentials of the dispute and see how it was resolved.

The Keynesian–Monetarist Controversy

The Keynesian–monetarist controversy is an ongoing dispute in macroeconomics between two broad groups of economists. **Keynesians** are macroeconomists whose views about the functioning of the economy represent an extension of the theories of John Maynard Keynes, published in Keynes' *General Theory* (see Our Advancing Knowledge, pp. 686–687). Keynesians regard the economy as being inherently unstable and as requiring active government intervention to achieve stability. They assign a low degree of importance to monetary policy and a high degree of importance to fiscal policy. **Monetarists** are macroeconomists who assign a high degree of importance to variations in the quantity of money as the main determinant of aggregate demand and who regard the economy as inherently stable. The founder of modern monetarism is Milton Friedman.

The nature of the Keynesian–monetarist debate has changed over the years. In the 1950s and 1960s, it was a debate about the relative effectiveness of fiscal policy and monetary policy in changing aggregate demand. We can see the essence of that debate by distinguishing three views:

◆ Extreme Keynesianism

◆ Extreme monetarism

◆ Intermediate position

Extreme Keynesianism The extreme Keynesian hypothesis is that a change in the money supply has no effect on the level of aggregate demand, and a change in government purchases of goods and services or in taxes has a large effect on aggregate demand.

There are two circumstances in which a change in the money supply has no effect on aggregate demand. They are

◆ A vertical investment demand curve

◆ A horizontal demand curve for real money

If the investment demand curve is vertical, investment is completely insensitive to interest rates. In this situation, a change in the money supply changes interest rates, but the change in interest rates does not affect aggregate planned expenditure. Monetary policy is impotent.

A horizontal demand curve for real money means that people are willing to hold any amount of money at a given interest rate—a situation called a **liquidity trap**. With a liquidity trap, a change in the money supply affects only the amount of money held. It does not affect interest rates. With an unchanged interest rate, investment remains constant. Monetary policy is impotent.

Extreme Keynesians assume that both of these conditions prevail. Notice that either one of these circumstances on its own is sufficient for monetary policy to be impotent, but extreme Keynesians suppose that both situations exist in reality.

Extreme Monetarism   The extreme monetarist hypothesis is that a change in government purchases of goods and services or in taxes has no effect on aggregate demand and that a change in the money supply has a large effect on aggregate demand. There are two circumstances giving rise to these predictions:

◆ A horizontal investment demand curve

◆ A vertical demand curve for real money

If an increase in government purchases of goods and services induces an increase in interest rates that is sufficiently large to reduce investment by the same amount as the initial increase in government purchases, then fiscal policy has no effect on aggregate demand. The outcome is complete crowding out. For this result to occur, either the demand curve for real money must be vertical—a fixed amount of money is held regardless of the interest rate—or the investment demand curve must be horizontal, in which case any amount of investment will be undertaken at a given interest rate.

Intermediate Position   The intermediate position is that both fiscal policy and monetary policy affect aggregate demand. Crowding out is not complete, so fiscal policy does have an effect. There is no liquidity trap and investment responds to interest rates, so monetary policy does indeed affect aggregate demand. This position is the one that now appears to be correct and is the one that we've spent most of this chapter exploring. Let's see how economists came to this conclusion.

Sorting Out the Competing Claims   The dispute among monetarists, Keynesians, and those taking an intermediate position was essentially a disagreement about the magnitudes of two economic parameters:

◆ The sensitivity of investment demand to interest rates

◆ The sensitivity of the demand for real money to interest rates

If investment demand is highly sensitive to interest rates or the demand for real money is hardly sensitive at all, then monetary policy is powerful and fiscal policy relatively ineffective. In this case, the world looks similar to the claims of extreme monetarists. If investment demand is very insensitive to interest rates, or the demand for real money is highly sensitive, then fiscal policy is powerful and monetary policy is relatively ineffective. In this case, the world looks similar to the claims of the extreme Keynesians.

By using statistical methods to study the demand for real money and investment demand and by using data from a wide variety of historical and national experiences, economists were able to settle this dispute. Neither extreme position turned out to be supported by the evidence, and the intermediate position won. The demand curve for real money slopes downward. So does the investment demand curve. Neither curve is vertical or horizontal, so the extreme Keynesian and extreme monetarist hypotheses are rejected.

This controversy is now behind us. Both fiscal and monetary policies are always under active consideration as you can see in Reading Between the Lines, pp. 808–809. The major unresolved issue that divides economists concerns the labour market, a controversy that we'll meet in the next chapter.

R E V I E W

T he relative effectiveness of fiscal and monetary policy depends on the sensitivity to interest rates of investment demand and the demand for money. Other things remaining the same, the more sensitive investment demand is to interest rates or the less sensitive the demand for money is, the smaller is the effect of a change in government purchases and the greater is the effect of a change in the money supply on equilibrium expenditure. The less sensitive investment demand is to interest rates or the more sensitive the demand for money is, the larger is the effect of a change in government purchases and the smaller is the effect of a change in the money supply on equilibrium expenditure. ◆

READING BETWEEN THE LINES

Spending cuts and tax increases in the 1993 federal and provincial budgets were predicted to halve the growth rate of Canada's real GDP from mid-1993 to mid-1994.

Whether the growth rate actually falls by such a large amount will depend on the actions of the Bank of Canada.

If the Bank of Canada lowers interest rates, some of the effects of the budgets can be offset.

THE FINANCIAL POST, MAY 22–24, 1993

Budgets hit recovery

By Jill Vardy

OTTAWA—The combined effect of the federal and provincial budgets will halve the growth rate of Canada's economy by the middle of next year, several leading economists warn.

That, in turn, will derail governments' economic and revenue forecasts and send their deficits skyward, said Carl Sonnen, vice-president of Informetrica Ltd....

Informetrica estimates that spending cuts and tax hikes in provincial budgets will slow growth in the country by two to three percentage points from mid–1993 to mid–1994—when the full impact of the budgets will be felt—and by as much as 1.5 points in the following 12 months.

Other economists agree with Informetrica's analysis. "In and of themselves their numbers are not outlandish," said Lloyd Atkinson, chief economist at Bank of Montreal.

But whether the impact is as severe as that depends on Bank of Canada governor John Crow, Atkinson said.

"If the Bank of Canada foresees that kind of weakness, they should be moving fairly aggressively to bring interest rates down further," he said.

So far, budgets have been brought down in Newfoundland, New Brunswick, Quebec, Ontario, Manitoba, Saskatchewan, Alberta and British Columbia. All contained spending cuts. Some, including Ontario's, Quebec's, New Brunswick's and Saskatchewan's, included tax increases.

The Finance Department predicts Canada's real gross domestic product will grow 2.9% this year and 4.6% in 1994. A Finance official says there are no plans to change those forecasts. But Finance Minister Don Mazankowski told reporters Thursday the Ontario budget could thwart economic growth. "We believe the recovery was at a stage where the imposition of additional taxation may very well have a stymying effect on the economy."

Sonnen said based on Finance's forecasts, growth from mid–1993 to mid–1994 would be around 4%. The provincial budget measures will likely pull that rate down to 1%–2%, he predicted....

Background and Analysis

In 1993, the Canadian economy was in the expansion phase of the business cycle and, with unchanged fiscal and monetary policy, real GDP was expected to grow from its 1993 level of $580 billion by about 4 percent to reach $600 billion by mid-1994.

Part (a) of the figure illustrates the economy in 1993. The aggregate expenditure curve was AE_{93} and equilibrium expenditure was $580 billion. With unchanged policy, the aggregate expenditure curve for 1994 would have been AE_a and equilibrium expenditure $600 billion.

The federal and provincial governments had large budget deficits in 1993 and took steps to cut those deficits. They cut spending and increased taxes. It was forecasted that these actions would lower aggregate expenditure to AE_b in part (a) and halve the growth of real GDP.

But suppose the Bank of Canada increases the money supply and that interest rates fall—say by a full percentage point as shown in part (b).

It is possible that an interest rate fall of this magnitude could increase investment by an amount sufficient to offset the smaller government spending and smaller consumer spending induced by higher taxes, and keep aggregate expenditure at AE_a.

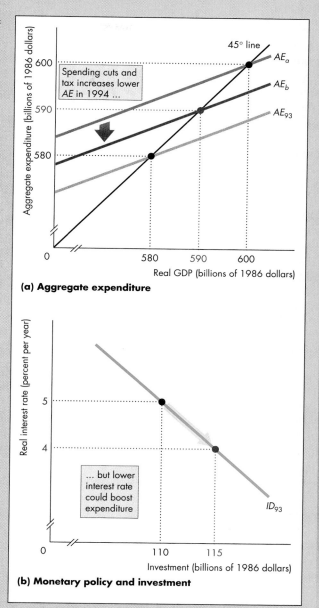

(a) Aggregate expenditure

(b) Monetary policy and investment

Influencing the Composition of Aggregate Expenditure

Aggregate expenditure can be increased either by an expansionary fiscal policy or by an increase in the money supply. An expansionary fiscal policy increases aggregate expenditure and raises interest rates. Increased expenditure increases income and consumption expenditure, but higher interest rates decrease investment. Hence if aggregate expenditure is increased by an expansionary fiscal policy, consumption expenditure increases and investment decreases. In contrast, an increase in the money supply increases aggregate expenditure and *lowers* interest rates. Again, increased expenditure increases income and consumption expenditure, but in this case lower interest rates also increase investment. Hence if aggregate expenditure is increased by an increase in the money supply, both consumption expenditure and investment increase. Thus the method whereby aggregate expenditure is increased affects the *composition* of expenditure.

Politics of Fiscal and Monetary Policy

The effects on the composition of aggregate expenditure resulting from different policies for changing aggregate expenditure are a source of tension between the various branches of government and influence the economy's long-term capacity for growth. Usually, the federal and provincial governments do not want the Bank of Canada to tighten monetary policy, which increases interest rates. Instead, they want to see the Bank of Canada steadily expanding the money supply, keeping interest rates as low as possible.

The Bank of Canada, on the other hand, frequently points to the importance of keeping government purchases of goods and services under control and keeping taxes sufficiently high to pay for those goods and services. It argues that unless the government increases taxes or cuts its expenditure, expansionary monetary policy cannot be pursued.

The choice of policy affects our long-term growth prospects because the long-term capacity of the economy to produce goods and services depends on the rate of capital accumulated—the level of investment. Expansionary fiscal policy that leads to a decrease in investment slows down the economy's long-term growth. But much government expenditure is on productive capital such as highways and on education and health care that increases human capital. Such expenditure increases the economy's long-term growth.

Real GDP, the Price Level, and Interest Rates

We've now studied the effects of fiscal and monetary policy on equilibrium expenditure and real GDP at a given price level. But the effects that we've worked out occur at each and every price level. Thus the fiscal and monetary policy effects that we've studied tell us about changes in aggregate demand and shifts in the aggregate demand curve.

When aggregate demand changes, both real GDP and the price level change. To determine the amounts by which each change, we need to look at both aggregate demand and aggregate supply. Let's now do this, starting with the short-run effects of fiscal and monetary policy.

The Short-Run Effects on Real GDP and the Price Level

When aggregate demand changes and the aggregate demand curve shifts, there is a movement along the short-run aggregate supply curve and both real GDP and the price level change. Figure 29.10 illustrates the change in real GDP and the price level that result from an increase in aggregate demand. Initially, the aggregate demand curve is AD_0, and the short-run aggregate supply curve is SAS. Real GDP is $600 billion, and the GDP deflator is 130.

Now suppose that changes in fiscal and monetary policy increase aggregate demand, shifting the aggregate demand curve to AD_1. At the initial price level (GDP deflator equal to 130) the quantity of real GDP demanded increases to $800 billion. But real GDP does not actually increase to this level. The reason is that the price level increases, bringing a decrease in the quantity of real GDP demanded. The increased aggregate demand puts upward pressure on the prices of all goods and services, and the GDP deflator rises to 135. At the higher price level, the real money supply decreases.

The decrease in the real money supply increases the interest rate, decreases investment, and decreases equilibrium expenditure and real GDP. The increase in real GDP from $600 billion to $800 billion is the result of the initial policy-induced increase in aggregate demand at a given price level;

The Long-Run Effects on Real GDP and the Price Level

The long-run effects of fiscal and monetary policy depend on the state of the economy when the policy action is taken. Again, we'll concentrate on an *increase* in aggregate demand. If, initially, unemployment is above its natural rate and real GDP is below its long-run level, fiscal and monetary policy can be used to restore full employment. We can use the example in Fig. 29.10 to illustrate this case.

Suppose, in Fig. 29.10, that long-run aggregate supply is $600 billion. The increase in aggregate demand moves the economy from below full-employment to full employment, and that is the end of the story. The short-run and long-run adjustments are the same. For example, expansionary monetary policy was used in 1983 and 1984 to move the Canadian economy out of a serious recession into a period of sustained expansion.

But a policy-induced increase in aggregate demand might occur when the economy is already at full employment with real GDP at its long-run level. What, then, are the long-run effects?

We can see the answers in Fig. 29.11. The long-run aggregate supply curve is *LAS*. Initially, the aggregate demand curve is AD_0, and the short-run aggregate supply curve is SAS_0. Real GDP is $600 billion, and the GDP deflator is 130.

Changes in fiscal and monetary policy increase aggregate demand, shifting the aggregate demand curve to AD_1. At the initial price level (GDP deflator equal to 130), the quantity of real GDP demanded increases to $800 billion—the increase we've already studied earlier in this chapter. But, as we've just seen, real GDP does not actually increase to this level. The higher price level decreases the real money supply and raises the interest rate. As a result, investment, equilibrium expenditure, and real GDP decrease. The new short-run equilibrium occurs at a real GDP of $750 billion and a GDP deflator of 135.

But real GDP is now above its long-run level and unemployment is below its natural rate. There is an inflationary gap. A shortage of labour puts upward pressure on wages. And as wages increase, the short-run aggregate supply curve begins to shift left-ward. It keeps shifting until it reaches SAS_1. The GDP deflator increases to 145 and real GDP returns to its long-run level. Thus the long-run effect of an expansionary fiscal and monetary policy at full employment brings a rising price level but no change in real GDP.

FIGURE 29.10

Policy-Induced Changes in Real GDP and the Price Level

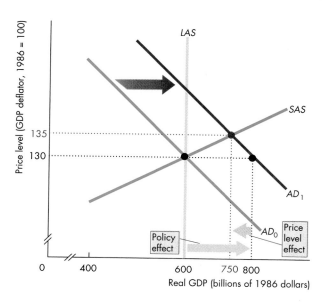

Initially aggregate demand is AD_0 and short-run aggregate supply curve is *SAS*. Real GDP is $600 billion and the GDP deflator is 130. Fiscal and monetary policy changes shift the aggregate demand curve to AD_1. At the initial price level (GDP deflator equal to 130), real GDP rises to $800 billion. But the price level increases, bringing a decrease in the real money supply. The decrease in the real money supply increases the interest rate, decreases investment, and decreases equilibrium expenditure and real GDP. The increase in real GDP from $600 billion to $800 billion is the result of the initial policy-induced increase in aggregate demand at a given price level. The decrease in real GDP from $800 billion to $750 billion is the result of the decrease in the real money supply induced by the higher price level.

---

and the decrease in real GDP from $800 billion to $750 billion is the result of the decrease in the real money supply induced by the higher price level.

The exercise that we've just conducted for an increase in aggregate demand can be reversed to see what happens when there is a policy-induced decrease in aggregate demand. In this case, real GDP decreases, and the price level falls.

The effects we've just worked out are short-run effects. Let's now look at the long-run effects of fiscal and monetary policy.

FIGURE 29.11

The Long-Run Effects of
Policy-Induced Changes in
Real GDP and the Price Level

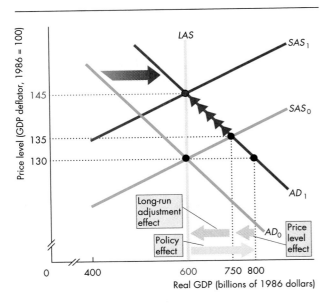

The long-run aggregate supply curve is *LAS*, and initially the aggregate demand curve is AD_0 and the short-run aggregate supply curve is SAS_0. Real GDP is $600 billion and the GDP deflator is 130. Fiscal and monetary policy changes shift the aggregate demand curve to AD_1. At the new short-run equilibrium, real GDP is $750 billion and the GDP deflator is 135. Because real GDP is above its long-run level, wages increase and the short-run aggregate supply curve begins to shift upward to SAS_1. At the new long-run equilibrium, the GDP deflator is 145 and real GDP is back at its original level.

R E V I E W

A policy-induced change in aggregate demand changes both real GDP and the price level. The amount by which each changes depends on aggregate supply. In the short run, both real GDP and the price level increase, but the increase in real GDP is smaller than what would occur at a fixed price level. In the long run, the effects of fiscal and monetary policy depend on the state of the economy when the policy action is taken. Starting from a position below long-run real GDP, expansionary fiscal and monetary policy increases both real GDP and the price level and restores full employment. But starting from full employment, an expansionary fiscal and monetary policy brings a rise in the price level and no change in real GDP. ◆

◆ ◆ ◆ ◆ We have now studied the detailed effects of fiscal and monetary policy on real GDP, interest rates, and the price level. We've seen what determines the relative effectiveness of fiscal and monetary policy and how the mix of these policies can influence the composition of aggregate expenditure. But we've also seen that the ultimate effects of these policies on real GDP and the price level depend not only on the behaviour of aggregate demand but also on aggregate supply. Our next task is to turn to aggregate supply and study the determination of long-run and short-run aggregate supply, employment, and unemployment.

S U M M A R Y

Money, Interest, and Aggregate Demand

Real GDP and the price level are determined by the interaction of *aggregate demand* and *aggregate supply* (Chapter 24). Fiscal and monetary policies influence *aggregate demand*. One component of aggregate expenditure, investment, varies with the interest rate. The higher the interest rate, other things remaining the same, the lower is investment, and hence the lower is the quantity of real GDP.

The interest rate is determined by equilibrium in the money market. The demand for real money depends on real GDP. The higher real GDP, other things remaining the same, the greater is the demand for real money and the higher is the interest rate. Therefore the interest rate depends on real GDP.

Real GDP and the interest rate are determined simultaneously such that the money market is in equilibrium and aggregate planned expenditure equals real GDP. (pp. 792–794)

Fiscal Policy and Aggregate Demand

Fiscal policy influences aggregate demand by changing autonomous expenditure. An expansionary fiscal policy increases autonomous expenditure and increases aggregate planned expenditure. The increase in aggregate planned expenditure increases equilibrium expenditure and sets up a multiplier effect that increases real GDP. These are the first round effects. The rising real GDP sets up a second round. The increasing real GDP increases the demand for money, and the interest rate rises. With a rise in the interest rate, investment decreases. A decrease in investment decreases autonomous expenditure and decreases aggregate planned expenditure. These second round effects work in the opposite direction to the first round effects but are smaller in magnitude. The outcome of an increase in government purchases is an increase in real GDP, a rise in the interest rate, and a decrease in investment.

The effect of higher interest rates on investment—the "crowding out" effect—might be complete. That is, the decrease in investment might be sufficient to offset the initial increase in government purchases. In practice, complete crowding out does not occur. An opposing effect is "crowding in," an increase in investment resulting from an increase in government purchases of goods and services. Such an effect may occur in a recession if fiscal stimulation brings expectations of higher future profits, if the government purchases capital that strengthens the economy, or if tax cuts stimulate investment.

Fiscal policy also influences aggregate demand through the foreign exchange rate. Expansionary fiscal policy increases interest rates and makes the value of the dollar rise against other currencies. When the dollar strengthens, Canadian net exports declines. (pp. 794–798)

Monetary Policy and Aggregate Demand

Monetary policy influences aggregate demand by changing the interest rate. An increase in the money supply lowers the interest rate and increases investment. The higher investment increases aggregate planned expenditure and sets up a multiplier effect in which real GDP starts to increase. This is the first round effect. Increasing real GDP sets up a second round effect in which the demand for money increases and the interest rate rises. A rise in the interest rate decreases investment and decreases aggregate planned expenditure. The second round effect works in the opposite direction to the first round effect but is smaller in magnitude. The outcome of an increase in the money supply is an increase in real GDP and a fall in the interest rate.

Monetary policy also influences aggregate demand through the foreign exchange rate. An increase in the money supply decreases the interest rate and makes the value of the dollar fall against other currencies. When the dollar weakens, Canadian net exports increases. (pp. 798–802)

The Relative Effectiveness of Fiscal and Monetary Policy

The relative effectiveness of fiscal and monetary policy on aggregate demand depends on two factors: the sensitivity of investment demand to the interest rate and the sensitivity of the demand for money to the interest rate. The more sensitive investment demand to the interest rate or the less sensitive the demand for money to the interest rate, the larger is the effect of a change in the money supply on aggregate demand. The less sensitive investment demand to the interest rate or the more sensitive the demand for money to the interest rate, the larger is the effect of fiscal policy on aggregate demand.

A Keynesian–monetarist controversy of the 1950s and 1960s concerned the relative effectiveness of fiscal and monetary actions in influencing aggregate demand. The extreme Keynesian position was that only fiscal policy affects aggregate demand and monetary policy is impotent. The extreme monetarist position was that only monetary policy affects aggregate demand and fiscal policy is impotent. As a result of statistical investigations, we now know that neither of these extreme positions is correct. The demand curve for real money and the investment demand curve both slope downward, and both fiscal and monetary policy influence aggregate demand.

The mix of fiscal and monetary policy influences the composition of aggregate demand. If aggregate demand increases as a result of an increase in the money supply, interest rates fall and investment increases. If aggregate demand increases as a result of an increase in government purchases of goods and services, interest rates rise and investment falls. These different effects of fiscal and monetary policy on aggregate demand create some political tensions. To keep aggregate demand in check and interest rates moderate, taxes must be high enough to support the level of government purchases. (pp. 802–810)

Real GDP, the Price Level, and Interest Rates

When aggregate demand changes, both real GDP and the price level change by amounts determined by both aggregate demand and aggregate supply. A policy-induced increase in aggregate demand shifts the aggregate demand curve rightward. The magnitude of the shift of the aggregate demand curve is equal to the effect of the policy change on aggregate demand at a given price level. In the short run, real

GDP and the price level increase. The rise in the price level decreases the real money supply, which increases the interest rate. Investment and real GDP decrease.

The long-run effects of fiscal and monetary policy depend on the state of the economy when the policy action is taken. Starting with unemployment above its natural rate and real GDP below its long-run level, expansionary fiscal and monetary policies increase real GDP and the price level and restore full employment. But starting at full employment with real GDP at its long-run level, a policy-induced increase in aggregate demand increases the price level and leaves real GDP unchanged. (pp. 810–812)

K E Y E L E M E N T S

Key Terms

Crowding in, 798
Crowding out, 798
International crowding out, 798
Keynesians, 806
Liquidity trap, 807
Monetarist, 806

Key Figures

Figure 29.1   Equilibrium Interest Rate and Real GDP, 793
Figure 29.2   First Round Effects of an Expansionary Fiscal Policy, 795

Figure 29.3   How the Economy Adjusts to an Expansionary Fiscal Policy, 796
Figure 29.5   First Round Effects of an Increase in the Money Supply, 799
Figure 29.6   How the Economy Adjusts to an Increase in the Money Supply, 800
Figure 29.8   The Effectiveness of Fiscal Policy, 803
Figure 29.9   The Effectiveness of Monetary Policy, 805
Figure 29.10 Policy-Induced Changes in Real GDP and the Price Level, 811
Figure 29.11 The Long-Run Effects of Policy-Induced Changes in Real GDP and the Price Level, 812

R E V I E W Q U E S T I O N S

1 Explain the link between the money market and the market for goods and services.

2 What are the first round effects of an increase in government purchases of goods and services?

3 What are the second round effects of an increase in government purchases of goods and services?

4 What is the outcome of an increase in government purchases of goods and services?

5 What role does the foreign exchange rate play in influencing aggregate demand when there is an expansionary fiscal policy?

6 What are crowding out, crowding in, and international crowding out? Explain how each occurs.

7 What are the first round effects of an increase in the money supply?

8 What are the second round effects of an increase in the money supply?

9 What is the outcome of an increase in the money supply?

10 What role does the foreign exchange rate play in influencing aggregate demand when there is a change in the money supply?

11 What factors determine the effectiveness of fiscal policy and monetary policy?

12 Under what conditions is fiscal policy more effective than monetary policy in stimulating aggregate demand?

13 Distinguish between the hypotheses of extreme Keynesians and extreme monetarists.

14 Explain the Keynesian–monetarist controversy about the influence of monetary policy and fiscal policy on aggregate demand.

15 Explain how the Keynesian–monetarist controversy in question 14 was settled.

16 Explain how fiscal policy and monetary policy influence the composition of aggregate demand.

17 Explain the effect of an increase in the money supply and expansionary fiscal policy on the price level and real GDP. Be careful to distinguish between the short-run and the long-run effect.

P R O B L E M S

1 In the economy described in Fig. 29.1, suppose the government decreases its purchases of goods and services by $150 billion.
a Work out the first round effects.
b Explain how real GDP and the interest rate change.
c Explain the second round effects that take the economy to a new equilibrium.

2 In the economy described in Fig. 29.1, suppose the Bank of Canada decreases the money supply by $150 billion.
a Work out the first round effects.
b Explain how real GDP and the interest rate change.
c Explain the second round effects that take the economy to a new equilibrium

3 The economies of two countries, Alpha and Beta, are identical in every way except the following: In Alpha, a change in the interest rate of 1 percentage point (for example, from 5 percent to 6 percent) results in a $1 billion change in the quantity of real money demanded. In Beta, a change in the interest rate of 1 percentage point results in a $0.1 billion change in the quantity of real money demanded.
a In which economy does an increase in government purchases of goods and services have a larger effect on real GDP?

b In which economy is the crowding out effect weaker?
c In which economy does a change in the money supply have a larger effect on equilibrium real GDP?

4 The economy is in a recession and the government wants to increase aggregate demand, stimulate exports, and increase investment. It has three policy options: increase government purchases of goods and services, decrease taxes, and increase the money supply.
a Explain the mechanisms at work under each alternative policy.
b What is the effect of each policy on the composition of aggregate demand?
c What are the short-run effects of each policy on real GDP and the price level
d Which policy would you recommend that the government adopt?

5 The economy is at full employment, but the government is disappointed with the growth rate of real GDP. It wants to stimulate investment and at the same time avoid an increase in the price level. Suggest a combination of fiscal and monetary policies that will achieve the government's objective.

APPENDIX

To
CHAPTER 29

◆

THE
IS–LM
MODEL OF
AGGREGATE
DEMAND

Equilibrium Expenditure and Real GDP

A ggregate planned expenditure depends on real GDP because consumption increases as real GDP increases. Aggregate planned expenditure also depends on the interest rate because investment decreases as the interest rate increases. These two influences give rise to the *IS* curve.

The *IS* Curve

The *IS curve* shows combinations of real GDP and the interest rate at which aggregate expenditure is at its equilibrium level—aggregate planned expenditure equals real GDP.

Figure A29.1 derives the *IS* curve. Part (a) is similar to Fig. 26.2 (p. 717). The 45° line shows all the points at which aggregate planned expenditure equals real GDP. Curves AE_a, AE_b, and AE_c are aggregate planned expenditure curves. Curve AE_a represents aggregate planned expenditure when the interest rate is 6 percent (row a of the table). Curve AE_b shows aggregate planned expenditure when the

interest rate is 5 percent (row b), and AE_c shows aggregate planned expenditure when the interest rate is 4 percent (row c).

There is just one expenditure equilibrium on each of these aggregate planned expenditure curves. On curve AE_a, the equilibrium point is a, where real GDP is $3 billion. The equilibrium point on curve AE_b is b, where real GDP is $4 billion. The equilibrium point on curve AE_c is c, where real GDP is $5 billion.

Figure A29.1(b) shows each expenditure equilibrium again but highlights the relationship between the interest rate and real GDP at the expenditure equilibrium. Its horizontal axis measures real GDP. Its vertical axis measures the interest rate. Points a, b, and c in part (b) illustrate the expenditure equilibrium at points a, b, and c in part (a). For example, point a tells us that if the interest rate is 6 percent, the expenditure equilibrium occurs at a real GDP of $3 billion. The continuous line through points a, b, and c is the *IS* curve.

Some relationships show "cause and effect." For example, the investment demand curve tells us the level of investment (effect) at a particular interest rate (cause). The *IS* curve is *not* a "cause and effect" relationship. It can be read in two ways. It tells us that if the interest rate is 6 percent, then aggregate planned expenditure equals real GDP only if real GDP is $3 billion. It also tells us that if real

FIGURE A29.1

Aggregate Planned Expenditure, Flow Equilibrium, and the *IS* Curve

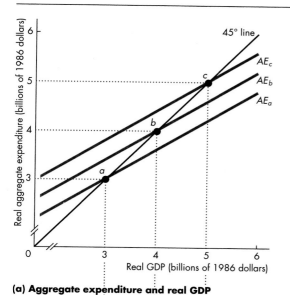

(a) Aggregate expenditure and real GDP

The table shows aggregate planned expenditure—the sum of autonomous expenditure and induced expenditure—that occurs at different combinations of the interest rate and real GDP. For example, if the interest rate is 6 percent and real GDP is $5 billion, aggregate planned expenditure is $4.2 billion (top right number). Flow equilibrium (equality of aggregate planned expenditure and real GDP) is shown by the green squares. Each of rows *a*, *b*, and *c* represents an aggregate expenditure schedule, plotted as the aggregate expenditure curves AE_a, AE_b, and AE_c, respectively, in part (a). Expenditure equilibrium positions are shown in part (a), where these *AE* curves intersect the 45° line and are marked *a*, *b*, and *c*. Part (b) shows these same equilibrium positions but highlights the combinations of the interest rate and real GDP at which they occur. The line connecting those points is the *IS* curve.

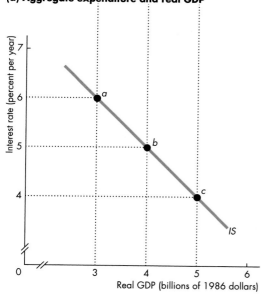

(b) The *IS* curve

Interest rate (percent per year)	Autonomous expenditure (billions of 1986 dollars)	Aggregate planned expenditure (billions of 1986 dollars)		
a 6	1.2	3.0	3.6	4.2
b 5	1.6	3.4	4.0	4.6
c 4	2.0	3.8	4.4	5.0

Induced expenditure	1.8	2.4	3.0
Real GDP (billions of 1986 dollars)	3.0	4.0	5.0

GDP is $3 billion, then the interest rate at which aggregate planned expenditure equals real GDP is 6 percent.

The *IS* curve shows combinations of the interest rate and real GDP at which aggregate expenditure is at its equilibrium level. To determine the interest rate and real GDP, we need an additional relationship between those two variables. That second relationship between interest rates and real GDP comes from equilibrium in the money market.

Money Market Equilibrium

T he quantity of money demanded depends on the price level, real GDP, and the interest rate. The quantity of money demanded is proportional to the price level. If the price level doubles, so does the quantity of money demanded. Real money is the ratio of the quantity of money to the price level. The quantity of real money demanded increases as real GDP increases and decreases as the interest rate increases.

The supply of money is determined by the actions of the Bank of Canada, the banks, and other financial intermediaries. Given those actions, and given the price level, there is a given quantity of real money in existence. Money market equilibrium occurs when the quantity of real money supplied is equal to the quantity demanded. Equilibrium in the money market is a stock equilibrium. Figure A29.2 contains a numerical example that enables us to study money market equilibrium.

Suppose that the quantity of money supplied is $3 billion. Also, suppose that the GDP deflator is 100, so that the quantity of real money supplied is also $3 billion. The real money supply is shown in the last row of the table. Money market equilibrium occurs when the quantity of real money demanded equals the quantity supplied—$3 billion. The quantity of real money demanded depends on real GDP and the interest rate. The table tells us about the demand for real money. Each row tells us how much real money is demanded at a given interest rate as real GDP varies, and each column tells us how much is demanded at a given real GDP as the interest rate varies. For example, at an interest rate of 6 percent and real GDP at $3 billion, the quantity of real money demanded is $2 billion. Alternatively, at an interest rate of 5 percent and real GDP at $4 billion, the quantity of real money demanded is $3 billion. The rest of the table is read in a similar way.

Money market equilibrium occurs when the quantity of real money demanded equals the quantity supplied, $3 billion in this example. The green squares in the table indicate positions of money market equilibrium—combinations of interest rate and

real GDP at which the quantity of money demanded is equal to the quantity supplied. For example, look at column *e*. Real GDP is $3 billion, and the quantity of real money demanded is $3 billion (equal to the quantity supplied) when the interest rate is 4 percent. Thus at real GDP of $3 billion and an interest rate of 4 percent, the money market is in equilibrium. At the other two green squares the interest rate is such that the quantity of real money demanded is $3 billion when real GDP is $4 billion and $5 billion respectively. That is, the green squares show combinations of the interest rate and real GDP at which the money market is in equilibrium.

The *LM* curve

The *LM curve* shows the combinations of real GDP and the interest rate at which the quantity of real money demanded equals the quantity of real money supplied. Figure A29.2 derives the *LM* curve. Part (a) shows the demand and supply curves for real money. The quantity supplied is fixed at $3 billion, so the supply curve *MS* is vertical. Each of the columns of the table labelled *d, e,* and *f* is a demand schedule for real money—a schedule that tells us how the quantity of real money demanded rises as the interest rate falls. There is a different schedule for each level of real GDP. These three demand schedules for real money are graphed as demand curves for real money in part (a) of the figure as MD_d, MD_e, and MD_f. For example, when real GDP is $3 billion, the demand curve for real money is MD_d. Money market equilibrium occurs at the intersection of the supply curve and the demand curves for real money at points *d, e,* and *f* in part (a).

Figure A29.2(b) shows each money market equilibrium again but highlights the relationship between the interest rate and real GDP at which an equilibrium occurs. Points *d, e,* and *f* in part (b) illustrate the money market equilibrium represented by the green squares in the table and by those similarly labelled points in part (a). The continuous line through these points is the *LM* curve. The *LM* curve shows the interest rate and real GDP at which money market equilibrium occurs when the real money supply is $3 billion.

Like the *IS* curve, the *LM* curve does not have a

FIGURE A29.2

The Money Market, Stock Equilibrium, and the *LM* Curve

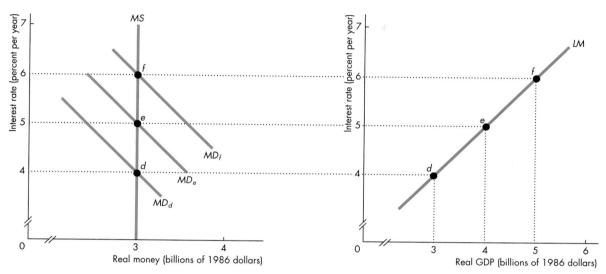

(a) Money market equilibrium

(b) The *LM* curve

The table shows the quantity of real money demanded at different combinations of the interest rate and real GDP. For example, if the interest rate is 6 percent and real GDP is $3 billion, the quantity of real money demanded is $2 billion (top left number). Stock equilibrium—equality between the quantity of real money demanded and supplied—is shown by the green squares. Each of columns *d*, *e*, and *f* represents a demand schedule for real money, plotted as the demand curves for real money MD_d, MD_e, and MD_f, respectively, in part (a). Money market equilibrium positions are shown in part (a), where these *MD* curves intersect the supply curve of real money *MS*, and are marked *d*, *e*, and *f*. Part (b) shows these same equilibrium positions but highlights the combinations of the interest rate and real GDP at which they occur. The line connecting these points is the *LM* curve.

Interest rate (percent per year)	Quantity of real money demanded (billions of 1986 dollars)		
6	2.0	2.5	3.0
5	2.5	3.0	3.5
4	3.0	3.5	4.0
Real GDP	3.0	4.0	5.0

Real money supply (billions of 1986 dollars)	3.0	3.0	3.0
	d	*e*	*f*

"cause and effect" interpretation. The *LM* curve illustrated in Fig. A29.2(b) tells us that if the quantity of real money supplied is $3 billion and real GDP is $3 billion, then for money market equilibrium the interest rate is 4 percent. It also tells us that if the quantity of real money supplied is $3 billion and the interest rate is 4 percent, then for money market equilibrium real GDP is $3 billion.

Equilibrium and Aggregate Demand

E quilibrium real GDP and the interest rate are shown in Fig. A29.3, which brings together the *IS* curve and the *LM* curve. This equilibrium is the point of intersection of the *IS* curve and *LM* curve. Point *b* on the *IS* curve is a point of expenditure equilibrium. The interest rate and real GDP are such that aggregate planned expenditure equals real GDP. Point *e* on the *LM* curve is a point of money market equilibrium. The interest rate and real GDP are such that the quantity of real money demanded equals the quantity of real money supplied. At this intersection point, there is both flow equilibrium in the goods market and stock equilibrium in the money market. The equilibrium interest rate is 5 percent and real GDP is $4 billion.

At all other points, there is either no expenditure equilibrium or the money market is not in equilibrium or both. At a point such as *a*, the economy is on its *IS* curve but off its *LM* curve. With real GDP at $3 billion and the interest rate at 6 percent, the interest rate is too high or real GDP is too low for money market equilibrium. Interest rates adjust quickly and would fall to 4 percent to bring about money market equilibrium, putting the economy at point *d*, a point on the *LM* curve. But point *d* is off the *IS* curve. At point *d*, with the interest rate at 4 percent and real GDP at $3 billion, aggregate planned expenditure exceeds real GDP. By checking back to the table in Fig. A29.1, aggregate planned expenditure is $3.8 billion, which exceeds real GDP of $3 billion. With aggregate planned expenditure larger than real GDP, real GDP will increase. But as real GDP increases, so does the demand for real money and so does the interest rate. Real GDP and the interest rate would rise, and continue to do so, until the point of intersection of the *IS* and *LM* curves is reached.

The Effects of a Change in Price Level on the *LM* Curve

The price level enters the *IS-LM* model to determine the quantity of real money supplied. To see how, first ask what happens if the price level, instead of being 100, is 120. The money supply is $3 billion. With a

GDP deflator of 100, the real money supply is also $3 billion. But if the GDP deflator is 120, the real money supply is $2.5 billion. (The real money supply is $3 billion divided by 1.2, which equals $2.5 billion.) For money market equilibrium we can see in the table of Fig. A29.2 what happens to the interest rate at a real GDP of $4 billion. With a GDP deflator of 120, the interest rate rises to 6 percent in order to decrease the quantity of real money demanded to $2.5 billion—equal to the real money supply. Thus with a GDP deflator of 120, an interest rate of 6 percent and real GDP of $4 billion become a point on the *LM* curve—point *g* in Fig. A29.4(a).

Next, suppose the GDP deflator is lower than in the original case—86 instead of 100. Now the real money supply becomes $3.5 billion ($3 billion divided by 0.86, which equals $3.5 billion). Again, for money market equilibrium we can see in the table of Fig. A29.2 what happens to the interest rate at a real GDP of $4 billion. With a GDP deflator of

---

FIGURE A29.3

IS-LM Equilibrium

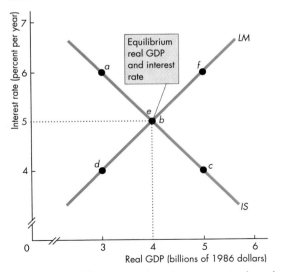

All points on the *IS* curve are points where aggregate planned expenditure equals real GDP. All points on the *LM* curve are points at which the quantity of real money demanded equals the quantity of real money supplied. The intersection of the *IS* curve and the *LM* curve determines the equilibrium interest rate and real GDP—5 percent and $4 billion. At this interest rate and real GDP, there is flow equilibrium in the goods market and stock equilibrium in the money market.

86, the interest rate falls to 4 percent in order to increase the quantity of real money demanded to $3.5 billion—equal to the real money supply. Thus with a GDP deflator of 86, an interest rate of 4 percent and real GDP of $4 billion become a point on the *LM* curve—point *h* in Fig. A29.4(a).

The *LM* Curve Shift   The example we have worked through tells us that there is a different *LM* curve for each price level. Figure A29.4(a) illustrates the *LM* curves for the three different price levels we have considered. The initial *LM* curve has the GDP deflator equal to 100. This curve has been relabelled as *LM*₀ in Fig. A29.4(a). When the GDP deflator is 120 and real GDP is $4 billion, the interest rate that achieves equilibrium in the money market is 6 percent. This equilibrium is shown as point *g* on curve *LM*₁ in Fig. A29.4(a). The entire *LM* curve shifts up to *LM*₁ in order to pass through point *g*. When the GDP deflator is 86 and real GDP is $4 billion, the interest rate that achieves equilibrium in the money market is 4 percent. This equilibrium is shown as point *h* on the curve *LM*₂ in Fig. A29.4(a). Again, the entire *LM* curve shifts downward to *LM*₂ in order to pass through point *h*.

The Aggregate Demand Curve Derived

Figure A29.4 derives the *AD* curve. Part (a) shows the *IS* curve and the three *LM* curves associated with the three different price levels (GDP deflators of 86, 100, and 120). When the GDP deflator is 100, the *LM* curve is *LM*₀. Equilibrium is at point *e* where real GDP is $4 billion and the equilibrium interest rate is 5 percent. If the GDP deflator is 120, the *LM* curve is *LM*₁. Equilibrium is at point *j* where real GDP is $3.5 billion and the interest rate is 5.5 percent. If the GDP deflator is 86, the *LM* curve is *LM*₂. Equilibrium is at point *k* where real GDP is $4.5 billion and the interest rate is 4.5 percent. At each price level there is a different equilibrium real GDP and interest rate.

Part (b) traces the aggregate demand curve. The price level is measured on the vertical axis of part (b) and real GDP on the horizontal axis. When the GDP deflator is 100, equilibrium real GDP is $4 billion (point *e*). When the GDP deflator is 120, equilibrium real GDP is $3.5 billion (point *j*). And when the GDP deflator is 86, real GDP demanded is $4.5 billion (point *k*). Each of these points corresponds to the same point in part (a). The line joining these points in part (b) is the aggregate demand curve.

FIGURE A29.4

Deriving the Aggregate Demand Curve

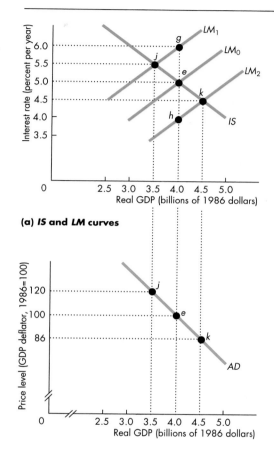

(a) IS and LM curves

In part (a), if the GDP deflator is 100, the *LM* curve is *LM*₀. If the GDP deflator increases to 120, the *LM* curve shifts leftward to *LM*₁. A lower real money supply requires a higher interest rate at each level of real GDP for money market equilibrium. For example, if real GDP is $4 billion, the interest rate has to increase from 5 percent to 6 percent (point *g*). If the price level falls, the real money supply increases and the *LM* curve shifts rightward to *LM*₂. If real GDP is $4 billion, the interest rate falls to 4 percent (point *h*) to maintain money market equilibrium. When the GDP deflator is 100, the *IS* and *LM* curves intersect at point *e*—real GDP of $4 billion. This equilibrium is shown in part (b) at point *e* on aggregate demand curve *AD*. This point tells us that when the GDP deflator is 100, the quantity of real GDP demanded is $4 billion. If the GDP deflator is 120, the *LM* curve is *LM*₁ and real GDP is $3.5 billion. A second point on the aggregate demand curve is found at *j*. If the GDP deflator is 86, the *LM* curve is *LM*₂, and real GDP is $4.5 billion. Another point on the aggregate demand curve is generated at point *k*. Joining points *j*, *e*, and *k* gives the aggregate demand curve.

Fiscal Policy and Aggregate Demand

A change in government purchases or in taxes shifts the *IS* curve and the aggregate demand curve. In Chapter 26, we worked out the magnitude of the change in aggregate planned expenditure resulting from a change in government purchases or in taxes when the interest rate is constant. In terms of the *IS-LM* model, these multiplier effects tell us how far the *IS* curve shifts. But the change in aggregate planned expenditure at a given interest rate is not the same thing as a change in aggregate demand. For, when aggregate planned expenditure changes, the interest rate usually changes as well and that has further effects on expenditure plans.

Figure A29.5 illustrates three different effects of a change in fiscal policy. In all three parts of the figure, the same fiscal policy action takes place. There is either a rise in government purchases or a cut in autonomous taxes that shifts the *IS* curve from IS_0 to IS_1. In part (a), the normal case, the *LM* curve slopes upward (LM_N). When the *IS* curve shifts, the interest rate increases and so does real GDP. But the increase in real GDP is smaller than the magnitude of the rightward shift in the *IS* curve. The reason is

that the higher interest rate leads to a decrease in investment and that decrease in investment partially offsets the initial increased spending resulting from the fiscal policy action.

In part (b), the *LM* curve is horizontal (LM_H). The *LM* curve is horizontal only if there is a "liquidity trap"—a situation in which people are willing to hold any quantity of money at a given interest rate. When the *IS* curve shifts rightward, real GDP increases by the same amount as the rightward shift of the *IS* curve. Interest rates stay constant. In this case, the multiplier effect of Chapter 26 still operates.

In part (c), the *LM* curve is vertical (LM_V). In this case, although the *IS* curve shifts rightward by exactly the same amount as in parts (a) and (b), real GDP stays constant. Here, the interest rate increases. The higher interest rate leads to a decrease in investment that exactly offsets the initial increase in expenditure resulting from the fiscal policy. There is complete crowding out. Complete crowding out occurs if the demand for real money is completely insensitive to interest rates. No matter what the interest rate, the quantity of real money demanded is a constant portion of real GDP.

FIGURE A29.5

Fiscal Policy and Aggregate Demand

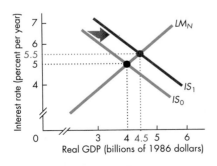

(a) Fiscal policy: normal case

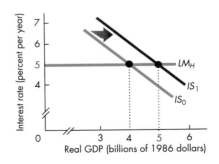

(b) Fiscal policy: maximum effect on GDP

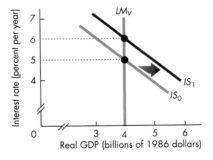

(c) Fiscal policy: no effect on GDP

An increase in government purchases or an autonomous tax cut shifts the *IS* curve rightward. The effects of fiscal policy on real GDP and the interest rate depend on the slope of the *LM* curve. In the normal case (part a), interest rates and real GDP rise. If there is a liquidity trap, the *LM* curve is horizontal (part b) and real GDP increases but interest

rates stay constant. If the demand for money is insensitive to interest rates, the *LM* curve is vertical (part c) and interest rates rise but real GDP stays constant. In this case, there is complete "crowding out." The higher interest rate leads to a cut in investment that exactly offsets the initial fiscal policy action.

Part (b) of the figure corresponds to the extreme Keynesian prediction, part (c) to the extreme monetarist prediction, and part (a) to the intermediate position.

Monetary Policy and Aggregate Demand

We saw earlier in this appendix that when the LM curve shifts because of a change in the price level, equilibrium real GDP changes and there is a movement along the aggregate demand curve. But a change in the money supply also shifts the LM curve. If the LM curve shifts because there is a change in the nominal money supply, then the aggregate demand curve shifts. The magnitude of the change in aggregate demand—the shift in the aggregate demand curve—depends on two factors: the size of the shift of the LM curve and the slope of the IS curve. Figure A29.6 shows three possible cases. In each case, the LM curve shifts rightward by the same amount, from LM_0 to LM_1. In part (a), the normal case, the IS curve slopes downward (IS_N). When the money supply increases, the interest rate falls, investment increases and real GDP increases.

In part (b), the IS curve is horizontal (IS_H). This situation arises if people change the timing of their investment whenever the interest rate rises above or falls below 5 percent. If the interest rate rises above 5 percent, all investment stops; if the interest rate falls below 5 percent, there is no limit to the amount of investment that people try to undertake. At 5 percent, any amount of investment will be undertaken. In this case, a change in the money supply shifts the LM curve and increases real GDP but leaves the interest rate unchanged.

In part (c), the IS curve is vertical (IS_V). This case arises if investment is completely insensitive to interest rates. People plan to undertake a given level of investment regardless of the interest cost involved. In this case, when the LM curve shifts, interest rates fall, but the lower interest rate does not stimulate additional expenditure, so real GDP stays constant.

Part (c) corresponds to the views of extreme Keynesians. A change in the money supply has no effect on real GDP. Part (b) corresponds to the predictions of monetarists. A change in the money supply has a large and powerful effect on real GDP. Part (a) is the intermediate position.

FIGURE A29.6

Monetary Policy and Aggregate Demand

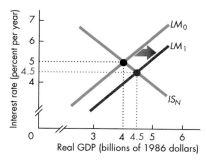

(a) Monetary policy: normal case

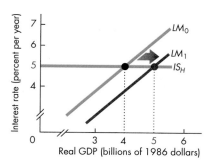

(b) Monetary policy: maximum effect on GDP

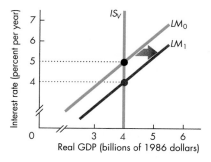

(c) Monetary policy: no effect on GDP

An increase in the money supply shifts the LM curve rightward. The effect of the monetary action on interest rates and real GDP depends on the slope of the IS curve. In the normal case (part a), interest rates fall and real GDP rises. The lower interest rates stimulate investment. In the special case (part b), the IS curve is horizontal. People don't care when they undertake their investment and will undertake any amount at an interest rate of 5 percent. The change in the money supply changes real GDP but leaves the interest rate constant. If investment demand is completely insensitive to interest rates (part c), the IS curve is vertical and a change in the money supply lowers interest rates but leaves real GDP unchanged. In this case, the lower interest rate has no effect on investment, so there is no initial injection of additional expenditure.

PART 11

AGGREGATE SUPPLY, INFLATION, AND RECESSION

Talking with Edmund Phelps

E dmund S. Phelps was born in Evanston, Illinois, in 1933 and is McVickar Professor of Political Economy at Columbia University. Professor Phelps was an undergraduate at Amherst College and obtained his Ph.D. from Yale in 1959. He was one of the initiators of New Macroeconomics—macroeconomics built on microeconomic foundations—and was the first to formalize the idea of the "natural rate of unemployment." Professor Phelps is a theorist—but a theorist who is driven by the desire to understand and explain the facts of unemployment and inflation and business cycles.

Why did you first study economics?

When I was going into my sophomore year at Amherst, my father prevailed on me to try a course in economics. I had guessed it was a dull subject that didn't get much beyond balance sheets or profit-and-loss statements, but I couldn't refuse my father's sole request. To my surprise, I took to the subject right away. The teacher and the textbook were part of the explanation. My professor, Jim Nelson, had a breezy style and was good at devising brain teasers for the weekly quizzes, and the textbook, by Paul Samuelson, was written in a brilliant style. I did very well, too, which was a reinforcement.

The other important point for me and a lot of students, I think, is that you are vaguely aware that you don't really have down how the various parts of the subject fit together. So you keep deciding to take one more course—until one day you find you've got a Ph.D.

What were the first questions that attracted your attention?

Even as a sophomore, I noticed that the microeconomics chapter on the theory of the firm talked about employment levels and relative prices in various industries being determined by supply and demand, while the macroeconomics chapter talked about employment as determined by aggregate demand plus some "story" about rigidity or stickiness of wages and prices. It turned out I spent a big chunk of my career working on that "story."

From thinking about the fundamental theoretical question, I started asking questions about the more applied areas of monetary and fiscal policy and public finance. What difference does it make what kind of inflation targets the monetary authorities adopt? Similarly, what difference does it make what fiscal policy is chosen? Or what tax rate structure is legislated?

These questions appealed to my interest, which went way back, in notions of the just state and the good society or, in economic terms, the optimum economy. The idea of economic justice, of just rewards for contributions to the output of the economy, is a flickering passion of mine. But there are very few economists around who respond to it as I do. It's a minority taste, I guess. Like opera.

How did you hit on the idea that there is a natural rate of unemployment—an equilibrium unemployment rate—that is independent of the inflation rate? Were you driven by the internal logic of the theory or by your observations of events?

I had read enough of earlier scholars—like Lerner and Fellner—to know that the idea of an equilibrium rate of unemployment that is not influenced by inflation had to be good economics. The problem was to develop, or at least sketch, the rudiments of a theory of how the natural rate is actually determined. Then I could develop a concrete, specific explanation of why steady inflation wouldn't affect the equilibrium rate.

How do you rate the predictive power of the natural rate theory?

I kept looking over my shoulder at each month's inflation rate in 1966 and 1967 when the unemployment rate had gotten pretty low. The inflation rate rose so slowly that I worried. Fortunately, the model looked better and better as we got to 1970, and statistical studies over subsequent years have given it mounting support.

The so-called "New Classical" approach of the 1970s in many ways followed your earlier work on wages in a setting of incomplete information. What is your evaluation of the contribution of the New Classicals?

On the one hand, I admired them very much for deriving such beautiful results so clearly. But I was a bit shocked that they accepted the idea of rational expectations so uncritically. And, like a lot of others, I was repelled by the imperious attitude that to be scientific, economics had to be done their way—that you don't question the faith.

Anyway, the New Classical models failed one empirical test after another. For example, they couldn't explain in a plausible way why the economy tends to come out of even short recessions as gradually as it does,—what's called the "persistence problem." Also, they couldn't explain why changes in the money supply that are perfectly anticipated by people have about as much effect on output and employment as money supply changes that are presumably unforeseen. There are two possible reasons for these failures. The first is that expectations are not generally rational. The

" The result is a labour market equilibrium in which not all workers can get the jobs they want and meet the qualifications . . ."

second is that wages and prices are not all reset simultaneously every month or quarter-year, contrary to the New Classical theory.

You are regarded as one of the founders of the New Keynesian school of macroeconomics. What is New Keynesian macroeconomics, and why do you find it attractive?

The New Keynesian school proposes that prices and wages are *not* all adjusted at the same time. When you introduce that possibility into your model, the average price level can adjust only gradually to monetary and real shocks to the economy. In other words, the effects of a shock are spread out over a long period of time. And even correctly foreseen shocks to the money supply are not offset by anticipatory changes in wages and prices.

At this time the New Keynesian model is still the model of choice for me and many others.

What is your evaluation of the real business cycle school?

The hope was that this school would show how the underlying equilibrium path of employment and output was disturbed by fundamental non-monetary factors. It would be the final achievement rounding out macroeconomic theory.

But it has not gotten as far as it could have because of its insistence on many of the fetishes of neoclassical theory plus some new self-inflicted constraints.

For example, they can't let go of the neoclassical feature of their models that all unemployment, or nonemployment, is basically voluntary because prices and wages are all market clearing. With only a little exaggeration, you can say that the natural rate of unemployment in their models is zero. Their only way of explaining fluctuations in employment is by explaining fluctuations in the length of the workweek that workers are willing to work.

It's a shame, really. Here are these technical wizards who have for some reason decided to turn their backs on the most important development within economic theory of the twentieth century. That is the rise of a modern theory of economic equilibrium based on asymmetric information, or private information. This theory explains that employees inflict damage on their employers, abusing their relationship by quitting frivolously or shirking unconscionably or arriving shamelessly unfit to work. Just about the only thing firms can do about it is to offer any new worker hired a better rate of pay to induce better behaviour. But this makes labour too expensive and hence causes some people not to be able to get jobs who otherwise could have. The result is a labour market equilibrium in which not all workers can get the jobs they want and meet the qualifications for because there is no way they can provide convincing information to a firm that they would not quit or shirk or be absent with the same frequency as the firm's existing employees—or be worse if the pay was worse.

What key principle of economics do you keep returning to in your own work?

Well, when I am wondering what economics suggests will be the consequences of some event or other, I keep rediscovering the importance of distinguishing between near-term and far-term effects. In trying to figure out the short-term or medium-term effects, I sooner or later realize I had better focus on the long-run effect first and then work backward to try to see what sort of short-run or medium-term scenario could lead to that long-run outcome. I guess the main principle is that the short term and the long term are distinct, though the one flows into the other. Any analysis of the consequences of an economic disturbance that focusses just on the short run or on the long run is apt to be misleading. And, being incomplete, it runs a big risk of also being wrong.

CHAPTER **30**

PRODUCTIVITY, WAGES, AND UNEMPLOYMENT

After studying this chapter, you will be able to

◆ Explain why productivity and real GDP grow

◆ Explain how firms decide how much labour to employ

◆ Explain how households decide how much labour to supply

◆ Explain how wages and employment are determined

◆ Derive the long-run and short-run aggregate supply curves

◆ Explain what makes aggregate supply fluctuate

◆ Explain why unemployment exists and why its rate fluctuates

N 1992, EACH HOUR OF WORK EARNED CANADIANS 20 percent more than it did in 1972. And over the same period, the number of Canadians with jobs grew by more than 50 percent. What makes our wages and the number of jobs grow? ◆ ◆ As our economy grows, it ebbs and flows through the business cycle, with employment and real GDP marching in step with each other. Sometimes the Canadian economy is in recession—real GDP has fallen. Such was the situation in 1990 when real GDP decreased by almost 4 percent. What makes real GDP sometimes decrease? ◆ ◆ Recently, Canadian National Railways announced that it will shed 10,000 jobs over three years to 1995. GM Canada will cut some 4,000 jobs. These are examples of a general trend towards fewer jobs in many industries. Because of this trend, and despite two years of growth in real GDP, Canadian unemployment continued upward throughout 1991 and 1992. At the beginning of 1993,

Incomes and Jobs

12 percent of the labour force was unemployed. What causes unemployment? Why don't the unemployed get jobs? And why is unemployment sometimes high?

◆ ◆ ◆ ◆ In this chapter, we'll look at productivity, wages, and the Canadian labour market. We'll discover what makes employment, productivity, and wages grow, why there is always some unemployment, and why the unemployment rate is sometimes high. Our study completes a further block in the macroeconomic jigsaw puzzle—the aggregate supply block. We'll return to the long-run and short-run aggregate supply curves that you met in Chapter 24 and see how those curves are related to the labour market.

Productivity and Income Growth

When we talk about *productivity*, we usually mean labour productivity—although we can measure the productivity of any factor of production. **Labour productivity** is measured as total output per person employed. To study the growth of labour productivity and its effects on wages, employment, and unemployment, we use the concept of the production function. A **production function** shows how output varies as the employment of inputs is varied. A **short-run production function** shows how output varies when the quantity of labour employed varies, holding constant the quantity of capital and the state of technology. Production functions exist for every kind of economic activity—building dams and highways or baking loaves of bread. But the production function that tells us about the relationship between *aggregate* employment and *aggregate* output is the short-run *aggregate* production function. The **short-run aggregate production function** shows how real GDP varies as the quantity of labour employed is varied, holding constant all other influences on production.

The table in Fig. 30.1 records part of an economy's short-run aggregate production function. In that table, we look at the aggregate quantity of labour, measured in billions of hours a year, over the range 15 billion to 35 billion. Through that range of employment, real GDP varies between $400 billion and $700 billion a year (measured in 1986 dollars).

The short-run aggregate production function (*PF*) is illustrated in the graph in Fig. 30.1. The labour input is measured on the horizontal axis, and real GDP is measured on the vertical axis. The short-run production function slopes upward, showing that more labour input produces more real GDP.

The Marginal Product of Labour

The **marginal product of labour** is the additional real GDP produced by one additional hour of labour input, holding all other influences on production constant. We calculate the marginal product of labour as the change in real GDP divided by the

FIGURE 30.1

The Short-Run Aggregate Production Function

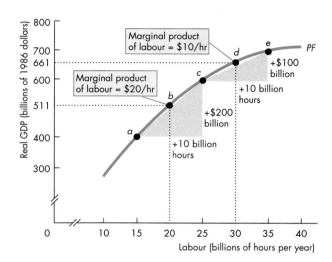

	Labour (billions of hours per year)	Real GDP (billions of 1986 dollars per year)
a	15	400
b	20	511
c	25	600
d	30	661
e	35	700

The short-run aggregate production function shows the level of real GDP at each quantity of labour input, holding all other inputs constant. The table lists five points on a short-run aggregate production function. Each row tells us the amount of real GDP that can be produced by a given labour input. Points *a* through *e* in the graph correspond to the rows in the table. The curve passing through these points traces the economy's short-run aggregate production function. The marginal product of labour is highlighted in the figure. As the labour input increases, real GDP increases but by successively smaller amounts. For example, a 10 billion hour increase in labour from 15 billion to 25 billion increases real GDP by $200 billion—a marginal product of $20 an hour. But a 10 billion hour increase in labour from 25 billion to 35 billion hours increases real GDP by only $100 billion—a marginal product of $10 an hour.

change in the quantity of labour employed. Let's do such a calculation, using Fig. 30.1.

When the labour input increases from 15 billion to 25 billion hours—an increase of 10 billion hours—real GDP increases from $400 billion to $600 billion, an increase of $200 billion. The marginal product of labour over this range is $20 an hour ($200 billion divided by 10 billion hours). Next, look at what happens at a higher level of labour input. When the labour input increases by 10 billion hours from 25 billion to 35 billion hours, real GDP increases, but by less than in the previous case—by only $100 billion. Now the marginal product of labour is $10 an hour ($100 billion divided by 10 billion hours).

The marginal product of labour is measured by the slope of the production function. Figure 30.1 highlights this fact. The slope of the production function at point b is $20 an hour. This slope is calculated as $200 billion (the change in real GDP from $400 billion to $600 billion) divided by 10 billion hours (the change in employment from 15 billion hours to 25 billion hours.) Similarly, the slope of the production function at point d is $10 an hour.

Diminishing Marginal Product of Labour

The marginal product of labour declines as the labour input increases. This phenomenon, apparent from the calculations we've just made and visible in the figure, is called the diminishing marginal product of labour. The **diminishing marginal product of labour** is the tendency for the marginal product of labour to decline as the labour input increases, holding everything else constant.

Diminishing marginal product of labour arises because we are dealing with a *short-run* production function. As the quantity of labour employed is varied, all other inputs are held constant. Thus, although more labour can produce more output, a larger labour force operates the same capital equipment—machines and tools—as does a smaller labour force. As more people are hired, the capital equipment is worked closer and closer to its physical limits, more breakdowns occur, and bottlenecks arise. As a result, output does not increase in proportion to the amount of labour employed. The marginal product of labour declines as more labour is hired. This feature is present in almost all production processes and is also present in the relationship between aggregate employment and aggregate output—real GDP.

A change in the quantity of labour brings a movement along the production function. A change in any other influence on production shifts the production function. Let's now look at these influences.

Economic Growth

Economic growth is the expansion of the economy's productive capacity. Economic growth results from two sources. They are

◆ Capital accumulation

◆ Technological change

Capital Accumulation   Every year, some of the economy's resources are devoted to accumulating new capital. Much of this capital takes the form of machines, production lines, and buildings. But a larger part takes the form of *human capital*. Human capital is acquired by attending school and by on-the-job experience. This last source of capital accumulation is now believed to be the largest single contributor to economic growth. Additional capital enables a given amount of labour to produce more output.

Technological Change   We also devote some of our resources to developing new technologies. Technological change has two stages, invention and innovation. **Invention** is the discovery of a new technique; **innovation** is the act of putting a new technique to work. Invention is the driving force behind technological change, but it is innovation that actually changes our productive capacity. Like capital accumulation, technological change also enables a given amount of labour to produce more output.

The Shifting Production Function   Because capital accumulation and technological change enable a given amount of labour to produce more output, they shift the short-run aggregate production function upward. Figure 30.2 illustrates such a shift. The curve labelled PF_{93} is the same as the production function in Fig. 30.1. During 1993 and 1994, new equipment is installed, labour becomes more skillful as a result of on-the-job experience, and new technologies are used. Some old, less productive capital wears out and is retired to the scrap heap. The net result is an increase in the productivity of the economy that results in an upward movement of the short-run aggregate production function to PF_{95}.

FIGURE 30.2

The Growth of Output

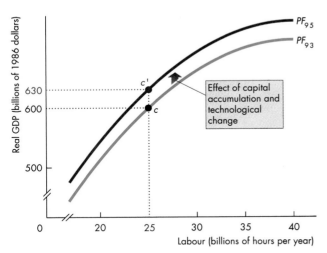

Output grows over time. The accumulation of capital and the adoption of more productive technologies make it possible to achieve a higher level of real GDP for any given labour input. For example, between 1993 and 1995 the production function shifts upward from PF_{93} to PF_{95}. A labour input of 25 billion hours produces $600 billion of real GDP in 1993 (point c) and $630 billion in 1995 (point c').

When 25 billion hours of labour are employed, the economy can produce a real GDP of $600 billion in 1993 (point c). By 1995, that same quantity of labour can produce $630 billion (point c'). Each level of labour input can produce more output in 1995 than in 1993.

Variable Growth Rates

Capital accumulation and technological change do not proceed at a constant pace. In some years, the level of investment is high and the capital stock grows quickly. In other years—recession years—investment decreases and the capital stock grows slowly. Also, there are fluctuations in the pace of technological innovation. These fluctuations in the pace of capital accumulation and innovation result in fluctuations in the magnitude of the upward shift in the short-run production from one year to another. But usually it shifts upward.

Occasionally, the short-run aggregate production function shifts downward—productivity decreases. Such a downward shift can be the result of a widespread drought, a disruption to international trade, an outbreak of civil disorder, or a war. A serious disruption to international trade occurred in 1974 when the Organization of Petroleum Exporting Countries (OPEC) placed an embargo on oil exports. This action deprived the industrialized world of one of its crucial raw materials. Firms could not obtain all the fuel they needed, and as a result the labour force was not able to produce as much output as normal. As a consequence, the short-run aggregate production function shifted downward in 1974.

Let's take a look at Canada's short-run aggregate production function and see what it tells about our productivity growth.

Canadian Productivity Growth

Figure 30.3 shows Canada's short-run aggregate production function. Concentrate first on the blue dots in this figure. There is a dot for each year between 1975 and 1993, and each one represents the values of real GDP and aggregate employment for a particular year. For example, the dot for 1975 tells us that in 1975 real GDP was $350 billion and labour hours were 17.4 billion; in 1993, real GDP was $572 billion and labour hours were 21.6 billion.

These two dots together with the other dots in the figure do not all lie on the same short-run aggregate production function. Instead, they each lie on their own short-run aggregate production function. Each year the stock of capital equipment and the state of technology change, so the economy's productive potential is usually higher than in the year before. The production function for 1975 is PF_{75} and that for 1993 is PF_{93}.

The 1993 short-run production function is almost 45 percent higher than the 1975 aggregate production function. This fact means that if employment in 1993 had been the same as it was in 1975, real GDP in 1993 would have been $507 billion. Equivalently, if employment in 1975 had been the same as it was in 1993, real GDP in 1975 would have been $395 billion.

The Productivity Slowdown

The short-run production function shifts upward over time because we become more productive— a given amount of labour produces an increased

FIGURE 30.3

The Canadian Short-Run Aggregate Production Function

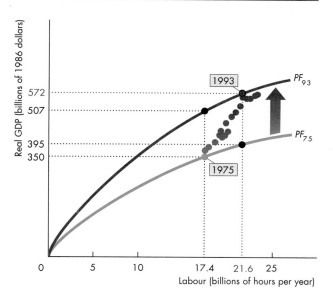

The dots in the figure show real GDP and aggregate hours of labour employed in Canada for each year between 1975 and 1993. For example, in 1975 labour input was 17.4 million hours and real GDP was $350 billion. In 1993, labour input was 21.6 million hours and real GDP was $572 billion. The dots do not lie on one short-run aggregate production function. Instead, the short-run aggregate production function shifts from year to year as capital accumulates and technologies change. The figure shows the short-run aggregate production functions for 1975 and 1993—PF_{75} and PF_{93}. The 1993 production function is almost 45 percent higher than that for 1975. For example, the 17.4 billion hours of labour that produced $350 billion of real GDP in 1975 would have produced $507 billion of real GDP in 1993. Similarly, the 21.6 billion hours of labour that produced $572 billion of real GDP in 1993 would have produced $395 billion of real GDP in 1975.

amount of output. But labour productivity does not grow at an even pace. During the late 1970s, we experienced a productivity slowdown.

There are several reasons for the slowdown in Canadian productivity growth during the 1970s. The two main ones are energy price shocks and changes in the composition of output. First, energy prices quadrupled in 1973–1974 and increased sharply again in 1979–1980, forcing firms to find energy-saving, labour-using, and capital-using methods of production. Second, as our economy expanded, the composition of output changed. Agriculture and manufacturing contracted and services expanded. Productivity growth is fastest in agriculture and manufacturing and slowest in services, so as the composition of output changed towards a greater emphasis on services, average productivity growth slowed down.

REVIEW

A production function tells us how the output that can be produced varies as inputs are varied. A short-run production function tells us how the output that can be produced varies as the employment of labour varies, holding everything else constant. The short-run aggregate production function tells us how real GDP varies as total labour hours vary. The marginal product of labour—the increase in real GDP resulting from a one-hour increase of labour input—diminishes as the labour input increases. ◆ ◆ The short-run production function usually shifts upward from year to year but, on occasion, it shifts downward. Capital accumulation and technological advances shift the short-run aggregate production function upward. Shocks such as droughts, disruptions of international trade, or civil and political unrest shift the production function downward. The short-run aggregate production function in Canada shifted upward by almost 45 percent between 1975 and 1993. ◆

We've seen that output in any year depends on the position of the short-run aggregate production function and on the quantity of labour employed. Even if the short-run aggregate production function shifts upward, it is still possible for output to fall because of a fall in employment. For example, in 1991 employment and real GDP fell as the economy went into recession. To determine the level of output, we need to understand not only the influences on the short-run aggregate production function but also those on the level of employment. And to determine the level of employment, we need to study the demand for and supply of labour and how the market allocates labour to jobs. We'll begin by studying the demand for labour.

The Demand for Labour

T he **quantity of labour demanded** is the number of labour hours hired by all the firms in an economy. The **demand for labour** is the quantity of labour demanded at each real wage rate. The **real wage rate** is the wage per hour expressed in constant dollars—for example, the wage per hour expressed in 1986 dollars. The wage rate expressed in *current dollars* is called the **money wage rate**. A real wage rate expressed in 1986 dollars tells us what today's money wage rate would buy if prices today were the same as in 1986. We calculate the real wage rate by dividing the money wage rate by the GDP deflator and multiplying by 100. For example, if the money wage rate is $18 and the GDP deflator is 120, the real wage rate is $15 ($18 divided by 120 and multiplied by 100 equals $15).

We can represent the demand for labour as a schedule or a curve. The table in Fig. 30.4 sets out an example of a demand for labour schedule. Row *b* tells us that at a real wage rate of $20.00 an hour, 20 billion hours of labour (a year) are demanded. The other rows of the table are read in a similar way. The demand for labour schedule is graphed as the demand for labour curve (*LD*). Each point on the curve corresponds to the row identified by the same letter in the table.

Why is the quantity of labour demanded influenced by the *real* wage rate? Why isn't it the *money* wage rate that affects the quantity of labour demanded? Also, why does the quantity of labour demanded increase as the real wage rate decreases? That is, why does the demand for labour curve slope downward? Let's answer these questions.

Diminishing Marginal Product and the Demand for Labour

Firms are in business to maximize profits. Each worker that a firm hires adds to its costs and increases its output. Up to a point, the extra output produced by the worker is worth more to the firm than the wages the firm has to pay. But each additional hour of labour hired produces less output than the previous hour—the marginal product of labour

FIGURE 30.4

Demand for Labour

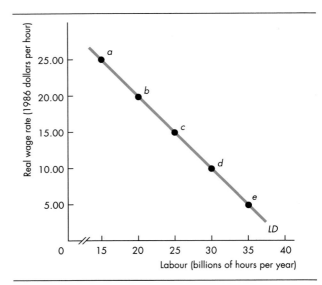

	Real wage rate (1986 dollars per hour)	Quantity of labour demanded (billions of hours per year)
a	25.00	15
b	20.00	20
c	15.00	25
d	10.00	30
e	5.00	35

The quantity of labour demanded increases as the real wage rate decreases, as illustrated by the labour demand schedule in the table and the demand for labour curve (*LD*). Each row in the table tells us the quantity of labour demanded at a given real wage rate and corresponds to a point on the labour demand curve. For example, when the real wage rate is $15 an hour, the quantity of labour demanded is 25 billion hours a year (point *c*). The demand for labour curve slopes downward because it pays firms to hire labour so long as its marginal product of labour is greater than or equal to the real wage rate. The lower the real wage rate, the larger is the number of workers whose marginal product exceeds that real wage rate.

diminishes. As the amount of labour employed increases and the capital equipment employed is constant, more workers have to use the same machines and the plant operates closer and closer to its physical limits. Output increases, but not in proportion to the increase in labour input. As the firm hires more workers, it eventually reaches the point where the revenue from selling the extra output produced by an additional hour of labour equals the hourly wage rate. If the firm hires even one more hour of labour, the extra cost incurred will exceed the revenue brought in from selling the extra output. The firm will not employ that additional hour of labour. It hires the quantity of labour such that the revenue brought in by the last hour of labour input equals the money wage rate.

To see why it is the *real* wage rate, rather than the money wage rate, that affects the quantity of labour demanded, let's consider an example.

The Demand for Labour in a Pop Factory

A pop factory employs 400 hours of labour. The additional output produced by the last hour hired is 11 bottles of pop. That is, the marginal product of labour is 11 bottles of pop an hour. Pop sells for 50¢ a bottle, so the revenue brought in from selling these 11 bottles is $5.50. The money wage rate is also $5.50 an hour. This last hour of labour hired brings in as much revenue as the wages paid out, so it just pays the firm to hire that hour of labour. The firm is paying a real wage rate that is exactly the same as the marginal product of labour—11 bottles of pop. That is, the firm's real wage rate is equal to the money wage rate of $5.50 an hour divided by the price of pop, 50¢ a bottle.

A Change in the Real Wage Rate   Let's work out what happens when the real wage rate changes. Suppose the money wage rate increases to $11 an hour while the price of pop remains constant at 50¢ a bottle. The real wage rate has now increased to 22 bottles of pop—equal to the money wage of $11 an hour divided by 50¢ a bottle, the price of a bottle of pop. The last hour of labour hired now costs $11 but brings in only $5.50 of extra revenue. It does not pay the firm to hire this hour of labour. The firm decreases the quantity of labour employed until the marginal product of labour brings in $11 of revenue. This occurs when the marginal product of labour is 22 bottles of pop—that is, 22 bottles at 50¢ a bottle sell for $11. The marginal product is again equal to the real wage rate. But to make the marginal product of labour equal to the real wage rate, the firm has to decrease the quantity of labour employed. Thus, when the real wage rate increases, the quantity of labour demanded decreases.

In the example we've just worked through, the real wage rate increased because the money wage rate increased with a constant output price. But the same outcome occurs if the money wage rate remains constant and the output price decreases. For example, if the wage rate remains at $5.50 an hour while the price of pop falls to 25¢ a bottle, the real wage rate is 22 bottles of pop. The firm hires the amount of labour that makes the marginal product of labour equal to 22 bottles.

A Change in the Money Wage Rate with a Constant Real Wage   To see why the money wage rate does not affect the quantity of labour demanded, suppose that the money wage rate and all prices double. The money wage rate increases to $11 an hour and the price of pop increases to $1 a bottle. The pop factory is in the same real situation as before. It pays $11 for the last hour of labour employed and sells the output produced by that labour for $11. The money wage rate has doubled from $5.50 to $11 an hour, but nothing *real* has changed. The real wage rate is still 11 bottles of pop. As far as the firm is concerned, 400 hours is still the right quantity of labour to hire. The money wage rate has changed, but the real wage rate and the quantity of labour demanded have remained constant.

The Demand for Labour in the Economy

The demand for labour in the economy as a whole is determined in the same way as in the pop factory. Thus the quantity of labour demanded depends on the real wage rate, not the money wage rate, and the higher the real wage rate, the smaller is the quantity of labour demanded.

We now know why the demand for labour curve slopes downward, but what makes it shift?

Changes in the Demand for Labour

When the marginal product of each hour of labour changes, the demand for labour changes and the demand for labour curve shifts. The accumulation of capital and the development of new technologies are constantly increasing the marginal product of each hour of labour. We've already seen one effect of such changes. They shift the short-run aggregate production function upward, as shown in Fig. 30.2. At the same time, they make the short-run aggregate production function *steeper*. Anything that makes the short-run production function steeper increases the marginal product of each hour of labour—that is, it increases the extra output obtained from one additional hour of labour. At a given real wage rate, firms will increase the amount of labour they hire until the revenue brought in from selling the extra output produced by the last hour of labour input equals the hourly wage. Thus, as the short-run aggregate production function shifts upward, the demand for labour curve shifts rightward.

In general, the demand for labour curve shifts rightward over time. But there are fluctuations in the pace at which the demand for labour curve shifts that match the fluctuations in the short-run aggregate production function. Let's look at the demand for labour in Canada and see how it has changed from 1975 to 1993.

The Canadian Demand for Labour

Figure 30.5 shows the average real wage rate and the quantity of labour employed in each year between 1975 and 1993. For example, in 1993 the real wage was $15.47 an hour (in 1986 dollars) and 21.6 billion hours of labour were employed.

The figure shows two demand for labour curves, one for 1975 and the other for 1993. Between 1975 and 1993, the production function shifted upward and the marginal product of labour increased. If the quantity of labour employed in 1993 had been the same as in 1975 (17.4 billion hours), the real wage rate would have been $17.03 an hour. If the quantity of labour employed in 1975 had been as high as that in 1993 (21.6 billion hours), the real wage rate in that year would have been only $10.31 an hour.

In some years, the changes in labour productivity are particularly large and news worthy. For an example, see Reading between the Lines on pp.838–839.

FIGURE 30.5

The Canadian Demand for Labour

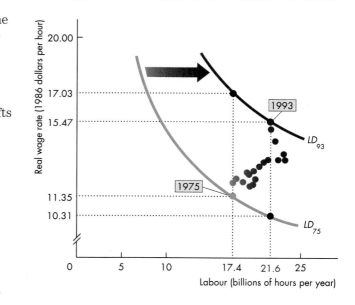

The figure shows the quantity of labour employed and the average real wage rate in Canada from 1975 to 1993. For example, in 1975 the real wage rate was $11.35 an hour and 17.4 billion hours of labour were employed. In 1993, the real wage rate was $15.47 an hour and 21.6 billion hours of labour were employed. These two points (and the dots for the years between them) do not lie on a single demand for labour curve. The demand for labour curve has shifted as a result of shifts in the short-run aggregate production function. The figure shows the demand curves for 1975 and 1993—LD_{75} and LD_{93}. Over time, the demand for labour curve has shifted rightward.

R E V I E W

The quantity of labour demanded is the quantity of labour hours hired by all firms in the economy. It depends on the real wage rate. For an individual firm, the real wage rate is the money wage rate paid to the worker divided by the price for which the firm's output sells. For the economy as a whole, the real wage rate is the money wage rate divided by the price level. The lower the real wage rate, the greater is the quantity of labour demanded. The demand for labour curve slopes downward. ◆ ◆ The demand for labour curve shifts because of shifts in the short-run aggregate production function. An increase in the capital stock or advances in technology embodied in the capital stock shift the short-run aggregate production function upward and increase the marginal product of labour. The demand for labour curve shifts rightward, but at an uneven pace. ◆

Let's now turn to the other side of the labour market and see how the supply of labour is determined.

The Supply of Labour

T he **quantity of labour supplied** is the number of hours of labour services that households supply to firms. The **supply of labour** is the quantity of labour supplied at each real wage rate.

We can represent the supply of labour as a schedule or a curve. The table in Fig. 30.6 shows a supply of labour schedule. For example, row *b* tells us that at a real wage rate of $10.00 an hour, 20 billion hours of labour (a year) are supplied. The other rows of the table are read in a similar way. The supply of labour schedule is graphed as the supply of labour curve (*LS*). Each point on the *LS* curve represents the row identified by the same letter in the table. As the real wage rate increases, the quantity of labour supplied increases. The supply of labour curve slopes upward.

But why does the quantity of labour supplied increase when the real wage rate increases? Because there is an increase in

◆ Hours per worker

◆ The participation rate

Hours per Worker

In choosing how many hours to work, a household has to decide how to allocate its time between work and other activities. If a household chooses not to work for an hour, it does not get paid for that hour. The opportunity cost of not working an hour is what the household really gives up by not working. It is all the goods and services that the household could buy with the hourly money wage. So the opportunity cost of an hour of time spent not working is the real hourly wage rate.

What happens to people's willingness to work if the real wage rate increases? Such a change has two opposing effects:

◆ A substitution effect

◆ An income effect

Substitution Effect The substitution effect of a change in the real wage rate works in exactly the

FIGURE 30.6

The Supply of Labour

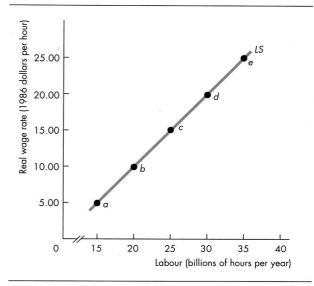

	Real wage rate (1986 dollars per hour)	Quantity of labour supplied (billions of hours per year)
a	5.00	15
b	10.00	20
c	15.00	25
d	20.00	30
e	25.00	35

The quantity of labour supplied increases as the real wage rate increases, as illustrated by the labour supply schedule in the table and the supply of labour curve (*LS*). Each row of the table tells us the quantity of labour supplied at a given real wage rate and corresponds to a point on the labour supply curve. For example, when the real wage rate is $15 an hour, the quantity of labour supplied is 25 billion hours a year (point *c*). The supply of labour curve slopes upward because households work longer hours, on the average, at higher real wage rates and more households participate in the labour force. These responses are reinforced by intertemporal substitution—the retiming of work to take advantage of temporarily high wages.

same way as a change in the price of tapes affects the quantity of tapes demanded. Just as tapes have a price, so does time. As we've just noted, the real hourly wage rate is the opportunity cost of an hour

Productivity Growth

THE FINANCIAL POST, MAY 18, 1993

Labor productivity shows strong gains

By Greg Ip

Labor productivity registered its biggest increase in eight years in 1992, thanks to extra spending on capital equipment and ongoing payroll cuts.

Real gross domestic product per person-hour worked rose 2.2% in 1992 after a 1.8% gain in 1991, Statistics Canada said yesterday, the biggest gain since productivity soared 4.1% in 1983 and 3.6% in 1984 after the 1981–82 recession.

The increase in labor productivity and a slowing in wage increases enabled business to slash growth in unit labor costs, to an eight-year low of 1.7% in 1992 compared to 3.8% in 1991....

The gains were even more impressive in manufacturing, where labor productivity soared 4.2% last year while unit labor costs did not grow at all.

Business achieved these gains by both cutting jobs and investing in equipment. Although the economy grew in 1992, hours worked fell 1.5% after falling 4% in 1991, and manufacturing chopped hours worked

by 3.6% after cuts of 7.2% in 1991 and 6.3% in 1990.

At the same time, business was increasing its capital stock rapidly, by 8% between 1989 and 1991....

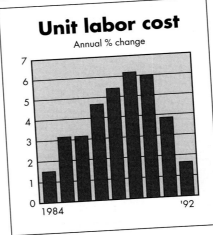

Unit labor cost
Annual % change

Source: Statistics Canada

The Essence of the Story

Real gross domestic product per person-hour worked rose 2.2% in 1992, its biggest increase in eight years. (Numbers for earlier years are: 1.8% in 1991, 4.1% in 1983, and 3.6% in 1984.)

The increase in labour productivity and a slowing in wage increases cut the growth in unit labour costs to 1.7% (another eight-year low) compared to 3.8% in 1991.

Labour productivity growth in manufacturing was even larger—4.2%—and unit labour costs did not grow at all.

Business achieved these gains by cutting work hours and increasing its stock of capital equipment.

Background and Analysis

In 1992, two factors increased labour productivity—an increase in the stock of capital and a decrease in the quantity of labour employed.

The figures illustrate how the growth in labour productivity occurred.

In part (a) of the figure, an increase in the capital stock shifted the short-run aggregate production function upward from PF_{91} to PF_{92}. As a result, output per hour of labour increased at all levels of employment.

In part (b) of the figure, the effect of the increase in the capital stock is seen as a shift in the demand for labour curve from LD_{91} to LD_{92}.

If employment had remained constant at its 1991 level, the *marginal product of labour* and the real wage rate would have increased from $14.15 an hour to $14.45 an hour—an increase of about 2 percent.

But the quantity of labour employed decreased—as shown by a movement along the demand for labour curve—so the marginal product of labour and the real wage rate increased by a further 2 percent to $14.75 an hour.

The percentage increases in labour productivity shown in part (b) are larger than those reported in the news article. They are based on the latest revised data at the time of writing.

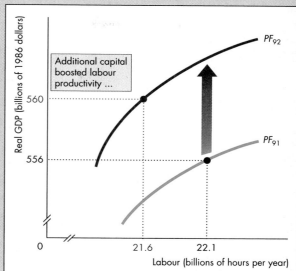

(a) Production function

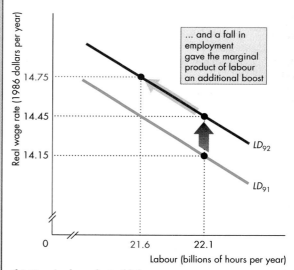

(b) Marginal product of labour

spent not working. A higher real wage rate increases the opportunity cost of time and makes time itself a more valuable commodity. This higher opportunity cost of not working encourages people to reduce their nonwork time and increase the time spent working. Thus, as the real wage rate increases, more hours of work are supplied.

Income Effect But a higher real wage rate also increases people's incomes. As you know, the higher a person's income, the greater is their demand for all types of goods and services. One such "good" is leisure—the time to do pleasurable things that don't generate an income. Thus a higher real wage rate also makes people want to enjoy longer leisure hours and supply fewer hours of work.

Which of these two effects dominates depends on each individual's attitude towards work and also on the real wage rate. Attitudes towards work, though varying across individuals, do not change much, on the average, over time. But the real wage rate does change and it brings changes in the quantity of labour supplied. At a very low real wage rate, the substitution effect is stronger than the income effect. That is, as the real wage rate increases, the inducement to substitute working time for leisure time is stronger than the inducement to spend part of a larger income on more leisure hours. As a consequence, as the real wage rate increases, the quantity of labour supplied increases.

At a high enough real wage rate, the income effect becomes stronger than the substitution effect. As the real wage increases, the inducement to spend more of the additional income on leisure time is stronger than the inducement to economize on leisure time.

Some people undoubtedly receive such a high real wage rate that a further increase would cause them to reduce their hours of work. But for most of us a higher real wage rate coaxes us to work more. Thus, on the average, the higher the real wage rate, the more hours each person works.

The Participation Rate

The **labour force participation rate** is the proportion of the working-age population that is either employed or unemployed (but seeking employment). For a variety of reasons, people differ in their willingness to work. Some people have more productive opportunities at home and so need a bigger inducement to quit those activities and work for

someone else. Other individuals place a very high value on leisure, and they require a high real wage to induce them to do any work at all. These considerations suggest that each person has a reservation wage. A **reservation wage** is the lowest wage at which a person will supply any labour. Below that wage, a person will not work.

Those people who have a reservation wage below or equal to the actual real wage will be in the labour force, and those who have a reservation wage above the real wage will not be in the labour force. The higher the real wage rate, the larger is the number of people whose reservation wage falls below the real wage rate and, hence, the larger is the labour force participation rate.

Reinforcing and strengthening the increase in hours worked per household and the labour force participation rate is an intertemporal substitution effect on the quantity of labour supplied.

Intertemporal Substitution

Households have to decide not only whether to work but also *when* to work. This decision is based not just on the current real wage but also on the current real wage relative to expected future real wages.

Suppose that the real wage rate is higher today than it is expected to be later on. How does this fact affect a person's labour supply decision? It encourages more work today and less in the future. Thus the higher today's real wage rate relative to what is expected in the future (other things being constant), the larger is the supply of labour.

Temporarily high real wages are similar to a high rate of return. If real wages are temporarily high, people can obtain a higher rate of return on their work effort by enjoying a smaller amount of leisure and supplying more labour in such a period. By investing in some work now and taking the return in more leisure time later, they can obtain a higher overall level of consumption of goods and services and of leisure.

R E V I E W

The opportunity cost of time is the real wage rate—the goods and services that can be bought with the income from an hour of work. An increase in the real wage rate, other things remaining the same, increases the supply of hours per worker and increases the labour force participation rate. A higher *current* real wage relative to the expected future real wage encourages people to supply more labour today and less in the future. ◆

We've now seen why, as the real wage rate increases, the quantity of labour supplied increases—why the supply of labour curve slopes upward. Let's next bring the two sides of the labour market together and study the determination of wages and employment.

Wages and Employment

We've discovered that as the real wage rate increases, the quantity of labour demanded declines and the quantity of labour supplied increases. We now want to study how the two sides of the labour market interact to determine the real wage rate, employment, and unemployment.

There is disagreement about how the labour market works, and this disagreement is the main source of current controversy in macroeconomics.

There are two leading theories about the labour market:

◆ Flexible wage theory

◆ Sticky wage theory

The flexible wage theory is based on the assumption that the labour market operates in a way similar to the markets for goods and services, with the real wage rate continuously and freely adjusting to keep the quantity of labour demanded equal to the quantity supplied. The sticky wage theory is based on the assumption that wage contracts *fix* the money wage rate—hence the name sticky wages. If the money wage rate is sticky, the real wage rate does not continuously adjust to keep the quantity of labour demanded equal to the quantity supplied. Let's look at these two theories, beginning with the flexible wage theory.

The Flexible Wage Theory

Most people's wages—*money wages*—are determined by wage contracts that run for at least one year and often for two or three years. Doesn't this fact mean that money wages are not flexible? Not necessarily. Money wage rates, even those fixed by wage contracts, can and do adjust upward or downward. For example, some workers receive bonus payments in good times and lose those bonuses in bad times. Some workers get overtime at high rates of pay in good times but only get work at the normal wage rate in bad times. Workers often get unusually rapid promotion to jobs with a higher wage rate in good times and get stuck on a lower rung of the promotion ladder in bad times. Thus fluctuations in bonuses, overtime pay, and the pace of promotion result in changes in the average wage rate even when wage rate schedules don't change.

The flexible wage theory assumes that these sources of wage adjustment are sufficient to achieve a continuous balance between the quantity of labour demanded and the quantity supplied.

Figure 30.7 illustrates the theory. The demand for labour curve is *LD* and the supply of labour curve is *LS*. This market determines an equilibrium real wage rate of $15 an hour and a quantity of labour employed of 25 billion hours. If the real wage rate is below its equilibrium level of $15 an hour, the quantity of labour demanded exceeds the quantity supplied. In such a situation, the real wage rate will rise since firms are willing to offer higher wages to overcome their labour shortages. The real wage rate will continue to rise until it reaches $15 an hour, at which point there will be no shortage of labour.

If the real wage rate is higher than its equilibrium level of $15 an hour, the quantity of labour supplied exceeds the quantity demanded. In this situation, households are not able to get all the work they want and firms find it easy to hire labour. Firms will have an incentive to cut the wage, and households will accept the lower wage to get a job. The real wage rate will fall until it reaches $15 an hour, at which point every household is satisfied with the quantity of labour it is supplying.

Changes in Wages and Employment   The flexible wage theory makes predictions about wages and employment that are identical to the predictions of the demand and supply model we studied in Chapter 4. An increase in the demand for labour shifts the demand for labour curve rightward and increases

FIGURE 30.7

Equilibrium with Flexible Wages

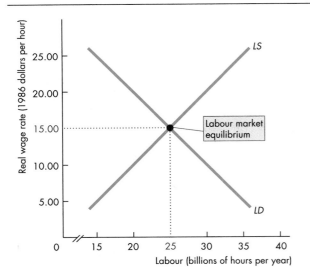

Equilibrium occurs when the real wage rate makes the quantity of labour demanded equal to the quantity supplied. This equilibrium occurs at a real wage rate of $15 an hour. At that real wage rate, 25 billion hours of labour are employed. At real wage rates below $15 an hour, the quantity of labour demanded exceeds the quantity supplied and the real wage rate rises. At real wage rates above $15 an hour, the quantity of labour supplied exceeds the quantity of labour demanded and the real wage rate falls.

both the real wage rate and the quantity of labour employed. A decrease in the demand for labour shifts the demand for labour curve leftward and decreases both the real wage rate and the quantity of labour employed. An increase in the supply of labour shifts the supply of labour curve rightward, lowering the real wage rate and increasing employment. A decrease in the supply of labour shifts the supply of labour curve leftward, raising the real wage rate and decreasing employment.

The demand for labour increases over time because capital accumulation and technological change increase the marginal product of labour. The supply of labour increases over time because the working-age population is steadily increasing. Rightward shifts in the demand for labour curve have generally been larger than shifts in the supply of labour curve so, over time, both the quantity of labour employed and the real wage rate have increased.

Aggregate Supply with Flexible Wages

The flexible wage theory of the labour market implies that the quantity of real GDP supplied is independent of the price level—that the aggregate supply curve is vertical. The reason is that as the price level changes, the money wage rate *always* adjusts to determine a real wage rate that brings equality between the quantity of labour demanded and the quantity supplied.

Figure 30.8 illustrates the derivation of the aggregate supply curve when wages are flexible. Part (a) shows the aggregate labour market. The demand and supply curves shown are the same as those in Fig. 30.7. The equilibrium, a real wage of $15 an hour and employment of 25 billion hours, is the same equilibrium that was determined in that figure.

Figure 30.8(b) shows the short-run aggregate production function. This production function is the one shown in Fig. 30.1. We know from the labour market (part a) that 25 billion hours of labour are employed. Part (b) tells us that when 25 million hours of labour are employed, real GDP is $600 billion.

Figure 30.8(c) shows the long-run aggregate supply curve. That curve tells us that real GDP is $600 billion regardless of the price level. To see why, look at what happens to real GDP when the price level changes.

Start with a GDP deflator of 100. In this case, the economy is at point *j* in part (c) of the figure. That is, the GDP deflator is 100 and real GDP is $600 billion. We've determined, in part (a), that the real wage rate is $15. With a GDP deflator of 100, the money wage rate (the wage rate in current dollars) is also $15 an hour.

What happens to real GDP if the GDP deflator falls from 100 to 80 (a 20 percent decrease in the price level)? If the money wage rate remains at $15 an hour, the real wage rate rises and the quantity of labour supplied exceeds the quantity demanded. In such a situation, the money wage rate will fall. It falls to $12 an hour. With a money wage rate of $12 and a GDP deflator of 80, the real wage rate is still $15 ($12 divided by 80 and multiplied by 100 equals $15). With the lower money wage rate but a constant real wage rate, employment remains at 25 billion hours and real GDP remains at $600 billion. The economy is at point *k* in Fig. 30.8(c).

What happens to real GDP if the GDP deflator rises from 100 to 120 (a 20 percent increase in the price level)? If the money wage rate stays at $15 an hour, the real wage rate falls and the quantity of

FIGURE 30.8

Aggregate Supply with Flexible Wages

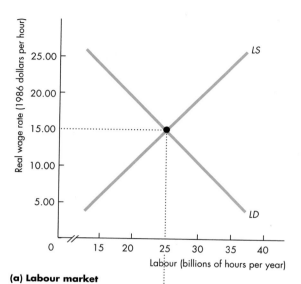

(a) Labour market

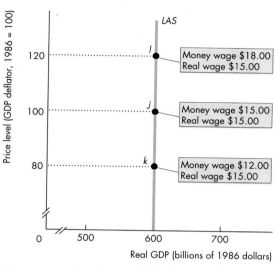

(c) Long-run aggregate supply curve

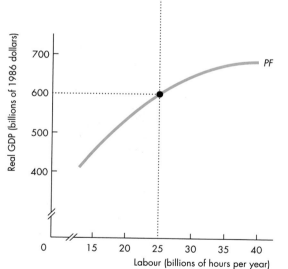

(b) Short-run aggregate production function

Labour market equilibrium determines the real wage rate and employment. The demand for labour curve (*LD*) intersects the supply of labour curve (*LS*) at a real wage rate of $15 an hour and 25 billion hours of employment (part a). The short-run aggregate production function (*PF*) and employment of 25 billion hours determine real GDP at $600 billion (part b). Real GDP supplied is $600 billion regardless of the price level. The long-run aggregate supply curve is the vertical line (*LAS*), in part (c). If the GDP deflator is 100, the economy is at point *j*. If the GDP deflator is 120, the money wage rate rises to keep the real wage rate constant at $15 an hour, employment remains at 25 billion hours, and real GDP is $600 billion. The economy is at point *l*. If the GDP deflator is 80, the money wage rate falls to keep the real wage rate constant at $15 an hour, employment remains at 25 billion hours, and real GDP is $600 billion. The economy is at point *k*.

labour demanded exceeds the quantity supplied. In such a situation, the money wage rate rises. It will keep rising until it reaches $18 an hour. At that money wage rate, the real wage rate is $15 ($18 divided by 120 and multiplied by 100 equals $15)

and the quantity of labour demanded equals the quantity supplied. Employment remains at 25 billion hours and real GDP remains at $600 billion. The economy is at point *l* in Fig. 30.8(c).

Points *j*, *k*, and *l* in part (c) all lie on the long-run aggregate supply curve. We have considered only three price levels. We could have considered any price level, and we would have reached the same conclusion: a change in the price level generates a proportionate change in the money wage rate and leaves the real wage rate unchanged. Employment and real GDP are also unchanged. The long-run aggregate supply curve is vertical.

Real Business Cycle Theory

In the flexible wage model of the labour market, the only sources of the business cycle—of fluctuations in real GDP and other economic aggregates—are shifts in the aggregate supply curve. A change in aggregate demand—a shift in the aggregate demand curve—brings a change in the price level but no change in real GDP. The view that aggregate supply fluctuations alone are responsible for the business cycle is called the **real business cycle theory**.

According to real business cycle theory, random fluctuations in the pace of technological change cause fluctuations in the pace of capital accumulation, so the short-run aggregate production function shifts upward at an uneven pace. These changes in the short-run aggregate production function change the demand for labour, shifting the demand for labour curve rightward, but again at an uneven pace. Population growth increases the supply of labour, and the supply of labour curve shifts rightward. But the uneven pace of technological change brings fluctuations in the real wage rate that are anticipated, to some degree, and so lead to changes in the supply of labour from intertemporal substitution.

These changes in the production function, the demand for labour, and the supply of labour change equilibrium employment, the real wage rate, and real GDP. They do so by shifting the long-run aggregate supply curve.

The general trend from the ongoing process of technological change is an increase in long-run aggregate supply. The aggregate supply curve shifts rightward, and real GDP increases. But the pace at which the long-run aggregate supply curve shifts rightward varies, leading to fluctuations in the growth rate of real GDP. Occasionally, the short-run production function shifts downward. When it does so, the demand for labour curve shifts leftward, employment falls, and the long-run aggregate supply curve shifts leftward, decreasing real GDP.

REVIEW

T he flexible wage theory of the labour market maintains that the money wage rate adjusts sufficiently freely to maintain continuous equality between the quantity of labour demanded and the quantity of labour supplied. In such an economy, the real wage rate, employment, and real GDP are independent of the price level. The aggregate supply curve is vertical. Fluctuations in employment, real wages, and real GDP occur because of fluctuations in the pace of technological change that bring fluctuations in the aggregate production function that, in turn, bring fluctuations in the demand for labour and the supply of labour. Occasionally, negative influences on the aggregate production function reduce employment and decrease real GDP. ◆

Let's now examine the sticky wage theory of the labour market.

The Sticky Wage Theory

Most economists, while recognizing the scope for flexibility in wages from bonuses and overtime wage rates, believe that these sources of flexibility are insufficient to keep the quantity of labour supplied equal to the quantity demanded. Basic money wage rates rarely adjust more frequently than once a year, so money wage rates are fairly rigid—sticky. Real wage rates change more frequently than do money wage rates because of changes in the price level, but according to the sticky wage theory these adjustments do not make real wages sufficiently flexible to maintain full employment.

The starting point for the sticky wage theory of the labour market is a theory of the determination of the money wage rate.

Money Wage Determination Naturally, firms like to pay as low a wage as possible, and workers like as high a wage as possible. But workers want to get hired, and firms want to be able to find labour. Firms recognize that if they offer too low a wage there will be a labour shortage. Workers recognize that if they try to achieve too high a wage there will be a shortage of jobs—excessive unemployment. The wage that balances off these opposing forces is the equi-librium wage—the wage that makes the quantity of labour demanded equal to the quantity supplied. But if money wages are going to be set for a year or more ahead, it will be impossible to achieve a continuous balance between the quantity of labour demanded and the quantity supplied. In such a situation, how is the money wage rate determined? It is set at a level designed to achieve an expectation or belief that, on the average, the quantity of labour demanded will equal the quantity supplied. Let's work out what that money wage rate is.

If the labour demand and supply curves are the same as those we used in Fig. 30.7, the real wage rate that achieves equality between the quantity demand-ed and quantity supplied is $15 an hour, as shown in Fig. 30.9. The money wage rate that this real wage rate translates into depends on the price level. But when firms and workers agree on a money wage rate for a future contract, they do not know what the price level is going to be. All they can do is base the con-tract on their best forecast of the future price level. Let's suppose that firms and their workers have the same expectations about the future. Suppose that they *expect* the GDP deflator for the coming year to be 100. That being the case, firms and workers will be ready to agree to a money wage rate of $15 an hour. That is, with an expected GDP deflator of 100, a money wage rate of $15 an hour translates into an expected real wage rate of $15 an hour.

Real Wage Determination   The real wage rate that actually emerges depends on the *actual* price level. If the GDP deflator turns out to be 100, as expected, then the real wage rate is $15 an hour, as expected. But many other outcomes are possible. Let's consid-er two of them, one in which the price level turns out to be higher than expected and one in which it turns out to be lower than expected.

First, suppose that the GDP deflator turns out to be 150. In this case, the real wage rate is $10 an hour. That is, a money wage rate of $15 an hour and a GDP deflator of 150 enable people to buy the same goods and services that a money wage rate of $15 an hour buys when the GDP deflator is 100.

Next, suppose that the GDP deflator turns out to be 75 instead of 100. In this case, the real wage rate is $20 an hour. A money wage rate of $15 an hour with a GDP deflator of 75 buys the same quantity of goods and services that a money wage rate of $15 an hour buys when the GDP deflator is 100.

FIGURE 30.9

A Labour Market with Sticky Money Wages

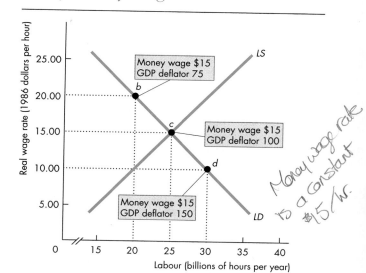

The labour demand curve is *LD* and the labour supply curve is *LS*. The money wage rate is set to achieve an expected balance between the quantity of labour demanded and the quantity supplied. If the GDP deflator is expected to be 100, the money wage rate is set at $15 an hour. The labour market is expected to be at point *c*. The quantity of labour employed is determined by the demand for labour. If the GDP deflator turns out to be 100, then the real wage rate is equal to $15 and the quantity of labour employed is 25 billion hours. The economy oper-ates at point *c*. If the GDP deflator turns out to be 75, then the real wage rate is $20 an hour and the quantity of labour employed falls to 20 billion hours. The economy operates at point *b*. If the GDP deflator is 150, then the real wage rate is $10 an hour and the quantity of labour employed increases to 30 billion hours. The economy operates at point *d*.

The three points *b*, *c*, and *d* in Fig. 30.9 illustrate the relationship among the price level, the money wage rate, and the real wage rate. The money wage rate is constant at $15 an hour, and the higher the price level, the lower is the real wage rate. But as the real wage rate varies, what determines the quan-tity of labour employed?

Employment with Sticky Wages   The sticky wage theory assumes that firms determine the level of employment. Provided that firms pay the agreed money wage rate, households supply whatever labour firms demand. These assumptions imply that the level of employment is determined by the demand curve for labour and that households are willing to be "off" their supply curves.

In Fig. 30.9, the money wage rate is $15 an hour. If the GDP deflator turns out to be 100 as expected, the real wage rate is $15 an hour and 25 billion hours of labour are employed (point c in the figure). If the GDP deflator turns out to be 75, the real wage rate is $20 an hour and the quantity of labour demanded and employed is 20 billion hours (point b in the figure). Households supply less labour than they would like to. If the GDP deflator turns out to be 150, the real wage rate is $10 an hour and the quantity of labour demanded and employed is 30 billion hours (point d in the figure). In this case, households supply more labour than they would like to.

It is easy to understand why a household might supply less labour, but why would it supply *more* labour than it would like to? In the long run, it would not. But for the duration of the existing contract, the household agrees to supply whatever quantity of labour the firm demands in exchange for a job and a guaranteed money wage rate.

Aggregate Supply with Sticky Wages

When money wages are sticky, the short-run aggregate supply curve slopes upward. Figure 30.10 illustrates why this is so. Let's start by looking at part (a), which describes the labour market. The three equilibrium levels of real wages and employment we discovered in Fig. 30.9 are shown again here. The money wage rate is fixed at $15 an hour. If the price level is 100, the real wage rate is also $15 an hour and 25 billion hours of labour are employed—point c. If the price level is 75, the real wage rate is $20 an hour and employment is only 20 billion hours—point b. If the price level is 150, the real wage rate is $10 an hour and employment is 30 billion hours—point d.

Figure 30.10(b) shows the short-run aggregate production function. We know from the labour market (part a) that at different price levels, different quantities of labour are employed. Part (b) tells us how these employment levels translate into real GDP. For example, when employment is 20 billion

hours, real GDP is $511 billion—point b. When employment is 25 billion hours, real GDP is $600 billion—point c, and when employment is 30 billion hours, real GDP is $661 billion—point d.

Figure 30.10(c) shows the aggregate supply curves. The long-run aggregate supply curve, LAS, is the one we've already derived in Fig. 30.8. The short-run aggregate supply curve, SAS, is derived from the labour market and production function we've just examined. To see why, first focus on point b in all three parts of the figure. At point b, the price level is 75. From the labour market (part a) we know that in this situation, the real wage is $20 an hour and 20 billion hours of labour are employed. At this employment level we know from the production function (part b) that real GDP is $511 billion. That's what point b in part (c) tells us—when the price level is 75, real GDP supplied is $511 billion. The other two points, c and d, are interpreted in the same way. At point d, the price level is 150 so the real wage rate is $10 an hour and 30 billion hours of labour are employed (part a). This employment level produces a real GDP of $661 billion. Points b, c, and d are points on the short-run aggregate supply curve.

The short-run aggregate supply curve intersects the long-run aggregate supply curve at the expected price level—where the GDP deflator is 100. At price levels higher than that expected, the quantity of real GDP supplied exceeds its long-run level, and at price levels lower than that expected, the quantity of real GDP supplied falls short of its long-run level.

Notice that the short-run aggregate supply curve, like the one in Chapter 24, is *curved*. As the price level rises, real GDP increases but the increments in real GDP become successively smaller. The straight-line SAS curve we are using is an approximation to this curve.

Fluctuations in Real GDP   All the factors that lead to fluctuations in long-run aggregate supply in the flexible wage theory apply to the long-run aggregate supply curve of the sticky wage theory. But in addition, employment and real GDP can fluctuate because of movements along the short-run aggregate supply curve. These movements occur because of changes in real wages resulting from changes in aggregate demand. The real wage rate changes in the sticky wage theory when the price level changes but the contractually determined money wage rate stays constant.

FIGURE 30.10

Aggregate Supply with Sticky Money Wages

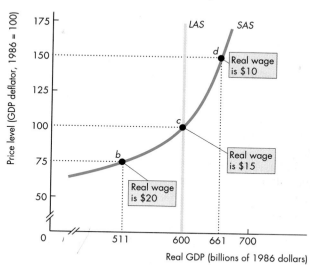

(c) Aggregate supply curve

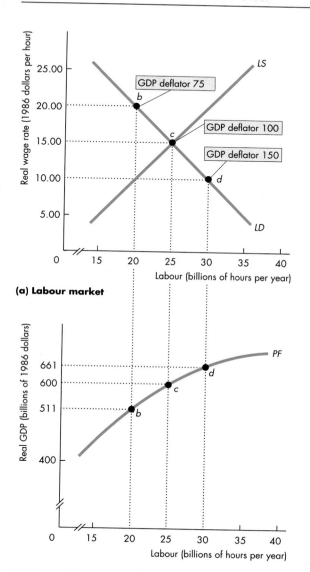

(a) Labour market

(b) Short-run aggregate production function

The money wage rate is fixed at $15 an hour. In part (a), the demand for labour curve (*LD*) intersects the supply of labour curve (*LS*) at a real wage rate of $15 an hour and 25 billion hours of employment. If the GDP deflator is 100, the economy operates at this point—*c*. In part (b), the short-run aggregate production function (*PF*) determines real GDP at $600 billion. This is long-run aggregate supply (*LAS*), in part (c). If the GDP deflator is 75, real wages are $20 an hour and the economy is at point *b*—employment is 20 billion hours (part a) and real GDP is $511 billion (part b). The economy is at point *b* on its short-run aggregate supply curve (*SAS*) in part (c). If the GDP deflator is 150, real wages are $10 an hour and the economy is at point *d*—employment is 30 billion hours (part a) and real GDP is $661 billion (part b). The economy is at point *d* on its short-run aggregate supply curve in part (c).

REVIEW

T he sticky wage theory assumes that the money wage rate is set on the basis of expectations about the price level over the course of the wage contract to make the expected quantities of labour demanded and supplied equal. The level of employment is determined by the demand for labour and the real wage rate. If the price level equals the expected price level, the quantity of labour demanded equals the quantity supplied. If the price level is lower than expected, the real wage is higher than expected and the quantity of labour demanded decreases. If the price level is higher than expected, the real wage is lower than expected and the quantity of labour demanded increases. Changes in the price level that bring changes in the level of employment result in changes in real GDP—movements along the short-run aggregate supply curve. ◆

We have studied the determination of wages and employment under two conditions—wages are flexible and wages are sticky. But when wages are sticky the number of workers hired can be less than the number hired when wages are flexible. What makes wages sticky? Why don't wages adjust to clear the labour market and keep the economy at full employment?

Why Wages Are Sticky

T here is no single, simple, consensus explanation for sticky wages. Instead, there are several possible explanations. The main ones are

◆ Minimum wage regulations
◆ Implicit risk-sharing contracts
◆ Incomplete price level information
◆ Menu costs

Let's look more closely at these explanations for wage stickiness.

Minimum Wage Regulations

Minimum wages are legislated by provincial and federal governments in Canada. These minimum wages are set at a level that is higher than what the market would determine. As a result of minimum wage regulations, the market wage cannot adjust downward to the level that makes the quantity of labour demanded equal to the quantity supplied.

This source of wage rigidity explains why the wages of the low paid are sticky. But it does not explain why the wages of the vast majority of workers whose wages exceed the legislated minimum wage are sticky.

Implicit Risk-Sharing Contracts

People dislike risk and buy insurance that compensates them if an unwanted bad outcome arises. Insurance against the risk of fire, auto accident, theft, and ill-health is commonplace. But one of the biggest risks we face is the loss of income from losing our job. And insurance companies don't offer policies that protect our incomes in the event of job loss.

But employers and employees can enter into implicit risk-sharing contracts that provide income insurance. An **implicit contract** is an informal arrangement that has the force of a formal written contract. An employment contract implicitly contains two transactions. The firm buys labour from the household and the household buys income insurance from the firm. The wage is "sticky" to protect the worker against fluctuating economic conditions. The household "pays" for income insurance in the form of a wage that is below what it would otherwise be in times of average or high demand. But the household benefits from the insurance by receiving a wage that is greater than it otherwise would be in times of low demand.

This explanation of sticky wages is actually an explanation of sticky *real* wages, not sticky *money* wages. If the price level changes, firms and workers with an implicit contract can easily see that the money wage rate must be changed to preserve the original implicit agreement. With sticky real wages and flexible money wages, the labour market does not reach an equilibrium in which the quantity of labour demanded equals the quantity supplied. But it does reach an equilibrium that does not depend on the price level. The aggregate supply curve is vertical.

Incomplete Price Level Information

The supply of labour depends on the real wage rate—the money wage rate divided by the price level. But when people decide how much labour to supply, they only know the money wage rate being offered. They don't know the prices of the goods and services they will buy with their wages. They don't know the real wage rate. So, to make a labour supply decision, they forecast the price level and base their decision on the *expected* real wage rate. The expected real wage rate is the money wage rate divided by the expected price level. On the other side of the labour market, firms know the prices they are getting for the goods and services they are producing, so they know the *actual* real wages they are paying.

These features of the labour market form the basis of a theory of partly sticky money wages suggested by Robert E. Lucas Jr. (see Our Advancing Knowledge, pp. 906–907. The theory is illustrated in Fig. 30.11. The labour market is shown in a diagram in which the *money* wage rate is measured on the vertical axis. The demand for labour depends on the *real* wage rate, so, when graphed against the money wage rate, there is a different demand curve for each price level. If the price level is 100, the demand curve is LD_0. If the price level is 200, the demand curve is LD_1, and if the price level is 50, the demand curve is LD_2. (We're using big differences in the price level in this example to make things as clear as possible.)

Notice that the demand curves LD_0, LD_1, and LD_2, are not parallel. That is because when the price level changes, the curve shifts by a fixed *percentage* amount. For example, if with a price level of 100 and a money wage rate of $15 an hour, the quantity of labour demanded is 25 billion hours a year, then that same quantity will be demanded at a price level of 200 and a money wage rate of $30 an hour or a price level of 50 and a money wage rate of $7.70 an hour.

The supply of labour depends on the *expected real* wage rate. So the position of the supply curve depends on the *expected price level*. The supply curve LS is that for an expected price level of 100. A change in the actual price that is not perceived or expected does not change the supply of labour and does not shift the labour supply curve.

If the actual price level equals the expected price level, the labour market equilibrium is at an

FIGURE 30.11

Incomplete Price Level Information

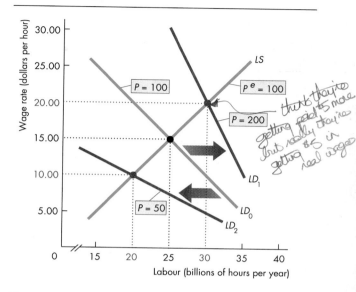

The vertical axis measures the *money* wage rate, so the position of the demand for labour curve depends on the price level. The demand for labour is LD_0 when the price level is 100, LD_1 when the price level is 200, and LD_2 when the price level is 50. The supply of labour depends on the expected real wage and the position of the supply curve depends on the expected price level. The supply curve LS is that for an expected price level of 100. Equilibrium is at the point of intersection of the demand and supply curves. When the price level is 100, employment is 25 billion hours and the real and nominal wage rate is $15 an hour. If the price level rises to 200, employment increases to 30 billion hours, the nominal wage rate rises to $20, the real wage rate falls, and the expected real wage rate rises. If the price level falls to 50, employment decreases to 20 billion hours, the nominal wage rate falls to $10, the real wage rate rises, and the expected real wage rate falls.

employment level of 25 billion hours and a real and nominal wage rate of $15 an hour, the same as in the flexible wage rate case. If the actual price level is 200, the money wage rate rises to $20 and employment increases to 30 billion hours. The *real* wage rate falls to $10 ($20 divided by 200 and multiplied by 100), and the expected real wage rate *rises* to $20. Because the actual real wage rate has fallen, there is an increase in the quantity of labour demanded and because the expected real wage rate has increased, there is an increase in the quantity of labour supplied.

If the actual price level is 50, the money wage rate falls to $10 and employment decreases to 20 billion hours. But the actual real wage rate *rises* to $20 ($10 divided by 50 and multiplied by 100), and the expected real wage rate *falls* to $10.

So, with incomplete information about the price level, employment changes as the price level changes. Because employment changes, so does the quantity of real GDP supplied. The short-run aggregate supply curve slopes upward.

Wages are sticky but they are not fixed. Wages change less than in proportion to the change in the price level. But the closer the expected price level is to the actual price level, the closer the predictions of this theory are to the flexible wage theory. With the Consumer Price Index being measured and widely publicized every month, this source of partial wage stickiness is not likely to play a major role in actual labour markets.

Menu Costs

When prices or wages are changed, some costs are incurred. The cost of changing a price or a wage rate is called a **menu cost**. The name comes from the simple fact that if a restaurant changes its prices, it must print a new menu and the cost of doing so is the cost of changing prices.

Menu costs in the labour market are large. They arise from the fact that most wages are determined as part of a contract negotiated collectively between a union and an employer, and that each party to the negotiations must spend considerable resources researching the demand and supply conditions and preparing the best possible strategy for a bargaining process. Because of these costs, contracts are renegotiated at infrequent intervals and, in the intervening period, wages are fixed or change along a pre-agreed path.

This explanation for sticky wages is the most convincing currently available, although an objection to it is that wage contracts could use cost-of-living adjustments at a small menu cost.

So far, we have been examining models of the labour market that determine employment and the wage rate. We have seen that in the sticky wage models, employment is not necessarily equal to the quantity of labour supplied. Such a situation looks like one of unemployment. But we have not explicitly studied unemployment. How is unemployment determined? This is our next question.

Unemployment

We discovered in Chapter 22 that unemployment is an ever present feature of economic life and that the unemployment rate sometimes rises to a level that poses a massive problem for millions of families (see pp. 599–604). Yet the labour market models we have just been studying seem to ignore this important phenomenon. They determine the real wage rate and aggregate hours of labour employed, but they don't say anything about *who* supplies the hours. Unemployment arises when some people in the labour force are working zero hours but are seeking work. Why does unemployment exist? Why does its rate vary?

There are four main explanations for unemployment:

◆ Job search
◆ Efficiency wages
◆ Insiders and outsiders
◆ Sticky wages

We'll examine the four explanations in turn.

Job Search

Suppose that a firm employs 400 hours of labour each week and has 10 workers, each working 40 hours. If the firm decides to cut back its production and reduce employment to 360 hours, it might either lay off one worker or cut the hours of each of its 10 workers to 36 hours a week. In most production processes, the profitable course for the firm is to lay off one worker and keep the remaining workers' hours constant. There is an optimum or efficient number of hours for each worker. Work hours in excess of the optimum level result in decreased output per hour as workers become tired. Employing a large number of workers for a small number of hours each also lowers output per hour, since workers take time to start up and there are disruptions to the production process caused by workers leaving and arriving. For these reasons, labour is an economically indivisible factor of production. That is, taking account of the output produced per hour, it pays firms to hire labour in indivisible lumps. As a consequence, when the demand for labour changes, the number of people employed changes rather than the number of hours per worker.

Being fired or laid off would not matter if an equally good job could be found right away. But finding a job takes time and effort—it has an opportunity cost. Firms are not fully informed about the potential workers available to them and households are not fully informed about the potential jobs available to them. As a consequence, both firms and workers have to search for a profitable match. Let's examine this source of unemployment.

Labour Market Stocks and Flows   Because households are incompletely informed about available jobs, they find it efficient to devote resources to searching for the best available job. Time spent searching for a job is part of unemployment. Let's take a closer look at this source of unemployment by examining the decisions that lead to labour market flows. Figure 30.12 provides a schematic summary of this discussion.

The working-age population is divided into two groups: those in the labour force and those not in the labour force. Those not in the labour force are full-time students, homemakers, and retirees. The labour force consists of two groups: the employed and the unemployed.

Decisions made by the demanders of labour and the suppliers of labour result in five types of flows that change the numbers of people employed and unemployed. The flows resulting from these decisions are shown by the arrows in the figure. Let's look at these decisions and see how the flows that result from them affect the amount of employment and unemployment.

First, there is a flow into the labour force as full-time students decide to quit school and homemakers decide to enter or re-enter the labour force. Initially, when such people enter the labour force, they are unemployed. These decisions result in an increase in the labour force and an increase in unemployment.

Second, there is a flow from employment to unemployment resulting from employers deciding to lay off workers temporarily or fire workers and from workers deciding to quit their current job to find a better one. These decisions result in a decrease in employment and an increase in unemployment but no change in the labour force.

Third, there is a flow from the labour force as employed people decide to quit their jobs to become

FIGURE 30.12

Labour Market Flows

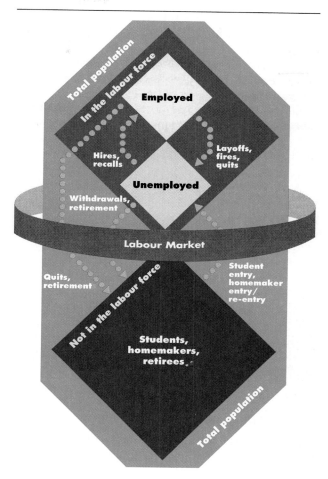

The working age population is divided into two groups: those in the labour force and those not in the labour force. The labour force comprises the employed and the unemployed. Flows into and out of the labour force and between employment and unemployment determine the number of people unemployed. New entrants from full-time schooling and re-entrants flow into unemployment. Flows from employment to unemployment result from fires, layoffs, and quits. Flows from unemployment to employment result from hires and recalls. Flows from the labour force occur as people decide to become homemakers, go back to school, or retire. Flows from the labour force also occur as unemployed people get discouraged by their failure to find a job.

homemakers, go back to school, or retire. These decisions result in a decrease in employment and a decrease in the labour force but no change in unemployment.

Fourth, there is a flow from the labour force as unemployed people give up the search for a job. These people are *discouraged workers* whose job search efforts have been repeatedly unsuccessful. These decisions to leave the labour force result in a decrease in unemployment and a decrease in the labour force.

Fifth, there is a flow from unemployment to employment as firms recall temporarily laid-off workers and hire new workers. These decisions result in an increase in employment, a decrease in unemployment, and no change in the labour force.

At any one moment, there is a stock of employment and unemployment. Over any given period, there are flows into and out of the labour force and between employment and unemployment. For example, in January 1993, there were 13.8 million people in the labour force—65.2 percent of the working-age population. Of these, 1.5 million (11 percent of the labour force) were unemployed and 12.3 million (89 percent of the labour force) were employed. Of the 1.5 million unemployed, 63.6 percent had been fired from their previous job or laid off, 7.8 percent had re-entered the labour force after a period of specializing in household production, 14.3 percent had voluntarily quit their previous job to seek a better one, and 8.5 percent were new entrants.

Unemployment with Flexible Wages

According to the flexible wage model of the labour market, all the unemployment that exists arises from the sources we've just reviewed. The unemployment rate is always equal to the natural rate of unemployment. There is a balance between the quantity of labour demanded and the quantity of labour supplied. But the quantity of labour supplied is the number of hours available for work at a given moment without further search for a better job. And the quantity of labour demanded is the number of hours that firms wish to hire at a given moment in time, given their knowledge of the individual skills and talents available. In addition to supplying hours for work, households also supply time for job search. Those people who devote no time to working and specialize in job search are the ones who are unemployed.

Figure 30.13 illustrates such a situation. The labour force—everyone who has a job and all those who are looking for one—is larger than the supply of

FIGURE 30.13

Unemployment with Flexible Wages

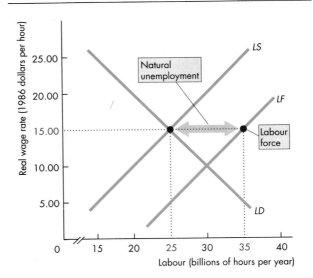

Some members of the labour force are immediately available for work at a given real wage rate, and this amount determines the supply of labour (*LS*). Other members of the labour force are searching for the best available job. Adding this quantity to the supply of labour gives the labour force curve (*LF*). Equilibrium occurs at the real wage rate that makes the quantity of labour supplied equal to the quantity demanded. The economy is at full employment and unemployment is at its natural rate.

labour. The supply curve of labour (*LS*) tells us about the quantity of labour available with no further job search. The labour force curve (*LF*) tells us about the quantity of labour available with no further job search plus the quantity of job search. In the figure, the quantity of labour supplied and the labour force increase as the real wage rate increases. But the quantity of job search, measured by the horizontal distance between the *LS* and *LF* curves, is constant. (This is an assumption. In real labour markets, the supply of job search may also increase as the real wage rate increases.)

Equilibrium in the labour market occurs at the real wage rate that makes the quantity of labour demanded equal to the quantity of labour supplied, not the labour force. Unemployment arises from the fact that information about jobs and workers is costly and that it takes time for people without work to find an acceptable job. According to the flexible wage theory, fluctuations in unemployment are caused by changes in the labour market flows that change the supply of labour, the labour force, and the demand for labour. These changes shift the *LS*, *LF*, and *LD* curves and change the natural rate of unemployment. The main influences are

◆ Demographic change

◆ Unemployment compensation

◆ Technological change

Demographic Change   The supply side of the labour market is influenced by the age distribution of the population. A large increase in the proportion of the population of working age brings an increase in the rate of entry into the labour force and a corresponding increase in the unemployment rate as the new entrants take time to find the best available jobs. Such a demographic change has influenced the Canadian labour market in recent years. A bulge in the birth rate occurred in the late 1940s and early 1950s, following World War II. This bulge resulted in an increase in the proportion of new entrants into the labour force during the 1970s. It resulted in a rightward shift in the *LS* curve, an even greater rightward shift in the *LF* curve, and an increase in the unemployment rate.

As the birth rate declined, the bulge moved to higher age groups and the proportion of new entrants into the labour force declined during the 1980s. During this period, the shift in the *LS* curve was larger than the shift in the *LF* curve, and the unemployment rate declined.

Unemployment Compensation   One of the most significant supply side events influencing unemployment is the establishment of generous unemployment compensation arrangements. The length of time that an unemployed person is willing to spend searching for a job depends, in part, on the opportunity cost of that search. With no unemployment insurance and no income during a spell of unemployment, an unemployed person faces a high opportunity cost of job search. In this situation, search is likely to be short and an unattractive job is likely to be accepted as a better alternative to continuing a costly search process. With generous unemployment insurance benefits, the opportunity cost of job search is low. In this situation, search is likely to be

prolonged. An unemployed worker will hold out for the ideal job.

Over the years, the opportunity cost of job search has fallen as unemployment insurance benefits have been increased and been extended to larger groups. As a result, the amount of job-search unemployment has steadily increased.

Technological Change   Cycles in unemployment arise from the fact that the scale of hiring, firing, and job quitting ebbs and flows with fluctuations in real GDP—with the business cycle. These labour market flows and the resulting unemployment are also strongly influenced by the pace and direction of technological change. When some firms and sectors of the economy are expanding quickly and others are contracting quickly, labour turnover increases. This means that flows between employment and unemployment and the pool of those temporarily unemployed increases at such a time. The relative decline of traditional industries in Quebec and the Maritimes and the expansion of new industries in Ontario and Alberta were a major source of flows of labour and of the rise in unemployment that occurred during the 1970s and early 1980s.

Job Creation and Job Destruction

The magnitude of changes in labour market flows can be seen by looking at some newly available data compiled by Steve Davis of the University of Chicago Business School and John Haltiwanger of the University of Maryland. Using data from individual plants in the manufacturing sector of the U.S. economy, they have painted a remarkable picture of the changing job scene in the United States. (We don't have the equivalent data for Canada, but it would be surprising if the picture here is very different from that in the United States.) The picture is shown in Fig. 30.14.

Look first at part (a), which shows the amount of job creation and destruction. On the average, close to 10 percent of all jobs in the United States disappear each year and a similar number of new jobs are created. Adding the jobs destroyed and created together gives a measure of the total amount of turnover in the U.S. labour market arising from this process—shown as "Sum" in the figure. Subtracting jobs destroyed from jobs created gives the change in the number of U.S. jobs—shown as "Net" in the figure. As you can see, the scale of U.S. job turnover

FIGURE 30.14

Job Creation, Job Destruction, and Unemployment

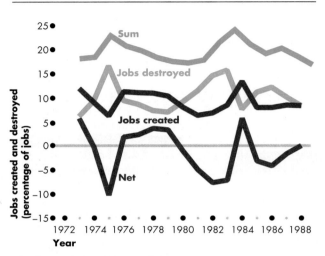

(a) Job creation and destruction rates

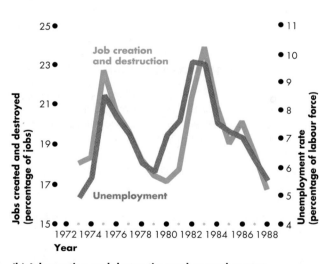

(b) Job creation and destruction and unemployment

On the average, close to 10 percent of existing U.S. jobs disappear each year (the curve labelled "Jobs destroyed" in part a) and a similar number of new jobs are created. The total amount of U.S. job creation and destruction (the curve labelled "Sum") and the rate of U.S. job creation minus the rate of U.S. job destruction (the curve labelled "Net") fluctuate. Those fluctuations follow a similar cycle to that in the U.S. unemployment rate (part b).

Source: Data kindly provided by Steve Davis and John Haltiwanger.

is not only large but also fluctuates a great deal. Part (b) shows how the fluctuations in job creation and destruction correspond with fluctuations in the U.S. unemployment rate.

Whether fluctuations in the job creation and job destruction rates cause fluctuations in the unemployment rate, or whether fluctuations in both the job creation and job destruction rate and the unemployment rate have a common cause is not known.

The next influences on the natural rate of unemployment that we'll examine arise from non-competitive features of the labour market.

Efficiency Wages

A firm can increase its labour productivity by paying wages above the competitive wage rate. The higher wage attracts a higher quality of labour, encourages greater work effort, and cuts down on the firm's labour turnover rate and recruiting costs. But the higher wage also adds to the firm's costs. So a firm offers a wage rate that balances productivity gains and additional costs. The wage rate that maximizes profit is called the **efficiency wage**.

The efficiency wage will be higher than the competitive equilibrium wage. If the wage was lower than the competitive wage, competition for labour would bid the wage up. With an efficiency wage above the competitive wage, some labour is unemployed and the employed have an incentive to perform well to avoid being fired.

The efficiency wage theory is not a theory of sticky wages. It is a theory of flexible wages set at a level that creates a permanent gap between the quantity of labour demanded and the quantity supplied. The efficiency wage theory relies on the costly job-search mechanisms we studied earlier in this chapter and can be viewed as one more reason why the natural rate of unemployment is not zero.

Insiders and Outsiders

Insider-outsider theory is an explanation of why firms don't hire new workers—outsiders—in a recession when unemployment is high. In particular, why don't they cut their wage costs by offering the unemployed a lower wage rate than that paid to their existing workers—insiders?

The explanation is that to be productive, new workers must receive on-the-job training from existing workers. If the existing workers provide such training to potential workers who are paid a lower wage, the insider's bargaining position would be weakened. So insiders will not train outsiders unless outsiders receive the same rate of pay as insiders.

When bargaining for a pay deal, unions represent insiders only, so the wage agreed exceeds the competitive wage. And there are always some workers—outsiders—who are unable to find work. Like the efficiency wage theory, this theory is a further reason why the natural rate of unemployment is positive.

According to the three theories of unemployment we have looked at, unemployment arises from the internal workings of the labour market. And fluctuations in the unemployment rate result from demographic, policy and technological change.

In contrast to these theories, the sticky wage theory of the labour market emphasizes fluctuations in *aggregate demand* as sources of fluctuations in unemployment. Let's see why.

Unemployment with Sticky Wages

With sticky money wages, unemployment might rise above or fall below the natural rate. If the real wage rate is above its full-employment level, the quantity of labour employed is less than the quantity supplied and unemployment is above its natural rate. Such a situation is shown in Fig. 30.15. The *LS* and *LF* curves are the same as those in Fig. 30.13 and the natural rate of unemployment is measured by the horizontal distance between those two curves.

The money wage rate is $15 an hour. If the GDP deflator is 75, the real wage rate is $20 an hour and the quantity of labour demanded is 20 billion hours. Unemployment is above its natural rate. If the GDP deflator is 120, the real wage rate is $12.50 an hour and the quantity of labour demanded is 27.5 billion hours. Unemployment is below its natural rate.

Fluctuations in aggregate demand bring fluctuations in the price level. These fluctuations move the economy (upward and downward) along its demand for labour curve. At the same time, unemployment fluctuates around its natural rate. According to the sticky wage theory, fluctuations in unemployment arise primarily from the mechanism just described. Changes in the real wage rate arising from a sticky money wage rate and a changing price level result in movements along the labour demand curve and movements along the short-run aggregate supply curve. The rates of job creation and job destruction

FIGURE 30.15

Unemployment with Sticky Money Wages

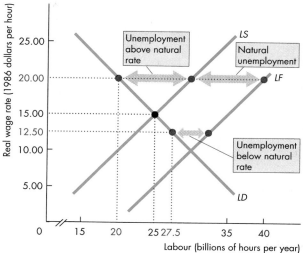

The money wage rate is $15 an hour. If the GDP deflator turns out to be 75, the real wage rate is $20 an hour. At this higher real wage rate, the quantity of labour demanded falls short of the quantity of labour supplied and unemployment is above its natural rate. If the GDP deflator turns out to be 120, the real wage rate is $12.50 an hour. At this lower real wage rate, the quantity of labour demanded exceeds the quantity of labour supplied and unemployment is below its natural rate. Fluctuations in the price level, with sticky money wages, cause fluctuations in the level of unemployment.

also fluctuate (as shown in Fig. 30.14), but those fluctuations are the result of aggregate demand fluctuations.

Economists who emphasize the role of sticky wages in generating fluctuations in unemployment usually regard the natural rate of unemployment as constant—or slowly changing. Fluctuations in the actual unemployment rate are fluctuations around the natural rate. Notice that this interpretation of fluctuations in unemployment contrasts with that of the flexible wage theory. The flexible wage model predicts that *all* changes in unemployment are fluctuations in the natural rate of unemployment.

If most of the fluctuations in unemployment *do* arise from sticky wages, then aggregate demand management can moderate those fluctuations in unemployment. By keeping aggregate demand steady so that the price level stays close to its expected level, the economy can be kept close to full employment.

◆ ◆ ◆ ◆ We have now studied the labour market and the determination of long-run and short-run aggregate supply, employment, wages, and unemployment. We've examined the forces that change aggregate supply, shifting the long-run and short-run aggregate supply curves. We've also examined the sources of productivity growth in the Canadian economy. Our next task is to bring together the aggregate demand and aggregate supply sides of the economy again and see how they interact to determine inflation and business cycles. We are going to pursue these tasks in the next two chapters.

S U M M A R Y

Productivity and Income Growth

The short-run aggregate production function tells us how real GDP varies as the aggregate quantity of labour employed varies with a given stock of capital equipment and given state of technology. As the labour input increases, real GDP increases but by diminishing marginal amounts. Capital accumulation and technological change lead to productivity growth that causes the short-run aggregate production function to shift upward over time. Occasionally the production function shifts downward because of negative influences such as restrictions on international trade. The Canadian short-run aggregate production function shifted upward by almost 45 percent between 1975 and 1993. (pp. 830–833)

The Demand for Labour

Firms choose how much labour to demand. The lower the real wage rate, the larger is the quantity of labour hours demanded. In choosing how much labour to hire, firms aim to maximize their profits. They achieve this objective by ensuring that the revenue brought in by an additional hour of labour equals the hourly wage rate. The more hours of labour that are employed, the lower is the revenue brought in by the last hour of labour. Firms can be induced to increase the quantity of labour hours demanded by either a decrease in the wage rate or an increase in the revenue brought in—by an increase in the price of output. Both a decrease in the wage rate and an increase in prices result in a lower real wage rate. Thus the lower the real wage rate, the greater is the quantity of labour demanded.

The relationship between the real wage rate and the quantity of labour demanded is summarized in the demand for labour curve, which slopes downward. The demand for labour curve shifts as a result of shifts in the short-run aggregate production function. (pp. 834–836)

The Supply of Labour

Households choose how much labour to supply. They also choose the timing of their labour supply. A higher real wage rate encourages the substitution of work for leisure (the substitution effect) and encourages the taking of more leisure (the income effect). The substitution effect dominates the income effect, so the higher the real wage rate, the more hours each worker supplies. Also, the higher the real wage rate, the higher is the labour force participation rate. A higher *current* wage relative to the expected future wage encourages more work in the present and less in the future—the intertemporal substitution effect. Taking all these forces together, the higher the real wage rate, the greater is the quantity of labour supplied.

The relationship between the real wage rate and the quantity of labour supplied is summarized in the supply of labour curve, which slopes upward. (pp. 837–841)

Wages and Employment

There are two theories of labour market equilibrium, one based on the assumption that wages are flexible and the other based on the assumption that they are sticky. Under the flexible wage theory, the real wage rate adjusts to ensure that the quantity of labour supplied equals the quantity demanded.

With flexible wages, the aggregate supply curve is vertical—the long-run aggregate supply curve. The quantity of real GDP supplied is independent of the price level. The long-run aggregate supply curve shifts as a result of shifts in the supply of labour curve and shifts in the short-run aggregate production function that lead to shifts in the demand for labour curve.

With sticky money wages, real wages do not adjust to balance the quantity of labour supplied and the quantity demanded. The money wage rate is set to make the expected quantity of labour demanded equal to the expected quantity supplied. The real wage rate depends on the contracted money wage rate and the price level. The level of employment is determined by the demand for labour, with households agreeing to supply the quantity demanded. Fluctuations in the price level relative to what was expected generate fluctuations in the quantity of labour demanded and in employment and real GDP. The higher the price level relative to what was expected, the lower is the real wage rate. The lower the real wage rate, the greater is the quantity of labour demanded and the greater is employment and real GDP.

With sticky money wages, the aggregate supply curve slopes upward—the short-run aggregate supply curve. The higher the price level, the higher is the quantity of real GDP supplied. (pp. 841–848)

Why Wages Are Sticky

The four main explanations for sticky wages are minimum wage regulations, implicit risk-sharing contracts, incomplete price level information, and menu costs.

Minimum wage laws set a minimum wage above the market wage.

Implicit risk-sharing contracts arise as a method of providing income insurance. Firms benefit by being able to hire labour at a lower wage rate on the average and households benefit by having a more certain income. This source of sticky wages explains sticky *real* wages but not sticky *money* wages.

With incomplete information about the price level, people base their labour supply decision on the *expected* real wage rate and the *expected price level*. A change in the price level brings a less than proportionate change in the money wage rate and a change in employment and output.

When prices or wages are changed, some costs—menu costs—are incurred. Menu costs in the labour market are large and result in infrequent changes in negotiated wage rates. (pp. 848–850)

Unemployment

The labour market is in a constant state of change or labour turnover. Labour turnover creates unemployment. New entrants to the labour force and workers re-entering after a period of household production take time to find a job. Some people quit an existing job to seek a better one. Some are laid off, and others are fired and forced to find another job. The pace of labour turnover is not constant. When technological change is expanding one sector and contracting another, labour turnover increases. Finding new jobs takes time and the process of adjustment may create overtime and unfilled vacancies in the expanding sector but unemployment in the contracting sector.

Even if wages are flexible, unemployment arising from labour-market turnover cannot be avoided. The unemployment rate arising from this source is the natural rate of unemployment. In labour markets with flexible wages, all fluctuations in unemployment are fluctuations in the natural rate arising from changes in the rate of labour turnover. The scale and cycles in the rates of job creation and job destruction are consistent with the flexible wage theory.

The natural rate includes unemployment arising from efficiency wages and insider-outsider relations. The efficiency wage is the wage that maximizes a firm's profit taking into account that a higher wage both increases cost and increases productivity. The efficiency wage exceeds the competitive market wage and results in unemployment. Those with jobs (insiders) are unwilling to train those without jobs (outsiders) unless the outsiders are paid the same wages as the insiders. And in negotiating their wages, the insiders take only their own interests into account. So they agree on a wage at which some outsiders would like to become insiders, and unemployment persists.

If wages are sticky, unemployment arises for the same reasons as in the case of flexible wages and for one additional reason. With sticky wages the real wage may not move quickly enough to keep the quantity of labour demanded equal to the quantity supplied. In such a case, an increase in the real wage rate can result in unemployment rising above its natural rate and a decrease in real wages can result in unemployment falling below its natural rate. (pp. 850–856)

KEY ELEMENTS

Key Terms

Demand for labour, 834
Diminishing marginal product of labour, 831
Economic growth, 831
Efficiency wage, 854
Implicit contract, 848
Innovation, 831
Invention, 831
Labour force participation rate, 840
Labour productivity, 830
Marginal product of labour, 830
Menu cost, 850
Money wage rate, 834
Production function, 830
Quantity of labour demanded, 834
Quantity of labour supplied, 837
Real business cycle theory, 844
Real wage rate, 834
Reservation wage, 840

Short-run aggregate production function, 830
Short-run production function, 830
Supply of labour, 837

Key Figures

Figure 30.1   The Short-Run Aggregate
              Production Function, 830
Figure 30.2   The Growth of Output, 832
Figure 30.7   Equilibrium with Flexible Wages, 842
Figure 30.8   Aggregate Supply with Flexible
              Wages, 843
Figure 30.9   A Labour Market with Sticky Money
              Wages, 845
Figure 30.10 Aggregate Supply with Sticky Money
              Wages, 847
Figure 30.13 Unemployment with Flexible
              Wages, 852
Figure 30.15 Unemployment with Sticky Money
              Wages, 855

REVIEW QUESTIONS

1 What is the relationship between output and labour input in the short run? Why does the marginal product of labour diminish?

2 If the short-run production function shifts from 1993 to 1995 by the amount shown in Fig. 30.2, what happens to the marginal product of labour between 1993 and 1995?

3 Explain why the demand for labour curve slopes downward.

4 Given your answer to question 2, does the demand for labour curve shift between 1993 and 1995? If so, in what direction and by how much?

5 Why does the labour force participation rate rise as the real wage rate rises?

6 How is the quantity of labour currently supplied influenced by the wage rate today relative to those expected in the future?

7 Explain what happens in a labour market with flexible wages when technological change increases the marginal product of labour for each unit of labour input.

8 In question 7, explain what happens to the long-run aggregate supply curve.

9 What are sticky wages?

10 Explain what happens in a labour market with sticky wages when technological change increases the marginal product of labour for each unit of labour input.

11 In question 10, explain what happens to the short-run aggregate supply curve.

12 Explain how unemployment can arise if wages are flexible.

13 Describe the main facts about the rates of job creation and job destruction.

14 Explain how unemployment fluctuates above its natural rate.

P R O B L E M S

Use the following information about an economy to answer problems 1 through 7. The economy's short-run production function is:

Labour (millions of hours per year)	Real GDP (millions of 1986 dollars per year)
1	38
2	54
3	68
4	80
5	90
6	98
7	104
8	108

Its demand and supply schedules for labour are:

Real wage rate (1986 dollars per hour)	Quantity of labour demanded (millions of hours per year)	Quantity of labour supplied (millions of hours per year)
3	8	4
5	7	5
7	6	6
9	5	7
11	4	8
13	3	9
15	2	10
17	1	11

1 If real wages are flexible, how much labour is employed and what is the real wage rate?

2 If the GDP deflator is 120, what is the money wage rate?

3 If the real wage rate is flexible, calculate the aggregate supply curve in this economy.

4 If money wages are sticky and the GDP deflator is expected to be 100, what is the money wage rate in this economy?

5 Find three points on the economy's short-run aggregate supply curve when the money wage rate is at the level determined in problem 4.

6 Calculate the real wage rate at each of the points you used in answering problem 5.

7 At what price level and level of employment do the short-run and long-run aggregate supply curves intersect?

8 There are two economies, each with *constant* unemployment rates but with a great deal of labour market turnover. In economy A, there is a rapid pace of technological change. Twenty percent of the labour force is either fired or quits every year and 20 percent is hired every year. In economy B, only 5 percent is fired or quits and 5 percent is hired. Which economy has the higher unemployment rate? Why?

9 There are two economies, Flexiland and Fixland. These economies are identical in every way except that in Flexiland, real wages are flexible and maintain equality between the quantities of labour demanded and supplied. In Fixland, wages are sticky but the money wage rate is set so that, *on the average*, the quantity of labour demanded equals the quantity supplied.

a Explain which economy has the higher average unemployment rate.

b Explain which economy has the largest fluctuations in unemployment.

CHAPTER **31**

INFLATION

After studying this chapter, you will be able to

◆ Explain how increasing aggregate demand can generate a price-wage inflation spiral

◆ Explain how decreasing aggregate supply can generate a cost-price inflation spiral

◆ Explain the consequences of unanticipated inflation

◆ Explain how people try to anticipate inflation

◆ Explain the consequences of anticipated inflation

◆ Explain the relationship between inflation and unemployment

◆ Explain the relationship between inflation and interest rates

◆ Explain the politics of inflation

N THE CLOSING YEARS OF THE ROMAN EMPIRE, EMPEROR Diocletian presided over a massive inflation. Prices increased at a rate of more than 300 percent a year. In 1993, as Russia attempted to introduce a market economy, President Boris Yeltsin struggled to contain a similarly massive inflation. Rapid inflations are also occurring in other Eastern European countries such as Ukraine and Poland as well as in many Latin American countries. Canada, too, has had a high inflation rate in its recent past—during the 1970s and early 1980s. But today Canada, along with most other rich industrial countries, has a low inflation rate. What causes inflation? Why does inflation sometimes become extremely rapid and at other times subside? ◆ ◆ To make good decisions we need good forecasts of inflation, and not for just next year but for many years into the future. How do people try to anticipate inflation? And how do expectations of inflation influence the economy? ◆ ◆ As the inflation rate rises and falls, the unemployment rate and interest rates also fluctuate. What is the connection between inflation and unemployment and between inflation and interest rates?

From Rome to Russia

◆ ◆ ◆ ◆ In this chapter, you will learn about the forces that generate inflation, the consequences of inflation, and the way that people try to forecast and therefore anticipate inflation. But first, let's remind ourselves of what inflation is and how its rate is measured.

Inflation and the Price Level

Inflation is a *process* of *rising prices*. It is not a one-time increase in the price level. If the price level is rising at 10 percent a year, the economy is experiencing inflation. If the price level rises by 10 percent and then stabilizes, the economy has experienced a one-time increase in the price level.

The inflation rate is measured as the percentage change in the price level. That is,

$$\text{Inflation rate} = \frac{\text{Current year's price level} - \text{Last year's price level}}{\text{Last year's price level}} \times 100.$$

Let's write this equation in symbols. We'll call this year's price level P_1 and last year's price level P_0, so that,

$$\text{Inflation rate} = \frac{P_1 - P_0}{P_0} \times 100.$$

For example, if the price level this year is 143 and the price level last year was 130, the inflation rate is 10 percent a year. That is,

$$\text{Inflation rate} = \frac{143 - 130}{130} \times 100$$

$$= \frac{13}{130} \times 100$$

$$= 10 \text{ percent a year.}$$

This equation shows the connection between the *inflation rate* and the *price level*. For a given price level last year, the higher the price level in the current year, the higher is the inflation rate.

Keep the distinction between the price level and the inflation rate clear. If the price level is *rising*, the inflation rate is *positive*. If the price level is *falling*, the inflation rate is *negative*. If the price level rises at a *faster* rate, the inflation rate *increases*. If the price level rises at a *slower* rate, the inflation rate *decreases*.

We are going to study the forces that generate inflation and the consequences of inflation. First, we'll study the effects of inflation on real GDP, real wages, and employment. Next, we'll examine the connection between inflation and unemployment. Finally, we'll look at the effects of inflation on interest rates. We'll discover that the effects of inflation on all these variables depends on whether the inflation is anticipated or unanticipated. **Anticipated inflation** is inflation that is correctly foreseen. **Unanticipated inflation** is inflation that is not foreseen—that takes people by surprise.

We'll begin by using the aggregate demand–aggregate supply model to study the sources of inflation. In that model, inflation can result from either an increase in aggregate demand or a decrease in aggregate supply. The economy follows a different course depending on which source of inflation is at work. We'll begin by studying the effects on inflation of an increase in aggregate demand.

Demand–Pull Inflation

The inflation resulting from an increase in aggregate demand is called **demand–pull inflation**. Such an inflation may arise from any individual factor that increases aggregate demand, but the main ones that generate *ongoing* increases in aggregate demand are

1. Increases in the money supply

2. Increases in government purchases

3. Increases in the price level in the rest of the world

When aggregate demand increases, the aggregate demand curve shifts rightward. Let's trace the effects of such an increase.

Inflation Effect of an Increase in Aggregate Demand

Suppose that last year the GDP deflator was 130 and real GDP was $600 billion. Long-run real GDP was also $600 billion. This situation is shown in

FIGURE 31.1

Demand-Pull Inflation

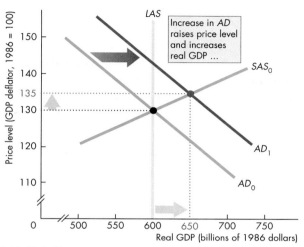

(a) Initial effect

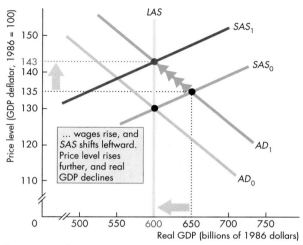

(b) Wages adjust

In part (a), the aggregate demand curve is AD_0, the short-run aggregate supply curve is SAS_0, and the long-run aggregate supply curve is LAS. The GDP deflator is 130 and real GDP is $600 billion, its long-run level. Aggregate demand increases to AD_1 (because the Bank of Canada increases the money supply or the government increases its purchases of goods and services). The new equilibrium occurs where

AD_1 intersects SAS_0. The economy experiences inflation (the GDP deflator rises to 135) and real GDP increases to $650 billion. In part (b), starting from above full employment, wages begin to rise and the short-run aggregate supply curve shifts gradually leftward towards SAS_1. The price level rises further, and real GDP returns to its long-run level.

Fig. 31.1(a). The aggregate demand curve is AD_0, the short-run aggregate supply curve is SAS_0, and the long-run aggregate supply curve is LAS.

In the current year, aggregate demand increases to AD_1. Such a situation arises if, for example, the Bank of Canada loosens its grip on the money supply, or the government increases its purchases of goods and services, or the price level rises in the United States. The economy moves to the point where the aggregate demand curve AD_1 intersects the short-run aggregate supply curve SAS_0. The GDP deflator increases to 135, and real GDP increases to $650 billion. The economy experiences 3.8 percent inflation (a GDP deflator of 135 compared with 130 in the previous year) and an increase in real GDP.

The situation that developed in the Canadian economy towards the end of the 1960s is a good example of the process we have just analysed. In those years, the main influence on aggregate demand in Canada and in much of the rest of the

world came from events in the United States. A large increase in U.S. government purchases on the Vietnam War and on social programs, together with an increase in the growth rate of the U.S. money supply, increased aggregate demand in the world economy. At the same time, the Bank of Canada loosened its own monetary policy and permitted the quantity of money to increase more quickly. As a consequence, the aggregate demand curve shifted rightward, the price level increased quickly, and real GDP moved above its long-run level.

The situation shown in Fig. 31.1(a) is not the end of the story. Let's see why not.

Wage Response

The economy cannot produce at above full-employment forever. With unemployment below its natural rate, there is a shortage of labour. Wages begin to increase, and the short-run aggregate supply curve starts to shift leftward. Prices rise further, and real

GDP begins to fall. With no further change in aggregate demand—the aggregate demand curve remains at AD_1—this process comes to an end when the short-run aggregate supply curve has shifted to SAS_1 in Fig. 31.1(b). At this time, the GDP deflator has increased to 143—a 10 percent increase over its initial level—and real GDP has returned to the level from which it started, its long-run level.

A Price–Wage Inflation Spiral

The inflation process we've just studied eventually comes to an end when, for a given increase in aggregate demand, wages have adjusted enough to restore the real wage rate to its full-employment level. But suppose that the initial increase in aggregate demand resulted from a government budget deficit financed by creating more and more money. If such a policy remains in place, aggregate demand will continue to increase year after year. The aggregate demand curve will keep shifting rightward, putting continual upward pressure on the price level. The economy will experience perpetual demand-pull inflation.

Figure 31.2 illustrates a perpetual demand-pull inflation. The starting point is the same as that shown in Fig. 31.1. The aggregate demand curve is AD_0, the short-run aggregate supply curve is SAS_0, and the long-run aggregate supply curve is LAS. Real GDP is $600 billion and the GDP deflator is 130. Aggregate demand increases, shifting the aggregate demand curve to AD_1. Real GDP increases to $650 billion, and the GDP deflator rises to 135. The economy is at an above full-employment equilibrium. There is a shortage of labour and the wage rate rises, shifting the short-run aggregate supply curve to SAS_1. The GDP deflator increases to 143, and real GDP returns to its long-run level.

But the money supply increases again by the same percentage as before and aggregate demand continues to increase. The aggregate demand curve shifts rightward to AD_2. The GDP deflator increases further, real GDP exceeds its long-run level, and the wage rate continues to rise. As the SAS curve shifts to SAS_2, the GDP deflator increases further to 157. As aggregate demand continues to increase, the price level rises continuously, generating a perpetual demand-pull inflation and a price-wage inflation spiral. Real GDP fluctuates between $600 billion and $650 billion.

FIGURE 31.2

A Price–Wage Inflation Spiral

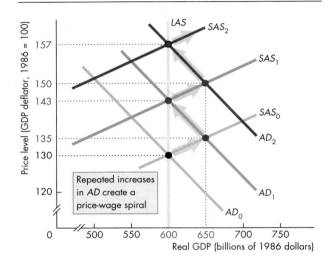

The aggregate demand curve is AD_0, the short-run aggregate supply curve is SAS_0, and the long-run aggregate supply curve is LAS. Real GDP is $600 billion and the GDP deflator is 130. Aggregate demand increases, shifting the aggregate demand curve to AD_1. Real GDP increases to $650 billion and the GDP deflator rises to 135. With the economy operating above full employment, the wage rate begins to rise, shifting the short-run aggregate supply curve leftward to SAS_1. The GDP deflator increases to 143 and real GDP returns to its long-run level. As aggregate demand continues to increase, the aggregate demand curve shifts to AD_2. The GDP deflator increases further, real GDP exceeds its long-run level, and the wage rate continues to rise. As the short-run aggregate supply curve shifts leftward to SAS_2, the GDP deflator increases to 157. As aggregate demand continues to increase, the price level rises, generating a perpetual demand-pull inflation. Real GDP fluctuates between $600 billion and $650 billion. But if aggregate demand increases *at the same time* as wages increase, real GDP remains at $650 billion as the demand-pull inflation occurs.

In the price-wage inflation spiral that we've just described, aggregate demand increases and wage increases alternate—first aggregate demand increases, then wages, then aggregate demand, and so on. If, after the initial increase in aggregate demand that took real GDP to $650 billion, aggregate demand continues to increase *at the same time* as the wage rate increases, real GDP remains above its long-run level at $650 billion as the demand-pull inflation proceeds.

Demand-Pull Inflation in Chatham   You may better understand the inflation process that we've just described by considering what is going on in a small part of the economy, such as a Chatham ketchup bottling plant. Initially, when aggregate demand increases, the demand for ketchup increases and the price of ketchup rises. Faced with a higher price, the ketchup plant works overtime and increases production. Conditions are good for workers in Chatham, and the ketchup factory finds it hard to hang onto its best people. To do so it has to offer higher wages. As wages increase, so do the ketchup factory's costs.

What happens next depends on what happens to aggregate demand. If aggregate demand remains constant (as in Fig. 31.1b), the firm's costs are increasing, but the price of ketchup is not increasing as quickly as its costs. Production is scaled back. Eventually, wages and costs increase by the same amount as the price of ketchup. In real terms, the ketchup factory is in the same situation as initially. The bottling plant produces the same amount of ketchup and employs the same amount of labour.

But if aggregate demand continues to increase, so does the demand for ketchup, and the price of ketchup rises at the same rate as wages. The ketchup factory continues to operate above full employment, and there is a persistent shortage of labour. Prices and wages chase each other upward in an unending price-wage spiral.

R E V I E W

Demand-pull inflation results from any initial factor that increases aggregate demand. The main such factors are an increase in the money supply, an increase in government purchases of goods and services, and an increase in the price level in the rest of the world. Initially, the increase in aggregate demand increases the price level and real GDP. With the economy operating at above full employment, the wage rate rises, decreasing short-run aggregate supply. If aggregate demand remains constant at its new level, the price level rises further and real GDP returns to its long-run level. If aggregate demand continues to increase, wages chase prices in an unending price-wage inflation spiral. ◆

Next, let's look at how shocks to aggregate supply can create inflation.

Supply Inflation and Stagflation

Inflation can result from a decrease in aggregate supply. The two main sources of a decrease in aggregate supply are

◆ An increase in wage rates

◆ An increase in the prices of raw materials

These sources of a decrease in aggregate supply operate by increasing costs, and the resulting inflation is called **cost-push inflation**.

Other things remaining the same, the higher the cost of production, the smaller is the amount produced. At a given price level, rising wage rates or rising prices of raw materials such as oil lead firms to decrease the quantity of labour employed and to cut production. This decrease in short-run aggregate supply shifts the short-run aggregate supply curve leftward. Let's see what that does to the price level.

Inflation Effect of a Decrease in Aggregate Supply

Suppose that last year the GDP deflator was 130 and real GDP was $600 billion. Long-run real GDP was also $600 billion. This situation is shown in Fig. 31.3. The aggregate demand curve was AD_0, the short-run aggregate supply curve was SAS_0, and the long-run aggregate supply curve was LAS. In the current year, a sharp increase in world oil prices decreases short-run aggregate supply. The short-run aggregate supply curve shifts leftward to SAS_1. The GDP deflator increases to 140, and real GDP decreases to $550 billion. The economy experiences 7.7 percent inflation (a GDP deflator of 140 compared with 130 in the previous year) and a contraction of real GDP—*stagflation*.

Aggregate Demand Response

When the economy is at an unemployment equilibrium such as that shown in Fig. 31.3, there is usually a call for policy actions to restore full employment. Such action can include an increase in government purchases of goods and services or a tax cut, but the most likely is a response from the Bank of Canada that increases the money supply. If the Bank of Canada does respond in this way, aggregate demand increases and the aggregate demand curve shifts rightward. Figure 31.4 shows an increase in aggregate demand that shifts the aggregate demand curve to AD_1 and restores full employment. But this happens at the expense of a yet higher price level. The price level rises to 143, a 10 percent increase over the original price level.

A Cost–Price Inflation Spiral

Suppose now that the oil producers, seeing the prices of everything they buy increase by 10 percent, decide to increase the price of oil yet again. Figure 31.5 continues the story. The short-run aggregate supply curve now shifts to SAS_2, and another bout of stagflation ensues. The price level

rises further to 154, and real GDP falls to $550 billion. Unemployment increases above its natural rate. If the Bank of Canada responds again with an increase in the money supply, aggregate demand increases and the aggregate demand curve shifts to AD_2. The price level rises even higher—to 160—and full employment is again restored. A cost-price inflation spiral results. But if the Bank of Canada does not respond, the economy remains below full employment until the initial price increase that triggered the stagflation is reversed.

You can see that the Bank of Canada has a dilemma. If it increases the money supply to restore full employment, it invites another oil price hike that will call forth a further increase in the money supply. Inflation will rage at a rate decided by the oil-exporting nations. If the Bank of Canada keeps the lid on money supply growth, the economy operates with a high level of unemployment.

FIGURE 31.3

Cost–Push Inflation

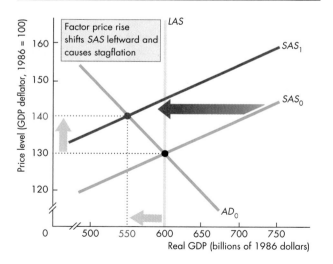

Initially, the aggregate demand curve is AD_0, the short-run aggregate supply curve is SAS_0, and the long-run aggregate supply curve is LAS. A decrease in aggregate supply (for example, resulting from an increase in the world price of oil) shifts the short-run aggregate supply curve to SAS_1. The economy moves to the point where the short-run aggregate supply curve SAS_1 intersects the aggregate demand curve AD_0. The GDP deflator increases to 140 and real GDP decreases to $550 billion. The economy experiences inflation and a contraction of real GDP—*stagflation.*

FIGURE 31.4

Aggregate Demand Response to Cost Push

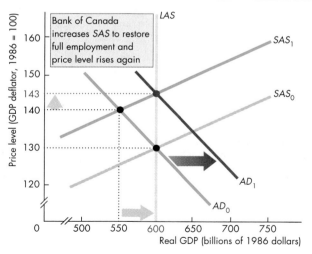

A decrease in aggregate supply shifts the short-run aggregate supply curve leftward to SAS_1. The GDP deflator rises from 130 to 140 and real GDP decreases from $600 billion to $550 billion. The economy experiences stagflation. It is stuck at an unemployment equilibrium. If the Bank of Canada responds by increasing aggregate demand to restore full employment, the aggregate demand curve shifts rightward to AD_1. The economy returns to full employment, but at the expense of higher inflation. The price level rises to 143.

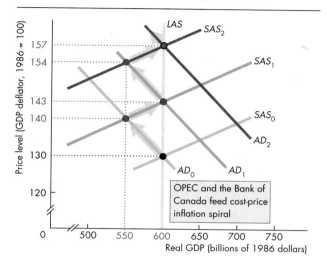

FIGURE 31.5

A Cost-Price Inflation Spiral

When a cost increase (for example, an increase in the world oil price) decreases short-run aggregate supply from SAS_0 to SAS_1, the GDP deflator rises to 140 and real GDP decreases to $550 billion. The Bank of Canada responds with an increase in the money supply that shifts the aggregate demand curve from AD_0 to AD_1. The GDP deflator rises again to 143 and real GDP returns to $600 billion. The cost increase is applied again, shifting the short-run aggregate supply curve to SAS_2. Stagflation is repeated—real GDP decreases to $550 billion and the GDP deflator now rises to 154. The Bank of Canada responds again, taking the aggregate demand curve to AD_2, and the cost-price inflation spiral continues as the price level rises to 157.

The Bank of Canada faced such a dilemma during the 1970s and early 1980s when OPEC pushed oil prices higher. At first, the Bank accommodated these price increases and inflation exploded. But during the early 1980s, the Bank decided not to respond to the oil price hike with an increase in the money supply. The result was a severe recession, but also an eventual fall in the inflation rate.

Cost-Push Inflation in Chatham   What is going on in the Chatham ketchup bottling plant when the economy is experiencing cost-push inflation? When the oil price increases, so do the costs of bottling ketchup. These higher costs decrease the supply of ketchup, increasing its price and decreasing the quantity produced. The ketchup plant lays off some workers. This situation persists until either the Bank of Canada increases aggregate demand or the price

of oil falls. If the Bank of Canada increases aggregate demand, as it did in the mid-1970s, the demand for ketchup increases and so does its price. The higher price of ketchup brings higher profits and the bottling plant increases its production. The ketchup factory rehires the laid-off workers. But if the Bank of Canada resists the pressure to increase aggregate demand, the price of oil eventually falls and ketchup production gradually increases.

R E V I E W

Cost-push inflation results from an increase in any factor such as the wage rate or the price of a key raw material that decreases aggregate supply. The initial effect of a decrease in aggregate supply is an increase in the price level and a decrease in real GDP—*stagflation*. If monetary or fiscal policy increases aggregate demand to restore full employment, the price level rises further. If aggregate demand remains constant, the economy stays below full employment until the initial price rise is reversed. If the response to stagflation is an increase in aggregate demand, a freewheeling cost-push inflation takes place at a rate determined by the speed at which costs are pushed upward. ◆

Anticipating Inflation

With demand-pull inflation, a persistent increase in aggregate demand creates a price-wage inflation spiral. With cost-push inflation, a persistent increase in factor prices accommodated by persistent increases in the money supply creates a cost-price inflation spiral. Regardless of whether the inflation is demand-pull or cost-push, the failure to correctly *anticipate* it results in unintended consequences that impose costs on firms and workers. Let's examine these consequences.

Labour Market Consequences of Unanticipated Inflation

Unanticipated inflation has two main consequences for the operation of the labour market. They are

◆ Redistribution of income

◆ Departure from full employment

Redistribution of Income   Unanticipated inflation redistributes income between workers and employers. In some situations, workers gain at the expense of employers and, in other situations, employers gain at the expense of workers.

If an unexpected increase in aggregate demand increases the inflation rate, then wages will not have been set high enough. Profits will be higher than expected, and wages will buy fewer goods than expected. Employers gain at the expense of workers. But if aggregate demand is expected to increase at a rapid rate and it fails to do so, workers gain at the expense of employers. In this situation, the anticipated inflation rate is higher than the actual inflation rate. Wages will be set too high and profits will be squeezed. Workers will be able to buy more with their income than was originally anticipated.

These redistributions between workers and employers create an incentive for both firms and unions to try to anticipate inflation correctly. Some other costs of unanticipated inflation fall on both workers and firms at the same time. These are the costs arising from departures from full employment.

Departure from Full Employment   Unanticipated inflation results in departure from full employment. You can confirm this proposition by looking again at Figs. 31.2 and 31.5. To see why departure from full employment imposes costs, let's return to the ketchup bottling plant in Chatham.

If the bottling plant and its workers are not anticipating inflation, but an inflation actually occurs, wages will be set too low and employment will increase above the full-employment level. The price of ketchup and of other goods increases initially but the wage rate doesn't change. The real wage rate falls and the bottling plant increases production. Workers begin to quit the bottling plant to find jobs that pay a higher real wage rate, one closer to that prevailing before the outburst of inflation. This outcome imposes costs on both the firm and the workers. The firm operates its plant at a high output rate and incurs overtime costs and higher plant mainte-

nance and parts replacement costs. The workers wind up feeling cheated. They've worked overtime to produce the extra output but, when they come to spend their wages, they discover that prices have increased, so their wages buy a smaller quantity of goods and services than was originally anticipated.

If the bottling plant and its workers anticipate a high inflation rate that does not occur, wages will be set too high, and unemployment will increase. Those workers keeping their jobs gain, but those who become unemployed lose. Also, the bottling plant loses because output and profits fall.

So unanticipated inflation imposes costs regardless of whether the inflation forecast turns out to be wrong on the up side or the down side. The presence of these costs creates an incentive to forecast inflation as accurately as possible—to correctly anticipate inflation. Let's now see how people make forecasts of inflation.

How People Forecast Inflation

People devote different amounts of time and effort to forecasting inflation. Some people specialize in forecasting inflation and make a living from it. They are economists who work for public and private macroeconomic forecasting agencies and firms.

Specialist forecasters stand to lose from wrong forecasts and have a strong incentive to make their forecasts as accurate as possible—minimizing the range of error and making them correct on the average. Also, organizations that stand to lose by making wrong forecasts devote a good deal of effort to checking the forecasts made by the specialists. For example, banks, labour unions, government departments, and most large private-sector producers of goods and services devote a lot of effort to making their own forecasts and comparing them with the forecasts of others. Specialist forecasters use vast amounts of data, which they analyse with the help of statistical models of the economy. The models they use are based on (but are more detailed than) the aggregate demand-aggregate supply model that you are studying in this book.

How Economists Predict People's Forecasts

Economics tries to predict the choices that people make. Since people's choices depend on their forecasts of phenomena such as inflation, we must predict their forecasts in order to predict their choices. How do economists go about that task?

They assume that people are as rational in their use of information when forming expectations as they are in all their other economic actions. Lacking crystal balls, people cannot always be right about the future. But they can use all the relevant information available to them to make their forecasting errors as small as possible. That is, they can make a rational expectation. A **rational expectation** is a forecast based on all the available relevant information. It has two features:

1. The expected forecast error is zero.

2. The range of the forecast error is as small as possible.

With an expected forecast error of zero, a rational expectation is right *on the average*. But it is not an accurate forecast. It has the same chance of being too high as it has of being too low.

The assumption that people don't waste information when they make their forecasts does not tell us what information they actually use. So we make one further assumption. They use the *information that economic theory predicts is relevant*. For example, to predict people's expectations of the price of orange juice, we use the economic model of demand and supply, together with all the available information about the positions of the demand and supply curves for orange juice. To make a prediction about people's expectations of the price level and inflation, we use the economic model of aggregate demand and aggregate supply.

Let's see how we can use the aggregate demand-aggregate supply model to work out the rational expectation of the price level.

Rational Expectation of the Price Level

We use the aggregate demand-aggregate supply model to forecast the price level in the same way that the meteorologist uses a model of the atmosphere to forecast the weather. But there is a difference between the meteorologist's model of the atmosphere and the economist's model of the economy. In the meteorologist's model, tomorrow's weather does not depend on people's forecast of it. In the economist's model, next year's price level *does* depend on people's forecast of it. To work out the rational expectation of the price level, we must

take acccount of this dependence of the actual price level on the forecasted price level.

We're going to work out the rational expectation of the price level, using Fig. 31.6 to guide our analysis. The aggregate demand-aggregate supply model predicts that the price level is at the point of intersection of the aggregate demand and short-run aggregate supply curves. To forecast the price level, therefore, we have to forecast the positions of these curves.

Let's begin with aggregate demand. To forecast the position of the aggregate demand curve, we must forecast all the variables that influence aggregate demand. Suppose that we have done this and our forecast of aggregate demand is given by the curve *EAD*, the *expected* aggregate demand curve.

Our next task is to forecast the position of the short-run aggregate supply curve. We know that the position of the short-run aggregate supply curve is determined by two things:

◆ Long-run aggregate supply

◆ The money wage rate

The short-run aggregate supply curve intersects the long-run aggregate supply curve at the full-employment price level. So we need a forecast of the position of the long-run aggregate supply curve. To make such a forecast, we must forecast all the factors that determine long-run aggregate supply. Suppose that we have made the best forecast we can of long-run real GDP and that we expect long-run aggregate supply to be $600 billion. The *expected* long-run aggregate supply curve is *ELAS* in Fig. 31.6.

The final ingredient we need is a forecast of the wage rate. Armed with this information, we have a forecast of the point on the *ELAS* curve at which the short-run aggregate supply intersects it. The forecast of the wage rate depends on how far ahead we are forecasting it. There are two cases to deal with:

◆ Rational expectations in the short run

◆ Rational expectations in the long run

Rational Expectations in the Short Run   In the short run, money wages are already set, so forecasting money wages is easy. The forecast is equal to the current actual wage rate. Given that fixed wage rate and the expected long-run aggregate supply curve *ELAS*, there is an expected short-run aggregate supply curve. In Fig. 31.6(a), such a curve is $ESAS_0$.

FIGURE 31.6

Rational Expectation of the Price Level

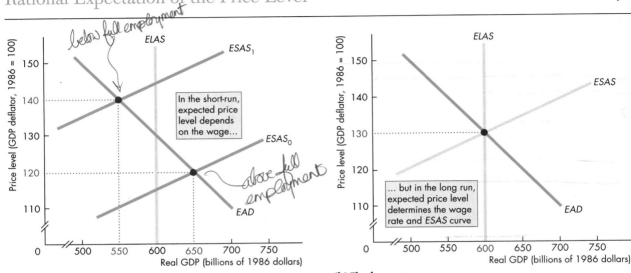

(a) The short run

(b) The long run

The rational expectation of the price level is the best available forecast. That forecast is constructed by forecasting the expected aggregate demand curve (*EAD*) and the expected short-run aggregate supply curve (*ESAS*). The rational expectation of the price level occurs at the point of intersection of curves *EAD* and *ESAS*. To forecast the position of *ESAS*, forecasts of the long-run aggregate supply curve *ELAS* and the wage rate are needed. In the short run (part a), wages are sticky and do not respond to price level expectations, so the position of the expected short-run aggregate supply curve depends on

ELAS and the fixed wage rate. With a low wage rate, the expected short-run aggregate supply curve is *ESAS*$_0$ and the rational expectation of the price level is 120. With a high wage rate, the expected short-run aggregate supply curve is *ESAS*$_1$ and the rational expectation of the price level is 140. In the long run (part b), wages are flexible and respond to the expected price level. The rational expectation of the price level is at the point of intersection of *EAD* and *ELAS*. The wage rate is determined by this expected price level, and the expected short-run aggregate supply curve is *ESAS*.

The rational expectation of the price level is the point of intersection of *EAD* and *ESAS*$_0$, a price level of 120. The rational expectation of inflation is calculated as the percentage amount by which the forecasted future price level exceeds the current price level. For example, if the current price level is 110, and next year's forecasted price level is 120, the expected inflation rate over the year is 9.1 percent.

There is also a rational expectation of real GDP. Given the wage rate and the expected short-run aggregate supply curve *ESAS*$_0$, the rational expectation is that real GDP will be $650 billion and the economy will be at an above full-employment equilibrium.

Figure 31.6(a) shows another case—one in which the expected short-run aggregate supply curve is *ESAS*$_1$. Here, the wage rate is higher. The rational expectation of the price level is determined at the

point of intersection of *EAD* and *ESAS*$_1$, an expected price level of 140. With a current price level of 110, the expected inflation rate over the year is 27 percent. The economy is expected to be at an unemployment equilibrium, with a real GDP of $550 billion.

Rational Expectations in the Long Run In the long run, wages are flexible and to forecast the position of the short-run aggregate supply curve we must first forecast the money wage rate. But the money wage rate is set to make the expected real wage rate give full employment. So to set the money wage rate, people use a forecast—a rational expectation—of the price level. There seems to be a problem here: to forecast the price level, we need a forecast of the wage rate; and to forecast the wage rate, we need a forecast of the price level.

The problem is solved by finding a forecast of

both the price level and the wage rate that are consistent with each other. There is only one such consistent forecast. It occurs when the forecasted wage rate makes the expected short-run aggregate supply curve $ESAS$ pass through the point of intersection of the expected aggregate demand curve and the expected long-run aggregate supply curve. This case is shown in Fig. 31.6(b). The forecasted price level is 130, determined at the intersection of the EAD and $ESAS$ curves. Here, we forecast the position of the short-run aggregate supply curve and the price level at the same time, and the two forecasts are consistent with each other.

Model, Theory, and Reality

The analysis we've just conducted shows how economists work out a rational expectation of the price level. But do real people use the same analysis to form their expectations of the price level? We can imagine that graduates of economics might, but it seems unrealistic to attribute such calculations to most people. Does this make the idea of rational expectations invalid?

The answer is no. In performing our calculations, we have built an economic model. That model does not describe the thought processes of real people. Its purpose is to make predictions about *choices*, not mental processes. The theory is that the forecasts people make, regardless of *how* they make them, are the same (on the average) as the forecasts that an economist makes using the relevant economic theory.

We've seen how unanticipated changes in aggregate demand and aggregate supply create inflation and impose costs. We've also seen how people try to anticipate inflation and avoid those costs. Let's next see how things work out when forecasts are correct—when people get lucky and correctly anticipate the future.

Anticipated Inflation

If people could correctly anticipate the future course of inflation, they would always set the money wage rate at its full-employment level.

Let's suppose that last year the GDP deflator was 130 and real GDP was $600 billion. Let's also suppose that the economy was at full employment and its long-run real GDP last year was $600 billion. Figure 31.7 illustrates the economy last year. The aggregate demand curve last year was AD_0, the

aggregate supply curve was SAS_0, and the long-run aggregate supply curve was LAS. Since the economy was in equilibrium at long-run real GDP, the actual price level equalled the expected price level.

To simplify the analysis, let's suppose that at the end of last year long-run real GDP was not expected to change, so that this year's expected long-run aggregate supply is the same as last year's. Let's also suppose that aggregate demand was expected to increase, so that the expected aggregate demand curve for this year is AD_1. We can now calculate the rational expectation of the price level for this year. It is a GDP deflator of 143, the price

FIGURE 31.7

Anticipated Inflation

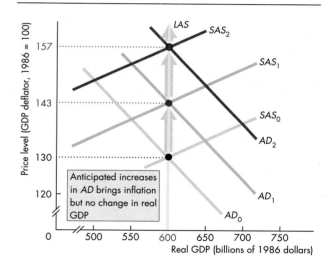

The actual and expected long-run aggregate supply curve (LAS) is at a real GDP of $600 billion. Last year, aggregate demand was AD_0, and the short-run aggregate supply curve was SAS_0. The actual price level was the same as that expected—a GDP deflator of 130. This year aggregate demand is expected to rise to AD_1. The rational expectation of the GDP deflator changes from 130 to 143. As a result, the short-run aggregate supply curve shifts up to SAS_1. If aggregate demand actually increases as expected, the actual aggregate demand curve AD_1 is the same as the expected aggregate demand curve. Equilibrium occurs at a real GDP of $600 billion and an actual GDP deflator of 143. The inflation is correctly anticipated.

In the next period, the process continues with aggregate demand increasing as expected to AD_2 and wages rising to shift the short-run aggregate supply curve to SAS_2. Again, real GDP remains at $600 billion and the GDP deflator rises, as anticipated, to 157.

level at which the new expected aggregate demand curve intersects the expected long-run aggregate supply curve. The expected inflation rate is 10 percent, the percentage change in the price level from 130 to 143.

Wages increase as a result of the expected inflation, and the short-run aggregate supply curve also shifts leftward. In particular, given that expected inflation is 10 percent, the short-run aggregate supply curve for next year (SAS_1) shifts upward by that same percentage amount (10 percent) and passes through the long-run aggregate supply curve (LAS) at the expected price level.

If aggregate demand turns out to be the same as expected, the actual aggregate demand curve is AD_1. The intersection point of AD_1 and SAS_1 determines the actual price level—the GDP deflator is 143. Between last year and this year, the GDP deflator increased from 130 to 143 and the economy experienced an inflation rate of 10 percent, the same as the anticipated inflation rate.

What caused the inflation? The immediate answer is the anticipated and actual increase in aggregate demand. Because aggregate demand was *expected* to increase from AD_0 to AD_1, the short-run aggregate supply curve shifted up from SAS_0 to SAS_1. Because aggregate demand actually did increase by the amount expected, the actual aggregate demand curve shifted from AD_0 to AD_1. The combination of the anticipated and actual shifts of the aggregate demand curve rightward produced an increase in the price level that was anticipated.

Only if aggregate demand growth is correctly forecasted does the economy follow the course described in Fig. 31.7. If the expected growth rate of aggregate demand is different from its actual growth rate, the expected aggregate demand curve shifts by an amount different from the actual aggregate demand curve. The inflation rate departs from its expected level and, to some extent, there is unanticipated inflation. It is this type of inflation that we studied in the first part of this chapter.

We've seen that when inflation is anticipated, the economy remains on its long-run aggregate supply curve. Does this mean that an anticipated inflation has no costs?

The Costs of Anticipated Inflation

An anticipated inflation at a moderate rate—a few per-cent a year—probably has a very small cost. But an anticipated inflation at a rapid rate is extremely costly.

Recall that inflation is the pace at which money loses its value. If money loses value at a rapid anticipated rate, it does not function well as a medium of exchange. In such a situation, people try to avoid holding money. They spend their incomes as soon as they receive them, and firms pay out incomes—wages and dividends—as soon as they receive revenue from their sales. During the 1920s, when inflation in Germany reached *hyperinflation* levels, rates in excess of 50 percent a month, wages were paid and spent twice in a single day! Also, at high anticipated inflation rates, people seek alternatives to money as a means of payment (for example, cigarettes or foreign currency). During the 1980s, when inflation in Israel reached 1,000 percent a year, the U.S dollar started to replace the worthless Israeli shekel. Also, in times of anticipated inflation, barter becomes more common.

The activities that are encouraged by a high anticipated inflation rate use valuable time and other resources. Instead of people concentrating on the activities at which they have a comparative advantage, they find it more profitable to search for ways of avoiding the losses that inflation inflicts.

In terms of the aggregate demand-aggregate supply model, a rapid anticipated inflation shifts the LAS curve leftward—it decreases long-run aggregate supply. The faster the anticipated inflation rate, the further leftward the LAS curve shifts.

There are many examples of costly anticipated inflations around the world, especially in South American countries such as Argentina, Bolivia, and Brazil, and in Russia and other Eastern European countries. The closest that Canada has come to experiencing a costly anticipated inflation was in the late 1970s and early 1980s, when the inflation rate exceeded 10 percent a year.

Stopping an Anticipated Inflation

An anticipated inflation can be stubborn and hard to stop. The monetary and fiscal policies that create inflation also create expectations of inflation that reinforce the inflationary effects of the policy. Also, people don't like to have their expectations disappointed, so if they anticipate a high inflation rate, they want a high inflation rate. Such was the situation in Canada in the late 1970s and early 1980s.

REVIEW

Decisions to work and produce are based on forecasts of inflation, but the returns to firms and workers depend on actual inflation. Wrong inflation forecasts impose costs on firms and workers. To minimize those costs, people make forecasts that use all available information. Such a forecast is called a *rational expectation*. To predict people's forecasts of the future price level, we use the aggregate demand-aggregate supply model. ◆ ◆ If people correctly anticipate changes in aggregate demand and aggregate supply, the result is anticipated inflation. If the anticipated inflation rate is moderate, real GDP is unchanged. But a rapid anticipated inflation diverts productive resources and decreases long-run aggregate supply. ◆

Inflation over the Business Cycle: The Phillips Curve

We've seen that a speedup in aggregate demand growth that is not fully anticipated increases both inflation and real GDP growth. It also decreases unemployment. Similarly, a slowdown in the growth rate of aggregate demand that is not fully anticipated slows down both inflation and real GDP growth and increases unemployment. We've also seen that a fully anticipated change in the growth rate of aggregate demand changes the inflation rate and has no effect on real GDP or unemployment. Finally, we've seen that a decrease in aggregate supply increases inflation and decreases real GDP growth. In this case, unemployment increases.

The aggregate demand-aggregate supply model we've used to obtain these results gives predictions about the level of real GDP and the price level. Given these predictions, we can work out how unemployment and inflation have changed. But the aggregate demand-aggregate supply model does not place inflation and unemployment at the centre of the stage.

An alternative way of studying inflation and unemployment focuses directly on their joint movements and uses a relationship called the Phillips curve. The Phillips curve is so named because it was popularized by New Zealand economist A.W. Phillips when he was working at the London School of Economics in the 1950s. A **Phillips curve** is a curve showing the relationship between inflation and unemployment. There are two time frames for Phillips curves:

◆ The short-run Phillips curve
◆ The long-run Phillips curve

The Short-Run Phillips Curve

The **short-run Phillips curve** is a curve showing the relationship between inflation and unemployment, holding constant:

1. The expected inflation rate

2. The natural rate of unemployment

Figure 31.8 shows a short-run Phillips curve *SRPC*. Suppose that the expected inflation rate is 10 percent a year and the natural rate of unemployment is 6 percent, point *a* in the figure. The short-run Phillips curve passes through this point. If the unemployment rate falls below its natural rate, inflation rises above its expected rate. This joint movement in the inflation rate and the unemployment rate is illustrated as a movement up the short-run Phillips curve from point *a* to point *b* in the figure. Similarly, if unemployment rises above the natural rate, inflation falls below its expected rate. In this case, there is movement down the short-run Phillips curve from point *a* to point *c*.

This negative relationship between inflation and unemployment along the short-run Phillips curve is explained by the aggregate demand-aggregate supply model. Suppose that, initially, inflation is anticipated to be 10 percent a year and unemployment is at its natural rate. This situation is illustrated by the aggregate demand-aggregate supply model in Fig. 31.7 and by the Phillips curve approach as point *a* in Fig. 31.8. Suppose that now an unanticipated increase in the growth of aggregate demand occurs. In Fig. 31.7 the aggregate demand curve shifts rightward more quickly than expected. Real GDP increases, the unemployment rate decreases, and the price level starts to increase at a rate faster

FIGURE 31.8

The Short-Run Phillips Curve

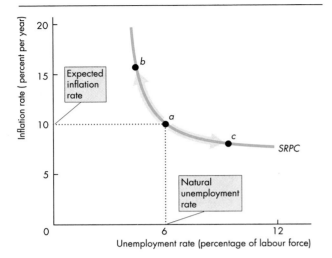

The short-run Phillips curve *SRPC* shows the relationship between inflation and unemployment at a given expected inflation rate and given natural unemployment. With an expected inflation rate of 10 percent a year and a natural rate of unemployment of 6 percent, the short-run Phillips curve passes through point *a*. An unanticipated increase in aggregate demand lowers unemployment and increases inflation—a movement up the short-run Phillips curve. An unanticipated decrease in aggregate demand increases unemployment and lowers inflation—a movement down the short-run Phillips curve.

than expected. The economy moves from point *a* to point *b* in Fig. 31.8. If the unanticipated increase in aggregate demand is temporary, aggregate demand growth slows to its previous level. When it does so, the process is reversed and the economy moves back to point *a* in Fig. 31.8.

A similar story can be told to illustrate the effects of an unanticipated decrease in the growth of aggregate demand. In this case, an unanticipated slowdown in the growth of aggregate demand reduces inflation, slows real GDP growth, and increases unemployment. The economy moves down the short-run Phillips curve from point *a* to point *c*.

The Long-Run Phillips Curve

The **long-run Phillips curve** is a curve showing the relationship between inflation and unemployment,

when the actual inflation rate equals the expected inflation rate. The long-run Phillips curve is vertical at the natural rate of unemployment. It is shown in Fig. 31.9 as the vertical line *LRPC*.

If the expected inflation rate is 10 percent a year, the short-run Phillips curve is $SRPC_0$. If the expected inflation rate falls to 8 percent a year, the short-run Phillips curve shifts downward to $SRPC_1$. At points *a* and *d*, inflation is equal to its expected rate and unemployment is equal to its natural rate. The distance by which the short-run Phillips curve shifts downward when the expected inflation rate falls is equal to the change in the expected inflation rate. Points *a* and *d* lie on the long-run Phillips curve *LRPC*. This curve tells us that any inflation rate is possible at the natural rate of unemployment.

FIGURE 31.9

The Short-Run and Long-Run Phillips Curves

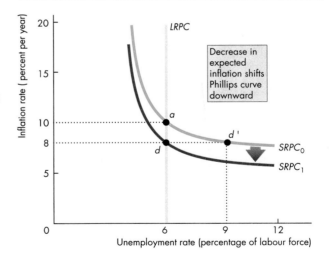

The long-run Phillips curve is *LRPC*, a vertical line at the natural rate of unemployment. A decrease in inflation expectations shifts the short-run Phillips curve down by the amount of the fall in the expected inflation rate. Here, when expected inflation falls from 10 percent a year to 8 percent a year, the short-run Phillips curve shifts from $SRPC_0$ to $SRPC_1$. The new short-run Phillips curve intersects the long-run Phillips curve at the new expected inflation rate at point *d*. With the original expected inflation rate (of 10 percent), an inflation rate of 8 percent a year would occur at an unemployment rate of 9 percent, at point d^1.

To see why the short-run Phillips curve shifts when the expected inflation rate changes, let's do an experiment. The economy is at full employment and a fully anticipated inflation is raging at 10 percent a year. The Bank of Canada and the government now begin a permanent attack on inflation by slowing money supply growth and cutting the deficit. Aggregate demand growth slows down and the inflation rate falls to 8 percent a year. At first, this decrease in inflation is unanticipated, so wages continue to rise at their original rate, shifting the short-run aggregate supply curve leftward at the same pace as before. Real GDP falls and unemployment increases. In Fig. 31.9, the economy moves from point a to point d' on the short-run Phillips curve $SRPC_0$.

If the actual inflation rate remains steady at 8 percent a year, eventually this rate will come to be expected. As this happens, wage growth slows down and the short-run aggregate supply curve shifts leftward less quickly. Eventually it shifts leftward at the same pace at which the aggregate demand curve is shifting rightward. The actual inflation rate equals the expected inflation rate and full employment is restored. Unemployment is back at its natural rate. In Fig. 31.9, the short-run Phillips curve has shifted from $SRPC_0$ to $SRPC_1$ and the economy is at point d.

Changes in the Natural Rate of Unemployment

The natural rate of unemployment changes for many reasons that are explained in Chapter 30 (pp. 853–854). A change in the natural rate of unemployment shifts both the short-run and the long-run Phillips curves. Such shifts are illustrated in Fig. 31.10. If the natural rate of unemployment increases from 6 percent to 9 percent, the long-run Phillips curve shifts from $LRPC_0$ to $LRPC_1$, and if expected inflation is constant at 10 percent a year, the short-run Phillips curve shifts from $SRPC_0$ to $SRPC_1$. Because the expected inflation rate is constant, the short-run Phillips curve $SRPC_1$ intersects the long-run curve $LRPC_1$ (point e) at the same inflation rate as the short-run Phillips curve $SRPC_0$ intersects the long-run curve $LRPC_0$ (point a).

The Phillips Curve in Canada

Figure 31.11 shows the relationship between inflation and unemployment in Canada. Begin by looking at part (a), a scatter diagram of inflation and unemploy-

FIGURE 31.10

A Change in the Natural Rate of Unemployment

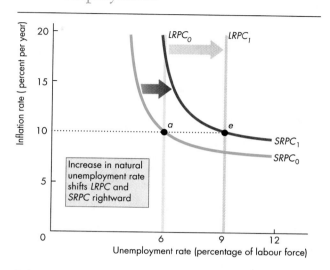

A change in the natural rate of unemployment shifts both the short-run and long-run Phillips curves. Here, the natural rate of unemployment increases from 6 percent to 9 percent, and the two Phillips curves shift rightward to $SRPC_1$ and $LRPC_1$. The new long-run Phillips curve intersects the new short-run Phillips curve at the expected inflation rate of 10 percent a year—point e.

ment since 1960. Each dot in the figure represents the combination of inflation and unemployment for a particular year. As you can see, there does not appear to be any clear relationship between inflation and unemployment. We certainly cannot see a Phillips curve similar to that shown in Fig. 31.8.

But we can interpret the data in terms of a shifting short-run Phillips curve. Figure 31.11(b) provides such an interpretation. Three short-run Phillips curves appear in the figure.

The short-run Phillips curve of the 1960s is $SRPC_0$. During the 1960s, the natural rate of unemployment was around 4 percent and the expected inflation rate was about 1 percent. The short-run Phillips curve started to shift upward during the late 1960s and early 1970s, and by 1974 it was $SRPC_1$. In this year, the natural unemployment rate was 9 percent and the expected inflation rate was 10 percent a year. The short-run Phillips curve shifted downward (not shown in the figure) in the late 1970s and then shifted upward again to $SRPC_1$ in

FIGURE 31.11

Phillips Curves in Canada

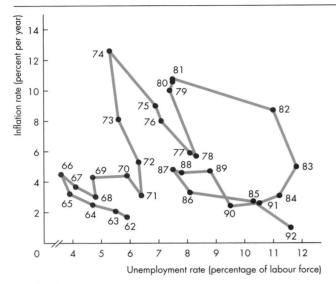

(a) The time sequence

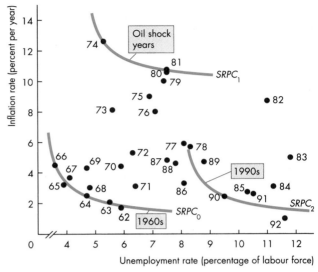

(b) Three Phillips curves

In part (a), each dot represents the combination of inflation and unemployment for a particular year in Canada. There is no clear relationship between the two variables. Part (b) interprets the data in terms of a shifting short-run Phillips curve. The short-run Phillips curve of the 1960s, when the expected inflation rate was 1 percent a year and the natural rate of unemployment was 4 percent, is $SRPC_0$. The short-run

Phillips curve then began to shift upward, and by 1974 it was $SRPC_1$. It shifted downward (not shown) and then upward again, and was back at $SRPC_1$ in 1980-1981. Through the 1980s, the expected inflation rate declined and the short-run Phillips curve shifted downward. By the early 1990s, it was $SRPC_2$.

1980-1981. Like 1974, these were years of extremely large oil price increases that had profound effects on both the natural rate of unemployment and the expected inflation rate. During the 1980s, the short-run Phillips curve shifted downward and by the early 1990s it was $SRPC_2$. At this time, the expected inflation rate was similar to its level in the early 1960s, but the natural unemployment rate remained high.

unemployment and results in a movement down the short-run Phillips curve. A change in the expected inflation rate shifts the short-run Phillips curve (upward for an increase in inflation and downward for a decrease in inflation) by an amount equal to the change in the expected inflation rate. A change in the natural rate of unemployment shifts both the short-run and the long-run Phillips curve rightward for an increase in the natural rate, and leftward for a decrease. The relationship between inflation and unemployment in Canada can be interpreted in terms of a shifting short-run Phillips curve. ◆

REVIEW

An unanticipated increase in the inflation rate decreases unemployment and results in a movement up the short-run Phillips curve. An unanticipated decrease in the inflation rate increases

So far, we've studied the effects of inflation on real GDP, real wages, employment, and unemployment. But inflation lowers the value of money and changes the real value of the amounts borrowed and repaid. As a result, interest rates are influenced by inflation. Let's see how.

Interest Rates and Inflation

T here have been large fluctuations in interest rates in Canada in recent years. In the early 1960s, corporations could raise long-term capital at interest rates of 5 percent a year. By the end of the 1960s, that interest rate had climbed to 8 percent a year. During the 1970s, the interest rates paid by firms for long-term loans fluctuated between 8 and 11 percent a year. During the early 1980s, interest rates hit close to 20 percent a year. They fell during the rest of the 1980s and by 1992 had returned to the levels of the late 1960s. Why have interest rates fluctuated so much and why were they so high during the late 1970s and early 1980s?

A major part of the answer to these questions is that the inflation rate also fluctuated and that interest rates fluctuated to compensate for the fall in the value of money. But the precise relationship between interest rates and inflation depends on whether inflation is anticipated or unanticipated. Let's begin by considering the effects of unanticipated inflation.

Interest Rates and Unanticipated Inflation

We'll work out the effects of inflation on interest rates by using Fig. 31.12. This figure is similar to Fig. 28.3 (p. 775), which explains the effects of the Bank of Canada's actions on interest rates.

Initially, the economy is at full employment and there is no inflation, and none is expected. The *real* quantity of money is $500 billion and the money supply curve is MS_0. The demand for money curve is MD_0 and the interest rate is 5 percent a year. This interest rate is both the *nominal* interest rate and the *real* interest rate. To see why, recall that

Real interest rate = Nominal interest rate − Inflation rate.

Because the inflation rate is zero, the real and nominal interest rates are the same.

To get an inflation going, the Bank of Canada must increase the quantity of money. Suppose that the Bank increases the quantity of money to $525 billion—a 5 percent increase—so the money supply curve shifts rightward to MS_1. The nominal interest rate falls to 4 percent a year.

FIGURE **31.12**

Money Growth, Inflation and the Interest Rate

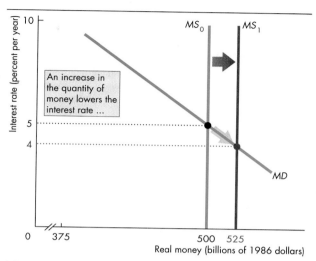

(a) Unanticipated increase in money

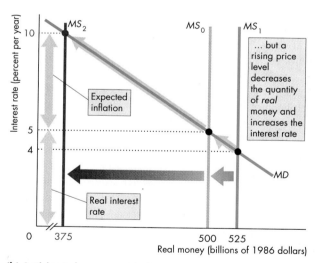

(b) Anticipated money growth

The demand for money curve is MD_0, the supply of money curve is MS_0, and the interest rate (*nominal* and *real*) is 5 percent a year. The Bank of Canada increases the quantity of money and the money supply curve shifts rightward to MS_1. In part (a), the nominal interest rate falls to 4 percent a year. In part (b), as the price level rises, the quantity of real money decreases and the interest rate returns to its original level. If the Bank continues to increase the money supply and if people anticipate the resulting inflation, the price level rises and the quantity of real money falls until the interest rate exceeds its original level by the anticipated inflation rate.

With a lower interest rate, aggregate planned expenditure increases and the aggregate demand curve shifts rightward. Both real GDP and the price level rise. The higher real GDP increases the demand for money (not shown in Fig. 31.12). The higher price level decreases the *real* quantity of money and the money supply curve shifts leftward. Both of these influences increase the interest rate.

With real GDP above its long-run level, wages begin to rise. As they do so, the short-run aggregate supply curve shifts leftward. The price level rises yet higher and real GDP decreases as the economy heads back towards full employment. When full employment is again restored, real GDP is back at its original level and the price level has increased by the same percentage as the money supply. Fig. 31.12(b) shows the effects of these events on the money market. The real quantity of money is back at its original level of $500 billion and the interest rate is back at 5 percent.

Interest Rates and Anticipated Inflation

If the Bank of Canada increases the quantity of money just once and then holds the quantity steady, the price level remains constant at its higher level and inflation returns to zero. But suppose that the Bank continues to increase the quantity of money by 5 percent a year and that people come to anticipate a resulting 5 percent a year inflation. (To keep things simple, we are ignoring growing long-run aggregate supply.) In these circumstances, people are not willing to hold bonds at an interest rate of 5 percent a year. Why not? Because the *real* interest rate has fallen.

People sell bonds and increase their demand for goods and services. As they do so, the price of bonds falls and the interest rate increases. At the same time, aggregate demand increases faster and the inflation rate speeds up to a rate that for a period exceeds the rate at which the quantity of money is increasing. The *real* quantity of money decreases further as the interest rate increases.

Only when interest rates have increased by enough to compensate bondholders for the anticipated falling value of money is a long-run equilibrium restored. Such an equilibrium is shown in Fig. 31.12(b). When the real money supply has decreased to MS_2 and the interest rate has increased to 10 percent, the *real* interest rate has returned to its original level of 5 percent a year.

Thus an unanticipated increase in the money supply brings a fall in interest rates. An anticipated and ongoing increase in the money supply increases interest rates. The decrease in interest rates following an increase in the money supply is an immediate but temporary response. The increase in interest rates associated with an increase in the growth rate of the money supply is a long-run response.

The Effect of Unanticipated Inflation on Borrowers and Lenders

Bondholders are lenders and bond issuers are borrowers. When inflation is unanticipated, the *real interest rate* falls and borrowers gain at the expense of lenders. You can appreciate this outcome by looking at the situation of Sue. Sue buys a bond for $5,000 that pays $250 interest after one year. The interest rate is 5 percent a year. At the end of the year, Sue plans to sell the bond and buy a car that today costs $5,250. She will have the $5,250 she needs made up of the $250 of interest plus her original $5,000.

If there is no inflation, Sue can buy the car. But suppose that prices rise during the year and a car that cost $5,250 at the beginning of the year costs $5,500 at the end of the year. Sue can't afford to buy the car at that price. Actually, Sue is as far away from being able to buy the car as she was at the beginning of the year. She's got more money, but everything now costs more. Sue has *really* made no interest income at all; and the bond issuer has *really* paid no interest. The *real interest rate* is zero.

Sue has lost $250 and the person to whom she lent $5,000 for the year has profited by $250.

The Effect of Anticipated Inflation on Borrowers and Lenders

We've seen that when inflation is anticipated, the *nominal interest rate* increases by an amount equal to the inflation rate, and the *real interest rate* remains constant. Anticipated inflation has no effect on borrowers and lenders. To see why, suppose that Sue (and all the other people buying and selling bonds) anticipates that inflation is going to be 10 percent.

If Sue anticipates a 5 percent inflation rate, she will not be willing to pay $5,000 for a bond that pays $250 in interest at the end of one year. In fact, if $250 is the yield that makes her (and other bondholders) willing to pay $5,000 for a bond when there is no inflation, then $2,500 is the price they will pay when inflation is anticipated to be 5 percent a year. Sue's nominal rate of return is then 10 percent a year and her real rate of return is 5 percent a year—a 10 percent nominal interest rate minus a 5 percent inflation rate equals a 5 percent real interest rate. With $5,000 to lend, Sue will buy *two* bonds for $2,5000 each. At the end of the year, she sells the two bonds for $5,000 and collects $500 in interest, so she has $5,500 with which to buy the car. Sue's income of $500 can be thought of as a real interest income of $250 and another $250 as compensation for the loss in the value of money. Sue *really* receives a 5 percent interest rate, and that's what the bond issuer *really* pays. The *real interest rate* is unchanged and is 5 percent, the same as when anticipated inflation rate is zero.

We've seen that an unanticipated inflation leads to a decrease in the real interest rate and that an anticipated inflation leads to an increase in the nominal interest rate and no change in the real interest rate. Therefore, the higher the anticipated inflation rate, the higher is the nominal interest rate. To the extent that inflation is in fact anticipated, interest rates and the inflation rate will move up and down together. Let's see if they do.

Inflation and Interest Rates in Canada

The relationship between nominal interest rates and the inflation rate in Canada is examined in Reading Between the Lines on pp. 880–881. And the relationship over a longer period is illustrated in Fig. 31.13. The interest rate measured on the vertical axis is that paid by the government on three-month loans. Each point on the graph represents a year in recent Canadian macroeconomic history between 1969 and 1992. The blue line shows the relationship between the nominal interest rate and the inflation rate if the real interest rate is constant at 3.5 percent a year, its actual average value in this period. As you can see, there is a positive relationship between the inflation rate and the interest rate, but it is not exact. As we have just seen, it is only *anticipated* inflation that influences interest rates. Thus only to the extent that a higher inflation rate is anticipated does it result in higher interest rates.

During the 1960s, both actual and expected inflation were moderate and so were nominal interest

FIGURE 31.13

Inflation and the Interest Rate

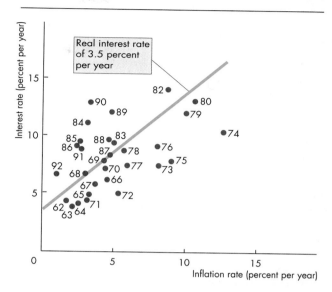

Other things remaining the same, the higher the expected inflation rate, the higher is the interest rate. A graph showing the relationship between interest rates and the actual inflation rate reveals that the influence of inflation on interest rates is a powerful one. Here, the interest rate is that paid by the big companies on three-month loans. Each point represents a year between 1962 and 1993.

Source: Inflation rate: Fig. 22.1. Interest rate: *Bank of Canada Review,* CANSIM Series B14017.

rates. In the early 1970s, inflation began to increase, but it was not expected to increase much and certainly not to persist. As a result, nominal interest rates did not rise very much at that time. By the mid-1970s, there was a burst of unexpectedly high inflation. Interest rates increased somewhat, but not by nearly as much as the inflation rate. During the late 1970s and early 1980s, inflation of close to 10 percent a year came to be expected as an ongoing and highly persistent phenomenon. As a result, nominal interest rates increased to around 15 percent a year. In 1984 and 1985, the inflation rate fell—at first unexpectedly. Interest rates began to fall but not nearly as quickly as the inflation rate. They rose again in 1989 and 1990, mainly because the Bank of Canada was pursuing a disinflationary monetary policy, and then continued to fall into the 1990s.

THE TORONTO STAR, JUNE 3, 1993

Can't just cut interest rates to spur economy, Crow insists

By Shawn McCarthy

OTTAWA—The Bank of Canada can't simply reduce interest rates to spur the economy and reduce deficits as provincial finance ministers have demanded, bank governor John Crow says.

"It isn't that simple," Crow said yesterday after appearing before a House of Commons committee.

The key to lower interest rates is growing confidence among investors—both foreign and Canadian—that inflation will not erode their savings, Crow said.

"There are many factors that go into interest rates beside what the Bank of Canada does. But what we do does matter and the most important thing we can do is provide a money policy that people can trust so they are prepared to lend at lower interest rates."

At a meeting with federal Finance Minister Don Mazankowski this week, his provincial counterparts argued the central bank has not done enough to get interest rates down.

Ontario Treasurer Floyd Laughren said the provinces "need some help on the monetary side to stimulate economic growth and job creation."

Quebec Finance Minister Gerard D. Levesque said he will press Crow for lower rates when the central bank governor meets with provincial treasurers this fall.

"What we are expecting from the Bank of Canada is a monetary policy that is compatible with the economic situation. We have to realize that interest rates are too high," Levesque said.

The Bank of Canada rate—which sets the trend for a whole host of consumer and business rates—has dropped to 5.06 per cent from a high of 14.05 per cent in May 1990.

But critics say that with inflation almost non-existent, the real interest rate remains far too high for such a weak economy.

Crow said it would be improper for him to forecast interest rates, but added that "the less inflation there is, the more likely it is interest rates will be down."...

Provincial finance ministers have demanded that Bank of Canada governor John Crow cut interest rates.

Governor Crow's response:

◆ The Bank of Canada can't simply reduce interest rates to spur the economy and reduce deficits.

◆ Lower interest rates will result from the greater confidence low inflation gives investors.

◆ The most important thing the Bank can do is provide a monetary policy that people can trust so they are prepared to lend at lower interest rates.

Background and Analysis

In its bid to achieve price level stability in Canada, the Bank of Canada severely restricted the growth rate of the money supply in 1990 and forced up interest rates.

At the beginning of 1991 (see part (a) of the figure), the bank rate stood at 11 percent a year and the inflation rate, at 7 percent a year, was much higher than the Bank of Canada wanted to see it.

But the economy was also in recession and the Bank expected inflation to fall, so it eased its tight money policy and allowed the bank rate to fall somewhat.

The Bank of Canada's tight money policy eventually brought a dramatic drop in the inflation rate in early 1992. And the bank rate continued to fall.

By mid-1992, the inflation rate turned upward slightly and the Bank of Canada was quick to push the bank rate up sharply, but temporarily.

Throughout its attempts to squeeze inflation out of the Canadian economy, the Bank of Canada has permitted the *real* bank rate—bank rate minus the inflation rate—to rise to unusually high levels. And this situation is what has disturbed the provincial finance ministers in the news article.

But by mid-1993, with inflation tamed and interest rates down, the real bank rate was back down to its 1991 level.

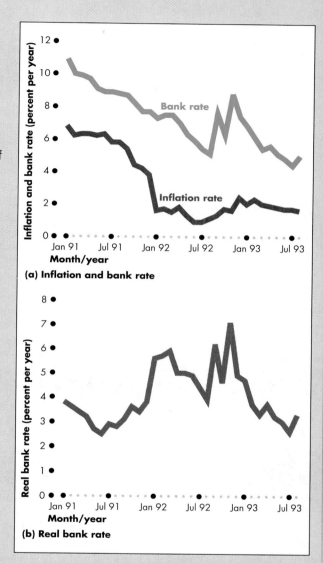

(a) Inflation and bank rate

(b) Real bank rate

The relationship between interest rates and the inflation rate is even more dramatically illustrated by international experience. For example, in recent years Chile has experienced an inflation rate of around 30 percent with nominal interest rates of about 40 percent. Brazil has experienced inflation rates of more than 200 percent a year with nominal interest rates also above 200 percent a year. At the other extreme, countries such as Japan and Belgium have low inflation and low nominal interest rates.

R E V I E W

An unanticipated inflation results in a fall in the real interest rate. An anticipated inflation results in an increase in the nominal interest rate and no change in the real interest rate. If most changes in the inflation rate are anticipated, the inflation rate and interest rates will move up and down together. This relationship is present in the Canadian data. ◆

The Politics of Inflation

We noted at the beginning of this chapter that inflation has plagued nations over many centuries, from the Roman Empire to modern Russia. (There are examples of inflation going back to the earliest civilizations.) What are the deeper sources of inflation that are common to all these vastly different societies? The answer lies in the political situation. There are three main political sources of inflation. They are

◆ Inflation tax

◆ Contest for income shares

◆ Errors in forecasting the natural unemployment rate

Let's look at each of these sources.

Inflation Tax

Inflation is not a tax in the usual sense. Governments don't pass inflation tax laws like income tax and sales tax laws. But inflation works just like a tax. One way in which a government can finance its expenditure is by selling bonds to the central bank. Not all governments have this privilege. In Canada, only the federal government does. It can get funds by selling bonds to the Bank of Canada. The provincial governments must sell their bonds to the public.

If the federal government sells bonds to the Bank of Canada, those bonds are paid for with new money—with an increase in the monetary base. When the government finances its expenditure this way, the quantity of money increases. So the government gets resources from inflation just as if it had increased taxes. And the holders of money pay this tax to the government. They do so because the real value of their money holdings decreases at a rate equal to the inflation rate.

Inflation is not used as a major source of tax revenue in Canada. But in some countries it is. The closing years of the Roman Empire and the transition years to a market economy in Russia and Eastern Europe are examples. In the case of the Roman Empire, the Empire had grown beyond its capacity to administer the collection of taxes on a scale sufficient to cover the expenditures of the government. In the case of Russia, the traditional source of government revenue was from state-owned enterprises. In the transition to a market economy, government revenue from these enterprises dried up, but expenditure commitments did not decline in line with this loss of revenue. In both cases, the inflation was used to finance expenditures.

In general, the inflation tax is used when conventional revenue sources are insufficient to cover expenditures and the larger the revenue shortfall, the larger is the inflation tax and the inflation rate.

Contest for Income Shares

Another possible political source of inflation is a contest among various groups for an increased share of the Gross Domestic Product. Suppose that one group with increased monopoly power over some factor of production exercises its power by increasing the price of the factor. The group might be a large labour union or an international cartel that controls a natural resource.

The initial effect of the factor price increase is stagflation. If the central bank responds with an increase in the money supply, prices rise, the monopoly's gain disappears, and the economy returns to full employment but at a higher price level. If the monopoly repeats its action, inflation ensues.

Inflation from this source will arise when there is a lack of consensus about the appropriate distribution of income and when there are changes in the degree of monopoly power of the owners of factors of production. This source of inflation probably occurs extremely rarely.

Errors in Forecasting the Natural Unemployment Rate

One objective of fiscal and monetary policy is to stabilize aggregate demand and keep the economy close to full employment. If demand increases too quickly, the economy overheats and inflation increases. If demand increases too slowly, recession occurs and inflation declines.

In judging the appropriate level of aggregate demand, the government and the Bank of Canada must make a judgment about long-run aggregate supply and the natural rate of unemployment. No one knows what the natural rate is, and its level must be estimated from the current state of the economy. When the natural rate of unemployment increases—and long-run aggregate supply grows at a slower rate—and when this change is not foreseen, aggregate demand grows too rapidly and the inflation rate increases. When the natural rate of unem-

ployment decreases—and long-run aggregate supply grows at a faster rate—and when this change is not foreseen, aggregate demand grows too slowly and the inflation rate decreases.

This source of changes in the inflation rate probably explains most of the *changes* in Canada's inflation rate during the past 30 years.

R E V I E W

Inflation stems from the political situation. Inflation is a source of government revenue—inflation is a tax. When conventional tax sources are inadequate, the inflation tax is used. Inflation could also arise as the outcome of a contest for bigger income shares among groups with some monopoly power. But most of the changes in inflation in Canada have resulted from changes in the natural unemployment rate—and changes in long-run aggregate supply—that could not be foreseen and that resulted in fiscal and monetary policies that were seen after the event to be inappropriate. ◆

◆ ◆ ◆ ◆ We have now completed our study of inflation and the relationships among the inflation rate, the unemployment rate, and the interest rate. Our next task, which we'll pursue in Chapter 32, is to see how the aggregate demand-aggregate supply model that we have used to study inflation also helps us to explore and interpret fluctuations in real GDP and explain recessions and depressions.

S U M M A R Y

Inflation and the Price Level

Inflation is a process of persistently rising prices. The price level rises when the inflation rate is positive and falls when the inflation rate is negative. The price level rises *faster* when the inflation rate *increases* and *slower* when the inflation rate *decreases*. Inflation can result from either rising aggregate demand or falling aggregate supply. The consequences of inflation depend on which of these

sources it springs from and whether it is *anticipated* or *unanticipated*. (p. 862)

Demand–Pull Inflation

Demand-pull inflation arises from increasing aggregate demand. Its origin can be any of the factors that shift the aggregate demand curve rightward. The main such factors are an increasing money supply, increasing government purchases of goods and services, and rising prices in the rest of the world. When the aggregate demand curve shifts rightward, other things remaining the same, both real GDP and the GDP deflator increase and unemployment falls. With a shortage of labour, wages begin to increase and the short-run aggregate supply curve shifts leftward, raising the GDP deflator still more and decreasing real GDP.

If aggregate demand continues to increase, the aggregate demand curve keeps shifting rightward and the price level keeps on rising. Wages respond, aggregate demand increases again, and a price-wage inflation spiral ensues. (pp. 862–865)

Supply Inflation and Stagflation

Cost-push inflation can result from any factor that decreases aggregate supply, but the main such factors are increasing wage rates and increasing prices of key raw materials. These sources of a decreasing aggregate supply bring increasing costs that shift the short-run aggregate supply curve leftward. Firms decrease the quantity of labour employed and cut back production. Real GDP declines and the price level rises. If no action is taken to increase aggregate demand, the economy remains below full employment until the initial price increase that triggered the stagflation is reversed.

Action by the Bank of Canada or the government to restore full employment (an increase in the money supply or in government purchases of goods and services or a tax cut) increases aggregate demand and shifts the aggregate demand curve rightward, resulting in a higher price level and higher real GDP. If the original source of cost-push inflation is still present, costs rise again and the short-run aggregate supply curve shifts leftward again. If the Bank of Canada or the government responds with another increase in aggregate demand, the price level rises even higher. Inflation proceeds at a rate determined by the cost-push forces. (pp. 865–867)

Anticipating Inflation

The decisions made by firms and households to produce and work are based on forecasts of inflation. But the actual levels of real GDP, real wages, and employment depend on actual inflation. Errors in forecasting inflation are costly and people have an incentive to anticipate inflation as accurately as possible.

Forecasters use data and statistical models to generate expectations and economists predict people's forecasts by using the rational expectations hypothesis—the hypothesis that inflation forecasts are made by using the aggregate demand-aggregate supply model together with all the available information on the positions of the aggregate demand and aggregate supply curves.

When changes in aggregate demand are correctly anticipated, inflation is anticipated, and if its rate is moderate, it does not affect real GDP, real wages, or employment. But a rapid anticipated inflation decreases long-run aggregate supply, real wages, and employment. (pp. 867–873)

Inflation over the Business Cycle: The Phillips Curve

Phillips curves describe the relationships between inflation and unemployment. The short-run Phillips curve shows the relationship between inflation and unemployment, holding constant the expected inflation rate and the natural rate of unemployment. The long-run Phillips curve shows the relationship between inflation and unemployment when the actual inflation rate equals the expected inflation rate. The short-run Phillips curve slopes downward—the lower the unemployment rate, the higher is the inflation rate, other things remaining the same. The long-run Phillips curve is vertical at the natural rate of unemployment—the natural rate hypothesis.

Changes in aggregate demand, with a constant expected inflation rate and natural rate of unemployment bring movements along the short-run Phillips curve. Changes in expected inflation bring shifts in the short-run Phillips curve. Changes in the natural rate of unemployment bring shifts in both the short-run and long-run Phillips curves.

There is no clear relationship between inflation and unemployment in Canada, but the joint movements in those variables can be interpreted in terms of a shifting short-run Phillips curve. (pp. 873–878)

Interest Rates and Inflation

Expectations of inflation affect nominal interest rates. The higher the expected inflation rate, the higher is the nominal interest rate. Borrowers will willingly pay more and lenders will successfully demand more, as the anticipated inflation rate rises.

Borrowing and lending and asset-holding plans are made consistent by adjustments in the real interest rate—the difference between the nominal interest rate and the expected inflation rate. (pp. 879–882)

The Politics of Inflation

Inflation is one source of revenue for the government—it is a tax—and its rate increases when the government has financial needs that exceed its ability to collect income taxes and sales taxes. Inflation can also arise from a contest for a bigger income share among groups with monopoly power. This source of inflation is uncommon. The most common source of inflation in Canada in recent years is errors in forecasting the natural unemployment rate. No one knows the magnitude of the natural unemployment rate, and its level must be estimated from the current state of the economy. Unforeseen increases in the natural rate of unemployment bring an increase in the inflation rate. (pp. 882–883)

KEY ELEMENTS

Key Terms

Anticipated inflation, 862
Cost-push inflation, 865
Demand-pull inflation, 862
Long-run Phillips curve, 874
Phillips curve, 873
Rational expectation, 869
Short-run Phillips curve, 873
Unanticipated inflation, 862

Key Figures

Figure 31.1   Demand–Pull Inflation, 863

Figure 31.2   A Price–Wage Inflation Spiral, 864
Figure 31.3   Cost–Push Inflation, 866
Figure 31.5   A Cost–Price Inflation Spiral, 867
Figure 31.6   Rational Expectation of the Price Level, 870
Figure 31.7   Anticipated Inflation, 871
Figure 31.8   The Short-Run Phillips Curve, 874
Figure 31.9   The Short-Run and Long-Run Phillips Curves, 874
Figure 31.12   Money Growth, Inflation, and the Interest Rate, 879
Figure 31.13   Inflation and the Interest Rate, 881

REVIEW QUESTIONS

1 Distinguish between the price level and the inflation rate.

2 Distinguish between anticipated and unanticipated inflation.

3 Distinguish between demand-pull inflation and cost-push inflation.

4 Explain how a price-cost inflation spiral occurs.

5 Explain how a cost-price inflation spiral occurs.

6 Why are wrong inflation expectations costly? Suggest some of the losses that an individual would suffer in labour markets and in asset markets.

7 What is a rational expectation? Explain the two features of a rational expectation.

8 What is the rational expectation of the price in
a   The short run?

b   The long run?

9 Explain how anticipated inflation arises.

10 What are the main factors leading to changes in aggregate demand that produce ongoing and persistent inflation?

11 How does a change in the quantity of money influence the interest rate
a   When it changes once and is unanticipated?
b   When its change is ongoing and anticipated?

12 What is the connection between expected inflation and nominal interest rates?

13 What does the short-run Phillips curve show?

14 What does the long-run Phillips curve show?

15 What have been the main shifts in the Canadian short-run Phillips curve during the 1970s, 1980s, and 1990s?

P R O B L E M S

1 Work out the effects on the price level of the following unexpected events:

a   An increase in the money supply
b   An increase in government purchases of goods and services
c   An increase in income taxes
d   An increase in investment demand
e   An increase in the wage rate
f   An increase in labour productivity

2 Work out the effects on the price level of the same events listed in problem 1 when they are correctly anticipated.

3 An economy's long-run aggregate supply is $4 billion, and it has the following expected aggregate demand and short-run aggregate supply curves:

Price level (GDP deflator)	Expected GDP demanded	Expected GDP supplied
	(billions of 1986 dollars)	
80	5	1
100	4	3
130	3	5
150	2	7

a   What is the expected price level?
b   What is expected real GDP?
c   Are wages expected to be fixed?

4 In the economy of problem 3, the expected price level increases to 130.

a   What is the new *SAS* curve in the short run when wages are fixed?
b   What is the new *SAS* curve in the long run when wages are flexible?
c   In parts (a) and (b), is real GDP expected to be above or below full employment?

5 In 1992, the expected aggregate demand schedule for 1993 is as follows:

Price level (GDP deflator)	Expected real GDP demanded (billions of 1986 dollars)
130	4.0
121	3.9
122	3.8
123	3.7
124	3.6

In 1992, the long-run real GDP is $3.8 billion and the real GDP expected for 1993 is $3.9 billion. Calculate the 1992 rational expectation of the price level for 1993 if the money wage rate

a   Is not expected to change.
b   Is expected to change to its long-run equilibrium level.

6 The economy in problem 5 has the following short-run aggregate supply schedule:

Price level (GDP deflator)	Real GDP supplied (billions of 1986 dollars)
130	3.2
121	3.5
122	3.8
123	4.1
124	4.4

a   Under what conditions is this short-run aggregate supply schedule consistent with your answer to problem 5?
b   Calculate the actual and expected inflation rate if the aggregate demand curve is expected to shift upward by 10 percent and if it actually does shift upward by that amount.

7 An economy has a natural rate of unemployment of 4 percent when its expected inflation is 6 percent. Its inflation and unemployment history is

Inflation rate (percent per year)	Unemployment rate (percentage of the labour force)
10	2
8	3
6	4
4	5
2	6

a   Draw a diagram of this economy's short-run and long-run Phillips curves.
b   If the actual inflation rate rises from 6 percent a year to 8 percent a year, what is the change in the unemployment rate? Explain why.
c   If the natural rate of unemployment rises to 5 percent, what is the change in the unemployment rate? Explain why it occurs.
d   In part (a), if the expected inflation rate falls to 4 percent a year, what is the change in the unemployment rate? Explain why.

CHAPTER 32

RECESSIONS
AND
DEPRESSIONS

After studying this chapter, you will be able to

◆ Describe the origins of Canada's 1990 recession

◆ Describe the course of expenditure, interest rates, and money as the economy contracts

◆ Describe the labour market in recession

◆ Compare and contrast the sticky wage and flexible wage theories of the labour market in recession

◆ Describe the onset of the Great Depression in 1929

◆ Describe the economy in the depths of the Great Depression between 1929 and 1933

◆ Compare the economy of the 1930s with that of today and assess the likelihood of another Great Depression

N OCTOBER 1929, AN UNPRECEDENTED STOCK MARKET crash signalled the start of the Great Depression. Overnight, the values of stocks and shares trading on Wall Street and Bay Street and in London, Paris, and Berlin fell by 30 percent. The four succeeding years witnessed the most severe economic contraction in recorded history. By 1933, real GDP had fallen by 30 percent and unemployment had increased to 20 percent of the labour force. What caused the Great Depression? ◆ ◆ In October 1987, the world's stock markets crashed again. The crash was so steep and widespread that it was dubbed a stock market "meltdown"—conjuring up images of Three Mile Island and Chernobyl. This stock market crash caused some commentators to draw parallels between 1987 and 1929. Are there similar forces at work today that might bring about a Great Depression in the 1990s? ◆ ◆ We experienced a serious recession in 1990. Real GDP fell by 3 percent

What Goes Up Must Come Down

and unemployment increased to 10 percent. In 1991 and 1992, real GDP began to grow but so slowly that unemployment continued to climb those years to a peak of 11.5 percent. What caused the 1990 recession and the sluggish recovery from it? Are all recessions triggered in the same way or is there a variety of causes?

◆ ◆ ◆ ◆ In this chapter, we'll use the macroeconomic tools we've studied in the previous chapters to explain economic contractions. We're going to unravel some of the mysteries of recession and depression and assess the likelihood of a serious depression such as that of the 1930s occurring again.

The Canadian Economy in the 1990s

The Canadian economy is experiencing hard times in the 1990s. How hard can be seen in Fig. 32.1. After almost a decade of expansion, real GDP reached a peak in the first quarter of 1990, and by the end of 1992 real GDP had not returned to that level. The contraction that lasted for a full year was a *recession*—a period of at least two quarters of falling real GDP. After the first quarter of 1991, Canada was technically not in a recession because real GDP was growing again. But the Canadian economy remained in a *depressed state*—real GDP was below its previous peak and unemployment continued to increase.

Figure 32.2 shows the seriousness of the situation. You can see in part (a) how real GDP per person has evolved during the 1990s and, in part (b), what has happened to unemployment. With the exception of one quarter in 1991, real GDP per person has *fallen* every quarter since the beginning of 1989. And from the beginning of 1990 to the end of 1992, unemployment increased every quarter.

FIGURE 32.1

Real GDP: 1989–1992

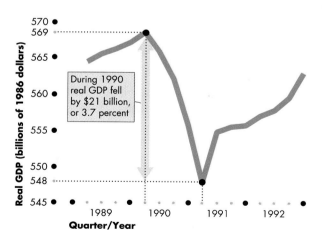

Real GDP reached a peak of $569 billion (1986 dollars) in the first quarter of 1990 and then began a year of decline during which it fell by 3 percent to $548 billion. Even after the recession was technically over and real GDP began to grow again, the growth rate was low and at the end of 1992 real GDP remained below its peak 1989 value.

Source: Statistics Canada, CANSIM series D20463.

FIGURE 32.2

Canada's 1990s Depression

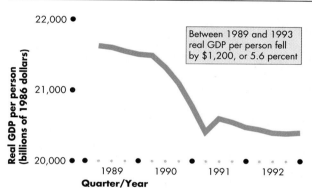

(a) Real GDP per person

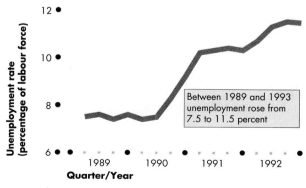

(b) Unemployment

The Canadian economy remained in a depressed state through 1992. Real GDP per person (part a) declined steadily each quarter from the beginning of 1989 to the end of 1992 with one exception (the second quarter of 1991). The unemployment rate (part b) kept on rising through 1991 and 1992 even though real GDP increased through these years.

Sources: Statistics Canada, Real GDP per person is CANSIM series D20463 divided by CANSIM series D1, and the unemployment rate is CANSIM series D767611.

We're going to study the origins of and mechanisms at work during Canada's 1990 recession and the forces that are preventing the economy from making a normal-speed recovery. We'll pay special attention to the labour market and to the central disagreement among economists about how the labour market works during an economic contraction. Let's begin with the origins of the 1990 recession.

The Origins of the 1990 Recession

Some recessions have their origins in shocks to aggregate supply, some in shocks to aggregate demand, and some in a combination of these shocks. Three forces were at work in Canada during 1990 that appear to have contributed to the recession and subsequent sluggish growth. They are

◆ The Bank of Canada's policy of price stability

◆ The Canada–United States Free Trade Agreement

◆ A slowdown in economic expansion in the United States

The Bank of Canada's Policy of Price Stability The Bank of Canada began to pursue the goal of price stability in 1988 (see Talking with John Crow on pp. 911–914). But because of the time lags involved in the operation of monetary policy, the policy began to bite in 1989 and to bite hard in 1990. The best evidence available suggests that the long-term effects of price stability will be extremely beneficial to Canadians. But its short-term effects are costly.

To achieve price stability, the Bank of Canada must slow the growth rate of the money supply. The extent to which the Bank did slow money growth can be seen in Fig. 32.3. The growth rate of the narrow definition of money, M1, slowed in 1989 and became negative—the quantity of money fell—during 1990. The growth rate of the broad definition of money, M2+, slowed more gently.

The Canada-United States Free Trade Agreement The first tariff cuts under the free trade agreement with the United States occurred on January 1, 1989, and the second phase of cuts came a year later. The gradual elimination of tariffs on most of Canada's trade with the United States will result in a rationalization of production activities on both sides of the border. The long-term effects of this rationalization are expected to be beneficial to Canada (and the

FIGURE 32.3

Money Supply Growth: 1989–1992

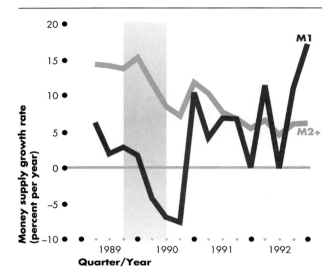

The Bank of Canada began to pursue the goal of price stability in 1988, and the money supply growth rate began to slow during 1989 and slowed even further during 1990. The narrow definition of money, M1, actually declined during 1990—its growth rate became negative.

Source: Bank of Canada, M1 is CANSIM series B1627 and M2+ is CANSIM series B1633.

United States). But like the Bank of Canada's price stability policy, tariff cuts impose costs in the short term. These costs arise because, initially, tariff cuts destroy more jobs that they create. Production cutbacks in the contracting sectors precedes production increases in the expanding sectors. The result is a temporary decrease in both short-run and long-run aggregate supply as structural unemployment increases.

The elimination of tariffs changes the profitability of businesses, bringing gains to some industries and firms and losses to others. It is easy to see who the immediate winners and losers are. But it is difficult to predict where the gains and losses will ultimately be when the new tariff structure has been in place for some time. As a result, tariff cuts bring an increase in uncertainty that decreases investment which, in turn, decreases aggregate supply.

A Slowdown in Economic Expansion in the United States   After its longest-ever period of peacetime expansion, U.S. real GDP growth began to slow in 1989 and 1990 and the United States went into recession in mid-1990, a quarter of a year behind Canada. You can see the performance of real GDP growth in the United States (and Canada) by looking at Fig. 32.4. You can see that the U.S. recession not only lagged behind Canada's recession but was also less severe than Canada's. Also, the U.S. recovery during 1991 and 1992 was more rapid than Canada's.

The slowdown of the U.S. economy brought slower growth in the demand for Canada's exports and resulted in lower export prices and lower export volumes.

These first two influences on Canada's 1990 recession operate by changing aggregate demand. The third influence, which we'll now examine, operates on both aggregate demand and aggregate supply.

Let's see how the events we've just described influenced the Canadian economy in 1990.

Aggregate Demand and Aggregate Supply in the 1990 Recession

The Canadian economy in the first quarter of 1990, on the eve of the 1990 recession, is shown in Fig. 32.5. The aggregate demand curve was AD_0 and the short-run aggregate supply curve was SAS_0. Real GDP was $569 billion, and the price level was 117.

The 1990 recession was caused by a decrease in both aggregate demand and aggregate supply. Aggregate demand decreased, initially, because of the slowdown in the growth rate of the quantity of

FIGURE 32.5

The 1990 Recession

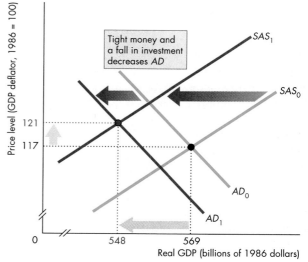

At the beginning of 1990, the economy was on its aggregate demand curve AD_0 and its short-run aggregate supply curve SAS_0, with real GDP at $569 billion and a GDP deflator of 117. Sectoral reallocations resulting from the Canada–United States Free Trade Agreement together with increases in the money wage rate decreased aggregate supply. The short-run aggregate supply curve shifted leftward to SAS_1. A decrease in the real quantity of money, a slowdown in the growth rate of the U.S. economy, and increased uncertainty and lowered profit expectations decreased aggregate demand. The aggregate demand curve shifted leftward to AD_1. The combination of a decrease in both aggregate supply and aggregate demand put the economy into recession. Real GDP decreased to $548 billion and the price level increased to 121.

FIGURE 32.4

U.S. and Canadian Real GDP Growth: 1989–1992

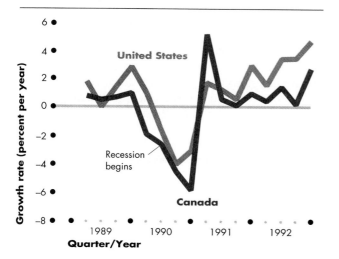

The United States had a recession in 1990, but Canada's recession preceded that in the United States by one quarter. The Canadian recession was deeper than that in the United States, and with the exception of the first quarter of 1991, the Canadian real GDP growth rate has remained below that of the United States.

Sources: Statistics Canada, CANSIM series D20463, and *Economic Report of the President,* 1993, Table B-3, p. 350.

money. This initial source was soon afterwards reinforced by the slowdown in the U.S. economy that brought a decline in the growth of exports. These two factors together with increased uncertainty arising from tariff cuts triggered a massive decline in investment. The resulting decrease in aggregate demand is shown by the shift of the aggregate demand curve leftward to AD_1. Aggregate supply decreased partly because of the effects of the free trade agreement and partly because money wages continued to increase throughout 1990 at a rate similar to that in 1989. This decrease in aggregate supply is shown in Fig. 32.5 as the shift in the short-run aggregate supply curve leftward to SAS_1. (The figure does not show the long-run aggregate supply curve.)

The effect of the decreases in aggregate supply and aggregate demand was a decrease in real GDP to $548 billion—a 3 percent decrease—and an increase in the price level to 121, a 3.4 percent increase.

Let's now look a bit more deeply at the forces that created the 1990 recession by going behind the aggregate demand and aggregate supply curves. We'll begin with aggregate demand.

Expenditure in the 1990 Recession

When the economy is in a recession, real GDP falls and real aggregate expenditure also falls. (Recall that real GDP and real aggregate expenditure are equal to each other.) Table 32.1 shows the components of aggregate expenditure in the first quarter of 1990 on the eve of the recession and the first quarter of 1991, when real GDP was at its lowest level.

You can see in the table that the largest component of aggregate expenditure is consumption

expenditure. During a recession, consumption expenditure falls, but usually it falls along a stable *consumption function*. The numbers in the table and the points plotted in Fig. 32.6(a) show that during Canada's 1990 recession, consumption expenditure remained very close to a consumption function in which the *marginal propensity to consume out of real GDP* was constant at 0.6.

The main component of aggregate expenditure that falls during a recession is investment. Investment falls for two reasons: interest rates increase, and profit expectations worsen. Figure 32.6(b) shows these two forces at work during the 1990 recession. In 1989, the *investment demand curve* was ID_{89}. When the real interest rate fell in the second quarter of 1989, the economy moved down along the investment demand curve. As the real interest rate increased in the second half of 1989, the economy moved back up the investment demand curve. In 1990, the investment demand curve shifted leftward as profit expectations declined. A further increase in the real interest rate during 1991 brought a movement up the new (lower) investment demand curve .

The decrease in investment from its peak in the second quarter of 1989 to its lowest value in the fourth quarter of 1990 was $23 billion—a decline of 19 percent. Such a decrease in investment has two effects. First, it decreases aggregate expenditure and aggregate demand. Second, it slows down the growth rate of the capital stock and the pace of innovation of new technologies. This aspect of the investment slowdown feeds back to slow down the growth of aggregate supply. But the effect of decreased investment on aggregate demand dominates.

TABLE 32.1

Aggregate Expenditure during the 1990 Recession

Year (quarter)	Real GDP			Components of aggregate expenditure						
				(billions of 1986 dollars)						
	Y	**= C**	**+**	**I**	**+**	**G**	**+**	**EX**	**–**	**IM**
1990(1)	569	= 341	+	113	+	129	+	161	–	177
1991(1)	548	= 329	+	104	+	129	+	158	–	17
Change	–21	= –12	+	–9	+	0	+	–3	–	–5
Percentage change	–3.7	= –3.5	+	–8.0	+	0	+	–1.9	–	–2.8

Source: Bank of Canada Review, Winter 1992–1993, Table H2.

FIGURE 32.6

Consumption and Investment: 1989–1992

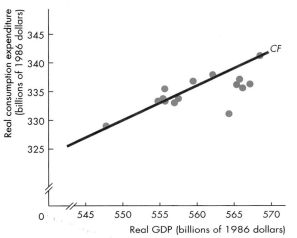

(a) The consumption function

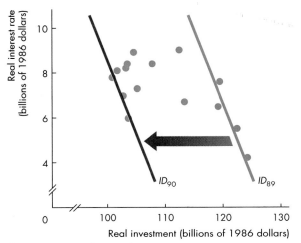

(b) Investment demand

Consumption expenditure (part a) remained remarkably close to the levels predicted by a stable consumption function. Consumption increased (decreased) when real GDP increased (decreased). These changes are described as movements along the consumption function. Investment (part b) changed because of changes in the real interest rate—movements along the investment demand curve—and because profit expectations changed—shifts in the investment demand curve.

Sources: Real GDP is CANSIM series D20463, consumption expenditure is CANSIM series D20488, investment is the sum of CANSIM series D20469, D20470, and D20471 plus the change in inventories, and the real interest rate is CANSIM series B14048 minus the annual percentage change in CANSIM series D20556. The consumption function and the investment demand curve are based on our assumptions and calculations.

The Money Market in the 1990 Recession

We've seen that the money supply growth rate slowed down in 1989 and that M1 actually decreased during 1990. We've also seen that the real interest rate increased. The increase in the real interest rate occurred partly because the inflation rate decreased, but also because the lower money supply increased the nominal interest rate. Figure 32.7 shows the money market during the 1990 recession and explains why the nominal interest rate increased.

In 1988, the *demand for money curve* was MD_{88}, the real money supply was MS_{88}, and the equilibrium interest rate was 9 percent a year. Between 1988 and 1989, the interest rate increased to 12 percent a year. This increase was the result of two forces. First, rising incomes increased the demand for money and the demand for money curve shifted rightward to MD_{89}. Second, the quantity of money increased, but at a pace slower than the price level. As a result, the *real* quantity of money decreased and the supply of money curve shifted leftward to MS_{89}. Because the demand for money increased, a small decrease in the supply of money was sufficient to result in a large increase in interest rates.

Between 1989 and 1990, interest rates increased again, but by only 1 percentage point to 13 percent a year. The quantity of real money decreased and the supply of money curve shifted leftward to MS_{90}—a much larger decrease than that of a year earlier. But in 1990, real GDP decreased so the demand for money also decreased. The demand for money curve shifted leftward to MD_{90}.

You can now work backwards through Figs. 32.7, 32.6, and 32.5 and see how the recession developed. Starting in Fig. 32.7, a decrease in the quantity of real money brought an increase in the interest rate. Both nominal and real interest rates increased and, in Fig. 32.6(b), investment decreased. The slowdown in the U.S. economy and the reallocation resulting from the tariff changes under the free trade agreement brought a further decline in investment, seen in Fig. 32.6(b) as a leftward shift in the investment demand curve. With a fall in investment, real GDP began to decrease. The fall in incomes decreased consumption expenditure, seen in Fig. 32.6(a). All these influences on aggregate demand shift the aggregate demand curve leftward in Fig. 32.5.

One of the main reasons people fear recession is because it brings high unemployment. What happens in the labour market during a recession? Why does unemployment increase?

FIGURE 32.7

The Money Market in 1990 Recession

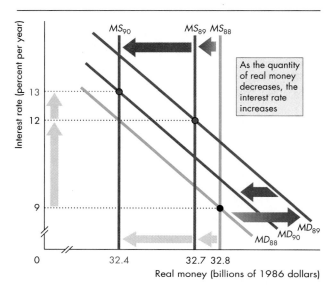

In 1988, the money supply curve was MS_{88} and the demand for money curve was MD_{88}. The interest rate was 9 percent. During 1989, the Bank of Canada slowed the growth rate of the money supply to a pace below the inflation rate, and the real money supply (M1 definition) decreased. The money supply curve shifted leftward to MS_{89}. Growing real income increased the demand for money, and the demand curve for money shifted rightward to MD_{89}. The interest rate, determined at the intersection of MD_{89} and MS_{89}, increased to 12 percent a year. In 1990, the Bank of Canada slowed the money supply growth rate even more and the money supply curve shifted leftward again to MS_{90}. In that year, *falling* real GDP decreased the demand for money and the demand curve shifted leftward to MD_{90}. The interest rate increased yet again, to 13 percent a year.

The Labour Market in the 1990s

In Fig. 32.2(b), the unemployment rate increased persistently from the beginning of 1990 to the end of 1992. Figure 32.8 shows two other facts about the labour market during this period—facts about employment and the real wage rate. The figure shows that employment hours (measured as billions of hours a year) are like a mirror image of the unemployment rate. While the unemployment rate increased, total hours worked fell. But throughout this process of rising unemployment and falling work hours, the real wage rate relentlessly increased.

There is controversy about how the labour market works and about its ability to act as a coordination mechanism to bring about an equality between the quantities of labour demanded and supplied. Let's see how we can interpret the events occurring in the Canadian labour market in the 1990s by using the sticky wage theory and the flexible wage theory.

Sticky Wage Theory

Figure 32.9 illustrates the sticky wage theory of the labour market. In the first quarter of 1990, the labour market operated at the point of intersection of LD_{90} and LS. The quantity of labour supplied and demanded was 23 billion hours and the wage rate was $13.65 an hour. There was some unemployment (not shown in the figure) but that unemployment

FIGURE 32.8

Employment and Real Wages: 1989–1992

Employment, measured on the right axis, was steady during 1989 at close to 23 billion hours a year. It then declined through the following two years to less than 22 billion hours a year. While employment was falling, real wages (measured on the left axis) were persistently rising.

Sources: Employment is Total Actual Hours Worked (all jobs) Canada, *Historical Labour Force Statistics,* Catalogue 71-201, p. 63. (The data were multiplied by 52 to give hours per year.) The real wage rate is CANSIM series D20002, Wages, salaries and supplementary labour income, deflated by CANSIM series D20556, the GDP deflator, and divided by the above hours variable.

FIGURE 32.9

The Labour Market in the 1990s: A Rigid Wage Interpretation

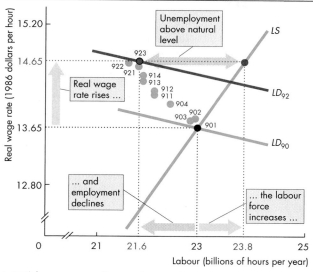

(a) Sticky wages and unemployment

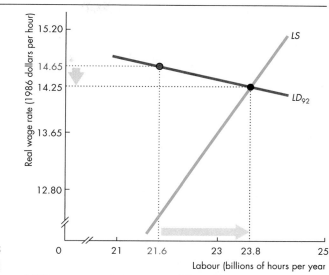

(b) Wage cut needed to restore full employment

The demand for labour curve in 1990 was LD_{90}. The supply curve in the first quarter of 1990 was *LS*. Wages and employment were at the intersection of LD_{90} and *LS* with a real wage rate of $13.65 an hour and 23 billion hours of labour being demanded and supplied. By 1992, increases in the marginal productivity of labour had increased the demand for labour and shifted the demand curve rightward to LD_{92}. The supply of labour remained constant (we assume) at *LS*. A money wage growth rate that exceeded the inflation rate increased the real wage rate to

$14.65 an hour. Employment decreased to 21.6 billion hours but the quantity of labour supplied increased to 23.8 billion hours. The difference between the quantity of labour demanded and the quantity supplied is the unemployment gap—the extent to which unemployment exceeds its natural rate.

Part (b) shows that a cut in the money rate to $14.25 an hour is necessary to reduce unemployment to its natural rate and restore full employment.

---

was frictional and the unemployment rate was equal to the natural rate.

Over the next three years, the demand for labour increased and the demand curve shifted rightward. Each of the blue dots in part (a) shows the real wage rate and employment level for the identified quarter. For example, the dot labelled 904 marks the employment level and the real wage rate in the fourth quarter of 1990. Each of these dots is on a demand curve for labour. By the end of 1992, the demand curve had shifted to LD_{92}.

The forces that increased the demand for labour over this period were the accumulation of capital and technological progress that increased the marginal product of labour. These forces produced an upward shift in the *short-run aggregate production function* as well as the rightward shift in the

demand for labour curve that we've just seen. The short-run aggregate production function and the demand for labour curve did not shift in a smooth way, changing by the same amount each quarter. In some quarters, such as the fourth quarter of 1990, the shift was large, while in other quarters, such as the third quarter of 1990, there was no shift. You can see these facts in the figure by noticing that the points labelled 902 and 903 are almost on top of each other (no shift), while the point labelled 904 lies above those points.

Over the period covered in Fig. 32.9, the labour force grew somewhat, but we'll *assume* that the labour supply curve remained at *LS*.

Figure 32.9(a) shows the situation at the end of 1992. The money wage rate had increased by 17 percent over its level in the first quarter of

1990, the price level had increased by 9 percent, and the real wage rate had increased by 8 percent to $14.65 an hour.

At this real wage rate, and with the demand for labour curve at LD_{92}, the quantity of labour demanded was 21.6 billion hours a year, 1.4 billion hours a year less than in the first quarter of 1990. The quantity of labour supplied *increased*—there was a movement along the supply of labour curve—from 23 billion hours a year to 23.8 billion hours a year, an increase of 0.8 billion hours a year.

The combined effect of a decrease in the quantity of labour demanded and an increase in the quantity supplied created an excess supply of labour of 2.2 billion hours a year—23.8 billion supplied minus 21.6 billion hours demanded.

The sticky wage theory regards the real wage rate as inflexible and incapable of changing by enough to maintain full employment. Figure 32.9(b) shows the wage change necessary to restore full employment. Here, if the real wage rate had increased to only $14.25, the quantity of labour demanded would have been 23.8 billion hours a year, the same quantity that is supplied at this real wage rate.[1]

Let's now see how the flexible wage theory interprets the labour market in the 1990s.

Flexible Wage Theory

Changes in economic aggregates such as the natural unemployment rate or total employment hours hide the deeper changes in the *structure* of the labour market. To interpret the changes in real wages and employment with a flexible wage theory, we must look behind the aggregates and examine these deeper changes.

The Structure of Employment and Unemployment

Figure 32.10 shows some of the changes that have taken place in employment in different parts of the economy. The horizontal axis measures the percentage change in employment between the first quarter of 1990 and the fourth quarter of 1992—the period during which the national unemployment rate was rising, the real wage rate was rising, and employment was declining. The vertical

axis measures the average unemployment rate over this same period. Each point in the figure refers to a sector. For example, the point labelled "construction" tells us that in the construction sector, employment fell by almost 2 percent and the unemployment rate was almost 22 percent. You can see that this sector has the highest unemployment rate and is the one in which employment contracted most. Other primary industries and manufacturing are also sectors that contracted quickly and have high unemployment rates. At the other extreme, finance, insurance, and real estate, agriculture, and community, business, and personal services, expanded employment and the unemployment rate was low.

Jobs are steadily disappearing in the declining sectors, new jobs are being created in the expanding sectors, and people are constantly on the move

FIGURE 32.10

Sectoral Unemployment and Changes in Employment

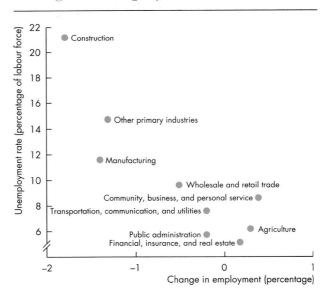

The sectors in which employment declines fastest, such as construction, other primary industries, and manufacturing, are the ones with the highest unemployment rate. The expanding sectors such as finance, insurance, and real estate, agriculture, and community, business, and personal services are the ones with the lowest unemployment rate.

Source: *Historical Labour Force Statistics*, Catalogue 71-201, pp. 48-51, and 427-30.

---

[1] The numbers here are the result of our assumptions about the degree of responsiveness of the quantities of labour demanded and supplied to a change in the real wage rate. Different assumptions give different numerical answers.

between the sectors. Let's see how the labour market copes with these changes and how, even with flexible wages, persistent unemployment can arise.

Two Labour Markets—Declining and Expanding

To study the forces at work in the labour market we need to look at both the expanding sectors and the declining sectors. We miss the action if we study only an aggregate labour market. Figure 32.11 shows two labour markets—one is expanding and the other is declining. Part (a) shows the labour market in the declining sectors and part (b) the expanding sectors. Initially, the two markets are of equal size (an assumption that makes it easier to learn how these markets work and how they relate to the national aggregates and averages).

Labour Supply in a Declining Sector   In a declining sector, jobs are constantly disappearing. The people who lose jobs have skills—human capital—that are specific to the jobs they've lost and of little value in the new expanding sectors. These people have a greater incentive to spend time searching for a new job in their old sector than to look for a job for which they know they are not trained in the expanding sector. But they believe that their skills are worth the wage rate they have recently earned and are not willing to take a job that pays much less, and they spend time searching for a job that is similar to the one they've lost. So, in the declining sectors, the quantity of labour supplied is highly responsive to a change in the real wage rate—a small percentage decrease in the real wage rate results in a large percentage

---

FIGURE 32.11

Labour Markets in the 1990s: Flexible Wage Interpretation

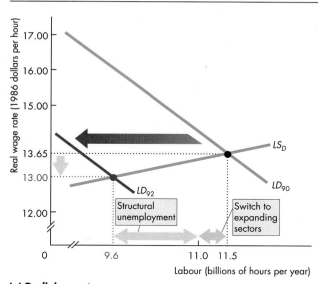

(a) Declining sectors

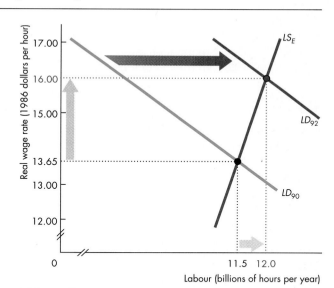

(a) Expanding sectors

The economy has two labour markets—the declining sectors and the expanding sectors. In part (a), the supply curve in the declining sectors is LS_D and, in part (b), the supply curve in the expanding sectors is LS_E. The demand curves for labour in 1990 in the two sectors are LD_{90} (in both parts). In 1990, the real wage rates were $13.65 in both sectors and employment was 11.5 billion hours in each sector. By 1992, the demand for labour had fallen in the declining sector and the demand curve had shifted leftward to LD_{92} in part (a). The real wage rate fell to $13.00 an hour and employment fell by 1.9 billion hours to 9.6 billion

hours a year. Over the same period, the demand for labour increased in the expanding sectors and the demand curve shifted rightward to LD_{92} in part (b). The real wage rate increased to $16.00 an hour, but employment increased by only 0.5 billion hours to 12 billion hours a year.

For the economy in aggregate, the real wage rate increased to $14.65 (the weighted average of the wages in the two sectors of the economy) and employment decreased by 1.4 billion hours. This decrease in employment was an increase in structural unemployment, as indicated in part (a).

decrease in the quantity of labour supplied. The supply curve LS_D in Fig. 32.11(a) reflects this fact.

Labour Supply in an Expanding Sector   In an expanding sector, jobs are constantly being created. The people who get those jobs must be attracted from other sectors and must have the desired skills—human capital. In some cases, they must be compensated for changing their geographical locations. So, in the expanding sector, a large percentage increase in the real wage rate is needed to bring forth a small percentage increase in the quantity of labour supplied. The supply curve LS_E in Fig. 32.11(b) reflects this fact.

Now let's see how these markets work to determine the wage rates and employment levels.

Demand, Equilibrium, and Change   Initially, the demand curves are LD_{90} in each labour market, and the two markets are in equilibrium at a real wage rate of $13.65 an hour and an employment level of 11.5 billion hours. Aggregate employment is 23 billion hours (2 x 11.5), and the average real wage rate is the same as in each market.

Now look at what happens when there is a change in the demand for labour such as occurred in Canada during 1990-1992. In the declining sector, the demand for labour decreases and the demand curve shifts leftward to LD_{92} in Fig. 32.11(a). The real wage rate falls, but not by much. Its equilibrium level is $13.00 an hour. The quantity of labour employed falls to 9 billion hours a year.

In the expanding sector, the demand for labour increases and the demand curve shifts rightward to LD_{92} in Fig. 32.11(b). The real wage rate increases to $16.00 an hour, and employment increases to 12 billion hours a year.

The average real wage rate is $14.65—a wage rate of $13.00 an hour for those in the declining sector (now 45 percent of the labour force) and $16.00 an hour for those in the expanding sector (now 55 percent of the labour force).

Aggregate employment decreases because the decrease in employment in the declining sector exceeds the increase in employment in the expanding sector. The people who lose their jobs in the declining sector fall into two groups. One group successfully switches to the expanding sector and to new jobs at a higher wage rate. In this example, 0.5 billion hours of labour switch between the sectors. Another group, 1.4 billion hours in this example, remains unemployed. This unemployment is *structural*

unemployment. And it persists until the people involved make the transition to new jobs in an expanding sector of the economy. But this transition takes a long time and is painful for those involved.

The average wage rate increases because the wage rate in the expanding sector increases by more than the wage rate in the declining sector decreases. The labour market is in equilibrium and the plans of demanders and suppliers of labour are coordinated.

Which Theory of the Labour Market Is Correct?

What exactly is the problem in deciding which theory of the labour market is correct? The essence of the problem is nicely summarized in Figs. 32.9 and 32.11. First, the facts are not in dispute. The average real wage rate in 1989 was $13.65 an hour. In 1992, the average real wage rate was $14.65. Employment in 1989 was 23 billion hours, and it fell to 21.8 billion hours in 1992.

Second, there is no disagreement about the demand for labour. The quantity of labour employed is determined by the profit-maximizing decisions of firms. That is, the quantity of labour employed depends on the real wage rate. Therefore, the level of employment and the real wage rate in each period represent a point on the demand for labour curve for that period. If we agree that the employment level and real wage rate are a point on the demand for labour curve, we can work out where the demand for labour curve is and what makes it shift. Thus there is not much disagreement among economists about the slope and position of the demand for labour curve.

But economists disagree about the supply of labour. Because a large amount of labour is supplied on long-term contracts and on wages and other terms that remain fixed for the duration of the contract, most economists believe that households are not normally operating on their supply of labour curve. Sometimes they are, but much of the time they are not. Furthermore, they believe that on the basis of evidence from variations in hours of work and wages, the quantity of labour supplied does not respond much to changes in real wage rates. In other words, they believe that the supply curve is like that shown in Fig. 32.9.

Other economists believe that the combination of the real wage rate and the level of employment not only represents a point on the demand for labour curve but also a point on the supply of labour curve. From this assumption they infer that the quantity of labour supplied in the declining sectors is highly responsive to real wage rates and that the supply of labour curve looks like that in Fig. 32.11(a).

No one has yet suggested a test that is sufficiently clear for all economists to agree on. The controversy will be settled when economists can agree on and implement a test of their competing views about the responsiveness of the quantity of labour supplied to a change in the real wage rate. Once such a test has been implemented, we'll be able to put this controversy (like the controversy about monetary and fiscal influences on aggregate demand that you met in Chapter 29) behind us. But until then, economists and students must live with the fact that we remain ignorant about an important issue at the heart of macroeconomics. This controversy is featured in Our Advancing Knowledge on pp. 906–907.

The Policy Issue   If the flexible wage theory is correct, there is only one aggregate supply curve—the vertical long-run aggregate supply curve. This fact means that any attempt to bring the economy out of recession by increasing aggregate demand—for example, by lowering interest rates and increasing the money supply or by expansionary fiscal policy— is doomed to failure and can result only in a higher price level (more inflation). Conversely, if the sticky wage theory is correct, the short-run aggregate supply curve slopes upward. An increase in aggregate demand, although increasing the price level somewhat, increases real GDP and will bring the economy out of a recession. Reading Between the Lines on pp. 902–903 takes a further look at these two possible consequences of fiscal or monetary stimulation in the Canadian recession of the early 1990s.

Another Great Depression?

Although the 1990 recession lasted for only one year, the Canadian economy remained depressed through 1992. The depressed conditions of the 1990s are a pale shadow of those of the 1930s, but the question remains: is there going to be another Great Depression? Of course, the answer to this question

is that no one knows. But we can try to assess the likelihood of such an event. Let's begin by asking some questions. What was the Great Depression like? Just how bad did things get in the early 1930s? What would the Canadian economy look like in 1999 if the events of 70 years earlier were to recur? Once we've charted the broad anatomy of the Great Depression, we'll examine why it happened and consider the question of whether it could happen again and how likely such an event would be.

What the Great Depression Was Like

At the beginning of 1929, the Canadian economy was operating at full employment and with only 2.9 percent of the labour force unemployed. But, as that eventful year unfolded, increasing signs of economic weakness began to appear. The most dramatic events occurred in October when the stock market collapsed, losing more than one-third of its value in two weeks. The four years that followed were years of monstrous economic depression— depression so severe that it came to be called the Great Depression—evident in Fig. 32.12.

The dimensions of the Great Depression can be seen in Fig. 32.12. That figure shows the situation on the eve of the Great Depression in 1929, when the economy was on its aggregate demand curve AD_{29} and short-run aggregate supply curve SAS_{29}. Real GDP was $42 billion and the GDP deflator was 15. (Real GDP at the end of the 1980s is some 11 times its 1929 level and the GDP deflator about 10 times its 1929 level.)

In 1930, there was widespread expectation that prices would fall, and wages fell. With lower wages, the short-run aggregate supply curve shifted leftward. But increased pessimism and uncertainty resulted in a drop in investment and in the demand for durables. Aggregate demand fell. In 1930, the economy went into recession as real GDP fell by about 7 percent. The price level also fell by a similar amount. (It was not unusual at that time for prices occasionally to fall.) When the price level is falling, the economy is experiencing *deflation*.

If the normal course of events had ensued in 1930, the economy might have remained in its depressed state for several months and then started a recovery. But 1930 was not a normal year. In 1930 and the next two years, the economy was further bombarded with huge negative demand shocks (the sources of which we'll look at in a moment). The aggregate demand curve shifted leftward all the way to AD_{33}. With a depressed economy, the price level was expected to fall and wages fell in line with those expectations. As a result, the short-run aggregate supply curve shifted leftward to SAS_{33}. But the size of the shift of the short-run aggregate supply curve was much less than the decrease in aggregate demand. As a result, the aggregate demand curve and the short-run aggregate supply curve intersected in 1933 at a real GDP of $30 billion and a GDP deflator of 12. Real GDP had fallen by almost 30 percent from its 1929 level and the price level had fallen by 20 percent.

Although the Great Depression brought enormous hardship, the distribution of that hardship was very uneven. One-fifth of the work force had no jobs at all. Also, at that time, there were virtually no organized social assistance and unemployment programs in place. So many families had virtually no income. But the pocketbooks of those who kept their jobs barely noticed the Great Depression. It's true that wages fell. But at the same time, the price level fell, and by almost exactly the same percentage amount as the fall in wages. Hence real wages remained constant. Thus those who had jobs continued to be paid a wage rate that had roughly the same buying power at the end of the Great Depression as in 1929.

You can begin to appreciate the magnitude of the Great Depression if you compare it with the 1990 recession. In 1990, real GDP fell by 3.7 percent. In comparison, from 1929 to 1933, it fell by 31 percent. A 1999 Great Depression of the same magnitude would lower income per person to its level of more than 20 years earlier.

FIGURE 32.12

The Great Depression

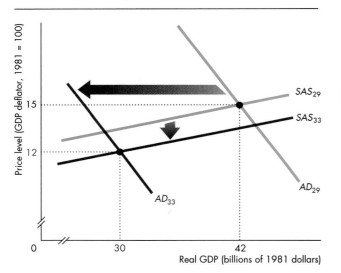

In 1929, real GDP was $42 billion and the GDP deflator was 15—at the intersection of AD_{29} and SAS_{29}. In 1930, increased pessimism and uncertainty resulted in a drop in investment, resulting in a decrease in aggregate demand. To some degree, this decrease was reflected in the labour market and wages fell, so the short-run aggregate supply curve shifted leftward. Real GDP and the price level fell. In the next three years, decreases in the money supply and investment lowered aggregate demand, shifting the aggregate demand curve to AD_{33}. Again, to some degree, the decrease in aggregate demand was reflected in lower wages, so the short-run aggregate supply curve shifted to SAS_{33}. By 1933, real GDP had fallen to $30 billion (70 percent of its 1929 level) and the GDP deflator had fallen to 12 (80 percent of its 1929 level).

Why the Great Depression Happened

The late 1920s were years of economic boom. New houses and apartments were built on an unprecedented scale, new firms were created, and the capital stock of the nation expanded. But these were also years of increasing uncertainty. The main source of increased uncertainty was international. The world economy was going through tumultuous times. The patterns of world trade were changing as Britain, the traditional economic powerhouse of the world, began its period of relative economic decline and new economic powers such as Japan began to emerge. International currency fluctuations and the introduction of restrictive trade policies by many countries (see Chapter 35) further increased the uncertainty faced by firms. There was also domestic uncertainty arising from the fact that there had been such a strong boom in recent years, especially in the capital goods sector and housing. No one believed that this boom could continue, but there was great uncertainty as to when it would end and how the pattern of demand would change.

This environment of uncertainty led to a slow-down in consumer spending, especially on new homes and household appliances. By the fall of 1929, the uncertainty had reached a critical level and contributed to the stock market crash. The stock market crash, in turn, heightened people's fears about economic prospects in the foreseeable future. Fear fed fear. Investment collapsed. The building industry almost disappeared. An industry that had been operating flat out just two years earlier was now building virtually no new houses and apartments. It was this drop in investment and a drop in consumer spending on durables that led to the initial decrease in aggregate demand.

The Deepening Depression   At this stage, what became the Great Depression was no worse than many previous recessions had been. What distinguishes the Great Depression from previous recessions are the events that followed between 1930 and 1933. But economists, even to this day, have not come to agreement on how to interpret those events. One view, argued by Peter Temin,[2] is that spending continued to fall for a wide variety of reasons—including a continuation of increasing pessimism and uncertainty. According to Temin's view, the continued contraction resulted from a leftward shift in the investment demand curve and a fall in autonomous expenditure. Milton Friedman and Anna J. Schwartz have argued that the continuation of the contraction was almost exclusively the result of the subsequent worsening of financial and monetary conditions.[3] According to Friedman and Schwartz, it was a severe cut in the money supply that lowered aggregate demand, prolonging the contraction and deepening the depression.

Although there is disagreement about the causes of the contraction phase of the Great Depression,

the disagreement is not about the elements at work but the degree of importance attached to each. Everyone agrees that increased pessimism and uncertainty lowered investment demand, and everyone agrees that there was a massive contraction of the real money supply. Temin and his supporters assign primary importance to the fall in autonomous expenditure and secondary importance to the fall in the money supply. Friedman and Schwartz and their supporters assign primary responsibility to the money supply and regard the other factors as being of limited importance.

The Components of Expenditure   Let's look at the contraction of aggregate demand a bit more closely. Table 32.2 shows the key facts about the composition of aggregate expenditure during the contraction years of the Great Depression. You can see that, just as in the 1990 recession, the main decline in expenditure was a decline in investment. During the Great Depression, investment almost disappeared. It is this decline in investment that Peter Temin emphasizes in his interpretation of the events. But monetary actions were also important. Let's examine these, beginning with a look at monetary forces in the United States.

Monetary Forces in the United States   In the United States between 1930 and 1933, there was a massive 20 percent contraction in the nominal money supply. This fall in the money supply was not directly induced by the Fed's actions. The *monetary base* (currency in circulation and bank reserves) hardly fell at all. But the bank deposits component of the money supply suffered an

---

[2] Peter Temin, *Did Monetary Forces Cause the Great Depression?* (New York, W. W. Norton, 1976).

[3] This explanation was developed by Milton Friedman and Anna J. Schwartz in *A Monetary History of the United States 1867–1960* (Princeton: Princeton University Press, 1963), ch. 7.

TABLE 32.2

Aggregate Expenditure during the Great Depression

Year	Real GDP		Components of aggregate expenditure								
			(billions of 1986 dollars)								
	Y	=	*C*	+	*I*	+	*G*	+	*EX*	–	*IM*
1929	42	=	27	+	10	+	7	+	9	–	11
1933	29	=	22	+	1	+	6	+	7	–	7
Change	–13	=	–5	+	–9	+	–1	+	–2	–	–4
Percentage change	–31	=	–19	+	–90	+	–14	+	–22	–	–36

Source: F.H. Leacy, *Historical Statistics of Canada*, 2nd. ed. (Ottawa: Statistics Canada and Social Science Federation of Canada, 1982).

Depression Persists

The Essence of the Story

A Statistics Canada survey of Canadian incomes showed that average family income after tax fell in 1990, 1991, and 1992.

The average family income in 1991 was 4.3% below its 1980 level.

But family size declined, so per capita income was unchanged.

Government cash transfers to families rose but taxes rose by more, so income after tax declined by more than income before tax.

The middle class was hit harder than either the rich or the poor, but the tax and transfer system moderated inequality.

Judith Maxwell attributed the fall in incomes to (among other factors) a slowdown in labour productivity growth in the 1970s and 1980s.

THE FINANCIAL POST, MAY 4, 1993

Gains from '80s boom are almost wiped out

By Greg Ip

Canadians saw 72% of the rise in their standard of living from the 1980s boom wiped out in the recession and are now worse off than in 1980, a Statistics Canada survey shows.

Average real family income after tax fell 2.6% in 1991 to $42,612 from 1990 in constant 1991 dollars, says StatCan's survey, published yesterday, after a 2.2% drop in 1990. Preliminary data suggest it fell further in 1992.

That left the average family with 4.3% less income than in 1980. Because family size declined, per capita family income was virtually unchanged.

Government cash transfers rose to 12% of the average family's income in 1991 from 7.9% in 1980. However, income tax rose to 19.8% in 1991 from 15.4% in 1980. Thus, incomes declined more after than before tax.

The middle class has been hit harder than either the rich or the poor, the survey indicates....

Judith Maxwell, associate director of the School of Policy Studies at Queen's University, attributed the decline in family incomes to the slowdown in labor productivity growth that began in the 1970s, the polarization of the labor market between high- and low-paying jobs, and marriage breakdown, which spread personal income over more households.

"The question is whether the growth we had in real incomes in the 1960s and 1970s was extraordinary, or is this slow-growth period extraordinary? We don't know what is normal."

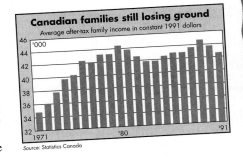

Canadian families still losing ground
Average after-tax family income in constant 1991 dollars

Source: Statistics Canada

Family real incomes in Canada fell in 1990, 1991, and 1992.

The main reason for the fall was a deep and prolonged recession, not low growth of labour productivity during the 1980s.

Figure 1 shows the severity of the recession as measured by real gross domestic product per adult (per Canadian aged 15 and over).

Figure 1 also shows that after-tax family income increased much more slowly than before-tax average income. The reasons: taxes went up and family size went down. But higher taxes paid for more public services, notably health and education.

But on any measure, incomes fell in 1990, 1991, and 1992. From the peak of 1989 to the trough of 1992, real income per person fell by 5.5 percent. In the previous (shorter) recession in 1982, real income per person fell by 4.5 percent.

Figure 2 gives two possible explanations for the 1990s recession.

In Fig. 2(a), a decrease in aggregate demand from AD_{89} to AD_{92} combined with a decrease in *short-run* aggregate supply from SAS_{89} to SAS_{92} lowered real GDP per adult (and increased the price level). Real GDP per adult could have been brought back to its 1989 level, with only a modest rise in the price level, with a fiscal or monetary policy stimulus package that increased aggregate demand to AD^*.

In Fig. 2(b), a decrease in aggregate demand from AD_{89} to AD_{92} combined with a decrease in *long-run* aggregate supply from LAS_{89} to LAS_{92} lowered real GDP per adult (and increased the price level). Real GDP would have been unchanged with a fiscal or monetary policy stimulus package, but the price level would have risen sharply.

With large budget deficits, the federal and provincial governments are unwilling to use fiscal stimulation, and with the overriding goal of price stability, the Bank of Canada is unwilling to risk monetary stimulation.

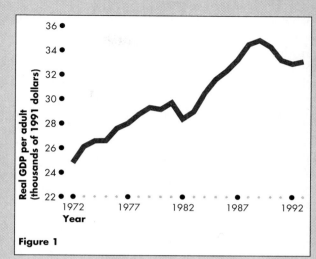

Figure 1

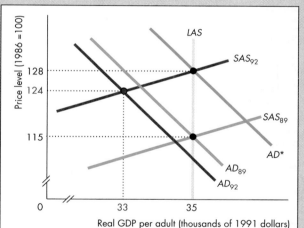

(a) Sticky wages

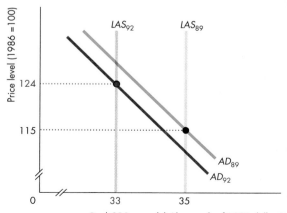

(b) Flexible wages—real business cycle

Figure 2

enormous collapse. It did so primarily because a large number of banks failed. The primary source of bank failure was unsound lending during the boom preceding the onset of the Great Depression. Fuelled by increasing stock prices and booming business conditions, bank loans expanded. But after the stock market crash and the downturn, many borrowers found themselves in hard economic times. They could not pay the interest on their loans and they could not meet the agreed repayment schedules. Banks had deposits that exceeded the realistic value of the loans that they had made. When depositors withdrew funds from the banks, the banks lost reserves, and many of them simply couldn't meet their depositors' demands to be repaid.

Bank failures feed on themselves and create additional failures. Seeing banks fail, people become anxious to protect themselves and so take their money out of the banks. Such were the events of 1930. The quantity of notes and coins in circulation increased and the volume of bank deposits declined. But the very action of taking money out of the bank to protect one's wealth accentuated the process of banking failure. Banks were increasingly short of cash and unable to meet their obligations.

Bank failure and the massive contraction of the money supply had two effects on the economy. First, the bank failures themselves brought financial hardship to many producers, increasing the business failure rate throughout the economy. At the same time, a sharp drop in the money supply kept interest rates high. Not only did nominal interest rates stay high, but with falling prices, real interest rates increased sharply. The real interest rate is (approximately) the difference between the nominal interest rate and the expected inflation rate. During the Great Depression, inflation was negative—the price level was falling. Thus the real interest rate equalled the nominal interest rate plus the expected rate of deflation. With high real interest rates, investment remained low.

Monetary Forces in Canada Monetary contraction also occurred in Canada, although on a less serious scale than in the United States. Our money supply declined in each of the contraction years of the Great Depression, but at a steady 5 percent a year in contrast to the whopping 20 percent in the United States. Also, no chartered bank in Canada failed, while bank failure was a severe problem in the United States.

The Stock Market Crash What role did the stock market crash of 1929 play in producing the Great Depression? It certainly created an atmosphere of fear and panic, and probably also contributed to the overall air of uncertainty that dampened investment spending. It also reduced the wealth of stockholders, encouraging them to cut back on their consumption spending. But the direct effect of the stock market crash on consumption, although a contributory factor to the Great Depression, was not the major source of the drop in aggregate demand. It was the collapse in investment arising from increased uncertainty that brought the 1930 decline in aggregate demand.

But the stock market crash was a predictor of severe recession. It reflected the expectations of stockholders concerning future profit prospects. As those expectations became pessimistic, the prices of stocks were bid lower and lower. That is, the behaviour of the stock market was a consequence of expectations about future profitability, and those expectations were lowered as a result of increased uncertainty.

Can It Happen Again?

Since, even today, we have an incomplete understanding of the causes of the Great Depression, we are not able to predict such an event or to be sure that it cannot occur again. But there are some major differences between the economy of the 1990s and that of the 1930s that make a severe depression much less likely today than it was 60 years ago. The most important features of the economy that make a severe depression less likely today are as follows:

◆ Bank deposit insurance

◆ The Bank of Canada's role as lender of last resort

◆ Taxes and government spending

◆ Multi-income families

Let's examine these in turn.

Bank Deposit Insurance In 1967, the government of Canada established the Canada Deposit Insurance Corporation (CDIC). The CDIC insures bank deposits up to $60,000 per deposit so that most depositors have no fear about the consequences of a bank failure. If a bank fails, the CDIC pays the deposit holders. Similar arrangements have been introduced in the United States, where deposits up to $100,000 are insured by the Federal Deposit Insurance Corporation. With government-insured bank deposits, one of the key events that turned a fairly ordinary recession into the Great Depression is most unlikely to occur. It was the fear of bank failure that caused people to withdraw their deposits from banks. The aggregate consequence of these individually rational acts was to cause the very bank failures that were feared. With deposit insurance, most depositors have nothing to lose if a bank fails and so have no incentive to take actions that are likely to give rise to that failure.

Although bank failure was not a severe problem in Canada during the Great Depression, it clearly was an important factor in intensifying the depression in the United States. And the severity of the U.S. recession certainly had an impact on Canada and the rest of the world.

Lender of Last Resort   The Bank of Canada is the lender of last resort in the Canadian economy. If a single bank is short of reserves, it can borrow reserves from other banks. If the entire banking system is short of reserves, banks can borrow from the Bank of Canada. By making reserves available (at a suitable interest rate), the Bank is able to make the quantity of reserves in the banking system respond flexibly to the demand for those reserves. Bank failure can be prevented, or at least contained to cases where bad management practices are the sources of the problem. Widespread failures of the type that occurred in the Great Depression can be prevented.

It is interesting to note, in this regard, that during the weeks following the October 1987 stock market crash, Fed Chairman Alan Greenspan and Bank of Canada Governor John Crow used every opportunity available to remind the world banking and financial community of their ability and readiness to maintain calm financial conditions.

Taxes and Government Spending   The government sector was a much less important part of the economy in 1929 than it has become today. On the eve of that earlier recession, government purchases of goods and services were less than 11 percent of GDP. In contrast, today they are more than 20 percent. Government transfer payments were around 5 percent of GDP in 1929. These items have grown to about 20 percent of GDP today.

A larger level of government purchases of goods and services means that when recession hits, a large component of aggregate demand does not decline. The most important economic stabilizer is government transfer payments. When the economy goes into recession and depression, more people qualify for unemployment insurance and social assistance. As a consequence, although disposable income decreases, the extent of the decrease is moderated by the existence of such programs. Consumption expenditure, in turn, does not decline by as much as it would in the absence of such government programs. The limited decline in consumption spending further limits the overall decrease in aggregate expenditure, thereby limiting the magnitude of an economic downturn.

Multi-Income Families   At the time of the Great Depression, families with more than one wage earner were much less common than they are today. The labour force participation rate in 1929 was around 55 percent. Today, it is 67 percent. Thus even if the unemployment rate increased to around 20 percent today, close to 54 percent of the adult population would actually have jobs. During the Great Depression, only 44 percent of the adult population had work. Multi-income families have greater security than single-income families. The chance of both (or all) income earners in a family losing their jobs simultaneously is much lower than the chance of a single earner losing work. With greater family income security, family consumption is likely to be less sensitive to fluctuations in family income that are seen as temporary. Thus when aggregate income falls, it does not induce a cut in consumption. For example, during the 1982 and 1990 recessions, as real GDP fell personal consumption expenditure actually increased.

For the four reasons we have just reviewed, it appears the economy has better shock-absorbing characteristics today than it had in the 1920s and 1930s. Even if there is a collapse of confidence leading to a fall in investment, the recession mechanism that is now in place will not translate that initial shock into the large and prolonged fall in real GDP and rise in unemployment that occurred more than 60 years ago.

Because the economy is now more immune to severe recession than it was in the 1930s, even a stock market crash of the magnitude of the one that occurred in 1987 had barely noticeable effects on spending. A crash of similar magnitude in 1929 resulted in the near collapse of housing investment and consumer durable purchases. In the period following the 1987 stock market crash, investment and spending on durable goods hardly changed.

UNDERSTANDING Business CYCLES

Economic activity has fluctuated between boom and bust for as long as we've kept records, and the range of fluctuations became especially pronounced during the nineteenth and early twentieth centuries. Understanding the sources of economic fluctuations has turned out to be difficult for two main reasons. First, there are no simple patterns. Every new episode of the business cycle is different from its predecessor in some important way. Some cycles are long and some short, some are mild and some severe. We never know with any certainty when the next turning point (down or up) is coming or what will cause it.

Second, resources are scarce even in a recession or depression. But at such times, large quantities of scarce resources go unemployed. A satisfactory theory of the business cycle must explain this fact. Why don't scarce resources *always* get fully employed?

There are plenty of simple, but wrong, theories of the business cycle. And when these theories are used to justify policies, they can create severe problems. For example, during the 1960s, recessions were believed to result from insufficient aggregate demand. The solution: increase government spending, cut taxes, and cut interest rates. Countries that pursued such policies most vigorously, such as the United Kingdom, found their economic growth rates sagging, unemployment rising, and inflation accelerating.

Today's new theory, real business cycle theory, predicts that fluctuations in aggregate demand have *no* effect on output and employment and that they only change the price level and inflation rate. But this theory ignores the *real* effects of financial collapse of the type that occurred in the 1930s. If banks fail on a large scale and people lose their wealth, other firms also begin to fail and jobs are destroyed. Unemployed people cut their spending, and output falls yet further. Demand stimulation may not be called for, but action to ensure that sound banks survive certainly is.

> "We don't want to manage the economy. And we don't think anybody else should take the job either."
>
> ROBERT E. LUCAS, JR.
> *Personal Interview*

From 1929 through 1933—the first four years of the Great Depression—unemployment swelled to 20 percent of the labour force. Prime Minister Richard Bennett's "solution" to the depression was to set up relief camps across the country in which people worked for low wages. By 1935, with no real relief from the depression in sight, desperate workers stopped work and took a symbolic train ride to Ottawa (pictured here). The mass unrest saw the end of the Bennett government and the return to office of William Lyon Mackenzie King. But a change of government did little to end the nation's economic ills and it was not until World War II began in 1939 that Canada saw the return to full employment.

How can it be that a building designed as a shop has no better use than to have its windows papered over and be left empty? Not enough aggregate demand, say the Keynesians. Not so, say the real business cycle theorists. Technological change has reduced the building's current productivity as a shop to zero. But its expected future productivity is sufficiently high that it is not efficient to refit the building for some other purpose.

All unemployment, whether of buildings or people, can be explained in a similar way. For example, how can it be that during a recession, a person trained as a shop clerk is unemployed? Not enough aggregate demand is one answer. Another is that the current productivity of shop clerks is low, but their expected future productivity is sufficiently high that it does not pay an unemployed clerk to retrain for a job that is currently available.

ROBERT E. LUCAS, JR.:

TODAY'S *Macroeconomic Revolutionary*

Many economists, past and present, have advanced our understanding of business cycles. But one contemporary economist stands out. He is Robert E. Lucas, Jr., of the University of Chicago. In 1970, then a 32 year-old professor at Carnegie-Mellon University, Lucas challenged the Keynesian theories of economic fluctuations and launched a macroeconomic revolution based on two principles: rational expectations and equilibrium. Like all scientific revolutions, the one touched off by Lucas was controversial. Twenty years later, the principle of rational expectations (whether right or wrong) is accepted by most economists. But the idea that the business cycle and unemployment can be understood as equilibria remains controversial and, for some economists, even distasteful. Lucas believes that we still know too little about the causes of the business cycle to be able to stabilize the economy.

None of this is to say that there might not be a deep recession or even a Great Depression in the 1990s (or beyond). But it would take a very severe shock to trigger one.

◆ ◆ ◆ ◆ We have now completed our study of the working of the macroeconomy. We've studied the macroeconomic model of aggregate demand and aggregate supply and we've learned a great deal about the workings of the markets for goods and services, labour, and money and financial assets. We have applied our knowledge to explain and understand the problems of unemployment, inflation, and business cycle fluctuations. ◆ ◆ In the next part of the book we will study two aspects of macroeconomic policy—the policies that governments can take to stabilize the economy and the policy towards the government's budget deficit.

SUMMARY

The Canadian Economy in the 1990s

The Canadian economy was in recession in 1990, and even by the end of 1992 real GDP had not returned to its pre-recession peak. Since the beginning of 1989, real GDP per person had *fallen* every quarter (except for one) and unemployment increased through 1992. Three forces contributed to the weak performance of the Canadian economy in the early 1990s: the Bank of Canada's price stability policy, the Canada–United States Free Trade Agreement, and a slowdown in economic expansion in the United States. The first two of these forces operated by decreasing aggregate demand and the third force operated by decreasing both aggregate demand and aggregate supply.

Consumption expenditure fell during the 1990 recession, but it remained very close to the consumption function, and the marginal propensity to consume out of real GDP was constant. Investment decreased sharply because the real interest rate increased and profit expectations decreased. The decrease in investment decreased aggregate demand and made the capital stock grow less quickly, and so decreased the growth rate of aggregate supply.

The increase in the real interest rate that lowered investment resulted from a lower inflation rate and a higher nominal interest rate. And the nominal interest rate increased because the Bank of Canada decreased the real money supply.

There is controversy about the behaviour of the labour market during a recession, and the 1990 recession can be interpreted by using either the sticky wage theory or the flexible wage theory. According to the sticky wage theory, the real wage rate got stuck at too high a level. As a result, when the economy went into recession, the quantity of labour supplied exceeded the quantity demanded. Even after the recession was over and real GDP was growing again, the real wage rate remained above the level necessary to give full employment. According to the flexible wage theory, when there is a decrease in the demand for labour, the quantity of labour supplied is highly responsive to changes in real wages. When the economy goes into recession, real wages fall a little and by enough to keep the quantity of labour demanded equal to the quantity supplied. Unemployment increases but the increase arises from increased job search activity associated with a higher degree of labour turnover. Macroeconomists have not yet found the acid test that enables them to resolve their dispute about the labour market mechanism in recession. (pp. 889–899)

Another Great Depression?

The Great Depression that began in 1929 lasted longer and was more severe than any before it or since. The Great Depression started with increased uncertainty and pessimism that brought a fall in investment (especially in housing) and spending on consumer durables. Increased uncertainty and pessimism also brought on the stock market crash. The crash added to the pessimistic outlook and further spending cuts occurred. In the United States, the financial system nearly collapsed. Banks failed and the money supply fell, resulting in a continued fall in aggregate demand. The Canadian financial system held up better, but the chaos in the United States hurt north of the border and throughout the world. Expectations of falling prices led to falling wages, but the fall in aggregate demand continued to exceed expectations and real GDP continued to decline.

The Great Depression itself produced a series of reforms that make a repeat of such a depression much less likely. The creation of the Bank of Canada as the lender of last resort and the introduction of federal deposit insurance both reduced the risk of bank failure and financial collapse. Higher taxes and government spending have given the economy greater resistance against depression, and an increased labour force participation rate provides a greater measure of security, especially for families with more than one wage earner. For these reasons, an initial change in either aggregate demand or aggregate supply is much less likely to translate into an accumulative depression than it did in the early 1930s. Thus even a stock market crash as severe as the one that occurred in 1987 does not lead to a collapse in aggregate demand. (pp. 899–908)

K E Y   E L E M E N T S

Key Figures

Figure 32.1   Real GDP: 1989–1992, 889
Figure 32.3   Money Supply Growth: 1989–1992, 890
Figure 32.4   U.S. and Canadian Real GDP Growth: 1989–1992, 891
Figure 32.5   The 1990 Recession, 891
Figure 32.6   Consumption and Investment: 1989–1992, 893

Figure 32.7   The Money Market in the 1990 Recession, 894
Figure 32.9   The Labour Market in the 1990s: A Rigid Wage Interpretation, 895
Figure 32.11 Labour Markets in the 1990s: Flexible Wage Interpretation, 897

R E V I E W   Q U E S T I O N S

1   Describe the changes in real GDP, real GDP per person, and unemployment that took place in Canada from the end of 1989 to the end of 1992.

2   What were the three forces that brought about Canada's recession in 1990?

3   Which of the forces that brought recession decreased aggregate demand, which decreased aggregate supply, and which decreased both aggregate demand and aggregate supply?

4   What happened to consumption expenditure in the 1990 recession and why?

5   What happened to investment in the 1990 recession and why?

6   Why did real interest rates increase during 1989 and 1990?

7   Describe the changes in employment and real wages in the 1990 recession.

8   What is the sticky wage theory of the labour market during a recession and how does this theory account for the events in Canada from 1990 to 1992?

9   What is the flexible wage theory of the labour market during a recession and how does this theory account for the events in Canada from 1990 to 1992?

10   When did the Great Depression occur?

11   Describe the changes in real GDP, employment and unemployment, and the price level that occurred during the Great Depression years of 1929 to 1933.

12   What were the main causes of the onset of the Great Depression in 1929?

13   What events in 1931 and 1932 led to the continuation and increasing severity of the fall in real GDP and the rise in employment?

14   What four features of today's economy make it less likely now than in 1929 that a Great Depression will occur? Why do they make it less likely?

P R O B L E M S

1 Analyse the changes in consumption expenditure during the 1990s by using the Canadian consumption function. Were the changes in consumption the result of shifts in the consumption function or movements along the consumption function?

2 Analyse the changes in investment during the 1990s by using the Canadian investment demand curve. Were the changes in investment the result of shifts in the investment demand curve or movements along the investment demand curve?

3 Analyse the changes in the interest rate during the lead-up to the 1990 recession by drawing a diagram of the money market showing shifts in the demand and supply curves for real money.

4 What monetary policy changes could have prevented interest rates from rising during 1989 and 1990? What would the effects of such actions have been on real GDP and the price level?

5 Between the end of 1989 and the end of 1992, real wages increased from $13.63 an hour to $14.65 an hour. Employment fell from 23 to 21 billion hours a year. How can these events be explained?
a   By the sticky wage theory
b   By the flexible wage theory

6 List all the features of the Canadian economy in 1994 that you can think of that are consistent with a pessimistic outlook for the mid-1990s.

7 List all the features of the Canadian economy in 1994 that you can think of that are consistent with an optimistic outlook for the mid-1990s.

8 How do you think the Canadian economy is going to evolve over the next year or two? Explain your predictions, drawing on the pessimistic and optimistic factors that you have listed in the previous two questions and on your knowledge of macroeconomic theory.

PART 12

MACROECONOMIC POLICY

Talking with John Crow

John Crow was born in London, England, in 1937 and studied economics at Oxford University where he obtained his B.A. in 1961. Immediately after graduating, he went to the International Monetary Fund (IMF) in Washington, D.C., where he remained, rising to become Chief of the North American Division, until he joined the Bank of Canada in 1973. He was governor of the Bank of Canada from 1987–94.

Mr. Crow propelled himself into the headlines with a lecture given at the University of Alberta in 1988 in which he said that the proper goal of monetary policy was to achieve and maintain "price stability." Robin Bade and Michael Parkin talked with John Crow about his work and the role of the Bank of Canada in stabilizing the Canadian economy.

What aspects of economics most excited you when you were a student at Oxford?

In fact I studied politics, philosophy, and economics—but half my studies were in economics. I "specialized" in economics because it seemed to shine a bright light on the real world. I found the concepts of economic analysis—especially trade, markets, and competitive outcomes—thoroughly illuminating and exciting. I'll just add that I found macroeconomics more appealing than microeconomics.

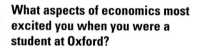

" 'specialized' in economics because it seemed to shine a bright light on the real world."

> "**I**f a meaningfully 'separate' central bank
> is to be useful, it must contribute sound money."

What attracted you to central banking?

In working at the IMF across a range of countries in North and South America, I was very much exposed to macroeconomic policy, lots of central banks, treasuries, and planning agencies. The offer of a position at the Bank of Canada was attractive because it was a fine institution that had a direct policy role, as opposed to the more indirect, or advisory, role played by the IMF.

Have you always believed that price stability is a desirable goal or is this a recent change of heart?

There's been not so much a "change of heart" as there's been a progression in my thinking. Look at the accumulation of evidence and the development of theory through the past twenty years or so. To my mind, it points monetary policy quite clearly in the direction of needing to be directed centrally at maintaining the purchasing value of money, if

it's going to be really useful to overall economic performance.

Another aspect of this is defining the proper role of a central bank. If a meaningfully "separate" central bank is to be useful, it must contribute sound money. Why else would one have a separate central bank?

Why did inflation get out of hand in the 1970s and 1980s?

Part of the reason was the running start into inflation that developed in the latter part of the 1960s. The view that prevailed at that time was that there really was a tradeoff with unemployment. Another part of the reason was the effect of the supply shocks, such as oil, that hit an already inflationary economy, and complicated greatly the task of monetary policy. For much of that period, monetary policy was playing catch-up.

Why has inflation fallen in so many countries during the past two or three years?

The groundwork was laid at the beginning of the 1980s when a consensus emerged that temporizing with inflation was a losing economic strategy. Monetary policies increasingly focussed on

> " **W**e've got the tools to run a Canadian monetary policy because we also have a flexible exchange rate regime."

combating inflation in the 1980s. This, combined with a virtual absence of supply shocks (perhaps because the world was, monetarily speaking, less inflationary to begin with), eventually produced results in lowering inflation.

Do you think the Bank of Canada should be mandated to achieve price stability?

Any institution needs to be accountable, and it can only be properly accountable if it has a clear mandate. As I have already suggested, the justification for a central bank with responsibility for monetary policy formulation must stem from the recognized desirability of preserving the value of money—price stability. So, any mandate, ideally, should reflect that.

How big an obstacle to stable prices is the federal government deficit?

It hasn't been in Canada. I can add that the Bank of Canada is not *required* to buy federal government debt. It only does so for monetary policy purposes.

Some people say that because Canada is a small open economy

appended to the larger U.S. economy, it cannot pursue its own inflation target independently of what the United States is doing. Do you agree?

Hardly. As a practical matter, we've got the tools to run a Canadian monetary policy because we also have a flexible exchange rate regime.

For example, if our dollar couldn't change in value against the U.S. dollar, inflation in Canada would obviously come to track very closely inflation developments stemming from the much bigger U.S. market. But because our dollar *can* adjust, we can control the pace of monetary expansion in Canada. This means

"**W**e can fundamentally
determine what kind of
inflation performance Canada
will experience . . . in the next
twenty years we will manage
to do better."

that we can fundamentally determine what kind of inflation performance Canada will experience—
for better or worse. To be more
concrete, over the past twenty
years Canada has managed to get
on average a worse inflation performance than the United States,
and this broadly accounts for the
depreciation of the Canadian
dollar over that period. Of course,
the object is not to do better or
worse than the United States on
inflation, but perhaps in the next
twenty years we will manage to
do better.

What kinds of work do economists do at the Bank of Canada?

Their work ranges over the whole
of macroeconomics, both domestic and international with, of
course, a heavy dose of monetary
and financial. Our economists
make regular contributions to the
academic literature, but their
work always stems from the
policy issues confronting the
Bank—from the functioning of
labour markets to the functioning
of money markets.

What sort of training does a student need to qualify for a job as an economist at the Bank?

These days, it seems that graduate work in economics is called
for—not necessarily in monetary
economics, and the students need
not necessarily have to obtain
a Ph.D. People often tell me that
being in one of our economics-
oriented departments is like being
in a special kind of graduate
school—economics with a policy
bent. In the end, how well you do
at the Bank depends on how good
you prove to be, not what you
came in with.

CHAPTER 33

STABILIZING THE ECONOMY

After studying this chapter, you will be able to

- ◆ Describe the goals of macro-economic stabilization policy
- ◆ Explain how the economy influences government popularity
- ◆ Describe the main features of fiscal policy since 1980
- ◆ Describe the main features of monetary policy since 1980
- ◆ Distinguish between fixed-rule and feedback-rule stabilization policies
- ◆ Explain how the economy responds to aggregate demand and aggregate supply shocks under fixed-rule and feedback-rule policies
- ◆ Explain why lowering inflation usually brings recession

WHEN UNEMPLOYMENT BECOMES A SERIOUS PROBLEM, people seek political action to jump-start the economy. And if action is not taken, leaders are often ditched as Brian Mulroney and Kim Campbell were in 1993. These Canadian politicians were not the first and will not be the last to suffer this fate. In 1979, with unemployment *and* inflation high by historical standards, the electorate ejected the Liberal government of Pierre Trudeau. And in 1984, with unemployment higher than ever before but with inflation having dramatically fallen, the electorate again rejected the Liberals (with John Turner the prime minister) and returned the Progressive Conservatives to power in a landslide election. How important is the economy in determining election outcomes?   ◆ ◆   The second half of the 1980s was a period of unimagined prosperity and macroeconomic stability. The early 1990s, in contrast, were years of slow income growth, high

Jump Start or Cruise Control?

unemployment, and recession. How were the stability and prosperity of the 1980s achieved? And what can be done to achieve a similar degree of success in the 1990s? Is there an economic equivalent of cruise control that can keep the economy moving forward at a steady pace?

◆ ◆ ◆ ◆   In this chapter, we're going to study the problems of stabilizing the Canadian economy—of avoiding inflation, high unemployment, and wildly fluctuating growth rates of real GDP. The chapter will give you a clearer and deeper understanding of the macroeconomic policy problems facing Canada today and of the political debate about those problems.

The Stabilization Problem

The stabilization problem is to deliver a macroeconomic performance that is as smooth and predictable as possible. Tackling this problem involves specifying targets to be achieved and then devising policies to achieve them. There are two main macroeconomic stabilization policy targets. They are

◆ Real GDP growth

◆ Inflation

Real GDP Growth

When real GDP grows less quickly than the economy's ability to produce, output is lost. When real GDP grows more quickly than the economy's ability to produce, bottlenecks arise. Keeping real GDP growth steady and equal to long-run aggregate supply growth avoids these problems.

Fluctuations in real GDP growth also bring fluctuations in unemployment. When unemployment rises above its natural rate, productive labour is wasted and there is a slowdown in the accumulation of human capital. If such unemployment persists, serious psychological and social problems arise for the unemployed workers and their families. When unemployment falls below its natural rate, expanding industries are held back by labour shortages. Keeping real GDP growth steady helps keep unemployment at its natural rate and avoids the waste and shortage of labour.

Fluctuations in real GDP growth contribute to fluctuations in our international trade balance. An international trade deficit enables us to purchase more goods and services than we have produced. But to do so we must borrow from the rest of the world and pay interest on our borrowing. An international trade surplus enables us to lend to the rest of the world and earn interest. But to do so we must purchase fewer goods and services than we have produced. In any given condition, there is an appropriate international trade balance and debt level. Keeping real GDP growth steady helps keep our balance of trade with the rest of the world and our international debt close to their desired levels.

Inflation

When inflation fluctuates unpredictably, money becomes less useful as a measuring rod for conducting transactions. Borrowers and lenders and employers and workers must take on extra risks. Keeping inflation steady and predictable avoids these problems.

Keeping inflation steady also helps keep the value of the dollar abroad steady. Other things remaining the same, if the inflation rate goes up by 1 percentage point, the dollar loses 1 percent of its value against the currencies of other countries. Large and unpredictable fluctuations in the foreign exchange rate—the value of the dollar against other currencies—make international trade and international borrowing and lending less profitable and limit the gains from international specialization and exchange. Keeping inflation low and predictable helps avoid such fluctuations in the exchange rate and enables international transactions to be undertaken at minimum risk and on the desired scale.

Figure 33.1 shows Canada's macroeconomic performance, as judged by two policy targets—real GDP growth and inflation. Here the red line is real GDP

FIGURE 33.1

Macroeconomic Performance:
Real GDP and Inflation

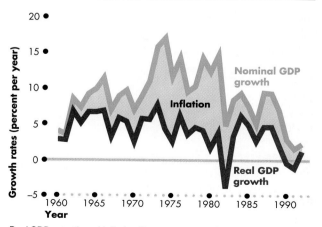

Real GDP growth and inflation fluctuate a great deal. During the 1970s, inflation mushroomed (the green area). This macroeconomic performance falls short of the goals of a stable real GDP growth rate and moderate and predictable inflation.

Source: Statistics Canada, CANSIM series D20000 and D20463.

growth and the green area is inflation. As you can see, our performance has fallen far short of stabilizing the economy. Why has the economy been so unstable? And can policy do better, making the next 30 years more stable than what is shown in Fig. 33.1? Answering these questions will occupy most of the rest of this chapter. Let's begin by identifying the key players and the policy actions they have taken.

Players and Policies

The two key players that formulate and execute macroeconomic stabilization policy are

◆ The government of Canada

◆ The Bank of Canada

The Government of Canada

The government of Canada implements the nation's fiscal policy, summarized in the federal budget. The **federal budget** is a statement of the federal government's financial plan, itemizing programs and their costs, tax revenues, and the proposed budget deficit or surplus.

Fiscal policy has three elements:

◆ Spending plans

◆ Tax laws

◆ Deficit

Spending Plans   The expenditure side of the budget is a list of programs with the amount that the government plans to spend on each program and a forecast of the total amount of government expenditure. Some expenditure items in the federal budget are directly controlled by government departments. Others arise from decisions to fund particular programs, the total cost of which depends on actions that the government can forecast but not directly control. For example, social welfare expenditure depends on the state of the economy and on how many people qualify for support. Farm subsidies depend on farm costs and prices.

Tax Laws   Parliament makes decisions about government revenue by enacting tax laws. As in the case of some important items of government expenditure, the government cannot control with precision the amount of tax revenue it will receive. The amount of tax paid is determined by the actions of the millions of people and firms who make their own choices about how much to work and spend and save.

Deficit   The difference between government spending and taxes is the government deficit. Every year since 1975, the federal government has had a deficit, and during the 1980s it became unusually large.

The Bank of Canada

The Bank of Canada is the nation's central bank. The main features of the Bank of Canada are described in Chapter 28. The Bank influences the economy by trading in markets in which it is one of the major participants. The two most important groups of such markets are those for government debt and for foreign currency. The Bank's decisions to buy and sell in these markets influence interest rates, the value of the dollar in terms of foreign currencies, and the amount of money in the economy. These variables that the Bank can directly influence in turn affect the conditions on which the millions of firms and households in the economy undertake their own economic actions.

Because the Bank's policymaking committee meets frequently and because the Bank operates daily in financial markets, monetary policy is used in an attempt to fine-tune the economy.

We've described the key players in the policy-making game. Let's now turn our attention to the policies they have pursued.

Fiscal and Monetary Policy Performance

Macroeconomic stabilization policy is strongly influenced by the constraints on the government and the Bank of Canada. The most important constraint is that arising from the effects of economic performance on voters in federal elections. To ensure adequate voter support to get re-elected, macroeconomic policy must deliver a macroeconomic performance acceptable to the electorate. What is an acceptable macroeconomic performance?

Macroeconomic Performance and Voter Behaviour

The effects of economic performance on voter behaviour have been studied most thoroughly by Ray Fair of Yale University. By studying the outcome of all the U.S. presidential elections between 1916 and 1984, Fair discovered that

◆ For each 1 percentage point *increase* in the real GDP growth rate, the incumbent political party gets a 1 percentage point *increase* in voter share.

◆ For each 3 percentage point *increase* in the inflation rate, the incumbent political party gets a 1 percentage point *decrease* in voter share.

There is no equivalent study of Canadian elections, but if we assume that our attitudes towards economic performance are similar to those of our neighbours, we can use Fair's discovery to calculate the predicted change in popularity (the change in

the percentage of votes that the incumbent is expected to receive in the next election) as follows:

$$\text{Change in popularity} = \text{Real GDP growth} - 1/3 \text{ Inflation rate} + \text{Other influences}$$

Politicians take actions that they believe will get them re-elected. That is, they take actions designed to increase the percentage of votes they receive. Among these actions are macroeconomic stabilization policies that increase real GDP growth and lower inflation. But a one percentage point increase in real GDP growth brings in as many additional votes as a three percentage point decrease in the inflation rate. Therefore politicians tend to favour policies that increase real GDP growth over those that decrease inflation.

Popularity and Economic Performance Since 1980

The macroeconomic performance of Canada since 1980, as measured by its predicted effects on the popularity of the incumbent party (but with other influences ignored) is shown in Fig. 33.2. The figure

FIGURE 33.2

Election Outcomes and the Economy

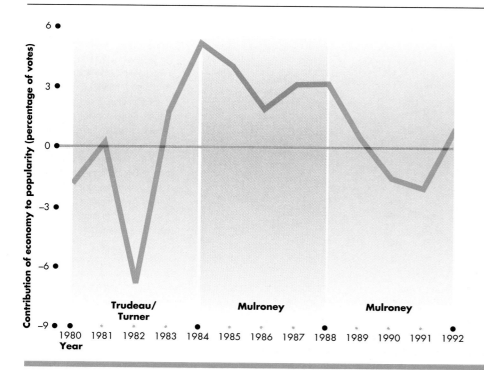

The outcome of a federal election depends partly on the performance of the economy. Faster real GDP growth and slower inflation generally improve the popularity of the incumbent party and improve its re-election chances.

Source: See Fig. 33.1 and our assumptions and calculations.

also gives information about the timing of federal elections and the outcomes of those elections, winners in red and losers in black.

Figure 33.2 shows that economic performance has been linked to federal elections. In 1980, slow growth and high inflation cost Joe Clark the election and helped to elect Pierre Trudeau. The Trudeau government was riding on an economic crest in the 1984 election, but the electorate had not forgotten the three preceding years of lacklustre performance and so favoured the Mulroney alternative. With a strong economy throughout his first term, Mulroney was easily re-elected in 1988, but a weak economy during his second term led to his fall in 1993.

The link between the economy and elections is sufficiently clear that the economic cycle has been called a political business cycle. A **political business cycle** is a business cycle whose origins are fluctuations in aggregate demand brought about by policies designed to improve the chance of a government being re-elected. Is the Canadian business cycle a political business cycle? And if it is, which policies have caused it—fiscal or monetary? Let's look at fiscal and monetary policy over the years since 1980.

Fiscal Policy since 1980   A broad summary of fiscal policy since 1980 is contained in Fig. 33.3. The figure also shows the three governments that were in office during these years. In the first period, when the Liberal party was in power first with Trudeau and then with John Turner as prime minister, government spending, taxes and the deficit all increased. But during the year immediately before the election, taxes were decreased. These actions can be seen as part of an attempt to get the economy growing again and establish conditions in which a successful election outcome is more likely.

But the deficit turned out to be a major concern for Canadians. One of the main tasks of the Progressive Conservative government of Brian Mulroney, elected in 1984, was to lower the deficit. This deficit reduction program was tackled on both sides of the budget equation. Spending was cut and taxes increased throughout Mulroney's first term. There is no appearance here of a government using fiscal policy to stimulate the economy. But there is such an appearance in the second Mulroney term as spending increased sharply as a percentage of GDP during the early 1990s.

FIGURE 33.3

The Fiscal Policy Record: A Summary

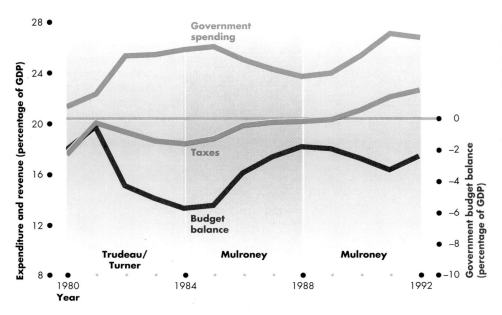

Fiscal policy is summarized here by the performance of government spending, taxes, and the deficit. Both spending and taxes have been on an upward trend and spending has persistently exceeded revenue, resulting in a deficit. Cycles in spending and taxes have occurred, but these cycles do not appear to have been created to improve re-election prospects.

Source: National Income and Expenditure Accounts, Catalogue 13-201, Statistics Canada, 1992, pp. 42-43 and our calculations.

Fiscal policy, then, has not followed a clear cycle that has contributed to the political business cycle. But what about monetary policy? Has it contributed to a political business cycle?

Monetary Policy since 1980 A broad measure of the influence of monetary policy is the growth rate of the money supply. Figure 33.4 shows such a measure, the growth rate of M2+. It also identifies the election years and terms of office of the two governors of the Bank of Canada during these years.

There are three distinct phases of monetary policy that almost coincide with the three political periods. During the Trudeau/Turner years, Governor Gerald Bouey was battling inflation, and the growth rate of the money supply decreased. Starting in 1984 and going through 1989, the money supply growth rate gradually increased. After 1989, when Governor John Crow began to pursue price stability, the money supply growth rate decreased again.

There is no evidence of a political business cycle here—in fact, almost the opposite. In each of the election years, the money supply growth rate has decreased and so has contributed to a slowing of the economy. Monetary policy has also been generally set to operate counter to fiscal policy. When government spending and the deficit were increasing in 1980-1984, money supply growth slowed down. When the deficit was being trimmed in 1984-1988, money supply growth speeded up. And when government spending and the deficit were running out of control again in 1989-1992, monetary policy was being severely tightened. But by 1993, the Bank of Canada was reluctant to take actions that would slow the pace of economic recovery—see Reading Between the Lines, pp. 922—923.

Alternative Stabilization Policies

Many different fiscal and monetary stabilization policies can be pursued, but they all fall into two broad categories:

◆ Fixed rules

◆ Feedback rules

FIGURE 33.4

The Monetary Policy Record: A Summary

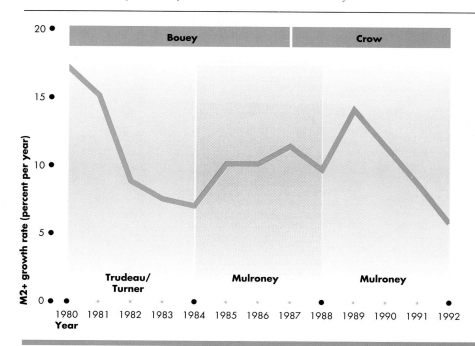

The monetary policy record is summarized here by the growth rate of M2+. The M2+ growth rate slowed during the Trudeau years when fiscal policy was expansionary, speeded up during Mulroney's first term when fiscal policy was contractionary, and became severely tight during Mulroney's second term when fiscal policy became expansionary again. There is no sign of monetary policy being used to stimulate the economy in time for a federal election.

Source: Bank of Canada, CANSIM series B1630.

Stabilizing the Canadian Economy

THE FINANCIAL POST, JUNE 10, 1993

Rates won't be forced up: Crow

By Heather D. Whyte

STOCKHOLM—The Bank of Canada doesn't feel the need to follow the U.S.'s lead if inflation pressures force up rates south of the border, according to governor John Crow.

In an exclusive interview with The Financial Post, Crow said that while changes in U.S. interest rates influence Canadian monetary policy, it is the fundamentals of the Canadian economy and financial markets—in combination with liquidity supplied by the Bank of Canada—that ultimately determine interest rates in Canada....

"The kind of productivity levels reported in Canada recently are helpful to maintaining strong rates of growth of the economy without creating excess demand or inflationary pressures" that the U.S. has, he said....

Several bankers attending the International Monetary Conference in Stockholm this week said they believe the Fed is under pressure to increase interest rates....

An increase in U.S. rates now would put some pressure on Canadian interest rates, Crow said. But because inflation is under control, he suggested Canada would not necessarily match a move in the U.S.

Crow...reiterated that the Bank of Canada's principal contribution to economic growth is maintaining price stability....

In mid-1993, renewed inflationary pressure in the United States led to the expectation of higher U.S. interest rates.

Higher U.S. rates put pressure on the Bank of Canada to increase Canadian rates.

But the Canadian economy was not experiencing the same inflation potential as the U.S. economy so the Bank of Canada did not see the need to match interest rate increases in the United States.

Bank of Canada governor John Crow said that the Bank's main contribution to economic growth is maintaining price stability.

In mid-1993, the U.S. economy was in the situation shown in part (a) of the figure. Real GDP was $5 trillion (1987 U.S. dollars) and was close to its full-employment level.

The U.S. aggregate demand curve was AD_0 and the short-run aggregate supply curve was SAS_0, and these curves intersected on the long-run aggregate supply curve LAS.

An increase in aggregate demand that shifts the aggregate demand curve to AD_1 would result in above full-employment. Wages would increase and the short-run aggregate supply curve would shift towards SAS_1. The price level would rise— inflation—and real GDP would return to $5 trillion.

The Fed (the U.S. central bank) might respond to this inflation threat with slower money growth and higher interest rates so as to hold aggregate demand at AD_0.

But higher U.S. interest rates would put upward pressure on Canadian interest rates as investors move their funds to the United States in search of higher returns.

The Bank of Canada would (according to governor Crow) resist matching higher U.S. interest rates because the Canadian economy is not under the same inflation threat as the U.S. economy.

As part (b) of the figure shows, the Canadian aggregate demand curve AD_C intersects the Canadian short-run aggregate supply curve SAS_C to the left of the long-run aggregate supply curve LAS_C. So any increase in aggregate demand in Canada would have a limited effect on prices and inflation and move real GDP closer to its full-employment level.

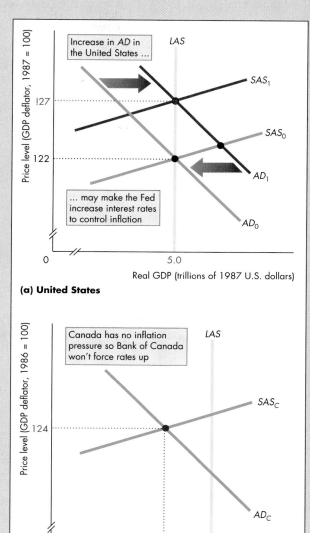

(a) United States

(b) Canada

Fixed Rules   A **fixed rule** specifies an action to be pursued independently of the state of the economy. There are many examples of fixed rules in everyday life. Perhaps the best known is the rule that keeps the traffic flowing by having us all stick to the right. The best-known fixed rule for stabilization policy is one that has long been advocated by Milton Friedman. He proposes setting the quantity of money growing at a constant rate year in and year out, regardless of the state of the economy. Inflation persists because continual increases in the money supply increase aggregate demand. Friedman proposes allowing the money supply to grow at a rate that keeps the *average* inflation rate at zero.

Feedback Rules   A **feedback rule** specifies how policy actions respond to changes in the state of the economy. An everyday example of a feedback rule is that governing your actions in choosing what to wear and whether to carry an umbrella. You base those actions on the best available forecast of the day's temperature and rainfall. (With a fixed rule, you either always or never carry an umbrella.) A stabilization policy feedback rule is one that changes policy instruments such as the money supply, interest rates, or even taxes, in response to the state of the economy. For example, the Bank of Canada pursues a feedback rule if an increase in unemployment causes it to engage in an open market operation aimed at increasing the money supply growth rate and lowering interest rates. The Bank also pursues a feedback rule if an increase in the inflation rate triggers an open market operation aimed at cutting the money supply growth rate and raising interest rates.

R E V I E W

Fiscal policy conducted by the government of Canada and monetary policy conducted by the Bank of Canada have generally been cyclical. But they have not followed a clear political cycle. Also, monetary policy has generally run counter to fiscal policy. When fiscal policy has stimulated aggregate demand, monetary policy has usually held aggregate demand in check. Policies based on either fixed rules or feedback rules may be used in an attempt to stabilize the economy. ◆

We'll study the effects of a fixed rule and a feedback rule for the conduct of stabilization policy by examining how real GDP growth and inflation behave under two alternative rules. We'll begin by studying shocks to aggregate demand. Such shocks can occur as a result of swings in business or consumer confidence in Canada or in other parts of the world.

Stabilization Policy and Aggregate Demand Shocks

We'll study an economy that starts out at full employment and has no inflation. Figure 33.5 illustrates this situation. The economy is on aggregate demand curve AD_0 and short-run aggregate supply curve *SAS*. These curves intersect at a point on the long-run aggregate supply curve, *LAS*. The GDP deflator is 130 and real GDP is $600 billion. Now suppose that there is a temporary fall in aggregate demand. Let's see what happens.

Perhaps investment falls because of a wave of pessimism about the future, or perhaps exports fall because of a recession in the rest of the world. Regardless of the origin of the fall in aggregate demand, the aggregate demand curve shifts leftward, to AD_1 in the figure. Wages don't change, so the short-run aggregate supply curve remains at *SAS*. Aggregate demand curve AD_1 intersects the short-run aggregate supply curve *SAS* at a GDP deflator of 125 and a real GDP of $550 billion. The economy is in a depressed state. Real GDP is below its long-run level and unemployment is above its natural rate.

Recall that we are assuming the fall in aggregate demand from AD_0 to AD_1 to be temporary. As confidence in the future improves, firms' investment picks up or, as economic recovery proceeds in the rest of the world, exports gradually rise, and the aggregate demand curve gradually returns to AD_0, but it takes some time to do so.

We are going to work out how the economy responds under two alternative monetary policies during the period in which aggregate demand gradually increases to its original level: a fixed rule and a feedback rule.

FIGURE 33.5

A Decrease in Aggregate Demand

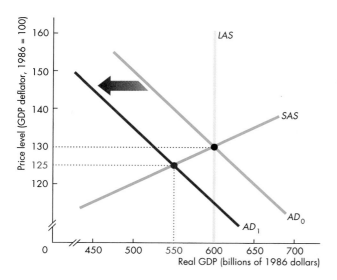

The economy starts out at full employment on aggregate demand curve *AD₀* and short-run aggregate supply curve *SAS*, with the two curves intersecting on the long-run aggregate supply curve *LAS*. Real GDP is $600 billion and the GDP deflator is 130. A fall in aggregate demand (due to pessimism about future profits, for example) unexpectedly shifts the aggregate demand curve to *AD₁*. Real GDP falls to $550 billion, and the GDP deflator falls to 125. The economy is in a recession.

Aggregate Demand Shock with a Fixed Rule

The fixed rule that we'll study here is one in which the level of government purchases of goods and services, taxes, and the deficit remain constant, and the money supply remains constant. Neither fiscal policy nor monetary policy responds to the depressed economy.

The response of the economy under this fixed-rule policy is shown in Fig. 33.6(a). When aggregate demand falls to AD_1, no policy measures are taken to bring the economy back to full employment. But recall that we are assuming that the decrease in aggregate demand is temporary and that it gradually increases to AD_0. As it does so, real GDP and the GDP deflator gradually increase. The GDP deflator gradually returns to 130 and real GDP to its long-run level of $600 billion, as shown in Fig. 33.6(a). Throughout this process, the economy

experiences more rapid growth than usual but beginning from a state of underemployment. Unemployment remains high until the aggregate demand curve has returned to AD_0.

Let's contrast this adjustment with what occurs under a feedback-rule policy.

Aggregate Demand Shock with a Feedback Rule

The feedback rule that we'll study is one in which government purchases of goods and services increase, taxes decrease, the deficit increases, and the money supply increases when real GDP falls below its long-run level. In other words, both fiscal policy and monetary policy become expansionary when real GDP falls below long-run real GDP. When real GDP rises above its long-run level, both policies operate in reverse, becoming contractionary.

The response of the economy under this feedback-rule policy is shown in Fig. 33.6(b). When aggregate demand falls to AD_1, the expansionary fiscal and monetary policies increase aggregate demand, shifting the aggregate demand curve to AD_0. Real GDP jumps back to its full-employment level and the GDP deflator jumps back to 130. As the other forces that increase aggregate demand kick in, fiscal and monetary policies become contractionary, holding the aggregate demand curve steady at AD_0. Real GDP is held steady at $600 billion and the GDP deflator remains at 130.

The Two Rules Compared

Under a fixed-rule policy, the economy goes into a recession and stays there for as long as it takes for aggregate demand to increase again under its own steam. Only gradually does the recession come to an end and the aggregate demand curve return to its original position.

Under a feedback-rule policy, the economy is pulled out of its recession by the policy action. Once back at its long-run level, real GDP is held there by a gradual, policy-induced decrease in aggregate demand that exactly offsets the increase in aggregate demand coming from private spending decisions.

The price level and real GDP fall and rise by exactly the same amounts under the two policies, but real GDP stays below its long-run level for longer with a fixed rule than it does with a feedback rule.

FIGURE 33.6

Two Stabilization Policies: Aggregate Demand Shock

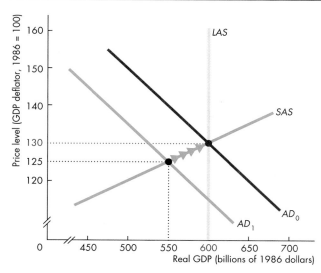

(a) Fixed rule

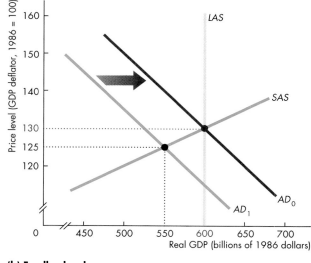

(b) Feedback rule

The economy is in a depressed state with a GDP deflator of 125 and real GDP of $550 billion. The short-run aggregate supply curve is *SAS*. A fixed-rule stabilization policy (part a) leaves aggregate demand initially at AD_1, so the GDP deflator remains at 125 and real GDP at $550 billion. As other influences gradually increase aggregate demand, the aggregate demand curve shifts back to AD_0. As it does, real GDP returns to $600 billion and the GDP deflator increases to 130.

Part (b) shows a feedback-rule stabilization policy. Expansionary fiscal and monetary policies increase aggregate demand, shifting the aggregate demand curve from AD_1 to AD_0. Real GDP returns to $600 billion and the GDP deflator returns to 130. Fiscal and monetary policies become contractionary as the other influences on aggregate demand increase its level. As a result, the aggregate demand curve is kept steady at AD_0 and real GDP stays at $600 billion.

So Feedback Rules Are Better?

Isn't it obvious that a feedback rule is better than a fixed rule? Can't the government and Bank of Canada use feedback rules to keep the economy close to full employment with a stable price level? Of course, unforecasted events—such as a collapse in business confidence—will hit the economy from time to time. But by responding with a change in tax rates, spending, and money supply, can't the government and the Bank of Canada minimize the damage from such a shock? It appears to be so from Fig. 33.6.

Despite the apparent superiority of a feedback rule, many economists remain convinced that a fixed rule stabilizes aggregate demand more effectively than a feedback rule. These economists assert that fixed rules are better than feedback rules because:

◆ Full-employment real GDP is not known.

◆ Policy lags are longer than the forecast horizon.

◆ Feedback policies are less predictable than fixed-rule policies.

Let's look at these assertions.

Knowledge of Full-Employment Real GDP   To decide whether a feedback policy needs to stimulate aggregate demand or retard it, it is necessary to determine whether real GDP is currently above or below its full-employment level. But full-employment real GDP is not known with certainty. It depends on a large number of factors, one of which is the level of employment when unemployment is at its natural rate. But there is uncertainty and disagreement about how the labour market works, so we can only estimate the natural rate of unemployment. As a result, there is uncertainty about the *direction* in which a feedback policy should be pushing the level of aggregate demand.

Policy Lags and the Forecast Horizon   The effects of a policy action taken today is spread out over the following two years. But no one is able to forecast that far ahead. The forecast horizon of the policy-makers is less than one year. Further, it is not possible to predict the precise timing and magnitude of the effects of policy itself. Thus a feedback policy that reacts to today's economy may be inappropriate for the state of the economy at that uncertain future date when the policy's effects are felt.

For example, suppose that today the economy is in recession. The Bank of Canada reacts with an increase in the money supply growth rate. When the Bank puts on the monetary accelerator, the first reaction is a fall in interest rates. Some time later, lower interest rates produce an increase in investment and the purchases of consumer durable goods. Some time still later, this rise in expenditure increases income, which in turn induces higher consumption expenditure. Later yet, the higher expenditure increases the demand for labour and eventually wages and prices rise. The sectors in which the spending increases occur vary and so does the impact on employment. It can take anywhere from nine months to two years for an initial action by the Bank to cause a change in real GDP, employment, and the inflation rate.

By the time the Bank's action is having its maximum effect, the economy might have experienced a shock to aggregate demand and moved to a new situation. For example, perhaps a world economic slowdown has added a new negative effect on aggregate demand that is offsetting the Bank's expansionary policy. Or perhaps a boost in business confidence has increased aggregate demand yet further, adding to the Bank's own expansionary policy. Whatever the situation, the Bank can only take the appropriate action today if it can forecast those future shocks to aggregate demand.

Thus to smooth the fluctuations in aggregate demand, the Bank of Canada needs to take action today, based on a forecast of what will be happening over a period stretching up to two years into the future. It is no use taking action a year from today to influence the situation that then prevails. It's too late.

If the Bank of Canada is good at economic forecasting and bases its policy actions on its forecasts, then the Bank can deliver the type of aggregate demand-smoothing performance that we assumed in the model economy we studied earlier in this chapter. But if the Bank takes a policy action that is based on today's economy rather than on the forecasted economy a year into the future, then that action will often be an inappropriate one.

When unemployment is high and the Bank of Canada puts its foot on the accelerator, it speeds the economy back to full employment. But the Bank cannot see far enough ahead to know when to ease off the accelerator and gently tap the brake, holding the economy at full employment. Usually it keeps its foot on the accelerator for too long and, after the Bank has taken its foot off the accelerator pedal, the economy races through full employment and starts to experience shortages and inflationary pressures. Eventually, inflation starts to take off and unemployment begins to fall. When inflation increases and unemployment falls below its natural rate, the Bank steps on the brake, pushing the economy back below full employment.

The Bank of Canada's own reaction to the current state of the economy has become one of the major sources of fluctuations in aggregate demand and the major factor that people have to forecast in order to make their own economic choices.

The problems for fiscal policy feedback rules are similar to those for monetary policy but are even more severe because of the lags in the implementation of fiscal policy. The Bank of Canada can take action relatively quickly. But before a fiscal policy action can be taken, the entire legislative process must be completed. Thus, even before a fiscal policy action is implemented, the economy may have moved on to a new situation that calls for a different policy to the one that is in the legislative pipeline.

Predictability of Policies   To make decisions about long-term contracts for employment (wage contracts) and for borrowing and lending, people have to anticipate the future course of prices—the future inflation rate. To forecast the inflation rate, it is necessary to forecast aggregate demand. And to forecast aggregate demand, it is necessary to forecast the policy actions of the government and the Bank of Canada.

If the government and the Bank of Canada stick to rock-steady, fixed rules for tax rates, spending programs, and money supply growth, then policy itself cannot be a contributor to unexpected fluctuations in aggregate demand.

In contrast, when a feedback rule is being pursued there is more scope for the policy actions to be unpredictable. The main reason is that feedback rules are not written down for all to see. Rather, they have to be inferred from the behaviour of the government and the Bank of Canada.

Thus with a feedback policy it is necessary to predict the variables to which the government and the Bank of Canada react and the extent to which they react. Consequently, a feedback rule for fiscal and monetary policy can create more unpredictable fluctuations in aggregate demand than a fixed rule.

Economists disagree whether those bigger fluctuations offset the potential stabilizing influence of the predictable changes the Bank of Canada makes. No agreed measurements have been made to settle this dispute. Nevertheless, the unpredictability of the Bank in its pursuit of feedback policies is an important fact of economic life. And the Bank does not always go out of its way to make its reactions clear.

It is not surprising that the Bank of Canada seeks to keep some of its actions behind a smoke screen. First, the Bank wants to maintain as much freedom of action as possible and so does not want to state too precisely the feedback rules that it will follow in any given circumstances. Second, the Bank is part of a political process and, although legally independent of the federal government, it is not immune to subtle influence from the government. For at least these two reasons, the Bank does not specify feedback rules as precisely as the one we've analysed in this chapter. As a result, the Bank cannot deliver an economic performance that has the stability we generated in the model economy.

To the extent that the Bank of Canada's actions are unpredictable, they lead to unpredictable fluctuations in aggregate demand. These fluctuations, in turn, produce fluctuations in real GDP, employment, and unemployment.

If it is difficult for the Bank of Canada to pursue a predictable feedback stabilization policy, it is probably impossible for the government. The government's stabilization policy is formulated in terms of spending programs and tax laws. Since these programs and laws are the outcome of a political process that is constrained only by the Constitution, there can be no effective way in which a predictable feedback fiscal policy can be adhered to.

REVIEW

Fixed-rule policies keep fiscal and monetary policies steady and independent of the state of the economy. Feedback policies cut taxes, increase spending, and speed up money supply growth when the economy is in recession and reverse these measures when the economy is overheating. Feedback rules apparently do a better job but we are not sure that is the case. Their successful use requires a good knowledge of the current state of the economy, an ability to forecast as far ahead as the policy actions have effects, and clarity and openness about the feedback rules being used. ◆

We reviewed three reasons why feedback policies may not be more effective than fixed rules in controlling aggregate demand. The evolution of views about aggregate demand stabilization is featured in Our Advancing Knowledge on pp.932–933. But there is a fourth reason why fixed rules are preferred by some economists—not all shocks to the economy are on the demand side. Advocates of feedback rules believe that most fluctuations do come from aggregate demand. Advocates of fixed rules believe that aggregate supply fluctuations are the dominant ones. Let's now see how aggregate supply fluctuations affect the economy under a fixed rule and a feedback rule. We will also see why those economists who believe that aggregate supply fluctuations are the dominant ones also favour a fixed rather than a feedback rule.

Stabilization Policy and Aggregate Supply Shocks

There are two reasons why aggregate supply fluctuations can cause problems for a stabilization feedback rule:

◆ Cost-push inflation
◆ Slowdown in productivity growth

In either of these situations, the economy experiences *stagflation*. Let's study the effects of alternative policies to deal with this problem.

Cost-Push Inflation

Cost-push inflation is inflation that has its origins in cost increases. The two most important potential sources of cost-push inflation are wage increases and increases in raw material prices. To proceed, a cost-push inflation must be accommodated by an increase in the money supply, which in turn increases aggregate demand. A monetary policy feedback rule makes cost-push inflation possible. A fixed rule makes such inflation impossible. Let's see why.

Consider the economy that is shown in Fig. 33.7. Aggregate demand is AD_0, short-run aggregate supply is SAS_0, and long-run aggregate supply is LAS. Real GDP is $600 billion and the GDP deflator is 130.

Now suppose that a number of labour unions, or the key suppliers of an important raw material such as oil, try to gain a temporary advantage by increasing the price at which they are willing to sell their

services—by increasing wages—or by increasing the price of the raw material. To make the exercise interesting, let's suppose that the people in question control a significant portion of the economy. As a consequence, when they increase the wage rate or the price of oil, the short-run aggregate supply curve shifts upward from SAS_0 to SAS_1.

Fixed Rule   Figure 33.7(a) shows what happens if the Bank of Canada follows a fixed rule for monetary policy and the government follows a fixed rule for fiscal policy. Suppose that the fixed rule is for zero money growth and no change in taxes or government purchases of goods and services. With these fixed rules, the Bank of Canada and the government pay no attention to the fact that there has been an increase in wages or raw material prices. No policy actions are taken. The short-run aggregate supply curve has shifted to SAS_1 but the aggregate demand

FIGURE 33.7

Stabilization Policy and Aggregate Supply: A Wage Increase

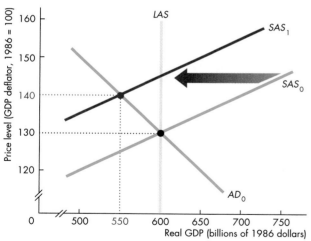

(a) Fixed rule

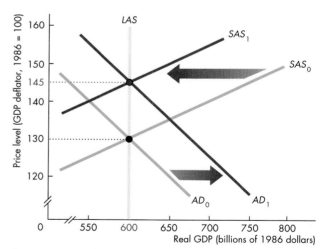

(b) Feedback rule

The economy starts out on AD_0 and SAS_0, with a GDP deflator of 130 and real GDP of $600 billion. A labour union (or a key supplier of raw materials) forces up wages (or the price of the raw material), shifting the short-run aggregate supply curve to SAS_1. Real GDP falls to $550 billion and the GDP deflator increases to 140. With a fixed rule (part a), the Bank of Canada and the government make no change to aggregate demand. The economy stays depressed until wages (or raw material

prices) fall, and the economy returns to its original position. With a feedback rule (part b), the Bank injects additional money and/or the government cuts taxes or increases spending, increasing aggregate demand to AD_1. Real GDP returns to $600 billion (full employment) but the GDP deflator increases to 145. The economy is set for another round of cost-push inflation.

curve remains at AD_0. The GDP deflator rises to 140, and real GDP falls to $550 billion. The economy is experiencing stagflation. Until wages or raw material prices fall, the economy will be depressed and will remain depressed. This decrease in wages or raw material prices may take a long time to come about. Eventually, however, the low level of real GDP will bring lower oil prices and wages—those very prices and wages whose increase caused the initial problem. Eventually, the short-run aggregate supply curve will shift back to SAS_0. The GDP deflator will fall to 130 and real GDP will increase to $600 billion.

Feedback Rule   Figure 33.7(b) shows what happens if the Bank of Canada and the government operate monetary and fiscal policy feedback rules. The starting point is the same as before—the economy is on SAS_0 and AD_0 with a GDP deflator of 130 and real GDP of $600 billion. Wages are increased and the short-run aggregate supply curve shifts to SAS_1. The economy goes into a recession, with real GDP falling to $550 billion and the price level increasing to 140. The monetary feedback rule is to increase the money supply growth rate when real GDP is below its long-run level. And the fiscal feedback rule is to cut taxes and increase government purchases when real GDP is below its long-run level. So, with real GDP at $550 billion, the Bank of Canada pumps up the money supply growth rate, Parliament passes a tax cut bill and a series of bills that increase spending, and the aggregate demand curve shifts to AD_1. The price level increases to 145 and real GDP returns to $600 billion. The economy moves back to full employment but at a higher price level.

The unionized workers or the raw material suppliers, who saw an advantage in forcing up their wages or prices before, see the same advantage again. Thus the short-run aggregate supply curve shifts up once more, and the Bank of Canada and the government chase it with increases in aggregate demand. The economy is in a freewheeling inflation.

Incentives to Push Up Costs   You can see that there are no checks on the incentives to push up costs if the Bank of Canada pursues a feedback rule of the type that we've just analysed. If some group sees a temporary gain from pushing up the price at which they are selling their resources and if the Bank of Canada and the government always accommodate to prevent unemployment and slack business conditions from emerging, then cost-push elements will have a free rein.

But when the Bank of Canada and the government pursue fixed-rule policies, the incentive to attempt to steal a temporary advantage by increasing wages or prices is severely weakened. The cost of higher unemployment and lower output is a consequence that each group will have to face and recognize.

Thus a fixed rule is capable of delivering a steady inflation rate (or even zero inflation), while a feedback rule, in the face of cost-push pressures, will leave the inflation rate free to rise and fall at the whim of whichever group believes a temporary advantage to be available from pushing up its wage or price.

Slowdown in Productivity Growth

Some economists believe that fluctuations in real GDP (and in employment and unemployment) are caused not by fluctuations in aggregate demand but by fluctuations in productivity growth. These economists have developed a new theory of aggregate fluctuations called real business cycle theory. **Real business cycle theory** is a theory of aggregate fluctuations based on flexible wages and random shocks to the economy's aggregate production function. The word "real" draws attention to the idea that it is real things (random shocks to the economy's real production possibilities) rather than nominal things (the money supply and its rate of growth) that are, according to that theory, the most important sources of aggregate fluctuations.

According to real business cycle theory, there is no useful distinction to be made between the long-run aggregate supply curve and the short-run aggregate supply curve. Because wages are flexible, the labour market is always in equilibrium and unemployment is always at its natural rate. The vertical long-run aggregate supply curve is also the short-run aggregate supply curve. Fluctuations occur because of shifts in the long-run aggregate supply curve. Normally, the long-run aggregate supply curve shifts rightward—the economy expands. But the pace at which the long-run aggregate supply curve shifts rightward varies. Also, on occasion, the long-run aggregate supply curve shifts leftward, bringing a decrease in aggregate supply and a fall in real GDP.

Economic policy that influences the aggregate demand curve has no effect on real GDP. But it does affect the price level. However, if a feedback policy is used to increase aggregate demand every time real GDP falls, and if the real business cycle theory is correct, the feedback policy will make price level fluctuations more severe than they otherwise would be. To see why, consider Fig. 33.8.

Imagine that the economy starts out on aggregate demand curve AD_0 and long-run aggregate supply curve LAS_0, at a GDP deflator of 130 and with real GDP equal to $600 billion. Now suppose that the long-run aggregate supply curve shifts to LAS_1. An actual decrease in long-run aggregate supply can occur as a result of a severe drought or other natural disaster or perhaps as the result of a disruption of international trade, such as the OPEC embargo of the 1970s.

Fixed Rule   With a fixed rule, the fall in the long-run aggregate supply has no effect on the Bank of Canada or the government and no effect on aggregate demand. The aggregate demand curve remains AD_0. Real GDP falls to $550 billion and the GDP deflator increases to 140.

Feedback Rule   Now suppose that the Bank of Canada and the government use feedback rules. In particular, suppose that when real GDP falls, the Bank of Canada increases the money supply and Parliament enacts a tax cut to increase aggregate demand. In this example, the money supply and tax cut shift the aggregate demand curve to AD_1. The policy goal is to bring real GDP back to $600 billion. But the long-run aggregate supply curve has shifted, long-run real GDP has decreased to $550 billion. The increase in aggregate demand cannot bring forth an increase in output if the economy does not have the capacity to produce that output. So real GDP stays at $550 billion but the price level rises still further—the GDP deflator increases to 150. You can see that in this case the attempt to stabilize real GDP using a feedback policy has no effect on real GDP but increases the price level.

We've now seen some of the shortcomings of using feedback rules for stabilization policy. Some economists believe that these shortcomings are serious and want to constrain the government and the Bank of Canada so that they use fixed rules. Others, regarding the potential advantages of feedback rules as greater than their costs, advocate the continued use of such policies but with a modification that we'll now look at.

Nominal GDP Targeting

Attempting to keep the growth rate of nominal GDP steady is called **nominal GDP targeting**. James

FIGURE 33.8

Stabilization Policy and Aggregate Supply: A Decrease in Productivity

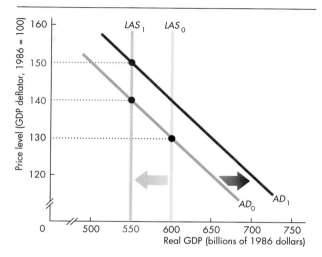

A decrease in productivity shifts the long-run aggregate supply curve from LAS_0 to LAS_1. Real GDP falls from $600 billion to $550 billion and the GDP deflator rises from 130 to 140. With a fixed rule, there is no change in the money supply, taxes, or government spending, so aggregate demand stays at AD_0, and that is the end of the matter. With a feedback rule, the Bank of Canada increases the money supply and/or the government cuts taxes or increases spending, intending to increase real GDP. Aggregate demand shifts to AD_1, but the long-run result is an increase in the price level—the GDP deflator rises to 150—with no change in real GDP.

Tobin of Yale University and John Taylor of Stanford University have suggested that nominal GDP targeting is a useful operating goal for macroeconomic policy.

The nominal GDP growth equals the real GDP growth rate plus the inflation rate. When nominal GDP grows quickly, it is usually because the inflation rate is high. When nominal GDP grows slowly, it is usually because real GDP growth is negative—the economy is in recession. Thus by keeping nominal GDP growth steady, it is hoped to avoid excesses of inflation and recession.

Nominal GDP targeting uses feedback rules. Expansionary fiscal and/or monetary actions increase aggregate demand when nominal GDP is below target, and contractionary fiscal and/or

EVOLVING Approaches to ECONOMIC STABILIZATION

When it comes to stabilizing the economy, people differ in their opinions about what's best. In 1960, almost every economist believed that Keynesian stabilization policies—fiscal and monetary demand management policies—could smooth out the business cycle. In that year, 30 of Canada's most prominent economists wrote to the minister of finance urging him to fire James Coyne, governor of the Bank of Canada, for refusing to pursue such policies.

Using the economic model described in Chapters 25 through 29, economists believed that by setting the levels of government purchases, taxes, and the money supply (or interest rates) at the appropriate levels, full-employment and steady economic expansion could be maintained indefinitely.

But there was always some scepticism that a small open economy sitting on the edge of the much larger U.S. economy could practise active stabilization policy with much success. This scepticism grew during the 1960s and 1970s as it became ever more clear that the Canadian and U.S. business cycles were inexorably linked.

Although it is now recognized that Canada cannot prevent economic fluctuations in the United States from rippling through its economy, there has been a return to an older view: Canada can control the value of its money and can use its monetary policy to pursue price stability.

This view was embodied in a jointly announced attack on inflation in 1991 by the then minister of finance, Michael Wilson, and governor of the Bank of Canada, John Crow. The monetary policy pursued since 1991 shows that Canada can indeed control its inflation rate. A large number of economists believe that the 1990s also show that monetary policy has a large effect on the Canadian business cycle and that the price of lower inflation was a severe and prolonged recession. Whether this evaluation is correct remains unclear for many other factors were at work—such as the tariff cuts under the Canada–United States Free Trade Agreement—that could have been responsible for Canada's persistent high unemployment in the early 1990s.

> "... the openness of the Canadian economy to the world economy ... restricts the possibilities of economic stabilization by domestic economic policies."
>
> HARRY G. JOHNSON
> *Essays in Monetary Economics*

The 1960s were the high years of Keynesian economic management, and a time of high drama in the management of the Canadian economy. In 1961, the governor of the Bank of Canada, James Coyne, was forced out of office by Prime Minister John Diefenbaker in a clash over who would make Canada's monetary policy, the Bank or the government. Coyne resigned, and the Bank of Canada Act was eventually rewritten with the intention of reducing the Bank's power. In practice, though, the Bank of Canada exercises considerable independence in its formulation and conduct of monetary policy.

John Diefenbaker

James Coyne

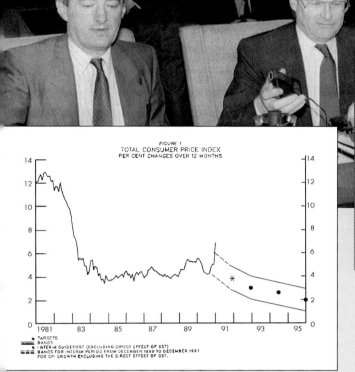

FIGURE 1
TOTAL CONSUMER PRICE INDEX
PER CENT CHANGES OVER 12 MONTHS

● TARGETS
▬ BANDS
▬ ▬ INTERIM GUIDEPOST (EXCLUDING DIRECT EFFECT OF GST)
▬ ▬ ▬ BANDS FOR INTERIM PERIOD FROM DECEMBER 1990 TO DECEMBER 1991
FOR CPI GROWTH EXCLUDING THE DIRECT EFFECT OF GST.

Bank of Canada Governor John Crow and former Finance Minister Michael Wilson (seen here at a meeting of the International Monetary Fund in Washington) collaborated in launching Canada's current monetary policy of price stability. The guidelines for achieving price stability have been surpassed and the problem facing the Bank of Canada in 1993 was to remain in the price stability zone while fostering a sustainable economic recovery.

HARRY JOHNSON VS. THE KEYNESIANS:

THE Brief Life of Fine-Tuning in Canada

Mabel Timlin

The ideas of John Maynard Keynes, developed in Britain in the 1930s, travelled quickly to Canada. A young Canadian, Robert Bryce, attended Keynes' lectures in Cambridge and subsequently became a leading economic mandarin in Ottawa. And by 1960, almost every economics professor was a Keynesian.

But the ideas of Keynes needed modification to be relevant to Canada. Mabel Timlin (1891–1976), a professor at the University of Saskatchewen, was one of the first to recognize this need. But it was Harry Johnson (1923–1977) who made the most significant contributions in this field. For almost twenty years until his premature death, Johnson was the most significant and prolific Canadian economist. Educated at the Universities of Toronto and Cambridge, he was simultaneously a professor at the London School of Economics and the University of Chicago. Johnson developed his own brand of macroeconomics—now absorbed into the mainstream—that applied to small, open, developing, and growing economies—to real-world economies. Along with fellow Canadian and Chicago colleague Robert Mundell, Johnson also developed what came to be called global monetarism—an application of the ideas of Milton Friedman to the global economy of interlinked, open trading nations.

Harry Johnson

monetary actions decrease aggregate demand when nominal GDP is above target. The main problem with nominal GDP targeting is that there are long and variable time lags between the identification of a need to change aggregate demand and the effects of the policy actions taken.

Macroeconomists are still debating the merits of the alternative policies for achieving stability.

Taming Inflation

S o far, we've concentrated on stabilizing real GDP either directly or indirectly and *avoiding* inflation. But often the problem is not to avoid inflation but to tame it. How can inflation, once it has set in, be cured? Let's look at some alternative ways.

A Surprise Inflation Reduction

To study the problem of lowering inflation, we'll use two equivalent approaches, aggregate demand-aggregate supply and the Phillips curve. You met the Phillips curve in Chapter 31 (pp. 873–879). The Phillips curve enables us to keep track of what is happening to both inflation and unemployment.

The economy is shown in Fig. 33.9. In part (a), it is on aggregate demand curve AD_0 and short-run aggregate supply curve SAS_0, with real GDP at $600 billion and the GDP deflator at 130. With real GDP at its long-run level (on the LAS curve), there is full employment. Equivalently, in part (b), the economy is on its long-run Phillips curve, $LRPC$ and short-run Phillips curve $SRPC_0$. Inflation is raging at 10 percent a year and unemployment is at its natural rate.

Next year, aggregate demand is *expected* to increase, shifting the aggregate demand curve in Fig. 33.9(a) to AD_1. Expecting this increase in aggregate demand, wages increase to shift the short-run aggregate supply curve to SAS_1. If expectations are fulfilled, real GDP remains at its long-run level and the GDP deflator rises to 143—a 10 percent inflation. In part (b), the economy remains at its original position.

But suppose the Bank of Canada tries to slow

down inflation to 5 percent a year. If it simply slows the growth of aggregate demand, the aggregate demand curve (in part a) shifts to AD_2. With no slowdown in the expected inflation rate, wage increases shift the short-run aggregate supply curve to SAS_1. Real GDP decreases to $550 billion and the GDP deflator rises to 140.4—an inflation rate of 8 percent a year. In Fig. 33.9(b), there is a movement along the short-run Phillips curve $SRPC_0$ as unemployment rises to 9 percent and inflation falls to 8 percent a year. The policy has succeeded in slowing inflation, but by less than desired and at a cost of recession. Real GDP is below its long-run level and unemployment is above its natural rate.

A Credible Announced Inflation Reduction

Suppose that instead of simply slowing down the growth of aggregate demand, the Bank of Canada announced its intention ahead of its action and in a credible and convincing way so that its announcement was believed. The lower level of aggregate demand becomes expected. In this case, wages increase at a pace consistent with the lower level of aggregate demand and the short-run aggregate supply curve (in Fig. 33.9a) shifts to SAS_2. When aggregate demand increases, shifting the aggregate demand curve to AD_2, the GDP deflator rises to 136.5—an inflation rate of 5 percent a year—and real GDP remains at its full-employment level.

In Fig. 33.9(b), the lower expected inflation rate shifts the short-run Phillips curve downward to $SRPC_1$, and inflation falls to 5 percent a year, while unemployment remains at its natural rate.

Inflation Reduction in Practice

The Bank of Canada has lowered the inflation rate on two occasions in recent years. You can see these episodes in Fig. 33.10. The first was in 1982-1985, the second in 1990-1992. On both occasions, the Bank's monetary policy action occurred in the face of wages that had been set at too high a level to be consistent with the growth of aggregate demand that the Bank subsequently allowed. The consequence was recession—a decrease in real GDP and a rise in unemployment. Couldn't the Bank have lowered inflation without causing recession by telling people far enough ahead of time that it did indeed plan to slow down the growth rate of aggregate demand?

FIGURE 33.9

Reducing Inflation

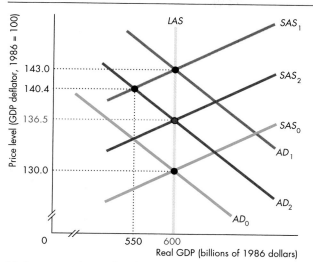

(a) Aggregate demand and aggregate supply

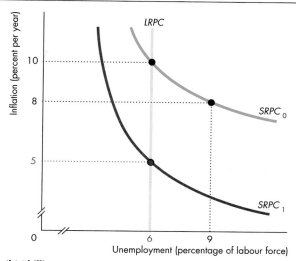

(b) Phillips curves

Initially, aggregate demand is AD_0 and short-run aggregate supply is SAS_0. Real GDP is $600 billion (its full-employment level on the long-run aggregate supply curve LAS). Inflation is proceeding at 10 percent a year. If it continues to do so, the aggregate demand curve shifts to AD_1 and the short-run aggregate supply curve shifts to SAS_1. The GDP deflator rises to 143. This same situation is shown in part (b) with the economy on the long-run Phillips curve $LRPC$ and the short-run Phillips curve $SRPC_0$.

Suppose the Bank of Canada tries to slow inflation to 5 percent a year. If the slowdown in aggregate demand growth is unexpected, the

aggregate demand curve (part a) shifts to AD_2, real GDP falls to $550 billion, and inflation slows to 8 percent (a GDP deflator of 140.4). In part (b), unemployment rises to 9 percent as the economy slides down $SRPC_0$.

If a credibly announced slowdown in aggregate demand growth occurs, the short-run aggregate supply curve (part a) shifts to SAS_2, the short-run Phillips curve (part b) shifts to $SRPC_1$, inflation slows to 5 percent, real GDP remains at $600 billion, and unemployment remains at its natural rate of 6 percent.

The answer appears to be no. The main reason is that people form their expectations of the Bank of Canada's action (like they form expectations about anyone's actions) on the basis of actual behaviour, not on the basis of stated intentions. And the Bank suffers from a time-inconsistency problem. A **time-inconsistency problem** occurs when a plan looks good when viewed from one point in time but bad when viewed from a different point in time. How many times have you told yourself that it is your firm intention to take off five unwanted kilograms, or to keep within your budget and put a few dollars away for a rainy day, only to discover that, despite your very best intentions, your old habits win out in the end? When this type of thing happens to you, you experience time inconsistency.

Forecasting the Bank of Canada's behaviour is

similar to forecasting your own behaviour (but it's more complicated in practice). To forecast the Bank's actions, people look at the Bank's past *actions*, not its stated intentions. Based on such observations, they try to work out what the Bank's policy is, forecast its future actions, and forecast the effects of those actions on aggregate demand and inflation. Because the Bank usually does not launch an all-out attack on inflation, it is not rational to forecast that the Bank will take such action, even if it announces its intention to do so.

A related problem is that even if the Bank does make a credible announcement of its intention to slow inflation, its tools for achieving its objective are imperfect and the Bank cannot guarantee not to undershoot or overshoot its declared targets. In the most recent attempt to achieve price stability,

FIGURE 33.10

Going for Price Stability

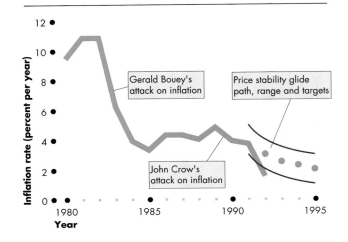

The Bank of Canada has attempted to lower the inflation rate on two occasions in the recent past, once in 1982-1985 and again in 1989-1992. On each occasion, the result was falling real GDP and rising unemployment. On both occasions, the Bank probably brought inflation down faster than it intended to. In the most recent period, it has undershot its previously announced target path.

the Bank published its targets and we now know that it brought inflation down much faster than it intended to.

A Truly Independent Bank of Canada

One suggestion for dealing with inflation is to make the Bank of Canada more independent and to charge it with the single responsibility of achieving and maintaining price level stability. Some central banks are more independent than the Bank of

Canada. The German and Swiss central banks are the best examples. Another example is the New Zealand central bank. All these central banks have the responsibility of stabilizing prices but not real GDP, and of doing so without interference from the government.

If an arrangement could be devised for making the Bank of Canada take a longer-term view concentrated only on inflation, it is possible that inflation could be lowered and kept low at a low cost.

REVIEW

U sually, when inflation is tamed, a recession results. The reason is that people form their expectations about policy on the basis of past policy actions. A more independent Bank of Canada pursuing only price stability could possibly achieve price stability with greater credibility and at lower cost. ◆

◆ ◆ ◆ ◆ We've now examined the main issues of stabilization policy. We've looked at the goals of stabilization policy, at the effects of the economy on political popularity, and at the fiscal and monetary policies pursued. We've seen how fixed and feedback rules operate under differing assumptions about the behaviour of the economy and why economists take different views on using these rules. We've also seen why lowering inflation usually is accompanied by recession. ◆ ◆ In the next chapter, we examine what many people believe is our economy's single most serious policy problem—the government's budget deficit ◆

SUMMARY

The Stabilization Problem

The stabilization problem is to keep the growth rate of real GDP steady (which also keeps unemployment

at its natural rate and prevents large international trade imbalances) and keep inflation low and predictable (which also avoids large fluctuations in the foreign exchange rate). (pp. 917–918)

Players and Policies

The key players in the formulation and execution of macroeconomic policy are the government of Canada and the Bank of Canada. The government makes fiscal policy and the Bank of Canada makes monetary policy.

Macroeconomic policy is influenced by the effects of macroeconomic performance on votes in federal elections. But there is no discernible attempt to use fiscal and monetary policy purely to get a government re-elected. Both fiscal policy and monetary policy have a cycle and each policy tends to counter the other.

The two broad types of stabilization policy are fixed rules and feedback rules. Fixed-rule policies are those that do not respond to the state of the economy, such as a constant growth rate of the money supply. Feedback-rule policies do respond to the state of the economy, stimulating activity in recession and holding activity in check in time of inflation. (pp. 918–924)

Stabilization Policy and Aggregate Demand Shocks

In the face of an aggregate demand shock, a fixed-rule policy takes no action to counter the shock. It permits aggregate demand to fluctuate as a result of all the independent forces that influence it. As a result, there are fluctuations in real GDP and the price level. A feedback-rule policy adjusts taxes, government purchases, or the money supply to offset the effects of other influences on aggregate demand. An ideal feedback rule keeps the economy at full employment, with stable prices.

Some economists argue that feedback rules make the economy less stable because they require greater knowledge of the state of the economy than we have, operate with time lags that extend beyond the forecast horizon, and introduce unpredictability about policy reactions. (pp. 924–928)

Stabilization Policy and Aggregate Supply Shocks

Two main aggregate supply shocks generate stabilization problems: cost-push inflation and a slowdown in productivity growth. A fixed rule minimizes the threat of and problems associated with cost-push inflation. A feedback rule reinforces cost-push inflation and leaves the price level and inflation rate free to move to wherever they are pushed. If productivity growth slows down, a fixed rule results in lower output (and higher unemployment) and a higher price level. A feedback rule that increases the money supply or cuts taxes to stimulate aggregate demand results in an even higher price level and higher inflation. Output (and unemployment) follows the same course as with a fixed rule.

By using feedback policies aimed at keeping nominal GDP growth steady—nominal GDP targeting—it is hoped to avoid excessive increases in inflation and decreases in real GDP growth. (pp. 928–934)

Taming Inflation

Inflation can be tamed, and at little or no cost in terms of lost output or excessive unemployment, by slowing the growth of aggregate demand in a credible and predictable way. But usually, when inflation is slowed down, a recession occurs. The reason is that people form their expectations about policy on the basis of actual behaviour, by looking at past actions, not by believing announced intentions. If the Bank of Canada could be made more independent and could pursue only a price stabilization goal, the cost of controlling inflation might be lower. (pp. 934–936)

K E Y E L E M E N T S

Key Terms

Federal budget, 918
Feedback rule, 924
Fixed rule, 924
Nominal GDP targeting, 931
Political business cycle, 920

Real business cycle theory, 930
Time-inconsistency problem 935

Key Figures

Figure 33.1   Macroeconomic Performance:
              Real GDP and Inflation, 917

Figure 33.3   The Fiscal Policy Record: A
              Summary, 920
Figure 33.4   The Monetary Policy Record: A
              Summary, 921
Figure 33.6   Two Stabilization Policies: Aggregate
              Demand Shock, 926

Figure 33.7   Stabilization Policy and Aggregate
              Supply: A Wage Increase, 929
Figure 33.8   Stabilization Policy and Aggregate
              Supply: A Decrease in Productivity,
              931
Figure 33.9   Reducing Inflation, 935

R E V I E W   Q U E S T I O N S

1 What are the goals of macroeconomic stabilization policy?

2 Describe the key players that formulate and execute macroeconomic policy? Explain the interaction between these players.

3 What is a political business cycle? Is there any evidence for a political business cycle in Canada since 1980?

4 Explain the distinction between a fixed-rule policy and a feedback-rule policy.

5 Analyse the effects of a temporary decrease in aggregate demand if a fixed rule is employed.

6 Analyse the behaviour of real GDP and the price level in the face of a permanent decrease in aggregate demand under

a   A fixed rule.

b   A feedback rule.

7 Explain the main problems in using fiscal policy for stabilizing the economy.

8 Why do economists disagree with each other on the appropriateness of fixed and feedback rules?

9 Analyse the effects of a rise in the price of oil on real GDP and the price level if the Bank of Canada employs

a   A fixed monetary rule.

b   A feedback monetary rule.

10 Explain nominal GDP targeting and why it reduces real GDP fluctuations and inflation.

11 Explain why the Bank of Canada's credibility affects the cost of lowering inflation.

P R O B L E M S

1 The economy is experiencing 10 percent inflation and 7 percent unemployment. Set out policies for the Bank of Canada and the government to pursue that will lower both inflation and unemployment. Explain how and why your proposed policies will work.

2 The economy is booming and inflation is beginning to rise, but it is widely agreed that a massive recession is just around the corner. Weigh the advantages and disadvantages of the government pursuing a fixed-rule and a feedback-rule fiscal policy.

3 The economy is in a recession and inflation is falling. It is widely agreed that a strong recovery is just around the corner. Weigh the advantages

and disadvantages of the Bank of Canada pursuing a fixed-rule and a feedback-rule monetary policy.

4 You have been hired by the prime minister to draw up an economic plan that will maximize the chance of his being re-elected.

a   What are the macroeconomic stabilization policy elements in that plan?

b   What do you have to make the economy do in an election year?

c   What policy actions would help the prime minister get re-elected?
    (In dealing with this problem, be careful to take into account the effects of your proposed policy on expectations and the effects of those expectations on actual economic performance.)

CHAPTER 34

THE FEDERAL DEFICIT

After studying this chapter, you will be able to

- ◆ Explain why, during the past decade, the federal government spent more each year than it raised in taxes
- ◆ Distinguish between debt and the federal deficit
- ◆ Distinguish between the *nominal* deficit and the *real* deficit
- ◆ Explain why the deficit appears to be larger than it really is
- ◆ Describe the different means available for financing the deficit
- ◆ Explain why the deficit makes the Bank of Canada's job harder
- ◆ Explain why a federal deficit can cause inflation
- ◆ Explain why a federal deficit can be a burden on future generations
- ◆ Describe the measures that are being taken to eliminate the federal deficit

E VERY SINGLE YEAR BETWEEN 1975 AND 1993, THE federal government spent more than it collected in taxes. During these eighteen years, the government's debt has grown to more than $400 billion. Why does the government have a deficit and growing debt? Is the deficit really as large as it appears? ◆ ◆ Some countries, such as Bolivia, Chile, Brazil, and Israel, have had large government deficits and runaway inflation. Do these experiences mean that Canada will eventually be the victim of rapid inflation? Does the deficit somehow make it harder, or even impossible, for the Bank of Canada to control the money supply and keep inflation in check? ◆ ◆ When we incur a personal debt, we accept a self-imposed obligation. When the nation incurs a debt, it imposes an obligation on its taxpayers. But the obligation does not end with the current taxpayers. It is passed on to their children and grandchildren. Does a government deficit impose a burden on future generations? ◆ ◆ There are two ways in which we can approach any problem: pretend it doesn't exist or try to identify its nature and solve it. How are we approaching the deficit? Are we sticking our heads in the sand like ostriches or are we taking steps that are likely to eliminate the deficit? What are the prospects for the future of the deficit?

Ottawa Spendthrifts

◆ ◆ ◆ ◆ In this chapter, we're going to study one of today's hottest economic topics. By the time you're through with this chapter, you'll be able to explain what the deficit is all about.

The Sources of the Deficit

W hat exactly is the deficit? The federal government's **budget balance** is equal to its total tax revenue minus its total expenditure in a given period of time (normally a year). Thus the government's budget balance is:

Budget balance = Revenue – Expenditure

The government's revenue consists of various types of taxes. Its expenditure is the sum of government purchases of goods and services, transfer payments, and interest on debt. If revenue exceeds expenditure, the budget balance is positive and the federal government has a **budget surplus**. If expenditure exceeds revenue, the budget balance is negative and the federal government has a **budget deficit**. If the budget balance is zero, in other words if tax revenue and expenditure are equal, the government has a **balanced budget**.

Government debt is the total amount of borrowing that the government has undertaken and the total amount that it owes to households, firms, and foreigners. Government debt is a stock. It is the accumulation of all the past deficits minus all the past surpluses. Thus, if the government has a deficit, its debt is increasing. If the government has a surplus, its debt is decreasing. If the government has a balanced budget, its debt is constant.

The Federal Budget: 1969–1992

Figure 34.1 shows the federal government's revenue, expenditure, and deficit from 1969 to 1992. As the figure illustrates, throughout this period the federal government had a budget deficit. The deficit climbed to 4.5 percent of GDP by 1978, and then slackened off through 1981. It grew again to a new peak of 6.8 percent of GDP in 1984. Between 1984 and 1990, the deficit declined, but it averaged 4.5 percent through the 1980s. The deficit increased again in the 1990 recession.

The effect of the deficit on the government's debt is shown in Fig. 34.2. So that you can see the government's debt in a slightly longer perspective, this figure begins in 1969. Also, to put the government's debt in perspective, we express it as a percentage of GDP. As you can see, federal government debt declined as a percentage of GDP through 1976. The ratio of debt to GDP in this year stood at its lowest point since World War II. The debt to GDP ratio increased slightly in the late 1970s and dramatically between 1981 and 1987. In the late 1980s, its growth continued, but at a more moderate rate. It grew quickly again in the 1990 recession.

[handwritten annotation: between 1975 & 1992]

FIGURE 34.1

The Deficit

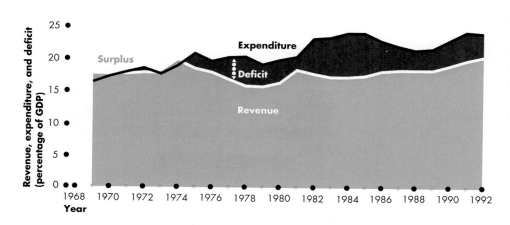

The figure records expenditure, revenue, and the deficit from 1969 to 1992. The deficit that first emerged in 1975 has persisted since that time.

Source: Bank of Canada Review, Table G1, Winter, 1992.

FIGURE 34.2

The Government Debt

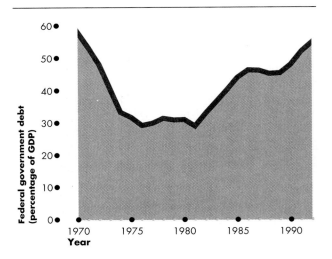

Government debt (the accumulation of past deficits minus past surpluses) declined through 1976. It remained fairly stable through 1981 but then increased sharply through 1985. Its growth slowed again in the second half of the 1980s and then sped up during the 1990 recession.

Source: Bank of Canada Review, Table G4, Winter, 1992.

Why did the government deficit appear in the 1970s, grow in the early 1980s, and remain high? The immediate answer is that in the 1970s and 1980s revenue declined and expenditure increased. But which sources of revenue decreased and which components of expenditure increased? Let's answer these questions by looking at revenue and expenditure in a bit more detail.

Federal Government Revenue

There are three broad categories of federal government revenue:

◆ Investment income

◆ Indirect taxes

◆ Income taxes

Investment income is the revenue received by the federal government from Crown corporations.

Indirect taxes are taxes on the goods and services that we buy. An example of an indirect tax is the Goods and Services Tax (GST). Income taxes include the taxes paid by individuals on their labour and capital incomes, taxes paid by companies on their profits, and taxes paid by foreigners on incomes earned in Canada. Figure 34.3(a) shows the levels and fluctuations in these taxes and in total taxes between 1975 and 1992. As you can see, total taxes decreased as a percentage of GDP between 1975 and 1979, increased through 1981 but then decreased through 1983. Most of the fluctuations were in income taxes. Investment income and indirect taxes remained relatively stable as percentages of GDP.

Federal Government Expenditure

We will examine federal government expenditure by dividing it into three categories:

◆ Purchases of goods and services

◆ Transfer payments

◆ Debt interest payments

The main item in the federal government's shopping basket is the purchase of goods and services for national defence. Other purchases of goods and services include items such as law and order and highways. Transfer payments include payments of social assistance and welfare benefits to households and subsidies to farms and other producers. Debt interest payments are paid by the government to the holders of its bonds—its outstanding debt.

Figure 34.3(b) shows the levels and fluctuations in these components of expenditure and in total expenditure between 1975 and 1992. As you can see, total expenditure remained fairly steady between 1975 and 1979 but increased between 1979 and 1984. It then declined slightly through 1989 before increasing again. Purchases of goods and services remained remarkably steady throughout this period but transfer payments grew steadily. The item that increased most persistently was debt interest. Once a persistent deficit had emerged, that deficit began to feed on itself. The deficit led to increased borrowing; increased borrowing led to higher interest payments; and higher interest payments led to a larger deficit.

FIGURE 34.3

Federal Government Revenue and Expenditure

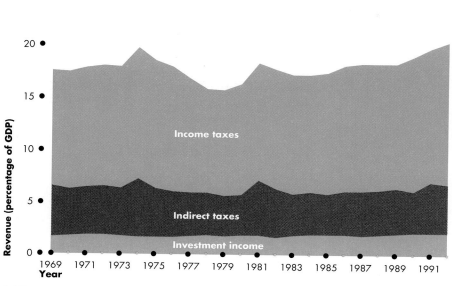

(a) Revenue

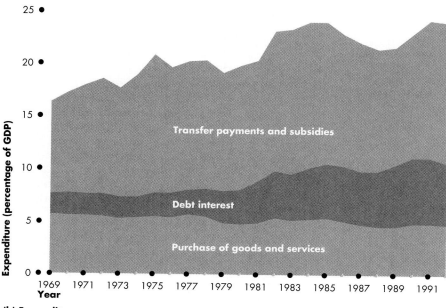

(b) Expenditure

Part (a) shows the three categories of federal government revenue: investment income, indirect taxes, and income taxes. Investment income (the income from Crown corporations) is a steady fraction of GDP. Indirect taxes fluctuate slightly and increased temporarily in 1974 and 1981. The largest item of government revenue and the one that fluctuates most is income taxes. There is no trend in federal government revenue but it fluctuates between 16 and 20 percent of GDP.

Part (b) shows the three categories of federal government expenditure: purchases of goods and services, debt interest, and transfer payments. Purchases of goods and services have been a steady and slightly declining percentage of GDP. Debt interest has increased most—the deficit feeding on itself. Transfer payments and subsidies have increased most strongly and have fluctuated most. It was the steady increase in transfer payments and subsidies combined with the sharp increase in debt interest that increased government expenditure.

Source: Bank of Canada Review, Table G1, Winter, 1992.

The Story of the Deficit

Until 1975, the federal government collected in taxes about the same amount as it spent on goods and services, transfer payments, and debt interest. In 1975, transfer payments increased sharply and tax revenue decreased. A deficit emerged.

But why did tax revenue fall and transfer payments increase in 1975? The event that triggered these changes was the energy crisis of the mid-1970s. The large increase in world energy prices was not permitted to feed through into energy prices in Canada. Instead, the government cut its own taxes on energy and increased its subsidies to those dependent on more costly energy. With the deficit in place, gradual decreases in income taxes, resulting mainly from the indexation of personal taxes, resulted in an ongoing deficit. The deficit was given a further boost in 1982 when transfer payments (mainly unemployment insurance payments) surged. The ongoing deficit, which increased debt, resulted in increasing interest payments that further fed the deficit. This has been the story of the deficit since the mid-1970s.

A Personal Analogy   Perhaps you will see more clearly why the deficit feeds on itself if you think in more personal terms. Suppose that each year you spend more than you earn. Your debt, let's say at the bank, rises each year. Therefore you owe the bank more in interest each year as a result of having a bigger debt outstanding. The government is in the same situation, but doesn't just borrow from banks. It borrows from anyone who buys the bonds that it issues—households, firms, the Bank of Canada, and foreigners. The government has been running a large deficit throughout the 1980s, so its outstanding debt has been rising and the interest payments on that debt have also been rising.

The Deficit and the Business Cycle

The size of the deficit is related to the phase of the business cycle through which the economy is passing. We defined the business cycle, in Chapter 22, as the ebbs and flows of economic activity measured by the percentage deviation of real GDP from trend. We also saw that fluctuations in the deviation of real GDP from trend match very closely fluctuations in

---

FIGURE 34.4

Unemployment and the Federal Deficit

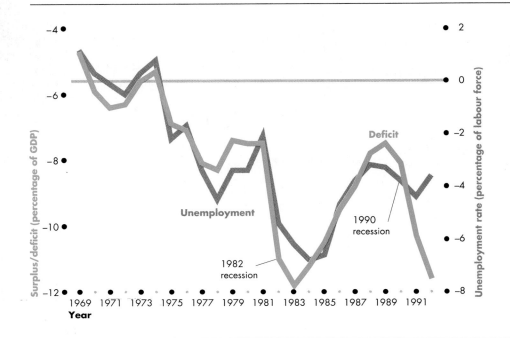

The business cycle—real GDP fluctuations—and the deficit move together. A recession leads to lower taxes and higher transfer payments and a higher deficit. A recovery leads to higher taxes, lower transfer payments, and a lower deficit. But despite the strong recovery in the 1980s, the deficit persisted. It increased again as the economy went into recession in 1990.

Source: Bank of Canada Review, Winter, 1992.

the deviation of unemployment from the natural rate.

To see the connection between the deficit and the business cycle, look at Fig. 34.4. This figure shows the federal deficit and the unemployment rate. As you can see, there is a remarkably close relationship between these two variables. When the unemployment rate increases, so does the deficit; when the unemployment rate decreases, so does the deficit.

Why does the deficit become larger when the economy goes into recession and unemployment increases? Part of the answer lies on the expenditure side and part on the tax revenue side of the government's account. The scale of government expenditure and tax revenue depends on the state of the economy. The government passes tax laws defining tax *rates*, not *dollars* to be paid in taxes. As a consequence, the tax revenue that the government collects depends on the level of income: if the economy is in a recovery phase of the business cycle, tax collections rise; if the economy is in a recession phase of the business cycle, tax collections fall.

Spending programs behave similarly. Many government programs are related to the state of well-being of individual citizens and firms. For example, when the economy is in a recession, unemployment is high, economic hardship from poverty increases, and a larger number of firms and farms experience hard times. Government transfer payments increase to respond to the increased economic hardship. When the economy experiences boom conditions, expenditure on programs to compensate for economic hardship declines.

In light of both of these factors, the deficit rises when the economy is in a depressed state and falls when the economy is in a state of boom. In order to take into account these facts, economists have developed a modified deficit concept called the cyclically adjusted deficit. The **cyclically adjusted deficit** is the deficit that would occur if the economy were at full employment. To measure the cyclically adjusted deficit, we calculate what tax revenue and expenditures would be if the economy were at full employment.

The Deficit in Recovery   From 1983 to 1989, the economy was in a prolonged and strong recovery. With unemployment declining, the deficit should have declined dramatically in these years. It declined but not as strongly as would have been expected given the strength of the recovery. It persisted around 3 percent, and the persistence of

a large deficit, even in the face of strong economic recovery, has led some observers to express grave concern about the potential effects of an ongoing deficit on the long-term health of the economy.

The Deficit in the 1990 Recession   During the 1990 recession, the deficit predictably increased as the growth of tax revenues slowed and spending on unemployment benefits and social programs increased. The deficit climbed from 3.5 percent in 1989 to 5 percent in 1991. The deficit remained high in the two years that followed and, when the provincial government deficits are added to the federal deficit, total government deficit was 7.5 percent of GDP in 1993—see Reading Between the Lines on pp. 946–947.

R E V I E W

The federal government deficit emerged in 1975 because the world oil shock resulted in a decrease in federal government revenue. The deficit persisted because revenue declined while expenditure increased only slightly. The deficit increased further in the early 1980s as a result of a sharp increase in government expenditure. *Welfare UI* Because the deficit persisted, debt and interest payment increased and the deficit fed on itself. A higher deficit led to higher debt, which in turn led to higher interest payments and a yet higher deficit. ◆ ◆ The deficit is related to the business cycle. Other things remaining the same, the stronger the economy, the smaller is the deficit. In the economic recovery of the 1980s, the relationship between the state of the economy and the deficit was broken, the deficit remaining large with the economy in a strong recovery. When the economy again went into recession in 1990, the deficit climbed to 5 percent of GDP. ◆

We've now seen when and how the deficit emerged and how it relates to the business cycle. But is the deficit really as bad as it looks? Can it really be true that in eight years the government debt increased by more than it did in the entire previous history of the nation? We'll now turn our attention to these questions.

Government Deficits

THE FINANCIAL POST, MAY 29–31, 1993

Canada's debt near $700B

By Catherine Harris

The eight provinces that have come down with budgets this spring are chopping their deficits by a total of $5.4 billion.

By itself, that sounds impressive. But it still leaves a total annual shortfall of $18.6 billion. And when that's combined with Ottawa's expected $32.6 billion deficit this year, we're left with government spending that's more than $50 billion greater than revenue intake.

And that's going to push up total federal and provincial government debt to $690 billion at March 31, 1994, according to calculations by Toronto Dominion Bank. That excludes Nova Scotia and Prince Edward Island (which delayed budgets until after their elections) and assumes deficit targets are met. These two would add on almost $7 billion to that total.

About half the planned decline in provincial deficits in 1993–94—$2.8 billion—is coming out of Ontario....

Some of the unhappiness with the budgets this year was with the tax increases, which could lower the incentive to increase earnings and instead raise the payoff in evading taxes and dampen revenue growth.

Canada's eight provinces with spring 1993 budgets (the two provinces with later budgets were Nova Scotia and Prince Edward Island) chopped their deficits by a total of $5.4 billion. Of this total, a cut of $2.8 billion was to come in Ontario.

The total provincial annual deficit after these cuts was projected to be $18.6 billion.

Adding Ottawa's projected deficit of $32.6 billion gave a total government sector deficit of more than $50 billion.

Total federal and provincial government debt was expected to reach $690 billion by March 31, 1994, according to the Toronto Dominion Bank.

Most of the deficit reduction took the form of tax increases rather than spending cuts.

Background and Analysis

In 1993, the total deficit of the federal and provincial governments was more than $50 billion—7.5 percent of GDP.

To some degree, this aggregate deficit was (and remains) a *structural deficit*—a deficit that could only be reduced by changing the structure of taxes, benefits, or government purchases of goods and services.

But part of the deficit arose from the fact that the Canadian economy was recovering from a deep and long recession and had not returned to its pre-recession growth path.

The effects of real GDP on the deficit is shown in part (a) of the figure. Government purchases plus debt interest payments do not change when real GDP changes and are shown by the horizontal line. Tax revenues *minus* transfer payments—*net taxes*—increase as real GDP increases and are shown by the upward-sloping line.

In 1993, with GDP at $680 billion, government purchases and debt interest exceeded net taxes by more than $50 billion.

With no changes in tax rates and in social programs that determine transfer payments, and with no change in government purchases plus debt interest, real GDP would have to increase to $900 billion (1993 dollars) to eliminate the deficit.

To rise to $900 billion, real GDP would have to grow by 3 percent a year for almost ten years.

If net taxes increased by 3 percent of GDP, the net taxes line would shift upward as shown in part (b) of the figure.

With this higher level of net taxes, budget balance would be achieved at a real GDP of $800 billion (1993 dollars), a level that would be attained after a mere five years of real GDP growth at a 3 percent annual rate.

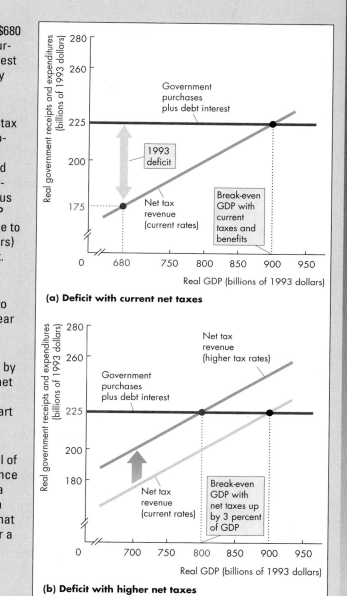

(a) Deficit with current net taxes

(b) Deficit with higher net taxes

The Real Deficit

Inflation distorts many things, not least of which is the deficit. To remove the inflationary distortion from the measured deficit, we need a concept of the real deficit. The **real deficit** is the change in the real value of outstanding government debt. The real value of outstanding government debt is equal to the market value of the debt divided by the price level. We are going to see how we can calculate the real deficit and how such a calculation changes our view of the size of the government's deficit. But before we do that, let's consider real deficits in more personal terms by examining the real deficit of a family.

The Real Deficit of a Family

In 1960, a young couple (perhaps your parents) ran a deficit to buy a new house. The deficit took the form of a mortgage. The amount borrowed to cover the deficit—the difference between the cost of the house and what the family had available to put down as a deposit—was $30,000. Today, the children of that couple are buying their first house. To do so, they also are incurring a deficit. But they're borrowing $120,000 to buy their first house. Is the $120,000 deficit (mortgage) of the 1990 house-buyer really four times as big as the deficit (mortgage) of the 1960 house-buyer? In dollar terms, the 1990 borrowing is indeed four times as big as the 1960 borrowing. But in terms of what money will buy, these two debts are almost equivalent to each other. Inflation in the years between 1960 and 1990 has raised the prices of most things to about four times what they were in 1960. Thus a mortgage of $120,000 in 1990 is really the same as a mortgage of $30,000 in 1960.

When a family buys a new home and finances it on a mortgage, it has a deficit in the year in which it buys the home. But in all the following years, until the debt has been paid off, the family has a surplus. That is, each year the family pays to the lender a sum of money, part of which covers the interest on the outstanding debt, but part of which *reduces* the outstanding debt. The reduction in the outstanding

debt is the household's surplus. Inflation has another important effect here. Because inflation brings higher prices, it also brings a lower real value of outstanding debts. Thus the real value of the mortgage declines by the amount paid off each year plus the amount wiped out by inflation. Other things remaining the same, the higher the inflation rate, the faster is the mortgage paid off, and the larger is the household's real surplus.

The Government's Real Deficit

This line of reasoning applies with equal force to the government. Because of inflation, the government's deficit is not *really* as big as it appears. To see how we can measure the deficit and correct for the distortion of inflation, we'll work through a concrete numerical example. First, look at Case A in Table 34.1—a situation in which there is no inflation. Government expenditure, excluding debt interest, is $17 billion and tax revenue is $20 billion. Thus, if the government didn't have interest to pay, it would have a surplus of $3 billion. But the government has outstanding debt of $50 billion and interest rates are running at 4 percent. Thus the government must pay $2 billion of debt interest (4 percent on $50 billion). When we add the $2 billion of debt interest to the government's other spending, we see that the government's total expenditure is $19 billion, so the government has a $1 billion surplus. The government's debt falls to $49 billion—the $50 billion outstanding at the beginning of the year is reduced by the surplus that the government has run. Ignore the last two rows of Table 34.1 for the moment.

Next, let's look at this same economy with exactly the same expenditure, tax revenue, and debt but in a situation in which there is a 10 percent *anticipated* inflation rate—Case B in Table 34.1. With 10 percent inflation anticipated, the market interest rate will not be 4 percent, but 14 percent. The reason why the interest rate is higher by 10 percentage points is that the real value of outstanding debt declines by 10 percent a year. Lenders—the households, firms, and foreigners that are buying government debt—know that the money they'll receive in repayment of the loans they make to the government will be worth less than the money they lend out. The government also recognizes that the money it will use to repay its debt will have a lower value than the money it borrows. Thus the government and the people from whom it borrows readily agree to a higher interest rate that compensates for these foreseen changes in the value of money. So, with a 14 percent interest rate, the government has to pay $7 billion in debt interest—14 percent of $50 billion. When the $7 billion of debt interest is added to the government's other spending, total expenditure is $24 billion, $4 billion more than tax revenue. Therefore the government has a deficit of $4 billion. At the end of the year, the government's debt will have increased from $50 billion to $54 billion.

TABLE 34.1

How Inflation Distorts the Deficit

	Case A	Case B
Government expenditure (excluding debt interest)	$17 billion	$17 billion
Tax revenue	$20 billion	$20 billion
Government debt	$50 billion	$50 billion
Market interest rate	4 percent	14 percent
Inflation rate	0 percent	10 percent
Real interest rate	4 percent	4 percent
Debt interest paid	$ 2 billion	$ 7 billion
Surplus (+)/deficit (–)	+$ 1 billion	–$ 4 billion
Government debt at end of year	$49 billion	$54 billion
Real government debt at end of year	$49 billion	$49 billion
Real surplus (+)/deficit (–)	+$ 1 billion	+$ 1 billion

Inflation distorts the measured deficit by distorting the debt interest payments made by the government. In this example, the real interest rate is 4 percent and government debt is $50 billion, so debt interest in real terms is $2 billion. With no inflation, Case A, the actual debt interest paid is also $2 billion. At 10 percent inflation, Case B, interest rates rise to 14 percent (in order to preserve a real interest rate of 4 percent), and debt interest increases to $7 billion. The deficit increases by $5 billion from a surplus of $1 billion to a deficit of $4 billion. This deficit is apparent, not real. With 10 percent inflation, the real value of the government's debt falls by $5 billion, offsetting the deficit of $4 billion and resulting in a $1 billion real surplus.

The only difference between the two situations we've just described is a 10 percent inflation rate. Real expenditure by the government and real tax revenue are the same and the real interest rate is the same in the two cases. But at the end of one year, government debt has increased to $54 billion in Case B and has fallen to $49 billion in Case A. Nevertheless the real debt is the same in the two cases. You can see this equality by keeping in mind that although government debt increases to $54 billion in Case B, the prices of all things have increased by 10 percent. If we deflate the government debt in Case B to express the debt in constant dollars instead of current dollars, we see that real government debt has actually fallen in Case B to $49 billion. ($54 billion divided by 1.1—1 plus the proportionate inflation rate—equals $49 billion.) Thus, even in Case B, the real situation is that there is a surplus of $1 billion. Inflation makes it appear that there is a $4 billion deficit when really there is a $1 billion surplus.

The numbers in Table 34.1 are, of course, hypothetical. They deal with two imaginary situations. But the calculations that we've just done provide us with a method of adjusting the federal government's deficit to eliminate the effects of inflation and reveal the real deficit. How important is it to adjust the federal government's deficit for inflation in order to obtain an inflation-free view of the deficit?

The Federal Government's Real and Nominal Deficit

Figure 34.5 provides an answer to the above question. It plots the nominal and real deficits of the federal government alongside each other. As you can see, the real deficit has not been as large as the nominal deficit, especially during the 1970s. The reason is that inflation was high during those years. Only when inflation declined in the mid-1980s, while interest rates remained high, did a large and persistent real deficit emerge.

You can see then that the distinction between the real and nominal deficit is an important practical distinction only when the inflation rate is high. Taking the distinction into account changes our view of the scale and seriousness of the deficit during the 1970s. But it does not change the story much in the second half of the 1980s and the 1990s.

FIGURE 34.5

The Real Deficit and the Nominal Deficit

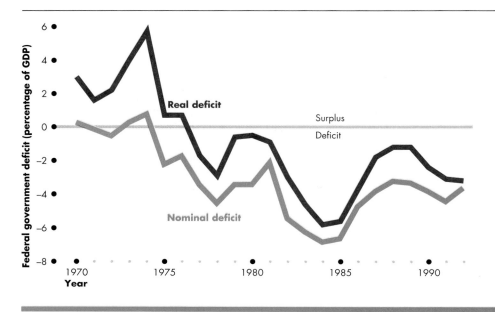

The real deficit removes the effects of inflation from interest rates and from the outstanding value of government debt. The real deficit and the nominal deficit follow a similar path, but the real deficit is smaller than the nominal deficit. Only when inflation declined in the 1980s did the two deficit measures move close together.

Source: *Bank of Canada Review*, Winter, 1992, and our calculations.

Deficits and Inflation

Many people fear government deficits because they believe deficits lead to inflation. Do deficits cause inflation? That depends on how the deficit is financed.

Financing the Deficit

To finance its deficit, the government sells bonds. But the effects of bond sales depend on who buys the bonds. If they are bought by the Bank of Canada, they bring an increase in the money supply. But if they are bought by anyone other than the Bank of Canada, they do not bring a change in the money supply.

When the Bank of Canada buys government bonds, it pays for them by creating new money (see Chapter 28, pp. 774–779). We call such financing of the deficit money financing. **Money financing** is the financing of the government deficit by the sale of

bonds to the Bank of Canada, which results in the creation of additional money. All other financing of the government's deficit is called debt financing. **Debt financing** is the financing of the government deficit by selling bonds to anyone (household, firm, or foreigner) other than the Bank of Canada.

Let's look at the consequences of these two ways of financing the deficit, starting with debt financing.

Debt Financing   First, suppose that the government borrows money by selling Treasury bonds to households and firms. In order to sell a bond, the government must offer the potential buyer a sufficiently attractive deal. In other words, the government must offer a high enough rate of return to convince people to lend their money.

Let's suppose that the going interest rate is 10 percent a year. In order to sell a bond worth $100 and cover its deficit of $100, the government must promise not only to pay back the $100 at the end of the year but also to pay the interest of $10 accumulated on that debt. Thus, to finance a deficit of $100 today, the government must pay $110 a year from today. In one year's time, in order simply to stand still, the government would have to borrow $110 to cover the cost of repaying, with interest, the bond that it sold a year earlier. Two years from today the government will have to pay $121—the $110 borrowed plus the 10 percent interest ($11) on that $110. The process continues with the total amount of debt and total interest payments mushrooming year after year.

Money Financing   Next, consider what happens if instead of selling bonds to households and firms, the government sells Treasury bonds to the Bank of Canada. There are two important differences in this case compared with the case of debt financing. First, the government winds up paying no interest on these bonds; second, additional money is created.

The government ends up paying no interest on bonds bought by the Bank of Canada because the Bank, although an independent agency, pays any profit it makes to the government. Thus, other things remaining the same, if the Bank receives an extra million dollars from the government in interest payments on government bonds held by the Bank, the Bank's profits increase by that same million dollars and flow back to the government. Second, when the Bank buys bonds from the government, it uses newly created money to do so. This newly created

money flows into the banking system in the form of an increase in the monetary base and enables the banks to create additional money by making additional loans. (See Chapter 27 and Chapter 28.)

As we studied in Chapter 24 and Chapter 31, an increase in the money supply causes an increase in aggregate demand. And higher aggregate demand eventually brings a higher price level. Persistent money financing leads to a continuously increasing aggregate demand and to inflation.

Debt Financing versus Money Financing   Figure 34.6 illustrates the extent to which debt financing and money financing have been used to cover the federal deficit in Canada over the past twenty years. As you can see, money financing has been used in a very limited way. It is true that in the 1970s and early 1980s, money financing increased, but there were times in the 1980s when the total amount of bond financing even exceeded the deficit itself. Thus in Canada, the large federal deficit has not, as yet, brought a large amount of money financing.

What are the pros and cons of financing a deficit by issuing debt or creating money? In comparing these two methods of financing the deficit, it is clear

FIGURE 34.6

Debt Financing versus Money Financing

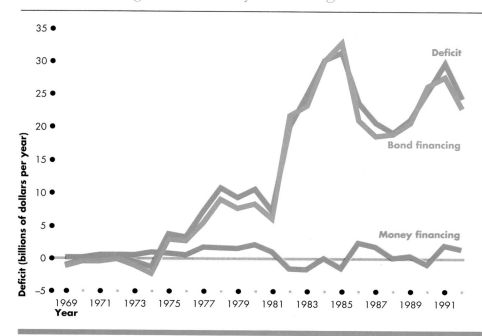

As the federal deficit mushroomed through the 1970s and 1980s, so also did the financing of that deficit by issuing debt. The use of money financing has been kept under tight control and in some years, such as 1983 and 1986, the amount of debt issued even exceeded the deficit.

Source: Figure 34.1 and *Bank of Canada Review,* CANSIM series B201.

that debt financing leaves the government with an ongoing obligation to pay interest—an obligation that gets bigger each year if the government keeps running deficits. When the government uses money financing, it pays its bills and that is the end of the matter. (The government pays interest to the Bank of Canada, but the Bank pays its profit to the government, so the government has no ongoing interest obligation.) There is a clear advantage from the government's point of view to use money financing rather than debt financing. Unfortunately, this solution causes inflationary problems for everybody else.

But the alternative, debt financing, is not problem free. Financing the deficit through bond sales to households, firms, and foreigners causes a mushrooming scale of debt and interest payments. The larger the scale of debt and interest payments, the bigger the deficit problem becomes, and the greater is the temptation to end the process of debt financing. Thus the temptation increases to finance the deficit by selling bonds to the Bank of Canada—

money financing. This ever-present temptation is what leads many to fear that deficits are inflationary even when they are not immediately money financed.

International Evidence

We have a large amount of experience from a wide variety of countries on the relationship between inflation and deficits. What does that experience tell us? Are deficits, in fact, inflationary?

This question is answered in Fig. 34.7. It contains data on inflation and deficits for 67 countries covering the 1980s. The countries are in three groups: Latin America (part a), European Community (part b), and 48 others (part c). The 67 countries are the only ones for which there are data on both inflation and the deficit for most of the 1980s.

First, notice the tremendous range of experience. The highest inflation rate was almost 1,600 percent per year—in Nicaragua (part a). The lowest inflation

FIGURE 34.7

Deficits and Inflation

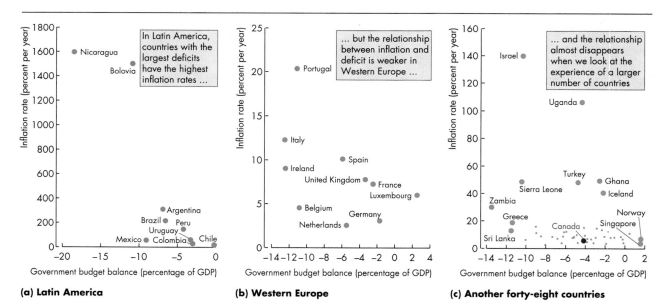

(a) Latin America   **(b) Western Europe**   **(c) Another forty-eight countries**

The relationship between the deficit and inflation is shown for 9 Latin American countries (part a), 10 countries in the European Community (part b), and 48 other countries—including Canada (part c). There is a tendency for large deficit countries to be high-inflation countries, but the correlation is weak.

Source: International Financial Statistics Yearbook, 1990. For each country, the dot shows its deficit (as a percentage of GDP) and inflation (GDP deflator) for the 1980s (or part decade where the full decade is not available).

rate was less than 3 percent—in the Netherlands (part b). The largest deficit was almost 20 percent of GDP—again in Nicaragua. The smallest deficit (actually a surplus) was more than 2 percent of GDP—in Luxembourg.

Second, look at the relationships between deficits and inflation. In the Latin American countries (part a), there is a clear tendency for these two variables to be correlated. The countries with the largest deficits (Nicaragua and Bolivia) have the highest inflation rates. The countries with the smallest deficits (Chile, Columbia, and Uruguay) have the lowest inflation rates. And countries with deficits between these have inflation rates that are intermediate as well (Argentina and Brazil). Only Mexico does not fit the pattern. Its inflation rate is lower than that in countries with much smaller deficits. In the European Community (part b), there is a similar, although somewhat weaker, relationship between deficits and inflation. And the relationship, although still present, is very loose for the countries shown in part (c).

Third, notice the position of Canada. Its deficit is in the middle of the pack but its inflation rate is among the lowest.

We have now reviewed the relationship between deficits and inflation. Deficits are not inevitably inflationary. But there is a correlation between deficits and inflation. And the larger the deficit and the longer it persists, the greater are the pressures and temptations to cover the deficit by creating money, thereby generating inflation.

Another common view about the deficit is that it places a burden on future generations. Let's now examine that view.

A Burden on Future Generations?

I t is a common and popular cry that "we owe it to our children to control the deficit." Is this popular view correct? How would the deficit place a burden on future generations?

We've already examined one burden that the deficit might place on future generations—the burden of inflation. But when people talk about the deficit as a burden on future generations, they usually mean something other than inflation. For example, somebody has to pay the interest on the huge national debt that the deficit creates. The government will pay the interest with money it takes from the people as taxes. Taxes will have to be raised. Won't those taxes burden future generations?

Wait, though: Doesn't the interest paid each year get financed with taxes collected each year? So how can the deficit be a burden to *future* generations? It might be a burden to some members of the future generation, but it must be a benefit to others, so that in the aggregate it evens out.

Although in the aggregate the interest paid equals the tax revenue collected, there may be important redistribution effects. For example, one feature of our present deficit is that some government debt is being bought not by Canadians but by American, European, and Japanese investors. So part of the future burden of the current deficit is that future Canadian taxpayers will have to provide the resources with which to pay interest to foreign holders of Canadian government debt.

There's another way in which today's deficit can make people poorer tomorrow: by slowing today's pace of investment and reducing the stock of productive capital equipment available for future generations. This phenomenon is called crowding out.

Crowding Out

Crowding out is the tendency for an increase in government purchases of goods and services to bring a decrease in investment (see Chapter 29, pp. 794–798). If crowding out does occur, and if government purchases of goods and services are financed by government debt, the economy will have a larger stock of government debt and a smaller stock of capital—plant and equipment. Unproductive government debt replaces productive capital.

Crowding out does *not* occur if

1. There is unemployment.
2. The deficit arises from the government's purchases of capital on which the return equals (or exceeds) that on privately purchased capital.

Crowding out *does* occur if

1. There is full employment.
2. The government purchases consumption goods and services or capital on which the return is less than that on privately purchased capital.

The Level of Employment   If there is full employment, increased government purchases of goods and services (and an increased deficit) must result in a decrease in the purchases of other goods and services. But if there is unemployment, it is possible that an increase in government purchases (and an increased deficit) could result in a decrease in unemployment and an increase in output. In such a case the deficit does not completely crowd out other expenditure. This possibility can only occur for short periods and when the economy is in recession.

Productive Government Purchases   Much of what the government purchases is productive capital. Highways, dams, airports, schools, and universities are obvious examples. But there are some not-so-obvious examples. Education and health care are investments in productive human capital. Defence expenditure protects both our physical and human capital resources and is also productive capital expenditure. To the extent that the deficit results from our acquisition of such assets, it does not crowd out productive capital. On the contrary, it contributes to it.

But it is possible for government purchases of consumption goods and services to crowd out productive capital. Let's see how.

How Crowding Out Occurs   For crowding out to occur, a deficit must result in less investment, so that future generations have a smaller capital stock than they otherwise would have had. This drop in the capital stock will lower their income and, in a sense, be a burden to them. (They will still be richer than we are, but not as rich as they would have been if they had a larger stock of productive machines.)

The scale of investment depends on its opportunity cost. That opportunity cost is the real interest rate. Other things remaining the same, the higher the real interest rate, the less firms will want to invest in new plant and equipment. For a government deficit to crowd out investment, the deficit must cause real interest rates to rise.

Some people believe that a deficit does increase

FIGURE 34.8

The Deficit, Borrowing, and Crowding Out

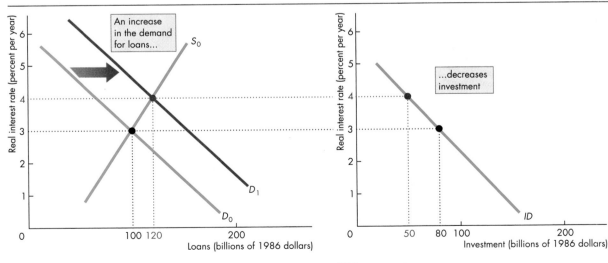

(a) The market for loans

(b) Investment

Part (a) shows the market for loans. The demand for loans is D_0 and the supply is S_0. The quantity of loans made is $100 billion and the real interest rate is 3 percent a year. Part (b) shows the determination of investment. At an interest rate of 3 percent a year, investment is $80 billion. The government runs a deficit and finances the deficit by borrowing. The government's increase in demand for loans shifts the demand curve to D_1. The interest rate rises to 4 percent a year and the equilibrium quantity of loans increases to $120 billion. The higher interest rate leads to a decrease in investment in part (b). The government deficit crowds out capital accumulation.

interest rates because the government's own borrowing represents an increase in the demand for loans with no corresponding increase in the supply of loans. Figure 34.8 shows what happens in this case. Part (a) shows the demand and supply curves for loans. Initially, the demand for loans is D_0 and the supply of loans is S_0. The real interest rate is 3 percent, and the quantity of loans made is $100 billion. Part (b) shows investment. At a real interest rate of 3 percent, investment is $80 billion. Now suppose that the government runs a deficit. To finance its deficit, the government borrows. The demand for loans increases and the demand curve for loans shifts from D_0 to D_1. There is no change in the supply of loans, so the real interest rate increases to 4 percent and the quantity of loans increases to $120 billion. Notice that the increase in the quantity of loans made is smaller than the increase in the demand for loans. That is, the demand curve shifts rightward by a larger amount than the increase in loans that actually occurs. The higher interest rate decreases investment and brings a smaller capital stock. Thus the increased stock of government debt crowds out some productive capital.

Does a deficit make real interest rates rise as shown in Fig. 34.8? Many economists believe so, and they have some pretty strong evidence to point to. Real interest rates in Canada in the last decade, in precisely the years in which we have had a large real deficit, have been higher than at any time in history. Furthermore, there is a general tendency for real interest rates and the real deficit to fluctuate in sympathy with each other.

It is this relationship in the data that leads some economists to predict that a higher real deficit means higher real interest rates, lower investment, and a smaller scale of capital accumulation. Because of its effects on real interest rates, the real deficit and the accumulation of paper debt crowds out the accumulation of productive physical capital. As a consequence, future output will be lower than it otherwise would have been, and so the deficit burdens future generations.

Ricardian Equivalence

Some economists do not believe that deficits crowd out capital accumulation. On the contrary, they argue, debt financing and paying for government spending with taxes are equivalent. The level of purchases of goods and services matters, but not the way in which it is financed.

The first economist to advance this idea (known as Ricardian equivalence) was the great English economist David Ricardo. Recently, Ricardo's idea has been given a forceful restatement by Robert Barro of Harvard University. Barro argues as follows: If the government increases its purchases of goods and services but does not increase taxes, people are smart enough to recognize that the government will increase taxes later in order to cover the increased spending and interest payments on the debt being issued today. In recognition of having to pay higher taxes later, people will cut their consumption now and save more. They'll increase their saving so that when the higher taxes are finally levied, sufficient wealth has been accumulated to meet those tax liabilities without a further cut in consumption. The scale of increased saving matches the scale of increased government spending.

Figure 34.9 illustrates this case. Initially, the demand for loans is D_0 and the supply of loans S_0. The real interest rate is 3 percent and the quantity

FIGURE 34.9

Ricardian Equivalence

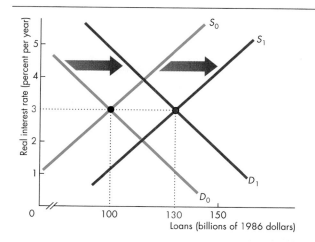

Initially, the demand for loans is D_0 and the supply of loans is S_0. The equilibrium quantity of loans is $100 billion and the real interest rate is 3 percent a year. An increase in the government deficit, financed by borrowing, increases the demand for loans, shifting the demand curve to D_1. Households, recognizing that the increased government deficit will bring increased future taxes to pay the additional interest charges, cut their consumption and increase their saving. The supply curve of loans shifts rightward to S_1. The equilibrium quantity of loans increases to $130 billion, but the real interest rate stays constant at 3 percent a year. There is no crowding out of investment.

of loans made is $100 billion. The government runs a deficit and finances that deficit by borrowing. The demand curve for loans shifts rightward to D_1. At the same time, using the reasoning of Ricardo and Barro, there is a decrease in consumption and an increase in saving. The supply of loans increases, shifting the supply curve rightward to S_1. The quantity of loans increases from $100 to $130 billion and the real interest rate stays constant at 3 percent. With no change in the real interest rate, there is no crowding out of investment.

Some economists argue that Ricardian equivalence breaks down because people take into account only the future tax liabilities that will be borne by themselves and not by their children and their grandchildren. Proponents of the Ricardian equivalence proposition argue that it makes no difference whether future tax liabilities are borne by those currently alive or by their descendants. If the taxes are borne by children and grandchildren, the current generation takes account of those future taxes and adjusts its own consumption so that it can make bequests on a large enough scale to enable those taxes to be paid.

Laying out the assumptions necessary for Ricardian equivalence leaves most economists convinced that the Ricardian equivalence proposition cannot apply to the real world. Yet there is a surprising amount of evidence in its support. In order to interpret the evidence, it is important to be clear that Ricardian equivalence does *not* imply that real interest rates are not affected by the level of government purchases. A high level of government purchases, other things remaining the same, brings a higher real interest rate. The Ricardian equivalence proposition implies that real interest rates are not affected by the way in which a given level of government purchases is financed. Regardless of whether government purchases are financed by taxes, or by borrowing, real interest rates will be the same.

Whether it is the deficit or the level of government purchases of goods and services that affects real interest rates remains unclear. If people do take into account future tax burdens (and not just their own but their children's and grandchildren's future tax burdens), then saving will respond to offset the deficit. The deficit itself will have little or no effect on real interest rates and capital accumulation. If people ignore the implications of the deficit for their own and their descendants' future consumption possibilities, the deficit will indeed increase real interest rates. The jury remains out on this question.

Eliminating the Deficit

Measures to eliminate the deficit can attack either the revenue side or the expenditure side of the government's budget. That is, there are two ways to eliminate the deficit:

◆ Reducing expenditure

◆ Increasing revenue

Reducing Expenditure

Throughout the modern history of most countries, government expenditure has increased as a percentage of GDP. The government of Canada has contained the growth of government expenditure more effectively than most governments. In most European countries, governments spend close to 50 percent of GDP and in the Netherlands expenditure was more than 53 percent of GDP at its peak in 1983.

Many components of government expenditure have a built-in tendency to increase at a faster pace than GDP. Two such components are education and health care. Even when these items are purchased privately, people spend a larger fraction of their incomes on them as incomes increase. When the government plays a significant role in the provision of these two goods, voter pressure for better provision of services is irresistible and the government has little choice but to increase its expenditures to meet voter demands. Only by "privatizing" these activities can the government's share of GDP be prevented from increasing.

In many European countries, the government is privatizing a variety of manufacturing operations. The Thatcher government in Britain (in the 1980s) even tried to limit its involvement in health care and health insurance. But there is much less scope for such privatization in Canada, for we have not taken the route of the Europeans in this regard.

In the early 1990s, one factor working against the tide of ever larger government expenditure is the "peace dividend"—the reduction in defence spending resulting from the end of the Cold War. It is possible that the peace dividend will finance enhanced health and other social programs without an increase in the overall level of government spending. But this dividend is likely to be short-lived. In the long run, growing incomes will bring higher expenditure.

Because of the difficulty of making significant reductions in government spending, many people take the view that the only way to eliminate the deficit is to increase government revenue. Let's now examine that option.

Increasing Revenue

Two approaches to increasing revenue have been proposed:

◆ Increase tax rates

◆ Decrease tax rates

Sounds paradoxical? Not really, when you remember that what the government wants to do is to increase its tax *revenue*. *Tax revenue* is the product of the tax rate and the tax base. A **tax rate** is the percentage rate of tax levied on a particular activity. The **tax base** is the activity on which a tax is levied. For example, the tax base for personal income tax is earned income minus some specified allowances.

There is ambiguity and disagreement about whether an increase in tax rates increases or decreases tax revenues. The source of the disagreement is something called the Laffer curve. The **Laffer curve** (named after Arthur Laffer, who first proposed it) is a curve that relates tax revenue to the tax rate. Figure 34.10 illustrates a hypothetical Laffer curve. The tax rate ranges between zero and 100 percent on the vertical axis. Tax revenue, measured in billions of dollars, is shown on the horizontal axis. If the tax rate is zero, then no tax revenue is raised. That is why the curve begins at the origin. As the tax rate increases, tax revenue also increases but only up to some maximum—*m* in the figure. In this example, once the tax rate has reached 40 percent, tax revenue is at its maximum. If the tax rate increases above 40 percent, tax revenue falls. Why does this happen?

Revenue falls because there is a fall in the scale of the activity that is being taxed. Suppose that the item in question is gasoline. With no tax, lots of people drive gas-guzzling cars and consume billions of litres a week. If gasoline is taxed, its price increases and the quantity bought declines. At first, the quantity bought decreases by a smaller percentage than the percentage increase in tax, and tax revenue increases. But there comes a point at which the decrease in the quantity demanded rises by a bigger

percentage than the increase in taxes. At that point, tax revenue begins to decline. People sell their gas-guzzlers, buy smaller cars, join car pools, and use public transportation. The tax rate goes up but the tax base goes down and tax revenue declines.

You can now see that whether a cut in the *tax rate* increases or decreases *tax revenue* depends on where we are on the Laffer curve. If we're at a point such as *a* in Fig. 34.10, a decrease in the tax rate results in an increase in tax revenue. But if we're at point *b*, a decrease in the tax rate results in a decrease in tax revenue. To increase tax revenue from point *b*, we have to increase the tax rate.

Economists and other observers argue about where we are on the Laffer curve for each of the various taxes. Some people suspect that for very highly

---

FIGURE 34.10

The Laffer Curve

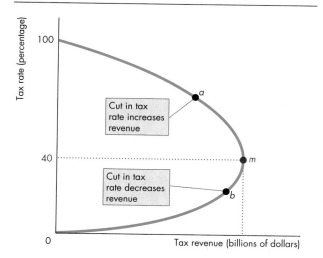

The Laffer curve shows the relationship between a tax rate and tax revenue. If the tax rate is 0 percent, the government collects no tax revenue. As the tax rate increases, the government's tax revenue also increases, but up to some maximum (*m*). As the tax rate continues to increase, tax revenue declines. At a tax rate of 100 percent, the government collects no revenue. Higher taxes act as a disincentive. The more heavily taxed is an activity, the less that activity is undertaken. When the percentage decrease in the activity is less than the percentage increase in the tax rate, we are at a point such as *b* and tax revenue rises. When the percentage decrease in the activity exceeds the percentage increase in the tax rate, we are at a point such as *a* and tax revenue decreases.

taxed commodities, such as gasoline, tobacco products, and alcohol, we are on the backward-bending part of the Laffer curve, so that an increase in the tax rate would decrease tax revenue. But hardly anyone believes this to be the case for the big revenue-raising taxes such as personal income taxes and sales taxes. It is much more likely, in the case of those taxes, that an increase in tax rates would increase tax revenue.

The second approach to increasing revenue is to reform taxes, lowering high marginal tax rates and perhaps introducing new taxes at low rates on activities not previously taxed.

The search for changes in taxes that will bring higher tax revenue is a permanent feature of our economic life and will always be with us, regardless of whether there is a deficit. But in a deficit situation, that search takes on a much greater urgency.

◆ ◆ ◆ ◆ We have now completed our study of macroeconomics and of the challenges and problems of stabilizing the economy. In this study, our main focus has been the Canadian economy. Occasionally, we have taken into account the linkages between Canada and the rest of the world, but international economic relations have not been our main concern. In the remaining chapters, we are going to shift our focus and study some vital international issues. First, in Chapter 35, we examine the international exchange of goods and services. Second, in Chapter 36, we study the financing of international trade and the determination of the value of our dollar in terms of other currencies. Third, in Chapter 37, we turn our attention to the problems of the developing countries of the Third World. Fourth. Finally, in Chapter 38, we examine economic systems in transition, such as those in the Soviet Union and China.

S U M M A R Y

The Sources of the Deficit

Until 1975, the federal government collected in taxes the same amount as it spent. In 1975, there was a sharp increase in transfer payments and a decrease in tax revenue, and a deficit emerged. The event that transformed the government's budget was the energy crisis of the mid-1970s. A large increase in world energy prices led the government of Canada to cut taxes on energy and increase subsidies to energy-dependent sectors. The deficit was worsened by decreases in income taxes resulting from the indexation of personal taxes in the 1970s and by a surge in transfer payments (mainly unemployment insurance payments) in the early 1980s. The deficit increased federal debt and resulted in increased interest payments that further fed the deficit.

The deficit fluctuates in sympathy with the business cycle. When the economy is in a recovery, taxes increase and transfer payments decrease as a percentage of GDP. The deficit declines. When the economy goes into recession, taxes decrease and transfer payments increase as a percentage of GDP, and so the deficit increases.

The deficit is large despite the fact that the economy has had a long, strong recovery. It is this fact that makes the current deficit a serious problem. (pp. 941–945)

The Real Deficit

Inflation distorts the deficit by overstating the real interest burden. Adjusting the deficit for this fact and measuring the real deficit lowers the deficit in the 1970s but makes little difference in the later 1980s. The cycles in the deficit remain the same, whether measured in real or current dollar terms. (pp. 948–950)

Deficits and Inflation

If deficits are money financed, they cause inflation. If they are debt financed, whether or not they cause inflation depends on how permanent they are. A temporary debt-financed deficit will have no inflationary effects. A permanent debt-financed deficit leads to inflation. It does so because the buildup of debt leads to a buildup of interest payments and a yet higher deficit. At some future date, the deficit will be money financed and the amount of money created will be larger, the longer the deficit persists and the more debt is issued. Fear of future inflation leads to a demand here and now for less government debt and less money. As a consequence, interest rates and inflation increase in anticipation of a future (and perhaps distant future) increase in money creation to finance the deficit. (pp. 950–953)

A Burden on Future Generations?

Whether the deficit is a burden on future generations is a controversial issue. Some economists believe that the deficit causes real interest rates to rise, thereby crowding out investment and reducing the amount of capital that we accumulate. As a consequence, future output will be lower than it otherwise would have been and future generations will be burdened with the effects of the deficit.

Other economists argue that government expenditure affects interest rates but the way in which that expenditure is financed does not. They suggest that if government spending is financed by borrowing, people will recognize that future taxes will have to increase to cover both the spending and the interest from the accumulated debt. And, in anticipation of those higher future taxes, saving will increase and consumption will decrease in the present. Thus the burden of increased government expenditure— not the burden of the deficit—is spread across all generations. (pp. 953–956)

Eliminating the Deficit

The deficit can be eliminated by reducing expenditure, by increasing revenue, or by a combination of the two. If social programs in Canada are to be maintained, there seems little scope for reducing expenditure. Increasing revenue could result from either increasing tax rates (if we are on the upward-sloping part of the Laffer curve) or decreasing tax rates (if we are on the backward-bending part of the Laffer curve). (pp. 956–958)

K E Y   E L E M E N T S

Key Terms

Balanced budget, 941
Budget balance, 941
Budget deficit, 941
Budget surplus, 941
Cyclically adjusted deficit, 945
Debt financing, 950
Government debt, 941
Laffer curve, 957
Money financing, 950
Real deficit, 948

Tax base, 957
Tax rate, 957

Key Figures

Figure 34.1   The Deficit, 941
Figure 34.4   Unemployment and the Federal Deficit, 944
Figure 34.5   The Real Deficit and the Nominal Deficit, 950
Figure 34.6   Debt Financing versus Money Financing, 951

R E V I E W   Q U E S T I O N S

1 List the main changes in taxes and government spending that are associated with the emergence of the federal government deficit.

2 Trace the events between 1980 and 1983 that resulted in an increase in the federal government's deficit.

3 What is meant by the cyclically adjusted deficit?

4 Distinguish between the real deficit and the nominal deficit.

5 In calculating the real deficit, which of the following would you do?

a   Value the interest payments in real terms and take into account the change in the real value of government debt.

b   Calculate the interest payments in nominal

terms and take into account the change in the real value of government debt.

c   Calculate the interest payments in real terms but ignore the change in the real value of outstanding government debt.

6   Explain how debt financing a deficit results in mushrooming interest payments.

7   Explain how, in a modern sophisticated financial system, the government finances its deficit by creating money.

8   Review the ways in which the deficit can be a burden on future generations.

9   Why do some economists argue that taxes and government debt are equivalent to each other so that the deficit does not matter?

10   What are the four main proposals for reducing government expenditure?

11   Why do some economists think that government revenue can be increased by cutting tax rates?

P R O B L E M S

1   You are given the following information about the economy of Spendland. When unemployment is at its natural rate, which is 5.5 percent, government spending and tax revenue are each 10 percent of GDP. There is no inflation. For each 1 percentage point increase in the unemployment rate, government spending increases by 1 percentage point of GDP and tax revenue falls by 1 percentage point of GDP.

Suppose that Spendland experiences a cycle in which the unemployment rate takes the following values:

Year	Unemployment rate
1	5
2	6
3	7
4	6
5	5
6	4
7	5

a   Calculate the actual deficit (as a percentage of GDP) for each year.

b   Calculate Spendland's cyclically adjusted deficit.

2   Government expenditure, excluding debt interest, on Day Dream Island is $8.5 billion. Taxes are $10 billion. The government has a $25 billion outstanding debt. Interest rates are 24 percent and there is a 20 percent inflation rate. Calculate the following:

a   The debt interest that the government pays

b   The government's budget surplus or deficit

c   The value of the government debt outstanding at the end of the year

d   The government's real deficit

e   The real value of its debt outstanding at the end of the year

3   The rate of return on private capital is 5 percent. The government is planning an increase in public health and welfare programs at an annual cost of $100 billion. These programs are expected to improve health and labour productivity, resulting in an increase in GDP of $50 billion a year. There is full employment.

a   What is the opportunity cost of the government program?

b   Does it make any difference to the opportunity cost if the program is financed by current taxes, borrowing, or money creation?

c   Will the program be a burden or a benefit to future generations if it is financed by borrowing?

PART 13

INTERNATIONAL ECONOMICS

**Talking
with
Laura
Tyson**

Laura Tyson was born in New Jersey in 1947. She was an undergraduate at Smith College and obtained her Ph.D. in economics from MIT in 1974. Dr. Tyson is Professor of Economics and Business Administration at the University of California at Berkeley and a consultant to the Council on Competitiveness. Her central area of work has been on the competitiveness and trade performance of the United States.

Professor Tyson, how did you get into economics?

I was immediately taken with economics when I first studied it as a sophomore in college. I was fascinated by both the international and public policy aspects: that is to say, how different countries try to solve their basic economic problems and how both the problems and countries relate to one another. I was also looking for a way to combine my analytic instincts with a public policy discipline, and economics was a wonderful match.

Most economists are free traders. But some, perhaps an increasing number, believe some measure of protectionism can help a developing country get off the ground. Where do you stand in the free trade versus protection debate for developing countries?

Like most economists, I consider myself to be a free trader. I believe that GATT has provided significant benefits to the world by breaking down many formal trade barriers. I'd like to see even more free trade. My studies of how countries interact suggest that free trade as an ideal does not exist; we're actually quite far from it. Countries have to push

very hard for change at the international level. At the same time, they have to use the domestic policies they have at their disposal to compensate for the fact that free trade doesn't exist.

Trade is of critical importance for bringing developing countries greater prosperity. Developing countries can't depend on aid or investment to the same extent they could in the past. They depend on trading in the world economy to increase their prosperity. They've become extremely dependent on their ability to find markets for their products.

Trade between poor and rich countries is likely to be based on different resource endowments, resulting in differences in comparative advantage. This is the kind of trade that traditional trade theory explains and the kind of trade that benefits both sides. When there exist big differences in development level and resource endowments, countries on both sides of the trading relationship stand to benefit by exploiting these differences and specializing in things that they are good at—their comparative advantage. So you have a powerful argument in favour of freer trade between developed and developing countries.

What about trade between developed countries such as Japan and the United States?

Much of the trade among the developed nations is not based on simple comparative advantage, because all of them are quite similar in underlying resource endowments and technological capabilities. Instead, such trade is often based on differences in product quality, design, reliability, and other non-price characteristics. Such trade takes place in imperfectly competitive markets in which competitive advantage and trade patterns can be manipulated by the market power of individual firms and the policy interventions of individual governments.

For informed national policy-making in such markets, the real choices are not simple choices between free trade and protection but choices about the appropriate combination of liberalization and government intervention that will improve national economic welfare while sustaining an open international trading system.

GATT must be overhauled to address the sources of trade friction among the developed countries. Rules about traditional border policies like tariffs and quotas are no longer enough. Deep interdependence among nations requires deep integration— the harmonization of significant national differences and the development of enforceable multilateral rules regulating such non-border policies as intellectual property protection, competition policy, and industrial targeting.

There appears to be an increasing tendency towards large regional trading blocs—the European Community and the North American Free Trade Area being the two most important. What are the benefits of large regional trading blocs such as these?

I think the benefits of trading blocs really are twofold. First, because of the benefits of freer trade and specialization, countries within a trading bloc are likely to grow faster. More rapid growth and increased prosperity within the bloc will, in turn, encourage imports from outside the bloc. This is called the "trade creation effect"—there will be new trade opportunities, even for countries that are not members of the bloc itself. Everybody benefits.

Second, a trading bloc can be a model for creating systemic change and establishing new multilateral rules. The politics of forming a free trade area are very complicated. If, over the course of decades, a group of countries such as those in Europe slowly develop a common set of rules and institutions, what they learn in the process can be a rich source of lessons and education for the rest of the world.

What are the dangers that result from the creation of these large regional blocs?

The possible costs of blocs are also, I think, twofold. First of all, there is what economists call "trade diversion" as opposed to trade creation. Trade diversion

> "**R**ules [among the developed countries] about traditional border policies like tariffs and quotas are no longer enough."

always occurs when a bloc is formed, because blocs are inherently discriminatory. The bloc by definition breaks down barriers within the bloc nations but not between them and the rest of the world. As a result, the formation of a bloc changes the incentives to trade, encouraging trade among the members of the bloc at the expense of trade between them and the rest of the world. For example, when France and Germany eliminate a barrier to trade between them, they have an incentive to trade more with one another and less with other countries like the United States, with whom trade barriers persist. This is the trade diversion effect.

The trade diversion effect works in conflict with the trade creation effect. On the one hand, the United States will be helped by the trade creation effect—if all of Europe grows faster, there will be a bigger market for the United States. On the other hand, the United States will be hurt by the trade diversion effect because an advantage it had before has now been diminished. Countries forming a bloc can mitigate the diversion effect or make it worse, depending on whether they raise or reduce the common barriers to trade with non-bloc members.

The second basic drawback to the creation of regional trading blocs is what might be called "attention diversion." Countries may expend so much energy and political capital working on their own bloc that they don't have any left to work on the GATT system. The collective effort of the United States, Europe, and Japan is required to improve GATT. But if the Europeans are so heavily engaged in attending to their own regional development, they may not have the political will or energy to commit to the collective problem-solving process.

What will trade barriers between Europe and the rest of the world look like over the next ten years?

That's an open question at this point. There's a big conflict in Europe between the liberalizers who want to see these barriers come down and those who really want to protect Europe for Europeans. It's not clear how that conflict will resolve, but it will be very sensitive to what happens to the world economy. If the world economy stays in a slow growth phase, it's more likely that we will see a protectionist outcome in Europe, as the Europeans strive to keep employment and production at home.

What are the challenges and opportunities created by the emerging new nations of Eastern Europe?

There are three major challenges. The first is macroeconomic stabilization. These economies must be rebuilt on a sound macroeconomic foundation. Fiscal deficits must be controlled, monetary and credit policies must contain inflationary pressure, and outstanding foreign debts must be repaid on a timely basis. Otherwise, macroeconomic crises will undermine the transition, as they have undermined the efforts of developing countries in other parts of the world to build prosperous market economies. The second challenge is restructuring the composition of the economic base. Because the Eastern European countries were inward looking and traded primarily with one another, they have inherited an industrial base that is not competitive by international standards. Many industries have to be scaled back dramatically and some closed down altogether because they simply do not meet the demands of the international marketplace. Additionally, many things must be put into place, such as the appropriate infrastructure of financial services and transportation services that do not exist. These countries do not have a whole series of industries and activities that support modern industrial economies. The last challenge is one of economic reform itself. By that I mean changing the institutions and policy environment in which individual consumers and producers make their decisions. Distinct from the challenge of economic restructuring, which changes the composition of the economy, this third challenge involves changing the basic institutions of the

> **"W**hen perfect markets don't exist, there may be a role for government intervention, since free trade does not always produce welfare-enhancing outcomes."

economy—for example, privatizing state-run institutions.

We now see after two years of economic reforms that the process itself is very slow. One can deal with macroeconomic crises rather quickly, although with considerable political risk because of the pain and austerity necessitated by macroeconomic stabilization. Reform and privatization, however, are not changes that can happen quickly. The problems are just too big and the solutions too few.

Now let's consider the opportunities. Many of the Eastern European countries are not that poor by international development standards. It sounds ridiculous when you think about the suffering going on there, but you have to contrast it with the suffering in other parts of the world. Their rel-

ative prosperity may permit the Eastern European countries to make a very difficult transition without getting derailed politically. Their second advantage is their location. Trade flows are still disproportionately the greatest between countries that are near one another. Therefore, the Eastern European countries benefit from being near Western Europe, which will shortly become the largest developed market in the world. Finally, these countries have highly educated work forces and are starting out with very high levels of skills. The ability of their workers to learn new skills quickly is enhanced by their high levels of educational achievement.

What are the key principles of economics that you find most useful in your work as an international economist?

I would start with comparative advantage. Students need to understand the benefits of specialization. They need to understand how differences in resource endowments and technologies can lead to differences in cost. Further, they need to recognize that not all countries can do everything well and that countries should specialize in those things they do relatively well.

I would go one step further because I'm a policy-oriented economist and say comparative advantage is to some extent inherited and to some extent created. The trick for national policymakers is to undertake policies that will either enhance the nation's comparative advantage or create

new advantage by creating new skills in the work force and new technologies.

It is also important for students and policymakers to understand the role of imperfect competition. Traditional comparative advantage theory is based on the notion of perfectly functioning markets, but almost all of the industries critical to trade among the developed countries have some of the features of imperfectly competitive markets. When perfect markets don't exist, there may be a role for government intervention, since free trade does not always produce welfare-enhancing outcomes.

How would you advise a student who is setting out on the study of economics and is interested in a career that emphasizes the international aspects of our subject?

I would advise students to study comparative economics as well as international economics because it's important to understand how national economies are organized and how they interact with one another. Since how countries organize to solve their economic problems is influenced by their politics, I would also suggest that students take a course or two in political science. They should also regularly read an international economic journal, like *The Economist* or the *Financial Times*. Finally, I strongly recommend that they either work or study abroad sometime during their college career. Studying at home is an imperfect substitute for living abroad when it comes to developing a real feel for differences among nations.

CHAPTER **35**

TRADING WITH THE WORLD

After studying this chapter, you will be able to

- ◆ Describe the trends and patterns in international trade
- ◆ Explain comparative advantage
- ◆ Explain why all countries can gain from international trade
- ◆ Explain how prices adjust to bring about balanced trade
- ◆ Explain how economies of scale and diversity of taste lead to gains from international trade
- ◆ Explain why trade restrictions lower the volume of imports and exports, and lower our consumption possibilities
- ◆ Explain why we have trade restrictions even though they lower our consumption possibilities

SINCE ANCIENT TIMES, PEOPLE HAVE STRIVED TO EXPAND

their trading as far as technology allowed. Marco

Polo opened up the silk route between Europe and

China in the thirteenth century. Today, container

ships laden with cars and machines, and Boeing

747s stuffed with farm-fresh food ply sea and air

routes, carrying millions of dollars worth of goods

and services. Why do people go to such great lengths to trade with those in other

nations? ◆ ◆ The wages earned by the workers in Indonesia and Hong Kong

are low compared with wages in Canada. Obviously, these countries can make

manufactured goods much more cheaply than we can. How can we possibly com-

pete with such countries? Are there any industries in which we have an advan-

tage? ◆ ◆ Tariffs—taxes on imported goods—have

been a source of government revenue in Canada since

before Confederation and were the centrepiece of Sir

John A. Macdonald's National Policy of the 1870s.

Silk Routes and Rust Belts

After World War II, a process of trade liberalization brought about a gradual

reduction of tariffs. What are the effects of tariffs on international trade? Why

don't we have completely unrestricted international trade?

◆ ◆ ◆ ◆ In this chapter, we're going to learn about international trade. We'll

discover how *all* nations can gain by each specializing in producing the goods and

services in which it has a comparative advantage and trading with other countries.

We'll discover that all countries can compete, no matter how high their wages.

We'll also explain why, despite the fact that international trade brings benefits to

all, countries restrict trade.

Patterns and Trends in International Trade

The goods and services that we buy from people in other countries are called **imports**. The goods and services that we sell to people in other countries are called **exports**. What are the most important things that we import and export? Most people would probably guess that a resource-rich nation such as Canada imports manufactured goods and exports raw materials. While that is one feature of Canada's international trade, it is not its most prominent feature. The vast bulk of exports *and* imports is manufactured goods. We sell automobiles, earth-moving equipment, aircraft, and electronic equipment, as well as raw materials and lumber products. We also import and export a huge volume of services—such as travel and freight and shipping services. Let's look at Canada's international trade in a recent year.

Canada's International Trade

Figure 35.1 provides a quick overview of the main components of Canada's exports (part a) and imports (part b). By far the biggest item in Canada's international trade is motor vehicles (including motor vehicle parts). Most of this trade crosses the border with the United States and is the result of an agreement, known as the Auto Pact, between these two countries. Automobiles and automobile parts are permitted to cross the border without any restriction and, in return for this freedom of movement, automobile manufacturers agree to undertake a sizeable amount of their manufacturing in Canada. Our second biggest export is, perhaps predictably, the products of the forestry industry—lumber

FIGURE 35.1

Canadian Exports and Imports: 1992

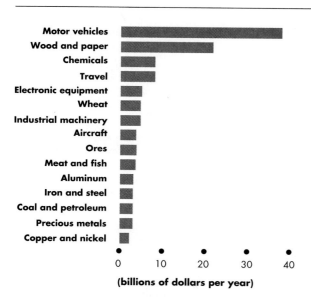

(a) Exports of goods and services

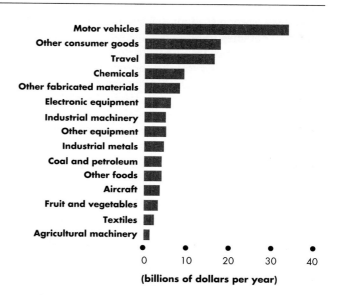

(b) Imports of goods and services

Canada exports and imports more motor vehicles and motor vehicle parts than any other individual category of goods or services. Lumber, pulp and paper, chemicals, and travel are also important exports;

consumer goods, electronic equipment, industrial machinery, and other equipment, as well as travel, are important imports.

Source: Summary of Canadian International Trade, Statistics Canada, December 1992.

and other forestry products including pulp and newsprint.

Motor vehicles are also our largest import. Other big import items are consumer goods, chemicals, electronic equipment, machinery, and other equipment. We also import a great deal of travel—Canadians travel abroad, buying the tourism services of other countries.

Trade in Services   Perhaps you are wondering why we call travel an export and an import. After all, we are not moving goods across the border in the same way that we are when we import or export a car. How do we export and import travel and other services? Let's look at some examples.

Suppose that you decided to vacation in France, travelling there on an Air France flight from Toronto. What you buy from Air France is not a good, but a transportation service. Although the concept may sound odd at first, in economic terms you are importing that service from France. Since you pay Canadian money to a French company in exchange for a service, it doesn't matter that most of your flight time is over the Atlantic Ocean. For that matter, the money you spend in France on hotel bills, restaurant meals, and other things is also classified as the import of services. Similarly, the vacation taken by a French student in Canada counts as an export of services to France.

When we import TV sets from South Korea, the owner of the ship that carries those TV sets might be Greek and the company that insures the cargo might be British. The payments that we make for the transportation and insurance to the Greek and British companies are also payments for the import of services. Similarly, when a Canadian shipping company transports newsprint to Tokyo, the transportation cost is an export of a service to Japan.

Geographical Patterns   Canada has important trading links with almost every part of the world except for Eastern Europe, where trade is almost nonexistent. Figure 35.2 gives a quick overview of the geographical pattern in Canada's international trade. As you can see, the vast bulk of that trade takes place across the U.S. border. Our trade with the countries of the European Community (the most important members being the United Kingdom, France, Germany, and Italy) is tiny in comparison and that with Japan is even smaller.

Figure 35.2 not only shows the volume of our exports and imports. It also illustrates our balance of trade. The **balance of trade** is the value of exports minus the value of imports. If the balance is positive, then the value of exports exceeds the value of imports and Canada is a **net exporter**. But if the balance is negative, the value of imports exceeds the value of exports and Canada is a **net importer**.

As you can see from Fig. 35.2, Canada exports more to the United States than it imports from that country. We are, therefore, a net exporter to the United States. Our balance of trade with the European Community is in the opposite direction. We are a net importer from that region. We are also net importers from Japan and other countries.

Trends in the Balance of Trade   International trade has become an increasingly important part of our economic life. We now both export and import much larger quantities of almost all goods and services than we did even a decade ago. There have also been important trends in the balance of our international trade. The balance of trade of goods and services is shown in Fig. 35.3. As you can see, in the period between 1970 and 1992, that balance has usually been positive—Canada has been a net exporter—but there were six years in which Canada was a net importer. These years were those immediately

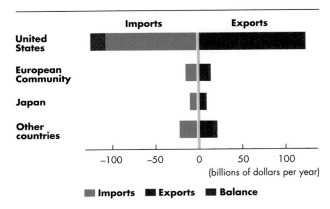

FIGURE 35.2

The Geographical Pattern of Canada's International Trade: 1992

The vast bulk of Canada's international trade is with the United States. We have a net export surplus with the United States, and a net export deficit with the European Community, Japan, and other countries.

Source: Bank of Canada Review, Winter 1992–1993, Table J3.

following the huge increase in world oil prices in the mid-1970s when the increased cost of imported oil temporarily threw our balance of trade into a deficit and in the early 1990s when the world economy was in recession.

Balance of Trade and International Borrowing

When people buy more goods and services than they sell, they must finance the difference by borrowing or by selling off some assets. When they sell more goods and services than they buy, they can use the surplus to make loans to others or to reduce their previous borrowing. This simple principle that governs the income and expenditure and borrowing and lending of individuals and firms is also a feature of our balance of trade. If we import more than we export, we must finance the difference by borrowing from foreigners or by selling some of our assets. When we export more than we import, we make loans to foreigners or repay our previous loans from foreigners.

This chapter does *not* cover the factors that determine the balance of trade and the scale of international borrowing and lending that finances that balance.[1] It is concerned with understanding the volume, pattern, and directions of international trade rather than its balance. So that we can keep our focus on these topics, we'll build a model in which there is no international borrowing and lending—just international trade in goods and services. We'll find that we are able to understand what determines the volume, pattern, and direction of international trade and also establish its benefits and the costs of trade restrictions within this framework. This model can be expanded to include international borrowing and lending, but such an extension does not change the conclusions that we'll reach here about the factors that determine the volume, pattern, and directions of international trade.

Let's now begin to study those factors.

---

[1] These matters are dealt with in Chapter 36.

FIGURE 35.3

Canada's Balance of Trade: 1970–1992

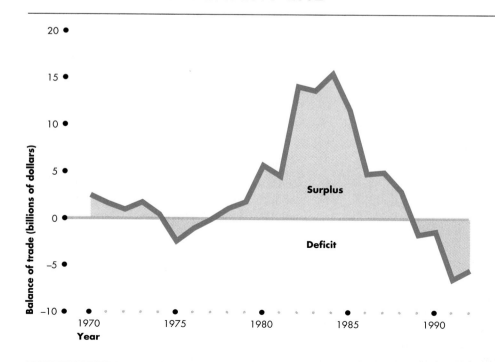

Canada's balance of trade in goods and services with the rest of the world fluctuates but is usually positive—we are a net exporter. But we had a deficit in the mid-1970s and from 1989 to 1992.

Source: Balance of Payments, Statistics Canada, 1992.

Opportunity Cost and Comparative Advantage

L et's apply the lessons that we learned in Chapter 3 about the gains from trade between Jane and Joe to the trade between nations. We'll begin by recalling how we can use the production possibility frontier to measure opportunity cost.

Opportunity Cost in Farmland

Farmland can produce grain and cars at any point inside or along the production possibility frontier shown in Fig. 35.4. (We're holding constant the output of all the other goods that Farmland produces.) The Farmers (the people of Farmland) are consuming all the grain and cars that they produce, and they are operating at point *a* in the figure. That is, Farmland is producing and consuming 15 million tonnes of grain and 8 million cars each year. What is the opportunity cost of a car in Farmland?

We can answer that question by calculating the slope of the production possibility frontier at point *a*. For, as we discovered in Chapter 3 (pp. 54–56), the slope of the frontier measures the opportunity cost of one good in terms of the other. To measure the slope of the frontier at point *a*, place a straight line tangential to the frontier at point *a* and calculate the slope of that straight line. Recall that the formula for the slope of a line is the change in the value of the variable measured on the *y*-axis divided by the change in the value of the variable measured on the *x*-axis as we move along the line. Here, the variable measured on the *y*-axis is millions of tonnes of grain and the variable measured on the *x*-axis is millions of cars. So the slope (opportunity cost) is the change in the number of tonnes of grain divided by the change in the number of cars. As you can see from the red triangle at point *a* in the figure, if the number of cars produced increases by 2 million, grain production decreases by 18 million tonnes. Therefore the slope is 18 million divided by 2 million, which equals 9. To get one more car, the people of Farmland must give up 9 tonnes of grain. Thus the opportunity cost of 1 car is 9 tonnes of grain. Equivalently, 9 tonnes of grain cost 1 car.

FIGURE 35.4

Opportunity Cost in Farmland

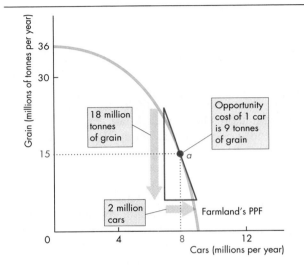

Farmland produces and consumes 15 million tonnes of grain and 8 million cars a year. That is, it produces and consumes at point *a* on its production possibility frontier. Opportunity cost is measured as the slope of the production possibility frontier. At point *a*, 2 million cars cost 18 million tonnes of grain. Equivalently, 1 car costs 9 tonnes of grain or 9 tonnes of grain cost 1 car.

Opportunity Cost in Mobilia

Now consider the production possibility frontier in Mobilia (the only other country in our model world). Figure 35.5 illustrates its production possibility frontier. Like the Farmers, the Mobilians (the people in Mobilia) consume all the grain and cars that they produce. Mobilia consumes 18 million tonnes of grain a year and 4 million cars, at point *a'*.

We can do the same kind of calculation of opportunity cost for Mobilia as we have just done for Farmland. At point *a'*, 1 car costs 1 tonne of grain or, equivalently, 1 tonne of grain costs 1 car.

Comparative Advantage

Cars are cheaper in Mobilia than in Farmland. One car costs 9 tonnes of grain in Farmland but only 1 tonne of grain in Mobilia. But grain is cheaper in Farmland than in Mobilia—9 tonnes of grain cost only 1 car in Farmland while that same amount of grain costs 9 cars in Mobilia.

FIGURE 35.5

Opportunity Cost in Mobilia

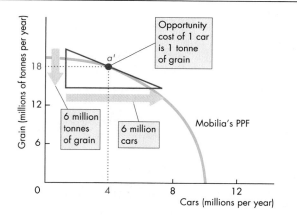

Mobilia produces and consumes 18 million tonnes of grain and 4 million cars a year. That is, it produces and consumes at point *a'* on its production possibility frontier. Opportunity cost is measured as the slope of the production possibility frontier. At point *a'*, 6 million cars cost 6 million tonnes of grain. Equivalently, 1 car costs 1 tonne of grain or 1 tonne of grain costs 1 car.

Mobilia has a comparative advantage in car production. Farmland has a comparative advantage in grain production. A country has a **comparative advantage** in producing a good if it can produce that good at a lower opportunity cost than any other country. Let's see how opportunity cost differences and comparative advantage generate gains from international trade.

The Gains from Trade

I f Mobilia bought grain for what it costs Farmland to produce it, then Mobilia could buy 9 tonnes of grain for 1 car. That is much lower than the cost of growing grain in Mobilia, where it costs 9 cars to produce 9 tonnes of grain. If the Mobilians buy at the low Farmland price, they will reap some gains.

If the Farmers buy cars for what it costs Mobilia to produce them, they will be able to obtain a car for 1 tonne of grain. Since it costs 9 tonnes of grain to produce a car in Farmland, the Farmers would gain from such an activity.

In this situation, it makes sense for Mobilians to buy their grain from Farmers and for Farmers to buy their cars from Mobilians. Let's see how such profitable international trade comes about.

Reaping the Gains from Trade

We've seen that the Farmers would like to buy their cars from the Mobilians and that the Mobilians would like to buy their grain from the Farmers. Let's see how the two groups do business with each other, concentrating attention on the international market for cars.

Figure 35.6 illustrates such a market. The quantity of cars traded internationally is measured on the horizontal axis. On the vertical axis we measure the price of a car, but it is expressed as its opportunity cost—the number of tonnes of grain that a car costs. If no international trade takes place, that price in Farmland is 9 tonnes of grain, indicated by point *a* in the figure. Again, if no trade takes place, that price is 1 tonne of grain in Mobilia, indicated by point *a'* in the figure.

The points *a* and *a'* in Fig. 35.6 correspond to the points identified by those same letters in Figs. 35.4 and 35.5. The lower the price of a car (in terms of tonnes of grain), the greater is the quantity of cars that the Farmers import from the Mobilians. This fact is illustrated in the downward-sloping curve that shows Farmland's import demand for cars.[2] The Mobilians respond in the opposite direction. The higher the price of cars (in terms of tonnes of grain), the greater is the quantity of cars that Mobilians export to Farmers. This fact is reflected in Mobilia's export supply of cars—the upward-sloping line in the figure.[3]

---

[2] The slope of Farmland's import demand curve for cars depends partly on the country's production possibility frontier and partly on the preferences of the citizens of Farmland.

[3] The slope of Mobilia's export supply curve of cars depends on that country's production possibility frontier and on the preferences of the citizens of Mobilia.

FIGURE 35.6

International Trade in Cars

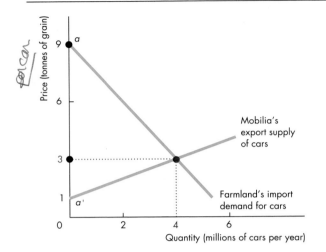

As the price of a car decreases, the quantity of imports demanded by Farmland increases—Farmland's import demand curve for cars is downward sloping. As the price of a car increases, the quantity of cars supplied by Mobilia for export increases—Mobilia's export supply curve of cars is upward sloping. Without international trade, the price of a car is 9 tonnes of grain in Farmland (point *a*) and 1 tonne of grain in Mobilia (point *a'*). With free international trade, the price of a car is determined where the export supply curve intersects the import demand curve—a price of 3 tonnes of grain. At that price, 4 million cars a year are imported by Farmland and exported by Mobilia. The value of grain exported by Farmland and imported by Mobilia is 12 million tonnes a year, the quantity required to pay for the cars imported.

The international market in cars determines the equilibrium price and quantity traded. This equilibrium occurs where the import demand curve intersects the export supply curve. In this case, the equilibrium price of a car is 3 tonnes of grain. Four million cars a year are exported by Mobilia and imported by Farmland. Notice that the price at which cars are traded is lower than the initial price in Farmland but higher than the initial price in Mobilia.

Balanced Trade

Notice that the number of cars exported by Mobilia—4 million a year—is exactly equal to the number of cars imported by Farmland. How does

Farmland pay for its cars? By exporting grain. How much grain does Farmland export? You can find the answer by noticing that for 1 car Farmland has to pay 3 tonnes of grain. Hence for 4 million cars it has to pay 12 million tonnes of grain. Thus Farmland's exports of grain are 12 million tonnes a year. Mobilia imports this same quantity of grain.

Mobilia is exchanging 4 million cars for 12 million tonnes of grain each year and Farmland is doing the opposite, exchanging 12 million tonnes of grain for 4 million cars. Trade is balanced between these two countries. The value received from exports equals the value paid out for imports.

Changes in Production and Consumption

We've seen that international trade makes it possible for Farmers to buy cars at a lower price than they can produce them for themselves. It also enables Mobilians to sell their cars for a higher price, which is equivalent to saying that Mobilians can buy grain for a lower price. Thus everybody seems to gain. Mobilians buy grain at a lower price and Farmers buy cars at a lower price. How is it possible for everyone to gain? What are the changes in production and consumption that accompany these gains?

An economy that does not trade with other economies has identical production and consumption possibilities. Without trade, the economy can only consume what it produces. But with international trade an economy can consume different quantities of goods from those that it produces. The production possibility frontier describes the limit of what a country can produce, but it does not describe the limits to what it can consume. Figure 35.7 will help you to see the distinction between production possibilities and consumption possibilities when a country trades with other countries.

First of all, notice that the figure has two parts, part (a) for Farmland and part (b) for Mobilia. The production possibility frontiers that you saw in Figs. 35.4 and 35.3 are reproduced here. The slopes of the two black lines in the figure represent the opportunity costs in the two countries when there is no international trade. Farmland produces and consumes at point *a* and Mobilia produces and consumes at point *a'*. A car costs 9 tonnes of grain in Farmland and 1 tonne of grain in Mobilia.

Consumption Possibilities   The countries' consumption possibilities with international trade are shown by the two red lines in Fig. 35.7. These lines in both parts of the figure have the same slope, and that slope is the opportunity cost of a car in terms of grain on the world market—3 tonnes per car. The *slope* of the consumption possibilities line is common to both countries because it is determined by the *world* price. But the position of a country's consumption possibilities line depends on its production possibilities. A country cannot produce outside its production possibility curve, so its consumption possibilities curve touches its production possibility curve. Thus Farmland could choose to consume what it produces, at point *b*, and not trade internationally or to trade internationally and consume at a point on its red consumption possibilities line.

Free Trade Equilibrium   With international trade, the producers of cars in Mobilia can now get a higher price for their output. As a result, they increase car production. At the same time, grain producers in Mobilia are now getting a lower price for their grain and so they reduce production. Producers in Mobilia adjust their output until the opportunity cost in Mobilia equals the opportunity cost in the world market. This situation arises when Mobilia is producing at point *b'* in Fig. 35.7(b).

But the Mobilians do not consume at point *b'*. That is, they do not increase their consumption of cars and decrease their consumption of grain. They sell some of their car production to Farmland in exchange for some of Farmland's grain. But to see

FIGURE 35.7

Expanding Consumption Possibilities

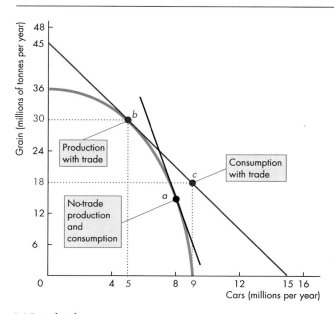

(a) Farmland

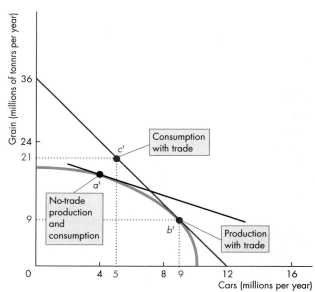

(b) Mobilia

With no international trade, the Farmers produce and consume at point *a* and the opportunity cost of a car is 9 tonnes of grain (the slope of the black line in part a). Also, with no international trade, the Mobilians produce and consume at point *a'* and the opportunity cost of 1 tonne of grain is 1 car (the slope of the black line in part b).

Goods can be exchanged internationally at a price of 3 tonnes of grain for 1 car along the red line. In part (a), Farmland decreases its production of cars and increases its production of grain, moving from *a*

to *b*. It exports grain and imports cars, and it consumes at point *c*. The Farmers have more of both cars and grain than they would have if they produced all their own consumption goods—at point *a*. In part (b), Mobilia increases car production and decreases grain production, moving from *a'* to *b'*. Mobilia exports cars and imports grain, and it consumes at point *c'*. The Mobilians have more of both cars and grain than they would have if they produced all their own consumption goods—at point *a'*.

how that works out, we first need to check in with Farmland to see what's happening there.

In Farmland, cars are now less expensive and grain more expensive than before. As a result, producers in Farmland decrease car production and increase grain production. They do so until the opportunity cost of a car in terms of grain equals the cost on the world market. They move to point *b* in part (a). But the Farmers do not consume at point *b*. They exchange some of their additional grain production for the now cheaper cars from Mobilia.

The figure shows us the quantities consumed in the two countries. We saw in Fig. 35.6 that Mobilia exports 4 million cars a year and Farmland imports those cars. We also saw that Farmland exports 12 million tonnes of grain a year and Mobilia imports that grain. Thus Farmland's consumption of grain is 12 million tonnes a year less than it produces and its consumption of cars is 4 million a year more than it produces. Farmland consumes at point *c* in Fig. 35.7(a).

Similarly, we know that Mobilia consumes 12 million tonnes of grain more than it produces and 4 million cars fewer than it produces. Thus Mobilia consumes at *c'* in Fig. 35.7(b).

Calculating the Gains from Trade

You can now literally "see" the gains from trade in Fig. 35.7. Without trade, Farmers produce and consume at *a* (part a)—a point on Farmland's production possibility frontier. With international trade, Farmers consume at point *c* (in part a)—a point *outside* the production possibility frontier. At point *c*, Farmers are consuming 3 million tonnes of grain a year and 1 million cars a year more than before. These increases in consumption of cars and grain, beyond the limits of the production possibility frontier, are the gains from international trade.

But Mobilians also gain. Without trade, they consume at point *a'* (part b)—a point on Mobilia's production possibility frontier. With international trade, they consume at point *c'*—a point *outside* the production possibility frontier. With international trade, Mobilia consumes 3 million tonnes of grain a year and 1 million cars a year more than without trade. These are the gains from international trade for Mobilia.

We've just seen that both Mobilia and Farmland gain from specialization and international trade. But is it really the case that countries can always gain? What if one country has low wages? Can't that country outsell the other? And what if the workers in one

country are more productive at making all goods? Why would such a country want to buy from a less productive country? These two questions are really two sides of the same question. Let's see why.

Wages and Costs

Suppose that the workers in Mobilia earn higher *real wages* than the workers in Farmland. How could the Mobilians compete with the low-wage Farmers in the international markets for cars and grain?

Real wages can be higher in Mobilia only if the Mobilian workers are more productive than the Farmland workers. For example, suppose one Mobilian worker can do the work of two Farmland workers. In this case, the real wage rate in Mobilia will be double that in Farmland. But the dollar cost of production will be the same in the two countries. That is, two workers in Farmland produce the same output and cost the same as one worker in Mobilia.

Productivity

If the workers in Mobilia are more productive than the workers in Farmland, Mobilia has an absolute advantage over Farmland. A country has an **absolute advantage** if its output per unit of inputs of all goods is higher than that of another country. With an absolute advantage, can't Mobilia outsell Farmland in all markets? Why, if Mobilia can produce all goods using fewer factors of production than Farmland, does it pay Mobilia to buy *anything* from Farmland?

We've just seen that more productive workers have higher real wages and the dollar cost of production is the same in the two countries. But it is not the dollar cost or the cost in terms of the factors of production employed that is relevant for determining the gains from trade. It does not matter how much labour, land, and capital are required to produce 1 tonne of grain or 1 car. What matters is how many cars must be given up to produce more grain or how much grain must be given up to produce more cars. That is, what matters is the opportunity cost of one good in terms of the other good.

Mobilia may have an absolute advantage in the production of all things, and Farmland may have lower wages, but neither country can have a comparative advantage in the production of all goods. The statement that the opportunity cost of cars in Mobilia is lower than in Farmland is identical to the statement that the opportunity cost of grain is higher in Mobilia than in Farmland. Thus *whenever opportunity costs diverge, every country has a comparative advantage in something.* All countries can potentially gain from international trade.

The story of the discovery of the logic of the gains from international trade is presented in Our Advancing Knowledge on pp. 976–977.

R E V I E W

W hen countries have divergent opportunity costs, they can gain from international trade. Each country can buy goods and services from another country at a lower opportunity cost than it can produce them for itself. Gains arise when each country increases its production of those goods and services in which it has a comparative advantage (of goods and services that it can produce at an opportunity cost that is lower than that of other countries) and exchanges some of its production for that of other countries. All countries gain from international trade. Every country has a comparative advantage in something. ◆

Gains from Trade in Reality

The gains from trade that we have just studied between Farmland and Mobilia in grain and cars are taking place in a model economy—in an economy that we have imagined. But these same phenomena are occurring every minute of every day in real-world economies. We buy cars made in Japan, and Canadian producers of grain sell large amounts of their output to Japanese households and firms. We buy airplanes and vegetables from U.S. producers and sell natural gas and forest products to Americans. We buy shirts and fashion goods from the people of Hong Kong and sell them machinery in return. We buy TV sets and VCRs from South Korea and Taiwan and sell them financial and other services as well as manufactured goods in return.

Thus much of the international trade that we see in the real world takes precisely the form of the trade that we have studied in our model of the world economy. But as we discovered earlier in this chapter, a great deal of world trade is heavily concentrated among industrial countries and primarily involves the international exchange of manufactured goods. Thus the type of trade that we have just analysed— exchanging cars for grain—although an important and clearly profitable type of trade, is not the most prominent type. Why do countries exchange manufactured goods with each other? Can our model of international trade explain such exchange?

Trade in Similar Goods

At first thought, it seems puzzling that countries would trade manufactured goods. Consider, for example, Canada's trade in cars and auto parts. Why does it make sense for Canada to produce cars for export and at the same time to import large quantities of cars from the United States, Japan, Korea, and Western Europe? Wouldn't it make more sense to produce all the cars that we buy here in Canada? After all, we have access to the best technology available for producing cars. Auto workers in Canada are surely as productive as their fellow workers in the United States, Western Europe, and the Pacific countries. Capital equipment, production lines, robots, and the like used in the manufacture of cars are as available to Canadian car producers as they are to any other. This line of reasoning leaves a puzzle concerning the sources of international exchange of similar commodities produced by similar people using similar equipment. Why does it happen? It happens for three reasons:

◆ Diversity of taste

◆ Economies of scale

◆ Transportation costs

Diversity of Taste The first part of the answer to the puzzle is that people have a tremendous diversity of taste. Let's stick with the example of cars. Some people prefer a sports car, some prefer a limousine, some a regular, full-size car, and some prefer a compact. In addition to size and type of car, there are many other dimensions in which cars vary. Some have low fuel consumption, some have high performance, some are spacious and comfortable, some have a large trunk, some have four-wheel drive, some have front-wheel drive, some have manual transmission, some have automatic transmission, some are durable, some are flashy, some have a radiator grill that looks like a Greek temple, and others look like a wedge. People's preferences across these many dimensions vary.

UNDERSTANDING the Gains from INTERNATIONAL TRADE

"Free trade, one of the greatest blessings which a government can confer on a people, is in almost every country unpopular."

LORD THOMAS MACAULAY
Essay on Mitford's History of Greece

Until the mid-eighteenth century, it was generally believed that the purpose of international trade was to keep exports in excess of imports and pile up gold. If gold were accumulated, it was believed, the nation would prosper; and if gold were lost through an international deficit, the nation would be drained of money and be impoverished. These beliefs are called *mercantilism*, and the *mercantilists* were pamphleteers who advocated with missionary fervour the pursuit of an international surplus. If exports did not exceed imports, the mercantilists wanted imports restricted.

In the 1740s, David Hume explained that as the quantity of money (gold) changes, so does the price level, and the nation's *real* wealth is unaffected. In the 1770s, Adam Smith explained that restricting imports lowers the gains from specialization and makes a nation poorer. Mercantilism was intellectually bankrupt.

Gradually, through the nineteenth century, the mercantilists' influence waned, and North America and Western Europe prospered in an environment of increasingly free international trade. But despite remarkable advances in economic understanding, mercantilism never quite died. It had a brief and devastating revival in the 1920s and 1930s, when tariff hikes brought about the collapse of international trade and accentuated the Great Depression. It subsided again after World War II with the establishment of the General Agreement on Tariffs and Trade (GATT).

But mercantilism lingers on. The often expressed view in Canada that we should restrict our imports and reduce our deficit is a modern manifestation of mercantilism. It would be interesting to have Hume and Smith comment on these views. But we know what they would say—the same things that they said to the eighteenth-century mercantilists. And they would still be right today.

In the eighteenth century, when mercantilists and economists were debating the pros and cons of free international exchange, the transportation technology available severely limited the gains from international trade. Sailing ships with tiny cargo holds took close to a month to cross the Atlantic Ocean. But the potential gains were large and so was the incentive to cut shipping costs. By the 1850s, the clipper ship had been developed that cut the time for the journey from Halifax to Liverpool to only 12 days. Half a century later, 10,000 tonnne steamships were sailing between Canada and England in just 4 days. As sailing times and costs declined, the gains from international trade increased and the volume of trade expanded.

The modern airplane and the container ship have revolutionized international trade and contributed to its continued expansion. Every day, dozens of cargo-laden 767s like this one fly between major Canadian cities and destinations across the Atlantic and Pacific oceans carrying high-value perishable cargoes such as flowers and fresh foods, as well as other urgent items. And millions of tonnes of goods cross the oceans in "containers"—metal boxes—packed into and piled on top of ships. Container technology has cut the cost of ocean shipping by economizing on handling and by making cargoes harder to steal, thereby lowering insurance costs. It is unlikely that there would be much international trade in goods such as television sets and VCRs without this technology.

FROM SMITH & RICARDO
To *GATT*

David Ricardo (1772–1832) was a highly successful 27 year-old stockbroker when he stumbled on a copy of Adam Smith's *Wealth of Nations* on a weekend visit to the country. He was immediately hooked and went on to become the most celebrated economist of his age and one of the all-time great economists. One of his many contributions was to develop the principle of comparative advantage, the foundation on which the modern theory of international trade is built. The example he used to illustrate this principle was the trade between England and Portugal in cloth and wine.

The General Agreement on Tariffs and Trade (GATT) was established as a reaction against the devastation wrought by beggar-my-neighbour tariffs imposed during the 1920s. But it is also a triumph for the logic first worked out by Smith and Ricardo.

The tremendous diversity in tastes for cars means that people would be dissatisfied if they were forced to consume from a limited range of standardized cars. People value variety and are willing to pay for it in the marketplace.

Economies of Scale   The second part of the answer to the puzzle is economies of scale. *Economies of scale* are present in many production processes and as a result, the larger the scale of production, the lower is the average cost of production. In such situations, larger and larger production runs lead to ever lower average production costs. Many manufactured goods, including cars, experience economies of scale. For example, if a car producer makes only a few hundred (or perhaps a few thousand) cars of a particular type and design, it has to use production techniques that are much more labour-intensive and much less automated than those actually employed to make hundreds of thousands of cars of a particular model. With small production runs and labour-intensive production techniques, costs are high. With very large production runs and automated assembly lines, production costs are much lower. But to obtain lower costs, the automated assembly lines have to produce a large number of cars.

It is the combination of diversity of taste and economies of scale that produces such a large amount of international trade in similar commodities. Diversity of taste and the willingness to pay for variety do not guarantee that variety will be available. It could simply be too expensive to provide a highly diversified range of different types of cars, for example. If every car bought in North America today were made in North America and if the present range of diversity and variety were available, production runs would be remarkably short. Car producers would not be able to reap economies of scale. Although the current variety of cars could be made available, it would be at a very high price, and perhaps at a price that no one would be willing to pay.

But with international trade, each manufacturer of cars has the whole world market to serve. Each producer specializes in a limited range of products and then sells its output to the entire world market. This arrangement enables large production runs on the most popular cars and feasible production runs even on the most customized cars demanded by only a handful of people.

The situation in the market for cars is also present in many other industries, especially those producing specialized machinery and specialized machine tools. Thus international exchange of similar but slightly differentiated manufactured products is a highly profitable activity.

This type of trade can be understood with exactly the same model of international trade that we studied earlier. Although we normally think of cars as a single commodity, we simply have to think of sports cars and sedans and so on as different goods. Different countries, by specializing in a few of these "goods," are able to enjoy economies of scale and, therefore, a comparative advantage in their production.

Transportation Costs   Although the combination of diversity of taste and economies of scale produces a large amount of international trade in similar commodities such as automobiles, it does not explain all the two-way trade in similar commodities. If you glance back at Fig. 35.1, you will perhaps be struck, for example, by the fact that we import and export large amounts of chemicals and also of crude petroleum. It is perhaps easy to understand why we both import and export a category of goods as broad as chemicals. After all, there are many different individual chemicals, some of which we export and others of which we import. But crude petroleum is crude petroleum—there are various grades of the product, but they do not differ all that much. Why do we import and export crude petroleum? The main part of the answer has to do with transportation costs. It is less costly to move petroleum in large tankers across the oceans than it is to transport it overland. Thus the petroleum consumed in Eastern Canada is imported along the Atlantic seaboard while petroleum used in the Western United States is imported from Alberta (and is therefore a Canadian export of crude petroleum).

Adjustment Costs

You've seen that comparative advantage and international trade bring gains. When the rich countries of the European Community, Japan, and the United States import raw materials from the Third World and from Australia and Canada, the rich importing countries gain and so do the exporting countries. When we buy cheap cars, TV sets, VCRs, shirts, and other goods from low-wage countries, both we and the exporters gain from the exchange.

But suppose a change in comparative advantage leads to an increase in our imports of cars and to a cut in domestic car production. Jobs in our car-producing sector disappear and many workers experience a painful adjustment process. Good new jobs take time to find and often people go through a period of prolonged search, putting up with inferior jobs and lower wages than they had before. Some older workers might never find a new job. In effect, they might be forced into retirement earlier than they would have wished.

Partly because of the costs of adjustment to changing international trade patterns, but partly also for other reasons, governments intervene in international trade, restricting its volume. Let's examine what happens when governments restrict international trade. We'll contrast restricted trade with free trade. We'll see that free trade brings the greatest possible benefits. We'll also see why, in spite of the benefits of free trade, governments sometimes restrict trade.

Trade Restrictions

Governments restrict international trade in order to protect domestic industries from foreign competition. The restriction of international trade is called **protectionism**. There are two main protectionist methods employed by governments:

◆ Tariffs

◆ Nontariff barriers

A **tariff** is a tax that is imposed by the importing country when a good crosses an international boundary. A **nontariff barrier** is any action other than a tariff that restricts international trade. Examples of nontariff barriers are quantitative restrictions and licensing regulations limiting imports. We'll consider nontariff barriers in more detail below. First, let's look at tariffs.

The History of Tariffs

The Canadian economy has always been protected by a tariff. The history of that tariff, from Confederation to 1992, is illustrated in Fig. 35.8. The figure shows tariffs as a percentage of total imports—the average tariff rate. As you can see, the average tariff rate climbed from the early 1870s to exceed 20 percent by the 1890s. The rate fluctuated but then steadily declined through the 1930s. After World War II, there was a stronger trend decline in tariff rates.

The reduction in tariffs followed the establishment of the General Agreement on Tariffs and Trade

FIGURE 35.8

Canadian Tariffs: 1867-1992

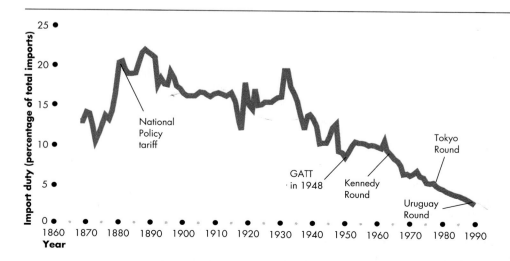

Canadian tariffs were in place before Confederation. Tariffs increased sharply in the 1870s and remained high until the 1930s. After World War II, tariffs declined more rapidly.

Source: Historical Statistics of Canada, Series G485, and Statistics Canada.

(GATT). The **General Agreement on Tariffs and Trade** is an international agreement designed to limit government intervention to restrict international trade. It was negotiated immediately following World War II and was signed in October 1947. Its goal is to liberalize trading activity and to provide an organization to administer more liberal trading arrangements. GATT itself is a small organization located in Geneva, Switzerland.

Since the formation of GATT, several rounds of negotiations have taken place that have resulted in general tariff reductions. One of these, the Kennedy Round that began in the early 1960s, resulted in large tariff cuts in the late 1960s. Yet further tariff cuts resulted from the Tokyo Round, which took place between 1973 and 1979, and the Uruguay Round of the late 1980s and early 1990s.

In addition to general tariff reductions, protection on trade with the United States has been reduced and will continue to be reduced under the provisions of the Canada-United States Free Trade Agreement, which came into effect on January 1, 1989.

Another development is an attempt to work out a free trade deal with Mexico that would create a large North American free trade area embracing Mexico, Canada, and the United States. Within Western Europe, trade barriers among the member countries of the European Community were virtually eliminated on January 1, 1993, creating the largest unified tariff-free market in the world.

The benefits of free trade, both in theory and in recent experience of the countries of the European Community, have given impetus to a series of talks among the countries of Central and South America aimed at creating a series of free-trade agreements among these countries and, even more ambitiously, free-trade between the American continents.

The talks taking place among the countries of North and South America underline the fact that despite a steady process of tariff reductions, trade among some countries and trade in some goods are still subject to extremely high tariffs. For example, if you want to buy a shirt from Hong Kong, you will pay a 25 percent duty on that import. Shoes from Brazil will also cost you an extra 23 percent in duty. A pearl ring or necklace from Japan will cost you 13 percent in duty. Import duties on automobiles from Japan run at 9.2 percent.

The temptation on governments to impose tariffs is a strong one. First, tariffs provide revenue to the government. Second, they enable the government to satisfy special interest groups in import-competing industries. But, as we'll see, free international trade brings enormous benefits that are reduced when tariffs are imposed. Let's see how.

How Tariffs Work

To determine the effects of tariffs and the effects of eliminating tariffs, such as the process under way as a result of the Canada-United States Free Trade Agreement, we need to know how tariffs work. To analyse how tariffs work, we're going to return to the example of trade between Farmland and Mobilia. We're going to work with this model economy rather than the real economy for two reasons. First, we'll find it easier to understand the basic principles involved in the working of tariffs and their elimination. Second, we are less emotionally involved in the affairs of the Farmers and Mobilians than we are in our own affairs. Thus we will be able to be more clear-headed in focusing on the purely economic aspects of the tariff issue.

Let's return, then, to Farmland and Mobilia. Suppose that these two countries are trading cars and grain in exactly the same way that we analysed before. Mobilia exports cars and Farmland exports grain. The volume of car imports into Farmland is 4 million a year, and a car sells on the world market for 3 tonnes of grain. Let's suppose that grain costs $1,000 a tonne so, equivalently, a car costs $3,000. Figure 35.9 illustrates this situation. The volume of trade in cars and their prices are determined at the point of intersection of Mobilia's export supply curve of cars and Farmland's import demand curve for cars.

Now suppose that the government of Farmland, perhaps under pressure from car producers, decides to impose a tariff on imported cars. In particular, suppose that a tariff of $4,000 per car is imposed. (This is a huge tariff, but the car producers of Farmland are pretty fed up with competition from Mobilia.) What happens?

The first part of the answer is obtained by studying the effects on the supply of cars in Farmland. Cars are no longer going to be available at the Mobilia export supply price. The tariff of $4,000 must be added to that price—the amount paid to the government of Farmland on each car imported. As a consequence, the supply curve in Farmland shifts upward by the amount of the tariff as shown in Fig. 35.9. The new supply curve is the curve labelled "Mobilia's export supply of cars plus tariff."

FIGURE 35.9

The Effects of a Tariff

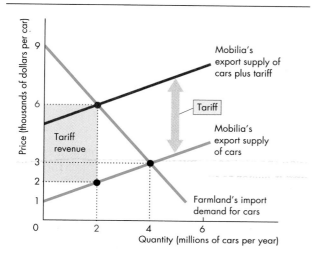

Farmland imposes a tariff on car imports from Mobilia. The tariff increases the price that the Farmers have to pay for cars. It shifts the supply curve of cars in Farmland upward. The distance between the original supply curve and the new one is the amount of the tariff. The price of cars in Farmland increases and the quantity of cars imported decreases. The government of Farmland collects a tariff revenue of $4,000 per car—a total of $8 billion on the 2 million cars imported. Farmland's exports of grain decrease since Mobilia now has a lower income from its exports of cars.

The next part of the answer is found by determining the new equilibrium. Imposing a tariff has no effect on the demand for cars in Farmland and so has no effect on Farmland's import demand for cars. The new equilibrium occurs where the new supply curve intersects Farmland's import demand curve for cars. That equilibrium is at a price of $6,000 a car with 2 million cars a year being imported. Imports fall from 4 billion to 2 million cars a year. At the higher price of $6,000 a car, domestic car producers increase their production. Domestic grain production decreases to free up the resources for the expanded car industry.

The total expenditure on imported cars by the Farmers is $6,000 a car multiplied by the 2 million cars imported ($12 billion). But not all of that money goes to the Mobilians. They receive $2,000 a car or $4 billion for the 2 million cars. The difference—$4,000 a car, or a total of $8 billion for the

2 million cars—is collected by the government of Farmland as tariff revenue.

Obviously, the government of Farmland is happy with this situation. It is now collecting $8 billion that it didn't have before. But what about the Farmers? How do they view the new situation? The demand curve tells us the maximum price that a buyer is willing to pay for one more unit of a good. As you can see from Farmland's import demand curve for cars, if one more car could be imported, someone would be willing to pay almost $6,000 for it. Mobilia's export supply curve of cars tells us the minimum price at which additional cars are available. As you can see, one additional car would be supplied by Mobilia for a price only slightly more than $2,000. Thus, since someone is willing to pay almost $6,000 for a car and someone is willing to supply one for little more than $2,000, there is obviously a gain to be had from trading an extra car. In fact, there are gains to be had—willingness to pay exceeds the minimum supply price—all the way up to 4 million cars a year. Only when 4 million cars are being traded is the maximum price that a Farmlander is willing to pay equal to the minimum price that is acceptable to a Mobilian. Thus restricting international trade reduces the gains from international trade.

It is easy to see that the tariff has lowered Farmland's total import bill. With free trade, Farmland was paying $3,000 a car and buying 4 million cars a year from Mobilia. Thus the total import bill was $12 billion a year. With a tariff, Farmland's imports have been cut to 2 million cars a year and the price paid to Mobilia has also been cut to only $2,000 a car. Thus the import bill has been cut to $4 billion a year. Doesn't this fact mean that Farmland's balance of trade has changed? Is Farmland now importing less than it is exporting?

To answer that question, we need to figure out what's happening in Mobilia. We've just seen that the price that Mobilia receives for cars has fallen from $3,000 to $2,000 a car. Thus the price of a car in Mobilia has fallen. But if the price of a car has fallen, the price of grain has increased. With free trade, the Mobilians could buy 3 tonnes of grain for 1 car. Now they can buy only 2 tonnes for 1 car. With a higher price of grain, the quantity demanded by the Mobilians decreases. As a result, Mobilia's import of grain declines. But so does Farmland's export of grain. In fact, Farmland's grain industry suffers from two sources. First, there is a decrease in the quantity of grain sold to Mobilia. Second, there is increased competition for inputs from the now expanded car industry. Thus the tariff leads to a contraction in the scale of the grain industry in Farmland.

It seems paradoxical at first that a country imposing a tariff on cars would hurt its own export industry, lowering its exports of grain. It may help to think of it this way: Foreigners buy grain with the money they make from exporting cars. If they export fewer cars, they cannot afford to buy as much grain. In fact, in the absence of any international borrowing and lending, Mobilia has to cut its imports of grain by exactly the same amount as the loss in revenue from its export of cars. Grain imports into Mobilia will be cut back to a value of $4 billion, the amount that can be paid for by the new lower revenue from Mobilia's car exports. Thus trade is still balanced in this post-tariff situation. Although the tariff has cut imports, it has also cut exports, and the cut in the value of exports is exactly equal to the cut in the value of imports. The tariff has no effect on the balance of trade—it reduces the volume of trade.

The result that we have just derived is perhaps one of the most misunderstood aspects of international economics. On countless occasions, politicians and others have called for tariffs in order to remove a balance of trade deficit or have argued that lowering tariffs would produce a balance of trade deficit. They reach this conclusion by failing to work out all the implications of a tariff. Because a tariff raises the price of imports and cuts the volume of imports, the easy conclusion is that the tariff strengthens the balance of trade. But the tariff also changes the *volume* of exports. The equilibrium effects of a tariff are to reduce the volume of trade in both directions and by the same value on each side of the equation. The balance of trade itself is left unaffected.

Learning the Hard Way   Although the analysis that we have just worked through leads to the clear conclusion that tariffs cut both imports and exports and make everyone worse off, Canadians have not found that conclusion easy to accept. Time and again in our history we have imposed high tariff barriers on international trade (as Fig. 35.8 illustrates). Whenever tariff barriers are increased, trade collapses. The most vivid historical example of this interaction of tariffs and trade occurred during the Great Depression years of the early 1930s when the world's largest trading nation, the United States, increased its tariffs, setting up a retaliatory round of

tariff changes in many countries. The consequence of this period of very high tariffs was an almost complete disappearance of world trade.

Let's now turn our attention to the other range of protectionist weapons—nontariff barriers.

Nontariff Barriers

There are two important forms of nontariff barriers:

◆ Quotas

◆ Voluntary export restraints

A **quota** is a quantitative restriction on the import of a particular good. It specifies the maximum amount of the good that may be imported in a given period of time. A **voluntary export restraint** is an agreement between two governments in which the government of the exporting country agrees to restrain the volume of its own exports. Voluntary export restraints are often called VERs.

Nontariff barriers have become important features of international trading arrangements in the period since World War II, and there is now general agreement that nontariff barriers are a more severe impediment to international trade than tariffs.

It is difficult to quantify the effects of nontariff barriers in a way that makes them easy to compare with tariffs, but some studies have attempted to do just that. Such studies attempt to assess the tariff rate that would restrict trade by the same amount as the nontariff barriers do. With such calculations, nontariff barriers and tariffs can be added together to assess the total amount of protection. When we add nontariff barriers to tariffs for Canada, the overall amount of protection increases more than threefold. Even so, Canada is one of the least protectionist countries in the world. Total protection in the European Community is higher, and it is higher still in Japan and other developed countries. The less developed countries and the so-called newly industrializing countries have the highest protection rates of all.

Quotas are especially important in the textile industries where there exists an international agreement called the Multifibre Arrangement, which establishes quotas on a wide range of textile products. Agriculture is also subject to extensive quotas. Voluntary export restraints are particularly important in regulating the international trade in cars between Japan and North America.

How Quotas and VERs Work

To understand how nontariff barriers affect international trade, let's return to the example of trade between Farmland and Mobilia. Suppose that Farmland imposes a quota on car imports. Specifically, suppose that the quota restricts imports to not more than 2 million cars a year. What are the effects of this action?

The answer is found in Fig. 35.10. The quota is shown by the vertical red line at 2 million cars a year. Since it is illegal to import more than that number of cars, car importers buy only that quantity from Mobilia producers. They pay $2,000 a car to the Mobilia producer. But what do they sell their cars for? The answer is $6,000 each. Since the import supply of cars is restricted to 2 million cars a year, people with cars for sale will be able to get $6,000 each for them. The quantity of cars imported equals the quantity determined by the quota.

FIGURE 35.10

The Effects of a Quota

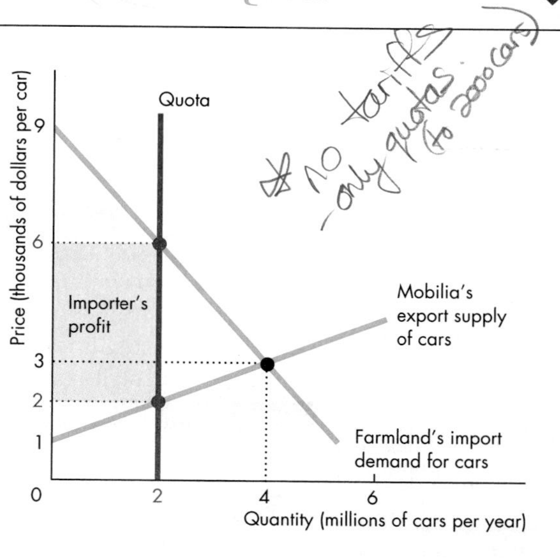

With free trade, Farmland imports 4 million cars a year from Mobilia. Farmland imposes a quota of 2 million cars a year on car imports from Mobilia. That quantity appears as the vertical line marked "Quota." Since the quantity of cars supplied by Mobilia is restricted to 2 million, the price at which those cars will be traded increases to $6,000 a car. Importing cars is profitable since Mobilia is willing to supply cars at $2,000 each. As a result, there is competition for import quotas—rent seeking.

Importing cars is now obviously a profitable business. An importer gets $6,000 for an item that costs only $2,000. Thus there is severe competition among car importers for the available quotas. It is the pursuit of the profits from quotas that economists call "rent seeking."

The value of imports—the amount paid to Mobilia—declines to $4 billion, exactly the same as in the case of the tariff. Thus, with lower incomes from car exports and with a higher price of grain, Mobilians cut back on their imports of grain in exactly the same way they did under a tariff.

The key difference between a quota and a tariff lies in who gets the profit represented by the difference between the import supply price and the domestic selling price. In the case of a tariff, that difference goes to the government. In the case of a quota, that difference goes to the person who has the right to import under the import-quota regulations.

A voluntary export restraint is like a quota arrangement where quotas are allocated to each exporting country. The effects of voluntary export restraints are similar to those of quotas but differ from them in that the gap between the domestic price and the export price is captured not by domestic importers but by the foreign exporter. The government of the exporting country has to establish procedures for allocating the restricted volume of exports among its producers.

R E V I E W

When a country opens itself up to international trade and trades freely at world market prices, it expands its consumption possibilities. When trade is restricted, some of the gains from trade are lost. A country may be better off with restricted trade than with no trade but not as well off as it could be if it engaged in free trade. A tariff reduces the volume of imports, but it also reduces the volume of exports. Under both free trade and restricted trade (and without international borrowing and lending), the value of imports equals the value of exports. With restricted trade, both the value of exports and the value of imports are lower than under free trade, but trade is still balanced. ◆

Why Quotas and VERs Might Be Preferred to Tariffs

At first sight, it seems puzzling that countries would ever want to use quotas and even more puzzling that they would want to use voluntary export restraints. We have seen that the same domestic price and the same quantity of imports can be achieved by using any of the three devices for restricting trade. However, a tariff provides the government with a source of revenue; a quota provides domestic importers with a profit; and a voluntary export restraint provides the foreigner with a profit. Why, then, would a country use a quota or a voluntary export restraint rather than a tariff?

There are two possible reasons. First, a government can use quotas to reward its political supporters. Under a quota, licences to import become tremendously profitable. So the government bestows riches on the people to whom it gives licences to import. Second, quotas are more precise instruments for holding down imports. As demand fluctuates, the domestic price of the good fluctuates but not the quantity of imports. You can see this implication of a quota by going back to Fig. 35.10. Suppose that the demand for imports fluctuates. With a quota, these demand fluctuations simply produce fluctuations in the domestic price of the import but no change in the volume of imports. With a tariff, fluctuations in demand lead to no change in the domestic price but to large changes in the volume of imports. Thus, if for some reason the government wants to control the quantity of imports and does not care about fluctuations in the domestic price, it will use a quota.

Why would a government use voluntary export restraints rather than a tariff or quota? The government may want to avoid a tariff or quota war with another country. If one country imposes a tariff or a quota, that might encourage another country to impose a similar tariff or quota on the exports of the first country. Such a tariff and quota war would result in a much smaller volume of trade and a much worse outcome for both countries. A voluntary export restraint can be viewed as a way of achieving trade restrictions to protect domestic industries but with some kind of compensation to encourage the foreign country to accept that situation and not retaliate with its own restrictions. Finally, VERs are often the only form of trade restriction that can be legally entered into under the terms of the General Agreement on Tariffs and Trade.

Dumping and Countervailing Duties

Dumping is the selling of a good in a foreign market for a lower price than in the domestic market or for a lower price than its cost of production. Such a practice can arise from discriminating monopoly seeking to maximize profit. Under GATT, dumping is illegal and antidumping duties may be imposed on foreign producers if Canadian producers can show that they have been injured by dumping.

Countervailing duties are tariffs that are imposed to enable domestic producers to compete with subsidized foreign producers. Often, foreign governments subsidize some of their domestic industries. Under the Special Import Measures Act, if Canada determines that a foreign government is unfairly subsidizing its exports to Canada, a countervailing duty may be imposed. Governments often subsidize some of their domestic industries, but defining what is a subsidy and what is a legitimate form of government aid (or simply a different government approach) can be a problem. The Canadian lumber industry offers an example. U.S. producers say it is subsidized, but Canadian governments, which own much of our timberland, say their method of renting it to producers simply differs from the U.S. method.

Why Is International Trade Restricted?

There are many reasons why international trade is restricted. We've just seen two reasons—to offset the effects of dumping and of foreign subsidies. Even in these cases, it does not obviously benefit a country to protect itself from cheap foreign imports. However, more generally, we've seen that international trade benefits a country by raising its consumption possibilities. Why do we restrict international trade when such restrictions lower our consumption possibilities?

The key reason is that consumption possibilities increase *on the average* but not everyone shares in the gain and some people even lose. Free trade brings benefits to some and costs to others, with total benefits exceeding total costs. It is the uneven distribution of costs and benefits that is the principal source of impediment to achieving more liberal international trade.

Returning to our example of international trade in cars and grain between Farmland and Mobilia, the benefits from free trade accrue to all the producers of grain and those producers of cars who would not have to bear the costs of adjusting to a smaller car industry. The costs of free trade are borne by those car producers and their employees who have to move and become grain producers.

The number of people who gain will, in general, be enormous compared with the number who lose. The gain per person will, therefore, be rather small. The loss per person to those who bear the loss will be large. Since the loss that falls on those who bear it is large, it will pay those people to incur considerable expenses in order to lobby against free trade. On the other hand, it will not pay those who gain to organize to achieve free trade. The gain from trade for any one individual is too small for that individual to spend much time or money on a political organization to achieve free trade. The loss from free trade will be seen as being so great by those bearing that loss that they *will* find it profitable to join a political organization to prevent free trade. Each group is optimizing—weighing benefits against costs and choosing the best action for themselves. The anti-free trade group will, however, undertake a larger quantity of political lobbying than the pro-free trade group.

Compensating Losers

If, in total, the gains from free international trade exceed the losses, why don't those who gain compensate those who lose so that everyone is in favour of free trade? To some degree, such compensation does take place. It also takes place indirectly as a consequence of unemployment compensation arrangements. But, as a rule, only limited attempts are made to compensate those who lose from free international trade.

The main reason why full compensation is not attempted is that the costs of identifying the losers would be enormous. Also, it would never be clear whether or not a person who has fallen on hard times is suffering because of free trade or for other reasons, and perhaps reasons largely under the control of the individual. Furthermore, some people who look like losers at one point in time may, in fact, wind up gaining. The young auto worker who loses his job in Windsor and becomes a computer assembly worker in Ottawa resents the loss of work and the need to move. But a year or two later, looking back on events, he counts himself fortunate. He's made a move that has increased his income and given him greater job security.

Political Outcome

The political outcome that emerges from this activity is one in which a modest amount of restriction on international trade occurs and is maintained. Politicians react to constituencies pressing for protection and find it necessary, in order to get re-elected, to support legislative programs that protect those constituencies. The producers of protected goods are far more vocal and much more sensitive swing-voters than the consumers of those goods. The political outcome, therefore, leans in the direction of maintaining protection.

Despite the political pressures for protection, the Canadian and U.S. governments have taken measures designed to secure greater gains from trade between the two countries. Let's take a look at the historical Canada–United States Free Trade Agreement.

The Canada–United States Free Trade Agreement

The Canada–United States Free Trade Agreement was signed in October 1987 following two years of intense negotiations and, on the Canadian side of the border, an intense political debate. First, let's look at the terms of the agreement.

Terms of Agreement

The main terms of the Canada–United States Free Trade Agreement are

- Tariffs to be phased out through 1999
- Nontariff barriers to be reduced
- Free trade in energy products, with energy resource sharing in times of national shortage
- More freedom of trade in services
- Future negotiations to eliminate subsidies
- Creation of a dispute-settling mechanism

Removal of Tariffs   Some tariffs were removed on January 1, 1989, when the free trade agreement became effective. Many other tariffs have now been

North American Free Trade

The Essence of the Story

Canadian producers have a 7 percent share of the Canada–U.S. market in manufacturing.

From 1981 to 1991, this market grew by $987.6 billion and Canada's share of the increase was 9 percent. So Canada's share of the total market increased.

Canada lost some of its domestic market—down from 66.8 percent during 1981–83 to 59.3 percent in 1989–91 but gained market share in the United States—up from 1.9 percent in 1981–83 to 2.6 percent in 1989–91.

Six industries—transportation equipment, food, chemicals, electrical equipment, electronics, and paper—accounted for more than half the gains in the combined market and for three-quarters of the gains in the U.S. market.

THE FINANCIAL POST, MARCH 4, 1993

Canada's market share up under free trade: StatCan

By Alan Toulin

OTTAWA—Canada has gained a larger share of North American merchandise trade in the three years since the Canada–U.S. free trade agreement was signed, according to a Statistics Canada study published yesterday....

During the 10-year period from 1981 to 1991, the supply of manufactured goods in the combined Canada-U.S. market grew to $3.165 trillion from $2.177 trillion.

Out of this $987.6 billion increase, Canada's share was $88.1 billion. U.S.-based manufacturers took $681.4 billion of the increase and foreign manufacturers took up the rest with $218.4 billion.

StatCan reported that Canada's share of the increase between the first three years of the decade and the last three years of the decade was just under 9%.

"Canada's share of the increase was just under 9%; its average share of the market was about 7%. Accordingly, Canada's share in the total supply of manufacturers to the combined market increased," the federal agency said.

However, as part of the reciprocal aspect of free trade, Canada lost market share in the domestic market. Canada's market share during [1981–1983] was 66.8%. By 1989–91, this share of market had declined to 59.3%.

But Canada offset this loss in domestic market share with large gains in the U.S. market, increasing its market share to 2.6% in 1989–91 from 1.9% during [1981–83]....

In its analysis of industries, StatCan reported that transportation equipment, food, chemicals, electrical and electronic and paper industries accounted for more than half the gains in the growth of the combined market.

"The same industries were responsible for three-fourths of the gains in the U.S. market."

Background and Analysis

The Canada–United States free trade agreement that came into effect on January 1, 1989, lowered trade barriers between Canada and the United States and increased the volume of trade between the two countries.

As a result, both countries gained. The figures show how from the Canadian perspective.

Figure 1 shows Canada's PPF for telephone equipment (electronics) and blue jeans (clothing). The figure also shows the international trading possibilities *before* the free trade agreement. Canada produces E_0 of electronics and C_0 of clothing. Canada exports electronics and imports clothing and consumes at point *a*.

Figure 2 shows what happens after the free trade agreement. Canada can buy clothing from the United States at a lower price and the United States can buy electronics from Canada for a lower price. But clothing prices fall by *a larger percentage* than electronics prices, so the international trade possibilities line gets steeper.

Canada increases its production of electronics and decreases its production of clothing. And Canada increases its exports of electronics and increases its imports of clothes.

Canadian consumption increases, and the move from point *a* to point *b* is the gain to Canadians from the free trade agreement.

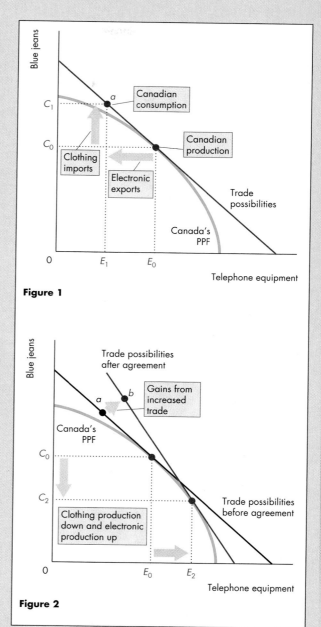

Figure 1

Figure 2

removed and others will be removed in a series of annual steps through 1999.

Nontariff Barriers   Nontariff barriers such as government procurement policies of buying local products are removed by the agreement. But most quotas, especially those that support agricultural policies in the two countries, remain in place.

Energy Products   Free trade in energy products existed before the free trade agreement, but the agreement ratified the intent to maintain that arrangement. The agreement that scarce energy resources will be shared in terms of national shortage became a controversial one. In effect, what the energy-sharing clause amounts to is an agreement that governments will not intervene in energy markets to prevent firms from selling their energy to the other country.

Trade in Services   International trade in services has been expanding more quickly than trade in manufactured goods in recent years. The free trade agreement, recognizing this factor and seeking to facilitate further expansion of trade in services between the United States and Canada, incorporates two principles: the *right of establishment* and *national treatment.* The right of establishment means that U.S. firms have the right to set up branches in Canada and Canadian firms have the right to set up operations in the United States. National treatment means that each country will treat firms and investors of the other country as if they were operating within its own borders.

Future Negotiations on Subsidies   In both the United States and Canada, there are many subsidies, especially to agricultural products. The presence of subsidies causes problems and makes it legitimate for the country importing subsidized goods to impose countervailing duties.

Effects of the Free Trade Agreement   Working out the effects of an agreement as complex as the Canada–United States Free Trade Agreement is difficult, and there is no general consensus on what the effects have been. The theory that you have studied in this chapter predicts that the removal of tariffs will produce an increase in the *volume* of international trade. That is, the theory predicts that Canadians will increasingly specialize in those activities at which they have a comparative advantage and Americans will specialize in a different range of

activities, and that the two countries will exchange a larger volume of goods and services.

As predicted, international trade between Canada and the United States did increase during the three years following the agreement. The increase in Canadian exports to the United States between 1989 and 1992 was 17 percent, while the increase between 1986 and 1989 was only 8 percent. Reading Between the Lines (pp. 986–987) looks at the effect of the agreement on Canada's share of merchandise trade.

Figure 35.11 shows some of the details of the changes in the pattern of trade with the United States. The industries shown in green are the ones in which trade was liberalized, and the industries shown in red are the ones in which protection did not change. You can see that following the agreement, Canada greatly increased its exports of advertising services, office and telecommunication equipment, paper, and transportation services. And its imports of meat and dairy products, communications services, clothing, furniture, and processed foods and beverages also increased by a large percentage.

These huge changes in exports and imports brought gains from increased specialization and exchange. But they also brought a heavy toll of adjustment. Thousands of jobs were lost in the declining sectors and new jobs were created in the expanding sectors. The amount of job destruction in the years following the free trade agreement was historically high, and the unemployment rate rose for three successive years. Only during the Great Depression did the rate of job destruction exceed that in the late 1980s and early 1990s. To what extent this high rate of job destruction was solely caused by the free trade agreement is unclear and controversial. But it is unquestionable that the free trade agreement made a large contribution.

◆ ◆ ◆ ◆ You've now seen how free international trade enables countries to gain from increased specialization and exchange. But you've also seen that when international specialization and exchange increase, a costly adjustment process must be endured. ◆ In the next chapter, we're going to study the ways in which international trade is financed and also learn why international borrowing and lending that permits unbalanced international trade arises. We'll discover the forces that determine the Canadian balance of payments and the value of the Canadian dollar.

FIGURE 35.11

The Changing Pattern of Canada–U.S. Trade

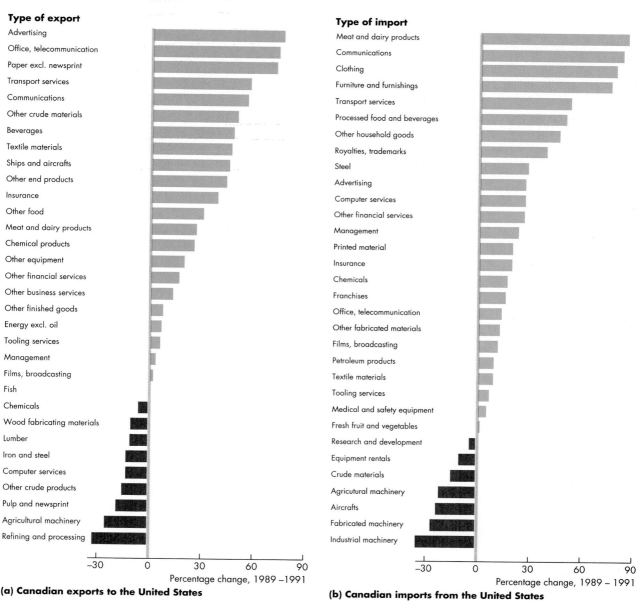

(a) Canadian exports to the United States

(b) Canadian imports from the United States

Between 1989 and 1991, Canadian exports to the United States of advertising services, office and telecommunication equipment, paper, transportation services, and communications services increased by more than 50 percent. An equally large percentage increase in Canada's imports from the United States occurred in meat and dairy products, communications, clothing, furniture, and processed foods and beverages.

Source: Daniel Schwanen, "Were the Optimists Wrong on Free Trade? A Canadian Perspective," C. D. Howe Institute Commentary, No. 37, Toronto, October 1992.

S U M M A R Y

Patterns and Trends in International Trade

Large flows of trade take place between rich and poor countries. Resource-rich countries exchange natural resources for manufactures, and resource-poor countries import their resources in exchange for their own manufactures. However, by far the biggest volume of trade is in manufactures exchanged among the rich industrialized countries. The biggest single Canadian export item is automobiles and automobile parts. These goods are also our biggest imports. Trade in services has grown in recent years. Total trade has also grown over the years. The Canadian balance of trade fluctuates but usually is positive—Canada is a net exporter. (pp. 967–969)

Opportunity Cost and Comparative Advantage

When opportunity costs differ between countries, the country with the lowest opportunity cost of producing a good has a comparative advantage in that good. Comparative advantage is the source of the gains from international trade. A country can have an absolute advantage, but not a comparative advantage, in the production of all goods. Every country has a comparative advantage in something. (pp. 970–971)

The Gains from Trade

Countries can gain from trade if their opportunity costs differ. Through trade, each country can obtain goods at a lower opportunity cost than it could if it produced all goods at home. Trading allows consumption to exceed production. By specializing in producing the good in which it has a comparative advantage and then trading some of that good for imports, a country can consume at points outside its production possibility frontier. Each country can consume at such a point.

In the absence of international borrowing and lending, trade is balanced as prices adjust to reflect the international supply and demand for goods. The world price is established at the level that balances the production and consumption plans of the trading parties. At the equilibrium price, trade is balanced and domestic consumption plans exactly match a combination of domestic production and international trade.

Comparative advantage explains the enormous volume and diversity of international trade that takes place in the world. But much trade takes the form of exchanging similar goods—one type of car for another. Such trade arises because of economies of scale in the face of diversified tastes. By specializing in producing a few goods, having long production runs, and then trading those goods internationally, consumers in all countries can enjoy greater diversity of products at lower prices. (pp. 971–979)

Trade Restrictions

A country can restrict international trade by imposing tariffs or nontariff barriers—quotas and voluntary export restraints. All trade restrictions raise the domestic price of imported goods, lower the volume of imports, and reduce the value of imports. They also reduce the value of exports by the same amount as the reduction in the value of imports.

All trade restrictions create a gap between the domestic price and the foreign supply price of an import. In the case of a tariff, that gap is the tariff revenue collected by the government. But the government raises no revenue from a quota. Instead, domestic importers who have a licence to import increase their profit. A voluntary export restraint resembles a quota except that a higher price is received by the foreign exporter.

Governments restrict trade to help the producers of the protected commodity and the workers employed by those producers. Because their gain is sufficiently large and the loss per consumer sufficiently small, the political equilibrium favours restricted trade. Politicians pay more attention to the vocal and active concerns of the few who stand to lose than to the quieter and less strongly expressed views of the many who stand to gain. (pp. 979–985)

The Canada–United States Free Trade Agreement

The Canadian-United States Free Trade Agreement, signed in October 1987, will phase out most tariffs on Canadian-U.S. trade through 1999. The agreement has reduced nontariff barriers, brought freer trade in energy products, freed up the trade in services, and created a dispute-settling mechanism. Future negotiations will attempt to reduce subsidies on both sides of the border.

The reductions in tariffs have brought a huge increase in volume of international trade between the two countries that is benefitting consumers but they have also brought a high rate unemployment that may persist for some time. (pp. 985–989)

K E Y   E L E M E N T S

Key Terms

Absolute advantage, 974
Balance of trade, 968
Comparative advantage, 971
Countervailing duties, 984
Dumping, 984
Exports, 967
General Agreement on Tariffs and Trade, 980
Imports, 967
Net exporter, 968
Net importer, 968
Nontariff barrier, 979
Protectionism, 979
Quota, 982

Tariff, 979
Voluntary export restraint, 982

Key Figures and Tables

Figure 35.1   Canadian Exports and Imports: 1992, 967
Figure 35.4   Opportunity Cost in Farmland, 970
Figure 35.5   Opportunity Cost in Mobilia, 971
Figure 35.6   International Trade in Cars, 972
Figure 35.7   Expanding Consumption Possibilities, 973
Figure 35.9   The Effects of a Tariff, 981
Figure 35.10 The Effects of a Quota, 983

R E V I E W   Q U E S T I O N S

1 What are the main exports and imports of Canada?

2 How does Canada trade services internationally?

3 Which items of international trade have been growing the most quickly in recent years?

4 What is comparative advantage? Why does it lead to gains from international trade?

5 Explain why international trade brings gains to all countries.

6 Distinguish between comparative advantage and absolute advantage.

7 Explain why all countries have a comparative advantage in something.

8 Explain why we import and export such large quantities of certain similar goods—such as cars.

9 What are the main ways in which we restrict international trade?

10 What are the effects of a tariff?

11 What are the effects of a quota?

12 What are the effects of a voluntary export restraint?

13 Describe the main trends in tariffs and nontariff barriers.

14 Which countries have the largest restrictions on their international trade?

15 Why do countries restrict international trade?

P R O B L E M S

1 Use Figs. 35.4 and 35.5 to calculate the opportunity cost of a car

a   In Farmland at the point on the production possibility frontier at which 2 million cars are produced.

b   In Mobilia when it produces 8 million cars.

2 The two countries in problem 1 do not trade. Farmland produces 2 million cars and Mobilia produces 8 million cars.

a   Which country has a comparative advantage in the production of cars?

b   If there is no trade between Farmland and Mobilia, how much grain is consumed and how many cars are bought in each country?

3 Suppose that the two countries in problem 2 trade freely.

a   Which country exports grain?

b   What adjustment will be made to the amount of each good produced by each country?

c   What adjustment will be made to the amount of each good consumed by each country?

d   What can you say about the price of a car under free trade?

4 Compare the total production of each good produced in problems 2 and 3.

5 Compare the situation in problems 2 and 3 with that analysed in this chapter (pp. 970–974). Why does Mobilia export cars in the chapter but import them in problem 3?

6 The following figure depicts the international market for soybeans.

a   What is the world price of soybeans if there is free trade between these countries?

b   If the country that imports soybeans imposes a tariff of $20 per tonne, what is the world price of soybeans and what quantity of soybeans gets traded internationally? What is the price of soybeans in the importing country? Calculate the tariff revenue.

7 If the importing country in problem 6(a) imposes a quota of 30 million tonnes, what is the price of soybeans in the importing country? What is the revenue from the quota and who gets this revenue?

8 If the exporting country in problem 6(a) imposes a VER of 30 million tonnes of soybeans, what is the world price of soybeans? What is the revenue of soybean growers in the exporting country? Which country gains from the VER?

9 Suppose that the exporting country in problem 6(a) subsidizes production by paying its farmers $10 a tonne for soybeans harvested.

a   What is the price of soybeans in the importing country?

b   What action might soybean growers in the importing country take? Why?

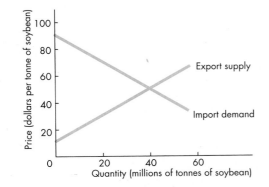

CHAPTER 36

THE BALANCE OF PAYMENTS AND THE DOLLAR

After studying this chapter, you will be able to

◆ Explain how international trade is financed

◆ Describe Canada's balance of payments accounts

◆ Explain why Canada is an international borrower

◆ Explain how the foreign exchange rate is determined and why it fluctuates

◆ Explain the relationship between interest rates in one country and another

◆ Explain why a flexible exchange rate brings monetary independence

FOR MOST OF US, ECONOMIC LIFE CENTRES ON THE COUNTRY in which we live. But for an increasing number of chief executive officers, marketing managers, lawyers, and many other professionals, the economy is the world—there is a global economy. ◆ ◆ Over the past four years, Canadians borrowed more than $100 billion from the rest of the world, $90 billion of which was to pay the interest on our previous debts. Why do we borrow from people in other countries? ◆ ◆ In 1973, it took one Canadian dollar to buy one U.S. dollar. But in 1986, it took 1.45 Canadian dollars to buy one U.S. dollar. What makes our dollar fluctuate in value against other currencies? Is there anything we can do to stabilize the value of the dollar? ◆ ◆ The world capital markets are becoming more integrated. As the Wall Street stock market rises and falls, so also do the stock markets in London, Paris, Tokyo, and Toronto. Interest rates in New York and Toronto rise and fall together. But the

The Global Economy

interest rates around the world vary enormously. For example, in early 1993, when the Canadian government was paying almost 10 percent a year on its borrowing, the Australian government was paying 13 percent, and the Japanese government 4 percent. Why aren't interest rates the same everywhere? And how can Canada pursue its own independent monetary policy in today's interdependent world?

◆ ◆ ◆ ◆ In this chapter, we're going to discover why our dollar fluctuates in value against other currencies and why interest rates around the world diverge.

Financing International Trade

When Eaton's imports Toshiba television sets from Japan, it does not pay for those TVs with Canadian dollars—it uses Japanese yen. When Benetton imports designer sweaters from Italy, it pays for them using Italian lire, and when a French power company buys a Candu reactor, it pays for it using Canadian dollars. Whenever we buy goods from another country, we use the currency of that country in order to make the transaction. It doesn't make any difference what item is traded—it might be a consumer good, a capital good, or even a firm.

We're going to study the markets in which transactions in different types of currency take place. But first we're going to look at the scale of international trading, borrowing, and lending and at the way in which we keep our records of these transactions. Such records are called balance of payments accounts.

Balance of Payments Accounts

Canada's **balance of payments accounts** record its international trading, borrowing, and lending. There are three balance of payments accounts:

◆ Current account

◆ Capital account

◆ Official settlements account

The **current account** records the receipts from the sale of goods and services to the rest of the world, the payments for goods and services bought from the rest of the world, net investment income paid to and received from non-residents, and net transfers (such as gifts to non-residents and foreign aid). By far the largest items in the current account are the receipts from the sale of goods and services to foreigners (value of exports) and the payments made for goods and services bought from foreigners (value of imports). The other items are relatively small. The current account balance is equal to exports of goods and services minus imports of goods and services plus net investment income plus net transfers.

The **capital account** records the amounts that Canadians lend to and borrow from non-residents. These transactions include direct investment (purchases of businesses) and portfolio investment (purchases of stocks and bonds). Lending to non-residents creates a Canadian claim, and borrowing from non-residents creates a Canadian liability. The capital account balance is equal to the increase in Canadian liabilities to non-residents minus the increase in Canadian claims on non-residents.

The **official settlements account** shows the change in the nation's official foreign exchange reserves. Official **foreign exchange reserves** are the federal government's and Bank of Canada's holdings of gold, foreign currencies, and Special Drawing Rights (SDRs) at the International Monetary Fund.[1] The double-entry bookkeeping system records an increase in reserves as a negative balance on the official settlements account and a decrease in reserves as a positive balance.

The sum of the balances on the three accounts equals zero. That is,

Current account balance + Capital account balance + Official settlements account balance = 0.

For example, if the current account balance is a $10 billion deficit and the capital account balance is a $9 billion surplus, the official settlements balance records a decrease in foreign exchange reserves (a positive number) of $1 billion. The current account deficit (–$10 billion) is matched by the capital account surplus (+$9 billion) plus the decrease in reserves (+$1 billion).

Canadian Balance of Payment in 1992   Table 36.1 shows the Canadian balance of payments accounts in 1992. As you can see from the table, Canada had a current account deficit of $28 billion in 1992. This deficit was made up of a deficit on the *balance of trade* (our exports of goods and services minus our imports of goods and services), a deficit on net investment income, and a zero balance on net transfers.

To cover our current account deficit, we borrowed from non-residents and used some of our reserves. The capital account surplus tells us that in 1992 we borrowed $17 billion more from non-residents than we lent to them. The official settlements account tells us that in 1992 we used $7 billion of

---

[1] Special Drawing Rights are international money created by the International Monetary Fund, which is described on p. 1003.

TABLE 36.1

Canada's Balance of Payments Accounts: 1992

	(billions of dollars)
CURRENT ACCOUNT	
Exports of goods and services	182
Imports of goods and services	−186
Net investment income	−24
Net transfers	0
Current account balance	−28
CAPITAL ACCOUNT	
Canadian claims on non-residents	−11
Canadian liabilities to non-residents	28
Capital account balance	17
Statistical discrepancy	4
OFFICIAL SETTLEMENTS ACCOUNT	
Decrease in official reserves	7

Source: Bank of Canada Review, Summer, 1993, Tables J1 and J2.

our foreign exchange reserves. The sum of these two amounts ($24 billion) exceeds the current account deficit because of measurement error and in 1992, the statistical discrepancy was $4 billion.

The numbers in Table 36.1 give you a snapshot of the balance of payments accounts in 1992. Figure 36.1 puts that snapshot into perspective by showing the balances on the three accounts from 1975 to 1992. As you can see, the current account balance is almost a mirror image of the capital account balance, and the official settlements balance is generally small compared with the balances on these other two accounts. A large current account deficit (and capital account surplus) emerged in the late 1980s and 1990s. And in the late 1980s, the official settlements balance also increased.

You might get a better understanding of the balance of payments accounts and the way they are linked together if you think about the balance of payments accounts of Joanne, a recent graduate.

Individual Analogy   Joanne's current account records her income from supplying the services of factors of production, her expenditure on goods and services, and her debt interest payments. In 1993, Joanne earned $25,000 from her work and $1,000 interest on her investments. Joanne's current account shows an income of $26,000. Joanne spent $18,000 on goods and services for consumption. She also bought an apartment, which cost her $60,000. She also paid $1,500 interest on her student loan. So Joanne's current account shows a total expenditure of $79,500. Joanne's income minus her expenditure is −$53,500 ($26,000 minus $79,500). So Joanne has a current account deficit of $53,500.

To pay for the expenditure of $53,500 in excess of her income, Joanne must either take a loan or use the money she has in the bank. Joanne took a loan of $50,000 to help buy her apartment. This borrowing appears in Joanne's capital account. With a current account deficit of $53,500 and a capital account surplus of $50,000, Joanne was still $3,500 short, so she used $3,500 from her own bank account. Her cash holdings decreased by $3,500.

Joanne's supply of factors of production is analogous to a country's supply of exports. Her purchases of goods and services including the apartment are analogous to a country's imports. The difference between these two items is analogous to a country's balance of trade. Joanne's interest income and payments are analogous to a country's net investment income. Joanne's housing loan—borrowing from someone else—is analogous to a country's foreign borrowing. The change in her own bank account balance is analogous to the change in a country's foreign exchange reserves. Because we've measured Joanne's transactions accurately, her accounts have a statistical discrepancy of zero.

Figure 36.1 shows that Canada's current account balance has almost always been in deficit since 1975. Let's look at the implications of persistent international deficits and surpluses.

International Borrowing and Lending

A country that has a capital account surplus is called a **net borrower**. The majority of countries are net borrowers including, in recent years, Canada, France, Italy, the United Kingdom, and the United States. But a small number of countries are net lenders.

A **net lender** is a country that has a capital

FIGURE 36.1

The Balance of Payments: 1975–1992

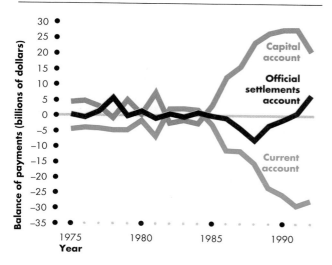

From 1975 to 1985, fluctuations in the balance of payments were relatively small but, after 1985, a large current account deficit emerged. With the exception of 1982-1984, the current account balance was negative. The capital account balance mirrors the current account balance. When the current account balance is positive, the capital account balance is usually negative—we lend to the rest of the world. When the current account balance is negative, the capital account balance is usually positive—we borrow from the rest of the world. Fluctuations in the official settlements balance are smaller than the fluctuations in the current account balance and the capital account balance.

Source: Bank of Canada Review, Summer 1993, Tables I2, J1, and J2.

account deficit. The oil-rich countries such as Kuwait and Venezuela, developed economies such as Japan and Germany, and developing countries such as Singapore and South Korea are net lenders.

A net borrower increases its liabilities or decreases its claims on non-residents. A net lender decreases its liabilities or increases its claims on non-residents. The sum of a nation's liabilities minus its claims on non-residents determines whether it is a debtor or creditor nation.

A **debtor nation** is a nation that during its entire history has borrowed more from the non-residents than it has lent to them. It has a stock of outstanding liabilities—debts—to non-residents that exceeds the

stock of its own claims on non-residents. A debtor nation is one whose net receipts of interest on debt are negative—interest payments made by it exceed the interest payments that it receives. Canada, France, Italy, and the United States are debtors. But the United Kingdom, although a net borrower in recent years, is not a debtor. It is a creditor.

A **creditor nation** is a nation that has lent more to non-residents than it has borrowed from them. It has a stock of outstanding debt to non-residents that is smaller than the stock of its own claims on non-residents. A creditor nation is one with positive net receipts of interest on debt—interest payments made to it exceed the interest payments that it makes. Japan is the largest creditor nation in the 1990s.

At the heart of the distinction between a net borrower/net lender and a debtor/creditor nation is the distinction between *flows* and *stocks*. Borrowing and lending are flows. They are the amounts borrowed and lent per unit of time. Liabilities and claims—debts—are stocks. They are the amounts owed at a point in time. The flow of borrowing and lending changes the stock of debt. But the outstanding stock of debt depends mainly on past flows of borrowing and lending, not on the current period's flows. The current period's flows determine the *change* in the stock of debt outstanding.

We've now described the balance of payments accounts and the relationships between international deficits and debts. Our next task is to see what determines a country's current account balance.

Current Account Balance

We've just seen that the current account balance is equal to exports of goods and services minus imports of goods and services plus net investment income plus net transfers. Of these items, by far the largest are exports and imports and it is fluctuations in exports and imports that bring fluctuations in the current account balance. The other items change only slowly.

To understand the forces that determine a country's current account balance and scale of its foreign borrowing or lending, we need to study the determination of exports and imports and the difference between them—net exports. And to determine net exports, we need to use the national income accounts that you studied in Chapter 23. Table 36.2 will refresh your memory and summarize the necessary calculations for you. Part (a) lists the national income variables that are needed, with their symbols. Their values in Canada in 1992 are also shown.

Part (b) presents two key national income equations. Equation (1) reminds us that gross domestic product is the sum of consumption expenditure, investment, government purchases of goods and services, and net exports (the difference between exports and imports). Equation (2) reminds us that aggregate income is used in three different ways—consumed, saved, or paid to the government as taxes (net of transfer payments). Equation (1) tells us how our expenditure generates our income. Equation (2) tells us how we dispose of that income.

Part (c) of the table takes you into new territory. It examines surpluses and deficits. We'll look at three surpluses/deficits—net exports, the government sector, and the private sector. To obtain these surpluses and deficits, first subtract equation (2) from equation (1) in Table 36.2. The result is equation (3). By rearranging equation (3), we obtain a relationship for net exports—exports minus imports—that appears as equation (4) in the table. Notice that net exports, in equation (4), is the sum of two components. The first is taxes minus government spending and the second is saving minus investment. These items are the surpluses/deficits of the government and private sectors.

The **government sector surplus or deficit** is the difference between taxes (net of transfers) and government purchases of goods and services. If taxes exceed government purchases, the government sector has a surplus. If taxes are less than government purchases, the government sector has a deficit. The government sector deficit is different from the federal government deficit, examined in Chapter 34 because it includes the federal, provincial, and local governments.

The **private sector surplus or deficit** is the difference between saving and investment. If saving exceeds investment, the private sector has a surplus to lend to other sectors. If investment exceeds saving, the private sector has a deficit that has to be financed by borrowing from other sectors.

As you can see from our calculations, net exports is equal to the sum of the government sector deficit and the private sector deficit. In Canada in 1992, the biggest of these two deficits was the government sector deficit—$46 billion. The net exports deficit was only $4 billion. These two deficits were offset by the private sector surplus, which was $50 billion.

Part (d) of Table 36.2 shows you how investment is financed. To increase investment, either private saving or the government sector surplus must increase or net exports must decrease.

The calculations that we've just performed are only bookkeeping. We've manipulated the national income accounts and discovered that net exports equals the sum of the deficits of the government and private sectors. But these calculations do reveal a fundamental fact—our net exports can change only if either our government sector deficit or the private sector deficit changes. This fact is often lost sight of in popular discussions of our net exports.

We've seen that our net exports is equal to the sum of the government sector deficit and the private sector deficit. But what determines those two deficits? Why doesn't the private sector have a surplus equal to the government sector deficit so that net exports are zero? Does an increase in the government sector deficit bring a decrease in net exports and an increase in the current account deficit?

FIGURE 36.2

The Twin Deficits: 1975–1992

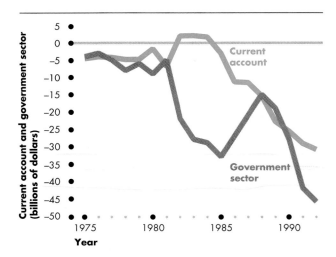

The twin deficits are the current account deficit and the government sector deficit. The relationship between these deficits is illustrated here. During the 1970s, the very late 1980s, and early l990s, these deficits moved together. During most of 1980s, they moved in opposite directions.

Sources: Current Account, see Fig. 36.1. Government Budget Deficit, Statistics Canada, CANSIM series D20193.

TABLE 36.2

The Current Account Balance, Net Foreign Borrowing, and the Financing of Investment

	Symbols and equations	Canadian values in 1992 (billions of dollars)
(a) VARIABLES		
Investment	I	111
Government purchases of goods and services	G	165
Exports of goods and services	EX	182
Imports of goods and services	IM	186
Saving	S	161
Taxes, net of transfer payments	T	119
(b) INJECTIONS AND LEAKAGES		
Injections	(1) $I + G + EX$	
Leakages	(2) $S + I + IM$	
Difference between (1) and (2)	(3) $0 = (I - S) + (G - T) + (EX - IM)$	
(c) SURPLUSES AND DEFICITS		
Net exports	(4) $EX - IM$	$182 - 186 = -4$
Government sector	(5) $T - G$	$119 - 165 = -46$
Private sector	(6) $S - I$	$161 - 111 = 50$
(d) FINANCING INVESTMENT		
Investment is financed by the sum of private saving,	S	161
net government saving,	$T - G$	−46
and net foreign saving.	$IM - EX$	4
That is,	(7) $I = S + (T - G) - (EX - IM)$	$111 = 161 - 46 - 4$

Source: National Income and Ecpenditure Accounts, Statistics Canada.

The Twin Deficits

You can see the answer to this question by looking at Fig. 36.2. In that figure, the government sector deficit is plotted alongside the current account deficit. As you can see, up to 1981, the current account deficit and the government sector deficit moved in close sympathy with each other. There was a clear tendency for the current account deficit to become larger when the government sector deficit became larger. But between 1982 and 1987, these two variables move a long way apart. By 1988, the current account deficit and the government sector deficit were close to each other again. The tendency for the two deficits to move together has given rise to the term *twin deficits*. The **twin deficits** are the government sector deficit and the current account deficit. But the twin deficits are not identical twins. There are independent variations in the two deficits that are not accommodated by variations in the private sector surplus. Let's see why.

Effects of Government Deficit on Private Surplus

As we've just seen, the private sector surplus is saving minus investment. One of the main influences on the level of saving is disposable income. Anything that increases disposable income, other things remaining the same, increases saving and increases the private sector surplus. The main influences on investment are the interest rate and expectations of future profits. Other things remaining the same, anything that lowers the interest rate or increases future profit expectations increases investment and decreases the private sector surplus.

Changes in taxes or government spending change the government sector deficit and influence disposable income and the interest rate. These changes, in turn, influence private sector saving and investment and hence change the private sector surplus. An increase in government purchases of goods and services or a tax cut—either of which increases the government sector deficit—tends to increase GDP and the interest rate. The higher GDP increases disposable income and stimulates additional saving. The higher interest rate dampens investment. Thus, to some degree, an increase in the government sector deficit induces an increase in the private sector surplus.

For an increase in the government sector deficit to lead to an increase in the private sector surplus, the government's actions must stimulate higher income and/or a higher interest rate. There are two factors that tend to limit these channels of influence. First, when the economy is operating close to full employment, the higher government sector deficit does not produce a higher level of real GDP. Second, internationally mobile capital lessens the effect of increased government spending on interest rates. Thus the two mechanisms by which an increase in the government sector deficit can increase the private sector surplus can be relatively weak.

Effects of Government Deficit on Current Account Deficit

Since the government sector deficit, the private sector deficit, and net exports sum to zero, any change in the government sector deficit that does not influence the private sector deficit must have its effect on net exports and the current account deficit. But how does that effect come about? The easiest way to see the effect is to consider what happens at full employment. An increase in government purchases or a tax cut leads to an increase in aggregate demand. But at full employment there are no spare resources to generate a comparable increase in output. So part of the increased demand spills over into the rest of the world and imports increase. Also, part of the domestic production going for export is diverted to satisfy domestic demand. Exports decrease. The rise in imports and the fall in exports decrease net exports and increase the current account deficit.

Of course, the economy does not always operate at full employment. Nor does foreign capital flow in at a fixed interest rate. Thus the link between the government sector deficit and the current account deficit is not a mechanical one.

Does the Current Account Deficit Matter?

Should Canada be concerned about its current account balance? Does it matter that Canada is a net borrower and a debtor? The answer depends on whether we borrow to finance investment or consumption. If we borrow to finance investments that yield more than the interest we must pay, borrowing is not a problem. But if we borrow to finance consumption, we must then make interest payments and eventually repay the loans out of future income. To do so, we must cut our consumption below the level that would have been attainable in the absence of borrowing.

Is Canada Borrowing for Consumption or Investment?

Up to 1981, Canada borrowed for investment. The scale of capital accumulation exceeded the scale of private saving and international borrowing. But between 1981 and 1988, Canada borrowed for consumption. During those years, capital accumulation was less than domestic saving plus foreign borrowing. In one year, 1985, we borrowed close to $25 billion to finance public and private consumption in excess of what our income could sustain. After 1985, our consumption of foreign loans declined. By 1988, Canada was again borrowing to finance investment. So the current account deficit certainly was a problem during the 1981–1988 but not always a problem.

REVIEW

Canada's current account deficit is financed by borrowing from non-residents or by using the nation's foreign exchange reserves. In the late 1980s and early 1990s, the Canadian current account moved into a large deficit and the capital account moved into a large surplus—Canada was a net borrower. Most of the time, Canada's international borrowing is used to finance investment but for a few years during the 1980s, foreign borrowing financed consumption. The current account deficit fluctuates in a way similar to the government sector deficit—the phenomenon of the twin deficits. ◆

Foreign Exchange and the Dollar

When we buy foreign goods or invest in another country, we must obtain some of that country's currency to make the transaction. When foreigners buy Canadian-produced goods or invest in Canada, they use Canadian dollars. We buy foreign currency and foreigners buy Canadian dollars in the foreign exchange market.

The **foreign exchange market** is the market in which the currency of one country is exchanged for the currency of another. The foreign exchange market is not a place like a downtown flea market or produce market. The market is made up of thousands of people—importers and exporters, banks, and specialists in the buying and selling of foreign exchange called foreign exchange brokers. The foreign exchange market opens on Monday morning in Hong Kong, which is still Sunday evening in Montreal. Figure 36.3 shows that as the day advances, markets open in Singapore, Tokyo, Sydney, Bahrain, Frankfurt, London (the largest market), New York, Toronto and, finally, Vancouver. One hour after the Vancouver market has closed, Hong Kong is open again for its next day of trading. Dealers around the world are continually in contact using computers linked by telephone and, on any given day, more than half a trillion dollars changes hands.

The price at which one currency exchanges for another is called a **foreign exchange rate**. For example, in June 1993 one Canadian dollar bought 83 Japanese yen. The exchange rate between the Canadian dollar and the Japanese yen was 83 yen per dollar. Exchange rates can be expressed either way. We've just expressed the exchange rate between the yen and the dollar as a number of yen per dollar. Equivalently, we can express it in terms of dollars per yen. That exchange rate, in June 1993, was $0.012 per yen.

The actions of the foreign exchange brokers make the foreign exchange market highly efficient. Exchange rates are almost identical no matter where in the world the transaction is taking place. If Canadian dollars are cheap in London and expensive in Tokyo, within a flash someone will place a buy order in London and a sell order in Tokyo, thereby increasing demand in one place and increasing supply in another, moving the prices to equality.

Foreign Exchange Regimes

Foreign exchange rates are of critical importance for millions of people. They affect the costs of our foreign vacations and our imported cars. They affect the number of dollars that we end up getting for the apples and wheat that we sell to Japan. Because of its importance, governments pay a great deal of attention to what is happening in foreign exchange markets and, more than that, take actions designed to achieve what they regard as desirable movements in exchange rates. There are three ways in which the government and the Bank of Canada can operate in the foreign exchange market—three foreign exchange market regimes. They are

◆ Fixed exchange rate

◆ Flexible exchange rate

◆ Managed exchange rate

A **fixed exchange rate** is an exchange rate the value of which is held steady by the country's central bank. For example, the Canadian government could adopt a fixed exchange rate by defining the Canadian dollar to be worth a certain number of units of some other currency and having the Bank of Canada take action to maintain that announced value. We'll study what those actions are below.

FIGURE 36.3

The Global Foreign Exchange Market

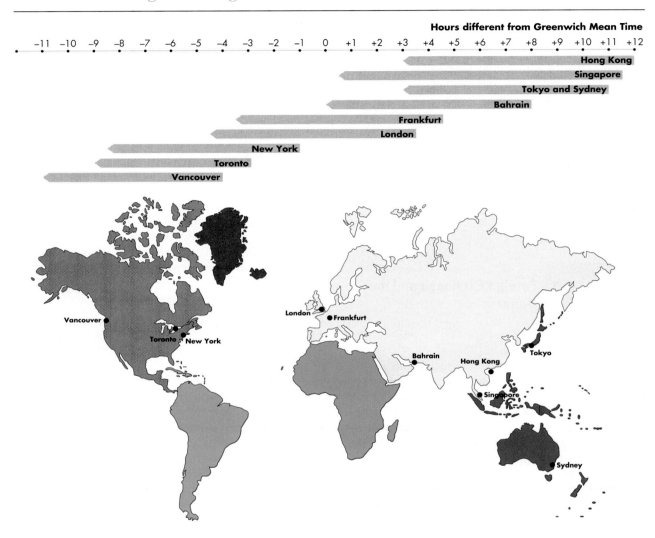

The foreign exchange market barely closes. The day begins in Hong Kong and as the globe spins, markets open up in Singapore, Tokyo, Sydney, Bahrain, Frankfurt, London, Toronto, and Vancouver. By the time the Vancouver market closes, Hong Kong is almost ready to begin another day.

Source: Based on a similar map in Steven Husted and Michael Melvin, *International Economics,* Harper & Row Publishers Inc., 1989, and data from *Euromoney,* April 1979, p. 14.

A **flexible exchange rate** is an exchange rate the value of which is determined by market forces in the absence of central bank intervention.

A **managed exchange rate** is an exchange rate the value of which is influenced by central bank intervention in the foreign exchange market. Under a managed exchange rate regime, the central bank's intervention does not seek to keep the exchange rate fixed at a pre-announced level but to dampen the fluctuations that might otherwise occur.

Recent Exchange Rate History

At the end of World War II, the major countries of the world set up the International Monetary Fund (IMF). The **International Monetary Fund** is an international organization that monitors balance of payments and exchange rate activities. The IMF, located in Washington, D.C., came into being as the result of negotiations between the United States and the United Kingdom during World War II. In July 1944, at Bretton Woods, New Hampshire, 44 countries signed the Articles of Agreement of the IMF. At the centrepiece of those agreements was the establishment of a worldwide system of fixed exchange rates between currencies. The anchor for this fixed exchange rate system was gold. One ounce of gold was defined to be worth US$35. All other currencies were pegged to the U.S. dollar at a fixed exchange rate. For example, the Japanese yen was set at 360 yen per U.S. dollar; the British pound was set to be worth US$4.80.

Canada's participation in the IMF's fixed exchange rate system was more limited than that of most other countries. From the creation of the system until 1962, Canada maintained a good deal of exchange rate independence. For most of the 1960s (1962 to 1970), Canada operated a fixed exchange rate as part of the IMF's system. Since 1970, Canada has allowed the foreign exchange value of its dollar to fluctuate. Sometimes those fluctuations have been almost completely freely determined by market forces, but most of the time Canada has had a managed exchange rate regime.

It was not only Canada that found problems with the fixed exchange rate regime of the international monetary system in the early 1970s. Although that system had served the world well during the 1950s and early 1960s, it came under increasing strain in the late 1960s and, by 1971, the system had almost collapsed. In the period since 1971, the world has operated a variety of flexible and managed exchange rate arrangements. Some currencies have increased in value, and others have declined. The Canadian dollar is among the currencies that have declined. The Japanese yen is the currency that has had the most spectacular increase in value.

Figure 36.4 shows what has happened to the foreign exchange value of the Canadian dollar since 1978. The orange line shows the value of the dollar against the Japanese yen. As you can see, the value of our dollar has fallen—the dollar has depreciated.

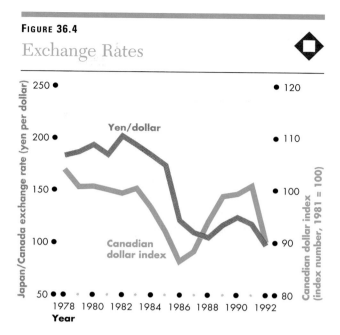

FIGURE 36.4

Exchange Rates

The exchange rate is the price at which two currencies can be traded. The yen-dollar exchange rate, expressed as yen per dollar, has fallen in value—the dollar has depreciated against the yen. An index of the value of the Canadian dollar against the G-10 currencies shows that the Canadian dollar has depreciated on the average against all G-10 currencies although it appreciated slightly in 1974, 1976, and 1987–1989.

Sources: Bank of Canada Review, CANSIM series B3407 and B3418.

Currency depreciation is the fall in the value of one currency in terms of another currency.

Although the dollar has depreciated in terms of the yen, it has not depreciated against all currencies. To calculate the value of the Canadian dollar against all other currencies on the average, the Bank of Canada calculates a Canadian dollar index against the G-10 currencies. The **Canadian dollar index against the G-10 currencies** is an index that measures the value of the Canadian dollar in terms of its ability to buy a basket of currencies of the group of countries known as G-10, where the weight placed on each currency is related to its importance in Canada's international trade. How the Canadian dollar has actually fluctuated against the G-10 currencies on the average in recent years is shown in Fig. 36.4. As you can see, in 1979, it depreciated; from 1979 to 1983, it remained steady; from 1983 to 1986, it depreciated; and after 1986 it appreciated.

What determines the foreign currency value of the dollar?

Exchange Rate Determination

T he foreign exchange value of the dollar is a price and, like any other price, is determined by demand and supply. But what exactly do we mean by the demand for and supply of dollars?

The quantity of dollars demanded in the foreign exchange market is the amount that people would buy on a given day at a particular exchange rate (price) if they found a willing seller. The quantity of dollars supplied in the foreign exchange market is the amount that people would sell on a given day at a particular exchange rate (price) if they found a willing buyer. What determines the quantities of dollars demanded and supplied in the foreign exchange market?

To answer this question, you need to think about the alternative to demanding and supplying dollars. For a demander of dollars, the alternative is to hang onto the foreign currency that would be exchanged for dollars. For a supplier of dollars, the alternative is to hang onto the dollars. So, holding dollars is the alternative to supplying dollars on the foreign exchange market. And holding foreign currency is the alternative to demanding dollars on the foreign market. The decision to buy or sell dollars is the same decision as that to hold dollars or foreign currency.

To understand the forces that determine demand and supply in the foreign exchange market, we need to study the factors that determine the decisions about the quantities of dollars (and other currencies) to hold. We'll begin by making clear what is meant by the quantity of dollars held.

The Quantity of Dollars

The **quantity of Canadian dollar assets** (which we'll call the **quantity of dollars**) is the stock of net financial assets denominated in Canadian dollars held outside the Bank of Canada and the government of Canada. There are three things about the quantity of dollars that need to be emphasized.

First, the quantity of dollars is a *stock*, not a *flow*. People make decisions about the quantity of dollars to hold (a stock) and about the quantities to buy or sell (flows) in the foreign exchange market. But it is

the decision about how many dollars to hold that determines whether people plan to buy or sell dollars.

Second, the quantity of dollars is a stock *denominated in Canadian dollars*. The denomination of an asset defines the units in which a debt must be repaid. It is possible to make a loan using any currency of denomination. The Canadian government could borrow in Japanese yen. If it did borrow in yen, it would issue a bond denominated in yen. Such a bond would be a promise to pay an agreed number of yen on an agreed date. It would not be a dollar debt and, even though the Canadian government issued the bond, it would not be part of the supply of dollars. Many governments actually do issue bonds in currencies other than their own. The Canadian government, for example, issues bonds denominated in U.S. dollars.

Third, the supply of dollars is a *net* supply—the quantity of assets *minus* the quantity of liabilities. This fact means that the quantity of dollars supplied does not include dollar assets created by private households, firms, financial institutions, or foreigners. The reason is that when a private debt is created, there is both an asset (for the holder) and a liability (for the issuer), so the *net* financial asset is zero.

The quantity of dollars includes only the dollar liabilities of the federal government *plus* the Bank of Canada. This quantity is equal to the government debt held outside the Bank of Canada plus the dollar liabilities of the Bank of Canada—the monetary base. That is,

$$\text{Quantity of dollars} = \begin{array}{c}\text{Government debt held}\\\text{outside the Bank of Canada}\\\text{+ Monetary base.}\end{array}$$

We've seen what dollar assets are. Let's now study the demand for these assets.

The Demand for Dollars

The law of demand applies to dollar assets just as it does to anything else that people value. The quantity of dollar assets demanded increases when the price of dollars in terms of foreign currency falls, and decreases when the price of dollars in terms of foreign currency rises. There are two separate reasons why the law of demand applies to dollars.

First, there is a transactions demand. The lower the value of the dollar, the larger is the demand for Canadian exports and the lower is our demand for imports. Hence the larger also is the amount of trade financed by dollars. Foreigners demand more dollars to buy Canadian exports and we demand fewer units of foreign currency and more dollars as we switch from importing to buying Canadian-produced goods.

Second, there is a demand arising from expected capital gains. Other things remaining the same, the lower the value of the dollar, the larger is the quantity of dollars demanded arising from the expectation of a capital gain. To see why, suppose that you expect the dollar to be worth 110 Japanese yen at the end of one year. If today the dollar is worth 120 yen, you're expecting the dollar to depreciate by 10 yen. But if today the dollar is worth 100 yen, you're expecting the dollar to appreciate by 10 yen. Other things remaining the same, the larger the expected appreciation of the dollar, the greater is the quantity of dollars demanded. But as the above example illustrates, for a given expected future exchange rate, the lower the value of the dollar today, the higher is its expected rate of appreciation (or the lower is its expected rate of depreciation).

Holding assets in a particular currency in anticipation of a gain in their value arising from a change in the exchange rate is the main influence on the quantity demanded of dollar assets and of foreign currency assets. The more a currency is expected to appreciate, the greater is the quantity of assets denominated in that currency that people want to hold.

Figure 36.5 shows the relationship between the foreign currency price of the Canadian dollar and the quantity of dollar assets demanded—the demand curve for dollar assets. When the foreign exchange rate changes, other things remaining the same, there is a movement along the demand curve.

Changes in the Demand for Dollars

Any other influence on the quantity of dollar assets that people want to hold results in a shift in the demand curve. Demand either increases or decreases. These other influences are

◆ The value of dollar payments

◆ The interest rate differential

◆ The expected future value of the dollar

The Value of Dollar Payments   By holding an inventory of dollars, people can avoid the transactions costs of converting assets in other currencies into dollars each time they need dollars to make a

FIGURE 36.5

The Demand for Dollar Assets

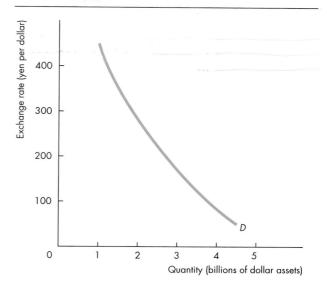

The quantity of dollar assets that people demand, other things remaining the same, depends on the exchange rate. The lower the exchange rate (the smaller the number of yen per dollar), the larger is the quantity of dollar assets demanded. The increased quantity demanded arises from an increase in the volume of dollar trade (the Japanese buy more Canadian goods and we buy fewer Japanese goods) and an increase in the expected appreciation (or decrease in the expected depreciation) of dollar assets.

payment. The larger the value of dollar payments, the larger is the inventory of dollars that people hold. An increase in the value of dollar payments increases the demand for dollars and shifts the demand curve for dollars rightward. And a decrease in the value of dollar payments decreases the demand for dollars and shifts the demand curve for dollars leftward.

The value of dollar payments changes when the *volume* of trade changes or when the Canadian *price level* changes. But the price level has two opposing effects. For a given volume of trade, a higher price level brings a higher value of trade and payments. But with prices in the rest of the world given, a higher price level lowers Canadian exports and decreases the volume of trade. So an increase in the price level, other things remaining the same, might increase or decrease the demand for dollars.

The Interest Rate Differential   The **interest rate differential** is the interest rate on dollar assets minus the interest rate on a foreign currency asset. People hold financial assets partly for convenience and partly to make a return—an interest income. An increase in the interest rate differential increases the demand for dollars and shifts the demand curve for dollars rightward. The interest rate differential can increase because the interest rate on Canadian dollar assets increases or because the interest rate on foreign currency assets decreases.

The Expected Future Value of the Dollar   If the dollar is expected to appreciate against other currencies, people will hold more dollar assets and fewer foreign-currency assets, other things remaining the same. An increase in the expected future value of the Canadian dollar increases the demand for dollars and shifts the demand curve for dollars rightward.

Table 36.4 summarizes the above discussion of the influences on the quantity of dollar assets that people demand.

TABLE 36.4

The Demand for Dollar Assets

THE LAW OF DEMAND

The quantity of dollar assets demanded

Increases if	*Decreases if*
◆ The foreign currency value of the dollar falls	◆ The foreign currency value of the dollar rises

CHANGES IN DEMAND

The quantity for dollar assets

Increases if	*Decreases if*
◆ The value of dollar payments increases	◆ The value of dollar payments decreases
◆ The interest rate differential increases	◆ The interest rate differential decreases

The Supply of Dollars

The quantity of dollar assets supplied is determined by the actions of the government and the Bank of Canada. We've seen that the quantity of dollars is equal to government debt plus the monetary base. Of these two items, the monetary base is by far the smallest. But it plays a crucial role in determining the supply of dollars, since the behaviour of the monetary base itself depends crucially on the foreign exchange rate regime in operation.

Under a fixed exchange rate regime, the supply curve of dollar assets is horizontal at the chosen exchange rate. The Bank of Canada stands ready to supply whatever quantity of dollar assets is demanded at the fixed exchange rate. Under a managed exchange rate regime, where the government wants to smooth fluctuations in the exchange rate, the supply curve of dollar assets is upward sloping. The higher the foreign exchange rate, the larger is the quantity of dollar assets supplied. Under a flexible exchange rate regime, a fixed quantity of dollar assets is supplied, regardless of their price. As a consequence, under a flexible exchange rate regime, the supply curve of dollar assets is vertical.

Changes in the Supply of Dollars

There are two ways in which the supply of dollar assets can change. They are

◆ The federal government has a deficit or surplus.

◆ The Bank of Canada buys or sells assets denominated in foreign currency.

When the federal government has a deficit, it borrows by issuing bonds. These bonds, denominated in Canadian dollars, are held by households, firms, financial institutions, foreigners, and the Bank of Canada. Bonds bought by the Bank of Canada are not part of the stock of dollar assets. But to buy the bonds, the Bank of Canada creates additional monetary base and this equivalent amount *is* part of the quantity of dollar assets. Thus when the Bank of Canada buys Canadian government debt, there is no change in the quantity of dollar assets, just a change in its composition.

The Bank of Canada can increase the quantity of dollars by buying assets denominated in foreign currency. If the Bank of Canada uses Canadian dollars to buy Japanese yen in the foreign exchange market,

TABLE 36.5

The Supply of Dollar Assets

SUPPLY

Fixed exchange rate regime
The supply curve of dollar assets is horizontal at the fixed exchange rate.

Managed exchange rate
In order to smooth fluctuations in the price of the dollar, the quantity of dollar assets supplied by the Bank of Canada increases if the foreign currency price of the dollar rises and decreases if the foreign currency price of the dollar falls. The supply curve of dollar assets slopes upward.

Flexible exchange rate
The supply curve of dollar assets is vertical.

CHANGES IN SUPPLY

The supply of dollar assets

Increases if	*Decreases if*
◆ The Canadian government budget is in deficit	◆ The Canadian government budget is in surplus
◆ The Bank of Canada buys assets denominated in foreign currency	◆ The Bank of Canada sells assets denominated in foreign currency

the monetary base increases by the amount paid for the yen.

The above discussion of the influences on the supply of dollar assets is summarized in Table 36.5.

The Market for Dollars

Let's now bring together the demand and supply sides of the market for dollar assets, and determine the exchange rate. Figure 36.6 illustrates the analysis.

Fixed Exchange Rate   First, consider a fixed exchange rate regime such as that from 1962 to 1971. This case is illustrated in Fig. 36.6(a). The supply curve of dollars is horizontal at the fixed exchange rate of 200 yen per dollar. If the demand curve is D_0, the quantity of dollar assets is Q_0. An increase in demand to D_1 results in an increase in

the quantity of dollar assets from Q_0 to Q_1 but no change in the yen price of dollars.

Flexible Exchange Rate   Next look at Fig. 36.6(b), which shows what happens under a flexible exchange rate regime. In this case, the quantity of dollar assets supplied is fixed at Q_0, so the supply curve of dollar assets is vertical. If the demand curve for dollars is D_0, the exchange rate is 200 yen per dollar. If the demand for dollars increases from D_0 to D_1, the exchange rate increases to 300 yen per dollar.

Managed Exchange Rate   Finally, consider a managed exchange rate regime, which appears in Fig. 36.6(c). Here, the supply curve is upward sloping. When the demand curve is D_0, the exchange rate is 200 yen per dollar. If demand increases to D_1, the yen value of the dollar rises but only to 225 yen per dollar. Compared with the flexible exchange rate case, the same increase in demand results in a smaller increase in the exchange rate when it is managed. The reason for this is that the quantity supplied increases in the managed exchange rate case.

Exchange Rate Regime and Official Settlements Balance   There is a connection between the foreign exchange rate regime and the balance of payments. The official settlements account of the balance of payments records the change in the country's official holdings (by the government and the Bank of Canada) of foreign currency. Under fixed exchange rates (as shown in Fig. 36.6a), every time there is a change in the demand for dollar assets, the Bank of Canada must change the quantity of dollar assets supplied to match it. When the Bank of Canada has to increase the quantity of dollar assets supplied, it does so by offering dollar assets in exchange for foreign currency. In this case, the official holdings of foreign exchange increase. If the demand for dollar assets decreases, the Bank of Canada has to decrease the quantity of dollar assets supplied. The Bank of Canada does so by buying dollars back and using its foreign exchange holdings to do so. In this case, official holdings of foreign exchange decrease. Thus, with a fixed exchange rate, fluctuations in the demand for dollar assets result in fluctuations in official holdings of foreign exchange.

Under a flexible exchange rate regime, there is no government or Bank of Canada intervention in the foreign exchange market. Regardless of what happens to the demand for dollars, no action is taken to

FIGURE 36.6

Three Exchange Rate Regimes

(a) Fixed exchange rate

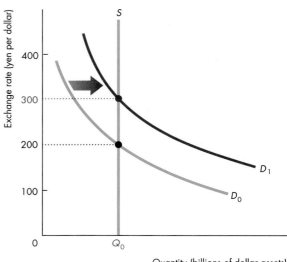

(b) Flexible exchange rate

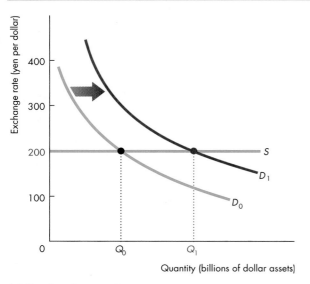

(c) Managed exchange rate

Under a fixed exchange rate regime (part a), the Bank of Canada stands ready to supply dollar assets or to take dollar assets off the market (supplying foreign currency in exchange) at a fixed exchange rate. The supply curve for dollar assets is horizontal. Fluctuations in demand lead to fluctuations in the quantity of dollar assets outstanding and to fluctuations in the nation's official holdings of foreign exchange. If demand increases from D_0 to D_1, the quantity of dollar assets increases from Q_0 to Q_1. Under a flexible exchange rate regime (part b), the Bank of Canada fixes the quantity of dollar assets so that their supply curve is vertical. An increase in the demand for dollar assets from D_0 to D_1 results only in an increase in the value of the dollar—the exchange rate rises from 200 to 300 yen per dollar. The quantity of dollar assets remains constant at Q_0. Under a managed exchange rate regime (part c), the Bank of Canada has an upward-sloping supply curve of dollar assets, so that if demand increases from D_0 to D_1, the dollar appreciates but the quantity of dollar assets supplied also increases—from Q_0 to Q_2. The increase in the quantity of dollar assets supplied moderates the rise in the value of the dollar but does not completely prevent it as in the case of fixed exchange rates.

change the quantity of dollars supplied. Therefore there are no changes in the country's official holdings of foreign exchange. In this case, the official settlements balance is zero.

With a managed exchange rate, official holdings of

foreign exchange are adjusted to meet fluctuations in demand but by less than under a fixed exchange rate. As a consequence, fluctuations in the official settlements balance are smaller under a managed floating regime than under a fixed exchange rate.

Why Is the Exchange Rate So Volatile?

We've seen times, especially recently, when the dollar-yen exchange rate has moved dramatically. On most of these occasions, the dollar has depreciated spectacularly, but on some occasions it has appreciated strongly.

The main reason why the exchange rate fluctuates so remarkably is that fluctuations in supply and demand are not always independent of each other. Sometimes a change in supply will trigger a change in demand that reinforces the effect of the change in supply. Let's see how these effects work by looking at two episodes.

1981 to 1982   From 1981 to 1982, the Canadian dollar appreciated against the yen, rising from 194 to 201 yen per dollar. Figure 36.7(a) explains why this happened. In 1981, the demand and supply curves were those labelled D_{81} and S_{81}. The foreign

exchange value of the dollar was 194 yen—where the supply and demand curves intersect. The period 1981 to 1982 was one of severe recession. This recession was brought about in part by the Bank of Canada pursuing a restrictive monetary policy. Interest rates rose sharply and the higher Canadian interest rates increased the demand for dollars. As a result, the demand curve shifted from D_{81} to D_{82}. The yen price of the dollar increased to 201 yen.

1985 to 1986   There was a spectacular depreciation of the dollar in terms of yen from 173 yen per dollar in 1985 to 120 yen per dollar in 1986. This fall came about in the following way. In 1985, the demand and supply curves were those labelled D_{85} and S_{85} in Fig. 36.7(b). The yen price of the dollar—the price at which these two curves intersect—was 173 yen per dollar. From 1982 to 1985, the Canadian economy experienced rapid growth in real GDP as it recovered from recession. But the government had a

---

FIGURE 36.7

Why the Exchange Rate Is So Volatile

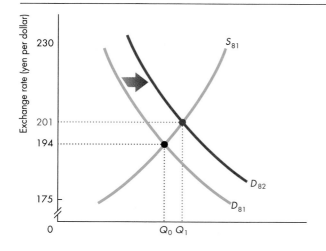

(a) 1981 to 1982

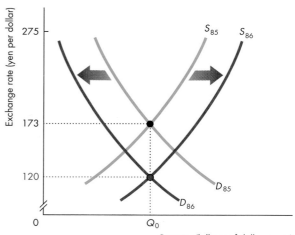

Quantity (billions of dollar assets)

(b) 1985 to 1986

The exchange rate is volatile because shifts in the demand and supply curves for dollar assets are not independent of each other. Between 1981 and 1982 (part a), the dollar appreciated from 194 to 201 yen per dollar. This appreciation arose because the supply curve of dollar assets shifted leftward and higher interest rates induced an increase in demand for dollar assets, shifting the demand curve rightward. The result was a large increase in the foreign exchange value of the dollar.

Between 1985 and 1986 (in part b), the Bank of Canada permitted the quantity of dollar assets to increase to sustain the long economic recovery. The supply curve shifted rightward. At the same time, interest rates decreased and expectations of further declines in the value of the dollar shifted the demand curve leftward. The result was a steep fall in the exchange rate, from 173 yen to 120 yen per dollar between 1985 and 1986.

large budget deficit which increased the supply of dollar assets. The supply curve shifted rightward from S_{85} to S_{86}. At the same time, the Bank of Canada was permitting the money supply to grow rapidly enough to keep the recovery going and interest rates in Canada began to fall. Also, expectations of future declines in the value of the dollar came to be widely held. As a consequence, the demand for dollar assets decreased from D_{85} to D_{86}. The result of this combined increase in supply and decrease in demand was a dramatic fall in the value of the dollar to 120 yen in 1986.

The Dollar and the Constitution Crisis of 1992

Between August and November 1992, the Canadian dollar depreciated by almost 10 percent against the U.S. dollar. You can see the path of the Canadian dollar against the U.S. dollar in Fig. 36.8. You can also see in Fig. 36.8 that the Bank of Canada used its foreign exchange reserves to buy dollars in an

attempt to stem the fall in the value of the dollar. Why did these events occur?

The most likely answer lies in the constitutional uncertainty arising from the referendum on the relationship between Quebec and the rest of Canada. Holders of Canadian dollar assets lowered their expectations of the future value of Canadian dollar assets because they feared that a break-up of Canada would bring lower real returns on Canadian investments. So many people dumped their Canadian dollar assets.

The effects of these actions are illustrated in Fig. 36.9, which shows the market for Canadian dollar assets against the value of the Canadian dollar in terms of U.S. dollars. In August 1992, the demand for Canadian dollar assets was D_0, the supply was S_0, and the exchange rate (at its highest value) was 84.6 U.S. cents per Canadian dollar. By November,

FIGURE 36.8

Reserves and the Dollar: 1992

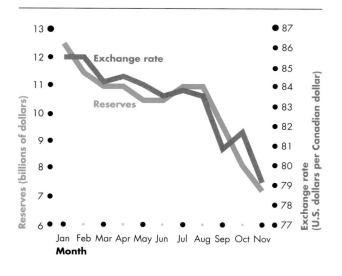

During the period August to November, 1992, the Canadian dollar depreciated by almost 10 percent against the U.S. dollar. At the same time, the Bank of Canada intervened heavily in the foreign exchange market in an attempt to moderate the fall.

Source: Bank of Canada Review, Winter, 1992–1993, CANSIM series B3400 and B3800.

FIGURE 36.9

The Foreign Exchange Market: 1992

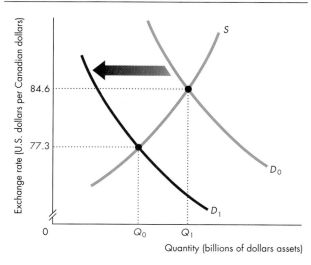

In August, 1992, the demand for Canadian dollar assets was D_0 and the supply was S. The exchange rate was 84.6 at its peak. A decrease in demand probably resulting from the uncertainty arising from the constitutional crisis of the fall of 1992 brought a decrease in the demand for Canadian dollar assets and the demand curve shifted leftward to D_1. The Bank of Canada operated a managed floating exchange rate regime and decreased the quantity of dollars supplied along its supply curve S. The dollar depreciated to 77.3 cents at its lowest point in November.

1992, the demand for Canadian dollars had decreased to D_1. The Bank of Canada was operating a managed floating regime and decreased the quantity of dollars supplied along the supply curve S_0. The exchange rate fell (the Canadian dollar depreciated) to 77.3 U.S. cents per Canadian dollar. If the Bank of Canada had not intervened in the foreign exchange market, the quantity of dollars supplied would have remained constant and the exchange rate would have fallen much further.

Another episode in which the Bank of Canada found it necessary to defend the dollar is studied in Reading Between the Lines on pp. 1014–1015.

R E V I E W

There are three possible foreign exchange rate regimes: fixed, flexible, and managed. Under a fixed exchange rate regime, the Bank of Canada pegs the exchange rate but the official settlements account of the balance of payments has to carry the burden of holding the exchange rate constant. A decrease in the demand for Canadian dollar assets and an increase in the demand for foreign currency assets has to be met by decreasing the country's foreign exchange reserves. Under a flexible exchange rate regime, the Bank of Canada does not intervene in the foreign exchange market. The official settlements balance is zero and the country's foreign exchange reserves do not change. Under a managed exchanged rate regime, the Bank of Canada smooths exchange rate fluctuations to a degree, but less strongly than under fixed exchange rates. Under a flexible or managed exchange rate regime, the exchange rate is determined by the demand for and supply of dollar assets. Fluctuations in supply often induce reinforcing fluctuations in demand, bringing severe fluctuations in the exchange rate. ◆

You've now seen how the foreign exchange value of the dollar is determined and studied the forces that make the exchange rate fluctuate. Let's now look at some linkages between the exchange rate, the prices of goods and services, and the interest rates on dollar assets and foreign-currency assets.

Exchange Rate, Prices, and Interest Rates

Arbitrage is the activity of buying low and selling high in order to make a profit on the margin between the two prices. Arbitrage affects the links among exchange rates, prices, and interest rates. An increase in demand forces the buying price up. An increase in supply forces the selling price down. The prices move until they are equal and there is no arbitrage profit available. An implication of arbitrage is the law of one price. The **law of one price** states that any given commodity will be available at a single price.

The law of one price has no respect for national borders or currencies. If the same commodity is being bought and sold on either side of the Detroit River, it doesn't matter that one of these transactions is being undertaken in Canada and the other in the United States and that one is using Canadian dollars and the other U.S. dollars. The forces of arbitrage bring about one price. Let's see how.

Arbitrage

Consider the price of a floppy disk that can be bought in either the United States or Canada. We will ignore taxes, tariffs, and transportation costs in order to keep the calculations simple, for these factors do not affect the fundamental issue.

Suppose that we can buy floppy disks in the United States for US$10 a box. Suppose that this same box of disks is available in Canada for C$15 a box. (The symbol US$ stands for the United States dollar and C$ for the Canadian dollar.) Where would it pay to buy disks—in Canada or in the United States? The answer depends on the relative costs of Canadian and U.S. money. If a U.S. dollar costs C$1.50, then it is clear that the price of the disks is the same in both countries. Americans can buy a box of disks in the United States for US$10 or they can use US$10 to buy C$15 and then buy the disks in Canada. The cost will be the same either way. The same is true for Canadians. Canadians can use C$15 to buy a box of disks in Canada or to buy US$10 and then buy the disks in the United States. Again, there is no difference in the price of the disks.

Suppose, however, that a U.S. dollar is less valuable than in the above example. In particular, suppose that a U.S. dollar costs C$1.40. In this case, it will pay to buy the disks in the United States. Canadians can buy US$10 for C$14 and therefore can buy the disks in the United States for C$14 a box compared with C$15 in Canada. The same comparison holds for Americans. Americans can use US$10 to buy C$14 but that would not be enough to buy the disks in Canada since the disks cost C$15 there. It therefore pays Americans also to buy the disks in the United States.

If the situation described above did prevail, there would be an advantage in switching the purchases of disks from Canada to the United States. Canadians would cross the border to buy their disks in the United States and keep on doing so until the Canadian price had fallen to C$14. Once that had happened, Canadians would be indifferent between buying their disks in Canada and in the United States. Arbitrage would have eliminated the difference in prices in the two countries.

Perhaps you are thinking that this is a pretty crazy example since Canadians don't rush down to the United States every time they want to buy a box of floppy disks. But the fact that there is a profit to be made means that it would pay someone to organize the importing of disks into Canada from the United States thereby increasing the number of disks available there and lowering their price. The incentive to undertake such a move would be present as long as disks were selling for a higher price in Canada than in the United States.

Purchasing Power Parity

Purchasing power parity occurs when money has equal value across countries. (The word *parity* simply means equality. The phrase *purchasing power* refers to the *value of money*. Thus *purchasing power parity* directly translates to *equal value of money*.) Purchasing power parity is an implication of arbitrage and of the law of one price. In the floppy disk example, when US$1 is worth C$1.50, US$10 will buy the same box of floppy disks that C$15 will buy. The value of money, when converted to common prices, is the same in both countries. Purchasing power parity thus prevails in that situation.

Purchasing power parity theory predicts that purchasing power parity applies to all goods and to price indexes of traded goods, not just to a single

"On the foreign-exchange markets today, the dollar fell against all major currencies and the doughnut."

good such as a floppy disk. That is, if any goods are cheaper in one country than in another, it will pay to convert money into the currency of that country, buy the goods in that country, and sell them in another. By such an arbitrage process, all prices are brought to equality.

But for many goods, the costs of moving between national markets is high and such goods are not traded internationally. A good that is not traded internationally is called a **nontraded good**. There are many examples of nontraded goods. Almost all the public services provided by the government are nontraded. And so are doughnuts—so when the dollar falls against other currencies, it falls against the doughnuts as well!

Arbitrage occurs not only in markets for goods and services but also in markets for assets. As a result, it brings about another equality or parity—interest rate parity.

Interest Rate Parity

Interest rate parity occurs when interest rates are equal across countries once the differences in risk are taken into account. Interest rate parity is a condition brought about by arbitrage in the markets for assets—markets in which borrowers and lenders operate.

At the beginning of this chapter, we noted some facts about interest rates in different countries. For example, in Canada, interest rates are lower than those in England. Suppose that it is possible to borrow in Toronto at an interest rate of 6 percent a year and lend in London at an interest rate of 12 percent a year. Isn't it possible, in this situation, to make a huge profit on such a transaction? In fact, it is not. Interest rates in Toronto and London are actually equal —interest rate parity prevails.

The key to understanding why the interest rates are equal is to realize that when you borrow in Toronto, you borrow *dollars*, and when you lend money in England—by placing it on deposit in a bank—you lend *pounds*. You are obliged to repay *dollars* but you will be repaid in *pounds*. It's a bit like borrowing apples and lending oranges. But if you borrow apples and lend oranges, you've got to convert the apples to oranges. When the loans become due, you've got to convert oranges back to apples. The prices at which you do these transactions affect the interest rates that you pay and receive. How many dollars you get for your pounds depends on the exchange rate when the loan is repaid. If the pound has fallen in value, you'll get fewer dollars than you paid in the first place.

The difference between the interest rates in Toronto and London reflects the change in the exchange rate between the dollar and the pound that, on the average, people are expecting. In this example, the average expectation is that the pound will fall against the dollar by 6 percent a year. So when you sell pounds to repay your dollar loan, you can expect to get 6 percent fewer dollars than you needed to buy the pounds. This 6 percent foreign exchange loss must be subtracted from the 12 percent interest income you earn in London. Thus your return from lending in London, when you convert your money back into dollars, is the same 6 percent that you must pay for funds in Toronto. Your profit is zero. Actually, you would incur a loss because you would pay commissions on your foreign exchange transactions.

In the situation that we've just described, interest rate parity prevails. The interest rate in Toronto— when the expected change in the value of the dollar is taken into account—is almost identical to that in London. If interest rate parity did *not* prevail, it would be possible to profit, without risk, by borrowing at low rates and lending at high rates. Such *arbitrage* actions would increase the demand for loans in countries with low interest rates, and their interest rates

would rise. And these actions would increase the supply of loans in countries with high interest rates, and their interest rates would fall. Such movements would restore interest rate parity very quickly.

A World Market

Arbitrage in asset markets operates on a worldwide scale and keeps the world capital markets linked in a single global market. This market is an enormous one. It involves borrowing and lending through banks, in bond markets, and in stock markets. The scale of this international business was estimated by Salomon Brothers, a U.S. investment bank, at more than one trillion U.S. dollars in 1986. It is because of international arbitrage in asset markets that the fortunes of the stock markets around the world are so closely linked. A stock market crash in New York makes its new low-priced stocks look attractive compared with high-priced stocks in Tokyo, Hong Kong, Zurich, Frankfurt, London, and Toronto. As a consequence, investors make plans to sell high in these other markets and buy low in New York. But before many such transactions can be put through, the prices in the other markets fall to match the fall in New York. Conversely, if the Tokyo market experiences rapid price increases and markets in the rest of the world stay constant, investors seek to sell high in Tokyo and buy low in the rest of the world. Again, these trading plans will induce movements in the prices in the other markets to bring them into line with the Tokyo market. The action of selling high in Tokyo will lower the prices there and the action of buying low in Frankfurt, London, Toronto, and New York will raise the prices there.

What you have just learned about arbitrage and its effects on prices and interest rates has implications for a country's monetary and financial independence. Let's explore this issue.

Monetary Independence

How does the Bank of Canada insulate the Canadian economy from the rest of the world? There is no perfect financial insulator. But there is a very effective one—a flexible exchange rate.

Independence with a Flexible Exchange Rate   By adopting a flexible exchange rate, Canadian monetary policy is geared towards Canadian objectives

Defending
the Dollar

THE MONTREAL GAZETTE, MAY 6, 1993

Bank of Canada dips deeply into dollar-defence fund

By Eric Beauchesne

OTTAWA—The Bank of Canada spent almost $1.4 billion U.S. rescuing the Canadian dollar last month in the wake of Finance Minister Don Mazankowski's stand-pat budget, according to government figures made public yesterday.

The dollar plunged more than a full cent from the mid-79-cent (U.S.) range to almost 78 cents following the April 26 budget and the subsequent downgrading of Ottawa's credit rating by a domestic bond-rating agency.

To offset the dumping of dollars by disappointed investors expecting a tough deficit-reduction budget, the bank dipped deeply into Ottawa's dollar-defence fund to buy up unwanted dollars....

The action, along with a temporary jump in interest rates, did stabilize the dollar, though at about one cent below its pre-budget level...

Holders of Canadian dollars were expecting the federal budget of April 1993 to cut the deficit.

The budget had no deficit reduction component, so investors started to sell the Canadian dollar.

To prevent the Canadian dollar from falling below 78 U.S. cents, the Bank of Canada spent almost $1.4 billion U.S. buying Canadian dollars.

The action, along with a temporary jump in interest rates, did stabilize the dollar at about one cent below its pre-budget level.

Background and Analysis

The Bank of Canada operates a *managed floating exchange rate regime.*

Before the federal budget of April 1993, the demand for Canadian dollars in the foreign exchange market was D_0. The supply curve for Canadian dollars was S. The Canadian dollar exchange rate was 79 U.S. cents per Canadian dollar.

After the budget, holders of Canadian dollars were disappointed by the lack of a deficit-reduction package in the budget.

Holders of Canadian dollars expected the federal government to finance its ongoing budget deficit with a sale of bonds.

They expected the bond sale would lead to higher interest rates and lower Canadian asset prices, so the demand for Canadian dollars decreased.

The Bank of Canada increased interest rates to prevent the demand for dollars from falling too far. But demand still decreased and the demand curve shifted leftward to D_1.

If the Bank of Canada had taken no further action and held the quantity of Canadian dollars at Q_0, the foreign exchange value of the Canadian dollar would have fallen. In the figure the fall is to 77 U.S. cents (an assumption).

To limit the fall in the dollar, the Bank of Canada intervened in the foreign exchange market and used its reserves of U.S. dollars to *buy* Canadian dollars.

This action decreased the quantity of Canadian dollars supplied—a movement along the supply curve S—and held the exchange rate at 78 U.S. cents.

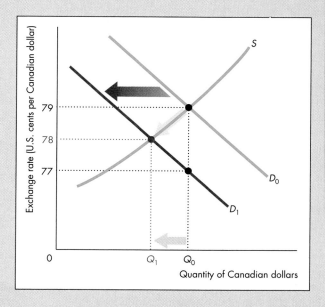

and does not respond to changes in U.S., European, or Japanese monetary policy. Suppose, for example, that the Federal Reserve in the United States increases the U.S. money supply growth rate by 5 percentage points (for example, from 3 percent a year to 8 percent a year). Eventually, inflation in the United States increases by 5 percentage points a year and U.S. interest rates also increase by 5 percentage points (see Chapter 31, p. 878, for an explanation of the influence of money supply growth on inflation and interest rates).

At the same time, the Bank of Canada makes no changes in its monetary policy—the money supply growth rate in Canada is held steady. With no increase in the money supply growth rate in Canada, there is no increase in the Canadian inflation rate. Prices in Canada continue to inflate at the same pace as before and the Canadian interest rate remains constant.

But with inflation in the United States higher than in Canada, there are some changes in the demand for U.S. and Canadian dollars. People know that the value of the U.S. dollar in terms of the goods and service it buys will fall. As a result, the demand for U.S. dollars decreases and the demand for Canadian dollars increases. The increase in the demand for Canadian dollars results in an appreciation of the Canadian dollar.

These forces will ensure that the Canadian dollar appreciates by the difference between the two inflation rates. Also, with an inflation rate differential that is plain for everyone to see, people expect the appreciation of the Canadian dollar to continue. As a consequence, the gap between interest rates in the United States and in Canada equals the expected rate of appreciation of the Canadian dollar.

We've seen how a flexible exchange rate brings monetary independence. Let's now see how a fixed exchange rate ties a country's hands and prevents it from pursuing an independent monetary policy.

Interdependence with a Fixed Exchange Rate

Suppose that Canada fixes its exchange rate against the U.S. dollar. The forces of arbitrage bring the prices of traded goods into line with each other on both sides of the U.S.-Canada border. If there is an increase in prices in the United States, there is an increase of the same percentage in Canada, other things remaining the same. Similarly, arbitrage in asset markets brings interest rates into equality in the two countries.

Now suppose that the U.S. money supply growth rate increases from 3 percent a year to 8 percent a year. This action eventually brings an increase in inflation in the United States of 5 percent a year. The higher inflation rate results in higher interest rates in the United States—by 5 percentage points. With higher inflation and higher interest rates in the United States, the forces of international commodity price and interest rate arbitrage bring higher inflation and higher interest rates to Canada. How does this occur? The higher U.S. prices lead to an increase in the demand for (cheaper) Canadian-produced goods and services which, in turn, leads to an increase in the demand for Canadian dollars. To keep the exchange rate fixed, the Bank of Canada intervenes in the foreign exchange market to increase the quantity of Canadian dollars supplied. It does so by buying foreign currency. As a result, Canada's monetary base increases, and the Canadian money supply increases. This increase in the Canadian money supply parallels the increase in the U.S. money supply and leads to higher inflation and interest rates in Canada.

In effect, Canada's inflation and interest rates are determined not by the Bank of Canada, but by the United States. To fix the value of the Canadian dollar against the U.S. dollar, the Bank of Canada must supply the quantity of Canadian dollars demanded at the price level and interest rate determined by U.S. monetary policy.

◆ ◆ ◆ You've now discovered what determines a country's current account balance and the foreign exchange value of its currency. You've also learned how international arbitrage links prices and interest rates in different countries. And you've seen how flexible exchange rates enable a country to pursue its own monetary policy goals.

In the final two chapters, we're going to look at some further global economic issues. First, in Chapter 37, we'll examine the problems faced by developing countries as they seek to grow. In Chapter 38, we'll look at the countries of Eastern Europe and China as they make the transition from planned economies to market economies.

SUMMARY

Financing International Trade

International trade, borrowing, and lending are financed using foreign currency. A country's international transactions are recorded in its balance of payments accounts. The current account records receipts and expenditures connected with the sale and purchase of goods and services, as well as net investment income, and net transfers to the rest of the world; the capital account records international borrowing and lending transactions; the official settlements account shows the increase or decrease in the country's foreign currency reserves.

Historically, Canada has been a net borrower from the rest of the world and is a debtor nation. Canada has used its international borrowing to develop its economic resources and increase its level of income.

The sum of net exports, the government sector deficit, and the private sector deficit is zero. Fluctuations in net exports produce the main fluctuations in the current account balance and they arise mainly from fluctuations in the government sector deficit. As the government sector deficit has persisted in the 1980s and 1990s, so has the current account deficit also grown. (pp. 995–1001)

Foreign Exchange and the Dollar

Foreign currency is obtained in exchange for domestic currency in the foreign exchange market. There are three types of foreign exchange rate regimes: fixed, flexible, and managed. When the exchange rate is fixed, the government declares a value for the currency in terms of some other currency and the Bank of Canada takes actions to ensure that the price is maintained.

A flexible exchange rate is one in which the central bank takes no actions to influence the value of its currency in the foreign exchange market. The country's holdings of foreign currencies remain constant and fluctuations in demand and supply lead to fluctuations in the exchange rate.

A managed exchange rate is one in which the central bank takes actions to smooth fluctuations that would otherwise arise but does so less strongly than under a fixed exchange rate regime. (pp. 1001–1003)

Exchange Rate Determination

The Canadian dollar exchange rate is determined by the demand for and supply of Canadian dollar assets in the world economy.

Other things remaining the same, the lower the exchange rate, the greater is the quantity of Canadian dollar assets demanded. The demand for dollars depends on the value of dollar payments, the interest rate differential, and the expected future value of the dollar.

The supply of Canadian dollar assets depends on the government's budget and the Bank of Canada's monetary policy and on the exchange rate regime. Under a fixed exchange rate, the Bank of Canada must stand ready to supply dollars and take in foreign currency or to remove dollars from circulation in exchange for foreign currency. The country's reserves of foreign currency fluctuate to maintain the fixed exchange rate. The supply curve is horizontal. Under a flexible exchange rate, the Bank of Canada does not intervene in the foreign exchange market and the supply curve of dollar assets is vertical. Under a managed exchange rate, the Bank of Canada intervenes in the foreign exchange market to limit exchange rate movements and the supply curve is upward sloping.

Fluctuations in the exchange rate occur because of fluctuations in demand and supply, and sometimes these fluctuations are large. Large fluctuations arise from interlinked changes in demand and supply. A shift in the supply curve often produces an induced change in the demand curve that reinforces the effect on the exchange rate. (pp. 1004–1011)

Exchange Rate, Prices, and Interest Rates

Arbitrage keeps the prices of goods and services that are traded internationally close to equality across all countries. Arbitrage also keeps interest rates in line with each other.

Interest rates around the world look unequal, but the appearance arises from the fact that loans are contracted in different currencies in different countries. To compare interest rates across countries, we have to take into account changes in the values of currencies. Countries whose currencies are appreciating have low interest rates; countries whose currencies are depreciating have high interest rates. If the rate of currency depreciation is taken into account, interest rates are nearly equal.

With a flexible exchange rate, a country can insulate itself from inflation and interest rate shocks coming from the rest of the world. If, in the face of a higher inflation rate in the rest of the world, domestic monetary policy is held steady, the domestic inflation rate stays constant. The currency appreciates and interest rates in the domestic economy stay below those in the rest of the world.

To achieve lower inflation and lower interest rates than other countries, it is necessary for the Bank of Canada to maintain a lower average growth rate of the Canadian money supply than the money supply growth rates that prevail in other countries. (pp. 1011–1016)

KEY ELEMENTS

Key Terms

Balance of payments accounts, 995
Canadian dollar index against the G-10 currencies, 1003
Capital account, 995
Creditor nation, 997
Currency depreciation, 1003
Current account, 995
Debtor nation, 997
Fixed exchange rate, 1001
Flexible exchange rate, 1002
Foreign exchange market, 1001
Foreign exchange rate, 1001
Foreign exchange reserves, 995
Government sector surplus or deficit, 998
Interest rate differential, 1006
Interest rate parity, 1012
International Monetary Fund, 1003
Law of one price, 1011
Managed exchange rate, 1002
Net borrower, 996

Net lender, 996
Nontraded good, 1014
Official settlements account, 995
Private sector surplus or deficit, 998
Purchasing power parity, 1014
Quantity of Canadian dollar assets, 1004
Quantity of dollars, 1004
Twin deficits, 998

Key Figures and Tables

Figure 36.1   The Balance of Payments: 1975-1992, 997
Figure 36.2   The Twin Deficits, 998
Figure 36.4   Exchange Rates, 1003
Figure 36.6   Three Exchange Rate Regimes, 1008
Table 36.2   The Current Account Balance, Net Foreign Borrowing, and the Financing of Investment, 999
Table 36.4   The Demand for Dollar Assets, 1006
Table 36.5   The Supply of Dollar Assets, 1007

REVIEW QUESTIONS

1   What are the transactions recorded in a country's current account, capital account, and official settlements account?

2   What is the relationship among the balance on the current account, the capital account, and the official settlements account?

3   Distinguish between a country that is a net borrower and one that is a creditor. Are net borrowers always creditors? Are creditors always net borrowers?

4   What is the connection between a country's current account balance and the government's budget deficit and the private sector deficit?

5 Why do fluctuations in the government budget balance lead to fluctuations in the current account balance?

6 Distinguish among the three exchange rate regimes: fixed, flexible, and managed.

7 Review the main influences on the quantity of dollars that people demand.

8 Review the influences on the supply of dollars.

9 How does the supply curve of dollars differ under the three exchange rate regimes?

10 Why does the dollar fluctuate so much?

11 What is arbitrage?

12 How does arbitrage lead to purchasing power parity?

13 What is interest rate parity?

14 How does interest rate parity come about?

15 How do flexible exchange rates insulate an economy from changes in inflation in the rest of the world?

P R O B L E M S

1 The citizens of Silecon, whose currency is grain, conduct the following transactions in 1990:

	Billions of grains
Imports of goods and services	350
Exports of goods and services	500
Borrowing from the rest of the world	60
Lending to the rest of the world	200
Increase in official foreign exchange reserves	10

a   Set out the three balance of payments accounts for Silecon.
b   Does Silecon have a flexible exchange rate?

2 You are told the following about Ecflex, a country with a flexible exchange rate whose currency is the band:

	Billions of bands
GDP	100
Consumption expenditure	60
Government purchases of goods and services	24
Investment	22
Exports of goods and services	20
Government budget deficit	4

Calculate the following for Ecflex:

a   Imports of goods and services
b   Current account balance
c   Capital account balance
d   Taxes (net of transfer payments)
e   Private sector deficit/surplus

3 A country's currency appreciates and its official holdings of foreign currency increase. What can you say about the following?

a   The exchange rate regime being pursued by the country
b   The country's current account
c   The country's official settlements account

4 The average annual interest rate in Japan is 4 percent; in Canada it is 6 percent; in Germany it is 9 percent; and in England it is 13 percent. What is the expected change over the coming year in each of the following?

a   The Canadian dollar against the Japanese yen
b   The British pound against the German mark
c   The Canadian dollar against the British pound
d   The Japanese yen against the German mark
e   The Canadian dollar against the German mark

PART 14

GROWTH, DEVELOPMENT, AND REFORM

Talking with Jeffrey Sachs

Jeffrey Sachs was born in Detroit in 1954 and has spent his entire university career at Harvard, first as an undergraduate and eventually as a professor. Today, however, Professor Sachs spends most of his time on airplanes or in Eastern Europe. He first began advising foreign governments on economic policy by helping Bolivia with hyperinflation in 1985. His name burst before the public with his work on Poland, but now he is increasingly associated with the economic reforms of Boris Yeltsin and the Russian Federation.

How did you get drawn into the Eastern European reform area?

I started my work in Eastern Europe in Poland at the time that Solidarity was legalized in the spring of 1989. I had been invited by the Communist government to give advice to them about their financial troubles. Events obviously went very fast because soon after legalization there was an election, which Solidarity won overwhelmingly. From that point on, I became an economic advisor to believers in Solidarity and helped them draft an outline of a radical economic reform program. Soon after that, a Solidarity government actually came to power, and I began to work on the implementation of economic reforms, which were widely viewed as the first and most comprehensive reforms in Eastern Europe. From there, I got to know reformers in all of the countries in the region and began to work closely with some Russian economists who are now senior members of the Yeltsin government. As democratization proceeded in Russia, these people invited me to help them develop their reform strategy.

Your name has been associated with the "big bang" or "cold turkey" approach to reform. Can you describe that approach and explain why you favour it over a more gradual and tentative one?

The basic idea is to start with the goal of the reform, such as to put in place a working capitalist system. Of course, it'll be a capitalist system that reflects the particular culture, history, tradition, and resources of the country. It is an attempt not to find a so-called "third way in" between the old system and the new system but to go fully towards the working capitalist model. In the case of Eastern Europe, the goal is even more explicit: to implement reforms that will make these countries harmonize with the economies of Western Europe so that in a short period of time—within a decade is their hope—they can actually become members of the European Community.

The essence of "big bang" is that it's important to move comprehensively and quickly towards the goal of a working capitalist economy because various aspects of the market economy are all interrelated. If one does just a piece of the reform but leaves much of the old system intact, the conflicts of the old and the new are likely to make things considerably worse rather than better.

What are the major pieces of the radical reform strategy that you're recommending to governments in Eastern Europe?

The reform strategy comes down to four components. The first is macroeconomic stabilization, because usually these countries start out in a deep macroeconomic crisis characterized by high inflation and intense shortages. Second is economic liberalization, which means ending central planning, trade quotas, and other barriers that cut the country off from the world market. The third part of the reform is privatization, which is the transfer of state property back to private owners. Those private owners could be individuals or they could be, as in the West, financial intermediaries like mutual funds or banks or pension funds that are in turn owned by individuals. When I say privatization, I use the word "transfer" rather than "sell" because selling state property is only one way to privatize. There are other ways, such as giving away the state property to workers, managers, or the public. The Eastern European countries are privatizing through a mix of sales and direct giveaways. The fourth part of the radical reform is the introduction of social safety nets, which provide protection for the most vulnerable parts of the society that are perhaps the hardest hit by the reform or are already suffering even irrespective of the reform. That means putting in place unemployment benefits, an adequate retirement system and heath care system, job training, public works spending, and so forth. Those are the four main pillars.

It's called "big bang" because you must move quickly on this. Probably the most dramatic part of all is the stabilization and liberalization phase, where subsidies are cut very quickly and price controls are eliminated. The result is usually a very dramatic one-time jump in prices. That starts off the reform.

How long does the reform process generally take?

Certain things can be done quickly, and others take more time. Stabilization and liberalization can be accomplished fast, or most parts of them. Freeing price controls, eliminating trade barriers, and cutting subsidies, for example, can all be done on the first day of the program, which is why it's sometimes called "shock therapy" or "cold turkey." Privatization, though, takes much longer. Some aspects of the fourth component of the reform strategy, the social safety net, can be done quickly. For example, pensions of retirees can be protected through budgetary allocation. An unemployment insurance system was started up very quickly in Poland, and it has worked adequately. Other parts of the social safety net, for instance, real reform of the health care system, are very complex and take a considerable amount of time to effect.

Even if the reforms go very quickly, the process of change that those reforms set loose will take years or even decades to work themselves out. What do I mean? The socialist system wasn't just messed up in terms of the organization of production and the ways that prices were set. It was also systematically misusing resources by putting tremendous overemphasis on heavy industrial production while neglecting other important parts of the economy, such as services and wholesale and retail trade. When you free up market forces, the market doesn't demand all the heavy industrial production that was built up in the past. This leads to unemployment, a drop in

demand, and people voluntarily quitting those industries to move into areas that were starved for people, resources, and capital in the past. You get a great boom in retail trade, for example, with tens of thousands of new shops opening up. The reforms set loose that process, but the corresponding shift of resources could take five, ten, fifteen, even twenty years to adjust.

Even within a big bang approach, presumably you can't literally do everything at once. What are the highest priorities?

The highest priority is to avoid real financial chaos. Poland, Yugoslavia, and Russia all fell into hyperinflation at the end of the Communist system. That meant that the new democratic governments' highest priority was to end the underlying conditions that were feeding the hyperinflation. If you can accomplish the financial stability, then I think the next highest priority is to have the rudiments of the private property system in place, such as a commercial code and laws for corporate enterprises, contracts, and protection of private property. Then the next priority is rapid privatization because until the enterprises are with real owners facing

proper incentives, one has to be sceptical that they'll be managed in an efficient and sensible way.

What are the earliest indicators of whether the reforms are beginning to take hold?

Of course, different things happen at different times. The first thing one looks for if an economy is trying to emerge from hyperinflation is stability of prices. After freeing prices and experiencing a significant one-time jump in the price level, this should not turn into ongoing high inflation but rather be followed by price stability.

Can the countries of Eastern Europe and the former Soviet Union evolve into democratic nations with market economies without economic aid from the West?

The whole history of radical economic change underscores the importance of financial assistance during the first critical years of reform. It takes many years for the real fruits of the reform to be widely evident in the society. Certain costs of the reform, however, such as closing down old inefficient enterprises, can become evident very quickly. It's during that crucial period between the introduction of the reforms and the time when they really are bearing fruit that lie the greatest dangers and also the greatest need for international assistance to help provide a cushion to living standards and a bolstering of the reform effort until the reforms really take hold.

The foreign assistance does not actually pay for the reconstruction of the country. It's never big enough. The Marshall Plan was not enough to really rebuild Europe, but what the Marshall Plan did was

to give the new democratic postwar governments time to put in place market-based policies so that they could take hold.

Whether it's postwar Germany or Japan, Mexico's turnaround in the 1980s, or Poland at the beginning of the 1990s, countries on the path to economic and political reform need help at the beginning. For Russia and the other states of the former Soviet Union, it will be the same. They will definitely need some years of Western and foreign help to keep their reforms on track and to make the living conditions tolerable.

What form will that aid take? Free-trading opportunities? Private investment? Government loans?

The form of aid has to be linked to the timetable of the reform process. At the beginning, say in the first year, the aid is inevitably of two sorts. First, humanitarian emergency assistance to make sure that food is getting to the table and that medical supplies are available. Second, stabilization assistance, or various kinds of financial support to help make the currency strong and to increase the flow of basic imports, which are needed just to keep the economy functioning. Russia has suffered a sharp decline in its own capacity to buy imports because its export earnings have fallen sharply in the past few years. They need help just to keep basic imports going, and by doing that you help strengthen the currency.

In later years, you want to get away from that kind of emergency stabilization support and put much more attention on project financing to get new enterprises going. One hopes these will become the major engine of economic growth in the future. Private investment, of course, is to be desired, but it will take many years to attract. Private investors first want to know the market, and then they wait to see signs that the reforms are working and that political stability is being achieved. The official support from government has to come first. Then the private money will flow in.

What are the economic principles that you find most valuable in dealing with the acute problems of Russia today?

The starting point for me is to recognize that all of the successful economies in the world have a shared core set of institutions. There are, of course, major differences across countries, but all of the advanced industrial economies share certain features—such as a currency that trades, that can be used to buy goods without facing fixed prices or shortages, and that is convertible internationally; an open trading system in which, with some exceptions, goods can be bought and sold from abroad on normal market terms; an economy based on private ownership not state ownership; a legal infrastructure that supports private ownership so that property rights are clearly defined and defensible. Things like that. It's that core of institutions that is so important to put into place.

What are the undergraduates studying economics in Russia today actually studying? Are they learning about demand and supply, competition and monopoly, aggregate demand and aggregate supply, and the role of money in creating inflation?

Of course, things are changing very fast. It was only a few years ago that ideas like market economy and private property were unfamiliar. What one sees now is incredible hunger to study and analyse the basic properties of market economies. There is no doubt, I think, in the minds of virtually everybody that the old system was a terrible failure and that what Russia should have is a normal economy like that which is in place in Western Europe, the United States, and Japan. The curricula are being revised with incredible speed to teach the standard economics that we also learn. Of course, students' attention is focussed not just on the well-functioning system but also on the problems of transitions.

What do you see as the major obstacles to economic development in Eastern Europe?

The major obstacle is that this is a time of great upheaval. The collapse of communism occurred, in part, because the old system had failed so thoroughly and people were in economic misery. So all this transformation is starting in the midst of a real economic crisis—a crisis that breeds confusion, fear, and anxiety. That confusion, fear, and anxiety can lead a whole country astray from its basic path of building up democratic market institutions. There are politicians waiting with messages attacking democracy, trying to take advantage of the anxieties of the people to win power. This could derail the reforms. If the new governments cannot deliver economic improvement, then I think risks to democracy will certainly exist. And once there is doubt about the basic direction of these changes, then things become unpredictable, but very hazardous results are possible. I don't think that's the likely outcome, but it's one of the reasons why I underscored the need for support, understanding, and a financial cushion from the West during this very critical and complicated stage of implementing the reforms.

Assuming that Russia does develop rapidly and solves its economic problems in the decade ahead, what are the major implications for the United States?

The overwhelming implication is that the chance for us to live in a peaceful world is enormously improved. We should not underestimate the difference that will mean to our own quality of life. The success of Russian democracy will make a huge difference to our security and, in financial terms, to our ability to divert our own resources from military spending to civilian use. Now, Russia's success with democracy depends a great deal on its success in overcoming this economic crisis. We know all too well that economic instability is one of the great dangers to a young democracy.

There are many, many other implications. The whole world will change, and I think vastly for the better. There will be a huge trading and investment opportunity when a country that covers one-sixth of the world's land mass, spanning over eleven time zones, becomes closely integrated with the rest of the world economy after having been cut off for seventy-five years. There will be important changes in trade patterns, investment opportunities, and global cooperation.

CHAPTER **37**

GROWTH
AND
DEVELOPMENT

After studying this chapter, you will be able to

- ◆ Describe the international distribution of income
- ◆ Explain the importance of economic growth
- ◆ Explain how the accumulation of capital and technological progress bring higher per capita incomes
- ◆ Describe the obstacles to economic growth in poor countries
- ◆ Explain the possible effects of population control, foreign aid, free trade, and demand stimulation on economic growth and development
- ◆ Evaluate policies designed to stimulate economic growth and development

HE WORLD'S POPULATION HAS PASSED 5 BILLION. THESE billions of people are unevenly distributed over the earth's surface. More than 4 billion live in the poor countries of Africa, Asia, and Central America, and only 1 billion in the rich industrial countries. It is estimated that by the year 2020, the world population will be 8.4 billion with close to 7 billion living in the poor countries and only 1.4 billion in the industrial countries. The poorest of countries, such as Ethiopia, are so poor that every day thousands of people die from an inadequate diet and disease. Why are some countries, like Ethiopia, chained to poverty? Why are there such differences in income between the poorest and richest countries? ◆ ◆ In 1946, after World War II ended, Hong Kong emerged from occupation by the Japanese as a poor colony of Britain. Occupying a cluster of overcrowded rocky islands, Hong Kong today is a city of vibrant, hardworking, and increasingly wealthy people. A simi-

Feed the World

lar story can be told of Singapore. Two and a half million people crowded into an island city nation have, by their dynamism, transformed their economy, increasing their average income more than sixfold since 1960. How do some countries manage to unshackle themselves from poverty? What do they have that other poor countries lack? Can their lessons be applied elsewhere?

◆ ◆ ◆ ◆ In this chapter, we'll study the economic problems facing the poor, developing countries. We'll also review some of the ideas people have advanced to speed up the growth of poor countries. We'll discover that some strategies help poor countries, but others have mixed results and may hinder their growth.

The International Distribution of Income

When we studied the distribution of Canadian income, we discovered that there is a great deal of inequality. As we will see, the differences in income within a country, large though they are, look insignificant when compared with the differences among nations. Let's see how world income is distributed among the nations.

Poorest Countries

The poorest countries are sometimes called underdeveloped countries. An **underdeveloped country** is a country in which there is little industrialization, limited mechanization of the agricultural sector, very little capital equipment, and low per capita income. In many underdeveloped countries, large numbers of people live on the edge of starvation. Such people devote their time to producing the supplies of food and clothing required for themselves and their families. They have no surplus to trade with others or to invest in new tools and equipment. One of the most publicized of the poor countries is Ethiopia, where thousands of people spend their lives trekking across parched landscapes in search of food.

Just how poor are the poorest countries? Twenty-seven percent of the world's population live in countries whose per capita incomes range between 4 and 9 percent of those in Canada. Although these countries contain 27 percent of the world's people, they earn only 6 percent of world income. These poorest of countries are located mainly in Africa.

Developing Countries

A **developing country** is one that is poor but is accumulating capital and developing an industrial and commercial base. The developing countries have a large and growing urban population and have steadily growing incomes. The per capita income level in such countries ranges between 10 and 30 percent of that in Canada. These countries are located in all parts of the world but many are found in Asia, the Middle East, and in Central America. Seventeen percent of the world's people live in these countries and earn 11 percent of world income.

Newly Industrialized Countries

Newly industrialized countries (often called NICs) are countries in which there is a rapidly developing broad industrial base and per capita income is growing quickly. Today, their per capita income levels approach 50 percent of those in Canada. Examples of such countries are Trinidad, Israel, and South Korea. Three percent of the world's people live in the newly industrialized countries and earn 3 percent of world income.

Industrial Countries

Industrial countries are countries that have a large amount of capital equipment and in which people undertake highly specialized activities, enabling them to earn high per capita incomes. These are the countries of Western Europe, Canada, the United States, Japan, Australia, and New Zealand. Seventeen percent of the world's people live in these countries and they earn 49 percent of world income.

Oil-Rich Countries

A small number of oil-rich countries have very high per capita incomes despite the fact that they are, in most other respects, similar to the poorest countries or developing countries. These countries have little industry, and indeed little of anything of value to sell to the world, except oil. Four percent of the world's people live in these countries and they earn 4 percent of world income. But that income is very unequally distributed within the countries: most of the people in these countries have incomes similar to those in the poorest countries, but a small number of people are extremely rich—indeed, among the richest people in the world.

Communist and Former Communist Countries

Close to 33 percent of the world's people live in communist countries or in countries that were formerly communist and are now making a transition towards capitalism. These countries earn 28 percent of world income. A **communist country** is a country in which there is limited private ownership of productive capital and of firms, limited reliance on the market as a means of allocating resources, and in which government agencies plan and direct the production and distribution of most goods and services. Rapid changes are taking place in many of these countries at the present time. We describe the economies of these countries, and the changes that are taking place, in Chapter 38.

Per capita incomes in these countries vary enormously. In China, per capita income is around 15 percent of that in Canada. China is a developing country. Per capita income in the former East Germany—now part of a reunited Germany—is almost 70 percent of that of Canada. Other countries in this category are the Czech and Slovak republics, Poland, Hungary, and the republics of the former Soviet Union. Some formerly communist countries, such as Romania, the states of the former Yugoslavia, and Bulgaria, have per capita incomes similar to those of the newly industrialized countries. Thus, within the communist and formerly communist countries, there is a great deal of variety in income levels and the degree of economic development.

The World Lorenz Curve

A **Lorenz curve** plots the cumulative percentage of income against the cumulative percentage of population. If income is equally distributed, the Lorenz curve is a 45° line running from the origin. The degree of inequality is indicated by the extent to which the Lorenz curve departs from the 45° line of equality. Figure 37.1 shows two Lorenz curves: one curve depicts the distribution of income among families in Canada, and the other depicts the distribution of average per capita income across countries.

As you can see, the distribution of income among countries is more unequal than the distribution of income among families within Canada. Forty percent of the world's people live in countries whose incomes account for less than 10 percent of the world's total. The richest 20 percent of the world's people live in countries whose incomes account for 55 percent of the world's total income. Inequality in income is even more severe than that apparent in Fig. 37.1, because the world Lorenz curve tells us only how unequal average incomes are among countries. Inequality within countries is not revealed by the world Lorenz curve.

Such numbers provide a statistical description of the enormity of the world's poverty problem. And they are *real* numbers. That is, the effects of differences in prices have been removed. To better appreciate the severity of the problem, imagine that your family has an income of 30 cents a day for each per-

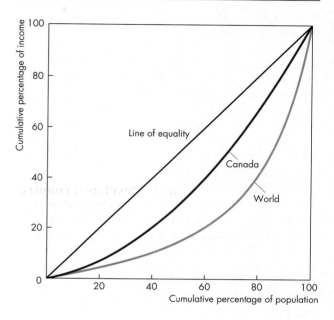

FIGURE 37.1

The World Lorenz
Curve: 1985

The cumulative percentage of income is plotted against the cumulative percentage of population. If income were distributed equally across countries, the Lorenz curve would be a straight diagonal line. The distribution of per capita income across countries is even more unequal than the distribution of income among families in Canada.

Sources: Robert Summers and Alan Heston, "A New Set of International Comparisons of Real Product and Price Levels; Estimates for 130 Countries, 1950-1985," *Review of Income and Wealth*, Series 34 (1988): 207-62; and Statistics Canada, *Income distribution by size in Canada:* 1991, Catalogue 13–207.

son. That 30 cents has to buy housing, food, clothing, transportation, and all the other things consumed. Such is the lot of more than a quarter of the world's people.

Although there are many poor people in the world, there are also many whose lives are undergoing dramatic change. They live in countries in which rapid economic growth is taking place. As a result of economic growth and development, millions of people now enjoy living standards undreamed of by their parents and inconceivable to their grandparents. Let's look at the connection between income levels and the rate of economic growth.

Growth Rates and Income Levels

P oor countries can and do grow into rich countries. Poor countries become rich countries by achieving high growth rates of real per capita income over prolonged periods of time. Over the years, a small increase in the growth rate, like compound interest, pays large dividends. A slowdown in the growth rate, maintained over a number of years, can result in a huge loss of real income.

The effects of economic growth on income levels is vividly illustrated by our own recent experience. In Canada in the early 1970s, aggregate income, measured by real GDP, was growing at more than 5 percent a year. After 1974, GDP growth slowed down. The actual path of Canadian GDP growth is shown in Fig. 37.2(a). The path that would have been followed if the pre-1974 growth trend had been maintained is also shown in that figure. By 1992, Canadian real GDP was $328 billion below—37 percent below—what it would have been if the pre-1974 growth rate had been maintained.

When poor countries have a slow growth rate and rich countries a fast growth rate, the gap between the rich and the poor widens. Figure 37.2(b) shows how the gap between Canada and many poor countries, such as Ethiopia, has widened over the years.

For a poor country to catch up to a rich country, it is necessary for its growth rate to exceed that of the rich country. In 1980, per capita income in China was 14 percent of that in Canada. Between 1975 and 1985, Canada experienced an average per capita income growth rate of 1.9 percent a year. If that growth rate is maintained and if per capita income in China also grows at 1.9 percent a year, China will remain at 14 percent of Canadian income levels forever. The gap will remain constant. If per capita income in Canada were to grow at 1.9 percent and if China could maintain a per capita income growth rate at twice that level—3.8 percent per year—China would catch up to Canada in per capita income levels in 2067. If China could do twice as well as that, maintaining an 8 percent per year growth rate in per capita incomes, the people of China would have income levels as high as those in Canada within your own lifetime—before 2020.

FIGURE 37.2

Growth Rates and Income Levels

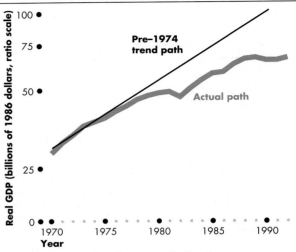

(a) Canadian output loss from growth slowdown

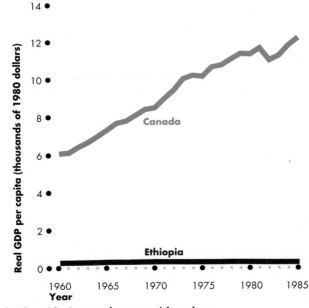

(b) The widening gap between rich and poor

A fall in the Canadian growth rate after 1974 (part a) has resulted in real GDP being almost $330 billion (37 percent) below its pre-1974 trend path. But with no growth, Ethiopia has fallen further behind Canada (part b).

Sources: Robert Summers and Alan Heston, "A New Set of International Comparisons of Real Product and Price Levels; Estimates for 130 Countries, 1950-1985," *Review of Income and Wealth*, Series 34 (1988): 207-62; and *National Income and Expenditure Accounts*, Statistics Canada, 1992.

A growth rate as high as 8 percent is not unknown. Japan's per capita income grew in excess of 10 percent a year, on the average, for almost 20 years following World War II. Recently China has, indeed, experienced per capita income growth of 12 percent a year, a rate which, if sustained, doubles per capita income every six years. Even the poorest countries in the world—those with per capita incomes of only 4 percent of those of Canada—would catch Canada in a matter of 40 or 50 years if they could achieve and maintain growth rates of this level.

The key, then, to achieving high per capita income is to attain and maintain a high rate of economic growth. That is how today's rich countries attained their high living standards. The poor countries of today will join the rich countries of tomorrow only if they can find ways of attaining and maintaining rapid growth.

Clearly, the question of what determines a country's economic growth rate is a vital one. What does determine a country's economic growth rate? Let's turn to an examination of this crucial question.

Resources, Technological Progress, and Economic Growth

In the aggregate, income equals the value of output. Thus, to increase average income, a country has to increase its output. A country's output depends on its resources and the techniques it employs for transforming these resources into outputs. This relationship between resources and outputs is the *production function*. There are three types of resource:

◆ Land

◆ Labour

◆ Capital

Land includes all the natural, nonproduced resources such as land itself, the minerals under it, and all other nonproduced inputs. The quantity of these resources is determined by nature, and countries have no choice but to put up with whatever natural resources they have. But countries do experience fluctuations in income as a result of fluctua-

tions in the prices of their natural resources. And at times those prices rise quickly, bringing temporary income growth. For example, in the late 1970s, resource-rich countries experienced rapid income growth as a result of rising commodity prices. But to achieve sustained income growth, countries have to look beyond their natural resources.

One such source of increased output is a sustained increase in *labour* resources. That is, a country can produce more output over the years simply because its working population grows. But for each successive generation of workers to have a higher *per capita* income than the previous generation, per capita output must increase. Population growth, on its own, does not lead to higher per capita output.

The resource most responsible for rapid and sustained economic growth is capital. There are two broad types of capital—physical and human. *Physical capital* includes such things as highways and railways, dams and irrigation systems, tractors and ploughs, factories, and buildings of all kinds. *Human capital* is the accumulated knowledge and skills of the working population. As individuals accumulate more capital, their incomes grow. Human capital accumulation is probably more important than physical capital in achieving rapid real income growth. As nations accumulate more capital per worker, labour productivity and output per capita grow.

To study the behaviour of per capita output, we use the per capita production function. The **per capita production function** shows how per capita output varies as the per capita stock of capital varies, in a given state of knowledge about alternative technologies. Figure 37.3 illustrates the per capita production function. Curve *PF* shows how per capita output varies as the amount of per capita capital varies. A rich country such as Canada has a large amount of per capita capital and a large per capita output. A poor country such as Ethiopia has hardly any capital and very low per capita output.

Capital Accumulation

By accumulating capital, a country can grow and move along its per capita production function. The greater the amount of capital (per capita), the greater is the output (per capita). But the fundamental *law of diminishing returns* applies to the per capita production function. That is, as capital per capita increases, output per capita also increases

FIGURE 37.3

The per Capita Production Function

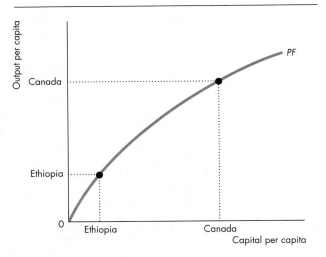

The per capita production function (*PF*) traces how per capita output varies as the stock of per capita capital varies. If two countries use the same technology, but one country has a larger per capita capital stock, that country will also have a higher per capita income. Suppose that Ethiopia and Canada each use the same technology. Ethiopia has a low per capita capital stock and low level of output per capita. Canada has a large per capita capital stock and a large per capita output rate.

but by decreasing increments. Thus there is a limit to the extent to which a country can grow merely by accumulating capital. Eventually, the country reaches the point at which the extra output from extra capital is not worth the effort of accumulating more capital. At such a point, it pays the country to consume rather than increase its capital stock.

But no country has yet reached such a point because the per capita production function is constantly shifting upward as a result of improvements in technology. Let's see how technological change affects output and growth.

Technological Change

Although rich countries have much more capital per capita than poor countries, that is not the only difference between them. Typically, rich countries use more productive technologies than do poor countries. That is, even if they have the same per

capita capital, the rich country produces more output than the poor country. For example, a farmer in a rich country might use a ten-horsepower tractor, whereas a farmer in a poor country might use ten horses. Each has the same amount of "horsepower" but the output achieved using the tractor is considerably greater than that produced by using ten horses. The combination of better technology and more per capita capital accentuates still further the difference between the rich and poor countries.

Figure 37.4 illustrates the impact that technological advance makes. Imagine that the year is 1867 and both Canada and Ethiopia (then called Abyssinia) use the same technology and have the same per capita production function, PF_{1867}. With a larger per capita stock of capital, Canada produces a larger per capita output in 1867 than does Ethiopia. By 1993, technological advances adopted in Canada, but not in Ethiopia, enable Canada to produce more output from given inputs. Canada's

FIGURE 37.4

Technological Change

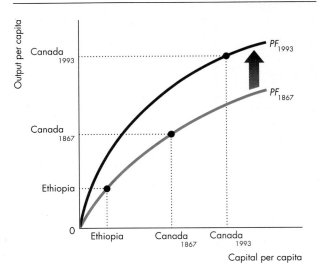

In 1867, Canada and Ethiopia have the same production function, PF_{1867}. By 1993, technological change has shifted the production function upward in Canada to PF_{1993}. Per capita income in Canada has increased from Canada$_{1867}$ to Canada$_{1993}$, partly because of an increase in the per capita capital stock and partly because of an increase in productivity arising from the adoption of better technology.

per capita production function shifts upward to PF_{1993}. Output per capita in Canada in 1993 is much larger than it was in 1867 for two reasons. First, the per capita stock of capital has increased dramatically; second, the techniques of production have improved, resulting in an upward shift in the production function.

FIGURE 37.5

Investment Trends

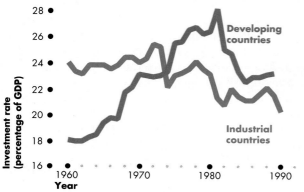

(a) Investment rates in industrial and developing countries

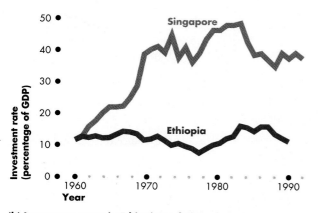

(b) Investment rates in Ethiopia and Singapore

The rate of investment in developing countries increased from 1960 to 1981 and then decreased. Investment in industrial countries was steady during the 1960s and early 1970s but fell after 1974 (part a). Investment in Singapore increased dramatically while that in Ethiopia was almost constant (part b). High investment in Singapore has led to rapid growth, while low investment in Ethiopia has led to low growth.

Source: International Monetary Fund, *International Financial Statistics Yearbook,* (1992).

The faster the pace of technological advance, the faster the production function shifts upward. The faster the pace of capital accumulation, the more quickly a country moves along its production function. Both of these forces lead to increased per capita output. A poor country becomes a rich country partly by moving along its production function and partly by adopting better technology, thereby shifting its production function upward.

Figure 37.5 illustrates the connection between capital accumulation and output growth. Capital accumulation is measured by the percentage of output represented by investment. (Recall that investment is the purchase of new capital equipment.) The figure shows what has been happening to investment over time in developing countries and industrial countries and in the two extreme cases—Singapore and Ethiopia. As you can see in part (a), the percentage of income invested by developing countries increased through 1981 and then began to decline. In industrial countries, the percentage of income invested has persistently declined, especially sharply since 1975. Fast-growing Singapore invests more than 40 percent of its income. Slow-growing Ethiopia invests less than 15 percent of its income. The source of Singapore's dramatic growth and of Ethiopia's almost static income level can be seen in part (b).

R E V I E W

T here is enormous inequality in the world. The poorest people in the poorest countries live on the edge of starvation. The poorest fifth of the world's people consume less than one-twentieth of total output and the richest fifth consume more than half the total output. Nations become rich by establishing and maintaining high rates of economic growth over prolonged periods. Economic growth results from the accumulation of capital and the adoption of increasingly efficient technologies. The more rapidly capital is accumulated and the more rapid is the pace of technological change, the higher is the rate of growth of output. Small changes in growth rates maintained over a long period of time make large differences to income levels. ◆

Obstacles to Economic Growth

The prescription for economic growth seems straightforward: poor countries can become wealthy by accumulating capital and adopting the most productive technologies. But if the cure for abject poverty is so simple, why haven't more poor countries become rich? Why are there so many poor people in the world today?

We do not know the answers to all these questions. If we did, we would be able to solve the problem of economic underdevelopment and there wouldn't be any poor countries. But we do understand some of the reasons for poverty and underdevelopment. The main ones are

◆ Absence of property rights and the rule of law

◆ Rapid population growth

◆ Low saving rate

◆ Heavy international debt burden

Let's examine these obstacles.

Absence of Property Rights and the Rule of Law

In the absence of private property rights and a stable legal environment, the incentives to work hard and to save and invest are weak. Establishing well-defined property rights and a legal system to protect those rights is a fundamental prerequisite for specialization and exchange and for the accumulation of capital. We take property rights and the rule of law for granted in Canada. But in many poor countries such rights are absent. Property is often confiscated at the whim of a political dictator, or wiped out by a sudden and unpredicted burst of rapid inflation. Crime is also rampant in many poor countries, and people are left to provide for their own security and protection.

In such conditions, there is vast inequality of wealth and living standards. Those with the power to steal, whether they are politicians or ordinary criminals, live lives of luxury while the masses of people struggle in abject poverty.

This prerequisite for economic development has been recognized by the World Bank and the International Monetary Fund as a crucial precondition for official international financial assistance. If this one problem can be solved in an adequate way, the other obstacles, although needing attention, can usually be dealt with. But in the absence of a solution to this problem, attempts to overcome other obstacles to development are likely to result in failure.

Rapid Population Growth

The second obstacle to economic development and sustained growth in per capita income is rapid population growth. In the past 20 years, world population has been growing at an average rate of 2 percent per year. At a population growth rate this high, world population doubles every 37 years. That population is now more than 5 billion. But the pattern of population growth is uneven. Rich industrial countries have relatively low population growth rates—often less than half a percent a year—while the poor, underdeveloped countries have high population growth rates—in some cases exceeding 3 percent a year.

Why is fast population growth an impediment to economic growth and development? Doesn't a larger population give a country more productive resources, permit more specialization, more division of labour, and therefore yet greater output? These benefits do indeed stem from a large population. But when the population is growing at a rapid rate and when a country is poor, there are two negative effects on economic growth and development that outweigh the benefits of a larger population. They are

◆ An increase in the proportion of dependants to workers

◆ An increase in the amount of capital devoted to supporting the population rather than producing goods and services

Some facts about the relationship between the number of dependants and population growth are shown in Fig. 37.6. The number of dependants is measured, on the vertical axis, as the percentage of the population under 15 years of age. As you can see, the higher the population growth rate, the larger is the percentage of the population under 15. In countries such as Canada, where the population growth rate is less than 1 percent per year, about

FIGURE 37.6

Population Growth and Number of Dependants

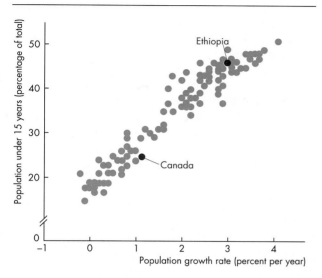

Each point represents a country. It shows the percentage of the population that is under 15 years of age (measured on the vertical axis) and the population growth rate (measured on the horizontal axis). The number of young people in the population is strongly influenced by the population growth rate. In slow-growing countries such as Canada, about one-fifth of the population is under the age of 15, while in fast-growing countries such as Ethiopia more than 40 percent of the population is under the age of 15.

Source: World Population Data Sheet of the Population Reference Bureau Inc., Washington, D.C., 1988.

one person in five (20 percent) is under the age of 15. In countries such as Ethiopia that have rapid population growth rates (3 percent per year or higher), close to one-half (50 percent) of the population is under the age of 15.

Let's see why there is a connection between the population growth rate and the percentage of young people in the population. A country might have a steady population because it has a high birth rate and an equally high death rate. But the same steady population growth could occur with a low birth rate and a low death rate. Population growth rates increase when either the birth rate increases or the death rate decreases. Historically, it is a fall in the death rate with a relatively constant birth rate that

has led to population explosions. The fall in the death rate mainly takes the form of a fall in the infant mortality rate, and it is this phenomenon that results in an enormous increase in the proportion of young people in the population.

In a country with a large number of young people, capital resources are directed towards providing schools, hospitals, roads, and housing rather than irrigation schemes and industrial capital projects. Such a use of scarce capital resources is obviously not wasteful and does bring great benefits, but it does not add to the economy's capacity to produce goods and services out of which yet additional capital accumulation can be provided.

Low Saving Rate

The third obstacle to rapid and sustained economic growth and development is a low saving rate. Poor people have so little income that they consume most of it, saving only a tiny amount. Saving is the major source of finance for capital accumulation and, as we have seen, capital accumulation is itself one of the main engines of economic growth. Let's investigate the connection between saving and the amount of capital that can be accumulated.

There are just three things that people can do with their income: consume it, save it, or pay it in taxes. That is,

$$\text{Income} = \text{Consumption} + \text{Saving} + \text{Taxes}.$$

An economy's output consists of consumption goods, capital goods, goods and services bought by the government, and net exports (exports minus imports). Expenditure on capital goods is investment, and expenditure on goods and services bought by the government is called government purchases of goods and services. Thus

$$\begin{aligned}\text{Income} = {}& \text{Consumption} + \text{Investment} \\ & + \text{Government purchases} \\ & + \text{Net exports.}\end{aligned}$$

The first of the above equations tells us that income minus consumption is equal to saving plus taxes. The second equation tells us that income minus consumption is equal to the value of investment plus government purchases plus net exports. Using these two equations, we then see that

$$\begin{aligned}\text{Saving} + \text{Taxes} = {}& \text{Investment} \\ & + \text{Government purchases} \\ & + \text{Net exports.}\end{aligned}$$

Or, with a small rearrangement of the terms,

Investment = Saving
– (Government purchases – Taxes)
– Net exports.

Government purchases minus taxes is the government budget deficit. So,

Investment = Saving
– Government budget deficit
– Net exports.

Net exports is related to the balance of payments current account surplus—more simply, the current account surplus. Specifically,

Net exports + Foreign aid – Debt interest payments
= Current account surplus.

But net exports makes a negative contribution to investment, so

– Net exports = Current account deficit
+ Foreign aid
– Debt interest payments.

We can rearrange the investment equation, therefore, as

Investment = Saving
+ Current account deficit
+ Foreign aid
– Debt interest payments
– Government budget deficit.

There are five influences on the pace at which a country can accumulate capital (can invest): saving, the current account deficit, and foreign aid contribute to investment, and the government budget deficit and debt interest payments to the rest of the world decrease the amount available for investment.

The fraction of income that people save depends on the income level. Very poor people save nothing. As income rises, some part of income is saved. The higher the income level, the higher is the proportion of income saved. These patterns in the relationship between income and saving crucially affect the pace at which a country can grow.

Heavy International Debt Burden

The fourth obstacle to economic development and sustained income growth is a large international debt burden. Poor countries often go into debt with the rest of the world and loans must be repaid and interest must be paid on the loans outstanding. To make debt repayments and interest payments, poor countries need a net export surplus—that is, a current account surplus. As we have just seen, when a country has a current account deficit, that deficit provides additional financial resources to domestic saving, enabling the country to accumulate capital at a faster pace than would otherwise be possible. A country that has a current account surplus is one that is accumulating capital at a slower pace than its domestic saving permits. Such a country uses part of its saving to accumulate capital—and thereby increases productivity—and uses the other part to pay interest on or repay loans from the rest of the world.

A poor country that borrows heavily from the rest of the world and uses the borrowing to invest in productive capital will not become overburdened by debt, provided the growth rate of income exceeds the interest rate on the debt. In such a situation, debt interest can be paid out of the higher income and there is still some income left over for additional domestic consumption or capital accumulation. Countries that borrow from the rest of the world and use the resources for consumption or invest in projects that have a low rate of return—lower than the interest rate on the debt—become overburdened by debt.

The burden of international debt became particularly onerous for many developing countries during the 1980s. For example, the Latin American countries have accumulated external debts of almost half a trillion dollars. Many of these debts were incurred during the 1970s when raw material prices were rising quickly. From 1973 to 1980, the prices of most raw materials increased on the average by close to 20 percent per year—a rate much higher than the interest rates on the foreign debt being accumulated. In such a situation, countries producing raw materials, hungry for capital, borrowed on an enormous scale. In the 1980s, raw material prices collapsed. Huge debts had been incurred, but the revenue with which to repay those debts was not coming in. To add a further burden, interest rates increased sharply during the 1980s. Today, because of the combination of sagging raw material prices and higher interest rates, many poor countries have a crippling burden of international debt.

The Underdevelopment Trap

The obstacles to economic development are so severe that some economists have suggested that there is a kind of poverty trap that applies to countries—the underdevelopment trap. The **underdevelopment trap** is a situation in which a country is locked into a low per capita income situation that reinforces itself. A low level of capital per worker (both physical and human capital) results in low output per worker. Low productivity in turn produces low per capita income. Low per capita income results in low saving. With low saving, there is a low rate of capital accumulation. Capital accumulation can barely keep up with population growth, so the stock of capital per worker remains low and the cycle repeats itself.

Overcoming the Obstacles to Economic Development

A variety of ways of breaking out of the underdevelopment trap have been suggested. They are

- Establishment of property rights and the rule of law
- Population control
- Foreign aid
- Removal of trade restrictions
- Aggregate demand stimulation

Let's look at each of these in turn.

Establishment of Property Rights and the Rule of Law

It is not a simple matter to overcome the lack of property rights and the rule of law. Some people benefit, and on a sumptuous scale, from running political dictatorships and confiscating the wealth created by the efforts of others. So, establishing a properly functioning property and legal system requires a political change—a change in the power structure of a country. To some degree, the inter-national institutions that have the power to make or withhold favourable loans can change the balance of power. And the World Bank and the International Monetary Fund do place a large weight on this matter before granting loans to the governments of poor countries.

All the economic growth success stories have been based on a strong adherence to private property rights and the rule of law. Countries such as Hong Kong and Singapore are the best examples. But even China, although remaining a political dictatorship, has established limited property rights and this change has been one of the crucial factors in speeding the growth of that country. We examine China more thoroughly in Chapter 38.

Population Control

Almost all developing countries use population control methods as part of their attempt to break out of the underdevelopment trap. Population control programs have two key elements: the provision of low-cost birth control facilities and the provision of incentives encouraging people to have a small number of children. These methods meet with some, but limited, success. One of the most highly publicized programs of population control is that employed in China. In that country, families are strongly discouraged from having more than one child. Despite this policy, the population of China continues to grow and forecasts suggest that by the year 2000 the population will have grown above its target level by an amount equal to five times the entire population of Canada. Thus, important though they are, population control methods are not the most likely to yield success in the fight against underdevelopment and poverty.

But to a large degree, if property rights and the rule of law are established and, if as a result, capital is accumulated and growth begins, automatic forces begin to operate to limit population growth. The most powerful of these forces is the rising opportunity cost of the time of women. As women's wages rise, more and more women choose to allocate more of their time to work and less to having children.

Foreign Aid

The idea that foreign aid helps economic development arises from a simple consideration. If a poor country is poor because it has too little capital, then by giving it aid, it can accumulate more capital and achieve a higher per capita output. Repeated applications of foreign aid year after year can enable a country to grow much more quickly than it could if it had to rely exclusively on its own domestic saving. By this line of reasoning, the greater the flow of foreign aid to a country, the faster it will grow.

Some economists suggest that foreign aid will not necessarily make a country grow faster. They argue that such aid consolidates the position of corrupt and/or incompetent politicians and that these politicians and their policies are two of the main impediments to economic development. Most people who administer foreign aid do not take this view. The consensus is that foreign aid does help economic development, but it is not a major factor. Its scale is simply too small to make a decisive difference.

A factor that has made a decisive difference in many countries is international trade policy. Let's now turn to an examination of the effects of international trade on growth and development.

Removal of Trade Restrictions

There is a steady political pressure in the rich countries in support of protection from imports produced with "cheap labour" in the underdeveloped countries. Some people also complain that buying from underdeveloped countries exploits low-wage workers. As a consequence, countries introduce tariffs, quotas, and voluntary restrictions on trade. How do such restrictions affect underdeveloped countries and how does the removal of such restrictions affect their growth and development?

To answer this question, consider the following example (which is illustrated in Fig. 37.7). Imagine a situation (such as that prevailing in the 1950s) in which the United States produces virtually all its cars. The automobile market in the United States is shown in part (a). The demand for cars is shown by curve D_{US} and the supply by curve S_{US}. The price of cars is P_{US} and the quantity produced and bought is Q_{US}.

Suppose that Mazda builds an automobile production plant in Mexico. The supply curve of cars produced in Mexico is shown in Fig. 37.7(b) as the curve S_M. What happens in the United States depends on U.S. international trade policy.

Suppose that the United States restricts the import of cars from Mexico. To make things as clear

as possible, let's suppose it bans such imports. In this case, Mexico produces no cars for export to the United States. The price of cars in the United States remains at P_{US} and the quantity remains at Q_{US}.

In contrast, let's see what happens if the United States engages in free trade with Mexico. (A trade accord, NAFTA, is, in fact, currently being negotiated.) To determine the price of cars and the quantities produced and bought in the United States, and the quantity produced in Mexico for export to the United States, we need to consider Fig. 37.7(c). The demand curve for cars in the United States remains D_{US} but the supply curve becomes S_W. This supply curve is made up of the sum of the quantities supplied both in the United States and Mexico at each price. Equilibrium is achieved in the U.S. market at a price of P_W and a quantity traded of Q_W. To see where these cars are produced, go back to parts (a) and (b). Mexico produces Q_M, the United States produces Q_P, and these two production levels sum to Q_W.

Mazda's Mexican plant increases its output of cars and its workers generate an income. The output of cars in the United States decreases. By permitting unrestricted trade with underdeveloped countries, rich countries gain by being able to buy goods that are imported at lower prices than would be possible if only domestic supplies were available. Developing countries gain by being able to sell their output for a higher price than would prevail if they had only the domestic market available to them.

Some of the most dramatic economic growth and development success stories have been based on reaping the gains from relatively unrestricted international trade. Countries such as Hong Kong and Singapore have opened their economies to free trade with the rest of the world and dramatically increased their living standards by specializing and producing goods and services at which they have a *comparative advantage*—which they can produce at a lower opportunity cost than other countries.

Aggregate Demand Stimulation

It is suggested that growth and development can be stimulated by expanding aggregate demand. The suggestion takes two forms. Sometimes it is suggested that if rich countries stimulate their own aggregate demand, their economies will grow more quickly and, as a consequence, commodity prices will remain high. High commodity prices help poor

FIGURE 37.7

International Trade and Economic Development

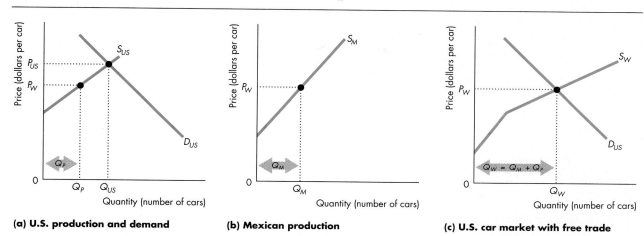

(a) U.S. production and demand   **(b) Mexican production**   **(c) U.S. car market with free trade**

The market for cars in the United States (part a) has demand curve D_{US} and supply curve S_{US}. The price of cars is P_{US} and the quantity produced and bought is Q_{US}. Mazda builds an automobile plant in Mexico and the supply curve of cars from that plant is S_M (part b). If the United States prohibits the import of cars from Mexico, the U.S. automobile market remains unchanged and Mexican output is zero. If the United States permits free international trade in cars with Mexico, the price in the U.S. market is P_W (part c) and the total quantity of cars bought in the United States is Q_W (W stands for "with trade"). Parts (a) and (b) show that at price P_W, Q_M cars are produced in Mexico and Q_P (P stands for "production") in the United States. Free international trade permits poor countries to sell their output for a price higher than they would otherwise receive and rich countries to buy goods for a price lower than they would otherwise pay.

countries and so stimulate their income growth and economic development. It is also suggested that poor countries can make themselves grow faster by stimulating their own level of aggregate demand.

Can stimulating aggregate demand in the rich countries help the poor countries? Can aggregate demand stimulation in poor countries help them grow? The answers to both of these questions are almost certainly no, but let's see why.

Changes in aggregate income can occur as a result of changes in either aggregate demand or aggregate supply. But aggregate demand changes affect output and income in the short run only. That is, when wages and other input prices are fixed, a change in aggregate demand changes both output and the price level. But in the long run, a change in aggregate demand leads to a change in the prices of goods and services and of factors of production. Once input prices have adjusted to a change in aggregate demand, income returns to its long-run level. Changes in per capita income in the long run can be brought about only by changes in per capita productivity—which results from changes in the stock of

per capita capital and the state of technology.

This aggregate demand–aggregate supply model applies to all countries, rich and poor alike. If rich countries persistently permit aggregate demand to grow at a pace faster than long-run aggregate supply, they will generate inflation. If they permit aggregate demand to grow at a pace similar to long-run aggregate supply, prices will be stable. In recent history, rich countries generated inflation. In the 1970s, inflation was rapid. Commodity prices increased quickly, enabling many developing countries to increase the pace of capital accumulation and income growth. In the 1980s, inflation was moderate. Raw material prices fell and brought the burden of large international debt for many developing countries.

Don't the facts of the 1970s and 1980s support the conclusion that rapid aggregate demand growth and inflation in the rich countries help the poor countries? They do not. Rather, they provide an example of what can happen, over a limited time period, when a growth rate of aggregate demand changes unexpectedly. In the 1970s, there was an unexpectedly rapid increase in aggregate demand, resulting in increasing inflation and increasing output growth. In the 1980s, there was an unexpectedly severe contraction of aggregate demand, resulting in falling inflation and a slowdown in output growth. Unexpected fluctuations in the inflation rate can produce fluctuations in output growth—as happened in the 1970s and 1980s. But sustained aggregate demand growth and steady inflation are not capable of producing sustained output growth.

Developing countries can make aggregate demand grow at a rapid or a moderate rate. The more rapidly aggregate demand grows relative to long-run aggregate supply, the higher is the inflation rate. Some developing countries inflate quickly and others slowly. But there is virtually no connection between the pace of their development and the inflation rate. As Fig. 37.8 illustrates, fast-growing Singapore, which invests more than 40 percent of its income each year, has a moderate inflation rate, while average-growing Ghana has the highest inflation rate of the developing countries—a rate in excess of 100 percent a year. Slow-growing Ethiopia, which invests only 10 percent of its income, has a moderate inflation rate. As you can see, the pace at which a developing country stimulates aggregate demand, affecting its inflation rate, has no appreciable effect on its growth rate of real income or its pace of economic development.

We've seen that to grow quickly, a country must accumulate capital at a rapid pace. To do so it must achieve a high saving rate and undertake foreign borrowing that is used in high-return activities. The most rapidly growing developing countries have a high pace of capital accumulation and obtain a high return on their capital by pursuing a free trade policy, thereby ensuring that they produce those goods and services in which they have a comparative advantage.

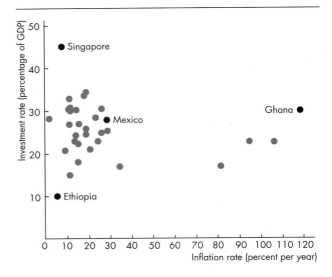

FIGURE 37.8

Inflation and Economic Growth

Each dot shows a developing country's investment level (as a percentage of GDP) plotted against its inflation rate. The data are average for 1960 to 1990. There is no discernible connection between a country's inflation rate and its pace of investment and economic growth. Fast-growing Singapore has a low inflation rate, as does slow-growing Ethiopia. Medium-growing Ghana has the highest inflation rate in the developing world.

Source: International Monetary Fund, *International Financial Statistics* (1991).

SUMMARY

The International Distribution of Income

There is enormous inequality in the international distribution of income. The poorest countries have average per capita income levels of 4 percent to 9 percent of that in Canada. Half of the world's population earns only 15 percent of world income and the richest 20 percent of the world's population earns 55 percent of world income. (pp. 1026–1027)

Growth Rates and Income Levels

Poor countries become rich by achieving and maintaining for prolonged periods high rates of per capita income growth. Rich countries grow at about 1.8 percent per year. Poor countries with a growth rate below 1.5 percent fall further behind. Poor countries that achieve a growth rate higher than 1.8 percent close the gap on the rich countries. High and sustained growth makes a dramatic difference in a short time span. If China can achieve and maintain a per capita income growth rate of 8 percent per year, the per capita income of China will catch up with that of Canada before 2020. (pp.1028–1029)

Resources, Technological Progress, and Economic Growth

Per capita income growth results from growth in per capita capital and technological change. The greater the fraction of income invested in new equipment and the faster the pace of technological change, the higher is the rate of economic growth. (pp. 1029–1031)

Obstacles to Economic Growth

There are four major obstacles to sustained economic growth and development: absence of property rights and the rule of law, rapid population growth, a low saving rate, and an international debt burden. The absence of an appropriate legal framework creates weak incentives for saving and capital accumulation. Rapid population growth results in there being a large proportion of young dependants in the population. A low saving rate results in a low rate of capital accumulation. A large international debt burden results in some savings having to be used to pay debt interest rather than to accumulate capital and improve productivity.

Low income results in low saving, which in turn results in low investment and low income growth. Many poor countries are caught in what appears to be an underdevelopment trap. (pp. 1032–1035)

Overcoming the Obstacles to Economic Development

The main ways of overcoming the obstacles to economic development are the creation of political and legal institutions able to enforce property rights, the implementation of population control measures, foreign aid, and the removal of trade restrictions. Of these, the most dramatic success stories have almost always involved creating the legal framework and expanding international trade.

The stimulation of aggregate demand, by either rich or poor countries, cannot contribute, in the long run, to economic growth and development. If aggregate demand grows at the same rate as long-run aggregate supply, prices are stable; if aggregate demand grows at a faster rate than long-run aggregate supply, prices rise—there is inflation. The rate of inflation does not appear to have a major influence on the rate of economic growth and development. (pp. 1035–1038)

KEY ELEMENTS

Key Terms

Communist country, 1026
Developing country, 1026
Industrial countries, 1026
Lorenz curve, 1027
Newly industrialized country, 1026
Per capita production function, 1029
Underdeveloped country, 1026
Underdevelopment trap, 1035

Key Figures

Figure 37.1 The World Lorenz Curve: 1985, 1071
Figure 37.4 Technological Change, 1030
Figure 37.5 Investment Trends, 1031
Figure 37.6 Population Growth and Number of Dependants, 1033

REVIEW QUESTIONS

1 Describe the main differences between the richest and poorest countries.

2 Compare the distribution of income among families in Canada with the distribution of income among countries in the world. Which distribution is more unequal?

3 What determines a country's per capita income level? What makes the per capita income level change?

4 Give an example of a country in which rapid economic growth has occurred and one in which slow economic growth has occurred. Which country has the higher investment rate?

5 Review the obstacles to economic growth.

6 Why is the lack of property rights an obstacle to economic growth?

7 Why is rapid population growth an obstacle to economic growth?

8 Describe the underdevelopment trap.

9 What are the main ways in which poor countries try to overcome their poverty?

10 Why does free trade stimulate economic growth and development?

11 Why doesn't demand stimulation improve a country's economic growth rate and development?

PROBLEMS

1 A poor country has 10 percent of the income of a rich country. The poor country achieves a growth rate of 10 percent per year. The rich country is growing at 5 percent per year. How many years will it take income in the poor country to catch up with that of the rich country?

2 Silecon is a poor country with no natural resources except sand. Per capita income is $500 a year and this entire income is consumed. Per capita income is constant—there is no economic growth. The government has a balanced budget and there are no exports or imports. One day, the price of silicon increases and Silecon is able to export sand at a huge profit. Exports soar from zero to $400 (per capita). Per capita income increases to $1,000 a year and per capita consumption increases to $600 a year. There are still no imports and Silecon has a balance of payments current account surplus of $400 per capita.

a What happens to investment and the growth rate in Silecon?

b If Silecon imports capital goods equal in value to its exports, what will be its investment?

c What will be Silecon's current account balance?

d If the government of Silecon runs a budget deficit of $100 (per capita), what will be its investment?

3 The per capita production function in Machecon is illustrated in the figure, and in year 1, Machecon has 1 machine per person.

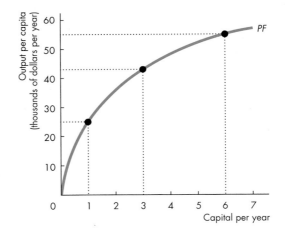

a What is per capita output in Machecon?

b If Machecon adds 1 machine per person to its capital stock during year 2, what is its new level of output and what is its output growth rate in year 2?

c In year 3, Machecon adds 1 more machine per person to its capital stock. What now is its output and what is its growth rate in year 3?

d If in year 4 Machecon adds no new machines to its capital stock, but a new technology becomes available that increases the productivity of each machine by 20 percent, what is the level of output in Machecon in year 4?

CHAPTER **38**

ECONOMIC SYSTEMS IN TRANSITION

After studying this chapter, you will be able to

- ◆ Describe the fundamental economic problem that confronts all nations

- ◆ Describe the alternative systems that have been used to solve the economic problem

- ◆ Describe the Soviet-style system of central planning

- ◆ Describe the economic problems confronting the former Soviet Union

- ◆ Describe the economic problems of other Eastern European countries

- ◆ Describe the process of economic change in China

- ◆ Describe and evaluate the alternative strategies for making the transition from a centrally planned to a market economy

EXTRAORDINARY EVENTS HAVE TAKEN PLACE IN EASTERN Europe. The Berlin Wall has fallen and Germany is reunited. The centrally planned economy of East Germany has been replaced by the market economic system of West Germany. Central planning has also been abandoned in Poland, Hungary, and the new Czech and Slovak republics. The Soviet Union has disintegrated and some of its former republics are independent nations while others are loosely linked in a Commonwealth of Independent States. These nations have abandoned central economic planning and are moving towards a market economy. The People's Republic of China is also undergoing massive economic change, gradually replacing its system of central planning with the market. ◆ ◆ Why are so many countries abandoning central economic planning and jumping on the market bandwagon? What are the problems that a country faces as it makes the transition to a market economy?

The Market Bandwagon

◆ ◆ ◆ ◆ This chapter brings you full circle and returns to the fundamental economic problem of scarcity and the alternative ways in which people cope with that problem. You've studied the way market economies such as our own operate. You are now going to look at the main alternative system that has been tried, that of socialist central planning. You are also going to look at the revolutionary process of change that is taking place during the 1990s as the centrally planned economies are making the transition towards market economies.

The Economic Problem and Its Alternative Solutions

The economic problem is the universal fact of scarcity—we want to consume more goods and services than the available resources make possible. The economic problem is illustrated in Fig. 38.1. People have preferences about the goods and services they would like to consume and about how they would like to use the factors of production that they own or control. Techniques of production—technologies—convert factors of production into goods and services. The economic problem is to choose the quantities of goods and services to produce (*what*), the ways to produce them (*how*), and the distribution of goods and services to each individual (*for whom*).

The production of goods and services is the objective of the economic system. But *what, how,* and *for whom* goods and services are produced depends on the way the economy is organized—on who makes which decisions. Different systems deliver different outcomes. Let's look at the main alternatives that have been used.

Alternative Economic Systems

Economic systems vary in two dimensions:

◆ Ownership of capital and land

◆ Incentive structure

Ownership of Capital and Land   Capital and land may be owned entirely by individuals, entirely by the state, or by a mixture of the two. The private ownership of capital and land enables individuals to create and operate their own firms. It also enables them to buy and sell capital, land, and firms freely at their going market prices. State ownership of capital and land enables individuals to control the use of these resources in state-owned firms but does not permit this control to be passed to others in a market transaction.

In practice, no economy has pure private ownership or pure and exclusive state ownership. For example, in an economy with widespread private ownership, the freedom to buy and sell firms is modified by the anti-trust laws. Also, national defence or

FIGURE 38.1

The Fundamental
Economic Problem

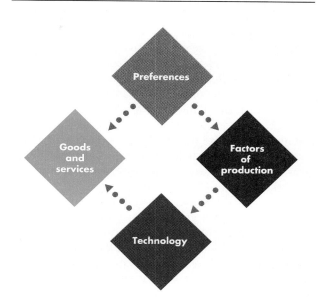

People have preferences about goods and services and the use of factors of production. Technologies are available for transforming factors of production into goods and services. People want to consume more goods and services than can be produced with the available factors of production and technology. The fundamental economic problem is to choose *what* goods and services to produce, *how* to produce them, and *for whom* to produce them. Different economic systems deliver different solutions to this problem.

the public interest may be invoked to limit private ownership. Such limitations operate to restrict the private ownership of beaches and areas of natural scenic beauty.

In an economy that has predominantly state ownership, individuals sometimes own small plots of land and their homes. Also, in many economies, private ownership and state ownership exist side by side. In such cases, the state acts like a private individual and buys capital, land, or even a production enterprise from its existing owner.

Incentive Structure   An **incentive structure** is a set of arrangements that induce people to take certain actions. Incentives may be created by market prices, by administered prices and administrative sanctions, or by a mixture of the two.

An incentive system based on market prices is one in which people respond to the price signals they receive and the price signals respond to people's actions. For example, suppose a severe frost wipes out the Florida orange crop one year. The supply of orange juice falls. As a result, the price of orange juice rises. Faced with the higher price, people have an *incentive* to economize on orange juice and they decrease the quantity demanded. At the same time, the higher price of orange juice induces an increase in the demand for apple juice, a substitute for orange juice. As a result, the prices of apples and apple juice also rise. With higher prices for orange juice and apple juice, orange and apple growers in other parts of the country and in other countries have an *incentive* to increase the quantity supplied.

An incentive system based on administered prices is one in which administrators set prices to achieve their own objectives. For example, a government might want everyone to have access to low cost bread. As a result, bread might be priced at, say, a penny a loaf. Under these circumstances, people have an *incentive* to buy lots of bread. Poor children might even use stale loaves as footballs! (This

use of bread apparently did actually occur in the former Soviet Union.) An incentive system based on administrative sanctions is one in which people are rewarded or punished in a variety of non-monetary ways to induce them to take particular actions. For example, a manager might reward a salesperson for achieving a sales goal with more rapid promotion, or with a bigger office. Alternatively, a salesperson might be punished for failing to achieve a sales goal by being moved to a less desirable sales district. When an entire economy is operated on administrative incentives, everyone, from the highest political authority to the lowest rank of workers, faces non-monetary rewards and punishments from their immediate superiors.

Types of Economic System   Economic systems differ in the ways in which they combine ownership and incentive arrangements. The range of alternatives is illustrated in Figure 38.2. One type of economic system is **capitalism**, a system based on the private ownership of capital and land and on an incentive system based on market prices. Another type of economic system is **socialism**, a system based on state ownership of capital and land and on an incentive based on administered prices or sanctions arising from a central economic plan.

FIGURE 38.2

Alternative Economic Systems

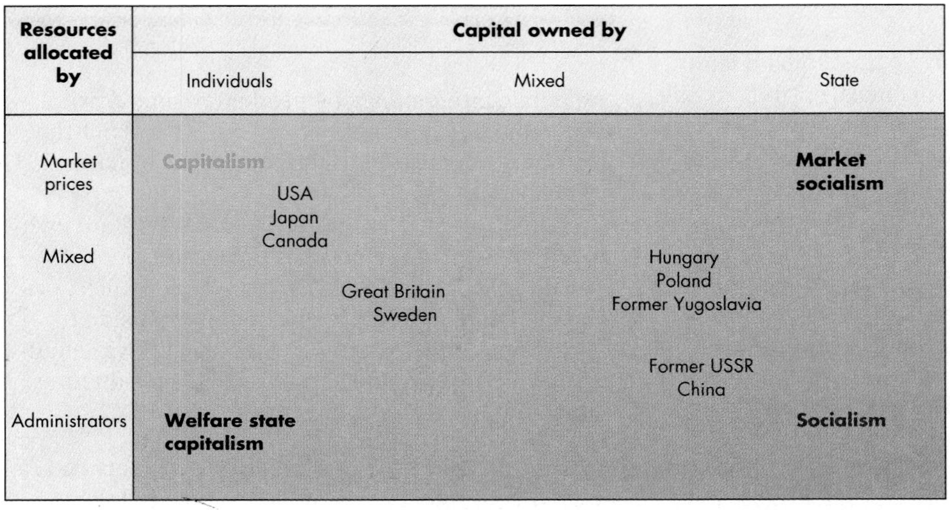

Resources allocated by	Capital owned by		
	Individuals	Mixed	State
Market prices	Capitalism USA Japan Canada		**Market socialism**
Mixed		Great Britain Sweden	Hungary Poland Former Yugoslavia
			Former USSR China
Administrators	**Welfare state capitalism**		**Socialism**

Under capitalism, individuals own capital—farms and factories, plant and equipment—and resources are allocated by markets. Under socialism, the state owns capital, and resources are allocated by a planning and command system. Market socialism combines state ownership of capital with a market allocation of resources. Welfare state capitalism combines private capital ownership with a high degree of state intervention in the allocation of resources.

Central planning is a method of allocating resources *by command*. A central plan for action is drawn up and the plan is implemented by creating a set of sanctions and rewards that ensure that the commands are carried out.

No country has used an economic system that precisely corresponds to one of these extreme types, but the United States and Japan come closest to being capitalist economies and the former Soviet Union and China before the 1980s came closest to being socialist economies. Socialism evolved from the ideas of Karl Marx (see Our Advancing Knowledge, pp. 1056–1057).

Some countries combine private ownership with state ownership and some combine market price incentives with administrative incentives and central planning. **Market socialism** (also called **decentralized planning**) is an economic system that combines state ownership of capital and land with incentives based on a mixture of market and administered prices. Hungary and the former Yugoslavia have had market socialist economies. In such economies, planners set the prices at which the various production and distribution organizations are able to buy and sell, and then leave those organizations free to choose the quantities of inputs and outputs. But the prices set by the planners respond to the forces of demand and supply.

Another combination is welfare state capitalism. **Welfare state capitalism** combines the private ownership of capital and land with state intervention in markets that modify the price signals to which people respond. Sweden, the United Kingdom, and other Western European countries are examples of such economies.

Alternative Systems Compared

Since all economic systems are made up of a combination of the two extreme special cases—capitalism and socialism—let's examine these two extreme types a bit more closely.

Capitalism   Figure 38.3 shows how capitalism solves the problem of scarcity. Households own the factors of production and are free to use those factors and the incomes they receive from the sale of their services in any way they choose. These choices are governed by their preferences. The preferences of households are all-powerful in a capitalist economy.

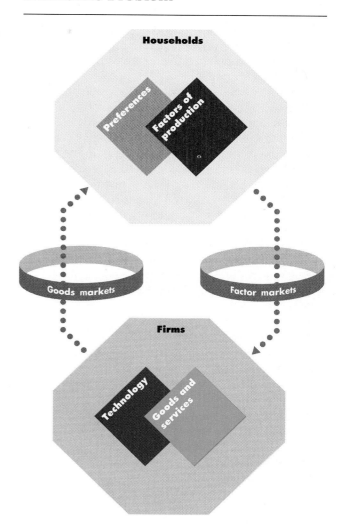

FIGURE 38.3

Capitalism's Solution to the Economic Problem

Under capitalism, the preferences of individual households dictate the choices that are made. Households own all the factors of production and sell the services of those factors in factor markets. Households decide which goods and services to consume and buy them in markets for goods and services. Firms decide which goods and services to produce and which factors of production to employ, selling their output and buying their inputs in the goods and factor markets. The markets find the prices that bring the quantities demanded and quantities supplied into equality for each factor of production and each good or service. Capitalism economizes on information because households and firms need to know only the prices of various goods and factors that they buy and sell.

Households choose the quantity of each factor of production to sell, and firms that organize production choose the quantity of each factor to buy. These choices respond to the prices prevailing in the factor markets. An increase in a factor price gives households an incentive to increase the quantity supplied and gives firms an incentive to decrease the quantity demanded. Factor prices adjust to bring the quantity of each factor supplied into equality with the quantity of each factor demanded.

Households choose the quantity of each good or service to buy and firms choose the quantity of each good or service to produce and sell. These choices respond to the prices confronting households and firms in the goods markets. An increase in the price of a good gives firms an incentive to increase the quantity supplied of that good and gives households an incentive to decrease the quantity demanded. Prices adjust to bring the quantity demanded and supplied into equality with each other.

Resources and goods and services flow in a clockwise direction from households to firms and back to households through the factors and goods markets. *What* is produced, *how* it is produced, and *for whom* it is produced is determined by the preferences of the households, the resources that they own, and the technologies available to the firms.

Nobody *plans* the capitalist economy. Doctors perform nearly miraculous life-saving surgery by using sophisticated computer-controlled equipment. The equipment is designed by medical and electronic engineers, programmed by mathematicians, financed by insurance companies and banks, and bought and installed by hospital administrators. Each individual household and firm involved in this process allocates the resources that it controls in the way that seems best for it. The firms try to maximize profit and the households try to maximize utility. And these plans are coordinated in the markets for health-care equipment, computers, engineers, computer programmers, insurance, hospital services, nurses, doctors, and hundreds of other markets for items that range from anaesthetic chemicals to apple juice.

When a surgeon performs an operation, an incredible amount of information is used. Yet no one possesses this information. It is not centralized in one place. The capitalist economic system economizes on information. Each household and firm needs to know very little about the other households and firms with whom it does business. The reason is that *prices convey most of the information they*

need. By comparing the prices of factors of production, households choose the quantity of each factor to supply. And by comparing the prices of goods and services, they choose the quantity of each to buy. Similarly, by comparing the prices of factors of production, firms choose the quantity of each factor to use, and by comparing the prices of goods and services, they choose the quantity of each to supply.

Socialism   Figure 38.4 shows how socialism solves the economic problem of scarcity. In this case, the planners' preferences carry the most weight. Those preferences dictate the activities of the production enterprises. The planners control capital and natural resources, directing them to the uses that satisfy their priorities. The planners also decide what types of jobs will be available, and the state plays a large role in the allocation of the only factor of production owned by households—labour.

The central plan is communicated to state-owned enterprises, which use the factors of production and the available technologies to produce goods and services. These goods and services are supplied to households in accordance with the central plan. The purchases by each individual household are determined by household preferences, but the total amount available is determined by the central planners.

A centrally planned economy has prices, but prices do not adjust to make the quantity demanded and supplied equal. Instead, they are set to achieve social objectives. For example, the prices of staple food products are set at low levels so that even the poorest families can afford an adequate basic diet. The effect of setting such prices at low levels is chronic shortages. The incentives that people respond to are the penalties and rewards that superiors can impose on and give to their subordinates.

R E V I E W

T he economic problem of *what, how,* and *for whom* to produce the various goods and services is solved in different ways by different economic systems. Capitalism solves it by permitting households and firms to exchange factors of production and goods and services in markets. Firms

FIGURE 38.4

Socialism's Solution to the Economic Problem

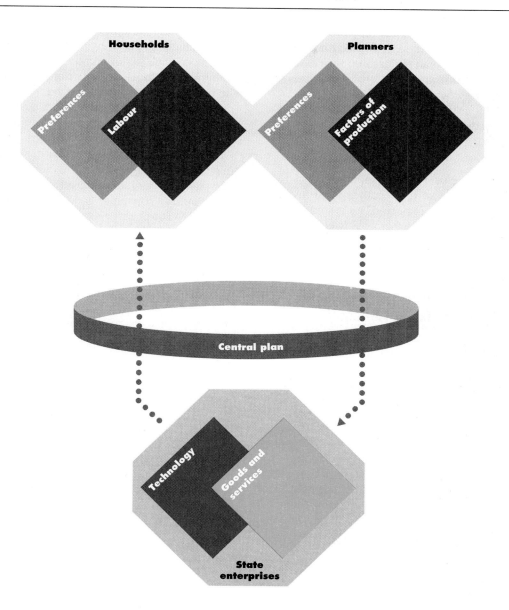

Under socialism, the preferences of the planners dictate the choices that are made. The planners control all the capital and natural resources owned by the state. They draw up plans and issue orders that determine how these resources will be used in the production of goods and services. Households decide which goods and services to consume and buy them in markets for goods and services. State enterprises produce the goods and services and employ the factors of production required by the central plan. The output of state enterprises is shipped to other enterprises in accordance with the plan or sold in the markets for goods and services. Prices are set by the planners to achieve social objectives and bear no relation to the quantities demanded and quantities supplied. Prices set at low levels for social reasons—as in the case of basic food products—result in chronic shortages.

produce the items that maximize their profits, households buy the goods that maximize their utility, and markets adjust prices to make buying and selling plans compatible. Socialism solves the economic problem by setting up a central planning system. The planners decide what will be produced and communicate their plans to state-owned enterprises. Incentives to fulfil the plan are created by a series of non-monetary rewards and sanctions. Each household decides what it wants to buy, but the total amount available is determined by the planners. Shortages, especially of basic staple food products, frequently arise. ◆

Let's now take a closer look at some socialist economies. We'll begin with the country that invented central planning and "exported" its system to the other socialist countries, the former Soviet Union.

Economic Change in the Former Soviet Union

The Soviet Union, or the Union of Soviet Socialist Republics (USSR), was founded in 1917 following the Bolshevik Revolution led by Vladimir Ilyich Lenin. The union collapsed and was replaced by the Commonwealth of Independent States (CIS) in 1991. The republics that make up the Commonwealth are resource-rich and diverse. Their land area is three times that of the United States; their population is approaching 300 million, 20 percent larger than that of the United States; they have vast reserves of coal, oil, iron ore, natural gas, timber, and almost every other mineral resource. (See the map on pp. 1052–1053.) They are republics of enormous ethnic diversity, with Russians making up 50 percent of the population and many European, Asian, and Arabic ethnic groups making up the other 50 percent.

History of the Soviet Union

A compact economic history of the Soviet Union appears in Table 38.1. Although the nation was founded in 1917, its economic management system was not put in place until the 1930s. The architect of this system was Joseph Stalin. The financial, manufacturing, and transportation sectors of the economy had been taken into state ownership and control by Lenin. Stalin added the farms to this list. He abolished the market and introduced a command planning mechanism, initiating a series of five-year plans that placed their major emphasis on setting and attaining goals for the production of capital goods. The production of consumer goods was given a secondary place and personal economic conditions were harsh. With emphasis on the production of capital goods, the Soviet economy grew quickly.

By the 1950s, after Stalin's death, steady economic growth continued, but the emphasis in economic planning gradually shifted away from capital goods towards consumer goods production. In the 1960s, the growth rate began to sag and by the 1970s and early 1980s, the Soviet economy was running into serious problems. Productivity was actually declining, especially in agriculture but also in industry. Growth slowed and, on some estimates, per capita income in the Soviet Union began to fall. It was in this situation that Mikhail Gorbachev came to power with plans to restructure the Soviet economy based on the idea of increased individual accountability and rewards based on performance.

As a unified political entity, the Soviet Union effectively disintegrated following an unsuccessful coup to topple former President Mikhail Gorbachev in August 1991. What emerged from that coup in 1992 was the loosely federated Commonwealth of Independent States. Political freedoms began to be enjoyed in the late 1980s under President Gorbachev's programs of *perestroika* (restructuring) and *glasnost* (openness). These political freedoms released nationalist and ethnic feelings that had been held in check for 50 years and created a virtual explosion of political activity. At the same time, the economies of the now independent republics underwent tumultuous change.

We are going to look at that change. But you will better appreciate the severity and nature of the problems posed by economic change if we first look at the way the Soviet Union operated before it abandoned its central planning system.

Soviet–Style Central Planning

Soviet style central planning is a method of economic planning and control that has four key elements:

TABLE 38.1

A Compact Summary of Key Periods in the Economic History of the Soviet Union

Period	Main economic events/characteristics
1917–1921 **(Lenin)**	◆ **Bolshevik Revolution** ◆ **Nationalization of banking, industry, and transportation** ◆ **Forced requisitioning of agricultural output**
1921–1924 **(Lenin)**	◆ **New Economic Policy (NEP), 1921** ◆ **Market allocation of most resources**
1928–1953 **(Stalin)**	◆ **Abolition of market** ◆ **Introduction of command planning and five-year plans** ◆ **Collectivization of farms** ◆ **Emphasis on capital goods and economic growth** ◆ **Harsh conditions**
1953–1970 **(Khrushchev to Brezhnev)**	◆ **Steady growth** ◆ **Increased emphasis on consumer goods**
1970–1985 **(Brezhnev to Chernenko)**	◆ **Deteriorating productivity in agriculture and industry** ◆ **Slowdown in growth**
1985–1991 **(Gorbachev)**	◆ **Perestroika—reforms based on increased accountability**
1991	◆ **Breakup of the Soviet Union**
1992	◆ **Creation of the Commonwealth of Independent States**

◆ Administrative hierarchy

◆ Iterative planning process

◆ Legally binding commands

◆ Taut and inflexible plans

Administrative Hierarchy   A large and complex hierarchy implements and controls the central economic plan that determines almost every aspect of

economic activity. A **hierarchy** is an organization arranged in ranks, each rank being subordinate to the one above it. At the top of an economic planning hierarchy is the highest *political* authority. Immediately below it is the economic planning ministry, the senior of a large number of ministries. Below the planning ministry are a large number of ministries that are responsible for the detailed aspects of production. For example, one ministry deals with engineering production, another with fruit and vegetables, and another with railway transportation. Responsibility for production processes is divided and subdivided yet further down to the level of the individual factories that carry out the production processes. For example, engineering is divided into light, heavy, electrical, and civil divisions. Light engineering is divided into departments that deal with individual product groups, such as ball bearings. And finally, ball bearings are manufactured in a number of factories. At each level of the hierarchy, there are superiors and subordinates. Superiors have absolute and arbitrary power over their subordinates.

Iterative Planning Process   An iterative process is a repetitive series of calculations that get closer and closer to a solution. Central planning is iterative. A plan is proposed and adjustments are repeatedly made until all the elements of the plan are consistent with each other. But a plan is not arrived at as the result of a set of neat calculations performed on a computer. Rather, the process involves a repeated sequence of communications of proposals and reactions down and up the administrative hierarchy.

The process begins with the issue of a big picture set of objectives or directives by the highest political authority. These directives are translated into targets by the planning ministry and retranslated into ever more detailed targets as they are passed down the hierarchy. Tens of millions of raw materials and intermediate goods featured in the detailed plans of the Soviet Union, which filled 70 volumes, or 12,000 pages, each year.

When the targets are specified as production plans for individual products, the factories react with their own assessments of what is feasible. Reactions as to feasibility are passed back up the hierarchy, and the central planning ministry makes the targets and reports of feasibility consistent. A good deal of bargaining takes place in this process, the superiors demanding the impossible and subordinates claiming requests to be infeasible.

Legally Binding Commands   Once a consistent (even if infeasible) plan has been determined by the planning ministry, the plan is given the force of law in a set of binding commands from the political authority. The commands are translated into increasing detail as they pass down the chain of command and are implemented by the production units in a way that most nearly satisfies the superiors of each level.

Taut and Inflexible Plans   In the former Soviet Union, the targets set by superiors for their subordinates were infeasible. The idea was that in the attempt to do the impossible, more would be achieved than if an easily attained task was set. The outcome of this planning process was a set of taut and inflexible plans. A taut plan is one that has no slack built into it. If one unit fails to meet its planned targets, all the other units that rely on the output of the first unit will fail to meet their targets also. An inflexible plan is one that has no capacity for reactions to changing circumstances.

Faced with impossible targets, factories produced a combination of products that enabled their superiors to report plan fulfilment, but the individual items produced did not meet the needs of the other parts of the economy. No factory received exactly the quantity and types of inputs needed, and the economy was unable to respond to changes in circumstances. In practice, the plan for the current year was the outcome of the previous year plus a wished-for but unattainable increment.

The Market Sector

Although the economy of the Soviet Union was a planned one, a substantial amount of economic activity took place outside the planning and command economy. The most important component of the market sector was in agriculture. It has been estimated that during the 1980s there were 35 million private plots worked by rural households in the USSR. These private plots constituted less than 3 percent of the agricultural land of the Soviet Union but produced close to 25 percent of total agricultural output and one-third of all the meat and milk. Some estimates suggested that the productivity on private plots was 40 times that of state enterprise farms and collective farms. Other economic activities undertaken by Soviet citizens outside the planning system were illegal.

Money in the Soviet Union

Money played a minor role in the economy of the Soviet Union. It was used in the market sector and in the state sector to pay wages and buy consumer goods and services. But all the transactions among state enterprises and between state enterprises and government took place as part of the *physical* plan, and money was used only as a means of keeping records. International trade was undertaken by the direct exchange of goods for goods—barter.

Soviet Economic Decline

Table 38.2 describes the growth performance of the Soviet economy between 1928 and 1990. The economy performed extraordinarily well before 1970. Growth rates of output in excess of 5 percent a year were achieved on the average for the entire period between 1928 and 1970, bringing an eight-fold increase in aggregate output over these years. The growth rate then began to fall. During the 1970s output expanded by 3.2 percent a year, and in the 1980s, growth collapsed to 2 percent a year between 1980 and 1986 and then to only 1 percent a year between 1986 and 1990. In 1990, the economy shrank by 4 percent.

Why did the economy perform well before 1970 and then begin to deliver successively slower growth rates? And what brought the virtual collapse of the Soviet economy during the 1980s? The combination and interaction of three features were responsible. They are

◆ Transition from investment to consumption economy

◆ External shocks

◆ Taut and inflexible plans

Transition from Investment to Consumption Economy

Before 1960, the Soviet economic planners concentrated on producing capital goods and maintaining a rapid rate of investment in new buildings, plant, and equipment. They ran the Soviet economy like a large corporation intent on rapid growth, putting all its profits into yet more growth. The central planning system is at its best when implementing such a strategy. The planners know exactly which types of capital they need to remove or reduce bottlenecks and can achieve a high rate of growth.

TABLE 38.2

Economic Growth Rates in the
Soviet Union

Years	Growth rates (percent per year)
1928–1937	5.4
1940–1960	5.7
1960–1970	5.1
1970–1979	3.2
1980–1986	2.0
1987	1.6
1988	4.4
1989	2.5
1990	–4.0

Economic growth in the Soviet Union was rapid between 1928 and 1970. During the 1970s, growth began to slow down, and the growth rate become successively lower until the early 1990s, when the economy began to contract.

Sources: Paul R. Gregory and Robert C. Stuart, *Soviet Economic Structure and Performance*, 2nd edition (New York: Harper and Row, 1981); U.S. Central Intelligence Agency, *USSR: Measures of Economic Growth and Development, 1950–1980*, U.S. Congress, Joint Economic Committee (Washington, D.C.: U.S. Government Printing Office, 1982); U.S. Central Intelligence Agency, "Gorbachev's Economic Program," Report to U.S. Congress, Subcommittee on National Security Economics, April 13, 1989 (Washington, D.C.: U.S. Government Printing Office, 1989); and The World Bank, *The Economy of the USSR* (Washington, D.C.:1990).

During the 1960s, the orientation of the Soviet economy began to change, with a relative increase in the production of consumer goods and services. By the 1970s and 1980s, this process had gone much further. A centrally planned economy does a very bad job at handling the complexities of producing a large variety of types, sizes, colours, designs, and styles of consumer goods. The planners need to collect and take into account more information than their computers can handle.

As a result, the planners order the wrong goods to be produced, creating surpluses of some and chronic shortages of others. Easy-to-produce plain white bread is available in excessive quantities at give-away prices and hard-to-produce blueberry muffins can't be found at any price. Surplus goods get wasted or used inefficiently, and increasing amounts of the resources that could be used to add to the economy's productive capital get diverted to meeting ever more desperate consumer demands. Gradually, economic growth vanishes.

External Shocks   The Soviet Union is the world's largest producer of crude oil and benefited enormously during the 1970s from the massive oil price increases. The extra revenue obtained from oil exports helped, during those years, to mask the problems just described. But the 1980s brought *falling* oil prices and exposed the problems of the Soviet Union in a sharp light.

During the late 1980s, the countries of Eastern Europe that had been the Soviet Union's traditional trading partners, embarked on their own transitions to market economies and began to look to the West for trading opportunities. As a consequence, the Soviet Union's sources of international trade collapsed.

Another major external shock was the escalation of the arms race. When the United States embarked on the "Star Wars" program, the implications for the Soviet defence program were devastating. Mounting an equivalent program would probably have been impossible, but even a smaller-scale response would have sapped the Soviet economy of its capacity to devote high-technology resources to meeting private consumption demands.

Taut and Inflexible Plans   A flexible economic system might have been able to deal with the switch to consumption goods production and the consequences of a changing world economic environment. But the Soviet economy was not flexible. On the contrary, with its system of taut planning and its unresponsive command structure, it was only able to attempt to produce the same bundle of goods as it had produced in the previous year. With less revenue from oil and other raw material exports, fewer imported inputs could be obtained. Imbalances in the central plan rippled through the entire economy disrupting the production of all goods and putting the system itself under enormous strain.

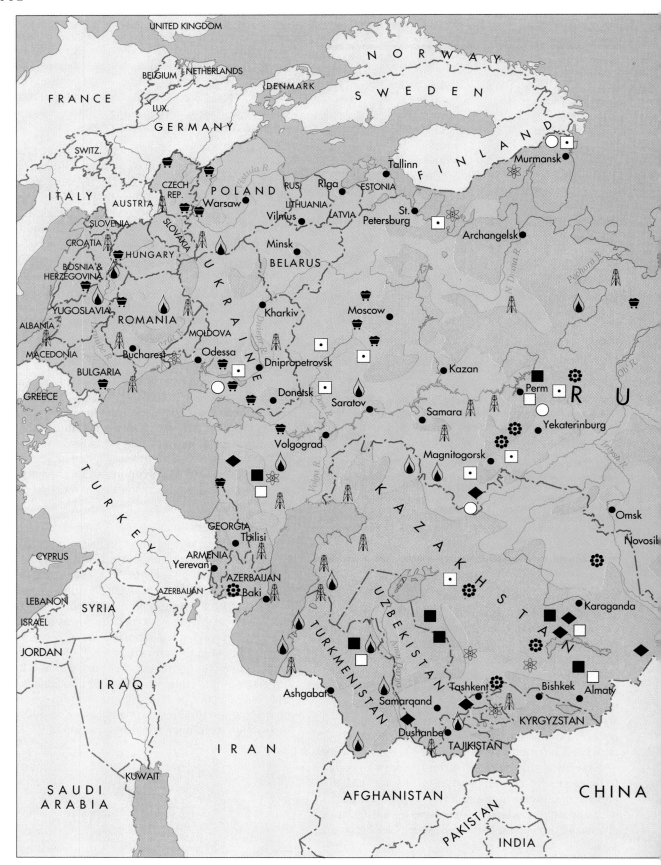

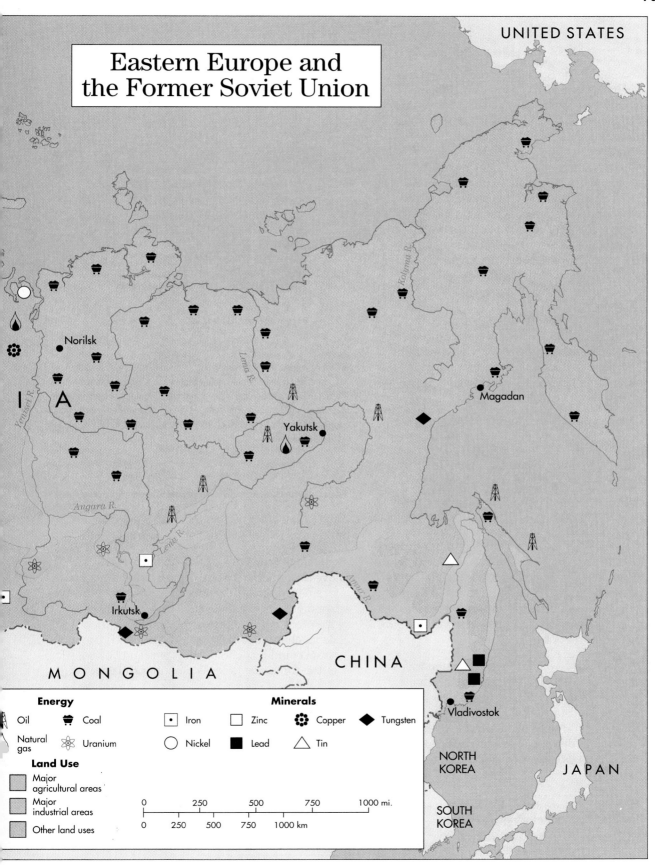

Eastern Europe and the Former Soviet Union

UNITED STATES

Norilsk

Magadan

Yakutsk

Yenisei R.

Lena R.

Kolyma R.

Angara R.

Lena R.

Amur R.

Irkutsk

MONGOLIA

CHINA

Vladivostok

NORTH KOREA

SOUTH KOREA

JAPAN

Energy

Oil   Coal

Natural gas   Uranium

Land Use

Major agricultural areas

Major industrial areas

Other land uses

Minerals

Iron   Zinc   Copper   Tungsten

Nickel   Lead   Tin

0   250   500   750   1000 mi.

0   250   500   750   1000 km

Living Standards in the Late 1980s

The problems of the Soviet economy are put in sharp focus in Figure 38.5, which compares the productivity and consumption levels of the former Soviet Union with those of the United States, Western Europe (Germany, France, and Italy), Japan, and Portugal.[1] As you can see, average worker productivity in the Soviet Union, measured by GDP per worker, is less than 40 percent of real GDP per worker in the United States and lags behind Western Europe and Japan. A similar picture is painted by comparing consumption per worker and consumption per person. The capitalist country whose productivity and consumption are most similar to that of the Soviet Union is Portugal.

Market Economy Reforms

By the end of the 1980s, there was widespread dissatisfaction throughout the Soviet Union with the economic planning system, and a process of transition towards the market economy began. This process had three main elements:

◆ Relaxing central plan enforcement

◆ Deregulating prices

◆ Permitting limited private ownership of firms

Relaxing Central Plan Enforcement   The transition in all three areas was one of gradual change. But the relaxation of central plan enforcement was the fastest and most far-reaching element of the transition. The idea was that by relaxing central control over the annual plan and permitting the managers of state enterprises greater freedom to act like the managers of private firms, enterprises would be able to respond to changing circumstances without having to wait for orders from the centre.

Deregulating Prices   Price deregulation was gradual and covered a limited range of products. Here, the idea was that by removing price controls the price mechanism would be able to allocate scarce resources to their highest-value uses. Shortages would disappear and be replaced by available but sometimes expensive goods and services.

---

[1] The article from which the data for Figure 38.5 were taken does not put Canada in the comparison, but you can regard the United States as being very similar to Canada on the variables displayed.

FIGURE 38.5

GDP and Consumption in the Soviet Union and Other Countries

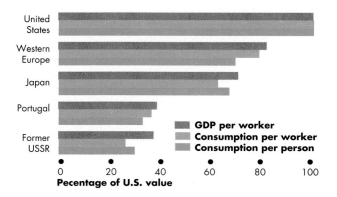

GDP per worker in the Soviet Union in the mid-1980s was less than 40 percent of its level in the United States and similar to the level in Portugal. Consumption per worker and consumption per person were even lower at less than 30 percent of the U.S. level. The Soviet Union lags considerably behind Western Europe and Japan in GDP and consumption level.

Source: Abram Bergson, "The USSR Before the Fall: How Poor and Why," *Journal of Economic Perspectives,* Volume 5, Number 4, Fall, 1991, pp. 29–44.

High prices would strengthen the inducement for producers to increase the quantities supplied.

Permitting Limited Private Ownership of Firms   The move towards the private ownership of firms was extremely gradual. The idea here was that enterprising individuals would be able to move quickly to seize profit opportunities, responding to price signals much more rapidly than the replaced planning system could respond to shortages and bottlenecks. But the transition process ran into problems.

Transition Problems

The three major problems confronting the republics of the former Soviet Union that complicate their transition to the capitalist market economic system are

◆ Value and legal systems alien to capitalism

◆ Collapse of traditional trade flows

◆ Fiscal crisis

Value and Legal Systems   Fifty years of socialist dictatorship have left a legacy of values and memories alien to the rapid and successful establishment of a capitalist, market economy. The political leaders and people of the former Soviet Union have no personal memories of free political institutions and markets. And they have been educated, both formally and informally, to believe in a political creed in which traders and speculators are not just shady characters but criminals. Unlearning these values will be a slow and perhaps painful process.

The legal system is also unsuited to the needs of a market economy in two ways. First, there are no well-established property rights and methods of protecting those rights. Second, and more important, there is no tradition of government behaving like individuals and firms before the rule of law. In the Soviet system, the government *was* the law. Its economic plan and the arbitrary decisions made by superiors at each level in the hierarchy was the only law that counted. Rational, self-promoting actions taken outside the plan were illegal. It will take a long time to establish a legal system based on private property rights and the rule of law.

Collapse of Traditional Trade Flows   A centrally administered empire has collapsed and its constituent republics have decided to create a loose federation. Such a political reorganization can have devastating economic consequences. The most serious of these is the collapse of traditional trade flows. The Soviet Union was a highly interdependent grouping of republics organized on a wheel-hub basis with Moscow (and to a lesser degree Leningrad—now St. Petersburg) at its centre. This view of the Soviet economy is shown in Fig. 38.6. The figure also shows the magnitude of the flows of goods from the republics through the Moscow hub.

The most heavily dependent republic, Belorussia, delivered 70 percent of its output to other republics and received a similar value of goods from the other republics. Even the least dependent republic, Kazakhstan, traded 30 percent of its production with the other republics. The vast amount of inter-republic trade, managed by the central planners and channelled through the Moscow hub, means that individual enterprise managers had (and still have) little knowledge of where their products end up being used or of where their inputs originate.

With the collapse of the central plan, managers must search for supplies and for markets. Until they have built new networks of information, shortages of raw materials and other material inputs will be common and a lack of markets will stunt production. This problem can be solved by the activities of specialist traders and speculators, but the emergence of this class of economic agent is likely to be slow because of political attitudes towards this type of activity.

The collapse of an economic empire does not inevitably lead to a collapse of traditional trade flows and an associated decline in production. But it usually has done so. The most similar collapse this century was that of the Austro-Hungarian Empire in 1919.

FIGURE 38.6

The Wheel-Hub Economy of the Soviet Union

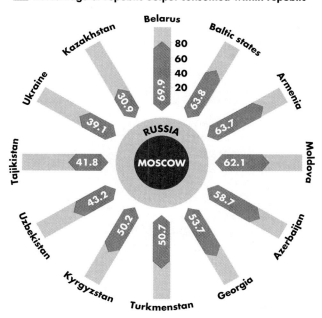

■ Percentage of republic output exported to other republics
■ Percentage of republic output consumed within republic

The Soviet economy was organized on a wheel-hub model. Vast amounts of goods and services were traded among the republics, but mainly through the Moscow hub. The percentages of production in each republic exported to other republics is shown along the spokes of the wheel.

Source: The Economy of the USSR, The World Bank, Washington, D.C., 1990, p. 51.

UNDERSTANDING the Limits of CENTRAL PLANNING

Our economy is a highly planned one. But it is not *centrally* planned. The planning takes place inside corporations. Nevertheless, some corporations are huge. Bell Canada Enterprises, for example, produces services of greater value than the gross domestic product of many countries. If it makes sense to plan the economy of Bell Canada, why doesn't it make sense to plan a national economy?

This question has puzzled and divided economists for many years. The answer given by Friedrich von Hayek is that an economy produces billions of different goods and services while a corporation, even a very large one, produces a very limited range of items. As a consequence, central planning requires the centralization of a vast amount of information that is extremely costly to collect. The market economizes on this information. Households and firms need to know only the prices of the range of goods and services that they buy and sell. No one needs to know every price. And no firm needs to know the technologies for producing anything beyond its area of specialization. Markets find the prices that make the plans of producers and consumers consistent.

But Hayek's answer leaves open another question. Why does Bell Canada plan? Why isn't the market used to allocate resources inside Bell Canada? This question was answered by Ronald Coase. Planning, he explained, economizes on transactions costs, while the market economizes on information costs. There is an optimal size of the planning unit (firm), and an optimal extent of the market for each activity.

The poor economic performances of the former Soviet Union, the other formerly planned Eastern European economies and China before 1978 suggest that planning was taken too far in those countries and that the scope of the market was too restricted. These countries were run like big firms, but the firms were too big.

> **"The more complicated the whole, the more dependent we become on that division of knowledge between individuals whose separate efforts are coordinated by the impersonal ... price system."**
>
> FRIEDRICH VON HAYEK
> *The Road to Serfdom*

Before 1978, the farms of China were operated as part of the national economic plan. The planners decided what would be produced and how the food would be distributed. Peasant farmers received an allocation of food but their rewards were unrelated to their efforts. Food production and living standards were low. In 1978, Deng Xiaoping reformed the farms. Families were permitted to take long-term leases on their land and to decide what to produce and where to sell their products. The result was a massive increase in food production and a rapid increase in the standard of living. By 1984, the farms had become so productive that China became an *exporter* of grain.

Deng Xiaoping's 1978 economic reforms have had dramatic effects on China's large cities and urban population. New laws that permitted the creation of private firms resulted in an explosion of new private enterprises—manufacturing a wide range of consumer goods and providing employment for people who were no longer needed on the increasingly efficient farms. By 1990, real income per person had increased to 2 times its 1978 level. Between 1982 and 1988, real income per person grew at a staggering 9.7 percent a year, almost doubling in six years. Many of the new private firms sell their outputs on world markets and, during the 1980s, China's exports grew at a much faster rate than GDP. By 1990, exports stood at 17 percent of GDP. If current trends continue, China will become the world's economic powerhouse in the twenty-first century.

AN *Alternative Economic Vision*

KARL MARX

Karl Marx (1818–1883) was a social scientist (political scientist, sociologist, and economist) of extraordinary breadth and influence. Born in Germany, he spent most of his adult life in London, using the British Museum as his workplace. With little income, life was harsh for Marx and his wife (his childhood sweetheart to whom he was devoted). Marx's major work in economics was *Das Kapital,* in which he argued that capitalism is self-destructive and will be replaced by a system with no private property and with a central plan in place of the market—a system he called "communism." Events have rejected Marx's theory, and his lasting contribution to modern economics is negligible. But his contribution to modern politics is substantial. "Marxism," a political creed based on Marx's ideas, thrives throughout much of the world today.

Like the Soviet Union, the Austro-Hungarian Empire was a centralized economic system organized with Vienna and Budapest as its hubs. There was a single currency and free trade. The empire was a great economic success, achieving rapid growth of living standards for its people. Following the collapse of the empire, tariffs were introduced, each country established its own currency, trade flows dried up, and economic growth declined.

Fiscal Crisis Under the central planning system of the Soviet Union, the central government collected taxes in an arbitrary way. One source of revenue was a tax on consumer goods, the rate of which was increased to eliminate shortages. With prices now being free to adjust to eliminate shortages, this source of government revenue has dried up. Another source (the major source) of revenue was the profits of the state enterprises. Since the state owned these enterprises, they also received the profits. With the collapse of central planning and the decentralization of control and privatization of state enterprises, this source of revenue has also declined.

Money played virtually no role in the Soviet Union's system of central planning. Workers received their wages in currency and used it to purchase consumer goods and services. But for the state enterprises and the government, money was just a unit for keeping records. With the collapse of central planning, money has become more important, especially for the government. With the loss of its traditional sources of revenue, and with no change in its spending, the government has a large budget deficit. It covers this deficit by printing money, and the result is inflation. The inflation rate during the final six months of the life of the Soviet Union—the first half of 1991—reached close to 200 percent, and it was on a rising path.

Inflation is not an inevitable accompaniment of the collapse of an economic empire, but like the collapse of trade flows, it has happened before. The rate of growth of the newly created currencies of Austria, Hungary, Poland, Romania, and Yugoslavia following the disintegration of the Austro-Hungarian Empire was extremely rapid and led in those countries to hyperinflation. In Poland, the hyperinflation reached an annual rate of 250 million percent.

REVIEW

The Soviet Union's system of central economic planning and state ownership was established in the 1930s. Under this system, a hierarchical administrative structure engaged in an iterative planning process to arrive at a consistent economic plan. The plan was implemented by the political authority issuing legally binding commands that were translated into ever greater detail as they were passed down the chain of command. ◆ ◆ In practice, the plans were infeasible and inflexible and required that each production unit better its previous year's achievement by a target (but infeasible) amount. The system performed well before 1970 but became steadily less effective during the 1970s and 1980s. The system's inflexibility could not cope with the transition from an investment to a consumption economy and with a series of external shocks. As a result, its growth rate slowed and eventually output began to decrease. ◆ ◆ A market reform process was begun that deregulated prices, permitted limited private ownership of firms, and relaxed the enforcement of the central plan. But the value and legal systems, the collapse of traditional trade flows, and a loss of tax revenue and inflation are making the transition extremely costly. ◆

Let's now examine economic transition in Eastern Europe.

Economic Transition in Eastern Europe

The formerly planned economies of Eastern Europe—Czechoslovakia, East Germany, Hungary, and Poland—are also making transitions to market economies. The processes being followed and the problems faced are similar to those of the former Soviet Union. But their problems, although severe, take different forms from those of the Soviet Union. The major differences arise from political factors. Let's take a brief look at the transition process in these countries.

East Germany

For East Germany, the transition from a centrally planned economy has been the most dramatic and the most complete. On October 3, 1990, East Germany united with West Germany. East Germany was a country with 16 million people, 26 percent of the population of West Germany, and with a GDP per person of less than 30 percent of that of West Germany. Even before the formal reunification of the two parts of Germany, East Germany had begun to dismantle its Soviet-style planning system and replace it with a market economy.

The former East Germany adopted the monetary system of West Germany, deregulated its prices, and opened itself up to free trade with its western partner. State enterprises were permitted to fail in the competition with western private firms, private firms were permitted to open up in the former East Germany, and a massive sell-off of state enterprises was embarked upon.

The process of selling state enterprises began by the creation of a state corporation called Treuhandanstalt (which roughly translates as "Trust Corporation"), which took over the assets of the almost 11,000 state enterprises. The idea was to sell off these enterprises in an orderly way over a period of a few years. By November 1991, Treuhandanstalt had disposed of more than 4,000 firms. Most of these firms had been sold to the private sector but about 900 firms were closed down or merged with other firms.

The loss of jobs resulting from this rapid shake-out of state enterprises was large. Even by July 1990, before the two Germanies were reunited, unemployment in East Germany had reached one-third of the labour force. The unemployment rate in the east will remain high for some years, but the safety net of the West German social security system will cushion the blow to individual workers and their families.

East Germany has no fiscal policy crisis and no inflation problem. It has adopted the West German taxation and monetary systems and has assured financial stability. But the transition for East Germany will last for several years, even though it will be the most rapid transition imaginable.

Czech Republic, Slovakia, Hungary, and Poland

The problems facing the Czech and Slovak republics, Hungary, and Poland differ in important ways, but share some common features. And these common features are similar to some of the problems faced by the Soviet Union that we've already seen. The most severe of these are the collapse of traditional trade flows and the loss of traditional sources of government revenue.

Czech and Slovak Republics   Czechoslovakia removed its Communist government in what was called the "Velvet Revolution" in November 1989 and almost immediately embarked on a program of economic reforms aimed at replacing its centrally planned economy with a market system.

The first step in the transition was the freeing of wages, prices, and interest rates. This step was accomplished quickly, but the emergence of well-functioning markets did not immediately follow. Financial markets were especially nervous and a shortage of liquidity created a financial crisis.

The second step in the transition was privatization. Czechoslovakia pursued a so-called two-track policy of "little privatization" and "big privatization." "Little privatization" is the sale or, where possible, the return to their former owners, of small businesses and shops. "Big privatization" is the sale of shares in the large industrial enterprises. One feature of this privatization process is the issue of vouchers to citizens that may be used to buy shares in former state enterprises.

Czechoslovakia's transition was slowed down by the decision of its people to divide the country into two parts and it has not yet reached the point of a positive economic payoff. Real GDP is growing, but very slowly, and unemployment is high.

Hungary   Hungary has been in a long transition towards a capitalist, market economy. The process began in the 1960s when central planning was replaced by decentralized planning based on a price system. It has also established a taxation system similar to that in the market economies. But the privatization of large-scale industry only began in the 1990s and is proceeding slowly.

Because of its extreme gradualism, Hungary's transition is much less disruptive than those in the other countries. But it is feeling the repercussions of the economic restructuring of the other Eastern European countries with which it has traditionally had the strongest trade links, so its rate of economic expansion has slowed substantially in recent years.

Poland   Severe shortages, black markets, and inflation were the jumping-off point for Poland's journey towards a market economy. This journey began in September 1989 when a non-communist government that included members of the trade union Solidarity took office. The new government has deregulated prices and black markets have gone. It has also pursued a policy of extreme financial restraint, bringing the state budget and inflation under control.

Privatization has also been put on a fast track in Poland. In mid-1991, the government announced its Mass Privatization Scheme. Under this scheme, the shares of 400 state enterprises were to be transferred to a Privatization Fund, the shares in which were to be distributed freely to the entire adult population. This method of privatization is like creating a giant insurance company that owns most of the production enterprises and that is in turn owned by private shareholders.

Here, we've described some of the detailed changes occurring in the economies of Eastern Europe as they make their transitions to market economies. Reading Between the Lines on pp. 1066–1067 takes one further look at this process and illustrates the process with the fundamental economic constraint, the production possibility frontier.

Although the transition to the market economy is changing Eastern Europe and the former Soviet Union, it has been going on for longer and has had more dramatic effects on living standards in China. Let's now look at this country.

Economic Transition in China

China is the world's largest nation. In 1990, its population was 1.2 billion—almost a quarter of the world's population. Chinese civilization is ancient and has a splendid history, but the modern nation—the People's Republic of China—dates only from 1949. A compact summary of key periods in the economic history of the People's Republic is presented in Table 38.3 and a map showing some of its key economic features is shown on pp. 1062–1063.

Modern China began when a revolutionary Communist movement, led by Mao Zedong, captured control of China, forcing the country's previous leader, Chiang Kai-shek (Jiang Jie-shi) to retreat to the island of Formosa—now Taiwan. Like the Soviet Union, China is a socialist country. But unlike the Soviet Union, China is largely nonindustrialized—it is a developing country.

During the early years of the People's Republic, the country followed the Soviet model of economic planning and command. Urban manufacturing industry was taken over and operated by the state and the farms were collectivized. Also, following the Stalin model of the 1930s, primary emphasis was placed on the production of capital equipment.

The Great Leap Forward

In 1958, Mao Zedong set the Chinese economy on a sharply divergent path from that which the Soviet Union had followed. Mao called his new path the Great Leap Forward. The **Great Leap Forward** was an economic plan based on small-scale, labour-intensive production. It paid little or no attention to linking individual pay to individual effort. Instead, a revolutionary commitment to the success of collective plans was relied upon. The Great Leap Forward was an economic failure. Productivity increased, but so slowly that living standards hardly changed. In the agricultural sector, massive injections of modern, high-yield seeds, improved irrigation, and chemical fertilizers were insufficient to enable China to feed its population. The country became the largest importer of grains, edible vegetable oils, and even raw cotton.

The popular explanation within China for poor performance, especially in agriculture, was that the country had reached the limits of its arable land and that its population explosion was so enormous that agriculture was being forced to use substandard areas for farming. The key problem was that the revolutionary and ideological motivation for the Great Leap Forward degenerated into what came to be called the Cultural Revolution. Revolutionary zealots denounced productive managers, engineers, scientists and scholars, and banished them to the life of the peasant. Schools and universities were closed and the accumulation of human capital was severely disrupted.

The 1978 Reforms

By 1978, two years after the death of Mao Zedong, the new Chinese leader, Deng Xiaoping, proclaimed major economic reforms. Collectivized agriculture

TABLE 38.3

A Compact Summary of Key
Periods in the Economic
History of the People's
Republic of China

Period	Main economic events/characteristics
1949	◆ People's Republic of China established under Mao Zedong
1949–1952	◆ Economy centralized under a new communist government
	◆ Emphasis on heavy industry and "socialist transformation"
1952–1957	◆ First five-year plan
1958–1960	◆ The Great Leap Forward: an economic reform plan based on labour-intensive production methods
	◆ Massive failure
1966	◆ Cultural Revolution: revolutionary zealots
1976	◆ Death of Mao Zedong
1978	◆ Deng Xiaoping's Reforms: liberalization of agriculture and introduction of individual incentives
	◆ Growth rates accelerated
1989	◆ Democracy movement; government crackdown

was abolished. Agricultural land was distributed among households on long-term leases. In exchange for a lease, a household agreed to pay a fixed tax and contracted to sell part of its output to the state. But the household made its own decisions on cropping patterns, the quantity and types of fertilizers and other inputs to use, and also hired its own workers. Private farm markets were liberalized and farmers received a higher price for their produce. Also, the state increased the price that it paid to farmers, especially for cotton and other nongrain crops.

The results of the reforms of Deng Xiaoping have been astounding. Annual growth rates of output of cotton and oil-bearing crops increased a staggering

fourteen-fold. Soybean production, which had been declining at an annual rate of 1 percent between 1957 and 1978, now started to grow at 4 percent a year. Growth rates of yields per hectare also increased dramatically. By 1984, a country that six years earlier had been the world's largest importer of agricultural products became a food exporter!

The reforms not only produced massive expansion in the agricultural sector. Increased rural incomes brought an expanding rural industrial sector that, by the middle 1980s, was employing one-fifth of the rural population.

China has gone even further and is encouraging foreign investment and joint ventures. In addition, China is experimenting with formal capital markets and now has a stock market.

Motivated partly by political considerations, China is proclaiming the virtues of what it calls the "one country, two systems" approach to economic management. The political source of this movement is the existence of two capitalist enclaves in which China has a close interest—Taiwan and Hong Kong. China claims sovereignty over Taiwan. As such, it wants to create an atmosphere in which it becomes possible for China to be "reunified" at some future date. Hong Kong, a British crown colony, is currently leased by Britain from China and that lease terminates in 1997. When the lease expires, Hong Kong will become part of China. Anxious not to damage the economic prosperity of Hong Kong, China is proposing to continue operating Hong Kong as a capitalist economy. With Hong Kong and Taiwan as part of the People's Republic of China, the stage will be set for the creation of other capitalist "islands" in such dynamic cities as Shanghai.

The results of this move towards capitalism in China are dramatically summarized in the country's real GDP growth statistics. Between 1978 and 1990, real GDP per person grew at an average rate of 7.2 percent a year—a 2.3 fold increase in income per person over the 12 year period. Between 1982 and 1988, real GDP per person grew at a staggering 9.7 percent a year, almost doubling in a six-year period. China is experiencing not only rapid growth of real income per person but also increasing international competitiveness. China now exports many goods which it previously imported—for example, wheat. And its exports have grown during the 1980s at a much faster rate than GDP, and by 1990 stood at 17 percent of GDP. How has China achieved this dramatic success?

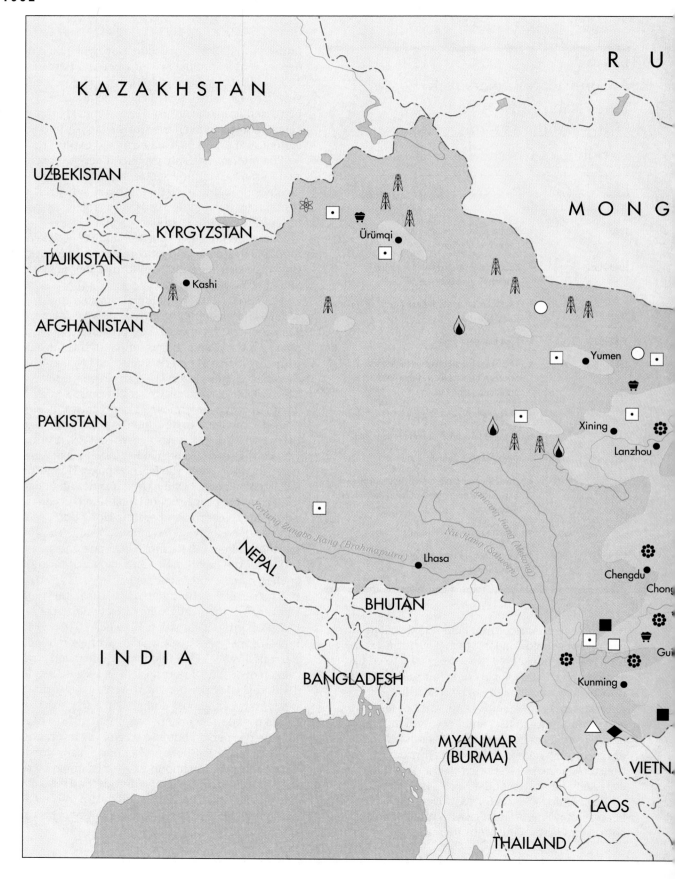

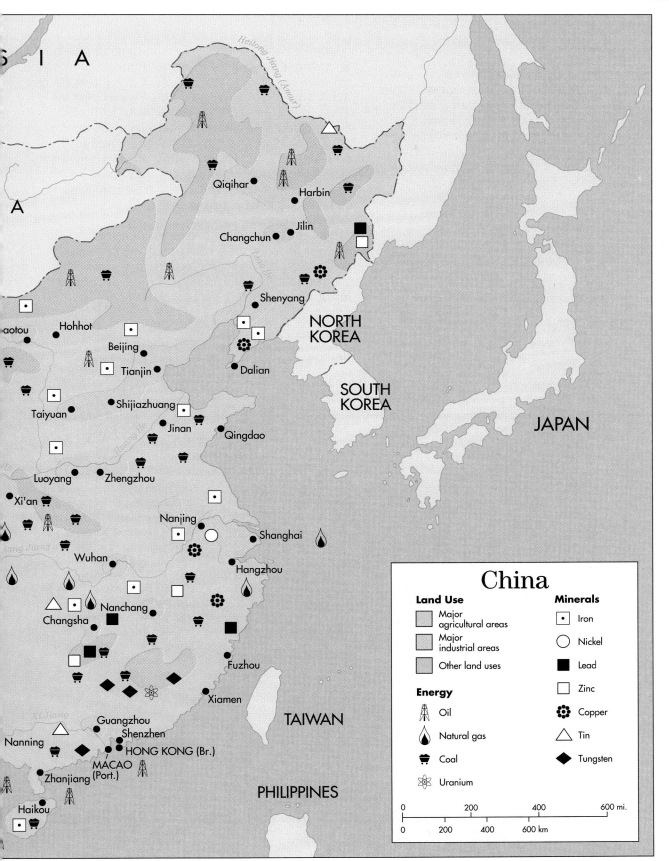

China

Land Use

- Major agricultural areas
- Major industrial areas
- Other land uses

Energy

- ⛏ Oil
- 💧 Natural gas
- ⛏ Coal
- ☢ Uranium

Minerals

- ▫ Iron
- ○ Nickel
- ■ Lead
- □ Zinc
- ❀ Copper
- △ Tin
- ◆ Tungsten

0   200   400   600 mi.

0   200   400   600 km

China's Success

To see how extraordinary China's success has been, look at Fig. 38.7. It shows the consequences of China and the United States maintaining their post-1978 average growth rates of real GDP per person. For the United States, that growth rate was a little over 1 percent a year and for China it was almost 8 percent a year. Maintaining these growth rates China catches up with the United States in a single generation by 2010. Even if China's growth slackens off to 5 percent a year, with no change in the U.S. growth rate, China catches up by 2030.

China's success in achieving a high rate of economic growth has resulted from four features of its reforms.[2] They are

◆ Massive rate of entry of new non-state firms

◆ Large increases in the productivity and profitability of state firms

◆ An efficient taxation system

◆ Gradual price deregulation

Entry of Non-State Firms   The most rapidly growing sector of the Chinese economy during the 1980s has been non-state industrial firms located typically in rural areas. This sector grew at an annual rate of 17.5 percent between 1978 and 1990. In 1978, this sector produced 22 percent of the nation's industrial output. By 1990, it was producing 45 percent of total industrial output. By contrast, the state-owned firms—the firms organized by the state under its national plan—shrank (relatively) from producing 78 percent of total output in 1978 to 55 percent in 1990.

The entry of new firms created a dramatic increase in competition both among the new firms and between the new firms and the state firms. This competition spurred both non-state and state firms into greater efficiency and productivity.

---

[2] This section is based on John McMillan and Barry Naughton, "How to Reform a Planned Economy: Lessons from China," Graduate School of International Relations and Pacific Studies, University of California, San Diego, 1991.

FIGURE 38.7

Economic Growth in China

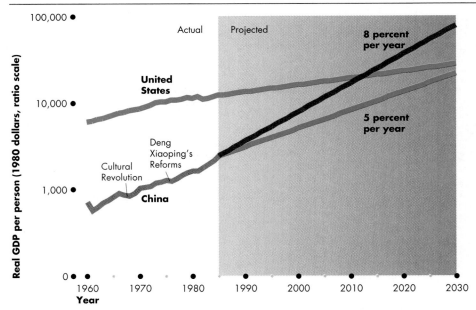

The growth of per capita income in China is strongly influenced by the economic system. During the Cultural Revolution, per capita income fell. Under a central planning and command mechanism in the early 1970s, per capita income grew at a moderate pace. Under capitalist methods of production in agriculture following the 1978 reforms, per capita income growth increased dramatically. If China continues to grow at the pace it has achieved since 1978, and if the United States also maintains its post-1978 growth rate, China will catch up with the United States in 2010. Even if China slows to a 5 percent growth rate, it will catch up with the United States in 2030.

Source: Alan Heston and Robert Summers, "A New Set of International Comparisons of Real Product and Price Levels: Estimates for 130 Countries, 1950-1985," *Review of Income and Wealth,* Series 34, vol. 1, 1988, pp. 1-25, Appendix B.

Increases in Productivity and Profitability of State Firms   China has not privatized its economy by selling off state firms. Instead, privatization has come from the entry of new firms. The state firms have continued to operate. But the government has a strong incentive to ensure that the state firms are profitable. If state firms make no profit, the government collects no taxes from them.

To achieve the greatest possible level of profit and tax revenue, the Chinese economic planners have changed the incentives faced by the managers of state enterprises to resemble those of the market incentives faced by the non-state sector. Managers of state-owned firms are paid according to the firm's performance—similar to managers in private firms.

The Chinese system gives incentives for managers of state enterprises to be extremely enterprising and productive. As a result of this new system the Chinese government is now able to auction off top management jobs. Potential managers bid for the right to be manager. The manager offering the best promise of performance is the one that gets the job.

Efficient Taxation System   Firms (both private and state firms) are taxed but the tax system is unusual and different from that in our own economy. Firms are required to pay a fixed amount of profit to the government. Once that fixed amount of tax has been paid, the firm keeps any additional profit beyond that point. In contrast, the Canadian corporate tax system requires firms to pay a fixed percentage of their profits in tax. Thus, in Canada, more profit means higher taxes while, in China, taxes are set independently of a firm's profit level. The Chinese system creates much stronger incentives than does our own system for firms to seek out and pursue profitable ventures.

Gradual Price Deregulation   China has not abandoned planning its prices. The socialist planning system keeps the prices of manufactured goods fairly high and keeps domestic prices higher than world prices. This pricing arrangement makes private enterprise production in China extremely profitable. In 1978, when the non-state sector was small, the profit rate in that sector was almost 40 percent—for every dollar invested 40¢ a year was earned. With such high profits there was a tremendous incentive for enterprising people to find niches and engage in creative and productive activity. The forces of com-

petition have gradually lowered prices; rates of return, by 1990, had fallen to 10 percent. But the price movements were gradual. There was no big bang adjustment of prices—no abandonment of the planning mechanism and introduction of a rip-roaring free market system.

Growing Out of the Plan

As a result of the reforms adopted in the 1970s and pursued vigorously since that time, the Chinese economy has gradually become a much more market-oriented economy and is, in effect, growing out of its central plan.[3] The proportion of the economy accounted for by private enterprise and market influenced prices has gradually increased and the proportion accounted for by state enterprises and planned and regulated prices has gradually decreased.

To sustain this process, changes in fiscal policy and monetary policy have been necessary. The reform of the economy has entailed the redesigning of the tax system. In a centrally planned economy the government's tax revenues come directly through its pricing policy. Also, the government, as the controller of all financial institutions, receives all of the nation's saving. When the central planning system is replaced by the market, the government must establish a tax collection agency similar to Revenue Canada. Also, it must establish financial markets so that the savings of households can be channelled into the growing private firms to finance their investment in new buildings, plant, and equipment.

Despite the reform of its tax system, the government of China spends more than it receives in tax revenue and covers its deficit by the creation of money. The result is a steady rate of inflation. But inflation in China is not out of control, as it is in the former Soviet Union, because the rapidly growing level of economic activity absorbs a great deal of the new money.

---

[3] Barry Naughton, *Growing Out of the Plan: Chinese Economic Reform*, 1978-90, Graduate School of International Relations and Pacific Studies, University of California, San Diego, 1992.

Success and Failure in Eastern Europe

The Essence of the Story

Hungary, the Czech Republic, and Poland are making economic reforms work.

Bulgaria, Romania, Slovakia, and Ukraine might make reforms work but have not done so yet.

Russia and other ex-Soviet states are not taking the steps necessary to reform their economies.

Reform has succeeded where state enterprises have been privatized on a mass scale, and where large numbers of private businesses have sprung up offering new jobs.

The key to success is accepting that public-sector jobs must become private-sector jobs as quickly as possible and that, in the transition, production will fall and unemployment rise.

THE GLOBE AND MAIL, FEBRUARY 20, 1993

The competition to go capitalist

By Peter Cook

Three years after the fall of the Berlin Wall, Eastern Europe is dividing into two camps. The division is economic, and separates those countries that are making reforms work and those that have failed to make the transition to capitalism.

In the successful category are Hungary, the Czech Republic and Poland, together with two promising but still lagging reformers, Romania and Bulgaria. In the second category are Russia and other ex-Soviet states, though an exception can be made for Ukraine, which has suddenly become a avid reformer. Slovakia, newly divorced from the Czech Republic, is rated a borderline reformer that will probably slip backward in the months ahead....

...reforms succeed best at the local or micro-economic level.

Some ex-communist economies have turned the corner because so many private businesses have sprung up offering new, viable jobs to replace the old, non-viable ones. Reform has been a success where this has happened, a failure where it has not....

In the early days, [where reform has succeeded] a lot of emphasis was put on mass privatization of existing big enterprises. Several countries, such as Poland and Hungary, have done better by liquidating or selling factories cheaply and quickly. The Czech Republic auctioned off some businesses, and is giving away others in a voucher scheme that is open to all its citizens.

However, it is not the old companies but the new ones that will give Poland its first taste of growth this year after four years of declining output; that have brought the unemployment rate in the Czech Republic below 3 per cent; and that has been responsible for Hungary's export boom to the West. For other countries following the model, the key is to accept that public-sector jobs must become private-sector jobs as quickly as possible and that, in the transition, production will fall and unemployment rise.

TROUBLED TRANSITION: EASTERN EUROPE'S NEW ECONOMIC MAP

Poland
Industrial production

Fall in 1989-92	Outlook 1993
-41%	+2%

Inflation	Unemployment rate
+35%	17%

Czech/Slovak Rep.
Industrial production

Fall in 1989-92	Outlook 1993
-35%	0%

Inflation	Unemployment rate
+16%	11%

Hungary
Industrial production

Fall in 1989-92	Outlook 1993
-38%	0%

Inflation	Unemployment rate
+15%	17%

Russia
Industrial production

Fall in 1989-92	Outlook 1993
-20%	-10%

Inflation	Unemployment rate
+3,000%	8%

Romania
Industrial production

Fall in 1989-92	Outlook 1993
-45%	-5%

Inflation	Unemployment rate
+95%	12%

Bulgaria
Industrial production

Fall in 1989-92	Outlook 1993
-46%	-4%

Inflation	Unemployment rate
+60%	15%

Data: Washington Economic Reports, OECD.

New York Times and The Globe and Mail

Background and Analysis

A planned, communist, economy produces on its production possibility frontier, but at the wrong point. It produces too many defence-related goods and capital goods and too few consumer goods and services.

In the figure (part a and b), the planned economy produces at point *a*. The production desired, and that which the market economy would give, is at point *c*. The problem is to get from *a* to *c*.

An unattainable ideal would be to slide around the PPF from *a* to *c*. Such a transition would take resources from the state planned sector and put them immediately to work in the private market sector.

In real economies, the first step to reform is to privatize the state enterprises and to free people to run their own businesses. Initially, talented people are spending most of their efforts setting up and organizing businesses rather than producing goods.

The initial consequence of this reorganization is unemployment. Production and employment fall in the state planned sector *before* they rise in the private market sector.

But a successful reform has incentives in place for private firms to make profits and hire labour. And as the process proceeds, output eventually grows faster in the private market sector than it falls in the state planned sector, and the economy moves towards point *c*, as shown in part (a) of the figure.

Where the state planning system is not replaced by private enterprise, output falls in the state sector, but it does not increase (or does not increase very quickly) in the market sector. So the economy gets stuck at a point such as *b* in part (b).

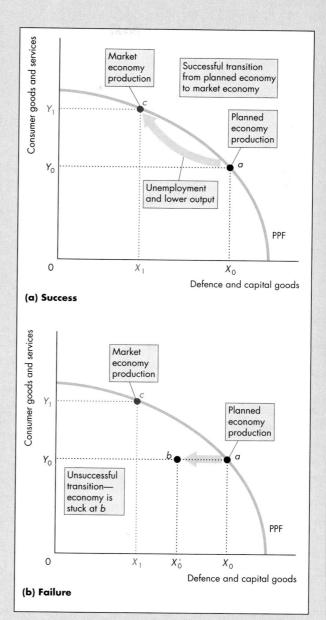

(a) **Success**

(b) **Failure**

Whether China has found a way of making the transition from socialism to capitalism in a relatively painless way is a controversial issue. The violent suppression of the democracy movement in Tiananmen Square in the summer of 1989 suggests that China may have bought economic gains at the expense of political freedom. Because China has retained a strong central government and only gradually changed its system, its experience is not directly useful to the struggling countries of Eastern Europe. But the experiment in comparative *economic* systems currently going on in China is one of the most exciting that the world has seen. Economists of all political shades of opinion will closely watch its outcome, and its lessons will be of enormous value for future generations—whatever those lessons turn out to be.

The Transition from Central Plan to Market

As the countries of Eastern Europe and China abandon their central planning systems, they must make a series of important choices. The key ones are

◆ The style of market economy to adopt

◆ The sequencing of reforms

◆ The speed of reforms

Styles of Market Economy

There is no unique type of market economy, and countries that formerly relied on central planning must choose from an array of possible models. The three main ones are

1. U.S.-style capitalism

2. Japanese-style capitalism

3. Welfare state capitalism

U.S.-Style Capitalism   No country relies on a pure, unregulated market mechanism to solve its economic problem. But the United States comes closer than

any other country to doing so. In the United States, individuals own the factors of production and decide how to use their factors to earn an income. They decide how much of their incomes to save to add to their capital resources, and how much to spend, and on which goods and services. These decisions by more than 250 million individuals are coordinated in markets. Governments (federal, state, and local) regulate these markets, provide public goods and services, and tax income and expenditure. Command mechanisms similar in kind to those used in the centrally planned economies are used in the government sector and by firms in their internal planning processes.

The other types of capitalism depart from the U.S. model mainly in the degree and nature of state intervention in the economy. But there are two distinct styles.

Japanese-Style Capitalism   Japan's economic performance since World War II has been called the "Japanese economic miracle." Emerging from war with an average income per person of less than one-fifth of that in Canada, Japan has transformed itself into an economic giant whose income per person now approaches that of our own. The most spectacular growth period occurred in the 25 years from 1945 to 1970, when per capita income increased eightfold. Today, Japan has a dominant position in world markets for cars and computers, audio and video equipment, and a range of "high-tech" commodities. The Japanese tourist is now as common a sight in London, Paris, and Rome as the U.S. tourist. And there are more Japanese visitors to the United States than U.S. visitors to Japan. What has led to this transformation of Japan into one of the world's richest and most powerful economies?

Three features of the Japanese economy have contributed to its dramatic success: reliance on free-market, capitalist methods; the small scale of government; and pro-business government intervention.

The economic system in Japan is like that in the United States. People are free to pursue their ideas, to own firms, to hire labour and other inputs, and to sell their outputs in relatively free markets.

The Japanese government is the smallest in the capitalist world. Average taxes and government spending account for slightly less than one-fifth of GDP. This contrasts with close to 30 percent in the United States and more than 40 percent in some Western European capitalist countries. A small scale of government means that taxes are low and, therefore, do not constitute a discouragement to work and to save and accumulate capital.

But the Japanese government does intervene in the economy, and its intervention is pro-business. The main vehicle for intervention is the Ministry of International Trade and Industry (MITI)—a government agency responsible for stimulating Japanese industrial development and international trade. In the years immediately following World War II, MITI encouraged the development of basic industries such as coal, electric power, shipbuilding, and steel. It used tariffs and quotas to protect these industries in their early stages of development, subsidized them, and ensured that capital resources were abundantly available for them. MITI is almost entrepreneurial in its activities. During the 1960s, with the basic industries in place, MITI turned its attention to helping the chemical and lighter manufacturing industries. In the 1980s, it helped Japanese industry dominate the world computer market.

MITI not only fosters the growth and development of industries. It also helps speed the decline of those industries that are not contributing to rapid income growth. For example, in the mid-1970s when the price of oil increased dramatically, the smelting of bauxite to create aluminum became inefficient in Japan. Within two years, Japan's bauxite-smelting industry had been closed down, and Japan was importing all its aluminum from Australia. By identifying industries for profitable growth and those for profitable decline, MITI helps speed the adjustment process in reallocating resources to take maximum advantage of technological change and trends in prices.

The result of Japan's economic system and government economic intervention has been a high rate of capital accumulation. There has also been a high rate of accumulation of human capital, especially in the applied sciences. In addition to a high rate of capital accumulation—both physical and human—there has been a high rate of technological advance with no inhibitions about using the best technologies available, wherever in the world they might have been developed.

Welfare State Capitalism   Capitalism in Western Europe is more heavily tinged with socialism than in either the United States or Japan. It is welfare state capitalism. The countries of Western Europe, many

of which now belong to the European Community, are basically capitalist market economies in the sense that most productive resources are owned by private individuals and most resources are allocated by individuals trading freely in markets for both goods and services and factors of production. But the scale of government, and the degree and direction of government intervention, is much larger in these countries than in the United States and Japan.

Government expenditure and taxes range between 40 and 50 percent of GDP in European countries. Tax rates this high create disincentives that result in less effort and lower saving rates than in countries with lower taxes. The European countries also have a large, nationalized industry sector. A **nationalized industry** is an industry owned and operated by a publicly owned authority that is directly responsible to the government. Railways, airlines, gas, electricity, telephones, radio and television broadcasting, coal, steel, banking and finance, and even automobiles are among the list of industries that are either wholly or partly publicly owned in some European countries. Nationalized industries are often managed on a command rather than market principle and usually are less efficient than privately owned, competitive firms.

Increasingly in recent years, European governments have been selling state-owned enterprises. The process of selling state-owned enterprises is called **privatization**. There has also been a retreat, in some countries, from very high tax rates. European countries, impressed by the economic success of Japan and the United States, have reached the conclusion that the greater reliance on capitalism in those economies is, in part, responsible for their economic success and they are seeking to emulate the more successful economies.

The Sequence of Reform

We've seen that socialism and capitalism differ along two dimensions: the ownership of capital and natural resources and the method of resource allocation. The features of a capitalist economy that must be adopted by a socialist economy if it is to make the transition are

◆ Private ownership of capital and natural resources

◆ Market determined prices

In making the transition from socialism to capitalism, a country must choose the order in which to adopt these capitalist features.

By placing firms in private ownership, a formerly socialist economy gets the benefits of strengthened incentives to put resources to work at their most profitable uses. Also, by permitting the free entry of new firms, the economy is able to reap the benefits of increased competition. Both the existing firms and new firms become more efficient. At the same time, the state loses its major source of revenue—the profits of state enterprises. Thus, as industry is privatized, a taxation system must be set up to enable the state to raise the revenue needed to provide public goods and services.

By freeing markets and allowing prices to be determined by supply and demand, a formerly socialist economy gets the benefits of price signals that reflect the relative scarcity of different goods and services. These signals get translated into changes in production. Those items whose prices rise most become highly profitable so their production increases fastest.

But often, the prices that rise the fastest are those on such basic staples as bread and milk. Because food items such as these are a very important part of the budget of the poorest families, when their prices increase sharply, there is great hardship. There is also likely to be political opposition to the reform process.

The Speed of Reform

Since reform brings turmoil, there is a case for doing it slowly—gradualism—and a case for doing it quickly, in a "big bang." The case for gradualism is that the adverse effects of reform are minimized and the transition can be managed and made smooth. The case for a big bang is that the socialist economy is a complete organism and it cannot function unless it is left intact. Remove one piece of the system and the rest ceases to function.

◆ ◆ ◆ The countries that we've studied in this chapter—the former Soviet Union, the countries of Eastern Europe, and China—are undergoing enormous political and economic change. These changes will have repercussions of historic proportions throughout the world economy of the 1990s. No one can foresee what the world economy of the mid-1990s will look like. ◆ ◆ But the world has seen change of historic proportions before. The transformation of the economies of formerly war-torn Germany and Japan into the economic powerhouses of today is one example. Throughout all this change—past, present, and future—our knowledge and understanding of the economic forces that produce the change and are unleashed by it has been gradually improving. There remains a great deal that we do not understand. But we have made a great deal of progress. The economic principles presented in this book summarize this progress and the current state of knowledge. As the world continues to change, you will need a compass to guide you into unknown terrain. The principles of economics are that compass!

SUMMARY

The Economic Problem and Its Alternative Solutions

The economic problem is the universal fact of scarcity. Different economic systems deliver different solutions to the economic problem of determining *what*, *how*, and *for whom* goods and services are produced. Alternative economic systems vary in two dimensions: ownership of capital and land and the incentives people face. Capital and land may be owned by individuals, by the state, or by a mixture of the two. Incentives may be created by market prices, by administered prices and administrative sanctions, or by a mixture of the two. Economic systems differ in the ways in which they combine ownership and incentive arrangements. Capitalism is based on the private ownership of capital and land and on market price incentives. Socialism is based on state ownership of capital and land and on administrative incentives and a central economic plan. Market socialism combines state ownership of capital and land with incentives based on a mixture of market and administered prices. Welfare state capitalism combines the private ownership of capital and land with state intervention in markets that change the price signals that people respond to. (pp. 1043–1048)

Economic Change in the Former Soviet Union

The Soviet Union was founded in 1917 and collapsed in 1991. The economy of the Soviet Union was based on a system of central planning that had four key elements: an administrative hierarchy, an iterative planning process, legally binding commands, and taut and inflexible plans. The Soviet Union had a market sector in which a substantial amount of economic activity took place, especially in agriculture. Money played only a minor role in the economy of the Soviet Union.

The Soviet economy grew extraordinarily quickly before 1970—in excess of 5 percent a year—but during the 1970s, and especially during the 1980s, output growth declined. By the early 1990s, the economy was shrinking. A combination of three features of the Soviet economy caused this deterioration in economic performance: the economy made a transition from being an investment economy to a consumption economy; the economy was hit by serious external shocks; and its taut and inflexible planning system was incapable of coping with these events.

By the end of the 1980s, the Soviet Union began a process of transition towards the market economy. This process had three main elements: the relaxation of central plan enforcement; the deregulation of prices; and the introduction of limited private ownership of firms. The transition was a process of gradual change, but it ran into severe problems. The most important were: value and legal systems alien to capitalism; the collapse of traditional trade flows; and the emergence of a large state budget deficit and inflation. (pp. 1048–1056)

Economic Transition in Eastern Europe

The formerly planned economies of Czechoslovakia, East Germany, Hungary, and Poland are also making transitions to market economies. East Germany's transition has been the most dramatic and the most complete. It has taken the form of a reunification of the two Germanies and the adoption by the former East Germany of West Germany's monetary and taxation system. Price deregulation and privatization have been rapid. The Czech and Slovak republics have deregulated wages, prices, and interest rates and are privatizing their industries by returning

small businesses and shops to their former owners and by issuing vouchers to their citizens that they may use to buy shares in former state enterprises. Hungary began the process of moving towards a market economy during the 1960s, when central planning was replaced by decentralized planning. Hungary has established a taxation system similar to that in the market economies. But the privatization of large-scale industry only began in the 1990s and is proceeding slowly. Poland has deregulated prices, pursued a policy of financial restraint that has brought inflation under control, and put privatization on a fast track. (pp. 1056–1058)

Economic Transition in China

Since the foundation of the People's Republic of China, economic management has been through turbulent changes. At first, China used the Soviet system of central planning. It then introduced the Great Leap Forward, which in turn degenerated into the Cultural Revolution. China at first grew quickly with heavy reliance on state planning and capital accumulation, but growth slowed and, at times, per capita income actually fell. In 1978, China revolutionized its economic management, placing greater emphasis on private incentives and markets. As a consequence, productivity grew at a rapid rate and per capita income increased.

China's success in achieving a high rate of economic growth has resulted from four features of its reforms: a massive rate of entry of new non-state firms; large increases in the productivity and profitability of state firms; an efficient taxation system; and gradual price deregulation. Whether China has found a way of making the transition from socialism to capitalism in a relatively painless way is a controversial issue. But the experiment in comparative *economic* systems currently going on in China is one of the most exciting that the world has seen. Economists of all political shades of opinion will closely watch its outcome, for its lessons will be of enormous value for future generations—whatever they turn out to be. (pp. 1058–1064)

The Transition from Central Plan to Market

In the transition from central planning to the market economy, three important choices must be made: the style of market economy to adopt, the sequencing of reforms, and the speed of reforms.

There are three main types of market economy to choose amongst: U.S.-style capitalism, Japanese-style capitalism, and welfare state capitalism. Two features of Japanese capitalism distinguish it from U.S. capitalism: its smaller scale of government and its pro-business government intervention. The capitalism of Western Europe, welfare state capitalism, is more heavily tinged with socialism than in either the United States or Japan. Government expendi-ture and taxes are much higher there—between 40 and 50 percent of GDP—and more of the manufac-turing sector is state-owned, that is, nationalized.

The main issue in the sequencing of reform is the order in which to privatize the ownership of capital and land and to deregulate prices. The main issue concerning the speed of reform is whether to go slowly—gradualism—or quickly—in a "big bang." (pp. 1064–1066)

K E Y   E L E M E N T S

Key Terms

Capitalism, 1044
Central planning, 1045
Decentralized planning, 1045
Great Leap Forward, 1058
Hierarchy, 1049
Incentive structure, 1043
Market socialism, 1045
Nationalized industry, 1065
Privatization, 1065
Socialism, 1044
Welfare state capitalism, 1045

Key Figures and Tables

Figure 38.1   The Fundamental Economic
                      Problem, 1043
Figure 38.2   Alternative Economic Systems, 1044
Figure 38.3   Capitalism's Solution to the Economic
                      Problem, 1045
Figure 38.4   Socialism's Solution to the Economic
                      Problem, 1047
Table 38.1   A Compact Summary of Key Periods in
                      the Economic History of the Soviet
                      Union, 1049
Table 38.3   A Compact Summary of Key Periods in
                      the Economic History of the People's
                      Republic of China, 1059

R E V I E W   Q U E S T I O N S

1 What is the fundamental economic problem that any economic system must solve?

2 What are the main economic systems? Set out the key features of each.

3 Give examples of countries that are capital-ist, socialist, market socialist, and welfare state capitalist. (Name countries other than those in Fig. 38.2.)

4 How does capitalism solve the economic prob-lem? What determines how much of each good to produce?

5 How does socialism solve the economic prob-lem? What determines how much of each good to produce?

6 How does market socialism determine the price and quantity of each good?

7 Why did the Soviet economy begin to fail in the 1980s?

8 What are the main features of the transition program in the former Soviet Union?

9 What are the main problems faced by the republics of the former Soviet Union?

10 What are the problems faced by the other Eastern European countries as they make the transi-tion to a market economy?

11 Review the main episodes in China's economic management since 1949.

12 Compare the economic growth performance of the United States and China. What do we learn from this comparison?

13 What are the lessons of the economic experi-ment that is going on in China?

GLOSSARY

Above full-employment equilibrium A situation in which macroeconomic equilibrium occurs at a level of real GDP above long-run real GDP.

Absolute advantage A person has an absolute advantage in production if that person has greater productivity than anyone else in the production of all goods. A country has an absolute advantage if its output per unit of inputs of all goods is larger than that of another country.

Aggregate demand The relationship between the aggregate quantity of goods and services demanded—real GDP demanded—and the price level—the GDP deflator—holding everything else constant.

Aggregate demand curve A curve showing real GDP demanded at each price level, holding everything else constant.

Aggregate demand schedule A list showing the quantity of real GDP demanded at each price level, holding all other influences on buying plans constant.

Aggregate expenditure curve A graph of the aggregate expenditure schedule.

Aggregate expenditure schedule A list of the level of aggregate planned expenditure generated at each level of real GDP.

Aggregate income The amount received by households in payment for the services of factors of production.

Aggregate planned expenditure The expenditure that economic agents (households, firms, governments, and foreigners) plan to undertake in given circumstances.

Aggregate quantity of goods and services demanded The sum of the quantities of consumption goods and services that households plan to buy, of investment goods that firms plan to buy, of goods and services that governments plan to buy, and of net exports that foreigners plan to buy.

Aggregate quantity of goods and services supplied The sum of the quantities of all final goods and services produced by all firms in the economy.

Anticipated inflation An inflation rate that has been correctly forecasted (on the average); inflation that is correctly foreseen.

Asset Anything of value that a household, firm, or government owns.

Assumptions The foundation on which a model is built.

Automatic stabilizer A mechanism that decreases the fluctuations in aggregate expenditure resulting from fluctuations in a component of aggregate expenditure.

Autonomous expenditure The part of

aggregate planned expenditure that is not influenced by real GDP.

Autonomous expenditure multiplier The amount by which a change in autonomous expenditure is multiplied to determine the change in equilibrium expenditure that it generates.

Average propensity to consume The ratio of consumption expenditure to disposable income.

Average propensity to save The ratio of saving to disposable income.

Axes The scale lines on a graph.

Balanced budget A government budget in which tax revenue and expenditure are equal.

Balanced budget multiplier The amount by which a change in government purchases of goods and services is multiplied to determine the change in equilibrium expenditure when taxes are changed by the same amount as the change in government purchases.

Balance of payments accounts A country's record of international trading, borrowing, and lending.

Balance of trade The value of exports minus the value of imports.

Balance sheet A statement that lists a firm's assets and liabilities.

Bank of Canada Canada's central bank.

Bank Rate The interest rate at which the Bank of Canada stands ready to lend reserves to the chartered banks.

Barter The direct exchange of goods and services for other goods and services.

Budget balance Total tax revenue minus the government's total expenditure in a given period of time (normally a year).

Budget deficit A government's budget balance that is negative—expenditure exceeds tax revenue.

Budget surplus A government's budget balance that is positive—tax revenue exceeds expenditure.

Business cycle The periodic but irregular up-and-down movement in economic activity, measured by fluctuations in real GDP and other macroeconomic variables.

Canadian dollar index against the G-10 currencies An index that measures the value of the Canadian dollar in terms of its ability to buy a basket of currencies of the group of countries known as G-10, where the weight placed on each currency is related to its importance in Canada's international trade.

Capital All the equipment, buildings, tools, and other manufactured goods used in production owned by a household, firm or government.

Capital account A record of a country's international borrowing and lending transactions.

Capital accumulation The growth of capital resources.

Capital goods Goods that are used in the production process and can be used many times before they eventually wear out.

Capital stock The stock of plant, equipment, buildings (including residential housing), and inventories.

Capitalism An economic system that permits private individuals to own capital resources and market allocation of resources.

Central bank A public authority charged with regulating and controlling a country's monetary and financial institutions and markets.

Central planning A method of allocating resources by command.

Ceteris paribus A Latin phrase that means other things being equal, or other things remaining constant.

Change in demand A shift of the entire demand curve that occurs when some influence on buyers' plans, other than the price of the good, changes.

Change in quantity demanded A movement along a demand curve that results from a change in the price of the good.

Change in quantity supplied A movement along the supply curve that results from a change in the price of the good.

Change in supply A shift in the entire supply curve that occurs when some influence on producers' plans, other than the price of the good, changes.

Chartered Bank A private firm chartered under the Bank Act of 1992 to receive deposits and make loans.

Closed economy An economy that has no links with any other economy.

Command economy An economy that relies on a command mechanism.

Command mechanism A method of determining *what*, *how*, and *for whom* goods and services are produced, using a hierarchical organization structure in which people carry out the instructions given to them.

Commodity money A physical commodity valued in its own right and also used as a means of payment.

Communist country A country in which

there is limited private ownership of productive capital and of firms, there is limited reliance on the market as a means of allocating resources, and government agencies plan and direct the production and distribution of most goods and services.

Comparative advantage A person has a comparative advantage in producing a good if he or she can produce that good at a lower opportunity cost than anyone else. A country has a comparative advantage in producing a good if it can produce that good at a lower opportunity cost than any other country.

Competition A contest for command over scarce resources.

Complement A good that is used in conjunction with another good.

Consumer Price Index An index that measures the average level of prices of the goods and services typically consumed by an urban Canadian family.

Consumption The process of using up goods and services.

Consumption expenditure The total payment made by households on consumption goods and services.

Consumption function The relationship between consumption expenditure and disposable income, other things remaining the same.

Consumption goods Goods that can be used just once.

Contraction A business cycle phase in which there is a slowdown in the pace of economic activity.

Convertible paper money A paper claim to a commodity (such as gold) that circulates as a means of payment.

Cooperation People working with others to achieve a common end.

Coordinates Lines running from a point on a graph perpendicularly to the axes.

Cost-push inflation Inflation that results from a decrease in aggregate supply, which increases costs.

Countervailing duty A tariff that is imposed to enable domestic producers to compete with subsidized foreign producers.

Creditor nation A country that has lent more to the rest of the world than other countries have borrowed from it.

Crowding in The tendency for an expansionary fiscal policy to increase investment.

Crowding out The tendency for an expansionary fiscal policy to increase interest rates, thereby reducing—crowding out—investment.

Currency The bills and coins that we use today.

Currency depreciation The fall in the value of one currency in terms of another currency.

Currency drain An increase in currency held outside the banks. A currency drain reduces the amount of additional money that can be created from a given increase in the monetary base.

Current account A record of receipts from the sale of goods and services to foreigners, the payments for goods and services bought from foreigners, and gifts and other transfers (such as foreign aid payments) received from and paid to foreigners.

Current account balance The trade balance (imports minus exports) plus the interest payments we receive from other countries, less interest payments we make to the rest of the world, plus net gifts.

Curve Any line on a graph, no matter whether it is straight or curved.

Cyclical unemployment The unemployment arising from the slowdown in the pace of economic expansion.

Cyclically adjusted deficit The deficit that would occur if the economy were at full employment.

Debt financing The financing of the government deficit by selling bonds to anyone (household, firm, or foreigner) other than the Bank of Canada.

Debtor nation A country that, during its entire history, has borrowed more from the rest of the world than it has lent to it. It has a stock of outstanding debt to the rest of the world that exceeds the stock of its own claims on the rest of the world.

Decentralized planning An economic system that combines state ownership of capital and land with incentives based on a mixture of market and administered prices.

Demand The entire relationship between the quantity demanded of a good and its price.

Demand curve A graph showing the relationship between the quantity demanded of a good and its price, holding everything else constant.

Demand for labour The quantity of labour demanded at each level of the real wage rate.

Demand for real money The relationship between the quantity of real money demanded and the interest rate, holding constant all other influences on the amount of money that people wish to hold.

Demand-pull inflation Inflation that results from an increase in aggregate demand.

Demand schedule A list of the quantities demanded at each different price when all

other influences on consumers' planned purchases are held constant.

Deposits Multiplier The amount by which an increase in bank reserves is multiplied to calculate the increase in bank deposits.

Depreciation The decrease in the value of the capital stock that results from wear and tear and the passage of time.

Depression A deep business cycle trough.

Desired reserves A bank's deposits multiplied by the desired reserve ratio.

Desired reserve ratio The ratio of reserves to deposits that banks plan to hold.

Developing country A country that is poor but is accumulating capital and developing an industrial and commercial base.

Diminishing marginal product of labour The tendency for the marginal product of labour to decline as the labour input increases, holding everything else constant.

Discouraged workers People who do not have jobs and would like to work but have stopped seeking work.

Disposable income Aggregate income plus transfer payments minus net taxes.

Dissaving Negative saving; a situation in which consumption expenditure exceeds disposable income.

Double coincidence of wants A situation that occurs when person A wants to buy exactly what person B is selling and person B wants to buy exactly what person A is selling.

Double counting Counting the expenditure on both the final good and the intermediate goods and services used in its production.

Dumping The sale of a good in a foreign market for a lower price than in the domestic market or for a lower price than its cost of production.

Econometric model A model economy with numerical values for the marginal propensities to consume and import, and for other economic parameters, which are estimated from data for an actual economy.

Economic activity What people do to cope with scarcity.

Economic growth The expansion of our production possibilities.

Economic theory A generalization that enables us to understand and predict the economic choices that people make.

Economic welfare A comprehensive measure of the general state of well-being and standard of living.

Economics The study of how people use

their limited resources to try to satisfy unlimited wants.

Economizing Making the best use of resources available.

Economy A mechanism that allocates scarce resources among competing uses.

Efficiency wage The wage rate that maximizes profit.

Endowment The resources that people have.

Equation of exchange An equation that states that the quantity of money multiplied by the velocity of circulation of money equals GDP—the price level multiplied by real GDP.

Equilibrium A situation in which everyone has economized—that is, all individuals have made the best possible choices in the light of their own preferences and given their endowments, technologies, and information—and in which those choices have been coordinated and made compatible with the choices of everyone else. Equilibrium is the solution or outcome of an economic model.

Equilibrium expenditure The level of aggregate planned expenditure that equals real GDP.

Equilibrium price The price at which the quantity demanded equals the quantity supplied.

Equilibrium quantity The quantity bought and sold at the equilibrium price.

Excess reserves A bank's actual reserves minus its desired reserves.

Expansion A business cycle phase in which there is a speedup in the pace of economic activity.

Expected inflation rate The rate at which people believe that the price level is rising.

Expenditure approach A measure of GDP obtained by adding together consumption expenditure, investment, government purchases of goods and services, and net exports.

Exports The goods and services that we sell to people in other countries.

Factor cost The value of a good measured by adding together the costs of all the factors of production used to produce it.

Factor incomes approach A measure of GDP obtained by adding together all the incomes paid by firms to households for the services of the factors of production they hire —wages, interest, rent, and profits.

Factor market A market in which the factors of production are bought and sold.

Factors of production The economy's productive resources—land, labour, and capital.

Federal budget A statement of the federal government's financial plan, itemizing programs and their costs, tax revenues, and the proposed deficit or surplus.

Feedback rule A rule that states how policy actions respond to changes in the state of the economy.

Fiat money An intrinsically worthless (or almost worthless) commodity that serves the functions of money.

Final goods and services Goods and services that are not used as inputs in the production of other goods and services but are bought by their final user.

Financial intermediary A firm that takes deposits from households and firms, makes loans to other households and firms and buys securities.

Firm An institution that buys or hires factors of production and organizes them to produce and sell goods and services.

Fiscal policy The government's attempt to influence the economy by using its spending and taxes.

Fixed exchange rate An exchange rate, the value of which is held steady by the country's central bank.

Fixed rule A rule that specifies an action to be pursued independently of the state of the economy.

Flexible exchange rate An exchange rate, the value of which is determined by market forces in the absence of central bank intervention.

Foreign exchange market The market in which the currency of one country is exchanged for the currency of another.

Foreign exchange rate The rate at which one country's money (or currency) exchanges for another country's money.

Foreign exchange reserves The federal government's and Bank of Canada's holdings of gold, foreign currencies and Special Drawing Rights at the International Monetary Fund.

Frictional unemployment Unemployment arising from normal labour turnover—new entrants are constantly coming into the labour market, and firms are constantly laying off workers and hiring new workers.

Full employment A state in which the quantity of labour demanded equals the quantity of labour supplied.

Full-employment equilibrium A macroeconomic equilibrium in which actual real GDP equals long-run real GDP.

GDP deflator A price index that measures the average level of the prices of all the goods and services that make up GDP.

General Agreement on Tariffs and Trade An international agreement that limits government intervention to restrict international trade.

Goods and services All the valuable things that people produce. Goods are tangible, and services are intangible.

Goods market A market in which goods and services are bought and sold.

Government An organization that provides goods and services to households and firms and redistributes income and wealth.

Government debt The total amount of borrowing that the government has undertaken and the total amount that it owes to households, firms, and foreigners.

Government deficit The total expenditure of the government sector minus the total revenue of that sector in a given period.

Government purchases multiplier The amount by which a change in government purchases of goods and services is multiplied to determine the change in equilibrium expenditure that it generates.

Government sector surplus or deficit The difference between taxes (net of transfers) and government purchases of goods and services. If taxes exceed government purchases, the government sector has a surplus; if taxes are less than government purchases, the government sector has a deficit.

Great Leap Forward An economic plan for postrevolutionary China based on small-scale, labour-intensive production.

Gresham's Law The tendency for bad money to drive good money out of circulation.

Gross domestic product The value of all final goods and services produced in the economy in a year.

Gross investment The amount spent on replacing depreciated capital and on net additions to the capital stock.

Hierarchy An organization arranged in ranks, each rank being subordinate to the one above.

Household Any group of people living together as a decision-making unit.

Human capital The accumulated skill and knowledge of human beings which arises from their training and education; the value of a person's education and acquired skills.

Implications The outcome of a model that follows logically from its assumptions.

Implicit contract An informal arrangement that has the force of a formal written contract.

Imports The goods and services that we buy from people in other countries.

Incentive structure A set of arrangements that induce people to take certain actions.

Indirect tax A tax paid by consumers when they purchase goods and services.

Induced expenditure The part of aggregate planned expenditure that varies as real GDP varies.

Industrial country A country that has a large amount of capital equipment and in which people undertake highly specialized activities, enabling them to earn high per capita incomes.

Inferior good A good the demand for which decreases when income increases.

Inflation An upward movement in the average level of prices.

Inflation rate The percentage change in the price level.

Inflationary gap Actual real GDP minus long-run real GDP when actual real GDP is above long-run real GDP.

Injections Expenditures that do not originate with households and that add to the circular flow of expenditure and income—investment, government purchases of goods and services, and exports.

Innovation The act of putting a new technique to work.

Intellectual property The intangible product of creative effort, protected by copyrights and patents. This type of property includes books, music, computer programs, and inventions of all kinds.

Interest rate differential The interest rate on dollar assets minus the interest rate on a foreign currency asset.

Interest rate parity A situation in which interest rates are equal across all countries once the differences in risk are taken into account.

Intermediate goods and services Goods and services that are used as inputs into the production process of another good or service.

International crowding out The tendency for an expansionary fiscal policy to decrease net exports.

International Monetary Fund An international organization that monitors the balance of payments and exchange rate activities.

International substitution effect The change in the quantity of real GDP demanded resulting from a change in the relative price of domestic goods and services and foreign goods and services.

Intertemporal substitution effect The change in the quantity of real GDP demanded resulting from a change in the relative price of goods now and in the future.

Invention The discovery of a new technique.

Inventories The stocks of raw materials, semifinished products, and unsold final goods held by firms.

Investment The purchase of new plant, equipment, and buildings and additions to inventories.

Investment demand The relationship between the level of planned investment and the real interest rate, holding all other influences on investment constant.

Investment demand curve A curve showing the relationship between the real interest rate and the level of planned investment, holding everything else constant.

Investment demand schedule The list showing the quantity of planned investment at each real interest rate, holding all other influences on investment constant.

Keynesian A macroeconomist who regards the economy as being inherently unstable and as requiring active government intervention to achieve stability.

Labour The brain power and muscle power of human beings.

Labour force The total number of employed and unemployed workers.

Labour force participation rate The proportion of the working age population that is either employed or unemployed (but seeking employment).

Labour productivity Total output per person employed.

Laffer curve A curve that relates tax revenue to the tax rate.

Land Natural resources of all kinds.

Law of one price A law stating that any given commodity will be available at a single price.

Leakages Income that is not spent on domestically produced goods and services—saving, taxes (net of transfer payments), and imports.

Liability Something that a firm owes to households and other firms.

Linear relationship The relationship between two variables depicted by a straight line on a graph. A linear relationship is one that has a constant slope.

Liquid asset An asset that is instantly convertible into a means of payment at a known price.

Liquidity trap A situation in which people are willing to hold any amount of money at a given interest rate—the demand curve for real money is horizontal.

Loan A commitment of a fixed amount of money for an agreed period of time.

Local credit union A cooperative organization operating under the Cooperative Credit Association Act of 1992, that receives deposits and makes loans.

Long-run aggregate supply The relationship between the aggregate quantity of final goods and services (real GDP) supplied and the price level (GDP deflator) when there is full employment.

Long-run aggregate supply curve A curve showing the quantity of real GDP supplied and the price level when there is full employment.

Long-run Phillips curve A curve showing the relationship between inflation and unemployment when the actual inflation rate equals the expected inflation rate.

Lorenz curve A curve that shows the cumulative percentage of income or wealth against the cumulative percentage of families or population.

M1 A measure of money that sums currency held outside banks, traveler's checks, demand deposits, and other checkable deposits such as NOW and ATS accounts.

M2+ A measure of money that sums M1, savings deposits, small time deposits, Eurodollar deposits, money market mutual fund shares held by individuals, and other M2 deposits.

Macroeconomic equilibrium A situation in which the quantity of real GDP demanded equals the quantity of real GDP supplied.

Macroeconomic long run A period that is sufficiently long for the prices of all the factors of production to have adjusted to any disturbance.

Macroeconomic short run A period during which the prices of goods and services change in response to changes in demand and supply but the prices of factors of production do not change.

Macroeconomics The branch of economics that studies the economy as a whole. Macroeconomics seeks to understand the big picture rather than detailed individual choices. In particular, it studies the determination of the overall level of economic activity — of unemployment, aggregate income, average prices and inflation.

Managed exchange rate An exchange rate, the value of which is influenced by central bank intervention in the foreign exchange market.

Marginal product of labour The additional real GDP produced by one additional hour of labour input, holding all other influences on production constant.

Marginal propensity to buy domestic goods and services The marginal propensity to consume out of real GDP minus the marginal propensity to import.

Marginal propensity to consume The fraction of the last dollar of disposable income that is spent on consumption goods and services.

Marginal propensity to consume out of real GDP The change in consumption expenditure divided by the change in real GDP.

Marginal propensity to import The fraction of the last dollar of real GDP spent on imports.

Marginal propensity to save The fraction of the last dollar of disposable income that is saved.

Marginal tax rate The fraction of the last dollar of income paid to the government in net taxes (taxes minus transfer payments).

Market Any arrangement that facilitates buying and selling of a good, service, factor of production, or future commitment.

Market economy An economy that determines *what*, *how*, and *for whom* goods and services are produced by coordinating individual choices through markets.

Market price The price that people pay for a good or service.

Market socialism An economic system that combines state ownership of capital and land with incentives based on a mixture of market and administered prices.

Means of payment The method of settling a debt.

Medium of exchange Anything that is generally acceptable in exchange for goods and services.

Menu cost The cost of changing a price or a wage rate.

Microeconomics The branch of economics that studies the decisions of individual households and firms and the way in which individual markets work. Microeconomics also studies the way in which taxes and government regulation affect the allocation of labour and of goods and services.

Mixed economy An economy that relies partly on markets and partly on a command mechanism to coordinate economic activity.

Monetarist A macroeconomist who assigns a high degree of importance to variations in the quantity of money as the main determinant of aggregate demand and who regards the economy as inherently stable.

Monetary base The amount of Bank of Canada notes in circulation, chartered banks' deposits at the Bank, and coins in circulation.

Monetary exchange A system in which some commodity or token serves as the medium of exchange.

Monetary policy The Bank of Canada's attempt to control inflation and the foreign exchange value of our currency and to moderate the business cycle by changing the quantity of money in circulation and adjusting interest rates.

Money Any commodity or token that can be passed on to others in exchange for goods and services.

Money financing The financing of the government deficit by the sale of bonds to the Bank of Canada, which results in the creation of additional money.

Money multiplier The amount by which a change in the monetary base is multiplied to determine the resulting change in the quantity of money.

Money wage rate The wage rate expressed in current dollars.

Multiplier The change in equilibrium real GDP divided by the change in autonomous expenditure.

Nationalized industry An industry owned and operated by a publicly owned authority that is directly responsible to the government.

Natural rate of unemployment The sum of frictional and structural unemployment, or the unemployment rate at which there is no cyclical unemployment.

Negative relationship A relationship between two variables that move in opposite directions.

Net borrower A country that is borrowing more from the rest of the world than it is lending to it; a country with a capital account surplus.

Net domestic income at factor cost The sum of all factor incomes.

Net domestic product at market prices The sum of all factor income plus indirect taxes less subsidies.

Net export function The relationship between net exports and Canadian real GDP, holding constant real GDP in the rest of the world, prices and the exchange rate.

Net exporter A country whose value of exports exceeds its value of imports—its balance of trade is positive.

Net exports The expenditure by foreigners on U.S.-produced goods minus the expenditure by U.S. residents on foreign-produced goods—exports minus imports.

Net importer A country whose value of imports exceeds its value of exports—its balance of trade is negative.

Net investment Gross investment minus depreciation.

Net lender A country that is lending more to the rest of the world than it is borrowing from it; a country with a capital account deficit.

Newly industrialized country A country in which there is a rapidly developing broad industrial base and per capita income is growing quickly.

Nominal GDP The output of final goods and services valued at current prices.

Nominal GDP targeting The attempt to keep the growth of nominal GDP steady.

Nominal money The quantity of money measured in current dollars.

Nonconvertible note A bank note that is not convertible into any commodity and that obtains its value by government fiat.

Nontariff barriers Any action other than a tariff that restricts international trade.

Nontraded good A good that cannot be traded internationally.

Normal good A good the demand for which increases as income increases.

Normative statement A statement about what *ought* to be. An expression of an opinion that cannot be verified by observation.

Official settlements account An account showing the change in a country's official foreign exchange reserves.

Open economy An economy that has trading and financial links with other economies.

Open market operation The purchase or sale of government of Canada securities by the Bank of Canada, designed to influence the money supply.

Opportunity cost The best forgone alternative.

Optimizing The process of balancing benefits against costs and doing the best within the limits of what is possible.

Origin The zero point that is common to both axes on a graph.

Output approach A measure of GDP that sums the value of output in each sector of the economy.

Peak The upper turning point of a business cycle, where an expansion turns into a contraction.

Per capita production function A curve showing how per capita output varies as the per capita stock of capital varies in a given state of knowledge about alternative technology.

Perpetuity A bond that promises to pay a certain fixed amount of money each year forever.

Phillips curve A curve showing the relationship between inflation and unemployment.

Political business cycle A business cycle whose origins are fluctuations in aggregate demand brought about by policies designed to improve the chance of the government being re-elected.

Positive relationship A relationship between two variables that move in the same direction. Such a relationship is shown by a line that slopes upward.

Positive statement A statement about what *is*. Something that can be verified by careful observation.

Preferences People's likes and dislikes and the intensity of those likes and dislikes.

Price index A measure of the average level of prices in one period as a percentage of their average level in an earlier period.

Price level The average level of prices as measured by a price index.

Private debt money A loan that the borrower promises to repay in currency on demand.

Private enterprise An economic system that permits individuals to decide on their own economic activities.

Private sector surplus or deficit The difference between saving and investment.

Privatization The process of selling publicly owned enterprises to private individuals and firms.

Production The conversion of land, labour, and capital into goods and services.

Production function The relationship showing how output varies as the employment if inputs is varied.

Production possibility frontier The boundary between those combinations of goods and services that can be produced and those which cannot.

Productivity The amount of output produced per unit of inputs used to produce it.

Property Anything of value that is owned.

Property rights Social arrangements that govern the ownership, use, and disposal of property.

Protectionism The restriction of international trade.

Purchasing power parity A situation that occurs when money has equal value across countries.

Quantity demanded The amount of a good or service that consumers plan to buy in a given period of time at a particular price.

Quantity of Canadian dollar assets The stock of net financial assets denominated in Canadian dollars held outside the Bank of Canada and the government of Canada.

Quantity of labour demanded The number of labour hours hired by all the firms in an economy.

Quantity of labour supplied The number of hours of labour services that households supply to firms.

Quantity supplied The amount of a good or service that producers plan to sell in a given period of time at a particular price.

Quantity theory of money The proposition that an increase in the quantity of money leads to an equal percentage increase in the price level.

Quota A restriction on the quantity of a good that a firm is permitted to produce or that a country is permitted to import.

Rational choice The choice that, among all possible choices, best achieves the goals of the person making the choice.

Rational expectation A forecast based on all the available relevant information.

Real business cycle theory A theory that aggregate supply fluctuations alone are responsible for the business cycle; theory of aggregate fluctuations based on flexible wages and random shocks to the economy's aggregate production function.

Real deficit The change in the real value of outstanding government debt.

Real GDP The output of final goods and services valued at prices prevailing in the base period.

Real interest rate The interest rate paid by a borrower and received by a lender after taking into account the change in the value of money resulting from inflation.

Real money The quantity of goods and services that money will buy.

Real money balances effect The change in the quantity of real GDP demanded resulting from a change in the quantity of real money.

Real wage rate The wage rate per hour expressed in constant dollars.

Recession A downturn in the level of economic activity in which real GDP falls in two successive quarters.

Recessionary gap Long-run real GDP minus actual real GDP when actual real GDP is below long-run real GDP.

Relative price The ratio of the price of one good to the price of another good.

Reservation wage The lowest wage rate at which a person or household will supply labour to the market. Below that wage, a person will not work.

Reserve ratio The fraction of a bank's total deposits that are held in reserves.

Reserves Cash in a bank's vault plus the bank's deposits with the Bank of Canada.

Saving Disposable income minus consumption expenditure.

Saving function The relationship between saving and disposable income, other things remaining the same.

Scarcity The universal state in which wants exceed the resources available to satisfy them.

Scatter diagram A diagram that plots the value of one economic variable associated with the value of another.

Security A marketable asset that can be sold at a moment's notice at a price that fluctuates.

Self-sufficiency A state that occurs when people produce only enough for their own consumption.

Short-run aggregate production function The relationship showing how real GDP varies as the quantity of labour employed varies, holding constant the inputs, including the capital stock and state of technology.

Short-run aggregate supply The relationship between the aggregate quantity of final goods and services (real GDP) supplied and the price level (the GDP deflator), holding everything else constant.

Short-run aggregate supply curve A curve showing the relationship between the quantity of real GDP supplied and the price level, holding everything else constant.

Short-run aggregate supply schedule A list showing the quantity of real GDP supplied at each price level, holding everything else constant.

Short-run Phillips curve A curve showing the relationship between inflation and unemployment, holding constant the expected inflation rate and the natural rate of unemployment.

Short-run production function The relationship showing how output varies when the quantity of labour employed varies, holding constant the quantity of capital and the state of technology.

Slope The change in the value of the variable measured on the y-axis divided by the change in the value of the variable measured on the x-axis.

Socialism An economic system based on state ownership of capital and land and on an incentive system based on administered prices or sanctions arising from a central economic plan.

Specialization Concentrating on the production of only one good or a few goods.

Standard of deferred payment An agreed measure that enables contracts to be written for future receipts and payments.

Store of value Any commodity or token that can be held and exchanged later for goods and services.

Structural unemployment The unemployment that arises when there is a decline in the number of jobs available in a particular region or industry.

Subsidy A payment made by the government to producers that depends on the level of output.

Substitute A good that can be used in place of another good.

Supply The entire relationship between the quantity supplied of a good and its price.

Supply curve A graph showing the relationship between the quantity supplied and the price of a good, holding everything else constant.

Supply of labour The quantity of labour supplied at each real wage rate.

Supply schedule A list of quantities supplied at different prices, holding everything else constant.

Tariff A tax that is imposed by the importing country when a good crosses an international boundary.

Tax base The activity on which a tax is levied.

Tax multiplier The amount by which a change in taxes is multiplied to determine the change in equilibrium expenditure that it generates.

Tax rate The percentage rate at which a tax is levied on a particular activity.

Technological progress The development of new and better ways of producing goods and services. **Technology** The method for converting endowments (the resources people have) into goods and services.

Time-inconsistency problem A situation that occurs when a plan looks good when viewed from one point in time, but bad when viewed from a different point in time.

Time-series graph A graph that measures time on the x-axis and the variable or variables in which we are interested on the y-axis.

Trade balance The value of exports minus the value of imports.

Transfer payments Payments made by the government to households under social programs, including pensions and unemployment benefits.

Transfer payments multiplier The amount by which a change in transfer payments is multiplied to determine the change in equilibrium expenditure that it generates.

Trend A general tendency for a variable to rise or fall.

Trough The lower turning point of a business cycle, where a contraction turns into an expansion.

Trust and Mortgage Loan Company A privately owned financial intermediary, operating under the Trust and Loan Companies Act of 1992, that receives deposits and makes loans and in addition acts as a trustee for pension funds and for estates.

Twin deficits The government sector deficit and the current account deficit.

Unanticipated inflation Inflation that catches people by surprise.

Underdeveloped country A country in which there is little industrialization, limited mechanization of the agricultural sector, very little capital equipment, and low per capita income.

Underdevelopment trap A situation in which a country is locked into a low per capita income situation that reinforces itself.

Underground economy All economic activity that is legal but unreported.

Unemployment A state in which there are qualified workers who are available for work at the current wage rate and who do not have jobs.

Unemployment equilibrium A situation in which macroeconomic equilibrium occurs at a level of real GDP below long-run real GDP.

Unemployment rate The number of people unemployed expressed as a percentage of the labour force.

Unit of account An agreed measure for stating the prices of goods and services.

Value added The value of a firm's output minus the value of the intermediate goods bought from other firms.

Value of money The amount of goods and services that can be bought with a given amount of money.

Velocity of circulation The average number of times a dollar of money is used annually to buy the goods and services that make up GDP.

Voluntary export restraint An agreement between two governments in which the government of the exporting country agrees to restrain the volume of its own exports. Voluntary export restraints are often called VERs.

Wants The unlimited desires or wishes that people have for goods and services.

Welfare state capitalism An economic system that combines the private ownership of capital and land with state interventions in markets that change the price signals that people respond to.

x-axis The horizontal line on a graph.

x-coordinate A line running from a point on a graph horizontally to the y-axis. It is called the x-coordinate because its length is the same as the value marked off on the x-axis.

y-axis The vertical line on a graph.

y-coordinate A line running from a point on a graph vertically to the x-axis. It is called the y-coordinate because its length is the same as the value marked off on the y-axis.

INDEX

Key concepts and pages where they are defined appear in boldface.

Above-full employment equilibrium, 662
Absolute advantage, 62, 974
Actual reserves, 749
Adjustment costs
   international trade and, 978-979
Advantage
   absolute, 62, 974
   comparative, 60, 971
Aggregate demand, 650, 650-656, 906-907
   aggregate expenditure and, 706
   changes in, 651-652, 655
   cost push inflation and, 865-866
   expectations and, 654
   feedback rules and, 925
   fiscal and monetary influences on, 792-812
   fiscal policy and, 652-653, 726-727, 822-823
   inflation and, 862-863
   international factors and, 653-654
   international substitution effect and, 652
   intertemporal substitution effect and, 652
   IS-LM model of, 824-828
   macroeconomic equilibrium and, 661-666
   monetary policy and, 653, 798-802, 823
   money and, 779-781
   real money balance effect and, 653-654
   recession and, 891-892
   recent trends in Canadian economy and, 666-672
   stimulation of economic growth and, 1036-1037
   time lags in influences on, 654-655
Aggregate demand curve, 650, 652-653
   derivation of, 821-822
   downward slope of, 651
   fiscal policy and, 822-823
   monetary policy and, 823-824
   shifts of, 655
Aggregate demand schedule, 650
   Aggregate demand shocks
   feedback rules and, 925
   fixed rules and, 925
   stabilization policy and, 924-928
Aggregate expenditure
   aggregate demand and, 706
   components of, 682-683, 810
   fluctuations in, 683
   output and income, 634
   real GDP and, 702-703
Aggregate expenditure curve, 702, 702-703
Aggregate expenditure schedule, 702, 702-703
Aggregate fluctuations
   changes in aggregate demand and, 663-665
   changes in aggregate supply and, 665-666
Aggregate income, 623
   aggregate expenditure, equality and, 624-625
Aggregate planned expenditure, 702
   price level and, 706-708
Aggregate quantity of goods and services demanded, 650
Aggregate quantity of goods and services supplied, 656

Aggregate supply, 656-661
   changes in, 667-668
   cost-push inflation and, 865, 929-930
   with flexible wages, 842-844
   long-run, 658-659, 660-661
   macroeconomic equilibrium and, 661-666
   money and, 779-781
   physical limit to real GDP and, 658
   recession and, 891-892
   recent trends in Canadian economy and, 666-672
   with sticky wages, 846-848
   short-run, 656-657, 659-661
   stabilization policy and, 928-934
   two economic time frames and, 656
Aggregate supply curve(s)
   long-run, 658
   shifts in, 659-661
   short-run, 656
Anticipated inflation, 607, 862, 871-873,
   costs of, 872
   effects on borrowers and lenders, 878-879
   interest rates and, 878
   problem of, 607
   stopping, 872
Arbitrage, 1011-1012
Asset, 746. *See also* Capital; Wealth
   liquid, 743
   prices of, interest rates and, 757-758
Assumptions, 19, 19-20
   ceteris paribus (other things being equal), 44-45
Automatic stabilizer, 725, 725-726
   government budget and, 725
Autonomous expenditure, 714
   change in, 716-717
Autonomous expenditure multiplier, 717
   See also Multiplier
Average propensity to consume, 688
Average propensity to save, 688
Axes, 29

Balanced budget, 941
Balanced budget multiplier, 723, 723-724
Balance of payments accounts, 995, 995-996
   Canada's, 995-996
   international borrowing and lending, 996-997
Balance of payments deficit, 594
Balance of trade, 968
   Canada's, 969
   international borrowing and, 969
Balance sheet, 746
   of Bank of Canada, 768-769
Balanced trade, 972
Bank(s)
   central, 765
   chartered, 746-747
   creation of money by, 749-752
   Bank of Canada, 765-769
   limit to lending, 749-751
Bank of Canada, 642, 765, 765-769, 784, 912-914, 932-933 *See also* Fiscal

   policy; Monetary policy; Stabilization policy in action, 775-778
   balance sheet of, 768-769
   federal government and, 766-767
   independent, 936
   international constraints on, 767
   open market operations of, 768
   origins of, 765
   policy tools of, 767-768
   predicting, 778
   stabilization problem and, 918
   structure of, 765-766
Bank of Canada Act, 932
Bank rate, 767
Bank reserves, monetary base and, 769-771
Barrow, Robert, 955, 956
Barter, 66, 738
Bergson, Abrum, 1054n
Borrower(s). *See also* Loans
   net, 996
   unanticipated inflation and, 878
Borrowing and lending, international, 996-997
Bouey, Gerald, 765, 775
Bryce, Robert, 687, 933
Buckley, A.H., 783n
Budget
   balanced, 941
   federal, 941-945. *See also* Budget deficit
Budget balance, 941
Budget deficit, 3, 913, **941**, 941-958
   business cycle and, 944-945
   crowding out, 953-955
   cyclically adjusted, 945
   eliminating, 956-958
   financing, 950-952
   future generations burden and, 953-956
   inflation and, 949, 950-953
   international evidence and, 952-953
   nominal, 949-950
   real, 948-950
   in recovery, 945
   Ricardian equivalence, 955-956
   sources of, 941-945
   story of, 944
   unemployment and, 944
Budget surplus, 941
Business cycle, 612, 612-616, 932 *See also* Real business cycle theory
   budget deficit and, 944-945
   inflation and, 615
   political, 920
   stock market and, 614-615
   unemployment and, 613
   Our Advancing Knowledge: Understanding Business Cycles, 906-907

Canada
   balance of payments in 1992, 995-996
   Bank of, 765-769
   borrowing for consumption or investment, 1000
   budget deficit in. *See* Budget deficit
   consumption function in, 690-691
   demand for labour in, 836
   demand for money in, 756-757

deposits multiplier in, 751
economic growth in, 832
economy from 1971-1992, 670-671
economy in 1990s, 889-899
economy in 1992 in, 666-667
exports and imports, 967
free trade agreement with the United
  States, 669
goods and services tax (GST), 559-563,
  669-672
growth, inflation, and cycles in 667-668
inflation and interest rates in, 879-882
inflation and money growth in, 783
insurance industry in, 467-468
international trade of, 967-969
investment demand in, 696-697
money today in, 742-745
multiplier in, 731-732, 773-774
national income and expenditure accounts,
  629-635
Phillips curve in, 875-876
Canada-United States free trade agreement,
  669, 932, 985-989
  changing pattern of Canada-U.S. trade, 989
  terms of, 985-989
**Canadian dollar index against the G-10
currencies, 1003**
Canadian economy in 1990s, 889-899
  aggregate demand and aggregate supply
    and, 891-892
  correct labour market theory and, 898-899
  depression and, 889
  expenditure and, 892
  flexible wage theory and, 896-898
  labour market and, 894
  money market and, 893
  recession and, 890-893
Canadian economy, recent trends and cycles
  in, 668-674
Canada-United States Free Trade
    Agreement and, 671
  evolving economy, 1971-1992, 670-671
  Goods and Services Tax and, 671-674
  growth, inflation, cycles and, 669-670
Capital account, 995
Capital accumulation, 57, 1029-1030
  technological change and, 57-58
Capital consumption. *See* Depreciation
Capital goods, 51
Capitalism, 66, 1044
  property rights in, 66
  socialism compared with, 1045-1046
  solution to economic problem and, 1045
  welfare state, 1045
Capital stock, 630
Central bank, 765
  independent, 766
  subservient, 766-767
Central planning, 1044
  transition to market plan from, 1068-1070
  Our Advancing Knowledge: Understanding
    the Limits of Central Planning, 1056-
    1057
Ceteris paribus (other things being equal),
  44, 44-45
Change in demand, 75-77, **77,** 92-93
changes in price and quantity traded and,
  84-85, 88-89

change in quantity demanded versus, 77
Change in price and quantity, predicting, 84-93
Change in supply, 79-82, **80,** 92-93
  changes in price and quantity traded and,
    85-88, 88-89
  change in quantity supplied versus, 80-81
Change in the quantity demanded, 77
Change in the quantity supplied, 80, 80-81
Chartered bank, 746, 746-747
Cheque(s), money measurement and, 743-744
China, economic transition in, 1060-1068
  gradual price deregulation and, 1065
  growing out of the plan, 1065-1068
  Great Leap Forward in, 1060
  map of, 1062-1063
  1978 reforms in, 1060-1064
  success and, 1064-1065
Circular flow, 623-629
  income and expenditure accounts and,
    623-629
  in simplified economy, 623-629
Circulation, velocity of. *See* Velocity of
  circulation
Closed economy, 16
Command economy, 15
Command mechanism, 14
Commodity money, 739, 739-740
Communist country, 1026,
Communist country, former, 1026-1027
Comparative advantage, 60, 962, **971**
  opportunity cost and, 970-971
Compensation of employees. *See* Earnings;
  Income(s); Wage(s)
Competition, 11,
Complement, 75
Constant GDP. *See* Real GDP
Consumer Price Index, 635, 636
  cost of living and, 639-640
Consumption, 51
  average propensity to consume and, 688
  international trade and, 972-974
  marginal propensity to consume and,
    688-690
  Soviet Union in, 1050-1051
Consumption expenditure, 594, 623,
    684-692
  average propensities to consume and to
    save and, 688
  Canadian consumption function and,
    690-691
  consumption function and saving function
    and, 684-688
  disposable income and, 684
  marginal propensities to consume and to
    save and, 688-690
  saving and, 684
Consumption function, 684
  Canadian, 690-691
  saving function and, 684
  Our Advancing Knowledge: Discovering
    the Consumption Function, 686-687
Consumption goods, 51
Contraction, 612
Convertible paper money, 740, 740-741,
  768
  fractional backing of, 740-741
Cooperation, 11
Coordinates, 29, 29-30

Coordination mechanism(s), 14-16
Cost(s)
  dollar, 10
  of factors. *See* Factor cost
  international trade, 974
  opportunity. *See* Opportunity cost
  time, 10
Cost-price inflation spiral, 866-867
Cost-push inflation, 865, 865-867, 929-930
Cost of living, Consumer Price Index and,
  639-640
Countervailing duty, 984
Cournot, Antoine-Augustin, 87
Coyne, James, 765, 766, 932
CPI. *See* Consumer Price Index
Credit cards, money measurement and,
  743-744
Creditor nation, 997
Crime
  unemployment and, 604
Crow, John 765, 778, 905, 921
  interview, 911-914
Crowding in, 798
Crowding out, 798, 953-955
  international, 798
Currency, 741
Currency depreciation, 1003
Currency drain, 770
Current account, 995
Current account balance, 616, 997-998
Current account deficit
  does it matter, 1000
  effects of government deficit on, 1000
Current dollar GDP. *See* Nominal GDP
Curve, 38
Cycles, growth and inflation in the Canadian
  economy, 667-668
Cyclical unemployment, 601
Cyclically adjusted deficit, 945
Czech Republic, economic transition in, 1059

Davis, Steve, 854n
Debt
  federal government, 941
Debt financing, 950, 950-951, 951-952
Debtor nation, 997
Decentralized federalism, 677
Decentralized planning, 1045
Decision maker, 13, 13-14
Decisions, 14
Deficit, 595, 677
  business cycle and, 944-945
  federal. *See* Budget deficit
  story of, 944
  sources of, 941-945
  Reading Between the Lines: Government
    Deficits, 946-947
Demand, 73, 73-77
  aggregate. *See* Aggregate demand
  for Canadian-dollar assets, 1004-1006
  change in, 440-441
  determining buying plans and, 73
  elasticity of. *See* Elasticity of demand
  income elasticity of. *See* Income elasticity of
    demand
  investment, 694-695
  for labour. *See* Demand for labour

law of, 73
  for money, 752-757
  price elasticity of. *See* Elasticity of demand
  quantity demanded and, 73
  willingness to pay and, 74
  Our Advancing Knowledge: Understanding
    the Laws of Demand and Supply, 86-87
  Reading Between the Lines: Demand and
    Supply In Action, 90-91
Demand curve, 73-74, **74**
  aggregate, 650, 652-653
  investment, 694
  movement along, 76-77
  shift in, 76-77
  willingness to pay and, 74, 83
Demand for labour, 834, 834-836
  in Canada, 836
  changes in, 835-836
  diminishing marginal product and, 834-835
  in economy, 835
Demand for money, 752-757
  in Canada, 756-757
  financial innovation and, 755-757
  influences on holding money and, 753-754
  interest sensitivity of investment demand
    and, 806
  motives for holding money and, 752-753
  real money and, 754, 755-757
  shifts in, 755
Demand-pull inflation, 862, 862-865
  effect of increase in aggregate demand on,
    862-863
  price-wage inflation spiral, 864-865
  wage response to, 863-864
Demand for real money, 754, 754-757
  curve, shifts in, 755
Demand schedule, 73, 73-74
Deposits multiplier, 751
Depreciation, 631
  of currency, 1003
Depression, 613, 906 *See also* Great
  Depression
  Canadian in 1990s, 889
  Reading Between the Lines: Depression
    Persists, 902-903
Desired reserves, 749
Desired reserve ratio, 749
Developing country, 1026
  Diefenbaker, John, 932
**Diminishing marginal product of labour,
  831**
  demand for labour and, 834-835
Discouraged workers, 599
Disposable income, 627, 684
Dissaving, 684
  Division of labour, 22
  Dollar, foreign exchange and, 1001-1003
  interest rates and, 779
  Reading Between the Lines: Defending
    The Dollar, 1014-1015
  Dollar assets
    demand for, 1004-1006
    market for, 1007-1008
    quantity of, 1004
    supply of, 1006-1007
Double coincidence of wants, 738
Double counting, 633
Dumping, 984

Dupuit, Arsène-Jules-Émile-Juvenal, 86, 87
Duties, countervailing, 984

Earnings, 7. *See also* Compensation rules;
    Income(s); Wage(s)
East Germany, 1059
Eastern Europe, 963, 1058-1060
  economic transition in, 1058-1060
  Czech Republic and Slovakia, 1059
  East Germany, 1059
  Hungary and Poland, 1059-1060
  map of, 1052-1053
  Reading Between the Lines: Success
    and Failure in Eastern Europe,
    1066-1067
Econometric models, 731
  of Canadian economy, 731
Economic accounting
  Our Advancing Knowledge: The Develop-
    ment of Economic Accounting, 642-643
Economic activity, 9, 9-10
Economic boom, 906
Economic equality, real GDP and, 644
Economic growth, 57, 57-60, **831,** 831-832
  in Canada, 832
  capital accumulation and technological
    growth and, 57-58, 831
  obstacles to, 1032-1035
  overcoming obstacles to, 1035-1038
  rates of, income levels and, 1028-1029
  in real world, 59-60
  technological change and, 831
  variable growth rates and, 832
Economic model,
  implications of, 20-21
  macroeconomic, 21
  microeconomic, 20-21
Economic problems, alternative solutions and,
    1043-1048
  alternative economic systems, 1043-1045
  alternative systems compared, 1045-1046
  socialism's solution to the economic
    problem, 1047
Economic science, 17-21
Economic stabilization
  Our Advancing Knowledge: Evolving
    Approaches to Economic Stabilization,
    932-933
Economic systems, 7, 1043-1066. *See also*
    Capitalism; Socialism
  alternatives and, 1043-1045
  in China, 1048-1050
  comparison of, 1045-1046
  fundamental economic problem and, 1043
  in Soviet Union, 1048-1056
  in Eastern Europe, 1058-1060
Economic theory, 18
  models and reality and, 21
Economic transition
  in Eastern Europe, 1058-1060
  in China, 1060-1068
  sequence of, 1069-1070
  speed of, 1070
Economic wealth
  Our Advancing Knowledge: Understanding
    the Sources of Economic Wealth, 22-23
Economic welfare, 640

Economics, 9,
  economic models and, 18-21
  observation and measurement in, 18
  positive and normative statements and,
    17-18
  theory and, 18
Economies of scale
  international trade and, 978
Economizing, 10
Economy, 12, 12-17
  closed, 16
  coordination mechanisms of, 14-16
  global, 16-17
  market, 16
  mixed, 16
  open, 16
  underground, 641
  Reading Between the Lines: Stabilizing
    The Economy, 922-923
Efficiency Wage, 854
Elasticity of demand, 677
Employment, 841-848. *See also* Unemployment
  flexible wage theory and, 841-844
  full, 601
  sticky wage theory and, 844-848
Endowment, 19
Environment, 7
Environmental damage, GDP and, 641
Equation of exchange, 781
Equilibrium, 20, 907
  above full-employment, 662
  aggregate demand and, 824-828
  economic, 827
  full-employment, 662
  labour market, 826
  long-run. *See* Long-run equilibrium
  macroeconomic. *See* Macroeconomic
    equilibrium
  money market. *See* Money market
    equilibrium
  short-run. *See* Short-run equilibrium
  unemployment, 662
Equilibrium expenditure, 704, 704-706
  actual expenditure, planned expenditure
    and real GDP and, 704
  convergence to equilibrium and, 704-706
  interest rate and, 792-794
  real GDP and, 816-818
  when planned expenditure equals real GDP,
    704-706
Equilibrium GDP, price level and, 727-731
Equilibrium price, 83, 83-84
Equilibrium quantity, 83, 83-84
European Community, 784, 962
Excess reserves, 749
Exchange
  equation of, 781
  medium of, 67, 738
  property rights and, 63-66
  real world, in the, 63-67
Exchange rate. *See* Foreign exchange rate
Expansion, 612
Expectations
  aggregate demand and, 654
  rational. *See* Rational expectations
Expected inflation rate, 607
Expenditure(s)
  aggregate. *See* Aggregate expenditure

autonomous. *See* Autonomous expenditure
circular flow of, 623-629
consumption. *See* Consumption
    expenditure
equilibrium. *See* Equilibrium expenditure
Federal government and, 942-943
induced, 714
recession and, 892
reducing, budget deficit and, 956-957
Expenditure accounts, circular flow and,
    623-629
Expenditure approach, 629, 629-630
Expenditure multipliers
autonomous expenditure, 714-718
induced expenditure, 714
marginal propensity to buy domestic goods
    and services, 714-716
multiplier effect, 716
multiplier, size of, 716-718
Exporter, net, 968
Exports, 700, **967**. *See also* International trade
exchange rate and, 802
net, 626, 700-702

Factor cost, 631
market price and, 631
net domestic income at, 631
Factor incomes approach, 630, 630-632
Factor market, 14
Factors of production, 14. *See also* Capital;
    Labour; Land
Fair, Ray, 919
Federal budget, 918
1969-1992, 941-942
Federal deficit . *See* budget deficit
Federal government
Bank of Canada and, 766-767
expenditure, 942-943
real deficit and, 948-950
real and nominal deficit, 949-950
revenue, 942-943
Feedback rules, 924
compared with fixed rules, 925-926
Fiat money, 741
Final goods and services, 608, 633-634
Financial innovation, 755-757
Financial intermediary, 745, 745-749
economic functions of, 747-749
financial legislation and, 747
Financing
debt, 950-952
of international trade, 995-1001
of the government deficit, 950-953
money, 950-952
Firm, 14, *See also* Corporation; Partnership;
    Sole proprietorship
collusive agreements among. *See* Collusive
    agreement
investment decisions and, 692-694
Fiscal policy, 677, 652, 825
    See also Stabilization policy
aggregate demand composition and,
    726-727, 794-798, 822-823
changes in aggregate demand and, 652-653
crowding in and, 798
crowding out and, 798
first and second round effects, 795-797

multipliers and, 722-726
politics of, 810
relative effectiveness of, 802-804
stabilization and, 918-921
Reading Between the Lines: Fiscal and
    Monetary Policy, 808-809
Reading Between the Lines: No Fiscal
    Stimulus?, 728-729
Fixed exchange rate, 1001
Fixed rule, 924
aggregate demand shock and, 925
compared with feedback rules, 925-926
Flexible exchange rate, 1002
Flexible wage theory, 841-844
aggregate supply with, 842-844
changes in wages and employment and,
    841-842
real business cycle theory and, 844
recession and, 896-898
unemployment and, 852-853
Forecasting inflation, 868-869
Foreign aid, economic growth and, 1035-1036
Foreign exchange, dollar and, 1001-1003
Foreign exchange market, 1001
Foreign exchange rate, 606, 1001
determination of, 1004-1011
exports and, 802
fixed, 1001
flexible, 1002
managed, 1002
prices, interest rates and, 1011-1016
recent history of, 1003
volatility of, 1009-1011
Foreign exchange reserves, 995
Free trade, 22, 961-962
Free trade agreement, Canada-U.S., 671, 677
    Reading Between the Lines: North
    American Free Trade, 986-987
Frictional unemployment, 600, 600-601
Friedman, Milton, 594, 686, 784, 806, 901,
    901n
Full employment, 601
macroeconomic equilibrium and, 662-663
Full-employment equilibrium, 662

Gains
from trade, 60-63, 971-979
Reading Between the Lines: The Gains
    from Specialization and Exchange,
    64-65
Gains from trade, 971-979
achieving, 61-62
adjustment costs and, 978-979
balanced trade and, 972
calculating, 974
changes in production and consumption,
    972-974
productivity and, 974-975
in reality, 975
reaping, 971-972
trade in similar goods, 975-978
wages and costs and, 974
Our Advancing Knowledge: Understanding
    the Gains From International Trade,
    976-977
GDP deflator, 635, 637-638
General Agreement on Tariffs and Trade,

678-679, 961-964, 976-977, **980**
*General Theory of Employment, Interest
    and Money*, 687
Global economy, 16
Goods, 51
capital, 51
complementary, 75
consumption, 51
final, 608, 633-634
inferior, 75
intermediate, 608, 633-634
market, 14
nontraded, 1012
normal. *See* Normal goods
public. *See* Public goods
substitute, 75
Goods and services, 51
Goods and services tax, 669-672
Goods market, 14
Government, 7, 14
competition policy and. *See* Competition
    policy
purchases of goods and services, 697
regulation by. *See* Regulation
stabilization policy and, 918
in welfare state capitalism, 1069
Government budget, automatic stabilizers and,
    725-726
Government debt, 941
Government deficit, 616
See also Budget deficit
current account deficit and, 1000
private surplus and, 1000
real, 948-950
Reading Between the Lines: Government
    Deficits, 946-947
Government purchases multiplier, 722
Government sector surplus or deficit, 998
Graphs, 29-45
independent variables and, 41
linear relationships and, 38
maximums and minimums and, 40-41
with more than two variables, 44-45
negative relationships and, 38-40
omitting origin and, 33-35
positive relationships and, 38-39
scatter diagrams and, 30-32
single-variable, 29
slope and, 42-44
time-series, 32-38
two-variable, 29-30
Reading Between the Lines: Graphs in
    Action, 36-37
Great Depression, 899-904, 976
reasons for, 900-904
repeat, 904-908
Great Leap Forward, 1060
Greenspan, Alan, 905
Gregory, Paul R., 1051n
Gresham, Thomas, 740
Gresham's Law, 740
Gross domestic product (GDP), 608,
    608-611
constant dollar. *See* Real GDP
current dollar. *See* Gross domestic product
equality of income and expenditure and,
    624-625

expenditure approach to measurement of, 629-630
factor incomes approach to measurement of, 630-632
net domestic product and, 631-632
nominal, 608
output approach to measurement of, 633-634
real. *See* Real GDP
simplified economy in, 625
Gross investment, 631
Growth, inflation, and cycles in Canadian economy, 667-668
Growth
  income levels and, 1028-1029
  obstacles to, 1032-1035

Hall, Robert, 686
Haltiwanger, John, 854n
Helliwell, John F., 732n
Heston, Alan, 1027n, 1028n
Hierarchy, 1049
Home production, 642
Household, 13
Human capital, 51, 604, 676. *See also* Labour
  unemployment and, 604
Human dignity, unemployment and, 604
Hume, David, 785, 976
Hyperinflation, 784-785

IMF. *See* International Monetary Fund
Implications, 19
Implicit contract, 848
Imports, 700, **967**. *See also* International trade
Importer, net, 968
Incentive structure, 1043-1044
Income *See also* Earnings; Wage(s)
  change in demand and, 75
  circular flow of, 623-629
  disposable, 684
  domestic. *See* Net domestic income
  growth rates and, 1028-1029
  unemployment and, 601-604
Income distribution. *See also* Income redistribution
  international, 1026-1027
  Lorenz curve for, 1027
Income growth, productivity and, 830-833
Income shares, contest for, 882-883
Income taxes
  transfer payments and, 725
Indirect tax, 631
Induced expenditure, 714
Industrial country, 1026
Industrial revolution, 22
Inferior good, 75
Inflation, 2, 8, **604**, 604-607, 912
  anticipated, 607, 862, 867-873
  budget deficit and, 949, 950-953
  business cycle and, 615, 873-876
  in Canada, 667-668, 783, 879-882
  causes of, understanding, 784-785
  changes in aggregate demand and, 862
  cost-price spiral, 866-867
  cost-push, 865

demand pull, 862-865
forecasting, 868-869
growth and cycles in Canadian economy, 667-668
high and variable, 607
interest rates and, 877-882
international evidence, 952-953
Phillips curve and, 873-876
politics of, 882-883
price level and, 635-640
as problem, 606-607
recent record of, 605-606
reduction, 934-936
relative price changes and, 638-639
stabilization problem and, 917-918
supply inflation and stagflation, 865-867
taming, 934-936
unanticipated, 607, 862, 868
value of money and, 606
Our Advancing Knowledge: Understanding the Causes of Inflation, 784-785
Reading Between the Lines: Inflation, 880-881
Inflation rate, 605
  expected, 607
  price level and, 604-605
Inflation tax, 882
Inflationary gap, 662
Information, asymmetric, 827
Injections, 627
Innovation, 831
  financial, 755-757
Insider-outsider theory, 854-855
Intellectual property, 63
Interest rates(s)
  dollar and, 779
  equilibrium expenditure and, 792-794
  exchange rate, prices and, 1011-1016
  inflation and, 877-882
  investment and, 692-694
  money supply and, 774-779
  real, 692-694
  real GDP and, 793
  real GDP, price level and, 810-812
Interest rate determination, 757-760
  asset prices and, 757-758
  money market equilibrium and, 758-759
Interest rate differential, 1006
Interest rate parity, 1012, 1012-1013
Intermediate goods and services, 608, 633-634
International borrowing and lending, 996-997
  balance of trade and, 969
  to consume or to invest, 1000
International competition, 2
International constraints on Bank of Canada, 767
International crowding out, 798
International debt, as obstacle to economic growth, 1034
International deficit, 616-617
International distribution of income, 1026-1027
  communist and former communist countries and, 1026
  developing countries and, 1026
  industrial countries and, 1026
  newly industrialized countries, 1026

oil-rich countries, 1026
poorest countries, 1026
world Lorenz curve and, 1027
International Monetary Fund, 678, 679, 687, 912, 933, **1003**

International substitution effect, 652
International trade, 8, 965-989. *See also* Foreign exchange rate
  Canada's, 967-969
  Canada-United States free trade agreement, 985-989
  financing, 995-1001
  gains from, 971-979
  opportunity cost and comparative advantage and, 970-971
  patterns and trends in, 967-969
  similar goods in, 975-978
  trade restrictions and, 979-985
  Our Advancing Knowledge: Understanding the Gains From International Trade, 976-977
Intertemporal substitution, 840
Intertemporal substitution effect, 652
Interviews
  Crow, John, 911-914
  Modigliani, Franco, 593-596
  Ostry, Sylvia, 676-679
  Phelps, Edmund, 824-827
  Sachs, Jeffrey, 1020-1023
  Solow, Robert, 1-4
  Tyson, Laura, 961-964
Invention, 831
Inventory(ies), 630
Investment, 623, 692-697
  expected profit and, 694
  firm's investment decisions and, 692-694
  gross, 631
  interest rates and, 692-694
  investment demand and, 694-695
  net, 631
  Reading Between the Lines: Investment Picks Up Slowly, 698-699
Investment demand, 694, 694-697
  in Canada, 696-697
  interest sensitivity of, 806
Investment demand curve, 694
Investment demand schedule, 694
IS curve, 816-818
IS-LM model, 816-823
  aggregate demand curve and, 821-824
  equilibrium interest rate and real GDP, 820
  IS curve and, 816-818
  LM curve and, 819-821
  money market equilibrium and, 819

Job creation and destruction, 853-854
Job search, 850-852
Johnson, Harry G., 932-933

Keynes, John Maynard, 686-687, 806, 933
Keynesian, 642, 806
  aggregate demand, theory of, 785
  extreme, 806
  monetarist controversy with, 806-810
  stabilization policies, 932

theories of economic fluctuations, 907
Kuznets, Simon, 686

Labour, 14. *See also* Human capital
  demand for. *See* Demand for labour
  marginal product of. *See* Marginal product
    of labour
  supply of. *See* Supply of labour
Labour force, 599
Labour force participation rate, 840
Labour market
  equilibrium, 826
  issues, 677
  job search and, 851-852
  in recession, 894-899
  theory, which correct, 898-899
  unanticipated inflation and, 868
Labour productivity, 830
Labour supply. *See* Supply of labour
Laffer, Arthur, 957
Laffer curve, 957
Land, 14
  supply of, 395-396
Lardner, Dionysius, 86, 87
Law of demand, 73
Law of supply, 78
Law of one price, 1011
Leacy, F.H., 600n, 783n, 901n
Leakages, 627
Lenders
  net, 996-997
  unanticipated inflation and, 878
Lending, international borrowing and, 996-997
Liability, 746
Linear relationship, 38
Liquid asset, 743
Liquidity trap, 807
Living standards, Soviet Union in late 1980s,
    1054
LM curve
  effects of change in price level on, 820-821
  money market equilibrium and, 819
Loan, 747. *See also* Borrower(s)
  money creation and, 749
Local credit union, 747
Long-run aggregate supply, 658
  changes in, 660-661
Long-run aggregate supply curve, 658
  shifts in, 663
Long-run Phillips curve, 874, 874-875
Lorenz curve, 1027
Lucas Jr, Robert E, 907

M1, 742, 742-743
M2, 742-743
M3, 742-743
M2+, 742, 742-743
Macroeconomic equilibrium, 661, 661-666
  change in aggregate demand and, 663-665
  change in short-run aggregate supply and,
    665-666
  determination of real GDP and price level
    and, 661
  full employment and, 662-663
Macroeconomic long-run, 656
Macroeconomic short-run, 656

Macroeconomic time frames, 658
Macroeconomics, 21
Managed exchange rate, 1002
Marginal product of labour, 830, 830-831
  diminishing, 831
Marginal propensity to buy domestic
    goods and services, 714-715
  multiplier and, 719-720
Marginal propensity to consume, 688,
    688-690
Marginal propensity to consume out of
    real GDP, 691
Marginal propensity to import, 714
Marginal propensity to save, 688-690, 688
Marginal tax rate, 725
Market(s), 14
  for Canadian-dollar assets, 1007-1008
  economy, 15-16
  entry into. *See* Entry
  exit from. *See* Exit
  factor, 14
  foreign exchange, 1001
  goods, 14
  stock. *See* Stock market
Market economy, 15
  reforms in Soviet Union, 1054
  styles of, 1068-1069
Market price, 631
Market socialism or decentralized
    planning, 1045
Market transactions, 642
Marshall, Alfred, 87
Marx, Karl, 642, 1057
Maximization
  of profit. *See* Profit maximization
Maximum, graphing, 40-41
Maxwell, Tom, 732n
McMillan, John, 1064n
Means of payment, 738
Measurement, 18
  of money, 742-743
  of opportunity cost, 54
  of unemployment, 599
Medium of exchange, 67, 738
Menu cost, 850
Mercantilism, 976
Microeconomics, 20
Minimum, graphing, 40-41
Minimum wage, 848
Ministry of International Trade and Industry,
    1069
Mixed economy, 16
Models. *See* Economic models
Modigliani, Franco, 686
  interview, 593-596
Monetarists, 594, 819
  extreme, 807
  Keynesian-monetarist controversy and,
    806-810
Monetary base, 768
  bank reserves and, 769-771
Monetary exchange, 67
Monetary independence, 1013-1016
  with fixed exchange rate, 1016
  with flexible exchange rate, 1013-1016
Monetary policy, 677, 653, 765, 825, 912-
    914, 932-933. *See also* Stabilization
    policy

aggregate demand and, 653, 823-824,
    798-802
  inflation, to lower and, 780
  politics of, 810
  relative effectiveness of, 804-806
  stabilization and, 918-921
  unemployment, to reduce, 780
  Reading Between the Lines: Fiscal and
    Monetary Policy, 808-809
  Reading Between the Lines: Monetary
    Policy Stimulus, 776-777
Money, 66, 67, 651, 738, 738-745
  Aggregate supply/aggregate demand model
    and, 779-781
  in Canada, 742-745
  commodity, 739-740
  creation of by banks, 749-752
  definition of, 738
  demand for. *See* Demand for money
  fiat, 741
  forms of, 739-741
  functions of, 738-739
  influences on holding, 753-754
  measurement of, 742-743
  as medium of exchange, 738
  motives for holding, 753-754
  nominal quantity of, 753
  paper, convertible, 740-741, 768
  price level and, 779-787
  private debt, 741
  quantity theory of, 781-786
  real, 651-652, 754-757
  Soviet Union, in, 1050
  as standard of deferred payment, 739
  as store of value, 739
  supply of. *See* Money supply
  as unit of account, 738-739
  value of, inflation and, 606
  velocity of circulation of, 781
Money financing, 950, 951-952
Money market equilibrium, 758-759, 818-820
  equilibrium interest rate and real GDP and,
    820
  LM curve and, 818-820
Money multiplier, 770, 770-771
  calculating, 773
  in Canada, 773-774
Money supply
  controlling, 769-774
  interest rates and, 774-779
Money wage rate, 834
Multiplier, 717
  automatic stabilizers and, 725-726
  balanced budget, 723-724
  in Canada, 731-732
  deposit, 751
  econometric models and, 731
  fiscal policy and, 722-726
  government purchases, 722
  greater than one, why, 720
  marginal propensity to buy domestic goods
    and services, 719-720
  money, 770, 771-774
  price level and, 726-731
  in recession and recovery, 731-732
  size of, 716-718
  tax, 723
  transfer payments, 722-723

Multiplier effect, 716
Mundell, Robert, 933

National Income and Expenditure, 642
   Accounts, 629-635
     expenditure approach, 629-630
     factor incomes approach, 630-632
     output approach, 633-634
National saving, 595
Nationalized industry, 1069
Natural rate of unemployment, 601
   errors in forecasting, 883
Naughton, Barry, 1064n, 1065n
Negative relationship, 38, 38-39
Net borrower, 996
Net domestic income at factor cost, 631
Net domestic product, gross domestic product
   and, 631-632
**Net domestic product at market prices,
   631**
Net exporter, 968
Net export function, 700, 700-702
Net export(s), 626, 700-702
Net importer, 968
Net investment, 631
Net lender, 996-997
New classical model/theory, 825-826
New Keynesian macroeconomics, 826
Newly industrialized countries, 1026
Nominal GDP, 608
   calculating, 637-638
   real GDP and, 608
Nominal GDP targeting, 931
Nominal income, 678
Nominal money, 753
Nonconvertible note, 768
Nontariff barrier, 979, 982-985
Nontraded good, 1012
Normal goods, 75
Normative statement, 17, 17-18
North American Free Trade, 962
   Reading Between the Lines: North
     American Free Trade, 986-987
Note, nonconvertible, 768

Observation, 18
OECD, 676-679
Official settlements account, 995
Oil-rich countries, 1026
Okun, Arthur, 604
Open economy, 16, 913, 933
Open-market operations, 768, 769, 770
   multiplier effect of, 771-773
Opportunity cost, 10
   best alternative foregone and, 10, 54
   comparative advantage and, 970-971
   farmland, in, 970
   increasing, 54-56
   international trade and, 970-971
   measuring, 54
   Mobilia, in, 970
   shape of production possibility frontier and,
     54
Optimizing, 10
Organization of Petroleum Exporting
Countries, 605-606

Origin, 29
   omitting, 33-35
Ostry, Sylvia (interview), 676-679
Other things being equal (*ceteris paribus*)
   assumption, 44
Our Advancing Knowledge
   The Development of Economic Accounting,
     642-643
   Discovering the Consumption Function,
     686-687
   Discovering the Laws of Supply and
     Demand, 86-87
   Evolving Approaches to Economic
     Stabilization, 932-933
   Understanding Business Cycles, 906-907
   Understanding the Causes of Inflation,
     784-785
   Understanding the Gains from International
     Trade, 976-977
   Understanding the Limits of Central
     Planning, 1056-1057
   Understanding the Sources of Economic
     Wealth, 22-23
Output. *See also* Production
   unemployment and, 601-604
   value of. *See* Gross domestic product
Output approach, 633, 633-634

Part-time workers, 599
Peak, 613
People's Republic of China. *See* China
Per capita production function, 1029,
   1029-1030
Perpetuity, 757
Petty, Sir William, 642, 644-645
Phelps, Edmund (interview), 824-827
Phillips, A.W., 873
Phillips curve, 785, 873
   in Canada, 875-876
   changes in natural rate of unemployment
     and, 875
   long run, 874-875
   short run, 873-874
Planning
   decentralized, 1045
   in Soviet Union, 1048-1050
Poland, economic transition in, 1059-1060
Policy lags, forecast horizon and, 927
Policy tools of the Bank of Canada, 767-768
Political business cycle, 920
Politics of inflation, 882-883
Population
   change in demand and, 75
   economic growth and, 1032-1033, 1035
Positive relationship, 38, 38-39
Positive statement, 17, 17-18
Poverty, 8. *See also* Wealth distribution
Preferences, 19
   change in demand and, 75
Price(s)
   change in demand and, 75, 84-85, 88-89
   change in supply and, 79, 85-89
   equilibrium, 83-84
   exchange rate and, 1011-1016
   expected future and change in demand, 75
   of factors of production. *See* Factor prices
   law of one price and, 1011

   market, 631
   as regulator, 82
   relative, 638
Price changes
   predicting, 84-93
   relative, inflation and, 638-639
Price deregulation in China, 1065
Price determination, 82-84
Price index, 604, 635-640
   calculating, 635
Price level, 604
   aggregate planned expenditure and,
     706-708
   equilibrium GDP and, 727-731
   incomplete information, sticky wages and,
     849-850
   inflation rate and, 605, 635-640, 862
   LM curve and, 824-825
   long run effects on, 811-812
   short run effects on, 810-811
   macroeconomic equilibrium and, 661
   multipliers and, 726-731
   rational expectation of, calculating, 869-871
   real GDP and, 706-708
   real GDP, interest rates and, 810-812
Price stability, 678, **912,** 933
Price-wage inflation spiral, 864-865
Private debt money, 741
Private enterprise, 66
Private sector surplus or deficit, 998
Private surplus, effects of government deficit
   on, 1000
Privatization, 1069
Production, 6-7, 51 *See also* Output
   international trade and, 972-974
Production function, 830
   short-run, 830
Production method. *See* Technique(s)
**Production possibility frontier,
   51,** 51-63
   model economy and, 51-53
   opportunity cost and, 54-56
   in real world, 56
   shape of, 54
   shifts in, 57-58
Productivity, 62
   absolute advantage and, 62-63
   growth in Canada, 832
   growth, slowdown in, 930-931
   income growth and, 830-833
   international trade and, 974-975
   labour, 830
Productivity Growth
   Reading Between the Lines: Productivity
     Growth, 838-839
Profit
   expected, investment and, 694
Property, 63
   intellectual, 63
Property rights, 63, 63-66
   absence of, 1032
   overcoming obstacles to economic growth
     and, 1035
   in private enterprise capitalism, 66
   world without, 63
Protectionism, 596, 961-962, **979**
Purchasing power parity, 1012

Quantity demanded, 73
change in, 77
change in demand versus, 77
determinants of, 73
Quantity of Canadian dollar assets, 1004
demand for, 1004-1006
market for, 1007-1008
supply of, 1006-1007
Quantity of labour demanded, 834
Quantity of labour supplied, 837
Quantity of real GDP demanded, changes in, 653
Quantity supplied, 78
determinants of, 78
Quantity theory of money, 781, 785
aggregate demand/aggregate supply model and, 781-782
historical evidence, 782-786
international evidence, 786
Quota(s), 982, 982-983
tariffs versus, 984

Rasminsky, Louis, 765
Rational behaviour, 596
Rational choice, 19
Rational expectation, 825, **869,** 869-871, 907
economists' predictions of, 868-869
of price level, calculating, 869-871
theory and reality and, 871
ding Between the Lines
993 recovery, 670-671
ng the dollar, 1014-1015
d supply in action, 90-91
ts, 902-903
licy, 808-809
ion and exchange,

government deficits, 946-947
graphs in action, 36-37
inflation, 880-881
investment picks up slowly, 698-699
monetary policy stimulus, 776-777
no fiscal stimulus?, 728-729
North American free trade, 986-987
productivity growth, 838-839
stabilizing the economy, 922-923
structural unemployment, 602-603
success and failure in Eastern Europe, 1066-1067
Real business cycle theory, 844, 906, **930**
Real deficit, 948, 948-950
of family, 948
of federal government, 948-950
nominal deficit and, 949-950
Real GDP, 608
aggregate economic activity, economic well-being and, 640-644
aggregate expenditure and, 702-704
benefits and costs of growth in, 609-611
calculating, 637-638
change in quantity demanded and, 651
economic equality and, 644
environmental damage and, 641
equilibrium expenditure and, 704-706, 816-818
fluctuations in, 609-611

household production and, 641
leisure time and, 641
long run aggregate demand and aggregate supply and, 811-812
macroeconomic equilibrium and, 661
omissions and, 644
physical limits to, 658
planned expenditure equal to, 704-706
price level expectations and, 706-708
price level, interest rates and, 810-812
record of, in Canada, 608-609
short-run aggregate demand and aggregate supply and, 810-811
stabilization problem and, 917
underground, 641
Real interest rate, 692
Reality
production possibilities and, 56
rational expectations and, 871
Real money, 651
Real money balances effect, 651
Real wage rate, 834
Recession, 613, 906
aggregate demand and aggregate supply and, 891-892
in Canada, 890-893
expenditure and, 892
money market and, 893
multiplier in, 731-732
Recessionary gap, 662
Recovery
multiplier in, 731-732
Reading Between the Lines: The 1993 Recovery, 670-671
Regulation *See also* Deregulation
property rights limited by, 66
Relative price, 638
Reservation wage, 840
Reserve ratio, 749
desired, 749
Reserves, 747
actual and desired, 749
excess, 749
Resource(s)
natural. *See* natural resource(s)
technological progress, economic growth and, 1029-1031
Revenue(s)
federal government, 942-943
Marginal. *See* Marginal revenue; Marginal revenue product
tax, increasing, 957-958
Ricardian equivalence, budget deficit and, 955-956
Ricardo, David, 955, **956,** 977
Rule of law
absence of property rights and, 1032
establishing, 1035

Sachs, Jeffrey (interview), 1020-1023
Sacks, Oliver, 24n
Saving, 627
average propensity to save and, 688
low rate of, as obstacle to economic growth, 1033-1034
marginal propensity to save and, 688-670
Saving function, 684

Scale economies. *See* Economies of scale; Increasing returns to scale
Scarcity, 9, 9-11
Scatter diagram, 30, 30-32
Schwartz, Anna J., 903, 903n
Security, 747
Self-sufficiency, 60
Service(s)
final, 608
intermediate, 608
Short-run aggregate production function, 830
Short-run aggregate supply, 656, 658-660
changes in, 659, 660-661
physical limit to real GDP and, 660
Short-run aggregate supply curve, 656
shifts in, 663
Short-run aggregate supply schedule, 656
Short-run Phillips curve, 873, 873-874
Short-run production function, 830
aggregate, 830
Slope, 42, 42-44
across arc, 44
calculating, 42-44
of curved line, 43
at point, 43-44
of straight line, 42-43
Slovak Republic, economic transition in, 1059
Smith, Adam, 22-23, 24, 976
Socialism, 1044
capitalism compared with, 1045-1047
market, 1045
solution to economic problem and, 1047
Solow, Robert (interview), 1-4
Soviet Union, former, 1048-1056
central planning, 1048-1050
economic decline in, 1050
history of 1048
living standards in late 1980s, 1054
map of, 1052-1053
market economy reforms, 1054
market sector, 1050
money in, 1050
transition from investment to consumption economy, 1050-1051
transition problems, 1054-1058
Specialization, 60
Stabilization policy, 917-918
aggregate demand shocks and, 924-928
aggregate supply and, 928-934
alternatives, 921-924
fixed and feedback rules and, 925-926
inflation and, 917-918
lags, forecast horizon and, 927
predictability of, 927-928
real GDP growth and, 917
Our Advancing Knowledge: Evolving Approaches to Economic Stabilization, 932-933
Standard of deferred payment, 739
Sticky wage theory, 825, 844-848
employment and, 845-846
implicit risk-sharing contracts and, 848
incomplete price level information and, 849-850
menu costs and, 850
minimum wage regulations and, 848
money wage determination and, 844-845

real wage determination and, 845
reason for sticky wages, 848-850
recession and, 894-896
short-run aggregate supply and, 846-848
unemployment and, 855-856
Stock
    capital, 630
Stock market
    business cycle and, 614-615
Store of value, 739
Structural unemployment, 601
    Reading Between the Lines: Structural
        Unemployment, 602-603
Stuart, Robert C., 1051n
Subsidy(ies), 631
Substitute, 75
Substitution *See also* Marginal rate of
        substitution
    international, 652
    intertemporal, 652
Summers, Robert, 1027n, 1028n
Supply, 78-82, 79
    aggregate. *See* Aggregate supply
    of capital. *See* Capital supply
    change in. *See* Change in supply
    of Canadian-dollar assets, 1006-1007
    determinants of, 78
    elasticity of. *See* Elasticity of supply
    of labour. *See* Supply of labour
    law of, 78
    minimum supply price and, 83-84
    quantity supplied and, 78, 80-81
    Our Advancing Knowledge: Understanding
        the Laws of Demand and Supply, 86-87
    Reading Between the Lines: Demand and
        Supply in Action, 90-91
Supply curve, 78, 78-82
    aggregate, 656-661
    minimum supply price and, 83-84
    movement along versus shift in, 80-81
Supply and demand, 86
Supply inflation, 865-867
    aggregate demand response and, 865-866
    aggregate supply and, 865
    cost-price inflation spiral and, 866-867
Supply of labour, 837, 837-841
    determination of hours per worker and,
        837-840
    intertemporal substitution and, 840
    participation rate and, 840
Supply schedule, 78

Tariff, 979
    effects of, 981
    history of, 979-980
    how work, 980-982
Tax base, 957
Tax multiplier, 723
Taxes. *See also* Income taxes

as automatic stabilizer, 725-726
    goods and services, 671-674
    indirect, 631
    inflation, 882
    property rights limited by, 66
Tax rate, 957
Technological progress, 57
    economic growth and , 57-58, 1029-1031
Technology, 19
Temin, Peter, 901, 901n
Time-inconsistency problem, 935
Time lags
    changes in aggregate demand and, 654-655
Time-series graph, 32, 32-38
    misleading, 33-35
    comparison of, 35-38
Timlin, Mabel, 933
Towers, Graham, 765, 766
Trade
    balance of, 968
    barriers, 961
    gains from, 60-63, 971-979
    international. *See* International trade
Trade balance, 616
Trade restrictions, 979-985
    compensating losers and, 985
    dumping and countervailing duties and, 984
    nontariff barriers and, 982-985
    political outcome of, 985
    reasons for, 984-985
    removal of, 1036
    tariffs and, 979-982
Transfer. *See* Income redistribution
Transfer payments, 625
Transfer payments multiplier, 722,
        722-723
Transition problems in former Soviet Union,
        1054-1058
Trend, 33
Trough, 612
Trust & Mortgage Loan company, 747
Twin deficits, 999
Tyson, Laura (interview), 961-964

Unanticipated inflation, 607, 862
    effect on borrowers and lenders, 878
    interest rates and, 877-882
    labour market consequences of, 868
    problem of, 607
Underdeveloped country, 1026
Underdevelopment trap, 1035
Underground economy, 641
Unemployment, 7-8, 599, 599-604, 850-856
    benefits and costs of, 601-604
    business cycle and, 613
    cyclical, 601
    efficiency wages and, 854
    federal deficit and, 944
    with flexible wages, 852-853

frictional, 600-601
    insiders and outsiders, 854-855
    job creation and job destruction, 853-854
    job search and, 850-852
    measuring, 599
    natural rate of, 601, 685
    record of, in Canada, 599-600
    with sticky wages, 855-856
    structural, 601
    types of, 600-601
    Reading Between the Lines: Structural
        Unemployment, 602-603
Unemployment equilibrium, 662
Unemployment rate, 599
    natural, 601, 875
Union of Soviet Socialist Republics. *See* Soviet
        Union
Unit of account, 738, 738-739
United States
    Canada-United States Free Trade
        Agreement, 671

Value added, 633
Value of money, 606
Variable(s)
    independent, 41
    linear relationship between, 38
    multiple, graphing relationship among,
        44-45
    negative relationship between, 38-40
    positive relationship between, 38-39
Velocity of circulation, 781
Volcker, Paul, 775
Voluntary export restraint, 982, 983-984

Wage(s). *See also* Compensation rules;
        Earnings; Income(s)
    employment and, 841-848
    flexible wage theory and, 841-844
    international trade and, 974
    sticky wage theory and, 844-850
    unrealistic expectations for, 599
Wants, 73
    double coincidence of, 66, 738
Waslander, H.E.L., 732n
Wealth, 8,
Welfare state capitalism, 1045, 1069
Wilson, Michael, 932-933

x-axis, 29
x-coordinate, 29

y-axis, 29
y-coordinate, 29